The readings in this book have been selected by a committee of British monetary economics teachers to provide a comprehensive introduction to recent work on the major aspects of the British financial structure. The extracts have been chosen to complement the standard textbooks, and they concentrate on studies which have attempted to use British data to develop and test monetary theory. The readings are grouped in seven sections: the demand for money, the supply of money, money and economic activity, financial intermediation, monetary efficiency, monetary policy, and debt management. Each section has a short introduction linking the extracts and showing their relation to other aspects of monetary economics.

The **Money Study Group** was formed in 1969. Its members are all monetary economists working in universities, banks, research institutes, and government departments, and the Group's purpose is to bring them together in seminars and conferences to discuss recent developments in the subject.

Harry G. Johnson, who is Chairman of the Money Study Group, is Professor of Economics at The London School of Economics and at the University of Chicago. His editorial committee consisted of: **M. J. Artis, D. R. Croome, N. J. Gibson, D. Laidler, M. H. Miller, A. R. Nobay, J. M. Parkin.**

READINGS IN BRITISH MONETARY ECONOMICS

Readings in British Monetary Economics

BY

H. G. JOHNSON
AND ASSOCIATES

CLARENDON PRESS · OXFORD
1972

Oxford University Press, Ely House, London W. 1

GLASGOW NEW YORK TORONTO MELBOURNE WELLINGTON
CAPE TOWN IBADAN NAIROBI DAR ES SALAAM LUSAKA ADDIS ABABA
DELHI BOMBAY CALCUTTA MADRAS KARACHI LAHORE DACCA
KUALA LUMPUR SINGAPORE HONG KONG TOKYO

PRINTED IN GREAT BRITAIN BY
WILLIAM CLOWES AND SONS LIMITED
LONDON, COLCHESTER AND BECCLES

CONTENTS

III. The Supply of Money

IV. Efficiency

V. Financial Intermediaries

VI. Debt Management

VII. Monetary Policy

FOREWORD

HARRY G. JOHNSON
Professor of Economics
The London School of Economics and Political Science
and The University of Chicago

THE Money Study Group was formed over a year ago, with the dual objectives of bringing together people in the United Kingdom concerned with understanding of and research into the British monetary system, whether as academic scholars, bank economists, or officials of the Bank of England and the Treasury, and promoting research on the British monetary and financial system. The main activities of the Group thus far have been directly or indirectly concerned with the organization of conferences and seminars on British monetary problems—the conferences being general assemblies of experts concerned with the field as a whole, and the seminars involving smaller groups of specialists in a particular problem area requiring special and more technical, theoretical, and empirical expertise. In all, three conferences were held during the Group's first two years of activity. The first of these, meeting in Hove in November 1969, marked the lapse of ten years from the publication of the *Radcliffe Report* and the conference papers surveyed subsequent developments in the monetary field, both in institutions and policy and in empirical and theoretical work. The second conference, held in Sheffield in September 1970, again centred on issues directly in the field of monetary economics whilst the third conference, organized in January this year and held in London, shifted the focus on to problems raised by the recent inflation.[1] The Group's seminars have met more frequently, generally in London.

In the course of these activities the academic participants became increasingly aware of a serious deficiency in the literature

[1] The proceedings of these conferences have been published in: Croome, D., and Johnson, H. G. (eds.), *Money in Britain* (Oxford, 1970); Clayton, G., Gilbert, J. C., and Sedgwick, R., *Monetary Theory and Monetary Policy in the 1970s* (Oxford, 1971); Johnson, H. G., and Nobay, A. R., (eds.) *The Current Inflation* (London, 1971).

on which they base their teaching. There are already some excellent collections of readings in the field of monetary economics—for example, those edited by Thorn and by Smith and Tiegen[2]—collections which make available to the student in convenient form materials drawn from widely scattered sources that are difficult, time-consuming, and sometimes impossible to locate in the average university library, and so enable him to study the best of contemporary thought and work on monetary problems. But such collections have all been assembled by American editors, and naturally and inevitably reflect both the institutional structure of the American monetary system and the policy problems that have concerned American monetary theorists and empirical workers over the years.

The present volume is an attempt to fill this gap, and to provide British students with a collection of readings that will at the same time instruct them on the general outlines of what is known and accepted and what is still controversial in monetary economics, and place the issues in the context of the existing British monetary system, with which they are familiar and with which in any case they will be concerned in their careers after graduation.

The articles included in the volume have been selected by a committee of seven young monetary economists, representing five major centres of teaching of monetary economics in Britain and including M. J. Artis, editor of the *National Institute Economic Review*, who as well as participating in making the selections, also contributed in a general editorial capacity. The editorial group has divided its selected material into seven chapters, with the aim in part of providing a structure for the book that could correspond to the structure of a lecture course in monetary economics, and in part of permitting teachers in cognate courses to use the relevant section of the book for reference purposes. The editors have also provided introductions to the various chapters, intended to orient the reader towards the place of the selections included within the field as a whole.

A book of selected readings is necessarily constrained by the availability of relevant published material. In the course of preparing the book, the editors became conscious of an important gap in the literature, as viewed from the standpoint of current issues of

[2] Thorn, R. S. (ed.), *Monetary Theory and Policy* (New York, 1961); Smith, W. L., and Tiegen, R. L. (eds.), *Readings in Money, National Income and Stabilization Policy* (London, 1965).

theory and policy, namely the absence of a good treatment of the international monetary aspects of and constraints on the conduct of British monetary policy. This is an important subject given both the increasing international mobility of capital and the changes that have occurred recently in ideas about the proper way of conducting monetary policy so as to improve the balance of payments. But, in the absence of readings on this topic appropriate to a separate section, the editors were reluctantly forced to conclude that they would have to leave this aspect of the subject uncovered in this volume, except for a few very brief remarks to be provided in this introduction.

There are in fact four major aspects of Britain's membership in an international monetary system of fixed exchange rates that need to be kept in mind in any thinking about British monetary policy at the present time.

The first is that, while the bulk of the literature is based on the assumption that the domestic monetary authorities have control of the supply of money, this is a closed-economy assumption that is not valid in an open economy connected by international trade and capital flows to a far larger world system. In pure theory, the inhabitants of an open economy can adjust their holdings of money to what they need and desire for the usual reasons of monetary theory, by either spending unwanted money on goods or securities in the world market, or alternatively by accumulating money through reduction of spending on current goods or capital assets. What the monetary authority controls, by its open market operations or its interest rate policy, is not the supply of money *per se* but the extent to which the domestic supply of money (determined by the demand for it) is backed by international reserves as contrasted with domestic securities. An easy money policy, in the form of relatively low interest rates and open market purchases of securities, leads towards an export of capital and a deterioration of the current account and hence a loss of international reserves, and vice versa. Hence in an open economy monetary policy has only a transitory impact on domestic activity and the money supply; its main impact is on the country's international reserves. Further, for current monetary analysis what matters is not so much the rate of change of the money supply which is the result of the interaction between monetary policy and the demand for money, but the rate of change of the volume of domestic credit extended by the banking system, which is a more reliable measure of what monetary policy is, and indicator of the trend of monetary policy. The problem remaining for economic analysts, in this theory, is to determine the time lags and the response mechanism within which the monetary authority has some freedom of independent action with respect to the money supply.

Second, in this theoretical context, there is the technical complication that, in the British institutional structure, the reserves are held by the Exchange Equalization Account, and financed by the sale of Treasury bills. In principle, therefore, a desire by the public, say to accumulate extra money through the balance of payments, could be frustrated by sales of securities from the Exchange Equalization Account to the market as the reserve inflow induced by the public's efforts to acquire cash accumulated in the Account. This would be the equivalent, in a direct-reserve-holding central bank, of a deliberate decision by that bank to 'sterilize' reserve acquisitions by offsetting open market sales of securities. Normally, one would expect the Bank of England, as a part of its stabilization operations in the government securities markets, to finance the acquisition of international reserves more or less automatically by monetary expansion. This expectation is in fact implicit in the agreement between the U.K. Government and the International Monetary Fund to limit the rate of domestic credit expansion reached after the disappointing early results of the 1967 devaluation. In any case, from a longer-run theoretical point of view this technical detail makes no difference to the general principle elaborated in the preceding paragraph.

Third, there is Britain's special position in the international monetary system resulting from the reserve currency role of sterling. Since overseas official holders of sterling, at least, typically hold it in the form of Treasury bills and other Government securities, their willingness to accumulate sterling balances is probably best thought of in the context of the other international arrangements by which Britain is able to borrow in order to prevent a balance-of-payments deficit and loss of reserves that would otherwise occur. In so far as foreigners, official and private, hold sterling in the form of actual money (mostly presumably bank deposits), their holdings add to the domestic demand for money which so to speak sets the 'budget constraint' on the monetary system's assets within which the central bank's policy determines the division between international reserves and domestic credit.

Finally, there is the question of the growth of the Euro-dollar market, and of the role of the City of London as its centre. The role of the Euro-dollar market in the international monetary system is a complex and controversial subject, too much so to be dealt with here. It can be said, however, that to the extent that Euro-dollar liabilities exceed Euro-dollar assets there is net borrowing by the United Kingdom from the rest of the world, in the same way as occurs through foreign holdings of sterling (this is to be distinguished from the current earnings derived from financial intermediation in Euro-dollars). But as Euro-dollar liabilities are not included in the U.K. money supply, they play no direct part in the British monetary system, as distinct from the financial system.

London School of Economics
20 *March* 1971

ACKNOWLEDGEMENTS

WE are grateful to all those publishers and authors who gave us permission to reprint from published work the selections which appear in this book. (Individual acknowledgements appear with the relevant reading.) Most of those concerned were generous enough to waive their claim to copyright fees, for which we are additionally and particularly grateful. Our thanks must also go to numerous teachers of monetary economics in universities up and down the country, who in response to our request, sent us their reading lists and offered suggestions for material that could usefully be reprinted in a book of readings such as this. Finally, we are grateful to Mr. S. Wanhill for his work in preparing the two indexes, and to the Clarendon Press for their co-operation and help in producing this book.

EDITORIAL NOTE

In reprinting the papers presented as readings in this volume, we interfered as little as possible with the original texts. The only paper to appear with substantive revision is Reading 9, a reprint of the article by D. Laidler and J. M. Parkin on 'The Demand for Money in the United Kingdom 1956–67', which first appeared in the *Manchester School*, September 1970. The nature of the revision made to the original version is explained in an introductory footnote on p. 181. In a book of this kind, however, it was felt to be important that references should be as full and accurate as possible, and in this spirit we have attempted to adjust the references cited in original papers to a standard which provides the necessary information. Apart from this, the liberties we have taken with the original papers have in general been confined to renumbering the tables, charts, and equations where appropriate and cross-referring where the original referred to a paper reprinted in the present volume, or where different sections of a particular paper appear in different chapters of this volume.

May 1971

For the Money Study Group:

M. J. Artis, National Institute of Economic and Social Research
D. R. Croome, Queen Mary College, London
N. J. Gibson, The New University of Ulster
D. Laidler, University of Manchester
M. H. Miller, London School of Economics
A. R. Nobay, University of Southampton
J. M. Parkin, University of Manchester

POSTSCRIPT

POTENTIALLY far-reaching changes in the British monetary system came about following the publication of new proposals by the Bank of England in May 1971, the general nature of which is outlined in a further postscript appended to the introduction of the section on Efficiency (page 284) where the relevance of the change is most obvious. Other sections of the book are, however, also affected in the sense that, where institutional data and the practice based on them are referred to, things are henceforth to be different. But it will be some time before new practices yield to *ex post* empirical analysis (as opposed to *a priori* speculation); in any case we did not choose articles for reprinting on the basis of their up-to-the-minute topicality but rather because of the more enduring contribution we felt they had to make in terms of analysis, methodology, or the advancement of our knowledge of important empirical magnitudes and relationships.

October 1971

I

MONEY AND ECONOMIC ACTIVITY

I

MONEY AND ECONOMIC ACTIVITY

EDITED BY
A. R. NOBAY

Introduction

THE publication of the Friedman–Mieselman study[1] on the relative stability of monetary velocity and the investment multiplier in the United States initiated an extensive and lively debate on the role and effectiveness of monetary policy in national income stabilization. An important feature of this debate is the extent to which it has called upon econometric investigation of the evidence, the bulk of the work, of course, being based upon data for the United States economy. In these empirical studies of money and economic activity, two distinct, though related sets of issues are involved; there are those which concern the economic rationale, specification, and interpretation of the results derived, and there are issues relating more specifically to the statistical or econometric characteristics of the methods of estimation employed in these studies.

In this chapter, we present a selection of studies which have attempted to evaluate the role of money in economic activity in the United Kingdom. Most of the papers presented here have attempted to estimate the effects of monetary variations on economic stabilization within the context of the reduced form estimation of the size and time-shape of the money multiplier. It would be useful, therefore, to provide a brief overview of the rationale and meaning of the money multiplier, together with the main issues that have been raised in these studies. Central to the monetarists' view of the

[1] Friedman, M., and Mieselman, D., 'The relative stability of monetary velocity and the investment multiplier in the United States, 1897–1958'; Research Study Two in *Stabilization Policies*, a series of research studies prepared for the Commission on Money and Credit (Englewood Cliffs, 1963).

relationship between the nominal quantity of money and the nominal level of income is the proposition that, whereas the demand for money is a demand for real balances and is an empirically well-established *endogenous* function of a few variables, the monetary authorities *exogenously* supply nominal quantities of money, and discrepancies between the two magnitudes are substantially reflected in real output and prices, i.e. nominal income.[2] Essentially, these 'reduced-form' studies are attempts to estimate these types of models by a single equation relating nominal income and money stock. Note that there are two substantive propositions involved here: one has to do with the existence of a stable demand for money function, and the other rests firmly on the proposition that the supply of money is exogenously determined.

Now, it is possible, within the context of the familiar Hicks–Hansen IS/LM framework to derive the 'reduced-form' of nominal income and money. Laidler, in an interesting paper which critically evaluates the ability of 'reduced-form' tests to discriminate between the 'Monetarist' and 'Keynesian' hypotheses, provides one such derivation of the reduced-form.[3] Additionally, the reader may refer to the introductory chapter of Smith and Tiegen's *Readings in Money, National Income and Stabilization Policy*. It is clear, that in such a formulation, the reduced-form coefficient of money reflects both the characteristics of the demand for money equation and of the expenditure function, and the essential differences between the 'Keynesian' and the 'Monetarist' positions are dependent on the relative coefficients on interest rates in the money demand and expenditure functions. Thus, a necessary and sufficient condition for a stable money multiplier is the existence both of a stable demand for money function, and of a stable expenditure function. The above analysis is based on a model where the money supply is assumed to be exogenous—the existence of a money supply function reduces the value of the money multiplier, to an extent which is dependent on the interest elasticity of the supply function.[4]

A substantial criticism voiced against the 'reduced-form'

[2] Money stock changes are emphasized, as they tend to reflect excess/deficient money balances on the assumption that the supply of money shifts erratically compared to a relatively stable demand for money.

[3] Laidler, D., 'The influence of Money in Economic Activity: a survey of some current problems' *in* Clayton, G., Gilbert, J. C., and Sedgwick, R. (eds.), *Monetary Theory and Monetary Policy in the* 1970*s* (Oxford, 1971), pp. 75–135.

[4] See, for instance, Tiegen, R., 'The demand for and supply of money' *in* Smith, W. L., and Tiegen, R. (eds.), op. cit.

approach to measuring the relationship of money to economic activity has been that whereas the money supply is taken to be exogenous, it has in fact to a large extent been influenced by economic activity itself—i.e. the money supply has been endogenous. If the monetary authorities attempt to peg interest rates, and this has generally been accepted to have been the case in the United Kingdom over the period of the studies included in this section, then the quantity of money ceases to be an exogenous variable.[5] It passively adjusts in order to maintain equilibrium in the money markets. Thus, far from having any causative role to play, the money supply merely reflects fluctuations elsewhere in the system. The consequences of this for the 'reduced-form' approach are obvious. In these circumstances what is required is a model, specified and estimated within the context of a simultaneous equation framework, which reflects and takes account of any two-way causation.

It will be obvious that the results presented in the studies reprinted in this chapter uniformly do not seem to establish a stable relationship between the quantity of money and the level of money income in the United Kingdom. But it would, on the other hand, seem fair to say that empirical investigation has gone far towards establishing the existence of a stable demand for money in this country. As mentioned earlier, in order to establish a stable relationship between the quantity of money and economic activity it is in addition necessary to establish relationships between expenditure and interest rates. It would be useful, therefore, to consider some of the evidence available for the United Kingdom on monetary variables in expenditure functions. In the Keynesian system the transmission mechanism linking monetary influences to income operates through the effects of interest rate variations via money supply changes, on investment, and via the usual multiplier on eventual changes in income. The *Radcliffe Report* rejected the use of money supply as a policy variable—the *Report's* assertion about the existence of close substitutes for money meant that variations in money supply would have rather little effect on interest rates, as (for example) a reduction in money supply would be offset by holdings of money substitutes, and interest rates would accordingly

[5] In a single equation, such as the 'reduced-form' estimation, one requirement of exogenous variables is that they do not respond to *current* movements in the endogenous variables. This follows from the statistical requirement that the exogenous variables be independent of the disturbance terms of the system.

rise very little (see para. 392 of the *Report*). The *Radcliffe Report* also employed a further line of attack in its virtual dismissal of the interest sensitivity of investment demand. This view was based upon the Committee's questioning of witnesses and use of business surveys. These general methods of verifying an interest effect are open to serious questioning, but then interest rates, generally, have been found to be insignificant in most empirical studies. In this respect, a recent paper by Martin Feldstein strongly indicates that the use of nominal interest rates, when theoretical considerations suggest that the real rate is the relevant variable, results in a substantial bias towards zero of the coefficient, with frequent opposite signs of the actual coefficients.[6] The incorporation of inflation expectations and the appropriate specification of the interest rate variable remain a serious problem in empirical estimation of interest rate effects. Nevertheless, and in view of the Feldstein findings, it is important to note that some of the recent studies on fixed and inventory investment in this country have indicated a significant role for interest rates in explaining these categories of expenditure. For instance, the study by Hines and Catephores of fixed investment finds an interest elasticity in the investment function of well above unity.[7] Probably more important, in the case of inventory investment, Trivedi is able to show that when relevant econometric techniques are employed in estimation procedures, significant interest elasticities are derived in both aggregated and disaggregated functions.[8] This result may be regarded as particularly significant in having been demonstrated for a sector which has traditionally been notorious for poor empirical results, certainly for monetary variables. So there seems reason to believe that improved econometric and specification procedures may well yield significant relationships between key expenditure and monetary variables.

It is instructive to note in passing, however, that in the absence of stable expenditure functions, i.e. where the IS function is liable to substantial disturbances, the optimal monetary policy indicated

[6] Feldstein, Martin, 'Inflation, specification bias and the impact of interest rates', *Journal of Political Economy*, vol. 78, no. 6, November/December 1970, pp. 1325–39.

[7] Hines, A. G., and Catephores, G., 'Investment in U.K. manufacturing industry, 1956–1967', *in* Heathfield, D. F., and Hilton, K. (eds.), *The Econometric Study of the U.K.* (London, 1970).

[8] See Trivedi, P. K., 'Inventory behaviour in U.K. manufacturing 1956–1967', *Review of Economic Studies*, vol. 37, no. 112, October 1970, pp. 517–36.

is the control of the money supply rather than control of the interest rate.[9]

The contributions that follow help to shed some light on the issues raised above. The issues and arguments are set out in excellent perspective in Reading 1. This provides essential background to the Barrett and Walters, and Artis and Nobay articles, which offer together results covering a long period of money multipliers. The second of the Bank of England papers (Reading 4) provides an interesting use of cross-correlogram analysis to investigate the timing relationships between movements in monetary and national income variables in the U.K. Finally, Dow, using an approach analogous to Tobin's use of the concept of the supply price of capital, sketches out the effect of changes in interest rates on the demand for real assets. When it is recalled that the U.K. authorities have, until recently, set interest rates as their intermediate monetary target, this essay provides an interesting explanation of the thrust of monetary (interest rate) policy on economic activity. The contributions between them provide an extensive bibliography on the subject. In addition to these the reader is referred to the articles listed below.

FURTHER READING

Friedman, M., 'A Monetary Theory of Nominal Income', *in* Clayton, G., Gilbert, J. C., and Sedgwick, R., *Monetary Theory and Monetary Policy in the* 1970*s* (Oxford, 1971), pp. 41–57.

Kaldor, N., 'The new monetarism', *Lloyds Bank Review*, no. 97, July 1970.

Laidler, David, 'The influence of money on economic activity: a survey of some current problems', *in* Clayton, G., Gilbert, J. C., and Sedgwick, R., *Monetary Theory and Monetary Policy in the* 1970*s* (Oxford, 1971), pp. 75–135.

Smith, W. L., and Tiegen, R. L. (eds.), *Readings in Money, National Income and Stabilization Policy* (London, 1965), chap. 1.

[9] See Poole, William, 'Optimal choice of monetary policy instruments in a simple stochastic macro-model', *Quarterly Journal of Economics*, vol. 84, no. 2, May 1970, pp. 197–216.

I

THE IMPORTANCE OF MONEY

THE BANK OF ENGLAND*

Definition and function

THE distinguishing characteristic of that set of assets which may be described as money is that they perform the function of a medium of exchange. This definition does not, however, allow for a clear-cut distinction in practice between those assets which should be regarded as money, and those which cannot be so treated. Cash and cheques drawn on banks are the means of payment for transactions which are generally acceptable in most developed economies, and this fact has led many to conclude that cash and demand deposits in banks are the only real monetary assets. There are, however, certain demand deposits, for example compensating balances held with banks in the United States, which cannot be freely used for transactions purposes. On the other hand possession of a balance on time deposit, or access to overdraft facilities, may allow a purchaser to draw a cheque on his bank account even when he has insufficient demand deposits to meet that cheque. A more fundamental point is that the set of assets which is acceptable as payment for transactions is not immutable over time; it has changed in the past and could do so again in the future. If people should find it economically advantageous to accept, and to proffer, other financial claims in payment for transactions, then the set of assets which is to be described as money will alter.

This difficulty in distinguishing exactly which set of assets most nearly accords with the definition of money, as set out above, has

* Extracts reprinted from the *Bank of England Quarterly Bulletin*, vol. 10, no. 2, pp. 159–80, 185–7, 197–8, by permission of the authors and publishers. The article was prepared in the Bank of England's Economic Section being largely the work of C. A. E. Goodhart, assisted, particularly in the preparation of the appendices, extracts from which are presented here, by A. D. Crockett. C. A. E. Goodhart, and A. D. Crockett are members of the Bank's research staff.

led some to emphasize other characteristics which monetary assets possess, for example 'liquidity' or 'money as a temporary abode of purchasing power'. Such alternative definitions have, in general, proved too indistinct for practical, and more particularly analytical, purposes. Others have argued, on *a priori* grounds, that one or another definition of money, though admittedly imperfect, is the best approximation to the underlying concept of money. Others again have argued that the matter can be determined empirically. If people should regard time deposits with deposit banks, but not time deposits with accepting houses, as close substitutes for demand deposits, then the former asset should be included in the definition of money and the latter asset excluded. To seek a definition in this way implies the expectation of finding a clear division whereby assets to be defined as money are close substitutes for each other, but markedly less close substitutes for all other—non-monetary—financial assets. Whether such a clear division is found in reality is considered later in this paper.

The function of money as a medium of exchange makes it a convenient asset to hold, because it enables the holder to avoid the time and effort which would otherwise have to be involved in synchronizing market exchanges (i.e. by barter). Convenience, particularly where it involves time saving, is something of a luxury. For this reason one might expect the demand for money, to provide such services, to rise by more than in proportion to the growth of real *per capita* incomes.[1] On the other hand, there are certain economies (of large scale) in cash management that can, in principle, be obtained as transactions get bigger and more frequent. This factor would result in the demand for money increasing by less than in proportion to the growth of real incomes.

The convenience to be enjoyed by holding money balances is only obtained at a cost—the cost, in effect, of not using the funds

[1] Holding additional money balances, as compared with bonds or equities whose capital value is subject to variation, tends to reduce the risk of unforeseen variation in the capital value of a portfolio of assets taken as a whole. In so far as risk avoidance is also something of a luxury, proportionately more money might be held in portfolios for this reason as people became more affluent. On the other hand, the development of the financial system has led to the introduction of a number of alternative capital-certain assets, in addition to money, which can be encashed at short notice. Therefore one would not expect the demand for money to have been strongly affected, at least in recent years, by the desire to avoid risk, because this motive can be equally well satisfied by holding alternative capital-certain assets yielding a higher return.

thereby tied up for purchases of more goods or alternative assets. As a broad principle, holders of money will adjust their holdings of money balances until the extra convenience from holding such balances just offsets the additional costs of having to make do with fewer other goods or assets. In order to bring about this adjustment, the money holder can, in principle, vary his purchases of anything else—financial assets, real capital goods, consumer goods—or of everything equally, in order to bring his money holdings into the desired balance with other possible uses of his funds.

In general, if the additional attraction (utility) of any good or asset does not match its cost, the main weight of the adjustment process falls, at least initially, upon changes in expenditures on close substitutes. If tomato soup seems to be getting rather expensive, the normal response is to buy less tomato soup and more oxtail soup, not less tomato soup and more company securities.

The transmission mechanism, whereby monetary influences affect decisions to spend generally, will be determined by the way in which people adjust their equilibrium portfolio of assets in response to a disturbance initiated, for example, by the intervention of the authorities in financial markets. These reactions, and therefore the transmission mechanism, will depend on which assets people view as particularly close substitutes for money balances.

The distinction between that theoretical approach to monetary analysis which may, perhaps unfairly, be termed 'Keynesian', and that approach which, equally unfairly, may be described as 'neo-quantity' or 'monetarist', turns mainly on divergent *a priori* expectations about the degree of substitution between money and other financial assets, and between financial assets and real assets. These differences are purposely exposed, and perhaps exaggerated, in the following sections, which provide a short résumé of the two approaches. As the points of contention between the two schools of thought can be reduced to issues that are, at least in principle, subject to empirical verification, it is not surprising that the results of the many statistical tests recently undertaken, mainly, however, using U.S. data, have brought many proponents of both views to modify their initial positions.

The transmission mechanism

'*Keynesian*' *analysis*

It is the conviction of Keynesian theorists that financial assets, particularly of a short-term liquid nature, are close substitutes for money, whereas goods and real assets are viewed as not being such close substitutes. In support of this position, Keynesians emphasize (a) the difficulty of defining which set of assets actually comprises the stock of money (which implies that such assets are similar in many respects), (b) the ease and simplicity with which a cash position can be adjusted at any given time by arranging the portfolio of financial assets to this end, and (c) the similarity of the character of financial assets adjoining each other in the liquidity spectrum ranging from cash at one end to, say, equities at the other.

If the authorities should bring about an increase in the money stock[2] by open-market operations,[3] for example, the extra convenience which such augmented money balances would provide would, other things being equal, not match the opportunity cost represented by the return available on other assets. Under such circumstances the adjustment back to a position of portfolio equilibrium would, according to Keynesian theory, take place mainly, if not necessarily entirely, by way of purchases of money substitutes, i.e. alternative liquid financial assets, rather than directly through purchases of goods and physical assets. This would raise the price and lower the yield on such financial assets, and would cause in turn further purchases of somewhat less liquid assets, further along the liquidity spectrum. The effect of a change in the money supply is seen to be like a ripple passing along the range of financial assets, diminishing in amplitude and predictability as it proceeds farther away from the initial disturbance. This 'ripple' eventually reaches to the long end of the financial market, causing a change in yields, which will bring about a divergence between the cost of capital and the return on capital.

The effect of changes in the money supply upon expenditure decisions is regarded, by Keynesians, as taking place almost

[2] As the authorities can, in theory, control the level of the money stock, it is customary in text books to treat the money stock as determined exogenously, that is to say, independently of the rest of the economic system, by the authroities. At a later stage in this paper, this method of treating the authorities' policy actions will be questioned.

[3] Open-market operations are undertaken in financial markets. Actions by the authorities to alter the money stock do not, therefore, affect everyone in the economy equally, but have their initial impact upon people and institutions active in such markets. It is quite possible that those active in such markets could have a higher interest-elasticity of demand for money than the average for the economy as a whole. The possible distributional effects of the particular nature of the authorities' monetary actions have received surprisingly little attention in the literature.

entirely by way of the changes in interest rates on financial assets caused by the monetary disturbance. This analysis, if true, has an immediate and obvious implication for monetary policy. It implies that monetary policy could be undertaken with greater certainty by acting directly to influence and to control interest rates than by seeking to control the money stock.[4]

In addition to the familiar cost-of-capital effect, the impact of changes in interest rates upon expenditures should be understood to include 'availability' effects and 'wealth' effects. Availability effects, in general, result from the presence of rigidities in certain interest rates and the consequent divergence of these rates from the more freely determined market rates (a good example of 'sticky' rates is provided by the Building Societies Association's recommended rates). In such cases a divergence of free market rates from the pegged rate may cause such large changes in the channels through which funds may flow that certain forms of credit may be rationed or entirely cut off. In those markets, such as housing, where credit subject to such effects is of great importance, the impact of availability effects can be considerable. The wealth effect occurs, in the main, because changes in interest rates alter the present value of existing physical assets. For example, if interest rates fall, the present value of physical assets will rise.[5] The ultimate owners of such real assets, very largely the holders of the company securities, will feel better off, and no-one will feel worse off.

Notwithstanding the theoretical argument, it for long seemed doubtful whether changes in interest rates had much effect on expenditure decisions, which appeared in general to be unresponsive to changes in interest rates. This implied, for Keynesians, that monetary policy could have little effect in influencing the level of expenditures; and this appreciation of the situation has been influential in conditioning the conduct of monetary policy in

[4] It is, however, the level of real interest rates that influences expenditure decisions, while the authorities can directly observe only nominal interest rates. In order to estimate the real cost of borrowing, the nominal rate of interest has to be adjusted by taking into consideration expectations of the prospective rate of inflation, the possible impact of tax arrangements and expectations of future levels of nominal interest rates themselves.

[5] In some cases there may also be a wealth effect following a fall in interest rates even when the financial asset held is not backed by real capital assets, as for example in the case of dead-weight national debt. In this instance a rise in the present value of these debt instruments—British government securities, etc.—to their holders should in theory be matched by a rise for the generality of taxpayers in the present value of their tax liabilities. In practice this is not likely to happen.

recent decades. In part this finding, of the lack of response to interest rate changes, may have been owing to the coincidence of movements of interest rates and of expectations about the future rate of price inflation, so that variations of real interest rates—even if usually in the same direction, perhaps, as nominal yields—have been much dampened. Indeed in those cases when the main cause of variations in the public's demand for marketable financial assets was changes in expectations of future price inflation, a policy of 'leaning into the wind'[6] by the authorities in, for example, the gilt-edged market would cause divergent but unobservable movements in real and nominal interest rates. If people became fearful of a faster rate of inflation and so began to sell gilts, support for the market by the authorities, who can in practice only observe nominal interest rates, would tend to prevent these rates rising sufficiently to reflect the more pessimistic view being taken of prospective inflation.

In recent years, however, more detailed empirical investigation has suggested the existence of some noticeable interest rate effects—though most of the work has used U.S. data, and the most significant effects have been found on State and local government expenditure, public utilities, and housing,[7] all of which are probably less sensitive to interest rate changes in the United Kingdom. There is, however, need for additional work in this country, to examine how changes in financial conditions affect expenditure decisions. Making use of the improved information that has become available during the last decade or so, further research in this field is being planned in the Bank. One recurrent problem is how to estimate the level of real interest rates, when only nominal rates can be observed.

The less that alternative financial liquid assets were felt to be close substitutes for money balances, the greater would the variation in interest rates on such assets need to be to restore equilibrium between the demand for and supply of money, after an initial

[6] i.e. absorbing stock when the gilt-edged market is weak, and selling stock when prices are rising.

[7] One of the most carefully researched studies of monetary effects in recent years came as part of the Federal Reserve—M.I.T. econometric model of the United States. The results of this study, reported by de Leeuw and Gramlich in the *Federal Reserve Bulletin*, June 1969, show a sizeable and fairly rapid wealth effect (via changes in stock exchange prices) on consumption, and a sizeable and fairly rapid cost-of-capital effect on residential construction. There is also a significant, but considerably lagged, cost-of-capital effect on business fixed investment. No evidence that inventory investment is sensitive to such monetary effects was found.

disturbance: the larger, therefore, would be the effect on expenditures, via changes in interest rates, of open-market operations undertaken by the authorities—given the climate of expectations in the economy. The greater the degree of substitution between money and other financial assets, the less would be the expected effect from any given change in the money supply. In conditions where other financial assets were very close substitutes for money balances, it would be possible, in principle, to envisage adopting a policy of enforcing very large changes in the money supply in order to affect the level of interest rates and thus expenditure decisions. But there would still be severe practical difficulties—for example, in maintaining an efficient and flexible system of financial intermediation—and such a policy would require considerable faith in the stability of the relationship between changes in the volume of money available and in the rate of interest.

If there were a high degree of substitution between money and other financial assets, which could be estimated with confidence, then a change in the money supply would have a small, but predictable, effect on interest rates on substitute financial assets. If financial assets were not good substitutes for money balances, on average, but the relationship seemed subject to considerable variation, then changes in the money supply would have a powerful but erratic effect.

There is, therefore, a close relationship between the view taken of the degree of substitution between money and alternative financial assets, and the stability of that relationship, and the importance and reliance that should be attached to control over the quantity of money. At one pole there is the view expressed in a passage in the *Radcliffe Report* 'In a highly developed financial system . . . there are many highly liquid assets which are close substitutes for money', so 'If there is less money to go round . . . rates of interest will rise. But they will not, unaided, rise by much . . .' (para. 392). It is only logical that the Committee should then go on to conclude that control over the money supply was not 'a critical factor' (para. 397). At the opposite pole there is the monetarist view, of which Professor Friedman is the best known proponent.

'*Monetarist*' *analysis*

In the monetarist view money is not regarded as a close substitute for a small range of paper financial assets. Instead money is regarded as an asset with certain unique characteristics, which cause it to be a substitute, not for any one small class of assets, but more generally for all assets alike, real or financial.

The crucial issue that corresponds to the distinction between the 'credit' [Keynesian] and 'monetary' [monetarist] effects of monetary policy is not whether changes in the stock of money operate through interest rates but rather the range of interest rates considered. On the 'credit' view, monetary policy impinges on a narrow and well-defined range of capital assets and a correspondingly narrow range of associated expenditures . . . On the 'monetary' view, monetary policy impinges on a much broader range of capital assets and correspondingly broader range of associated expenditures.[8]

In simple terms this means that if someone feels himself to be short of money balances, he is just as likely to adjust to his equilibrium position by foregoing some planned expenditure on goods or services, as by selling some financial asset. In this case the interest-elasticity of demand for money with respect to any one asset, or particular group of assets, is likely to be low, because money is no more, nor less, a substitute for that asset—real or financial—than for any other. More formally, all goods and other assets which are not immediately consumed may be thought of as yielding future services. The relationship between the value of these future services and the present cost of the asset can be regarded as a yield, or rate of return, which is termed the 'own-rate of interest' on the asset concerned. Keynesians and monetarists agree that asset-holders will strive to reach an equilibrium where the services yielded by a stock of money (convenience, liquidity, etc.) are at the margin equal to the own-rate of interest on other assets. Keynesians by and large believe that the relevant own-rate is that on some financial asset, monetarists that it is the generality of own-rates on all other assets. Keynesians, therefore, expect people to buy financial assets when they feel that they have larger money balances than they strictly require (given the pattern, present or prospective, of interest rates), whereas monetarists expect the adjustment to take place through 'direct' purchases of a wider range of assets, including physical assets such as consumer durables.

According to a monetarist's view the impact of monetary policy will be to cause a small, but pervasive, change on all planned

[8] Friedman and Meiselman, 'The relative stability of monetary velocity and the investment multiplier in the United States, 1897–1958', Research Study Two in *Stabilization Policies*, Englewood Cliffs, 1964, p. 217. This section provides an excellent statement of the theoretical basis of the monetarist viewpoint.

expenditures, whether on goods or financial assets. The impact of changes in the quantity of money will be widely spread, rather than working through changes in particular interest rates. A rise in interest rates, say on national savings or on local authority temporary money, would not cause a significant reduction in the demand for money—because these assets are not seen as especially close substitutes for money balances. Such changes in interest rates would rather affect the relative demand for other marketable assets, including real assets. Expenditure on assets, real and financial, is viewed as responding quite sensitively to variations in relative own-rates of interest; indeed monetarists generally regard most expenditure decisions as responding more sensitively to variations in interest rates than Keynesians are prone to believe. The generalized effect of monetary policy in influencing all own-rates of interest will, however, tend to be outweighed in each individual case by factors special to that asset (changes in taste, supply/demand factors particular to that market, etc.), so that no single interest rate can be taken as representing adequately, or indicating, the overall effect of monetary policy. As monetary changes have a pervasive effect, and as their effect is on relative 'real' rates, it is a fruitless quest to look for *the* rate of interest—particularly the rate on any financial asset—to represent the effect of monetary policy.

The crucial distinction between the monetarists and the Keynesians resides in their widely differing view of the degree to which certain alternative financial assets may be close substitutes for money balances; and in particular whether there is a significantly greater degree of substitution between money balances and such financial assets than between money balances and real assets. An example may help to illustrate the importance of this difference of view. Assume that the authorities undertake open-market sales of public sector debt (effectively to the non-bank private sector). The extreme Keynesian would argue that interest rates would be forced upwards by the open-market sales (and by the resulting shortage of cash in relation to the volume of transactions to be financed). Interest rates would not rise by much, however, because an increase in rates on financial assets, such as finance house deposits, which were close substitutes for money, would make people prepared to organize their affairs with smaller money balances. The authorities would, therefore, have reduced the money supply without much effect on financial markets. Because expenditure decisions would be affected, not directly by the fall in the quantity of money, but only by the second round effect of changes in conditions in financial markets, there would be little reason to expect much reduction in expenditures as a result—both because the interest rate changes would be small and because of the apparent insensitivity of many forms of expenditure to such small changes in interest rates.

The extreme monetarist would agree that interest rates on financial assets would be forced upwards by the initial open-market sales. This increase in rates would not, however, tend to restore equilibrium by making people satisfied to maintain a lower ratio of money balances to total incomes, or to wealth. The initial sales of financial assets (as part of the open-market operation), resulting in higher interest rates, would only bring about a short-run partial equilibrium in financial markets. In other words, because of the fall in their price, people would wish to hold more of these financial assets, and this would be achieved through the open-market sales. But the counterpart to the desire to hold more of the cheaper financial assets would not, probably, be to hold smaller money balances, but rather to hold less of other goods. It follows, therefore, that open-market transactions enable people to make the desired changes in their portfolio of non-monetary financial assets, but leave them holding too little money. Full equilibrium, in the market for goods as well, would only be re-established when the desired ratio of money balances to incomes was restored. This would be achieved (and could only be achieved) by a reduction in real expenditures. Which expenditures would be cut back would depend on the response to the changing pattern, overall, of prices (yields) on the full range of assets, set in motion by the initial monetary disturbance. In sum, monetary policy, by causing a reduction in the quantity of money, would bring about a nearly proportionate fall in expenditures elsewhere in the economy. In the meantime interest rates, initially forced upwards by the authorities' activities in undertaking open-market sales, would have drifted back down, as the deflationary effect of the restrictive monetary policy spread over the economy, affecting both the demand for capital (borrowing) in the markets and the rate of price inflation.

Thus, if alternative financial assets were very close substitutes for money balances, monetary policy (in the restricted sense of operating on the quantity of money in order to alter rates of interest) would be feeble; if they were not, it could be powerful. The issue is almost as simple as that. Furthermore, as was pointed out earlier, if people appear to treat all liquid, capital-certain, assets as close substitutes for each other, it makes it extremely difficult to attach any useful meaning to that sub-set of such assets which may be arbitrarily defined as money. Thus, the questions of the definition and of the importance of money each hang on the empirical issue of whether it is possible to identify a sub-set of liquid assets with a high degree of substitutability among themselves, but with a much lower degree of substitutability with other alternative liquid financial assets. Whatever the composition of this sub-set, it must include those assets commonly used for making payments, namely cash and demand deposits.

Testing the alternative views

The first stage in any exercise to establish the importance of control over the money stock must, therefore, be an attempt to discover whether money is a unique financial asset, without close substitutes, or is simply at one end of a continuous liquidity spectrum, with a number of very close substitutes. The empirical findings on this matter should help to settle the major difference between the theoretical position of the Keynesians on the one hand and the monetarists on the other. The usual method of estimating the extent of substitution between any two assets is to observe the change in the quantities of the two assets demanded as the relative price (rate of interest) on these assets varies, other things being equal. In the case of money balances, where there is no explicit interest paid on cash and current accounts, the normal procedure, to test whether money is a close substitute for other financial assets, is to examine how much the quantity of money demanded varies in response to changes in the price (rate of interest) of other financial assets, which are thought to be potentially close substitutes. If the demand for money should be shown to vary considerably in response to small changes in the price (rate of interest) of alternative financial assets, this finding would be taken as strong evidence that money was a close substitute for such assets. This relationship is usually described, and measured, in terms of the interest-elasticity of demand for money, which shows the percentage change in the money stock associated with a given percentage change in interest rates on alternative assets. A high interest-elasticity implies that a large percentage fall in money balances would normally accompany a small percentage rise in interest rates on alternative financial assets, and so suggests a high degree of substitution.

There have been in the last decade a large number of statistical investigations designed, *inter alia*, to provide evidence on the degree to which 'money', usually defined as currency and bank demand deposits—M_1—or as currency plus bank demand and time deposits —M_2—is a close substitute for other financial assets. A survey of this evidence is presented in Appendix I. [See Reading 6.] Most of these empirical studies are concerned to discover the factors that influence and determine the demand for money. In these studies on the nature of the demand for money, the total of money balances is usually related to the level of money incomes and the rate of interest ruling on some alternative financial asset, for example, on Treasury bills. Alternatively, the ratio of money balances to money incomes (the inverse of the income velocity of money) may be taken in place of the total of money balances, as the variable to be 'explained'. In most important respects, these two methods of approach are interchangeable. There are, however, a considerable number of optional variations in the precise manner in which these equations are specified, which form the subject of fierce debate for the *cognoscenti*.

In particular there is dispute over the form of the income (or wealth) variable which should be related to the demand for money. This issue is, however, peripheral to the question of the extent of substitution between money balances and other financial assets. Evidence on this latter question is deduced from the statistical results of fitting these equations and examining the estimated coefficient measuring the apparent change in money balances associated with a change in interest rates, which is interpreted as the interest-elasticity of demand for money.

Most of the statistical work of this kind has been done using data from the United States,[9] but the results of similar studies using U.K. data[10] give broadly confirmatory results, though there seems, perhaps, some tendency for the estimated stability of the relationships and the statistical significance of the coefficients to be slightly

[9] The source of the monetary data used in these studies is shown in each case in the selected survey of empirical results presented in Appendix I. [See Reading 6.]

[10] The results of work using U.K. data are also presented in Appendix I, including some early results of studies under way in the Economic Section of the Bank. [See Reading 7.]

less. Considering, however, that these studies cover a number of differing periods and employ a range of alternative variables, the main results of these exercises show a fair similarity and constancy in both the United States and the United Kingdom.

The conclusion seems to be, quite generally, that there is a significant negative relationship between movements in interest rates and money balances (i.e. that the higher the interest rate, the lower will be the quantity of money balances associated with any given level of money incomes), but that the interest-elasticity of demand appears to be quite low. The results, as shown in Table A of Appendix I, generally lie within the range –0·1 to –1·0.[11] This range is, however, rather wide. An interest-elasticity of –1 means that an upwards movement in interest rates of 10 per cent, for example from 4·0 to 4·4 per cent (not from 4 to 14 per cent), would be associated with a decline in money balances of 10 per cent. At present levels, this would amount to £1,500 million, which would imply a considerable response of money balances to changing interest rates. On the other hand, an interest-elasticity of –0·1 would imply a much smaller response, of only £150 million. This range, however, exaggerates the diversity of the findings, because the intrinsic nature of the data causes the estimated interest-elasticities to vary depending on the particular form of the relationship tested. If M_2 (money supply defined to include time deposits), rather than M_1 is the dependent variable, the estimated interest-elasticity will be lower, because part of the effect of rising interest rates will be to cause a shift from current to time deposits. If short-term rates rather than long-term rates are used, the estimated elasticity will also be lower because the variations in short-term rates are greater. If the data are estimated quarterly rather than annually, there again appears to be a tendency for the estimated elasticity to fall, probably because full adjustment to the changed financial conditions will not be achieved in as short a period as one quarter. In fact statistical studies using annual data with M_1 as the dependent variable and a long-term rate of interest as an explanatory variable do tend to given an estimate for the interest-elasticity of demand for money nearer to the top end of the range of results, and those with M_2 and a short-term rate of interest will tend to give an estimate nearer the bottom end. Even so, there still remains quite a considerable range of difference in the results

[11] [See Reading 6, pp. 130–2.]

estimated on a similar basis, but with data for different periods or for different countries.

The findings, however, do seem sufficiently uniform to provide a conclusive contradiction to the more extreme forms of both the Keynesian and the monetarist theories. The strict monetarist theory incorporated the assumption of a zero interest-elasticity of demand for money, so that adjustment to a (full) equilibrium after a change in money balances would have to take place entirely and directly by way of a change in money incomes (rather than by way of a variation in interest rates). On the other hand, the estimated values of the interest-elasticity are far too low to support the view that the result of even a substantial change in the money supply would be merely to cause a small and ineffectual variation in interest rates.

The area of agreement

The considerable efforts expended upon the statistical analysis of monetary data in recent years have produced empirical results that have limited the range of possible disagreement, and have thus brought about some movement towards consensus. It is no longer possible to aver, without flying in the face of much collected evidence, that the interest-elasticity of demand for money is, on the one hand, so large as to make monetary policy impotent, or, on the other hand, so small that it is sufficient to concentrate entirely on the direct relationship between movements in the money stock and in money incomes, while ignoring inter-relationships in the financial system.

Any summary of the area of agreement must inevitably be subjective. Nevertheless the following propositions would, perhaps, be widely accepted:

(i) The conduct of monetary policy by the authorities will normally take place by way of their actions in financial markets, or through their actions to influence financial intermediaries. To this extent it is really a truism, but nevertheless a useful truism, to state that the initial effects of monetary policy will normally occur in the form of changes in conditions in financial markets.

(ii) Monetary policy, defined narrowly to refer to operations to alter the money stock, will normally have quick and sizeable initial effects upon conditions in financial markets. It is not true that operations to alter the money stock would only cause a small change in interest rates without any further effect, nor that the velocity of money will vary without limit.

(iii) Open-market sales of debt by the authorities raise the return, at the margin, both on holdings of money balances and on holdings of financial assets. Any subsequent effect on expenditures, on the demand for real assets, results from the attempt to restore overall portfolio balance, so that rates of return on all possessions are equal at the margin. In this sense monetary policy is always transmitted by an interest rate effect.

(iv) The initial effect of monetary policy upon nominal interest rates may tend to be reversed after a period. For example, any increased demand for physical assets, encouraged by the lower rates of return on financial assets (including money balances), will stimulate additional borrowing in financial markets, thus driving up interest rates again, and the extra money incomes generated by such expenditures will cause an additional demand for money balances. If the increased demand for physical goods leads to a faster expected rate of price inflation, the resulting rise in nominal returns from holding financial assets and money balances will be reduced in real terms, so that the subsequent increase in nominal interest rates will have to be all the greater to achieve equilibrium.

(v) The strength of monetary policy depends mainly on the elasticity of response of economic decision-makers—entrepreneurs, consumers, etc.—to a divergence between the rates of return on financial assets, including the return on money balances, and the rate of return on real assets. Some empirical studies of the elasticity of response of various kinds of expenditures—company fixed investment, stock-building, house-building, consumer spending on durable goods, etc.—have found evidence, particularly when working with U.S. data, that demand does respond significantly to variations in nominal interest rates. But these estimated effects, although significant statistically, do not seem to be very large, and they appear to be subject to lengthy time-lags in their operation.

(vi) Although these statistical findings, of the fairly slight effect of variations in nominal interest rates on expenditures, are widely accepted, the inference that monetary policy is relatively impotent is not generally accepted. It is argued, and is becoming widely agreed, that variations in nominal interest rates may be a poor indicator of changes in real rates. As was already suggested in proposition (iv), an expansionary monetary policy is consistent with, and can lead directly to, rising nominal rates of interest, while real rates remain at low levels. If nominal rates of interest do provide a poor index of monetary conditions, many of the studies purporting to estimate the effect of changes in financial variables on expenditures become subject to serious error. This raises the problem of how to measure approximately variations in the real rates of interest facing borrowers and lenders, as these cannot be simply observed from available data.

A qualification

The evidence from the empirical studies shows that there is a statistically significant association between variations in the size of the money stock and in interest rates on alternative financial assets. This relationship is, however, neither particularly strong nor stable.[12] These results are often interpreted as evidence that money balances and such financial assets are not especially close substitutes, and that there may also be a significant degree of substitution between money balances and other assets, including real assets. This, taken together with the much closer statistical association between the money stock and economic activity, induces belief in the importance of controlling the money stock.

The observed loose association between changes in interest rates and in the money stock may, however, be due in part to another cause. It may well be that the relationship between interest rates and the demand for money is obscured by the volatile nature of expectations about the future movement of prices of marketable assets. Most of the statistical studies of the demand for money have related the total of money balances to the calculated yield to redemption of marketable financial assets, e.g. Treasury bills or gilt-edged stocks. This procedure implicitly assumes that the redemption yield is a good guide to the expected yield over the holders' relevant planning period; an assumption which will be generally invalid. People may, at certain times and in certain conditions, expect prices in the market to continue changing in the same direction as in the (recent) past for some (short) time (i.e. they hold extrapolative expectations). Or they may expect past price movements to be reversed over some future period, usually

[12] Although the ratio of the estimated value of the coefficient of the interest-elasticity of demand to the estimated standard error of that value (as measured by the *t* statistic), is large enough in almost all cases to show that the coefficient is significantly different from zero, the confidence interval frequently covers rather a wide range.

when this implies some return to a 'normal' level of prices (i.e. they hold regressive expectations).[13]

If people expect a fall in the price of an asset to continue even for a short time, and sell because of that expectation, then the calculated yield to redemption would be rising, while the real yield over the immediate short future could well be falling. This could mean that the effect of rising interest rates in causing some people to economize on money balances was being partly offset, or more than offset, by their effect in causing others to go liquid in anticipation of even higher rates. If market expectations were volatile, one might expect to observe quite large swings in interest rates associated with small changes in the level of money balances, or vice versa, sometimes even in a perverse direction (i.e. that rises in interest rates would be associated with increases in desired money balances). This result need not, however, imply that such financial assets were not good substitutes for money, but rather that the calculated yields did not always provide a good unbiased approximation to the true yields on which investors based their portfolio decisions.

There are, therefore, certain complications involved in the use of the yield (to maturity) on any marketable asset, with a varying capital value, as an index of the opportunity cost of holding money. It should, however, be feasible to observe more accurately the true relative return on holding assets with a fixed capital value—for example building society shares and deposits, national savings, local authority temporary money[14]—rather than money, because there is no problem of estimating the expected change in capital values.[15]

[13] It is quite possible, indeed probably fairly common, to find that expectations of price changes in the near future are generally extrapolative, while expectations for price changes in the more distant future are regressive.

[14] If there are additional penalties imposed for encashment of an asset before some predetermined time period has elapsed, then the alternative yields on such assets cannot be properly estimated without further knowledge of the expected holding periods. Moreover in some cases the rates offered, for example on building society shares and deposits, can be varied at short notice, while in other cases the rates may be fixed over the expected holding period. These are, however, probably lesser complications.

[15] An exercise is under way in the Economic Section of the Bank which attempts to estimate the extent to which persons, and companies, vary their holdings of money, as a proportion of their portfolio of assets whose capital value is certain in money terms, as relative interest rates (on these fixed value assets) change. It is hoped that it will be possible to produce estimates of the elasticity of substitution (for persons and companies separately) between all pairs of capital-certain assets, including money balances. The preliminary results of this exercise have already been reported in a paper on 'Substitutions between assets with fixed capital

It is still, however, difficult to refer to *the* opportunity cost of holding money because, when interest rates are generally increasing—and widely expected to continue increasing—the expected return (over the near future) on holding marketable assets may be falling, at the same time as the return on alternative capital-certain assets is rising.

It might, perhaps, be thought otiose to distinguish between these alternative reasons (volatile expectations or a limited degree of substitution) for finding a low response of the demand for money balances to changes in interest rates. As long as open-market operations cause a significant change in interest rates in financial markets, where the initial effect must occur, it could be argued that the fundamental reason for this reaction, whether it be a low extent of substitution or volatile expectations, was of secondary importance: what mattered was that the change could be foreseen and was large. On the other hand, in so far as market expectations of a volatile nature are regarded as having an important influence on developments in the market, the emphasis of policy under actual working conditions of uncertainty and changing circumstances will be inevitably transferred to market management, away from simple rules of operation on monetary quantities. Furthermore the importance, indeed the existence of any useful definition, of money depends largely on finding a break (of substitution) in the liquidity spectrum between money and other financial assets. If the finding of a fairly low interest-elasticity of demand is not taken as incontrovertible evidence of such a break in the spectrum, the issue of the central importance of the money stock as compared with some wider set of financial assets (even, perhaps, the much maligned concept of liquidity) remains open. It may indeed be questioned whether it is helpful to assign crucial importance to any one single financial variable. The need is to understand the complete adjustment process.

values', read by A. R. Latter and L. D. D. Price at the Association of University Teachers of Economics meeting in April 1970 in Belfast. Only short series of quarterly data are available, going back to 1963, and the sectoral allocation of the various assets is not adequate for the exercise in hand in some respects. For these and other reasons, the preliminary results of this exercise must be treated as extremely tentative. These results, however, suggest an interest-elasticity of demand for current accounts, the main component of M_1, of about 0·5, which is higher than the estimates in some other studies of the demand for money using U.K. data, but which remains well within the range of results obtained in a number of studies using U.S. data, as reported in Appendix I. [Reading 6.]

The stability of the income velocity of money

It is not possible to observe with any clarity either the real rates of return on asset holdings, which decision-makers in the economy believe that they face, or the precise process of portfolio adjustment. It is, therefore, difficult to chart and to measure the transmission of the effects of monetary policy. If, however, the sole aim of monetary policy is to affect the level of money incomes, it does not necessarily matter whether it is possible to observe and to understand the transmission mechanism in detail. It is enough to be able to relate the response of a change in money incomes to a prior change in the level of the money stock.

The statistical evidence

So the next stage in the analysis is usually to examine the direct statistical relationship between changes in the money stock and changes in money incomes. As was to be expected—for such a result would be predicted by almost all monetary theorists, irrespective of their particular viewpoint—movements in the money stock and movements in money incomes are closely associated over the long term. Over the last fifty or so years the demand for money appears to have grown at more or less the same rate as the growth of incomes. There have, however, been long spells within this period during which money balances have been growing faster or slower than money incomes. The American evidence suggests that money balances were growing at a faster rate than incomes before 1913, and the reverse has been the case for both the United States and the United Kingdom since about 1947.

The apparent fall in the velocity of circulation of money in the early part of this century in the United States may have been due to higher incomes enabling people to acquire proportionately more of the convenience (mainly in carrying out transactions) which the holding of larger money balances allows. The recent rise in velocity, in both the United Kingdom and the United States, may in turn have been brought about by people, especially company treasurers, seeking to obtain the benefit of economies in monetary management, spurred on by the rise in interest rates.

Alternatively these trends may have been associated with underlying structural changes, for example in the improvement of communications, in the change to a more urban society, in the growth and increasing stability of the banking system, in the emergence of non-bank financial intermediaries issuing alternative liquid assets and competitive services, and in technical developments in the mechanism for transmitting payments. In general it is not possible to ascribe the changing trends in the relative rates of growth of money balances and money incomes to any one, or any group, of these factors with any certainty; nor is it possible to predict when the trend of several years, or decades even, may alter direction. By definition, however, these trend-like movements are slow and quite steady. Only at or near a turning point is the relationship between movements in money incomes and in the stock of money balances likely to be misjudged.

The existence of a significant statistical relationship between these two variables does not of itself provide any indication of the causal mechanism linking the two series. The monetarists, though, usually argue that the money stock has been determined exogenously, meaning that the money supply is determined without regard to the value of the other vairables, such as money incomes and interest rates, within the economic system. As the money stock is thus assumed to be determined in such a fashion that changes in money incomes do not influence changes in the money stock, it follows that the existence of a statistical relationship between changes in the money stock and changes in money incomes must be assumed to reflect the influence of changes in the money stock on incomes.[16]

For the moment this basic assumption that the money stock is determined exogenously will be accepted, so that the relationship between changes in the money stock and in money incomes can be treated as cause and effect, running from money to money incomes. On this assumption it is possible to measure both the extent of the effect of a change in the money supply upon money incomes and the extent of variation in this relationship.[17] These results

[16] In a slightly more sophisticated version of this approach the cash (reserve) base of the monetary system (the cash reserves of the banks, including their deposits with the central bank, together with currency held by the public outside the banking system—high-powered money in Professor Friedman's terminology) is taken as exogenously determined while certain functional relationships (e.g. the public's desired cash/deposit ratio), which determine the total volume of the money stock consistent with a given cash base, are treated as behavioural relationships influenced by other variables in the system (i.e. they are endogenous). This minor variation in the approach makes no fundamental difference to the analysis.

[17] The empirical results of such an exercise are reported in Appendix II. *[The relevant extract appears on* *pp. 39–43 below.]*

generally show that the residual variation in the relationship between changes in the money stock and in money incomes is large as a proportion of short-run changes in these variables—over one or two quarters—but much smaller as a proportion of longer-run changes, over two or more years.

The interpretation, which has been drawn by monetarists from similar work done in the United States, is that the statistical significance of the relationship between changes in the money stock and in money incomes provides evidence of the importance of monetary policy. But the considerable extent of residual variation in the relationship, especially in the short term, combined with the likely existence of long and possibly variable time-lags in operation, prevents monetary policy—in the restricted sense of control over the money supply—being a suitable tool for 'fine tuning' purposes. From this appreciation of the statistical results comes Professor Friedman's proposal for adopting a rule of maintaining a constant rate of growth in the money stock.

In Keynesian theory changes in the money supply initially affect interest rates on financial assets, and these interest-rate variations subsequently influence the demand for capital goods (investment). Once the level of autonomous expenditure is set,[18] the level of money incomes is determined through the multiplier process. As monetary policy is but one factor affecting the level of autonomous expenditures, in particular fixed investment, one should, perhaps, expect to see a closer relationship between autonomous expenditures and money incomes than between the money stock and money incomes. The monetarists instead believe that expenditures on all goods and assets are pervasively affected by monetary policy (though the transmission process can still be regarded as taking place through interest rate changes in the process of restoring portfolio equilibrium). Thus, if the stock of money remains the same, an increase in demand at one point in the economy ('autonomous' or 'induced'; indeed the monetarists are sceptical about the value of this distinction) will have to be broadly matched by a fall in demand elsewhere in order to maintain equilibrium. Therefore they would expect changes in money incomes to vary more closely with exogenous changes in the money supply than with autonomous

[18] 'Autonomous' is defined as meaning those expenditures, generally taken to be exports, government expenditures, and fixed investment, that are not largely determined by the contemporaneous value of other variables within the economic system.

expenditures. The next step is usually to see which relationship appears to have a closer statistical fit. A commentary on, and critique of, such exercises is given in Appendix I [pp. 39–43 below]; it is suggested there that such exercises do not provide a satisfactory method of discriminating between the alternative theories.

The crux of this whole approach, of drawing conclusions from the statistical relationship between movements in the money stock and in money incomes, lies in the assumption that the money supply, or more precisely the monetary base,[19] is exogenously determined. This assumption allows a simple statistical association to be translated into a causal sequence. Is this crucial assumption justified? Clearly some of the factors which result in changes in the money supply/monetary base are endogenous (i.e. determined by the contemporaneous value of other variables within the economic system). Thus a large domestic borrowing requirement by the central government or a balance of payments surplus tends to enlarge the money supply. As a large borrowing requirement (fiscal deficit) and balance of payments surplus also result in expansionary pressures in the economy, there are reasons to expect increases in money incomes and in the money stock to be associated, without there being any necessary causal link running from money to money incomes.

But, in theory, a central bank can undertake such open-market operations that, whatever the extent of increase in the money supply/monetary base caused by endogenous, income-associated factors, the final level of the money supply is whatever the central bank wants it to be. In this sense the level of the money supply can be a policy instrument. A policy instrument is not, however, *ipso facto* an exogenous variable; it would only be so if policy were not influenced by the contemporaneous (or anticipated) value of other variables within the system, such as the level of incomes and interest rates. This clearly is not the case.

Obviously, if an increase in incomes causes the authorities to alter the money supply/monetary base, then the existence of a simple statistical association between movements in money incomes and in the money supply does not allow one to distinguish the strength of the intertwined causal mechanisms. In order to investigate

[19] The monetary base includes those assets that either are, or could be, used by the banks as cash reserves. It consists of the cash reserves of the banks, including their deposits with the central bank, together with currency held by the public outside the banking system.

whether this raises a serious problem, it is necessary to examine the factors which have apparently led the authorities to cause, or to accept, changes in the money supply/monetary base.

In the United Kingdom a general aim of policy has been to reduce the size of variations in interest rates, while at the same time moving towards a pattern of rates that would seem appropriate in the overall economic context. In so far as a policy of stabilization of financial markets is pursued, the money supply must tend to vary with money incomes—without necessarily having any causal effect on incomes. An increase in incomes relative to money balances will cause some tightening of liquidity; people will be induced to sell financial assets to restore their liquidity, thus pushing interest rates up; the authorities, to a greater or lesser extent (depending on their view about the preferred pattern of interest rates), will 'lean into the wind' and take up these assets; the money supply increases. There may even be a tendency for changes in market conditions to precede changes in money incomes, in so far as people are able to predict changes in the rate of inflation and activity accurately, and to make their asset dispositions in the light of their expectations. If this were the case an increase in inflationary pressures would be preceded by weakness in financial markets and an increase in the money supply.

There is little doubt that changes in the levels of certain key variables within the system (income levels and interest rates, for example) have brought about changes in the money supply. Therefore the money supply is not exogenous, and the statistical association between changes in the money supply and in money incomes cannot be advanced as evidence in itself of the importance of a quantitative monetary policy. Moreover, as the statistical relationships derived from the past depended on the particular kind of policy aim pursued by the authorities over the period considered, there would be no guarantee of their exact continuation in the future, should that policy be altered. In other words, although velocity has been fairly stable in the past this would be no guarantee of its stability in the future if the authorities chose to alter the rules of the game.

Post hoc, ergo propter hoc?

There is, therefore, a two-way relationship between movements in the money stock and in money incomes, with causal influences running in both directions. It may, however, still be possible to isolate and to estimate the strength of the causal relationships separately. It will be easiest to do so if the interactions are not simultaneous, but consecutive. Thus, if the money supply responds to changes in money incomes only after a time-lag, or if money incomes respond to changes in the money stock only after a time-lag, it may be possible to distinguish the separate relationships.

In particular, if changes in the money stock cause changes in money incomes, then changes in the money stock would be expected to precede the resulting changes in money incomes with perhaps a rather long lead, depending on the duration of the transmission process. If, however, money stock variations result in part automatically from increases in autonomous expenditures—for example in exports, fiscal expenditures or investment—and in part from the authorities' response to pressures in financial markets, then money incomes would be expected to rise more or less simultaneously with the stock of money. Thus, investigation of the extent to which changes in the money stock lead, or lag, changes in money incomes could be of considerable importance in any attempt to distinguish the main direction of causality.

The preliminary results of research done in the Bank suggest that, in the United Kingdom, movements in the money stock have preceded movements in money incomes. The pattern of this lead/lag relationship is, however, intriguing, for the relationship between the two series appears to be bimodal, i.e. to have two peaks. There was a fairly strong correlation between the two series when the monetary series had a very short lead over money incomes, of about two or three months. There seemed to be a further peak in the correlations indicating a much longer time-lag, with changes in the money stock leading changes in money incomes by some four to five quarters. The correlations were generally stronger when the monetary series used was narrowly defined (M_1 rather than M_2).

There have been a fairly large number of other statistical studies attempting to determine whether changes in the money stock do have a significant lead over changes in money incomes. The tests have used different series, from different countries, over different time periods, and the lag relationships have been estimated in different ways. Practically without exception they show that changes in the money stock appear to lead changes in money incomes, but the calculated length of lead has varied quite widely between the various studies, though to some extent this may have been due to the different forms in which the relationship was estimated. Professor

Friedman, for example, has claimed that there is evidence of a long and variable time-lag in movements of incomes after variations in the money stock. Other recent statistical work on this subject, both in the United Kingdom and in the United States, has tended rather to suggest that the interval by which the change in the money stock precedes the change in money incomes is quite short, a matter of months rather than of quarters.

A statistically significant lead, therefore, seems to exist even if it is quite short. Does this, then, make it possible to disentangle the causal effects of changes in money supply on money incomes, from those running in the opposite direction? It does not follow that the series which appears to lead always causes the change in the following series. There is a close association between visits to travel agents and tourist bureaux and trips abroad. The visit to the agent precedes the trip abroad, but does not cause it—though it facilitates it. Rather, the desire for travel abroad causes the initial visit to the travel agent. Analogously, desires for increased expenditure may be preceded by an accumulation of cash necessary to finance that expenditure. The demand for such additional money balances will cause pressure on financial markets, and so the authorities, seeking to maintain interest rates within some broad range, may in part accommodate the demand.

It is, however, unlikely that such accumulation of cash would take place far in advance of planned expenditures, for if the balances to be spent were at all sizeable it would be generally economic to lend them at interest on higher yielding assets in the meantime. From this source, a lead of money stock over money incomes of only a few weeks might, perhaps, be expected; though rather longer in the United States where the custom of making loans (together with compensating balances), rather than overdrafts, could distort the observed timing between changes in money incomes and money balances.

There are, indeed, a number of other hypotheses which are consistent with a situation in which changes in the money stock precede, but do not cause, subsequent changes in money incomes. However, in the absence of evidence to the contrary, a consistent lead is a prima facie indication of causation.

Most detailed investigations, however, of the effects on expenditures resulting from interest-rate changes (including wealth effects) show quite long average time-lags of the order of one or two years between changes in the monetary base and changes in expenditures.[20] Furthermore, Professor Friedman suggested that changes in monetary conditions affect expenditures only after a long and variable lag. If the duration of the transmission process, whereby changes in monetary conditions affect money incomes, is as long as these studies suggest, it would seem implausible to attribute the finding of a fairly strong relationship between the money stock and money incomes with a very short lead mainly to the impact of monetary changes on money incomes.

The preliminary results of studies made in the Bank which indicated that the lag pattern in the relationship between the money stock and money incomes was a dual one—a very short lead of two to three months and a much longer lead of four to five quarters—further suggested that the relationship between these series might result from the existence of separate causal relationships, each with its own lag pattern, whereby the levels of the money stock and money incomes approached a joint equilibrium.[21]

These findings do not make possible any confident measurement of the relative contributions of the adjustment of the money stock to changes in money incomes, or of the adjustment of money incomes to changes in the money stock, toward the simple overall statistical association between the two series. Even so, some of these results, particularly the observed relationship between bank advances and investment, seem to suggest that changes in monetary conditions do have a significant effect upon expenditures. Equally,

[20] See, for example, the F.R.B.–M.I.T. model as reported by F. de Leeuw and E. M. Gramlich in 'The Channels of Monetary Policy', *Federal Reserve Bulletin*, June 1969. Tables 1 and 2, pp. 487–8.

[21] In order to examine this proposition further, the series were disaggregated into their main components to discover whether the estimated relationships between the component series were significantly different from those of the aggregate series. The preliminary results of this exercise, which is still in hand, suggested that this was indeed the case. The relationship between the money stock and consumption appeared to be strongest when the two series were synchronous. The relationship between the money stock and investment suggested that changes in the money stock preceded investment with a long lead of some four to five quarters. When the monetary series was disaggregated into two components—advances to the private sector and other assets (mainly holdings of public sector debt)—movements in bank advances appeared to have a long lead over movements in money incomes, while the relationship between holdings of public sector debt and money incomes was strongest when the two series were synchronous. Indeed the relationship between the two series when bank holdings of public sector debt led money incomes was, perversely, negative. Finally, an examination of the relationship between bank advances and investment suggested the presence of a long (four to five quarters) lead over investment.

other results do not remove scepticism of the view that the simple relationship between movements in the money stock and in money incomes could be interpreted entirely, or even mainly, in terms of the direct impact of monetary conditions upon money incomes.

It follows that these studies of the simple statistical relationship between movements in the money stock and in money incomes can by themselves provide very little information about the strength of monetary policy. The statistical relationship is quite close, but this may reflect to a very large extent the accommodation of movements in the money supply to autonomous changes in money incomes (given the authorities' policy aims and operational techniques). If the authorities should make an abrupt change in their operations (altering the 'rules of the game') the old-established regularities might cease to apply.

Conclusions

The monetary authorities are in a position to alter financial conditions decisively by their operations in certain key financial markets. These market operations can have a considerable influence upon interest rates and also upon the climate of expectations. The existence of financial intermediaries other than banks, which are not so closely controlled, does not, in practice, prevent the authorities from bringing about sharp and considerable changes in financial conditions. Rather the danger is the other way around—namely, that aggressive actions by the authorities in markets subject to volatile reactions could cause exaggerated and excessive fluctuations in financial conditions.

The effect of these operations in financial markets is to cause disequilibria in portfolios. Expansionary monetary policy (narrowly defined to refer to operations to increase the money stock) will cause rates of return on a very wide range of assets, including stocks of all real goods, to be higher, at the margin, than the return available on money balances and other financial assets. In this general sense, monetary policy is transmitted to expenditure decisions via interest rates.

Attempts to measure the effect on expenditures of changes in interest rates on financial assets have on occasions shown these effects to be significant, though relatively small and often subject to long time-lags. There are, however, reasons for believing that these studies may underestimate the strength of monetary policy.

In particular, most of these studies use calculated nominal rates of return as an indicator of the impact of monetary policy. Expenditure decisions, however, are affected by relative real interest rates, and these cannot be directly observed. A strongly expansionary monetary policy, which would maintain low real rates of interest, might well be associated, after an initial decline, with rising nominal interest rates.

On the other hand, attempts to measure the effects of monetary policy by correlating changes in the money stock with changes in money incomes probably greatly overestimate the strength of monetary policy. There is a two-way relationship between these variables. It is not correct to regard changes in the money stock as having been determined independently of changes in money incomes; for example, the actions of the authorities in financial markets, which will directly affect the money supply, will usually be strongly influenced by current and expected future developments in the economy. Attempts to disentangle this two-way interaction by considering, for example, the lead/lag relationship, reinforce the view that monetary policy has some causal impact on money incomes, but do not allow this to be clearly isolated and quantified.

Monetary policy is not an easy policy to use. The possibility of exaggerated reactions and discontinuities in application must condition its use. We are not able to estimate the effects of such policy, even in normal circumstances, with any precision. Such effects may well be stronger than some studies undertaken from a Keynesian approach, relating expenditures to changes in nominal interest rates, would suggest, but weaker than some of the monetarist exercises may be interpreted as implying. Furthermore there are probably quite long time-lags in the operation of monetary policy, before it affects most kinds of expenditure. These considerations underline the difficulties of using monetary policy for short-run demand management.

A particular problem, perhaps, is to distinguish what the thrust of monetary policy is at any time. Indeed, it may be harder to decipher what effect monetary policy is having at any moment than to decide what effect should be aimed at. The level of nominal interest rates is not a good indicator of the stance of monetary policy. Rising nominal interest rates are quite consistent with falling real rates of interest. Professor Friedman has argued that the rate of change of the money supply would be a better indicator of the thrust of monetary policy than variations in the level of nominal rates. To the extent that price stability ceases to be an accepted norm, and expectations of inflation, or even accelerating inflation, become widespread, this claim that the rate of growth of the money stock may be a better indicator of the direction of policy than the level of interest rates takes on a certain merit. As, however, there will always be multiple objectives—for example the balance of payments, the level of employment, the distribution of expenditure, etc.—no single statistic can possibly provide an adequate and comprehensive indicator of policy. And basing policy, quasi-automatically, upon the variations in one simple indicator would lead to a hardening of the arteries of judgement.

[EXTRACT FROM APPENDIX I]

The relative stability of Keynesian and monetary multipliers

As noted earlier, a further means of testing the relative importance of Keynesian and monetarist hypotheses of income determination is provided by estimates of the direct relationship between incomes and money on the one hand and between incomes and autonomous expenditures on the other. This approach is open to the objection that it tests only a very simple representation of the underlying models, ignoring the improvements and refinements suggested by theoretical developments. As Johnson [7] has noted this may be defended on the grounds that the 'test of a good theory is its ability to predict something large from something small, by means of a simple and stable theoretical relationship'; but it is nevertheless quite possible that the relative explanatory power of simple equations may be a poor guide to the explanatory power of more complex equations derived as reduced forms from a set of interacting relationships.

More specifically, such an approach requires that the explanatory variables introduced should be the main exogenous variables influencing the economy, and that they should not themselves be functionally related to the dependent variables, or else erroneous conclusions may be reached. In general, a single equation model, which is not derived as a reduced form from a full set of structural equations, may be open to question as to whether the explanatory variables included are, indeed, truly exogenous. In particular, these tests of the monetarists' hypothesis hang crucially on the assumption that the money supply is exogenously determined, a question which is treated more fully in the main paper.

Quite apart from these problems with the specification of single equations, such equations can only provide information on the behaviour of one variable—albeit a variable of great significance to the economy. No government can possibly be content to rely on a model which only provides a forecast of, say, money income. It is essential to be able to make an informed and consistent judgement on a whole range of other variables, for example, productivity, inflation, unemployment, the balance of payments, the allocation of resources between various kinds of expenditure, etc. Furthermore, the authorities need to have some understanding of the route whereby they affect money incomes by changing their policy instruments. For example, it makes a difference whether monetary policy has its effect overwhelmingly on, say, private housebuilding, or more widely over all forms of expenditure. For this reason a proper test of the adequacy of the alternative models must be whether they can provide information on the behaviour of all the variables which are of concern to the authorities and to economists.

The pioneering comparison of Keynesian and monetary models was that of Friedman and Meiselman [**6**] in their research study for the Commission on Money and Credit. Using U.S. data for a 62-year period (1897–1958), which was divided into a number of sub-periods, they found that consumers' expenditure was more closely linked with the money stock than with autonomous expenditure in every period except the depression years. For the post-war period, when quarterly data were available, the picture was much the same, though neither hypothesis was at all successful in explaining quarterly *changes* in gross national product (G.N.P.). However, in the long run, velocity appeared to be more stable than at least one definition of the autonomous expenditure multiplier.

But Ando and Modigliani [**2**], using a definition of autonomous expenditure that was more in line with modern theory, obtained an explanation of consumers' expenditure which was better[22] than the one Friedman and Meiselman had detected using monetary variables. Their main argument, however, was methodological—namely, that to say the average value of the monetary multiplier had been more stable than the autonomous expenditure multiplier over a long run of years did not necessarily make it a particularly useful policy tool. Stabilization policy would need to take into

[22] As judged by the higher coefficient of determination.

account a much wider body of knowledge about how economic variables interacted; there was no reason to treat Keynesian and monetary measures as alternatives, nor any justification for picking a single independent variable—which was anyway not always truly independent—to represent each type of policy.

The same criticisms could be applied to a similar study based on U.K. data undertaken by Barrett and Walters [4], which, however, did not produce any very conclusive results. When levels of data were used, there was little to choose between the alternative hypotheses; though both achieved quite high correlation coefficients because of strong trends in all series. When first differences of data were used, the estimated explanatory power (as measured by the coefficient of determination) of both hypotheses was low, though the autonomous expenditure 'explanation' of consumers' expenditure was somewhat better than the monetary explanation for the inter-war years; and the monetary explanation was better before 1914 (when, however, the data are not entirely reliable). Barrett and Walters also showed that when money and autonomous expenditures were jointly considered as predictors of consumers' expenditure, the coefficient of determination was significantly increased, suggesting that, whether or not it is the major determinant, money does play some significant role.

A slightly different approach, followed by Andersen and Jordan [1] compared the impact on G.N.P. of fiscal and of monetary measures respectively. Given the limitations of single-equation models, the tests used were subtle ones. Changes in G.N.P. were separately related to changes in the full-employment budget balance, to changes in the money supply, and also to changes in the money base, which was assumed to be more nearly exogenous than the money supply.

The results obtained by Andersen and Jordan on U.S. data indicated that monetary changes had an impact on G.N.P. which was greater, more certain and more immediate than that of fiscal changes. de Leeuw and Kalchbrenner [8] challenged these conclusions on the grounds that the independent variables had been mis-specified; but although the alternative definitions proposed appeared to re-establish a role for fiscal policy, the case made by Andersen and Jordan for the importance of monetary factors was not refuted. Davis [5], however, showed that if the period to which the tests related was split into two equal sub-periods, the earlier part of the period (1952–60) showed very little relationship between money and incomes; the relationship discovered in the latter period (1960–68) might well have been due to common trends among the variables during these years.

For the United Kingdom, Artis and Nobay [**3**] have carried out tests very similar to those of Andersen and Jordan. In their study, fiscal policy was found to be more effective than monetary policy; but again little confidence can be attached to the results, because, as the authors themselves point out, these are critically dependent on the assumption that the authorities' fiscal and monetary policy actions are not functionally related to the level of money incomes. As much of the purpose of government action is to reduce deviations of actual incomes from some desired level, these assumptions must be suspect. Thus, if policy is used to offset a change in G.N.P. deriving from another source, it appears as though the policy measure has no effect. Perfect anti-cyclical fiscal policy would produce the *statistical* conclusion that fiscal policy was impotent.

[EXTRACT FROM APPENDIX II]

Money multipliers

Although it is clearly of considerable importance to understand the factors governing the demand for money, the estimation of a demand-for-money equation does not immediately provide any indication of the response of an economy to changes in the money stock.

In this connection, it is more relevant to consider relationships where income is the dependent variable, and money the explanatory variable. Despite the many shortcomings of such a highly simplified approach, which are discussed in more detail in the main paper[23] and in [the preceding extract from] Appendix I, it may be of interest to see whether such an approach provides any general indications about the strength and predictability of the relationship between the money stock and income levels.

Using the same data and definitions as in the earlier part of this appendix [see Reading 7], two separate models were tested:

$$Y_t = a_0 + a_1 M_t + a_2 Y_{t-1} + u_t \tag{1}$$

and

$$Y_t = a_0 + a_1 M_t + a_2 M_{t-1} + \cdots + a_8 M_{t-7} + v_t \tag{2}$$

[23] See pp. 26–34.

TABLE I

Estimated first difference forms of equation (2)

Money series	Estimated coefficients of: Constant	ΔM_0	ΔM_{-1}	ΔM_{-2}	ΔM_{-3}	ΔM_{-4}	ΔM_{-5}	ΔM_{-6}	ΔM_{-7}	Estimated money multiplier[a]	Coefficient of determination	Standard error of estimate	Durbin–Watson statistic
					Dependent variable—G.D.P.								
M_1	77·1		0·42	−0·38	0·40		0·33	−0·27		0·50	0·216	70·6	2·69
			(0·15)	(0·16)	(0·15)		(0·15)	(0·15)					
(1957: 2–1969: 3)	Suppressed	0·35	0·28		0·49		0·63	−0·39	0·45	1·81	0·565	83·7	2·17
		(0·17)	(0·18)		(0·15)		(0·17)	(0·20)	(0·18)				
M_2	64·6	0·25					0·37	−0·29		0·33	0·086	76·1	2·72
		(0·14)					(0·17)	(0·16)					
(1957: 2–1969: 3)	Suppressed	0·34			0·27		0·49	−0·45	0·27	0·92	0·629	77·3	2·47
		(0·12)			(0·15)		(0·16)	(0·19)	(0·16)				
M_3	91·7			0·19	−0·36	0·27		[b]	[b]	0·10	0·343	73·9	2·79
				(0·13)	(0·13)	(0·13)							
(1964: 3–1969: 3)	Suppressed			0·28	−0·31	0·32	0·20	[b]	[b]	0·49	0·742	74·4	2·54
				(0·11)	(0·12)	(0·12)	(0·11)						

Dependent variable—industrial output													
M_1	21·9	0·11	0·17	0·15		0·12				0·55	0·276	37·0	1·82
		(0·05)	(0·05)	(0·06)		(0·06)							
(1953: 2– 1969: 3)	Suppressed	0·14	0·22	0·18	0·12	0·15	0·09			0·90	0·588	39·0	1·64
		(0·06)	(0·06)	(0·06)	(0·06)	(0·06)	(0·06)						
M_2	14·9		0·22		0·10					0·32	0·212	38·6	1·53
			(0·06)		(0·07)								
(1953: 2– 1969: 3)	Suppressed	0·09	0·22		0·14					0·45	0·585	39·1	1·49
		(0·07)	(0·07)		(0·06)								
M_3	−57·0	0·08	0·09	0·23		0·12		[b]	[b]	0·53	0·516	34·2	1·46
		(0·06)	(0·05)	(0·06)		(0·06)							
(1964: 3– 1969: 3)	Suppressed		0·07	0·20				[b]	[b]	0·27	0·772	36·3	1·51
			(0·05)	(0·05)									

Note: Standard errors of the estimated coefficients are shown in brackets.

[a] The sum of the estimated coefficients of ΔM_0 to ΔM_{-7}, measuring the expected effect of a change in the money stock during the first eight quarters from its occurrence.

[b] These variables were not included in the estimation.

Both these equations were subject to very severe multicollinearity problems when estimated in levels, and little confidence could be attached to the results obtained. Using first differences of the data, no role for money could be detected in the estimated form of equation (1), which embodies an exponential adjustment lag. As a result attention was concentrated on equation (2).

This was estimated in two forms: with and without a constant term.[24] All variables whose estimated coefficients were not significantly different from zero at the 20 per cent probability level were excluded. In addition to the series for G.D.P. used in the estimation of the demand-for-money functions reported earlier in this appendix, a variable attempting to measure the output of the industrial sector of the economy was used—consisting of the index of industrial production converted to current prices by the wholesale price index.[25] The estimates of all these equations are given in Table 1. Both in terms of the coefficients of determination and of the shape of the lag-profiles, the industrial output variable performs much better than the G.D.P. measure. This suggests that money may have a closer association with industrial activity than with other sectors of the economy—private and government services and agriculture.

The 'official' definition of the money stock, M_3, appears to give the best explanation of changes in output whichever output measure is used, but this may be due to the fact that the data for M_3 cover a rather shorter time-period, during which there may have been a chance stability in the relationship. It will be recalled that M_3 performed no better than M_1 and M_2 in the estimates of the demand-for-money functions reported earlier.

In those equations in Table 1 where the constant term is suppressed, the estimated coefficients of the independent variables are generally increased, because some of the influence of the (normally positive) constant term is being attributed to them, and so the estimates of the long-run money multiplier tend to be larger.[26] Without a convincing explanation of what determines the size of the constant term, it is impossible to say which of the two estimates

[24] The transformation of equation (2) into first difference form does not yield a constant term. The existence of a non-zero constant term would imply that income would rise (or fall) at a steady rate if the money stock were unchanged.

[25] The resulting series was expressed in £ millions.

[26] The coefficients of determination of equations estimated with and without the constant term should not be compared directly.

of the long-run multiplier is the more accurate. Indeed, the possibility cannot be dismissed that the apparent connection between changes in money and changes in output is merely a reflection of cyclical influences acting on both variables, with no direct causal connection.

REFERENCES

[1] Andersen, L. C., and Jordan, J. L., 'Monetary and fiscal actions: a test of their relative importance in economic stabilization', *Federal Reserve Bank of St Louis Monthly Review*, vol. 50, no. 11, November 1968.

[2] Ando, A., and Modigliani, F., 'The relative stability of monetary velocity and the investment multiplier', *American Economic Review*, vol. 60, no. 4, pp. 693–728. See also other papers on the subject in the same issue.

[3] Artis, M. J., and Nobay, A. R., 'Two aspects of the monetary debate', *National Institute Economic Review*, no. 49, August 1969, pp. 33–51.

[4] Barrett, C. R., and Walters, A. A., 'The stability of Keynesian and monetary multipliers in the United Kingdom', *Review of Economics and Statistics*, vol. 48, no. 4, November 1966, pp. 395–405.

[5] Davis, R. G., 'How much does money matter?', *Federal Reserve Bank of New York*, June 1969.

[6] Friedman, M., and Meiselman, D., 'The relative stability of monetary velocity and the investment multiplier in the United States, 1897–1958', *Stabilization Policies*, Research Study Two in a series of research indices prepared for the Commission on Money and Credit (London, 1963), pp. 165–268.

[7] Johnson, H. G., 'Recent developments in monetary theory: a commentary', *in* Croome, D. R., and Johnson, H. G. (eds.), *Money in Britain* (Oxford, 1970), pp. 83–114.

[8] de Leeuw, and Kalchbrenner, J., 'Monetary and fiscal actions: a test of their relative importance in economic stabilization—comment', *Federal Reserve Bank of St. Louis Monthly Review*, vol. 51, no. 4, April 1969.

2

THE STABILITY OF KEYNESIAN AND MONETARY MULTIPLIERS IN THE UNITED KINGDOM

C. R. BARRETT *and* A. A. WALTERS*

Introduction

A CHALLENGING attack on Keynesian orthodoxy has been launched by Friedman and Meiselman.[1] They compare a simple form of the Keynesian hypothesis with a simple version of the quantity theory. The Keynesian model they examine is:

$$Y^d = C + A$$
$$C = kY^d + k'$$

i.e.,

$$C = \frac{k}{1-k}A + \frac{k'}{1-k}$$

where Y^d = disposable income,[2]
C = consumption, and
A = autonomous expenditure.

The time series of consumption is explained as a consequence of autonomous expenditure.

* Reprinted from the *Review of Economics and Statistics*, vol. 48, no. 4, November 1966, pp. 395–405, by permission of the authors and publisher. C. R. Barrett is at the University of Birmingham and A. A. Walters is Cassel Professor of Economics at the London School of Economics.

[1] Friedman, F., and Meiselman, D., 'The Relative Stability of Monetary Velocity and the Investment Multiplier in the United States, 1897–1958', *Stabilization Policies*. Series published by the Commission on Money and Credit (Englewood Cliffs, 1963).

[2] Actually, corporate undistributed profits are included in Y^d.

The quantity theory hypothesis relates the level of consumption in money terms to the nominal quantity of money. This is, of course, a variant of the normal quantity theory where the level of money income is determined by the amount of money. By subtracting investment from the dependent variable, one makes the quantity theory formulation directly comparable to its Keynesian rival. Money exerts its influence on consumption directly or via elements of autonomous expenditure such as investment.

With a different definition of 'autonomous expenditure', we get rather different results for United Kingdom data. Specifically, the monetary hypothesis is more successful for our early period up to the First World War, while the inter-war years are a strongly Keynesian period. After the Second World War, neither model has very high explanatory power, while for the overall period, there is a slightly better fit with autonomous expenditure.

Exogeneity of money

The usual quantity theory relates income to the money stock, assuming that money is exogenous and determined by the government. In practice, one also expects a relationship in the opposite direction.

In principle, the government can control the stock of money by controlling the reserves of the banking system. When reserves consist of cash, the cost of obtaining cash, the central bank's rate of discount, can be made prohibitive. Or, alternatively, cash acquired by the banking system at the 'penal rate' can be offset by open market operations. If reserves consist of 'liquid assets' appropriately defined, banks may be able to obtain these from the non-bank private sector by bidding up prices, but the government can again offset these operations. Banks, however, are left with some flexibility, perhaps tending to hold excess reserves in times of depression and utilizing these when business revives, so that they can accommodate customers while minimizing capital losses through sales of government securities. Within limits, they may vary their liquidity ratios. For most of the period considered, these were a bit more flexible than they are today.

A different consideration is that government policy has, in the past, focused more on interest rates than on the money stock. Governments usually have some interest in maintaining 'orderly markets', since stability in the prices of government securities adds to their attraction, high rates make servicing the public debt expensive, and unstable rates of interest may affect business confidence. The private sector gets supplied with its cash requirements, given the official policy on interest rates. The official view is likely to exclude too much variability, but remains sensitive to the foreign exchange position.

There are several ways in which the level of income may affect the money stock. First, bank deposits may reflect changes in private and government demand for credit. Suppose the demand for credit, as a consequence of higher income, is greater than the supply. In a free market, the rate of interest moves to equate supply and demand for loanable funds,[3] but if a higher rate of interest is contrary to government policy, the central bank may make it possible for the banking system to create new loanable funds by increasing its reserves. A persistently high level of demand for credit, for example during a war, may require a steady rise in the stock of money. Money then is dependent on elements of expenditure which we have called autonomous, and to a limited extent on consumption via the demand for consumer credit. The form of the quantity theory used makes consumption a function of money, so that the effects of autonomous expenditure on money raise the question of a spurious relationship when autonomous expenditure is excluded from the equation, but not when it is included. In this case, we are left with consumption affecting money through consumer credit, but the effect is probably not large.

Another way in which money may be related to the level of income is through governments practising counter cyclical policy. This would mean some negative relationship between income and money and might exaggerate the measured impact of money on expenditure. It would also involve the relationship between money and consumption, since consumption and income are highly correlated.

For some of the periods examined by Friedman and Meiselman, it is clear that the government, through the Federal Reserve Board, was influencing the quantity of money—controlling at least the minimum reserves of the banking system. It might be argued that the quantity of money was a consequence of the Federal Reserve Board's judgement of the difference between expected income and

[3] Prices of government securities may be particularly unstable in the face of a constant money stock, since other forms of credit such as bank loans tend to be conventionally priced. The 'lock-in' effect does exert some counter influence.

prices and desired income and prices. Friedman, however, has shown elsewhere that the Board's behaviour is not nicely determined by counter cyclical requirements.

A third way in which money may be linked to income is through the international regulatory mechanism. Under an old-fashioned gold standard system, for example, the level of the money stock is partly a consequence, as well as a cause, of the level of activity. Again, the argument may be applied to money and consumption. High consumption means high imports, less goods available for export, and, hence, a deterioration in the balance of payments. The stock of money is affected, since it is related to the gold reserves, and, assuming that the demand for money is interest-elastic, in raising short-term rates to replenish the reserves, the central bank maintains the stock of money below its initial level.

In the United Kingdom, over the period considered in this paper, there was a large variation in monetary conditions. During the early years up to 1914, Britain was on a not-very-close approximation to a classical gold standard. Domestic crises were met by the 'Lombard Street' rule of lending without stint. At the same time, the stock of money depended on a gold reserve base, which had to be maintained by adjusting the Bank Rate. With a deteriorating foreign exchange position, the Bank Rate was frequently used for this purpose. The balance of payments, then, affected the stock of money, especially since, as has been shown elsewhere,[4] the demand for money was interest-elastic over this period. If the balance of payments depended partly on the levels of domestic consumption and prices, the money stock was influenced by consumption, itself a function of money. However, it is safe to assume that many of the foreign exchange disturbances were brought about by exogenous forces such as a failure of harvests, a capital export boom, etc. Therefore, it seems fair to give the stock of money a high degree of exogeneity.

During the inter-war years the situation was rather less clear. Until 1925, the quantity of money was regulated with the long-run aim of getting back on the gold standard. Monetary stringency was a consequence of this policy, not of inflation. A reduction in the price level was not followed by easy money. The pseudo gold standard conditions persisted until 1931 when the period of cheap

[4] Walters, A. A., and Kavanagh, N. J., 'Demand for Money in the United Kingdom 1877–1962' (Birmingham University Discussion Paper, Series A, no. 48, 1964). [See Reading 8.]

money began. It is probably wrong to regard the stock of money after 1931 as exogenous to domestic conditions, and hence consumption.

We examine below the possibility of a lag in the effect of money on consumption. This helps to separate the creation of money by the government in response to existing or immediately past domestic conditions from the lagged effects of money on consumption. This partly solves the problem of the exogeneity of money, though it does not solve the problem of interpretation completely because of autocorrelation in the series for consumption. It is worth noting that it is the period before the First World War which fits a quantity theory best.

Definition of autonomous expenditure

There are more theoretical and practical problems in defining autonomous expenditure for the purpose of Keynesian analysis. Friedman and Meiselman take the text-book version treating investment, the excess of exports over imports and a suitably defined government deficit as exogenous. For policy purposes, it is clear that control of any of these elements gives some control over the level of income. But this does not necessarily mean that in the historical record the government has, in fact, determined these exogenously, or that these magnitudes were determined by outside forces.

In the *General Theory*, Keynes argued that investment was largely autonomous. In her recent work in the Keynesian tradition, Mrs Robinson makes investment depend on the 'animal spirits' of entrepreneurs. Aginst this view, accelerator theorists believe that much of investment is determined by expectations about future demand, and that these expectations are best measured by past changes in output. Here we keep to the simple assumption that private investment is exogenous.

Imports and exports depend partly on the relationship between foreign and domestic prices, and the levels of domestic and foreign demand. Imports are clearly related to domestic demand. For example, suppose an increase in investment generates an increase in demand for goods and services, some of which is directed towards imports, especially as home prices rise. Exports are likely to fall at the same time, so that with imports up and exports down, the increase in investment is partly offset by a fall in investment abroad. We are left, however, with increased income and imports, and reduced exports. It is possible, therefore, that imports are positively, and exports negatively, related to income, and hence the excess of exports over imports negatively related. This means that the balance of the current overseas account is a consequence of domestic multipliers. On the other hand, if variations in imports and exports are largely due to overseas disturbances which are independent of the domestic behaviour of the United Kingdom, or perhaps due to chance variations in the United Kingdom such as bad harvests, changes in tastes, etc., we are justified in taking the overseas balance as an autonomous, though uncontrolled, variable. We do not have separate figures for imports over the period considered, but examination of the data does not reveal a negative relationship between the overall balance of payments and income. Consequently, we make the balance autonomous. In other words we argue that foreign disturbances and opportunities, and exogenous variations in circumstances at home, were much more important than variations in domestic incomes in determining the level of overseas investment.

A question of endogeneity also arises with respect to the behaviour of the government. The expenditure of public authorities is for the most part determined independently of the level of income. On the other hand, revenue of public authorities and transfers may be regarded as endogenous. On the revenue side of the combined public authorities' account, receipts from taxation are a consequence of tax rates applied to current incomes and expenditures. Although the government determines the tax rates, the actual receipts are largely a result of the level of income. Since direct taxation is progressive, an increase of income, which does not involve a redistribution to low income groups, gives a more than proportionate increase in revenue from direct taxation, given the tax rates. For customs and excise duties, since luxury goods are highly taxed, a similar relationship is likely to hold. Against this, local authorities' revenue from rates increases less than proportionately to higher income. For total public authorities' revenue it seems a good approximation to make it a linear function of income.

With transfers it is less safe to assume a linear relationship with income. Net transfers abroad from the private sector are small enough to be neglected, leaving transfers from the government to the private sector. One expects variations in unemployment benefits to be in the opposite direction to income changes, and much more than proportionate in size. Other transfers, like pensions, are unlikely to vary much with income. We assume that net transfers to the private sector are linearly related to income, probably negatively, so that public authorities' revenue and net transfers from the private sector together are a positive linear function of income.

Hence the basic difference between Friedman and Meiselman's definition and ours is that we consider public authorities' revenue endogenous, i.e., a linear function of gross national product.[5] Apart from theoretical reasons for our definition, it is more convenient given those United Kingdom data which are available over a long period.

Consider a three-sector model consisting of government, private sector and abroad. Let suffixes denote the direction of purchasing payments and double suffixes the origin and direction of transfer payments, e.g., *Ca* represents consumers' expenditure on imported goods and services.

Expenditure:

Consumers' expenditure	$C = Cp + Cg + Ca$
Gross private domestic investment	$I = Ip + Ia$
Government expenditure	$G = Gp + Gg + Ga$
Exports	$E = Ep.$

Expenditure generating consumers' expenditure:

$$= Cp + Ip + Gp + Ep$$
$$= C + I + G + E - N - (Cg + Gg)$$

where

$$N = \text{Imports} = Ca + Ia + Ga.$$

Allowance for transfers: Net transfers from the private sector (including taxation)

$$T = Tpg + Tpa - Tgp - Tap.$$

Assume

$$T + Cg + Gg = tY + t'$$

[5] It seems that a number of economists have taken this objection to the Friedman–Meiselman formulation. Professors Modigliani and Ando, and Mayor and Andrano have produced papers arguing this point.

where t, and t' are constants,

$$\begin{aligned} Y &= \text{Gross national product} \\ &= C + I + G + E - N \\ C &= k(C + I + G + E - N - tY - t') + k' \\ &= k(1 - t)(C + I + G + E - N) + (k' - kt') \\ &= \frac{k(1 - t)}{1 - k(1 - t)}(I + G + E - N) + k'', \end{aligned}$$

and k, k', and k'' are constants.

Consequently, we define autonomous expenditure as

$$I + G + (E - N) = Y - C.$$

Note that (a)

$$T + Cg + Gg = tY + t' \qquad (1)$$

expresses the assumption that public authorities' revenue is endogenous. Hence gross public authorities' revenue, including inter-department or nationalized industry payments, has been taken as endogenous. It is assumed that expenditure on government produced goods and services, $(Cg + Gg)$, is either linearly related to G.N.P. or small enough to be neglected.

(b) The factor t increases over long periods, but this is not of serious consequence. For example, suppose $k = 0{\cdot}2$, initially $t = 0{\cdot}05$ and finally, $t = 0{\cdot}1$. With k constant, the multiplier varies from 0·235 to 0·220.

Some quantity theory expectations

With a simple quantity theory hypothesis:

$$\begin{aligned} Y^d &= \alpha M + \alpha_0 \\ Y^d &= C + A. \end{aligned}$$

Hence,

$$C = \alpha M - A + \alpha_0.$$

In other words, if the demand for money depends on disposable income, and not consumption, in this simple model, the expected value of the coefficient of autonomous expenditure when consumption is regressed on money and autonomous expenditure is minus one. If the value of the coefficient exceeds minus one, this is evidence of the existence of a Keynesian effect. This suggests it is misleading to interpret $r_{CA.M} = 0$ as the null hypothesis for the Keynesian theory.

To see this point more clearly, suppose we have a linear combination of both Keynesian and monetary models, i.e., let us suppose that the real world is 100δ per cent Keynesian and $100(1-\delta)$ per cent pure monetary, where $0 \leqslant \delta \leqslant 1$. Then we get:

Monetary equation:

$$C = \alpha M - A + \alpha_0$$

Keynesian equation:

$$C = \gamma A + \gamma_0$$

Combined equation:

$$\begin{aligned} C &= \delta(\gamma A + \gamma_0) + (1-\delta)(\alpha M - A + \alpha_0) \\ &= (1-\delta)\,\alpha M + [\delta(\gamma + 1) - 1]\,A + \text{constants.} \end{aligned}$$

It is still not easy to interpret the precise implications of the coefficients of the combined equation. Consider, for example, the monetary case where $\delta \to 0$. If the coefficient of autonomous expenditure is close to zero, the Keynesian multiplier must be very large! A near zero coefficient for autonomous expenditure may thus be consistent with a very large pseudo Keynesian multiplier, even in a 'pure' monetary model. One simple interpretation appears if the model is 'pure' Keynesian with $\delta = 1$. Then we have the result: γ = coefficient of autonomous expenditure. This is one of the few 'natural' interpretations.

Suppose, however, one argues, as do Friedman and Meiselman, that part of any positive relationship between consumption and autonomous expenditure is due to the fact that autonomous expenditure is itself positively related to money.[6] One should then eliminate the effect of money from the autonomous expenditure variable. The model then becomes:

$$Y^d = \alpha M + \alpha_0$$

$$Y^d = C + A$$

$$A = \beta M + A^*$$

[6] Empirical tests on United States data show the relationship is slight except for the inter-war years.

where A^* is *true* autonomous expenditure (i.e., autonomous of the stock of money). Then

$$C = (\alpha - \beta)\, M - A^* + \alpha_0.$$

Whether $r_{CA.M}$ is positive or negative depends on the covariance over time of the deviations from the mean of A^* and $C - (\alpha - \beta)\, M$. Consider the simple stochastic model

$$Y^d = \alpha M + \alpha_0 + u$$

where u is a random variable with zero mean. This is a statistical version of the simple quantity theory. Suppose also that autonomous expenditure is related to money via a stochastic relationship. Then

$$A = \beta M + \beta_0 + v$$

where v is a random variable with zero mean. We can write the quantity theory equation as:

$$C + \beta M + \beta_0 + v = \alpha M + \alpha_0 + u.$$

Thus

$$C = (\alpha - \beta)\, M - \beta_0 + \alpha_0 + (u - v).$$

The disturbance is the term $(u - v)$ in this equation.

One may consider with Friedman and Meiselman that the null hypothesis is a zero correlation between the residual of the regression of C on M, treating A implicitly as part of the residual, and the residual of the regression of A on M, i.e., $u - (A - \bar{A})$ and v. The covariance is

$$\sum uv - \sum (A - \bar{A})\, v = \sum uv - \sum v^2$$

since v is the residual in the elementary regression of A on M. Thus, the condition for a zero partial correlation coefficient $r_{CA.M}$ is that

$$\sum uv = \sum v^2.$$

This implies that an increase in truly autonomous expenditure, holding money constant, is associated with a higher income. This is because, in this case, the increase in truly autonomous expenditure does not effect consumption. Therefore, it increases income by the increase in autonomous expenditure. In other words, $r_{CA.M} = 0$ is a Keynesian case with a multiplier of unity.

Now consider the case where $r_{CA.M} > 0$. It follows that

$$\sum uv > \sum v^2.$$

Clearly this is the Keynesian case with a multiplier exceeding unity. If, on the other hand, $r_{CA.M} < 0$, we get

$$\sum uv < \sum v^2.$$

Of course, $\sum uv$ may still be positive though less than $\sum v^2$. If $0 < \sum uv < \sum v^2$, then we can interpret the result as a Keynesian model with a multiplier positive but less than unity. Thus, $r_{CA.M} < 0$ is consistent with a weak Keynesian multiplier. It does not imply a perversion of the autonomous expenditure effect.

Lags in the system

Lags may be introduced into both quantity theory and Keynesian models on the basis of Friedman's permanent income hypothesis. Friedman has effectively argued that consumption depends on permanent income which is in turn determined by current and past incomes. With permanent income proportional to a geometrically weighted average of past incomes, we get

$$C_t = \gamma Y_t + \mu C_{t-1} \tag{1}$$

where Y_t is gross national product with our definition of autonomous expenditure, and disposable income with Friedman and Meiselman's definition. Consumption in year t depends on autonomous expenditure in year t and consumption in the previous year $(t-1)$.

The alternative monetary multiplier model is also one suggested by Friedman. The demand for money is related to permanent income, which is again proportional to a geometrically weighted average of past incomes.

$$M_t^d = v(Y_t + \lambda Y_{t-1} + \lambda^2 Y_{t-2} + \cdots). \tag{2}$$

If the economy is always on the demand curve, the supply of money, taken as exogenous, determines the level of income, i.e.,

$$Y_t = \frac{1}{v}(M_t - \lambda M_{t-1}). \tag{3}$$

In principle, then, one should include in the monetary model the past year's money stock as a determinant of this year's income.[7]

[7] The empirical implications of the permanent income model of the demand for money have been discussed in detail in Walters, A. A., 'Professor Friedman on the Demand for Money', *Journal of Political Economy*, vol. 73, no. 5 (October 1965), pp. 545–51.

We can put these two alternative models into a form useful for our tests.

Keynesian model:

$$C_t = \frac{1}{1-\gamma}(\gamma A_t + \mu C_{t-1}), \text{ from (1)} \tag{4}$$

where $\gamma > 0$ and $0 < \mu < 1$.

Monetary model:

$$C_t = \frac{1}{\nu}(M_t - \lambda M_{t-1}) - A_t, \text{ from (3)} \tag{5}$$

where $\nu > 0$ and $0 < \lambda < 1$.

One interesting aspect of these equations is that when we use the permanent income hypothesis for the demand for money, a negative relationship between consumption and autonomous expenditure, as well as a negative association of consumption with the level of the money stock in the previous year, is implied. In the Keynesian model, the coefficient of autonomous expenditure is positive. Again, in the monetary model the expected value of the coefficient of A_t is minus one and *not* zero.

To test these models by a single equation technique requires that one take a linear combination of the two models and examine the fitted coefficients. Thus with $0 \leqslant \delta \leqslant 1$, we multiply the Keynesian model by δ and the monetary model by $(1-\delta)$ and add:

$$C_t = \frac{\delta\gamma}{1-\gamma}A_t + \frac{\delta\mu}{1-\gamma}C_{t-1} + \frac{1-\delta}{\nu}M_t - \frac{(1-\delta)\lambda}{\nu}M_{t-1} - (1-\delta)A_t. \tag{6}$$

A one equation test of the model would thus fit the equation

$$C_t = \alpha_1 M_t + \alpha_2 M_{t-1} + \alpha_3 A_t + \alpha_4 C_{t-1} \tag{7}$$

where

$$\alpha_1 = \frac{1-\delta}{\nu}$$

$$\alpha_2 = -\left(\frac{1-\delta}{\nu}\right)\lambda$$

$$\alpha_3 = \frac{\delta}{1-\gamma} - 1$$

$$\alpha_4 = \frac{\delta\mu}{1-\gamma}.$$

The test will then depend on the values of the coefficients α_i ($i = 1, 2, 3, 4$). If $\delta = 0$, then we expect the coefficients to take values:

$$\alpha_1 > 0$$
$$\alpha_2 < 0$$
$$\alpha_3 = -1$$
$$\alpha_4 = 0.$$

This is the outcome of a pure monetary process where the multiplier effects of the current year's autonomous expenditure and the past year's consumption have been ousted by the money variables. Again, in the pure monetary case, the coefficient of autonomous expenditure is minus one. This is curious, but, on the assumptions made, it is correct expectation for this coefficient. As before, a value of zero for α_3 does not imply that there are no Keynesian effects. On the contrary, it implies that some positive value should be attributed to the coefficient δ. If, for example, the value of γ is that revealed by Stone's researches,[8] i.e., $\gamma = 0{\cdot}56$, a value of zero for α_3 would give

$$0 = \frac{\delta}{1 - 0{\cdot}56} - 1$$

i.e., $\delta = 0{\cdot}44$. This implies that the model is '44 per cent Keynesian'.

A more profound and satisfactory test would try to trace the whole complex chain of reactions from an exogenous change in expenditure, say 'animal spirits' investment, to effects on consumption, prices, and the balance of trade. Then, with interim effects on investment via the accelerator, to loss of gold and foreign currency requiring monetary stringency, the effects of induced investment, and perhaps a down-turn due to monetary stringency, credit rationing, and the playing out of the accelerator effect. A complete dynamic model is beyond present statistical resources.

Since our money series is end-of-year, consumers' expenditure has been lagged six months behind money for most of our tests. Examination of the data suggests that this is a reasonable lag, and a six-month lag is also rather inconclusively suggested by Friedman and Meiselman's tests on quarterly data. Some tests were also

[8] Stone, Richard, 'Private Saving in Britain, Past, Present and Future', *Manchester School*, vol. 32 (May 1964), pp. 79–112.

carried out with two yearly averages of the end-of-year series to make the money variable concurrent with the expenditure variables, and the results are included. A less comprehensive series, averages of monthly figures, based on clearing bank net deposits, gave results similar to those for the end-of-year series.

Inter-relationship of money and autonomous expenditure

The two explanatory variables are likely to be correlated for several reasons:

(1) Private domestic investment is partly financed by borrowing from the banks, an inflation of whose assets is liable to be reflected in comparable changes in deposits.

(2) Public authorities' expenditure is related to public authorities' deficit spending, some of which may be financed by borrowing from the non-financial institution private sector, but the rest of which (apart from overseas borrowing) must be financed by borrowing from the financial institutions or increasing currency in circulation with the public. Banks are either directly affected or advance more to other financial institutions, and both increases in bank assets and in currency are reflected in money. The mechanism by which banks are persuaded to take up government bonds may include making more liquid assets available.

(3) Exports are also partly financed by bank borrowing, under Export Credit Guarantee Department arrangements or otherwise. Considering the likelihood of multicollinearity, the standard errors when both variables are included in the equation are small. One advantage of the six-month lag is that it minimizes the risk of multicollinearity. While consumers' expenditure is related to money at the end of the previous year, changes in money due to changes in autonomous expenditure are not registered until the end of the current year.

The series

The expenditure figures are largely Feinstein's latest estimates as published in 'The Times Review of Industry', June 1964. The First World War gap has been filled with figures taken from the 'Abstract of Historical Statistics' by Mitchell and Dean, but these are used in only one of the periods considered, namely 1879 to

1938. These First World War figures are rough. For gross national product, for example, Prest's estimates of net national income, based on bank clearings, have been raised proportionately.

The starting point is 1878 because the Kavanagh end-of-year money series begins in 1877. The money series is a new one, separately compiled from the year 1891, in the course of collecting an aggregate United Kingdom bank balance sheet for the period 1891 to 1962. These figures, based on exploratory work done by N. J. Kavanagh, have slightly wider coverage than the Kavanagh money series. They include the joint stock banks of England and Wales, Scotland and, until the end of 1918, Southern Ireland; the three Northern Irish banks from the end of 1919; 'The Economist's' private banks, and the joint stock banks of the Isle of Man and the Channel Islands until included among the joint stock banks of England and Wales; Yorkshire Penny Bank, British Bank of Northern Commerce and Hambros, Birmingham Municipal Bank, and the banking departments of the Cooperative Wholesale Society and the Scottish Cooperative Wholesale Society. In addition, notes and coin have been included throughout. The figures are as far as possible end of year, but occasionally balance sheets with varying dates over the year, or on 31 March of the following year, have had to be used. The earlier Kavanagh series figures have been spliced onto this series.

The break with the exclusion of Southern Ireland has been made consistent with the expenditure series, but apart from this, movements in the series are close to those in the Kavanagh series.

As well as the money series described, we have experimented with a wider definition of money, with similar but not as good results. This series consists of currency, bank deposits, Post Office and Trustee Savings Banks' deposits, building societies' shares and deposits and hire purchase finance companies' deposits. We have also tried two alternative definitions of autonomous expenditure. Defining it as net national product minus consumers' expenditure is theoretically justifiable, since then we assume that consumers, given their money balances, divide receipts between consumption and saving after allowance for depreciation has been made. However, much worse results were obtained with this definition; one possible explanation being that net national product figures are not as accurate as gross national product figures. Secondly, we tried taking gross domestic investment only as autonomous, and again results did not confirm this choice.

The periods

Five periods have been examined:

1878–1914, 1920–38, and 1948–63;
1878–1914;
1921–38;
1948–63; and
1879–1938.

The Second World War years have been completely excluded due to their exceptional nature, involving shortages, rationing, patriotic appeals to save, and general economic dislocation. Similarly, the First World War years have been excluded from all but one of the periods. The points at which rough normality is taken to be resumed were determined by examination of the data, but there is doubt how much of the post-war period can be taken as normal.

The empirical results

Transformation to logarithms is used to make the earlier figures comparable with the later, and results are also given for the logarithmic series differenced to eliminate trend.

A

Definitions

$C(t)$ = Consumers' expenditure in year t,

$M(t-1)$ = Money at end of year $t-1$, and

$A(t) = Y(t) - C(t)$, where $Y(t) = GNP$ at market prices,

= Autonomous expenditure in year t.

Logarithms are denoted by small letters.

$$\delta^2/S^2 = \text{Durbin Watson statistic.}$$

1878–1914, 1920–38, and 1948–63:

$$c(t) = \underset{(0{\cdot}09)}{1{\cdot}54} + \underset{(0{\cdot}011)}{0{\cdot}860}\, m(t-1)$$

$$\bar{R}^2 = 0{\cdot}988 \qquad \delta^2/S^2 = 0{\cdot}22$$

$$c(t) = \underset{(0{\cdot}08)}{3{\cdot}06} + \underset{(0{\cdot}012)}{0{\cdot}739}\, \alpha(t)$$

$$\bar{R}^2 = 0{\cdot}983 \qquad \delta^2/S^2 = 0{\cdot}32$$

$$\Delta c(t) = \underset{(0{\cdot}0024)}{0{\cdot}0109} + \underset{(0{\cdot}132)}{0{\cdot}456}\, \Delta m(t-1)$$

$$\bar{R}^2 = 0{\cdot}139 \qquad \delta^2/S^2 = 0{\cdot}89$$

$$\Delta c(t) = \underset{(0{\cdot}0012)}{0{\cdot}0125} + \underset{(0{\cdot}037)}{0{\cdot}214}\, \Delta \alpha(t)$$

$$\bar{R}^2 = 0{\cdot}328 \qquad \delta^2/S^2 = 1{\cdot}53$$

For the overall period, there is a much better fit with autonomous expenditure in the case of differences, and less autocorrelation for the autonomous expenditure equations.

$$c(t) = \underset{(0{\cdot}08)}{2{\cdot}16} + \underset{(0{\cdot}037)}{0{\cdot}486}\, m(t-1) + \underset{(0{\cdot}032)}{0{\cdot}328}\, \alpha(t)$$

$$\bar{R}^2 = 0{\cdot}995 \qquad \delta^2/S^2 = 0{\cdot}39$$

$$r^2_{12\cdot3} = 0{\cdot}714 \qquad r^2_{13\cdot2} = 0{\cdot}607$$

$$\Delta c(t) = \underset{(0{\cdot}0022)}{0{\cdot}0053} + \underset{(0{\cdot}106)}{0{\cdot}406}\, \Delta m(t-1) + \underset{(0{\cdot}033)}{0{\cdot}204}\, \Delta \alpha(t)$$

$$\bar{R}^2 = 0{\cdot}442 \qquad \delta^2/S^2 = 1{\cdot}45$$

$$r^2_{12\cdot3} = 0{\cdot}181 \qquad r^2_{13\cdot2} = 0{\cdot}361$$

When both autonomous expenditure and money are included in the equation, autonomous expenditure again has a relatively smaller standard error in the difference case, but even in the difference equation, both coefficients are significant, R^2 is reasonably high and there is little autocorrelation. The coefficients suggest that a one per cent increase in the money stock at the end of a year leads to a 0·4 per cent increase in consumers' expenditure the following year, while a one per cent increase in autonomous expenditure causes a 0·2 per cent increase the same year. The partial correlation coefficients, however, indicate much greater variability in autonomous expenditure than in money over the period.

Later, it is shown that the overall period consists of three very different periods, so that more significance is to be attached to the regressions for each separately.

1878–1914:

$$c(t) = 2{\cdot}27 + 0{\cdot}595\, m(t-1) + 0{\cdot}181\, \alpha(t)$$
$$(0{\cdot}17)\quad (0{\cdot}057) \qquad\qquad (0{\cdot}041)$$

$$\bar{R}^2 = 0{\cdot}983 \qquad \delta^2/S^2 = 0{\cdot}49$$

$$r^2_{12\cdot3} = 0{\cdot}763 \qquad r^2_{13\cdot2} = 0{\cdot}367$$

$$\Delta c(t) = 0{\cdot}0031 + 0{\cdot}576\, \Delta m(t-1) + 0{\cdot}087\, \Delta\alpha(t)$$
$$(0{\cdot}0020)\quad (0{\cdot}088) \qquad\qquad (0{\cdot}031)$$

$$\bar{R}^2 = 0{\cdot}579 \qquad \delta^2/S^2 = 1{\cdot}87$$

$$r^2_{12\cdot3} = 0{\cdot}564 \qquad r^2_{13\cdot2} = 0{\cdot}197$$

Money is much more significant than autonomous expenditure before the First World War. The coefficients for money are higher than for the overall period, those for autonomous expenditure are lower, but still significant. The worse fit with autonomous expenditure may be partly caused by inaccuracies in the data, since before the First World War, the money series is likely to be more accurate than the autonomous expenditure series. However, we get a high $\bar{R}^2$ and little autocorrelation for the difference equation.

1921–1938:

$$c(t) = 5{\cdot}41 + 0{\cdot}163\, m(t-1) + 0{\cdot}232\, \alpha(t)$$
$$(0{\cdot}40)\quad (0{\cdot}063) \qquad\qquad (0{\cdot}030)$$

$$\bar{R}^2 = 0{\cdot}900 \qquad \delta^2/S^2 = 1{\cdot}95$$

$$r^2_{12\cdot3} = 0{\cdot}312 \qquad r^2_{13\cdot2} = 0{\cdot}803$$

$$\Delta c(t) = -0{\cdot}0027 + 0{\cdot}250\, \Delta m(t-1) + 0{\cdot}194\, \Delta\alpha(t)$$
$$(0{\cdot}0012)\quad (0{\cdot}133) \qquad\qquad (0{\cdot}038)$$

$$\bar{R}^2 = 0{\cdot}678 \qquad \delta^2/S^2 = 1{\cdot}89$$

$$r^2_{12\cdot3} = 0{\cdot}202 \qquad r^2_{13\cdot2} = 0{\cdot}650$$

Initially, the year 1920 was included in this sample, but this was found to be an error. When it was excluded, much higher correlation coefficients were obtained, even with autonomous expenditure alone, and the money variable became significant.

For this period, the R^2s are exceptionally high[9] and there is little autocorrelation in either equation. The inter-war years are strongly Keynesian, considering the much better fit and higher partial correlation coefficient with autonomous expenditure in each case. The money coefficient is smaller than the autonomous expenditure coefficient in the logarithmic regression, but larger in the logarithmic difference regression, indicating once again greater variability in the autonomous expenditure variable. For the difference regression, the money coefficient is less than half, and the autonomous expenditure coefficient more than twice, what they were in the period 1878–1914.

1948–1963:

$$c(t) = -2{\cdot}12 + 0{\cdot}763\, m(t-1) + 0{\cdot}523\, \alpha(t)$$
$$(0{\cdot}93) \quad (0{\cdot}137) \qquad\qquad (0{\cdot}041)$$

$$\bar{R}^2 = 0{\cdot}996 \qquad \delta^2/S^2 = 1{\cdot}21$$

$$r^2_{12\cdot3} = 0{\cdot}700 \qquad r^2_{13\cdot2} = 0{\cdot}925$$

With differences of logarithms we get no positive results for this period. For the logarithmic equation, the standard errors are reasonably small and δ^2/S^2 fairly high, but the results with differences suggest that the high correlation for logarithms is largely trend. For what it is worth, the fit with autonomous expenditure is noticeably better and its partial correlation coefficient higher.

1879–1938:

$$c(t) = 1{\cdot}95 + 0{\cdot}702\, m(t-1) + 0{\cdot}115\, \alpha(t)$$
$$(0{\cdot}09) \quad (0{\cdot}032) \qquad\qquad (0{\cdot}031)$$

$$\bar{R}^2 = 0{\cdot}988 \qquad \delta^2/S^2 = 0{\cdot}91$$

$$r^2_{12\cdot3} = 0{\cdot}894 \qquad r^2_{13\cdot2} = 0{\cdot}191$$

$$\Delta c(t) = -0{\cdot}0047 + 0{\cdot}838\, \Delta m(t-1) + 0{\cdot}087\, \Delta\alpha(t)$$
$$(0{\cdot}0035) \quad (0{\cdot}116) \qquad\qquad (0{\cdot}041)$$

$$\bar{R}^2 = 0{\cdot}541 \qquad \delta^2/S^2 = 1{\cdot}66$$

$$r^2_{12\cdot3} = 0{\cdot}484 \qquad r^2_{13\cdot2} = 0{\cdot}076$$

The results for this period come closest to a quantity-theory hypothesis, though we have shown earlier that under a simple

[9] There is little upward trend.

quantity-theory hypothesis, a negative coefficient for autonomous expenditure is expected, whereas both coefficients of autonomous expenditure are significantly positive. The money coefficients are higher even than for the 1878–1914 period as a consequence of including the inflationary war years. Over these years, autonomous expenditure was abnormally high to pay for the war,[10] whereas consumers' expenditure was partly held in check, although it rose steeply in money terms as a consequence of inflation. We have elsewhere excluded the war years from our periods.

B

Definitions are the same as in section A excepting: $M(t)$ = Two yearly averages of end-of-year money series.

1878–1914:

$$\underset{}{\Delta c(t)} = \underset{(0{\cdot}0041)}{0{\cdot}0030} + \underset{(0{\cdot}168)}{0{\cdot}507}\,\Delta m(t) + \underset{(0{\cdot}041)}{0{\cdot}088}\,\Delta\alpha(t)$$

$$\bar{R}^2 = 0{\cdot}243 \qquad \delta^2/S^2 = 2{\cdot}37$$

$$r^2_{12\cdot3} = 0{\cdot}216 \qquad r^2_{13\cdot2} = 0{\cdot}122$$

1921–1938:

$$\Delta c(t) = \underset{(0{\cdot}0017)}{-0{\cdot}0044} + \underset{(0{\cdot}204)}{0{\cdot}472}\,\Delta m(t) + \underset{(0{\cdot}040)}{0{\cdot}166}\,\Delta\alpha(t)$$

$$\bar{R}^2 = 0{\cdot}708 \qquad \delta^2/S^2 = 2{\cdot}07$$

$$r^2_{12\cdot3} = 0{\cdot}276 \qquad r^2_{13\cdot2} = 0{\cdot}553$$

For these tests, the money figures were averaged to make the money variable concurrent with the expenditure variables. As expected, the problem of multicollinearity increased, shown by the relatively large size of three of the four standard errors. The measured money effect for the inter-war years did become stronger. However, the degree of exogeneity of money is likely to be less for concurrent figures. One important result is that $\bar{R}^2$ for the period before the First World War is less than half of what it was with money leading consumption by six months, while it is about the same for the inter-war years. This is some confirmation for the lag chosen.

[10] Autonomous expenditure figures for the war years are also very unreliable.

Permanent income model[11]

1878–1914:

$$\Delta c(t) = 0{\cdot}0040 + 0{\cdot}568\, \Delta m(t) - 0{\cdot}171\, \Delta m(t-1)$$
$$(0{\cdot}0040)\quad (0{\cdot}116)\qquad (0{\cdot}137)$$
$$+\, 0{\cdot}078\, \Delta \alpha(t) + 0{\cdot}172\, \Delta c(t-1)$$
$$(0{\cdot}033)\qquad (0{\cdot}164)$$
$$\bar{R}^2 = 0{\cdot}436 \qquad \delta^2/S^2 = 2{\cdot}04$$
$$\lambda = 0{\cdot}03 \qquad \mu = 0{\cdot}16$$

1921–1938:

$$\Delta c(t) = 0{\cdot}0049 + 0{\cdot}118\, \Delta m(t) - 0{\cdot}092\, \Delta m(t-1)$$
$$(0{\cdot}0014)\quad (0{\cdot}087)\qquad (0{\cdot}088)$$
$$+\, 0{\cdot}128\, \Delta \alpha(t) + 0{\cdot}256\, \Delta c(t-1)$$
$$(0{\cdot}026)\qquad (0{\cdot}106)$$
$$\bar{R}^2 = 0{\cdot}788 \qquad \delta^2/S^2 = 1{\cdot}55$$
$$\lambda = 0{\cdot}78 \qquad \mu = 0{\cdot}23$$

1878–1914 and 1921–1938:

$$\Delta c(t) = 0{\cdot}0052 + 0{\cdot}378\, \Delta m(t) - 0{\cdot}050\, \Delta m(t-1)$$
$$(0{\cdot}0019)\quad (0{\cdot}078)\qquad (0{\cdot}084)$$
$$+\, 0{\cdot}101\, \Delta \alpha(t) + 0{\cdot}109\, \Delta c(t-1)$$
$$(0{\cdot}022)\qquad (0{\cdot}100)$$
$$\bar{R}^2 = 0{\cdot}506 \qquad \delta^2/S^2 = 1{\cdot}87$$
$$\lambda = 0{\cdot}13 \qquad \mu = 0{\cdot}10$$

The sizes of the standard errors make the estimation of the coefficients in the Keynesian and monetary permanent income models uncertain.

Summary

Our results suggest that both money and autonomous expenditure have been important factors in the determination of aggregate consumption. When these two are made the explanatory variables in the consumption function, high correlations are obtained for both the period before the First World War and the inter-war years.

[11] See above for definitions of symbols.

In a simple model, it is not possible to isolate exogenous factors completely, but with some reservations concerning the exogeneity of the explanatory variables, results are still striking enough to be considered significant.

Money seems to have had special importance in the relatively full-employment conditions up to the First World War. With high unemployment between the wars, and prices falling for most of the period, autonomous expenditure accounted for most of the variability in consumption. The explanatory power of both variables declines for the postwar economy. It is possible that these years are exceptional because of large liquid balances and rationing, but other reasons make one hesitate to extrapolate results for the earlier periods to modern developed economies. One is the increasing interference of the government, which by controlling the terms and availability of investment and consumer credit, and the incidence of taxation, can bring about substitution between consumption and investment. A second consideration is the development of money substitutes. The growth of financial institutions and better financial markets increases the quantity and variety of assets which can easily be exchanged for money or used as collateral in borrowing. The combined model may all the same be applicable to less developed economies.

The findings of this paper are different from those of Friedman and Meiselman. With a more orthodox definition of autonomous expenditure they found the monetary multiplier far more stable than the Keynesian multiplier. Our definition seems more satisfactory, both from initial considerations and in view of results. (We believe others in America are working on a different definition too.)[12]

Some similarities between Friedman and Meiselman's results and ours exist. It was shown above that with a quantity theory hypothesis, the expected value of the coefficient of autonomous expenditure in the regression of consumption on money and autonomous expenditure is negative. Friedman and Meiselman obtained negative coefficients for the years before the First World War, which is also the time we find closest to a quantity theory, though for the United Kingdom the coefficient for autonomous expenditure is significantly positive. For later periods, excluding war

[12] For some published results, see Hester, Donald, 'Keynes and the Quantity Theory: A Comment on the Friedman–Meiselman C.M.C. Paper', *Review of Economics and Statistics*, vol. 46, no. 4, November 1964.

years, they found positive coefficients, contrary to a pure quantity theory, and strong Keynesian effects for some of the inter-war years. The war years have been excluded from most of the periods tested in this paper and possibly results in Friedman and Meiselman's paper for periods including war years should be viewed with caution.[13]

The way in which economic theory develops seems to depend very much on economic conditions. The classical economists of the nineteenth century were more pragmatic than we sometimes think, given the economic climate, while in spite of much political resistance, the inter-war years gave us Keynesian ideas. In modern developed economies both Keynesian and quantity theories are changing in character, and our results confirm that this is necessary. With full employment, the Keynesian approach has become a dynamic theory of inflation based on aggregate supply and demand, while the greater marketability of assets leads quantity theorists into an examination of the effects on expenditure of wealth.

[13] This point is also made by Hester, ibid.

3

THE ATTEMPT TO REINSTATE MONEY

M. J. ARTIS *and* A. R. NOBAY*

Introduction

IT is now ten years since the publication of the *Radcliffe Report* (Report of the Committee on the Working of the Monetary System (Cmnd. 827)), and once again the role of monetary operations is in the forefront of discussion of macro-economic policy.

This turn of events is shot through with elements of paradox. One of the immediate reasons behind the revival of interest in monetary policy is the (alleged) deficiency of fiscal economic management policies; yet the Radcliffe Committee was itself created because of a parallel disillusionment with the previous performance of monetary policy. Again, the main focus of the current revival of interest in monetary policy is the relevance of the money supply; yet of all the aims and objects of monetary policy, control of the money was listed by the *Radcliffe Report* as about the least important. Finally, the current fashion in monetary indicators rests heavily on the recent development of comprehensive financial data, a development for which the *Radcliffe Report*—sceptical as it was of monetary policy's role—can take the main credit.

While the main reason for re-examining the part which should be played by monetary policy stems from a disillusionment with the efficacy of fiscal policies, the form of the debate has been heavily influenced by the lines of research pursued by adherents of the so-called 'Chicago School', and by the analytical procedures of the

* Extract reprinted from Artis, M. J., and Nobay, A. R., 'Two aspects of the monetary debate', *National Institute Economic Review*, no. 49, August 1969, pp. 33–42, by permission of the authors and publishers. M. J. Artis is at the National Institute of Economic and Social Research and is editor of its *Economic Review*; A. R. Nobay is at the University of Southampton.

International Monetary Fund. These two influences are certainly distinct in character; but both have in common an association with the quantity theory of money, and either—if accepted—could make for a sharp change in the focus of economic policy.

Indeed, this process seems already to have begun in Britain. The latest statement of government policy, contained in the Letter of Intent, characterizes the Government's intentions in terms not only of a target for the balance of payments and a figure of the Government's borrowing requirement—familiar concepts—but also of a maximum figure for 'domestic credit expansion' (DCE), a monetary concept quite new in its application to the United Kingdom.

The circumstances point to the need for an article of an expository character, which describes the nature of the main propositions being advanced in the debate about monetary measures and the evidence adduced in their support.

This, in fact, is the main purpose of the present article. In view of the expansion of monetary research in this country and of the already massive literature in the United States, it was tempting to cast the net widely, but limitations of time and space oblige us to leave aside much that is important and to confine our attention to two main groups of issues; these are, first, the attempt to reinstate money, and second, the concept of domestic credit expansion and its relation to money supply [for the latter, see Reading 31].

The background

A considerable mass of empirical research work has gone into attempts to reinstate the quantity theory of money (or, as some of the protagonists have more modestly described it, to re-establish that 'money matters'). These efforts have been met with an abundance of critiques and rebuttals, which have themselves resulted in counter-rebuttals; and much of the time the argument in the learned journals has been conducted at an unusually high temperature. It is virtually impossible, in the circumstances, to present a summary which is both fair and comprehensive. All that is attempted in the opening parts of this section is to give a very brief summary of the main issues involved, couched so far as possible in neutral and antiseptic terms; but it is only fair to record that it thereby fails to do full justice to the complexity of some of the issues involved, and to the passions aroused by them.

A useful simplification is to draw the following distinctions between the chief lines of argument pursued by the monetary school. First, there is an early body of work mainly devoted to indicating the length and variability of the time lags in the operation of monetary influences; the most prominent contribution here is that of Friedman and Schwartz [**21**]. Then there is a further body of work mainly devoted to trial comparisons between simple 'Keynesian' and 'quantity theory' models of the economy. The seminal contribution here is that of Friedman and Meiselman [**18**]. Finally, there is the slightly different line of argument developed recently by Andersen and Jordan [**2**], which seeks to compare the effectiveness of monetary and fiscal *policies* (where once again considerations of the time lags involved is an important side-issue).

The basic points which the protagonists of the monetary school sought to establish in the earliest of the three main bodies of work distinguished in the previous paragraph concerned both the length of the lag between changes in monetary factors and changes in the level of economic activity, and its great variability. Whilst the article by Friedman and Schwartz [**21**] represented the first published comprehensive account of these factors, there had been earlier contributions by Friedman on the same subject, which led in 1960–61 to an exchange of views between him and Culbertson in the *Journal of Political Economy* [**9**, **10**, **16**]. The major points of contention then, as later in the critique by Kareken and Solow [**27**], concerned the way in which the lag was measured, and the interpretation to be attached to the evidence of association between 'money' and 'economic activity'—and in particular, whether such evidence justified the inference of a 'causal' relationship running from 'money' to 'economic activity'.

The measurement of the lag in the Friedman–Schwartz contribution proceeded essentially from an inspection of time series of growth rates of the money supply against turning points in economic activity. Friedman and Schwartz concluded that the troughs and peaks in the cycles of economic activity lagged by 12–18 months (respectively) behind previous troughs or peaks in the rate of growth of money supply. However, these average lags concealed great instability: the standard deviation of the twelve-month lag between troughs was six months; and of the eighteen-month lag between peaks, seven months. The first main point at issue in the exchange with Culbertson, and later in the critique by Kareken and Solow concerned the identification of the lag.

The critics argued that if there were a close association between money supply and economic activity, the causal link might well go the other way—changes in economic activity causing the money supply to adapt itself accordingly. Suppose that this adaptation occurred with little delay; then, their argument went, the peak in economic activity will be preceded by a phase of faster *growth* in economic activity; so it must also be preceded by a phase of faster growth in the money supply. Thus one would expect to find a lag of the kind identified by Friedman and Schwartz between changes in the rate of growth of the money supply and subsequent peaks or troughs in economic activity. But this would not be proof that the former caused the latter; on the contrary the association could equally well indicate a causation the other way round.

Although, in his exchange with Culbertson, Friedman cited some reasons of statistical convenience for measuring the lag in the way described, the other reasons cited then and developed later in his contribution with Schwartz turned on a particular economic rationale of the transmission of monetary influences to the 'real' economy, a rationale which—if accepted—would validate the procedures employed. This matter of the acceptance, or otherwise, of a rationale, underlies much of the debate which has ensued since then; without a plausible and acceptable account of the mechanisms involved, no amount of statistical measurement can (nor should) be conclusive in gaining acceptance for the 'monetary' model.

The next development of the monetarist 'view' occurred with the publication of an article by Friedman and Meiselman [**18**] which sought to confront two simple models of the economy—a quantity theory model, on the one hand, and an autonomous expenditures ('Keynesian') model, on the other. The form which this exercise took, in brief, was to compare the performance of 'money supply' and of 'autonomous expenditures' in explaining the level of consumption. Data were used over a long period of time, from 1897 to 1958, for the main calculations. In this confrontation, Friedman and Meiselman claimed to demonstrate the superiority of their quantity theory model over their autonomous expenditures model. A substantial volume of critical work was provoked by this contribution; (see in particular the articles by Hester [**24**, **25**], Ando, and Modigliani [**4**, **5**], and Deprano and Mayer [**13**, **14**], and the replies by Friedman and Meiselman [**19**, **20**]). Probably the most important criticisms raised were: that the confrontation of single equation models was not and could not be a valid test of any substantial macro-economic hypothesis (and that the Keynesian framework had yielded complicated structural elaborations and econometric models superior to the simplified autonomous expenditure model used by Friedman and Meiselman); that, in any case, their specification of autonomous expenditures was inappropriate and different specifications yielded different, and in some cases superior results; and that the relative performance of the monetary and autonomous expenditures models (especially when the latter were adjusted to different definitions) differed greatly in different time periods, and in particular that in more recent periods the monetary model had no clear superiority, and on some definitions of 'autonomous expenditures' was inferior. Again, some critics raised the question whether association of economic variables like consumption with money permitted any unique causal inference.

All the empirical work mentioned so far referred to various periods in the history of the United States. Barrett and Walters [**8**] subsequently published an application of the Friedman–Meiselman procedure (slightly amended) to the United Kingdom. As in the Friedman–Meiselman case, the task was to explain consumption (or changes in it) by reference to money supply or autonomous expenditures (or changes in them). Barrett and Walters laid greatest stress on the results of equations relating changes in consumption to changes in money supply or autonomous expenditures; they concluded that there were considerable differences in the periods they examined. The greater significance of money in the period 1878–1914 was reversed in the 'inter-war years' (1921–1938) which were strongly 'Keynesian'; and for the post-war period 1948–1963, they reported that they were unable to obtain good results for either money or autonomous expenditures. This led them to suggest that certain features of the modern economy—in particular the development of a range of assets performing as close substitutes for money and government control of investment and consumer finances—probably made the application of the simple models employed untenable in the modern context.

The most recent development of the monetarist view has been the work of Andersen and Jordan of the St. Louis Federal Reserve Bank [**2**]. They set out to test the relative effectiveness and time lags associated with monetary and fiscal policy. In the context of recent economic policy in the United States this departure was of course a timely one; and its results—given acceptance of the economic judgements and statistical procedures applied—demonstrated a more powerful effect of monetary policy than of fiscal policy, and failed to confirm that fiscal measures were either faster-acting or more reliable than monetary measures.

Criticism has already been published of the Andersen–Jordan analysis, notably in articles by De Leeuw and Kalchbrenner [12] and by Davis [11].[1] Some of this criticism runs along lines already familiar from critiques of the earlier developments of the monetarist view. For example, the very simplicity of the equations tested by Andersen and Jordan has been characterized as a defect in itself: this echoes an earlier criticism of the Friedman–Meiselman approach. The basic form of the equations employed was to relate quarterly changes in GNP to quarterly changes in monetary and fiscal policy variables, plus a constant term, determined by the estimation procedure and taken as representing (the average of) all other influences on GNP in so far as these were not reflected in the fiscal and monetary policy variables themselves. That the specified variables standing in for fiscal and monetary policy might not be free of such influences, as they should be, was the burden of a main part of the critical argument brought to bear on the analysis. Andersen and Jordan employed as measures of fiscal policy, changes in the 'full employment' budget surplus, and 'full employment' expenditures and revenues, and as measures of monetary policy, changes in money supply and in the monetary base (currency plus bank reserves adjusted for legal reserve requirements). Criticisms of these measures most importantly involved the characterization of monetary policy: it was argued that the change in money supply (and perhaps the change in monetary base) was not an appropriate exogenous variable, but partly reflected influences running from GNP to money. It was also shown that the relative performance of fiscal and monetary policy, as characterized, varied according to the period chosen (Andersen and Jordan used quarterly data for the period 1952 I—1968 II) and that assertions about the relative lags in effectiveness turned on the statistical method of estimation employed.

As a preliminary summing up, it seems fair to assert that the monetarist school have succeeded, at a minimum, in establishing the fact of a 'gross' association (to use the felicitous expression of a recent participant in the debate—see [11]) between money and macro-economic variables like consumption or GNP and economic activity generally. Although the extent to which even this minimal

[1] But see Andersen, L. C., and Jordan, J. L. [2] for a counter-reply.

claim holds good depends upon a weighting of different periods in history (recent or long past), it is an achievement which readily explains the extent to which, in popular and much informed opinion, the monetarist view has been able recently to make the running—especially given the embarrassment in which more orthodox views of economic policy, both here and in the United States, have been finding themselves. Alternative explanations of the apparent failure of orthodox policies and the forecasting techniques associated with them have been to some extent crowded out in consequence.

But the full claims of the monetarist school extend far beyond demonstrating a gross association of money with 'economic activity'; in the monetarist view this demonstration is a confirmation, rather, of an underlying theoretical view. That view is more sophisticated than the naive quantity theory, which requires short-term stability in the income velocity of circulation to establish a direct and proportional relationship between money supply and income. Such stability does not exist, certainly not within the narrow tolerances required for policy purposes. The new view is less sharply defined; but at its core there is still the assertion that money supply (or changes in it, or its rate of growth) is the primary causative factor leading to fluctuations in income. However, far from running their course quickly, the causal influences take a long, and varying, time to act themselves out. Hence the central assertion about the primacy of money supply does not result in a policy prescription for 'fine-tuning' by the monetary authorities; the forecasting ability which this prescription would require, especially given the variability of the time lags involved, does not exist. Friedman has argued, on the contrary, that the characteristics of monetary influences make out a good case for the policy makers to eschew—as a matter of policy—attempts at discretionary 'fine-tuning'; instead they should rest content with ensuring a steady rate of growth in money supply [**17**].

Some problems

The gap between the demonstration of a 'gross' association of money and economic activity and the radical changes in policy suggested is obviously a large one, and seems likely to remain so until the important questions of the primacy and exogeneity of money and the 'transmission mechanism' are settled.

This question whether the supply of money should be regarded as exogenous is a fundamental one. Unfortunately, the term 'exogenous' tends to be used in more than one way. In text book expositions it is common to make the demand for money endogenous—dependent on other economic variables—and then to assert that the supply of money is fixed by the 'authorities', i.e. the Government or the Central Bank as the case might be. In so far as the supply of money cannot be other than the authorities allow it to be, it is to that extent 'exogenous' or 'autonomous'; but it is open to the authorities deliberately to adopt a passive or 'accommodating' policy whereby, for example, they invariably increase or decrease the supply of money in response to changes in demand. Such a policy might be appropriate if the authorities wish to stabilize interest rates.[2] In such a case the money supply becomes, in terms of model specification *de facto* endogenous.

This does not mean that in such circumstances changes in the money supply, when they occur, cease to have the kind of influences which are expected from them when the changes are strictly exogenous; but because the changes are not independent of fluctuations in national income, statistical procedures to test this independent influence are likely to give a biased estimate of it. In other words, it is likely to be difficult to sort out the impact of income on money, from the impact of money on income (or, alternatively, to sort out the dependence of each on some third factor). In principle, a set of relationships is needed to resolve the different effects, and this requires a much more detailed analysis. Detailed econometric work on the financial sector and its relationships with the rest of the economy is still something of a novelty.[3]

The related issue is that of the transmission mechanism: how, and by what routes, does a change in money supply affect income? The single-equation approach casts no light on the various possible ways in which changes in money supply might spill over into the determination of expenditure and income; it has not for example, allowed any testing of the proposition that a given change in money supply might have different effects according to the change in its asset

[2] This is not the only example of an endogenous money supply. For example, an automatic gold standard system would have a similar effect. If exports and incomes rise, *ceteris paribus* so does money supply.

[3] However, in the United States work is now proceeding on a complex econometric model which is specifically designed to cast light on the efficacy of monetary and fiscal policy. Reports on this system, known as the Federal Reserve—M.I.T. model, have appeared in recent issues of the *Federal Reserve Bulletin*.

counterpart (thus, changes in money supply underpinned by increased bank advances might be associated with different effects from a change in money supply underpinned by increased bank holdings of government bonds). This area remains still to be explored. The sketch of the transmission mechanism offered by Friedman and Schwartz [**21**] interestingly seemed to offer changes in interest rates as the avenue through which money supply changes exerted their effects. Expenditures would be influenced as the result of a chain of financial asset substitutions, which would eventually lead to a substitution between current services and real assets and between new and old real assets. An increase in money supply leading to reduced interest rates in one sector of the financial market, for example, would spread to other parts of the financial market and lead to a rise in the price of existing real assets relative to the price of newly produced real assets—so leading to new investment in capital equipment and consumer durables. There is nothing in such a description of the transmission mechanism to offend the Keynesian account of 'how money works'; indeed, certain other possibilities seemed to be left out—wealth and distribution effects,[4] and induced changes in the degree of credit rationing, for example. The main doubts have arisen on the score of whether changes in interest rates can be expected to exert the scale of effect which the single equation estimates imply, and what role is played by interest rates in equating the demand for, and supply of money. Whilst few, if any, economists have ever doubted that changes in money supply should have *some* effect upon the 'real' economy, there has been scepticism about their *scale*. This scepticism has in particular rested upon an inability to verify sizeable responses of capital spending to changes in interest rates.[5] The second question is that of the role played by interest rates in the demand for money. The view with which the monetarist school is generally identified on this point is that interest rates play a rather negligible role[6]—in sharp contrast with received Keynesian theory,

[4] These would incorporate that part of any change in the money supply which involved an increase in net real wealth (increased claims on the Government, though really a special case of distribution effects, are usually accounted as such) as well as any induced effects on asset values which influence debtors and creditors unevenly.

[5] But the quality of the evidence used has been questioned more recently (see, for example, White [**31**], or in a particular case, Gurley's review of the evidence taken by the Radcliffe Committee on this point, [**23**]).

[6] See Friedman [**15**].

and a considerable body of empirical work.[7] Thus, *vis-à-vis* the 'Keynesian' view, the monetarist school appears to make much stronger claims for interest rates in adjusting expenditures, but a much weaker one for interest rates in equating the supply of, and demand for, money. Hence money is altogether more potent in the monetarist view than in 'Keynesian' economics.[8]

There is undoubtedly a great deal more we need to know about the importance of monetary influences and how they work. Whilst one insistent criticism of the monetary school has been that it has not yet illuminated the issue in sufficient detail, it probably is true to say that the development of its work has pointed up an area of comparative neglect in applied macro-economics, and so provided an overdue stimulus to work in this area. At the same time, the single-equation approach retains the seductiveness of simplicity: and in the remaining part of this section—for what they may be worth—we set out the results of some calculations of this type in which we attempted to apply the approach used by Andersen and Jordan.

Monetary and fiscal policy: single equation tests

As an experiment, we have attempted to replicate with United Kingdom data the kinds of test employed by Andersen and Jordan in evaluating fiscal and monetary policy in the United States.

Whilst on the formal level the results of this experiment are the reverse of some of those obtained by Andersen and Jordan (in brief, fiscal policy works faster and performs better in explaining changes in GDP than measures of monetary policy), we have to report that we have little confidence in them. An important reason for our lack of confidence is a doubt about the method itself: the regressions we ran related quarterly changes in GDP to changes in various selected measures of fiscal and monetary policy (and, in some cases, lagged values of the change in GDP itself). We doubt

[7] See, as isolated examples, Latané [**28**], or for the U.K. the work by Ball [**6**].

[8] The term 'Keynesian' here, as elsewhere in this section is used with trepidation. Exegetical work on the 'General Theory' can undoubtedly point up a number of differences between modern orthodox ('Keynesian') economics and the economics of Keynes as in the 'General Theory'. A particularly noteworthy development which may be mentioned in passing is the development in modern economics of financial theory involving a greater complication of assets than envisaged by Keynes and embracing the activities of financial institutions other than banks.

whether these equations can properly be held to represent a 'reduced form' of a structural system unless the characteristics of that system are specified in advance. At any rate, without such a prior specification, it is not really possible to determine what the signs and size of the coefficients attached to the variables 'should be', nor how far they should be interpreted as representing an effect of monetary or fiscal policy variables on GDP rather than the other way around. The single equation tests seem to us more correctly interpreted simply as measures of association. A second difficulty we encountered was in the use of the Almon technique[9] to estimate the lags involved; the assumptions which have to be made in deploying this technique appear to be very restrictive, and the results rather arbitrary. Thirdly, we have certain reservations about the reliability of the data we employed. The measures we used are described below; one of them—which we describe as 'broad money supply'—was designed to be like the official definition of money supply, with the exception that we excluded certain money holdings (those of Government and financial institutions). The official series is available only for the period 1963–68, and the earlier figures had to be reconstructed from available data, and by methods which—though the best we could manage in a limited period of time—are far from perfect.[10] So there are particularly serious doubts about the reliability of this series. We also found some difficulty in estimating the concept of the 'full employment budget surplus' and the series for revenues and expenditures, so that these figures also are less than perfect.

The variables employed

The regressions were run over the period 1958–67 III, using quarterly data, and with one important exception the range of variables employed was similar to that employed by Andersen and Jordan in their study. The dependent variable was throughout the change in GDP at current prices, and we employed for this purpose, a 'compromise' measure of GDP which averages out the rather distinct differences in quarterly movements thrown up by the three independent estimates of GDP (income, expenditure, and output).[11]

[9] See Almon, Shirley [1].

[10] We also experimented with another version of 'broad money supply', designed to be identical with the official definition. Similarly rough in construction, it turned out to perform less well than the version described in the text.

[11] We inflated a compromise series of real GDP back to current price values.

The 'monetary policy' variables, changes in which were used as the independent variables, included what we describe as 'narrow' money supply and 'broad' money supply, bank advances and two measures of the monetary (cash) base corresponding to the 'narrow' and 'broad' money supply definitions. The 'narrow' money supply was defined as cash in circulation plus London Clearing Banks' net deposits[12] (i.e. including both deposit and current accounts), and the corresponding monetary base as cash in circulation plus the clearing banks' holdings of cash and deposits with the Bank of England (excluding Special Deposits). The 'broad' money supply was defined as the official money supply less holdings of deposits by Government and financial instutitions[13] and this had to be reconstructed for previous periods, as explained above. (It would be a great help if an officially constructed quarterly series were made available for a longer period.) The broad money base accordingly included the cash and deposits at the Bank of England of all banks together with cash in circulation. The bank advances measure employed was total London Clearing Bank advances.

On the fiscal side, we constructed a series for full employment government receipts and expenditures, and the full employment budget surplus, for use in the equations. The concept of the full employment budget surplus is designed to measure the *ex ante* 'drag' exerted by fiscal policy, by measuring what the surplus would be at a given defined level of utilization of resources (conveniently, at full employment levels); then the higher the level of surplus, the greater is the drag, and the more restrictive is fiscal policy. The surplus would be the difference, in the full employment position, between expenditures and receipts (tax revenues). We encountered some difficulty in measuring the necessary tax revenue functions, which seemed to display a great deal of variability; on the expenditures side we made two changes to the actual level of government spending in order to estimate full employment expenditures. First, we took into account the fact that unemployment benefit payments

[12] Perhaps a more customary working definition of a narrow money supply would also include net deposits with the Scottish and Northern Irish banks. The R^2 between changes in such a series and the one actually used is, however, at the 0·99 level.

[13] This definition was employed for the usual reasons adduced in the case of government holdings, and because it was felt that the argument normally used to exclude inter-bank deposits might well extend to other financial institutions. As noted on p. 83, footnote 23, however, we also experimented with a series designed to be identical with the officially defined money supply.

vary with different levels of employment; secondly, we assumed that other government expenditures in the full employment position would occupy the same share in total expenditures as they did in the actually observed position.[14]

We also introduced another measure of 'fiscal' policy, which we call 'Governmental fiscal measures'. This series is derived from the approach of Hopkin and Godley [**26**],[15] and measures the (cumulated) impact of the 'first round' effects on GDP of defined taxation changes;[16] it also includes the estimated impact of changes in hire-purchase terms, which makes it a measure, strictly, of something rather broader than purely fiscal actions. It corresponds rather well to a measure of those policy actions which are taken for granted in orthodox descriptions of British economic policy as being the effective tools of demand management (omitting only an estimate of the impact of bank advances restrictions).

All data were seasonally unadjusted and expressed in £ million (current). Experimentation with seasonal dummy variables showed them to be insignificant.

The results: the initial step

As an initial step we employed a stepwise regression programme,[17] with a view to establishing the most important explanatory variables, and seeing whether we could estimate appropriate lags. The attraction of the stepwise programme was that it systematically introduced the independent (and lagged dependent) variables in order of their explanatory power.[18]

An excerpt from the step-wise regression results is shown in Table 1. The explanatory variables are shown in order of the entry

[14] What one assumes about this—or alternatively about the whole composition of national expenditure on full employment output—of course reacts back on the estimate of tax revenue.

[15] And has been elaborated by Shepherd and Surrey [**29**].

[16] These are, broadly, all taxation changes with a principal direct or indirect effect on persons. Thus the measure includes all changes in rates of purchase and income tax, SET and corporation tax, but excludes changes in investment grants, and any estimate of the investment impact of measures which affect both companies and persons (as, for example, in the case of corporation income tax).

[17] This programme is designated U.C.L.A. B.M.D. 029.

[18] The programme introduces the variables in order of the difference they make to the remaining error sums of squares at each successive stage. Put in another way, it introduces the variable with the highest F ratio amongst the variables not already chosen in previous steps. It is required only to specify F values to be achieved for a variable to be included.

TABLE I

Step-wise regression results (a)

Equation (1)

$$\Delta GDP = 122{\cdot}0 - \underset{(5\cdot9)}{0{\cdot}7}\,(\Delta GDP_{-1}) + \underset{(6\cdot1)}{11{\cdot}6}\,(\Delta GFM_{-1}) + \underset{(4\cdot7)}{0{\cdot}5}\,(\Delta ADV_{-5}) + \underset{(5\cdot1)}{0{\cdot}8}\,(\Delta FER) - \underset{(3\cdot8)}{0{\cdot}5}\,(\Delta GDP_{-2}) + \underset{(2\cdot6)}{0{\cdot}2}\,(\Delta BMS_{-4})$$

$R^2 = 0{\cdot}73$ S.E. $= 47{\cdot}1$ D.W. $= 1{\cdot}8$

Equation (2)

$$\Delta GDP = 161{\cdot}1 - \underset{(4\cdot1)}{0{\cdot}7}\,(\Delta GDP_{-1}) + \underset{(3\cdot4)}{8{\cdot}3}\,(\Delta GFM_{-1}) + \underset{(2\cdot8)}{0{\cdot}4}\,(\Delta ADV_{-5}) - \underset{(2\cdot0)}{0{\cdot}3}\,(\Delta GDP_{-2}) - \underset{(0\cdot3)}{0{\cdot}01}\,(\Delta BMS_{-4})$$

$R^2 = 0{\cdot}48$ S.E. $= 64{\cdot}1$ D.W. $= 1{\cdot}5$

Equation (3)

$$\Delta GDP = 160{\cdot}6 - \underset{(4\cdot4)}{0{\cdot}7}\,(\Delta GDP_{-1}) + \underset{(3\cdot6)}{8{\cdot}3}\,(\Delta GFM_{-1}) + \underset{(2\cdot8)}{0{\cdot}4}\,(\Delta ADV_{-5}) - \underset{(2\cdot1)}{0{\cdot}3}\,(\Delta GDP_{-2})$$

$R^2 = 0{\cdot}48$ S.E. $= 63$ D.W. $= 1{\cdot}5$

Equation (4)

$$\Delta GDP = 97{\cdot}0 + \underset{(3\cdot0)}{9{\cdot}3}\,(\Delta GFM_{-1}) - \underset{(2\cdot3)}{7{\cdot}0}\,(\Delta GFM_{-2})$$

$R^2 = 0{\cdot}23$ S.E. $= 73{\cdot}9$

Equation (5)

$$\Delta GDP = 77{\cdot}6 + \underset{(3\cdot6)}{10{\cdot}8}\,(\Delta GFM_{-1}) - \underset{(2\cdot8)}{8{\cdot}3}\,(\Delta GFM_{-2}) + \underset{(1\cdot9)}{0{\cdot}2}\,(\Delta ADV_{-4})$$

$R^2 = 0{\cdot}31$ S.E. $= 70{\cdot}9$

(a) The symbols have the following meanings: GDP = gross domestic product; GFM = government fiscal measures; ADV = advances; FER = full employment budget receipts; BMS = broad money supply. Other symbols have their usual meaning. For further explanations, see text.

Quarterly changes are indicated by the symbol Δ; *t*-ratios are shown in brackets below the coefficients.

determined by the programme, and the different equations represent the result of the different restrictions we chose to set upon the variables which could be called in by it.

Equation (1) represents the result of allowing the programme to choose freely from among the independent variables described above (and their lagged values) and, as well, to choose lagged values of the independent variable (ΔGDP). For an equation in terms of quarterly changes, the R^2 of this first equation is satisfactorily high (and a plot of calculated and actual values of the change in GDP shows that it picks up all the main turning points also). In these terms, and in terms of the significance of the coefficients (which is satisfactory here), this equation is certainly much better than those we report on later, where the Almon lag technique was employed. Two monetary variables—advances (ΔADV) and broad money supply (ΔBMS)—appear in this equation, and fiscal policy is represented by Government fiscal measures (ΔGFM) and by full employment receipts (ΔFER). However, the sign of the coefficient for full employment receipts appears to be *a priori* 'wrong'. We noticed repeatedly, in both these and the later 'Almon' regressions that whereas most of the lagged values of full employment receipts had the 'correct' (negative) signs, the signs of the contemporaneous value, and the first lagged value were usually positive. It is arguable that this represents in part an induced effect of the changes in GDP on full employment receipts, through systematic changes in the composition of expenditures on actual and (by construction) full-employment GDP. Thus, for example, a sharp increase in GDP associated with a rise in consumption will tend automatically to raise current tax revenues because consumption is a highly taxed form of expenditure and it will tend to raise the 'full employment' estimate as well, because of the assumption that the proportionate composition of expenditure in full employment GDP in a particular quarter will be identical with that of the actual composition. The opposite might be expected to occur for analogous reasons in a period of low growth in GDP. Whilst there is a real sense in which changes in the composition of expenditure, at unchanged rates of tax, do make fiscal policy more or less restrictive, reflection on this point certainly suggests that it may be erroneous to 'expect' a negative sign on the full employment receipts variable.[19]

[19] Nor is it clear, incidentally, that the expected sign on broad money supply is positive for all lagged values. Walters [**30**], for example, has pointed out that

However, equation (2) represents the result of dropping full employment receipts from the regression. The effect was to give a poorer overall fit, and to render the coefficient of broad money supply insignificant.

Accordingly, in equation (3), we dropped both full employment receipts and broad money supply. The programme did not choose any substitute variables on the specifications given.

In equation (4), we restricted the range of variables to those that seemed most important for the exercise: government fiscal measures and broad money supply. And we relaxed the statistical requirements except for specifying that only lagged values up to five quarters and no more could be chosen. The result was the exclusion of the money supply variable. In equation (5), where the variables were restricted to government fiscal measures and bank advances, again with a five-quarter limit on the introduction of lagged values, bank advances entered but at a level just short of statistical significance.

In the last two equations, as in other equations containing only the government fiscal measures and one of the monetary measures we found that the sign of the fiscal variable alternated from positive when lagged one quarter, to negative for greater lags. This would be consistent with the suggestion (among others) that fiscal measures have a fairly immediate and powerful effect on expenditures and GDP, but that in subsequent periods there is some compensating adjustment for an initial over-reaction.

It was hoped that the step-wise regressions containing lagged dependent variables along with current and lagged independent variables would allow estimates to be made of the lag structure.[20] Unfortunately, the size and sign of the lagged GDP terms proved unsuitable material for this exercise; but an estimate of the average lags can be made. Using equations (1) and (2), it can be estimated that the average lag with which fiscal measures exert their effect is shorter than is the lag in effect of broad money supply.[21] This

on certain assumptions about the demand for money, a negative sign could be expected on one lagged term.

[20] On the basis of the rational distribution lag.

[21] The average lag can be measured as $a = \dfrac{b + 2c}{1 - b - c} + m$, where b and c are the coefficients of the lagged dependent terms, and m is the lag of the independent variables (see Griliches [**22**]). Thus with respect to equation (1), the average lag of fiscal measures is 0·2 of a quarter, and for broad money supply, 3·2 quarters; given the variance of the average, the order of the lags seems broadly appropriate.

relative difference is confirmed in the Almon regressions reported below.

The Almon regressions

In the next stage of the work, we ran a second set of regressions, relating the change in GDP to changes in the two variables which the earlier work showed to be the most promising representatives of fiscal and of monetary policy.[22] These proved to be government fiscal measures and broad money supply: the other possibilities were eliminated. In particular, the other monetary measures, with the partial exception of bank advances, seemed to be very much weaker contenders than broad money supply. This was in a way unfortunate since the quality of the broad money supply series is rather suspect.[23]

In choosing to calculate the regression coefficients with the use of the Almon lag technique we were following closely the example of Andersen and Jordan. The technique is essentially one of interpolating unknown coefficients on the basis of a restricted set of actual estimates; and any interpolation technique involves some more or less arbitrary and restrictive assumptions. In this case, various restrictions were tested and the results reported are those which appeared 'best' on statistical criteria of significance. The results did, however, show considerable variability according to the precise assumptions made.

The basic set of results is given in Table 2. Equations (6) and (7) included both government fiscal measures and broad money supply, but with different specifications about the maximum lags and different interpolation points. The differences in the results represent differences caused by these changes in assumption. Equation (8) is a regression of the change in GDP on changes in

[22] We also conducted some experiments with other measures, which confirmed our initial choice.

[23] As indicated earlier, however, we did experiment with an alternative 'broad money supply', constructed to assemble the official money supply. When this was employed in the Almon regressions it gave rather similar results to those reported for BMS here, in terms of the size and sign of coefficients—the lag profile was in general terms quite similar. Significance was smaller, however, and one side effect was to reduce the size attributable to the GFM multiplier (see Table 3). In the step-wise regressions (Table 1), it performed less well than narrow money supply (NMS), but NMS also was found in the Almon regressions to have the slower-acting characteristic *vis-à-vis* the GFM measures, that was common to both the BMS measures.

government fiscal measures alone and equation (9) employs broad money supply alone. Unlike the results reported by Andersen and Jordan, those given here contain extremely little explanatory power, and R^2, even for equations in changes, is uniformly very low.

TABLE 2

Results of the Almon regressions, with changes in GDP (ΔGDP) as dependent variable[(a)]

	Equation (6)		Equation (7)		Equation (8)	Equation (9)
Quarter	ΔGFM	ΔBMS	ΔGFM	ΔBMS	ΔGFM	ΔBMS
0	1·86	−0·03	4·67	−0·08	2·70	−0·01
	(0·93)	(0·43)	(1·55)	(−0·74)	(1·10)	(−0·23)
1	1·58	0·02	2·64	−0·02	1·06	0·02
	(1·09)	(0·26)	(1·19)	(−0·22)	(0·65)	(0·33)
2	0·37	0·07	−0·42	0·07	−0·75	0·07
	(0·26)	(0·91)	(−0·23)	(0·79)	(−0·95)	(0·83)
3	−0·56	0·09	−1·41	0·14	−0·66	0·07
	(−0·27)	(1·10)	(−0·75)	(1·22)	(−0·36)	(0·97)
4			0·17	0·14	1·29	
			(0·12)	(1·11)	(0·95)	
5			2·21	0·09	2·93	
			(0·88)	(0·78)	(1·27)	
N	4		6		6	4
Q	3rd		4th		4th	3rd
R^2	0·07		0·134		0·083	0·034
S.E.	82·2		83·9		83·4	81·3
D.W.	2·9		3·1		3·0	2·8

(a) The number opposite *N* indicates the length of the polynomial employed for the Almon interpolation, *Q* the order; *t*-ratios are shown in brackets. All other symbols have their usual meaning or are defined in Table 1.

The 'wrong' signs—on simple *a priori* reasoning—are again evident for government fiscal measures lagged more than one quarter, and the same applies to contemporaneous values of changes in broad money supply. But as before, it can be observed that the specification of the 'right' signs is not in fact straightforward;[24] and one consequence of the signs estimated—that fiscal measures are depicted as quicker-acting than monetary measures—is intuitively plausible. This was one of the conclusions which it seemed could be drawn from the step-wise regression results; it is displayed graphically in Chart 1, where the 'beta coefficients' calculated from equation (6) have been plotted. These 'beta coefficients' are the regression coefficients (reported in Table 2)

Chart 1. Measures of lag response[(a)]

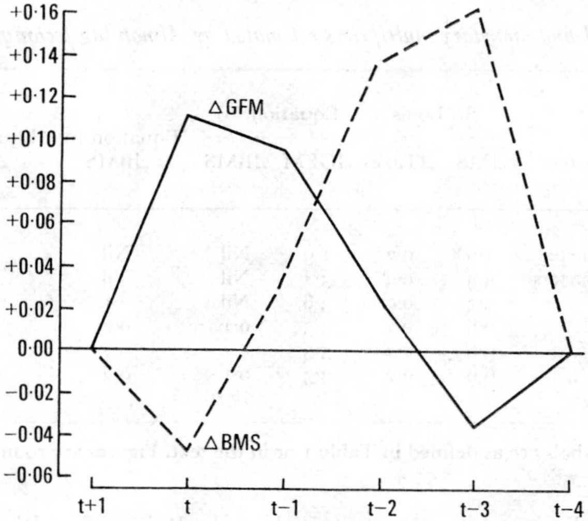

(a) The beta coefficients of equation (6), Table 2, for changes in government fiscal measures (ΔGFM) and changes in broad money supply (ΔBMS).

standardized for the variation in each of the two series (ΔGFM, ΔBMS) relative to the variation of changes in GDP (ΔGDP). This standardization makes them comparable as measures of the relative contribution of each variable to changes in GDP. In this

[24] A general point which may be made here is that this study employs quarterly changes. The time path and length of adjustment processes, and the role of expectations may well be such as to suggest an expectation of sign on lagged values different from that which would be appropriate to an analysis of annual changes, where it could be assumed that the adjustment processes would work themselves out within the period.

connection it may be important to note that the sum of the beta coefficients for BMS is slightly greater than that for GFM; but the fiscal measures variable is faster-acting.[25]

It is interesting to see that when changes in GDP are regressed exclusively upon changes in the fiscal policy variable or upon changes in broad money supply (equations (8) and (9)), all the terms in the fiscal measure equation (8) prove significant, whereas only two of those in the broad money supply equation (9) are significant.

TABLE 3

Fiscal and monetary multipliers estimated by Almon lag technique[(a)]

	St. Louis		Equation (6)		Equation (9)	Equation (8)
Elapsed time	ΔMS	ΔTaxes	ΔGFM	ΔBMS	ΔBMS	ΔGFM
After 1 quarter	1·6	0·2	1·9	Nil	Nil	2·7
,, 2 quarters	3·5	0·2	3·4	Nil	Nil	3·8
,, 3 ,,	5·3	0·2	3·8	Nil	0·1	3·0
,, 4 ,,	6·6	0·2	3·3	0·1	0·2	2·3
,, 5 ,,	6·6	0·2	3·3	0·1	0·2	3·6
,, 6 ,,	6·6	0·2	3·3	0·1	0·2	6·6

(a) Symbols are as defined in Table 1 or in the text. Figures are rounded.

The Almon regressions permit the calculation of multipliers for the total effect of the two measures, obtained by simply summing the regression coefficients. These are shown in Table 3 alongside those computed for two of the most nearly comparable measures in the Andersen–Jordan study.[26] It will be seen that the multiplier effects are reversed in relative size for the United Kingdom, where the fiscal multipliers are large and the money multipliers small, compared with the estimates for the United States which emerge from

[25] The chart shows time in quarters, measured from the position *t*, the present. The relatively high betas for ΔGFM in the current and immediately preceding quarters (t, t_{-1}) indicate its 'faster-acting' characteristic, compared with the coefficient for ΔBMS which is highest for t_{-3}.

[26] These were not directly quoted by them, but appear in a recent article by Davis [11].

the study by Andersen and Jordan:[27] indeed it happens, quite fortuitously, that the results are *precisely* reversed.

Conclusion

The results of the regressions presented would, if they were accepted as valid reduced forms, perhaps suggest that it is fiscal measures (at least in the representation they have been given) rather than monetary measures which are the more powerful and certainly the quicker-acting. One result obtained which is intuitively plausible is that fiscal measures work quickly whilst monetary measures may have a more delayed effect. That this may be true for the United Kingdom and not for the United States is, of course, possible. However, we should not want to claim much for any of the results of this kind of exercise; it is more salutary in underlining the defects of the procedure (and in our case also the available data) than in the results it produces. In general, the level of statistical explanation was not high; but there are other reasons for caution in accepting at their face value the results of this sort of analysis. These principally concern the evasion of the problem of specifying a structural model which the use of quasi-reduced form single equations implies. Some notable work on fiscal policy of the appropriate kind has already been published;[28] but much remains to be done in the financial sector.

REFERENCES

[1] Almon, S., 'The distributed lag between capital appropriations and expenditures', *Econometrica*, vol. 33, no. 1, January 1965.

[2] Andersen, L. C., and Jordan, J. L., 'Monetary and fiscal actions: a test of their relative importance in economic stabilisation', *Federal Reserve Bank of St. Louis Review*, vol. 50, no. 11, November 1968.

[3] Andersen, L. C., and Jordan, J. L., 'Reply', *Federal Reserve Bank of St. Louis Review*, vol. 51, no. 4, April 1969.

[4] Ando, A., and Modigliani, F., 'Velocity and the investment multiplier', *American Economic Review*, vol. 55, no. 4, September 1965.

[27] Davis, however, in his critique of the Andersen–Jordan study, pointed out that the large-scale M.I.T. Federal Reserve model gave much bigger multipliers for fiscal measures, and smaller ones for monetary measures than those obtained by Andersen and Jordan. See [11], pp. 121–3.

[28] We are thinking here of the work of Balapoulos [7].

[5] Ando, A., and Modigliani, F., 'Rejoinder', *American Economic Review*, vol. 55, no. 4, September 1965.

[6] Ball, R. J., 'Some econometric analysis of the long-term rate of interest in the United Kingdom, 1921–61', *The Manchester School of Economic and Social Studies*, vol. 33, no. 1, January 1965.

[7] Balopoulos, E. T., *Fiscal policy models of the British economy* (Amsterdam, 1967).

[8] Barrett, C. R., and Walters, A. A., 'The stability of Keynesian and monetary multipliers in the United Kingdom', *Review of Economics and Statistics*, vol. 48, no. 4, November 1966.

[9] Culbertson, J. M., 'Friedman on the lag in effect of monetary policy', *Journal of Political Economy*, vol. 68, no. 6, December 1960.

[10] Culbertson, J. M., 'The lag in effect of monetary policy: Reply', *Journal of Political Economy*, vol. 69, no. 5, October 1961.

[11] Davis, R. G., 'How much does money matter?', *Federal Reserve Bank of New York, Monthly Review*, June 1969.

[12] De Leeuw, F., and Kalchbrenner, J., 'Monetary and fiscal actions: a test of their relative importance in economic stabilisation—Comment', *Federal Reserve Bank of St. Louis Review*, vol. 51, no. 4, April 1969.

[13] Deprano, M., and Mayer, T., 'Autonomous expenditures and money', *American Economic Review*, vol. 55, no. 4, September 1965.

[14] Deprano, M., and Mayer, T., 'Rejoinder', *American Economic Review*, vol. 55, no. 4, September 1965.

[15] Friedman, M., 'The demand for money: some theoretical and empirical results', *Journal of Political Economy*, vol. 67, no. 4, August 1959.

[16] Friedman, M., 'The lag in effect of monetary policy', *Journal of Political Economy*, vol. 69, no. 5, October 1961.

[17] Friedman, M., 'The role of monetary policy', *American Economic Review*, vol. 57, no. 1, May 1968.

[18] Friedman, M., and Meiselman, D., 'The relative stability of monetary velocity and the investment multiplier in the United States, 1897–1958'. Stabilization policies, a series of research studies prepared for the Commission on Money and Credit (Englewood Cliffs, 1963).

[19] Friedman, M., and Meiselman, D., 'Reply to Donald Hester', *The Review of Economics and Statistics*, vol. 61, no. 4, November 1964.

[20] Friedman, M., and Meiselman, D., 'Reply', *American Economic Review*, vol. 55, no. 4, September 1965.

[21] Friedman, M., and Schwartz, A. J., 'Money and business cycles', *The Review of Economics and Statistics*, vol. 45, no. 1, part 2, Supplement: February 1963.

[22] Griliches, Z., 'Distributed lags: a survey', *Econometrica*, vol. 35, no. 1, January 1967.

[23] Gurley, J. G., 'The Radcliffe Report and Evidence', *American Economic Review*, vol. 50, no. 4, September 1960.

[24] Hester, D. D., 'Keynes and the quantity theory: a comment on the Friedman–Meiselman CMC paper', *The Review of Economics and Statistics*, vol. 46, no. 4, November 1964.

[25] Hester, D. D., 'Rejoinder', *The Review of Economics and Statistics*, vol. 46, no. 4, November 1964.

[26] Hopkin, W. A. B., and Godley, W. A. H., 'An analysis of tax changes', *National Institute Economic Review*, no. 32, May 1965.

[27] Kareken, J., and Solow, R., 'Lags in monetary policy', *Stabilisation policies*, a series of research studies prepared for the Commission on Money and Credit (Englewood Cliffs, 1963).

[28] Latané, H. A., 'Cash balances and the interest rate—a pragmatic approach', *Review of Economics and Statistics*, vol. 36, no. 4, November 1954.

[29] Shepherd, J. R., and Surrey, M. J. C., 'The short-term effects of tax changes', *National Institute Economic Review*, no. 46, November 1968.

[30] Walters, A. A., 'The demand for money—the dynamic properties of the multiplier', *Journal of Political Economy*, vol. 75, no. 3, June 1967.

[31] White, W. H., 'Interest inelasticity of investment demand: the case from business attitude surveys re-examined', *American Economic Review*, vol. 46, no. 4, September 1956.

4

TIMING RELATIONSHIPS BETWEEN MOVEMENTS OF MONETARY AND NATIONAL INCOME VARIABLES

THE BANK OF ENGLAND*

ONE way of viewing the impact of monetary policy on the economy is to see it as affecting the private sector's holdings of real and financial assets. By their actions in financial markets, changing interest rates and the relative quantities of financial assets, the monetary authorities can bring about a divergence between the private sector's desired portfolio of assets and its actual portfolio. Subsequent attempts by the private sector to restore the desired portfolio balance will involve sales and purchases of assets, both financial and real, which will have repercussions on income flows. Although there is considerable agreement on the value of this insight, there is much less agreement on how best it should be applied to forecasting and policy-making.

On the one hand, it is argued that certain relationships in the economic system are far more dominant and stable than others, and that if these relationships can be established with a substantial degree of statistical significance, the precise nature of the transmission mechanism by which one variable affects another is of secondary importance to the policy-maker. This seems to have been, broadly speaking, the methodological approach adopted in the research undertaken by the Federal Reserve Bank of St. Louis.[1]

* Reprinted from the *Bank of England Quarterly Bulletin*, vol. 10, no. 4, pp. 459–68, by permission of the publisher. The article was prepared in the Bank of England's Economic Section, being largely the work of A. D. Crockett, who is on the bank's research staff.

[1] See, for example, Andersen, L. C., and Jordan, J. L., 'Monetary and fiscal actions: a test of their relative importance in economic stabilization', *Federal Reserve Bank of St. Louis Review*, vol. 50, no. 11, November 1968, pp. 11–24;

On the other hand, it can be argued that this kind of simple single-equation relationship that is not derived as a reduced form from a more complex model is more likely to produce faulty answers should the basic ground-rules of the system change.[2] If the monetary authorities change their open-market tactics, for example, an equation which ignores the route by which open-market operations work through the financial system to the real economy may be unsuccessful in forecasting the consequences of such action. For this reason, it is argued that the transmission mechanism must be explicitly spelt out through the specification of a multi-equation model.

The choice boils down to one of heuristic simplicity against logically rigorous complexity. This paper presents the results of an analysis of correlation undertaken to determine average leads and lags between various monetary and expenditure series.[3] It has two main objectives, corresponding to the two broad approaches described above. In the first place, it provides information about the existence (and perhaps as important, the non-existence) of certain lead/lag relationships that may be useful in forecasting and analysis. Secondly, it provides some basic source material that may be of use in the building of more complex models. Theories must explain facts, and without a greater knowledge of the facts that have to be explained—such as timing relationships between economic variables—theorizing will tend to be a very hit-and-miss affair.

It is widely appreciated and recognized that a simultaneous relationship between two variables can tell nothing about the direction of any causal link. Two series can be highly correlated because changes in the first series are causing changes in the second, or vice versa, or because some third factor is causing changes in both series. It is not, perhaps, so widely appreciated that a lead or lag of one variable over another is also no evidence of causality. The circulation of Christmas cards rises before Christmas; this does not mean that the circulation of cards has caused Christmas.

Keran, M. W., 'Monetary and fiscal influences on economic activity—the historical evidence', *Federal Reserve Bank of St. Louis Review*, vol. 51, no. 11, November 1969, pp. 5–23.

[2] See Appendix I to the article 'The importance of money' which appeared in the *Bank of England Quarterly Bulletin*, vol. 10, no. 2, June 1970, p. 185.

[3] Some of these results were referred to in 'The importance of money', see footnote 2.

However, the inability of correlation studies to establish the nature of a causal relationship is not a defect peculiar to them. It is shared by all statistical methods. It is a truism—but not one that is always in the forefront of the mind—to say that, while statistical testing can disprove hypotheses, it cannot prove them. All the same, the finding of a close association whereby changes in one series are followed by changes in another series would at least appear to be evidence consistent with a theory about causal relationships. This evidence will be strengthened if there is a plausible economic explanation for the lag, and no comparably plausible alternative explanation. And although the pattern of linkages will ultimately have to be much more precisely specified, and estimated using regression techniques, correlations can give valuable initial indications of the possible nature of the transmission mechanism.

Furthermore, even if the existence of a regular lead does not allow causality to be imputed without further research, it may enable any such regular relationship to be used as a leading indicator, assuming that the general structure of the system remains unchanged. For these reasons it is of some considerable interest to inspect whether monetary aggregates lead certain income and expenditure variables.

In the present study therefore, the relationships between monetary and national income series have been tested to discover the nature and stability of the timing relationships. Tests have also been performed with disaggregated money stock data. This is of particular interest because an important unresolved area of debate is whether the origin of a change in the money stock is relevant to its impact on expenditure. Monetarist studies[4] generally assume that the particular source of changes in the money stock is immaterial; but others[5] have suggested that the way in which a monetary change is brought about may significantly affect its impact on final demand. Finally expenditure data have also been disaggregated, in a fairly simple way, to see whether different

[4] See, for example, Friedman, Milton, and Meiselman, David, 'The relative stability of monetary velocity and the investment multiplier in the United States, 1897–1958', *Stabilization policies*, C.M.C. Research Papers 1963, pp. 165–268; Andersen, L. C., and Jordan, J. L., see footnote 1, p. 90; Keran, M. W., see footnote 1, p. 90.

[5] Tobin, James, 'The monetary interpretation of history', *American Economic Review*, June 1965, pp. 464–85; Silber, W. L., 'Velocity and bank portfolio composition', *Southern Economic Journal*, October 1969, pp. 147–52.

categories of expenditure are similarly related to possible monetary stimuli, particularly in regard to lag structures.

Methods used

In what follows, the principal method used to analyse the stability of relationships between two series is the cross-correlogram.[6] A cross-correlogram is a series of coefficients of correlation which can range between +1·0 and −1·0 and which measure the closeness of association (positive or negative) between two series with a given lead or lag.[7] With quarterly observations for about fifteen years (as used in most of the charts in this paper), the correlation is significant if it is greater than ±0·25;[8] but it is perhaps more informative to look at the general shape of the correlogram rather than individual correlations, which will themselves be inter-correlated.[9] If, for example, two variables tend to move cyclically, the peak of the cross-correlogram would show the average lead or lag of one series over the other. Thus, in the example chart, the most significant relationship is a positive one where the first series leads the second by two quarters; but there is also a rather less strong negative relationship where the first series lags the second by five quarters.

[6] The spectral analysis was also used, and J. P. Burman provided statistical guidance in the application of both methods. The results of the spectral analysis, together with a description of the technique are given in the appendix.

[7] Mathematically, for N observations of two variables, x_t and y_t, each with zero mean, the cross-correlogram is the series:

$$r_k = C_k/\sqrt{V_1 V_2},$$

where

$$C_k = \frac{1}{N-k}\sum_t x_t y_{t-k} \quad \text{and} \quad V_1 = \sum_t x_t^2/N, \quad V_2 = \sum_t y_t^2/N$$

for $k = -m, \ldots, 0, \ldots, m$, where m is small compared with N. (The range of summation in the expression for C_k is truncated at one end if k is positive and the other end if k is negative.)

[8] The 'significance' of a correlation is measured by the probability of such a correlation arising by chance between two unrelated series: in this paper, significance is measured at the 5% level, i.e. there is only a 1 in 20 possibility of getting a correlation of ±0·25, or above, by chance.

[9] This is because the individual correlations, though estimated separately, are based on the same run of data. If there is autocorrelation in the original series the separate observations will not be independent.

In dealing with series which have strong common trends, a high correlation will be observed, without there necessarily being any close causal connection. For example, employment in the computer industry would probably be closely linked, in a purely statistical

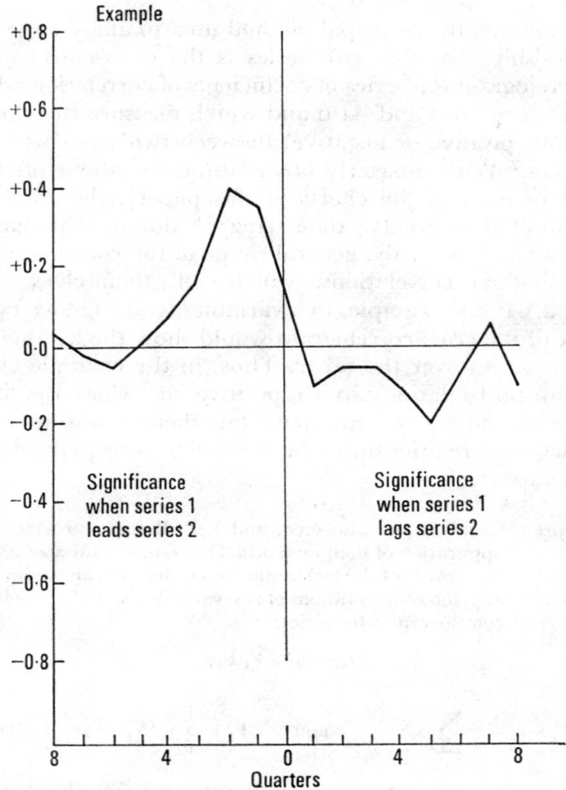

sense, with the number of tourists visiting Britain, but the link would be a coincidental one. During the past twenty-five years, monetary and national income statistics have both tended to rise over time, and a simple correlation between the two might tend to exaggerate the strength of the link between the two phenomena. It might also obscure the precise timing of any lead or lag relationship. To reduce this possibility, the relationships plotted in this paper are based on data with trends removed.[10]

Although the removal of trends is desirable in order to reduce the possibility of spurious correlation, it is nevertheless possible—indeed, with money and income series, probable—that the existence of common trends *does* owe something to a causal link. This being the case, the correlations will tend to underestimate the strength of any such causal link between the two series.

One final point is worthy of mention. An objective of trend removal is to make series more 'stationary' in the statistical sense. One possible consequence of achieving this is that there may be some counterbalancing of positive and negative correlations between 'stationary' series.[11] If two series move in regular cycles which, even though out of phase, are of approximately the same length, then more or less equal positive and negative correlations between them would tend to occur at timings determined by the cycle itself. Simple correlation analysis would not enable one to distinguish which series was leading and which was lagging. Indeed, it would serve as a reminder that a regression analysis which *did* specify a particular direction of causation between such cyclically dominated series would risk imputing causality that did not necessarily exist. However, cycles are not perfectly regular and, this being so, it is quite possible that there will be a unique point of maximum correlation. It will then be easier to say which series leads the other, though the nature of any causal connection will

[10] The technique of trend removal was to convert data to log form, to remove a linear trend, and then to use an autoregressive transformation, as described by Marc Nerlove in *Spectral Comparisons of two seasonal adjustment procedures*, Technical Report No. 2, 1964, Institute for Mathematical Studies in Social Sciences, Stanford University. Other methods of trend removal were tried: straightforward first differences produced series with somewhat larger residual variance; the autoregressive transformation without removing a linear trend gave much larger residual variance and series that were obviously not stationary. The results using these alternative methods are not reported here. However, it should be noted that the correlograms did prove rather sensitive to the particular method of trend removal used: where straightforward first differences were employed, the observed correlations tended to be lower than those reported in this paper, although the general shape of the correlograms was similar.

[11] This may be seen intuitively by considering that, when one observation in a series is above trend, the average of all other observations must, by definition, be below trend. Thus if there is a positive correlation between one series and synchronous observations in another series, the sum of the correlations with *non-synchronous* observations must be negative.

still be a matter of speculation, based on the most plausible economic explanation.

Results

There are a number of issues in monetary economics where theory suggests a clear hypothesis which may be tested against the data (e.g. that the demand for money responds negatively to a change in interest rates). In other cases, theory gives much less guidance, and these issues can only be resolved pragmatically. For example, the question of whether the money supply should be confined to currency and demand deposits, or extended to include time deposits, is generally acknowledged to be an empirical matter. It could also be argued that, as there is quite wide agreement that changes in the money stock affect expenditure through an interest rate type mechanism,[12] it is an empirical matter whether interest rates or money stocks most accurately measure that effect. On the one hand, interest rates have the disadvantage that they can be measured only in particular markets, and do not take account of changes in inflationary expectations; on the other, the money stock/expenditure relationship is subject to unforeseen changes in the demand-for-money function.

Another important issue is whether monetary policy should be concerned simply with the volume of banks' liabilities (the money stock) or whether it should attempt also to influence the structure of banks' asset portfolios (bank lending). It is sometimes claimed that market imperfections, such as rationing of bank loans, make control over bank lending to the private sector a strategic variable in counter-cyclical policy.[13]

Finally, there is debate whether monetary changes affect the overall level of demand without having any particular systematic effect on the *distribution* of output (a 'monetarist' view), or whether such changes affect first of all the demand for investment goods, and only rather more indirectly, consumption expenditures.

[12] 'The crucial issue that corresponds to the distinction between the "credit" and "monetary" effects of monetary policy is not whether changes in the stock of money operate through interest rates, but rather the range of interest rates considered...' Friedman and Meiselman, p. 217, see footnote 1, p. 92.

[13] See, for example, *Radcliffe Report, Committee on the Working of the Monetary System*, Cmnd 827, August 1959, Chap. VI.

The above questions suggest that it would be interesting to analyse the following correlations:

(a) Monetary aggregates and expenditure aggregates.
(b) Monetary components and expenditure aggregates.
(c) Monetary aggregates and expenditure components.
(d) Monetary components and expenditure components.

(i) *Monetary aggregates and expenditure aggregates*

Chart 1 plots the cross-correlogram for two definitions of money against gross domestic product.

The two definitions of money used are:[14]

(i) M_N: a 'narrow' definition, including currency in circulation plus net current account deposits at London clearing banks, and

(ii) M_B: a 'broader' definition, comprising currency plus all net deposits at London clearing banks.

G.D.P. is measured as the arithmetic average of G.D.P. estimates based on income and expenditure data.

Both definitions of money are positively related to movements in G.D.P. when changes in the quantity of money precede changes in G.D.P. by several quarters. Using a narrow definition of money, the peak relationship is $r = 0{\cdot}34$ with money leading G.D.P. by four quarters. With a broad definition, the peak is $r = 0{\cdot}18$, with a five-quarter lead. The 'narrow' definition of money shows a more pronounced downward slope from left to right, suggesting that the lead of changes in the stock of money over changes in money incomes is clearer when money is narrowly defined. On the basis of this evidence it would seem that, at least as an indicator, it is the stock of 'money-as-a-medium-of-exchange' that is the most important to look at.

As noted earlier, correlation analysis does not provide any direct evidence about the direction of causality; but if the causal link was merely one of the stock of money passively accommodating to changes in incomes, it is hard to see why cycles in money should precede cycles in G.D.P. by such a large interval. It seems more likely that there are other cyclical factors at work, which may or

[14] The official definitions of money supply (see Table 12 of the annex) were not used because of the considerably shorter run of data available.

may not include a causal link from money to G.D.P. The negative correlation between changes in G.D.P. and changes in the money supply some three quarters later seems unlikely to be due to a direct

Chart 1

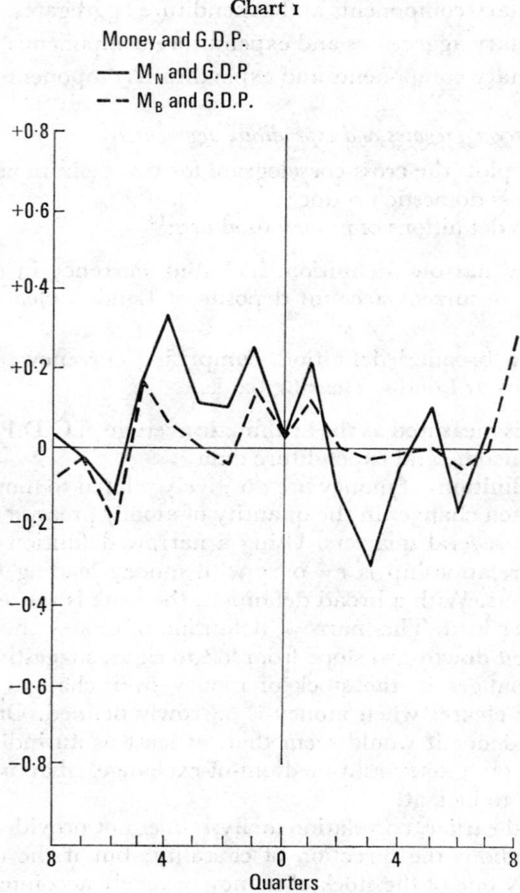

Note: In the charts, the correlation coefficient for a synchronous association between the two series is shown in the centre of each diagram. Points to the left of the centre show the correlation coefficient when the first series mentioned leads the second by the number of quarters indicated. Similarly, points to the right of the centre denote the first series lagging the second by the period indicated amount.

Chart 2

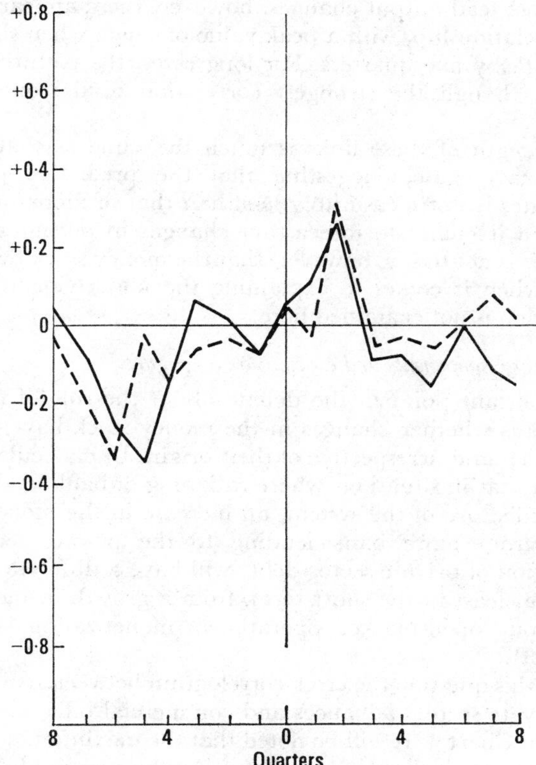

causal link, and more consistent with the theory that both money and output are responding to other cyclical forces.

Chart 2 plots the cross-correlogram for interest rates and G.D.P. For short-term interest rates,[15] there is a significant positive relationship with G.D.P. after a lag of two quarters. This probably

[15] The local authority three-month deposit rate was used as a proxy for all short-term rates. For the first two years of the period, when these data were not available, changes were assumed to be the same as in Treasury bill rates.

occurs because in the short run changes in demand tend to pull interest rates in the same direction; the authorities may resist or moderate this change for a while, thus possibly delaying the full effect on interest rates being felt for some months. When interest rate changes lead output changes, however, there appears to be a negative relationship, with a peak value of –0·33 when short rates lead G.D.P. by five quarters. For long rates, the picture is much the same, though the strongest correlation occurs one quarter earlier.

The strength of these links is much the same as that using a monetary aggregate, suggesting that the predictive power of interest rates is not measurably less than that of monetary aggregates when it comes to forecasting changes in output around a trend. This is not to say, however, that the money stock may not be superior when it comes to explaining the underlying trend, but that question is not examined here.

(ii) *Monetary components and expenditure aggregates*

An important point in the debate about the role of monetary aggregates is whether changes in the money stock have the same effect on demand, irrespective of their origin. In particular, it may be argued that in situations where rationing of bank lending is an important feature of the system, an increase in the money supply resulting from more bank lending to the private sector (the monetization of private sector debt) will have a different effect on demand, at least in the short term, from a growth in money that results from open-market operations (monetization of public sector debt).

To test this question the cross-correlogram between bank lending to the private sector (advances and commercial bills) and G.D.P. is shown in Chart 3. It will be noted that the maximum correlation ($r = 0{\cdot}34$) is much the same as that using the narrow definition of money supply, and that the chart has a similar lead/lag pattern.

Why should changes in advances lead changes in national income by a sizeable margin? It would probably be widely assumed that under the overdraft system, an advance and the expenditure it financed would take place simultaneously. However, if bank borrowing is a preferred form of debt—and it has certainly been the case that bank credit has been cheaper in recent years than most alternative forms of borrowing—then it is conceivable that easier access to bank credit will initially give rise to repayment of

other forms of debt. This might then result in a general easing of the credit situation and possibly a lowering of interest rates, which would combine to induce an increase in effective demand after a

Chart 3

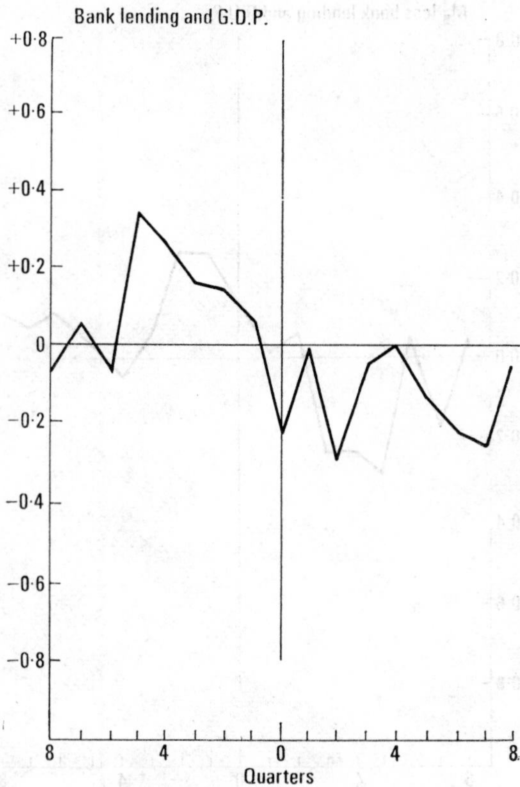

lag. However, it could also be the case that Chart 3 simply reflects time lags in the effect of other policy measures. Economic 'packages' often include measures to stimulate or restrain bank lending; so that if the package takes time to have its full effect on final demand, there might appear to be a lead of bank advances over G.D.P. that did not reflect any direct link.

Chart 4 shows the cross-correlogram between income and bank assets other than advances and commercial bills—a total which could alternatively be described as the component of the money

Chart 4

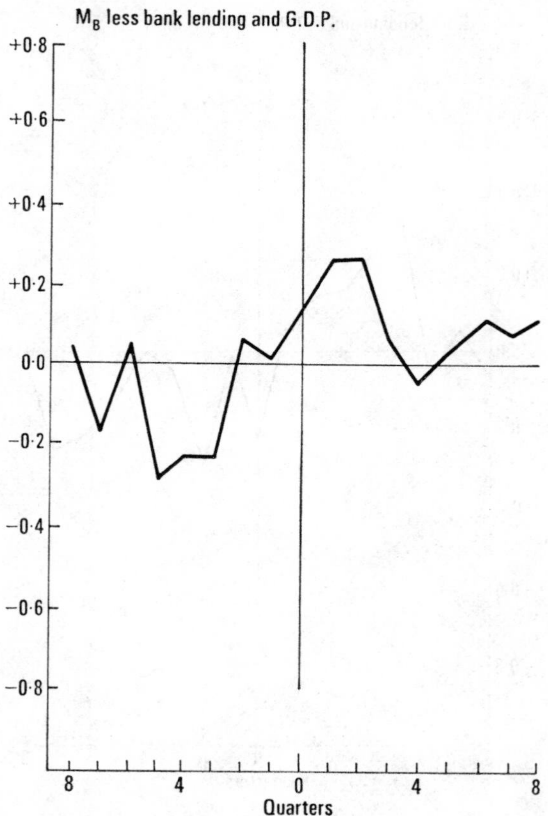

supply based on the monetization of public sector debt.[16] There is a significant negative relationship between such assets and subsequent changes in G.D.P. which, taken with the results in Chart 3, implies that the assets in which banks invest additional

[16] Although not all these other assets are public sector debt.

deposits could be of significance for subsequent changes in income. This may well reflect the fact that, in 1955, bank lending was, for historical reasons, abnormally low, so that in expansionary phases,

Chart 5

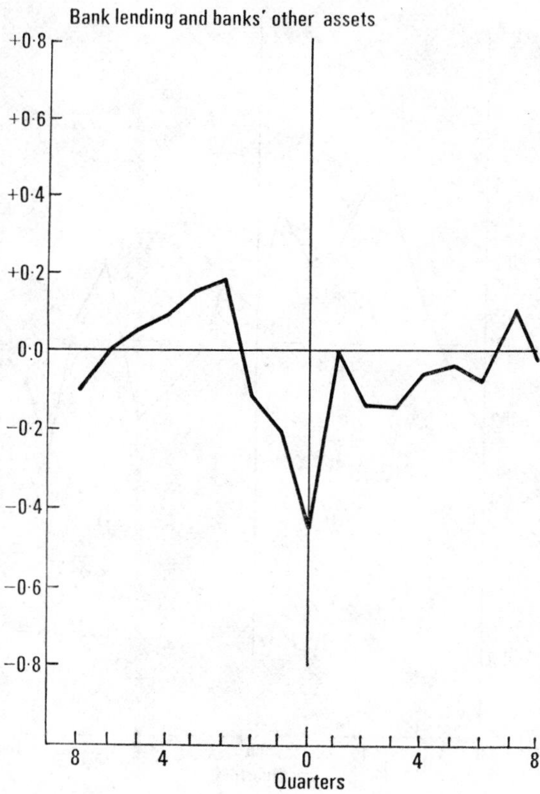

banks have been concerned to add to their advances by running down—or temporarily refraining from adding to—their other investments. In periods of quantitative credit restraint, on the other hand, banks will have been inhibited from making advances and will have tended to employ additional resources in public sector debt to a greater than normal extent.

Chart 5 shows that advances and commercial bills are, in fact (and as might be expected from inspection of Charts 3 and 4)

Chart 6

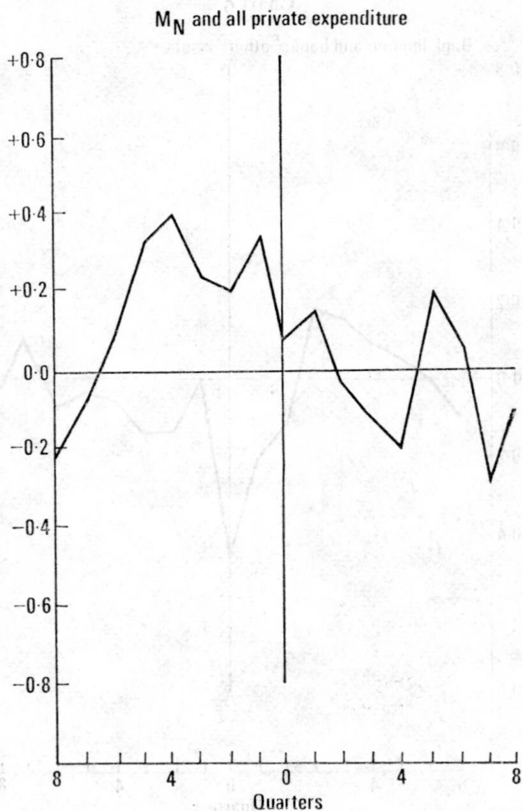

negatively associated with simultaneous changes in the banks' holdings of other assets.

(iii) *Monetary aggregates and expenditure components*

In so far as financial factors—whether measured as monetary aggregates or as credit aggregates—are measurably related to expenditure, the question arises whether the relationship is the same with all categories of expenditure. Monetarists generally

Chart 7

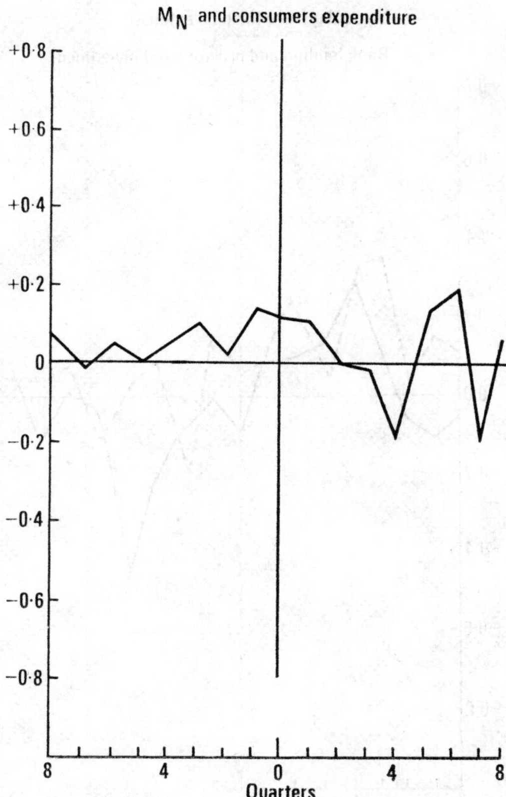

seem to expect that variations in monetary quantities will exercise a pervasive effect on demand,[17] while the distribution of income and expenditure will be largely influenced by other factors,

[17] See Friedman and Meiselman, footnote 1, p. 92.

including fiscal policy. The empirical studies,[18] and the theoretical analysis of those following a Keynesian income-expenditure

Chart 8

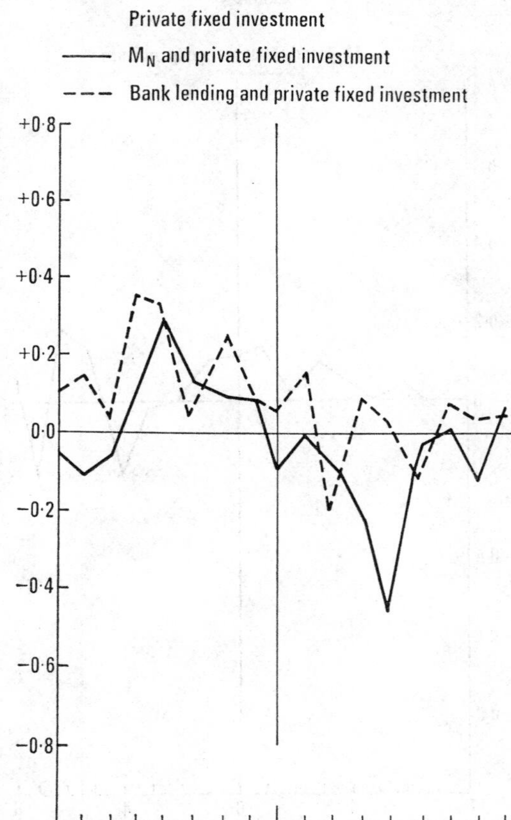

approach, on the other hand, would suggest that the main impact of financial factors would fall on investment (including investment

[18] See, for example, 'The Federal Reserve—M.I.T. econometric model', de Leeuw, Frank, and Gramlich, Edward, *Federal Reserve Bulletin*, January 1968, pp. 11–40.

Chart 9

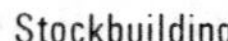

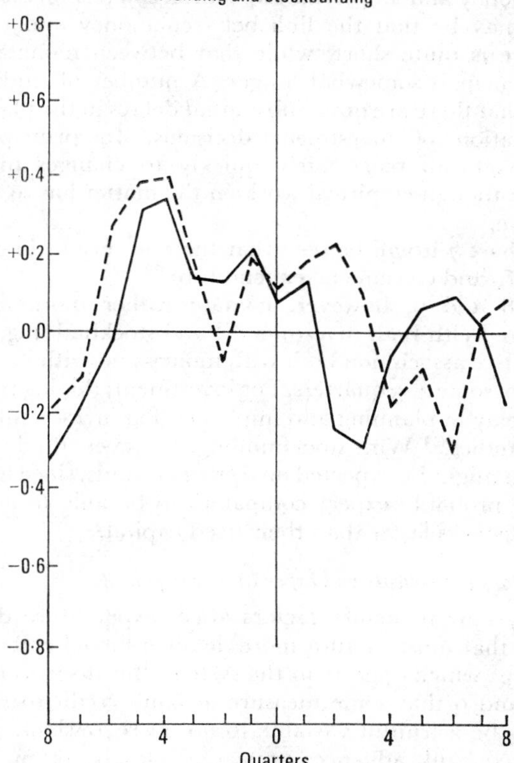

in durables),[19] while other categories of expenditure would be less directly affected.[20]

[19] Keynesian theory might also suggest that stockbuilding would be responsive to changes in financial conditions. In practice, it has proved very difficult to establish such a relationship empirically.

[20] Though in so far as changes in financial conditions gave rise to a change in investment, which then affected consumption (via the multiplier), there could be a *statistical* association between financial factors and other components of demand.

Charts 6–9, therefore, plot the relationship between various financial indicators, and, respectively, all private expenditure, and its components: consumers' expenditure, investment and stockbuilding. There is a noticeable 'twin peak' in the relationship between money and all private expenditure, a possible explanation of which may be that the link between money and consumers' expenditure is quite short, while that between monetary factors and investment is somewhat longer. A number of studies[21] have indicated that there are quite substantial delays in the planning and implementation of investment decisions. In principle, stockbuilding ought to react fairly quickly to changes in financial conditions; though empirical work on the matter has so far proved inconclusive.

From Chart 7 it will be seen that there is very little correlation between M_N and consumers' expenditure.[22]

Charts 8 and 9, however, contain rather more meaningful correlations. With both investment[23] and stockbuilding, there is a strong positive association both with money and with bank lending after a lag of some 4–5 quarters. For investment, this lag is consistent with the delay in planning and implementing investment indicated by other studies.[24] With stockbuilding, however, the lag is rather longer than might be expected on *a priori* grounds, since in principle one would probably expect companies to be able to adjust their holdings of stocks faster than their fixed capital.

(iv) *Monetary components and expenditure components*

Precisely how monetary factors affect expenditure decisions is something that must await a more detailed model embodying the relationships which operate in the system. But it seems likely from Charts 8 and 9 that some measure of bank credit to the private sector may be a fruitful variable to use in regressions. In each of these charts, bank advances appear as closely, or more closely, linked with subsequent changes in expenditure than does the

[21] See, for example, articles by Burman, J. P., Hines, A. G., and Catephores, G., *in* Heathfield, D. F., and Hilton, K. (eds.), *The econometric study of the United Kingdom* (London, 1970); and Almon, Shirley 'The distributed lag between capital appropriations and expenditures', *Econometrica*, vol. 33, no. 1, January 1965.

[22] The correlation was rather higher (though not quite significant at the 5 per cent level) when the broad definition of money was used.

[23] The national income definition of investment, used here, does not include investment in consumer durables.

[24] See, for example, Burman, footnote 21 above.

money stock. Thus whatever the long-run relationships, the transmission mechanism in the short run will probably have to take account of credit as well as purely monetary factors.

Conclusion

Although timing relationships cannot prove causality,[25] the length of the observed lead or lag may be consistent with certain hypotheses and not with others. Bearing in mind the necessary caveats, we may hazard the following tentative conclusions:

(i) Even when trends in the data are removed, the money stock, narrowly defined, seems to be positively related to subsequent changes in expenditure.

(ii) There appears, however, to be little to choose between monetary, credit and interest rate variables, as indicators of subsequent changes in G.D.P.

(iii) Investment appears to be more strongly related to changes in financial conditions than are the other components of expenditure.

In general it seems doubtful whether the strength of the observed association between monetary and real variables is great enough to support the view that control of monetary aggregates should be the main weapon of counter-cyclical macro-economic policy.

[25] See Tobin, J. L., and Brainard, W. C., 'Pitfalls in financial model building', *Papers and proceedings of the American Economic Association*, May 1963, pp. 99–122, for a forcible demonstration of this.

5

INTEREST RATES AND THE DEMAND FOR REAL ASSETS

J. C. R. Dow*

THE argument so far has sought to show how the monetary authorities can affect the price of financial securities and hence the rate of interest on them. It is now necessary to show how the demand for real and financial assets are interrelated. Keynes's 'liquidity preference' theory—the contention that the rate of interest represents 'the reward for parting with liquidity'—was developed in conscious opposition to the 'classical' doctrine that the rate of interest is 'the factor which brings the demand for investment and the willingness to save into equilibrium with one another'.[1] But he also believed that the 'rate of current investment will be pushed to the point where there is no longer any class of capital-asset of which the marginal efficiency exceeds the current rate of interest'.[2] These two articles of belief—as stated—are inconsistent. For the latter contention is equivalent to saying that bonds and real assets are substitutes for each other as far as the investor is concerned; and from this it follows that not only does the price of bonds affect the demand for real assets, but also that all the factors affecting the demand for real assets affect the price of bonds. Since Keynes wrote it has been one of the vexed questions of economics whether the rate of interest is a monetary phenomenon, or alternatively, is a creation of the real forces of 'productivity and thrift': in fact it must surely be both.

* Extract reprinted from Dow, J. C. R., *The Management of the British Economy 1945–60* (Cambridge, 1964), pp. 314–21, by permission of the author and publishers. J. C. R. Dow is Assistant Secretary-General at the Organization for European Co-operation and Development (OECD) in Paris.

[1] Keynes, J. M., *The General Theory of Employment, Interest and Money* (1936), pp. 167, 175.

[2] Ibid., p. 136.

The best way of describing the effect of changes in interest rates on the demand for real assets is in terms of changes in the price of assets; for, in the market for assets, it is the *price* of assets that is determined. The price of *new* capital assets, being dependent on current costs of production, may be taken as given from the present point of view. The price of *existing* real assets, on the other hand—in so far as there is a market price for second-hand houses, shops, offices, factories, machinery and vehicles—is not unrelated to the price of financial securities, and the two must to some extent vary in sympathy. A rise in bond prices therefore raises the price of old real assets relatively to their replacement cost; and thus makes it more desirable to maintain or add to the existing stock, i.e. it increases investment demand to some degree.

In operating on the composition of the National Debt as between money and bonds, the authorities are thus in effect, though at several removes, operating on a vast market—on nothing less than the demand to hold the stock of national wealth. The different categories of assets range in a sort of spectrum from money and bills, through bonds and equities, to real assets. At first sight it may seem difficult to believe that manipulations at the 'monetary' end of the spectrum have large effects on the market for real assets. In order to illustrate the orders of magnitude, it is convenient first to give a highly simplified picture, in which the differences between different capital goods are ignored, so that it is possible to speak of 'the stock' of real capital. To show the effect of monetary action, it is also necessary to have an idea of the other forces affecting the demand for real assets.

Interest-rate effects, though usually discussed in terms of savings and investment should properly be framed in terms of the stock of capital. Thus there may be reasons to think that if the stock of capital were greatly increased (the state of 'technique' being assumed as given), the 'rate of return' would fall: but there is no reason to think it would fall off quickly. Since the annual rate of investment is small in relation to the stock, there is therefore no reason to think that the rate of *investment* affects the yield materially.[3]

[3] The illegitimate transition in Keynes's argument in *The General Theory* from 'stocks' to 'flows' has already been pointed out [Chap. XI.4, p. 286 n. in Dow's book]. Thus Keynes concluded on this point that 'for each type of capital we can build up a schedule, showing by how much investment in it will have to increase within the period, in order that its marginal efficiency should fall to any given figure' (Keynes (1936), p. 136). His argument admittedly depended partly on the consideration that pressure on production facilities would raise the supply

The yield on capital expressed as a ratio of the replacement cost of capital assets can therefore at any one time be taken as given for all practical purposes.

The argument about saving (as already noted)[4] also needs to be formulated in terms of the desire to hold assets. People start by owning assets, and the alternatives open to them include not merely the possibility of adding to their assets, but of living off their capital: thus to speak only of decisions to save obscures the range of choice to be explained. That savings should be positive, and that communities should add fairly steadily to their economic wealth, seems an almost invariable concomitant of economic progress. It is difficult to believe that the precise level of interest rates has much affected the process of accumulation, which has surely to be explained rather in terms of the advantages of being wealthy. Moreover even if it were true that a higher interest rate, for instance, increased saving (as Marshall believed), it would still be true (as Marshall added) 'that the annual investment of wealth is a small part of the already existing stock, and that therefore the stock would not be increased perceptibly in any one year by even a considerable increase in the annual rate of saving'.[5] The desire to hold wealth, rather than to dissipate it in dis-saving, cannot then depend critically on the rate of interest.

It may be concluded that, at any moment of time, the rate of return on new additions to the stock of capital is what it is; and that the stock which people desire to maintain is what it is more or less irrespective of the rate of return. Their desired stock may however change for other reasons: with the passage of time, it normally grows, and it is affected by the actions of the monetary authorities. The present plane of argument leaves out many qualifications but contains the essentials needed to show the effect of monetary intervention.

Figure 1 shows the equilibrium position at a point in time.[6] The 'productivity of capital' curve (CC) can be expressed directly in 'real' terms: the curve shows the return (R) on capital (K) expressed as a ratio of the *replacement* cost. This falls only slowly as

price of capital goods—a short-term 'disequilibrium' consideration best ignored on the present plane of argument.

[4] See Chap. XI.3 [Dow, op. cit.].

[5] Marshall, A., *Principles of Economics* (1920) (1938 ed.), p. 236.

[6] Compare the discussion in Hicks, J. R., 'Thoughts on the Theory of Capital—The Corfu Conference', *Oxford Econ. Pap.*, June 1960, pp. 125–6. Figure 1 follows Hicks's notation.

the stock is increased. The demand to hold assets is insensitive with respect to the rate of return so defined (and so would in these terms be represented by a vertical line). The 'demand for assets' curve (*MM*) on the diagram relates the *volume* of assets desired to be held to the rate of return (*r*) expressed as a ratio of the *market value* of existing assets (which may be above or below the replacement cost). This curve, while nearly vertical, probably falls to the left.[7]

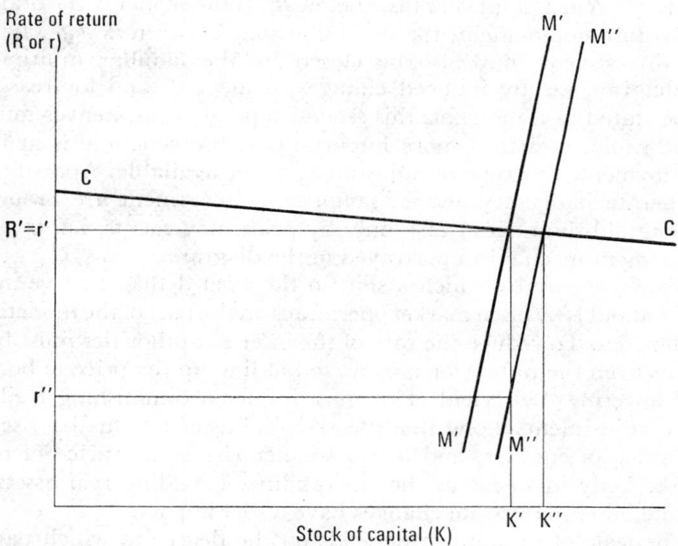

FIG. 1. *Productivity of capital (CC) and desire to hold real assets (MM)*

In stationary equilibrium, people would desire to maintain the capital stock at its present size: the market price would equal the replacement cost ($r' = R'$), so that it paid neither to add to the capital stock (K') nor to run it down. Now suppose that people

[7] Hicks argues that 'in the classical conception' we should think of *MM* as a *horizontal* line, but he later gives reasons for supposing that it should be drawn sloping downwards very sharply.

One reason for believing that the curve is not absolutely vertical is that the demand to hold assets is probably to some extent a demand for a certain *value* of assets. The quantity of assets demanded should therefore vary inversely with the price of assets; or directly with *r*, the return expressed as a ratio of the price.

want to increase their stock of assets (i.e. to save) and this is not immediately matched by an increase in the stock of assets (i.e. by investment). This is represented on the diagram by the shift from $M'M'$ to $M''M''$. One adjustment to close this disequilibrium would be for asset prices to be bid up, so providing an incentive to investment. The fall in the 'money' rate of interest to r'' implies a rise in asset prices, which causes an expansion of the capital stock from K' to K'', which in turn brings an eventual return to a position where $r = R$ at a point very little below R'. If the economy is working below full employment, the disequilibrium between *ex ante* saving and investment may also be closed by the familiar multiplier mechanism, i.e. by induced changes in income; and for reasons to be stated in a moment, this second type of adjustment is much more rapid, and thus more important. If the economy is at full employment, this type of adjustment is not available. Apart from deliberate budgetary action, saving and investment are brought into equilibrium—if at all—only by price movements, i.e. by the adjustment mechanism portrayed in the diagram.

Now one way by which a shift in the asset demand curve may come about is by open market operations on the part of the monetary authorities. To reduce the rate of the interest authorities must buy bonds from the public for money, so bidding up the price of bonds and lowering their yield. This must induce a diminishing trail of price adjustments along the 'spectrum' of assets: a smaller rise in the price of equities, and a still smaller rise in the price of real assets. Only in so far as the desirability of holding real assets is affected do interest-rate changes have a real impact.

The scale of the impact depends on the degree to which paper securities and real assets are substitutes. In practice, the degree of substitution is small; but it cannot be entirely negligible. If substitutability were perfect, the intervention of the authorities would have the same effect as if the authorities were buying not bonds but real assets. It is for instance conceivable that the banks should increase the public's holding of money by making loans against the security of real property, i.e. by monetizing part not of the National Debt but of the national wealth, or in effect by making 'open market purchases' of real property. There would then be an additional demand for real property coming from the banks in addition to the previously existing demand to hold real assets on the part of the public—which would analytically amount to a shift in the MM curve.

It may be helpful at this point to give some idea of the possible scale of action by the monetary authorities. In a country like the United Kingdom with a large National Debt, the possible range of action is large. All the following figures refer to the years 1953–55.[8] For these years the volume of money held by the public has been estimated at £9 billion; and the value of floating debt and British government bonds (not held by the banks or by the government itself) has been estimated at about £9 billion also. This compares with about £14 billion for the value of the liabilities of public and private non-financial companies;[9] and about £22 billion for the value of real assets other than those owned by the government.[10] The total net assets held by the private sector, excluding its holding of money, but including its holding of National Debt, were therefore of the order of £31 billion.

The ratio of the money supply to the national product fell (as there defined) from 0·7 in 1947 to a little under 0·5 in 1953–55 (and fell more by 1960). Suppose that this had not happened, but that the government had issued more money as national income rose and reduced its debt in inverse correspondence. The public's holding of money in 1953–55 would then have been almost half as large again, or £4 billion larger; and the value of National Debt £4 billion smaller. This is appreciable in relation to the public's total holding of financial *plus* real assets of £31 billion: had the money-income ratio been kept constant, this total would have been smaller by fifteen per cent. The price it was willing to pay for assets—chiefly financial assets, but also to some extent real assets—might therefore be expected to have been appreciably higher.

This gives some idea of the authorities' possible range of action: in principle, this could be much wider than the actual change over these seven years. The conclusion must be that operations of the open market type can be more than minor manipulations of the monetary end of the 'spectrum' of assets, and can represent sizeable additions to or subtractions from the demand for non-monetary assets. But though in the short run the authorities may effectively manipulate the level of yields and asset prices, in the long run one

[8] See Morgan, E. V., *The Structure of Property Ownership in Great Britain*, especially Table 65 (1960).

[9] This excludes the liabilities of foreign companies and British companies operating abroad.

[10] The real assets of the central government, the local authorities and the public corporations were put at another £8 billion.

would expect this to set up forces which restored rates or yields to something like their original level—a level determined by the real productivity of capital.

This account of the mechanism of adjustment, based on the distinction between the market price of real assets and their replacement value, is however a vast simplification of reality. The market for financial securities and for real assets is far from being one market. The financial capital market is often said to be imperfect: the property market is at least equally so, and that for most other sorts of real assets is so imperfect that one can hardly speak of there being a market at all.

If the market were as perfect as implied hitherto, small changes in asset prices (induced let us say by the actions of the monetary authorities) would induce sizeable adjustments to the stock of capital. Again, if the market were perfect, the adjustments would be rapid, so that one would see extreme variations in the rate of investment. Indeed, if the market were perfect, no discrepancy between *ex ante* saving and investment could arise. In practice, the market does not operate in this way; investment is by no means so sensitive. The notion that *ex ante* saving and investment may differ, so that excess demand may emerge, is a keystone of modern macro-economic theory: it is clear that the pricing system is *not* perfect enough to eradicate such divergencies, and that the idea of excess demand is based on a valid intuition.

The reason for the imperfection of the market for real assets is that their productiveness, and hence their value, depends very much on who it is that is putting them to use. Most capital goods are therefore, in this sense, highly specific: they have a higher value in their present use than elsewhere. They may have some value if sold separately; but if their 'second-hand' price falls, it does not necessarily reflect a low value in use, nor necessarily imply that it is less economic for their present owners to replace them when worn out.

The converse also holds. Real assets tend to be managed by those who think they can make best use of them; but there are so many uncertainties that their productivity is very difficult even for those managing them to judge. Consequently, probably profitable lines of investment are not exploited to the full immediately. The *management* of property is part and parcel of getting a profit; and, being a demanding task, entrepreneurs extend their commitments only gradually, making a second investment only when a first has proved successful.[11] A rise in second-hand asset prices, therefore, does not necessarily imply that entrepreneurs find it worthwhile to extend their investment.

The market price of real assets, in short, is a poor reflection of their value in use. The fact that real assets are not interchangeable among themselves means also that as a class they are not good substitutes for paper assets. It follows that the authorities are able within wide limits to vary the rate of return on interest-bearing paper assets (by themselves buying and holding more or less) without greatly affecting the demand for real assets. There is little immediate tendency to bring the market rate into equilibrium with the return on real assets. Indeed, when the riskiness of capital is allowed for, the 'return' on real assets becomes a misty and subjective entity.

The theoretical conclusion is then this: in the short-term, the rate of interest is primarily a 'monetary' phenomenon determined by the forces of liquidity preference as described by Keynes. Since paper securities and real assets are poor substitutes, there is no rigid link between the returns on each. Precisely because of this, it is relatively easy—and also relatively useless—for the authorities to vary the rate of interest. Nevertheless, the division between paper and real assets is not absolute. Hence the fact that real assets yield a return may still be regarded as the reason for there being a positive rate of interest at all: it is for this reason that the government cannot borrow free, but has to pay interest on its debt. Even in the short term, this link with real forces will cast its shadow before it, by providing some vague norm for the expectation of the market, so preventing security prices departing too far from what the market expects real forces will eventually dictate they should be.[12]

Equities also provide a bridge between the two markets. Since equities are 'standardized' real assets, they are fairly close substitutes for bonds; so that, in the absence of dividend changes, equity prices and bond prices move closely parallel.[13] But dividends —or expected dividends—bear some relation to firms' profits.

[11] See the discussion of the 'principle of increasing risk' in Chap. XI.4 [Dow, op. cit.].

[12] See discussion in §1 above [Dow, op. cit., pp. 223–227]. The market opposition to cheap money in 1947 probably sprang in part from the feeling that interest rates were lower than could be maintained.

[13] See for instance Sahni, I. M. (1951), 'A Study of Share Prices, 1918–1947', *Yorkshire B.*, February 1951.

Hence changes in profits affect the rate of interest on paper assets.[14]

There being a significant connection between the two markets, it follows that at least in the long term it matters what the authorities do to interest rates. If it is true that, in the long term, 'real' forces tend to predominate in fixing the level of interest rates, this is so only because in the long term the effects on the stock of capital can be expected to be appreciable. The effectiveness of monetary intervention is to be measured not by how greatly interest rates can be changed, but by how far even small effects on interest rates affect the volume of capital which the community wishes to maintain.

[14] Empirical confirmation of this conclusion is provided by Khusro, A. H. in 'An Investigation of Liquidity Preference', *Yorkshire Bulletin of Economic and Social Research*, vol. 4, no. 1 (January 1952), p. 1. It is however disputed. Mr Kennedy, for instance, attempting to reinstate a purely Keynesian view, has recently argued that, while expected dividend increases (arising from the expectation of continued inflation) 'must lead to an alteration in the relative yields of bonds and equities, there is no reason why equilibrium should not be restored by a rise in equity prices rather than by a fall in bond prices' (Kennedy, C. [1960], 'Inflation and the Bond Rate', *Oxford Econ. Pap.*, October 1960, p. 272). Khusro's results suggest, on the contrary, that in such a case bond yields in fact rise and bond prices fall.

II

THE DEMAND FOR MONEY

II

THE DEMAND FOR MONEY

EDITED BY
D. LAIDLER

Introduction

IT will be apparent from the preceding chapter of this book that a stable demand for money function is a necessary though not sufficient condition for variations in the quantity of money to have a stable and predictable effect on the level of economic activity. This particular relationship has probably been studied more intensively than any other in monetary economics, and it seems possible to make certain broad generalizations about it that hold true not only for Britain, but for other countries as well, notably the United States where a great deal of empirical work has been done.

First there does seem to exist, and to have existed at least since the end of the nineteenth century when available data begin, a reasonably stable relationship between the demand for cash balances and a few other variables. The description 'reasonably stable relationship' here means both that the demand for money seems to vary with these other variables so systematically as to make it virtually impossible to explain the apparent interrelationships as chance occurrences, and that the actual quantitative values of the parameters of the functions implied by these observed relationships have remained reasonably steady over time. These parameters have not remained constant, of course, but changes in them have been slow rather than sudden.

Thus, far from being something that can vary almost without limit, as the Radcliffe Committee claimed, the income velocity of circulation—the ratio of the quantity of money to national income—turns out mainly to vary systematically with the level of 'expected' or 'permanent' income and the rate of return on assets other than money. The main results on these issues are surveyed in the first item reprinted in this chapter (Reading 6), while the other three items reprinted here are themselves empirical studies of the behaviour of the demand for money function in the United Kingdom. The earliest study, by Kavanagh and Walters, shows that a stable demand for money relationship has existed at least since the end of the nineteenth century, while the other two selections deal specifically with the post-Second World War period. The latter studies both show that, in dealing with data generated in this period, it is vital to take account of time lags in the relationship both as regards the way in which money holders form their assessment of 'expected' or 'permanent' income on the basis of current income experience, and as regards the pace at which they choose to bring their money holdings back into equilibrium after a disturbance. Only when these lags are allowed for can the same kind of relationships that are apparent in Kavanagh and Walters's long-run study be seen to underlie the post-war data. This is particularly interesting in view of the difficulty that Barrett and Walters (see Reading 2 above) had in tracing the same stable money multiplier relationships for post-war years as they had discovered to hold for the earlier period.

Having said all this though, a caveat is in order. The studies in question leave a number of problems unsolved. Kavanagh and Walters, for example, find the inter-war period easier to deal with than other times; Laidler and Parkin's work, unlike the other two studies, could find no important role for the interest rate to play. These, and other discrepancies, imply that we still have a lot to learn about the demand for money function in the United Kingdom. These studies certainly do not provide grounds for attributing to the quantity of money a unique role in the determination of the level of economic activity. They do, however, strongly suggest that money plays too important a role for it to be ignored or relegated to secondary status. Though they stop far short of establishing the quantity of money as the sole tool of macro-economic policy, in this writer's judgement they go a long way towards rehabilitating the quantity of money as one potentially important instrument whereby macro-economic activity can be influenced.

We have chosen to concentrate mainly on empirical studies of the U.K. in this chapter of the book since basic theoretical articles both on the role of the demand for money function in the transmission of the effects of monetary policy and on the nature of the function itself are readily available elsewhere, as are empirical studies of the relationship in other economies, particularly the United States. The attached bibliography lists a sample of items that might well be read in conjunction with this section of the book.

FURTHER READING

General Overview of the Problem Area

Laidler, D. E. W., *The Demand for Money: Theories and Evidence* (Scranton, Pa., 1969).

Theories of the Demand for Money

Baumol, W. J., 'The Transactions Demand for Cash—An Inventory Theoretic Approach', *Quarterly Journal of Economics*, vol. 66, no. 4, November 1952, pp. 544–56.

Friedman, M., 'The Quantity Theory of Money, A Restatement' *in* Friedman, M. (ed.), *Studies in the Quantity Theory of Money* (Chicago, Ill., 1956).

Keynes, J. M., *The General Theory of Employment, Interest and Money* (London and New York, 1936), Chap. 15.

Tobin, J., 'Liquidity Preference as Behaviour Towards Risk', *Review of Economic Studies*, vol. 25, no. 67, February 1958, pp. 65–86.

Representative Empirical Studies

Feige, E., 'Expectations and Adjustments in the Monetary Sector', *American Economic Review*, vol. 57, no. 2, Papers and Proceedings, May 1967, pp. 462–73.

Fisher, D., 'The Demand for Money in Britain: Quarterly Results 1951–1967', *The Manchester School*, vol. 36, no. 4, December 1968, pp. 329–44.

Hynes, A., 'The Demand for Money and Monetary Adjustments in Chile', *Review of Economic Studies*, vol. 34, no. 3, July 1967, pp. 285–94.

Meltzer, A. H., 'The Demand for Money: The Evidence from the Time Series', *Journal of Political Economy*, vol. 71, no. 3, June 1963, pp. 219–46.

6

THE DEMAND FOR MONEY: THE EVIDENCE OF EMPIRICAL INVESTIGATIONS

The Bank of England*

Professor Friedman [10] has redefined the Quantity Theory as a theory of the demand for money. Many economists have therefore turned to the estimation of the money demand function (and its analogue, the velocity function) to test the theories advanced by monetarists. These tests have been designed to throw light on a number of issues, some of which—for example, the appropriate definition of money, whether income or wealth is the main determinant of desired money balances, and whether money is a luxury good—are not the really critical issues in the current debate between 'Keynesians' and 'monetarists'.[1] Other questions are, however, vitally important to this debate, and in this review the following are isolated:

(i) the basic predictability of the demand for money;
(ii) the role of interest rates in the demand-for-money function; and
(iii) the relative importance of short-term and long-term interest rates in explaining the demand for money.

* Extracts reprinted from 'The importance of money' (Appendix I), *Bank of England Quarterly Bulletin*, vol. 10, no. 3, June 1970, pp. 181–5, 188–90, by permission of the publisher. The article was prepared in the Bank of England's Economic Section, being largely the work of C. A. E. Goodhart assisted, particularly in the preparation of the appendices, by A. D. Crockett. Both Goodhart and Crockett are currently members of the Bank's research staff.

[1] As in the main paper /pp. 8–39 of Reading 1/, the terms 'Keynesian' and monetarist' are used to characterize views that would not necessarily be held by all, or even most, members of each school of thought.

Empirical tests have been successful in partially confirming some, at least, of the monetarists' theories. This has encouraged further work designed to compare the stability of Keynesian and monetary relationships.

The predictability of the demand for money

Although there is nothing in Keynes' work to suggest that the demand for money should be unpredictable (except at very low interest rates), a widespread feeling grew up among Keynesians in the post-war period that the availability of money substitutes would render the money–income relationship too volatile to be of much practical use for economic management or forecasting. This was the view that was challenged by the monetarists. Friedman and Schwartz, in their monetary history of the United States [**12**], demonstrated that real income and real money balances were connected in a reasonably predictable way over the period 1867–1959. Since then, the work of Meltzer [**22**], Chow [**5**], Laidler [**17**], and Courchene and Shapiro [**7**], among others, have borne out the contention that the demand-for-money function for the United States is fairly well determined over the long period, with coefficients of determination[2] in the range 0·9–0·99. The pioneering long-range study for the United Kingdom carried out by Kavanagh and Walters [**16**], for the period 1877–1961, established a coefficient of determination of 0·98 in the demand-for-money function.

It is, however, relatively easy to establish an apparently close-fitting relationship when there are strong trends in both dependent and independent (explanatory) variables. A possibly more searching test of the strength of the basic relationship is its predictability when estimated using changes in, rather than levels of, the data. Using changes reduces dramatically the coefficient of determination. For example, in Laidler's very comprehensive study based on U.S. data, the coefficient of determination in a typical equation was lowered from 0·99 to 0·51 when the data were transformed into first differences (i.e. changes). For U.K. data, the coefficient of 0·98 by Kavanagh and Walters, noted above, was reduced to 0·49 by first differencing.

[2] The coefficient of determination, or R^2 statistic, is the proportion of the variance of the dependent variable in an equation which can be associated with, or 'explained' by, changes in the independent variables.

The use of lagged dependent variables[3] is another way by which the danger of inferring false relationships from trend-dominated variables can be reduced, though similar dangers are raised in interpreting the lagged term. Most tests using lagged dependent variables [including the models reported in Reading 7] have shown the estimated coefficient of the lagged variable to be highly significant, while the explanatory power of other variables has been correspondingly lower. One explanation of these findings is the presence of time-lags in the process by which a dependent variable adjusts to an equilibrium; but an equally plausible one is the existence of first order serial correlation in the residuals;[4] both influences are probably present to some extent.

The empirical evidence suggests that the demand for money is more predictable than, say, the Radcliffe Committee would have imagined, but probably not predictable enough to be used as an instrument of short-term policy. Furthermore the predictability of the relationship in a period when control of the money supply was not a major feature of policy will not necessarily be a good guide to its predictability under conditions when it was more actively used.

The role of interest rates in the demand-for-money function

The next important point of dispute is the relationship between the level of interest rates and the quantity of money. Many Keynesians have supposed that the interest-elasticity of the demand for money would be relatively high[5] whilst monetarists have believed the elasticity would be low, because money was seen by them as a general substitute for all assets, rather than a specific substitute for interest-bearing financial assets.

In his early writings, Friedman [**11**] conceded that interest rates

[3] Where one of the factors explaining the level of the dependent variable is its level in the previous time period.

[4] The residuals associated with any estimated relationship are defined as:

$$u_t = y_t - \hat{y}_t$$

where y_t = the observed value of the dependent variable at time t

$\hat{y}_t$ = the value of the dependent variable at time t calculated from the estimated relationship.

First order serial correlation in the residuals is the correlation between u_t and u_{t-1}.

[5] See for example the *Radcliffe Report* [**24**].

might feature in the demand-for-money function but, on the basis of empirical work, contended that in practice they did not. Thus, it was argued that the observed relationship between money and incomes must be a 'direct' one. It has since been shown, however, that interest rates do play a significant role in the demand for money. Of all the studies of this subject published since Friedman's, and which are noted in Table A, only those by Heller [**15**] for the United States, and by Fisher [**8**] for the United Kingdom indicate an inability to find a significant role for interest rates.[6] The volume of evidence is now quite widely accepted, at least among Keynesians and some monetarists, as contradicting the view that 'only money matters'. However, the fact that interest rates are significant in the demand-for-money function undermines only the extreme version of the quantity theory, namely that there is a fixed short-term link between the stock of money and money incomes. It leaves open the question of the *relative* importance of income and interest rates in determining desired money holdings.

Nearly all the work that has been done on *levels* of data has shown income to be much more important than interest rates in determining the demand for money. Partial coefficients of correlations[7] are not generally given, but it may reasonably be inferred that incomes are more important from the fact that the margins of error in the estimates of coefficients are relatively much lower for income variables than for interest rates.[8]

That this should be so in the long term is not surprising, because there are long-term trends in both incomes and money. It is in this context more revealing to look at models which are estimated in first difference form (using changes, rather than levels, of data), or with the use of a lagged dependent variable. The study of U.S. data by Laidler [**17**] showed that the significance of an income variable was much reduced when the data were transformed into first

[6] See footnote 12 on p. 129 for a possible explanation of Heller's finding.

[7] The partial coefficient of correlation measures the degree of association between two variables, after allowing for the impact of other variables in the equation. Another means of measuring the relative strength of two separate effects is by beta coefficients (see Goldberger [**13**]).

[8] It is convenient to compare margins of error by the use of *t* statistics (the ratio of an estimated coefficient to its estimated standard error). In general, the smaller the *t* statistic, the more subject is the estimated coefficient to sampling fluctuations (random errors), and conversely the higher the *t* statistic. It is because of sampling fluctuations that a non-zero coefficient may be recorded even though the true value of the coefficient may be zero.

differences, though it was still somewhat greater than that of the interest rate variable. Hamburger [**14**], in a study using logarithmic first differences, found that the coefficient on incomes became insignificant.

Once a role has been conceded to interest rates the question becomes one of how large an interest-elasticity is consistent with according primary importance to money. There is no unambiguous answer to this question, since it hinges on the meaning that is given to words such as 'large', 'primary', etc. This is an example of how the two theories have, partly as a result of empirical testing, drawn together.

The numerical value of the interest-elasticity[9] that has been observed has generally been found to lie in the range −0·1 to −1·0. This is quite a wide band, but part at least of the variation is due to the different forms in which the demand-for-money function has been tested. Some economists, following the letter of Keynes, have used the bond rate in their equations as the opportunity cost of holding money. Others, recognizing that Keynes was using a restrictive theoretical model, have suggested that in practice short-term financial assets are more likely to be thought of as substitutes for money, and so have used a short-term rate of interest. Short-term and long-term rates are closely linked as to the direction of movements; but fluctuations in short-term rates are perhaps two to three times larger. Thus, it is to be expected that a higher interest-elasticity will have been observed for long-term rates than for short-term rates.

Another difference lies in the definition of money which has been used. The usual definition in the United States restricts money to currency and demand deposits; but certain monetarists, particularly Friedman, have argued that the definition should be widened to include time deposits, on the grounds that these too are a 'temporary abode of purchasing power'. It is to be expected that the narrower definition would probably have the greater interest-elasticity, because the wider definition includes assets bearing a yield which moves broadly in line with other market rates.

[9] The most commonly used measure of interest-elasticity measures approximately the percentage change in money balances resulting from a one per cent change in interest rates, a one per cent change being a change from, say, 4 to 4·04 per cent. To produce equations with constant interest-elasticities, interest rates are usually put directly into logarithmic form. This implies that a change in interest rates from, say, ½ to 1 per cent would have the same effect as a change from 4 to 8 per cent.

For these reasons it is, perhaps, to be expected that models using a narrow definition of money and a long-term rate of interest would yield the highest interest-elasticities, and that those with a wide definition and a short-term rate of interest would yield the lowest elasticities. This is broadly the picture which emerges from the empirical results presented in Table A, certainly for those based on annual data. The highest[10] estimates of interest-elasticity are those of Meltzer [**22**], Brunner and Meltzer [**3**], Chow [**5**] and Courchene and Shapiro [**7**]; all are derived on the basis of the narrow definition of money and a long-term interest rate, and none is below –0·7. Laidler [**17**] specifically set out to test the relative elasticities using different specifications; and Tobin [**26**] did much the same thing using a velocity function. Using annual U.S. data from 1892–1960,[11] Laidler produced elasticity estimates ranging from –0·16 using a wide definition of money and short-term interest rates as an argument, to –0·72 using a narrow definition of money and long-term interest rates. Tobin's estimates were much the same, ranging from –0·12 to –0·55.

For the United Kingdom, the only study of note using annual levels of the money stock is that of Kavanagh and Walters [**16**]. They used a wide definition of money, and a long-term interest rate, and obtained an elasticity of –0·30 for the period 1877–1961; and of –0·50 for the period 1926–61. The relationships between interest-elasticities estimated using U.S. data suggest, perhaps, that had a short-term interest rate been used, the estimated elasticity for the shorter period would have been closer to –0·2.

Thus, despite the superficial appearance of diversity, most of the work done with long runs of annual data produces a fairly consistent picture. The elasticity of currency and demand deposits with respect to long-term interest rates is probably about –0·7, and with respect to short-term interest rates about –0·25. For a wider definition of money, the relevant figures are slightly lower, and seem to depend more on the particular specification of the model.

Those studies which have used quarterly data have tended to produce lower estimates for the interest-elasticity of the demand for money. Heller [**15**] was unable to detect any significant influence of long-term interest rates[12] on the demand for money and, when

[10] In the sense of being furthest from zero.

[11] The data for money on a narrow definition are available only from 1919.

[12] These results, however, are partly due to the fact that the estimation period chosen includes the years prior to 1951 when interest rates were pegged. If these years are excluded, both long and short rates become highly significant.

TABLE A

For reasons of space, this selection of empirical work has had to be extremely compressed. As far as possible, representative equations have been chosen from the work of each author, though often other equations have produced somewhat different coefficients. No reference is made to the other variables, besides interest rates, included in the equations.

Where the equations contain lags, the implied long-run elasticity is given; these equations are marked † and no *t* statistic is given as its meaning would be ambiguous.

Author	Data used	Definition of money[a]	Interest rate used	Interest-elasticity[b]	*t* statistic[c]
	Demand-for-money equations				
Bronfenbrenner and Mayer [2]	Annual: U.S.: 1919–56	Narrow	Short	−0·33	†
Chow [5]	Annual: U.S.: 1897–1958	Narrow	Long	−0·73	17
Meltzer [22]	Annual: U.S.: 1900–58	Narrow	Long	−0·92	22
”	”	Broad	Long	−0·48	10
”	Annual: U.S.: 1930–58	Narrow	Long	−1·15	12
”	”	Broad	Long	−0·70	7
Brunner and Meltzer [3]	Annual: U.S.: 1930–59	Narrow	Long	−1·09	19
”	”	Broad	Long	−0·73	15
Laidler [17]	Annual: U.S.: 1919–60	Narrow	Short	−0·21 (−0·11)	12 (3)
”	”	Narrow	Long	−0·72 (−0·33)	12 (3)
”	Annual: U.S.: 1892–1960	Broad	Short	−0·16 (−0·10)	16 (5)
”	”	Broad	Long	−0·25 (−0·26)	4 (3)

Lee [21]	Annual: U.S.: 1951–65	Narrow	Short	−0·41	4
”	”	Broad	Short	−0·67	3
Motley [23]	Annual: U.S.: 1920–65 (Households only)	Broad	Short	−0·16	5
Courchene and Shapiro [7]	Annual: U.S.: 1900–58	Narrow	Long	−1·00	16
”	”	Broad	Long	−0·58	10
Teigen [25]	Quarterly: U.S. 1946–59	Narrow	Long	−0·07	†
”	Annual: U.S.: 1924–41	Narrow	Long	−0·20	†
Heller [15]	Quarterly: U.S.: 1947–58	Narrow	Short	−0·12	4
”	”	Broad	Short	−0·18	4
”	”	Narrow	Long	*	..
”	”	Broad	Long	*	..
Hamburger [14]	Quarterly: U.S.: 1952–60 (Households only)	Narrow	Long	−0·16	2
”	”	Narrow	Equity yield	−0·13	3
Kavanagh and Walters [16]	Annual: U.K.: 1880–1961	Broad	Long	−0·31 (−0·22)	3 (3)
”	Annual: U.K.: 1926–61	Broad	Long	−0·50 (−0·25)	6 (3)
Fisher [8]	Quarterly: U.K.: 1955–67	Narrow	Short	−0·11	†
”	”	Broad	Short	*	†
”	”	Narrow	Long	−0·3	†
”	”	Broad	Long	*	†
Laidler and Parkin [18]	Annual: U.K.: 1953–67	Broad	Short	−0·26	†
Bank of England [1]	Quarterly: U.K.: 1955–69	Narrow	Short	−1·05	†
”	”	Narrow	Long	−0·80	†
”	”	Broad	Short	−0·09	†
”	”	Broad	Long	−0·35	†

TABLE A—*continued*

Author	Data used	Definition of money[a]	Interest rate used	Interest-elasticity[b]	t statistic[c]
	Velocity equations				
Latané [**19**]	Annual: U.S.: 1919–52	Narrow	Long	−0·80	..
Latané [**20**]	Annual: U.S.: 1909–58	Narrow	Long	−0·77	..
Christ [**6**]	Annual: U.S.: 1892–1959	Narrow	Long	−0·72	..
Meltzer [**22**]	Annual: U.S.: 1950–58	Narrow	Long	−1·8	30
,,	,,	Broad	Long	−1·3	20
Tobin [**26**]	Annual: U.S.: 1915–59	Broad	Short	−0·12	7
,,	,,	Narrow	Short	−0·24	9
,,	,,	Broad	Long	−0·24	6
,,	,,	Narrow	Long	−0·55	10
Frazer [**9**]	Quarterly: U.S.: 1948–65	Narrow	Long	−0·8	27
,,	,,	Broad	Long	−0·37	12
Kavanagh and Walters [**16**]	Annual: U.K.: 1877–1961	Broad	Long	−0·20 (−0·44)	2 (6)
,,	Annual: U.K.: 1923–61	Broad	Long	−0·55	9

* Not significant, or wrong sign.
.. Not available.
[a] The 'narrow' definition of money is usually currency plus demand deposits; 'broad' money includes time deposits.
[b] Values shown in brackets are obtained using first differences.
[c] The *t* statistic is the ratio of the estimated coefficient to its estimated standard error.

he used short-term rates, the estimated long-run elasticity fell between −0·1 and −0·2. Hamburger [**14**] used two interest rates (the equity yield and the long-term bond yield) in his study of the demand for money of the household sector, and the sum of their coefficients was about −0·3. Teigen's work [**25**], undertaken in the framework of a simultaneous equations model, produced long-run elasticities of less than −0·1; though when a similar equation for annual data was estimated, an elasticity of nearly −0·2 was recorded.

The use of quarterly data has presented a number of problems. Chief among these is the existence of time-lags in the adjustment process, the correct specification of which becomes of greater importance when quarterly rather than annual data are used. These time-lags are presumably not due primarily to imperfections in financial markets, because it is relatively easy to move into and out of money balances. It seems more likely that money holders take time to adjust their behaviour after changes in their incomes and in relevant interest rates.

Fisher [**8**], and Laidler and Parkin [**18**] found that the results of their quarterly models using U.K. data were much improved by the inclusion of lagged terms.[13] Furthermore, the coefficient of the lagged terms was generally large and significant, indicating quite long adjustment lags. A study using quarterly data for the period 1955–68, which is reported in more detail in Appendix II, bears out these conclusions. On average, around two-fifths of the adjustment of money balances towards a new equilibrium seems to take place within the first year.

The existence of time-lags in the demand-for-money function implies that the restoration of equilibrium after an increase in the money supply would require a much greater change in the other variables (income and interest rates) in the short term than in the long term. This is because, at a point in time, the demand for money depends primarily on past values of incomes and interest rates (which by definition cannot be changed) and only to a relatively small extent on current values of these variables. It is, therefore, changes in current values of either income or interest rates which must in the first instance take the strain of adjustment to an exogenous monetary change. If the role of interest rates in the demand for money is considered to be of secondary importance, the response of incomes to a monetary change should be larger in the short run

[13] It should be noted, however, that this improvement may owe something to serial correlation in the basic equation, as well as to the existence of time-lags.

than in the long run, as Friedman [11] acknowledges; however, other evidence which he has produced [12] suggests that in practice changes in the money stock do not appear to affect income until after quite a long and variable time-lag. This inconsistency disappears if a transmission mechanism working via interest rates is postulated. If the demand for money responds slowly to changes in income and interest rates, a change in the stock of money could have a rapid and powerful effect on interest rates, which in turn could have a lagged effect on expenditure, causing income changes to follow an initial change in the money supply. Under these conditions, Burstein [4] has argued that rigid pursuit of a money supply target might lead to unnecessarily wide fluctuations in interest rates and hence in incomes.

The relative importance of long-term and short-term interest rates in the demand-for-money function

If money is simply the most liquid in a spectrum of assets, one would expect the demand for it to be most closely related to the yield on near substitutes, that is to say, on other short-term assets. If, on the other hand, money is an asset that is fundamentally different from other assets there is no reason to expect the demand for it to be any more closely related to the yield on short-term than on long-term assets. These two hypotheses may perhaps be empirically distinguished by testing whether a short-term or a long-term interest rate gives rise to the highest coefficient of determination in a demand-for-money function. Laidler [17] suggests a further test: if the demand function for money is stable, the 'right' interest rate would be expected to show the same relationship to the demand for money in different time periods while the 'wrong' one need not.

Many of the studies noted in this appendix do not provide any direct evidence on this issue. Those that do, however, tend to support the view that in the United States money has been a closer substitute for short-term than for longer-term assets. Laidler finds that using the wide definition of money, the coefficient of determination is much greater for short-term rates than for long-term rates; though in first differences, the superiority of short-term rates is less marked. He also found that when his data were divided into sub-periods, the estimates of interest-elasticity were much more stable with respect to short-term rates than to longer-term rates. Confirmation is provided by the work of Heller [15] who, using quarterly data for the post-war period, detects a significant elasticity for short-term interest rates but not for long-term rates.[14] Lee [**21**], using differential rather than absolute rates, finds that the yield on savings and loan shares (an asset which may be thought of as being very close to money on the liquidity spectrum) explains the demand for money, under either a narrow or broad definition, better than the yield on longer-term assets.

The results of the study set out in Appendix II,[15] which reports the estimation of demand-for-money equations from data for the United Kingdom, left almost nothing to choose between long-term and short-term rates. Long-term rates were marginally more significant when the definition of money was restricted to currency plus clearing bank deposits; but the short-term (local authority) rate appeared slightly better at explaining changes in money as defined in the Central Statistical Office's *Financial Statistics*. This may result from the deposits of the 'other' banks being more directly competitive with rates in the local authority market. When first differences were used, however, the short rate performed markedly better than the long rate. The estimated values of the coefficients corresponded much better with values recorded using levels, and the significance of the estimates was considerably greater.

Tobin's results [**26**] (based on Friedman's data) also suggest that there is little to choose between long-term and short-term rates, with long-term rates being marginally more successful in explaining the demand for 'narrow' money, and short rates slightly better for 'wide' money.

REFERENCES

[**1**] Bank of England, Appendix II to this paper *[see Reading 7]*.

[**2**] Bronfenbrenner, Martin, and Mayer, Thomas, 'Liquidity functions in the American economy', *Econometrica*, October 1960, pp. 810–34.

[**3**] Brunner, Karl, and Meltzer, A. H., 'Some further investigations of demand and supply functions for money', *Journal of Finance*, May 1964, pp. 240–83.

[**4**] Burstein, M. L., *Economic Theory Equilibrium and Change* (London, 1968).

[**5**] Chow, G. C., 'On the long-run and short-run demand for money', *Journal of Political Economy*, April 1966, pp. 111–31.

[**6**] Christ, C. F., 'Interest rates and "portfolio selection" among liquid assets in the U.S.', *Studies in memory of Yehunda Grunfeld* (Stanford, 1963).

[14] Though see footnote 12 on p. 129.

[15] *[Reading 7]*.

[7] Courchene, T. J., and Shapiro, H. T., 'The demand for money: a note from the time series', *Journal of Political Economy*, October 1964, pp. 498–503.

[8] Fisher, Douglas, 'The demand for money in Britain: quarterly results 1951–67', *The Manchester School of Economic and Social Studies*, December 1968, pp. 329–44.

[9] Frazer, W. J., 'The demand for money, statistical results and monetary policy', *Schweizerische Zeitschrift für Volkswirtschaft und Statistik*, March 1967.

[10] Friedman, Milton, 'The quantity theory of money: a restatement', *in* Friedman, M. (ed.), *Studies in the quantity theory of money* (Chicago, Ill., 1956), pp. 3–21.

[11] Friedman, Milton, 'The demand for money: some theoretical and empirical results', *Journal of Political Economy*, August 1959, pp. 327–51.

[12] Friedman, Milton, and Schwartz, A. J., *A monetary history of the United States* 1867–1960' (Princeton, 1963).

[13] Goldberger, A. S., *Econometric theory* (New York, 1966), pp. 197–200.

[14] Hamburger, M. J., 'The demand for money by households, money substitutes, and monetary policy', *Journal of Political Economy*, December 1966, pp. 600–23.

[15] Heller, H. R., 'The demand for money: the evidence from the short-run data', *Quarterly Journal of Economics*, May 1965, pp. 291–303.

[16] Kavanagh, N. J., and Walters, A. A., 'Demand for money in the U.K. 1877–1961: some preliminary findings', *Bulletin of the Oxford University Institute of Economics and Statistics*, May 1966, pp. 93–116. /Reading 8/.

[17] Laidler, David, 'The rate of interest and the demand for money—some empirical evidence', *Journal of Political Economy*, December 1966, pp. 543–55.

[18] Laidler, David, and Parkin, Michael, 'The demand for money in the United Kingdom 1956–67: preliminary estimates', University of Essex Discussion Paper (unpublished). /Reading 9/.

[19] Latané, H. A., 'Cash balances and the interest rate: a pragmatic approach', *Review of Economics and Statistics*, November 1954.

[20] Latané, H. A., 'Income velocity and interest rates: a pragmatic approach', *Review of Economics and Statistics*, November 1960.

[21] Lee, T. H., 'Alternative interest rates and the demand for money: the empirical evidence', *American Economic Review*, December 1967, pp. 1168–81.

[22] Meltzer, A. H., 'The demand for money: the evidence from time series', *Journal of Political Economy*, June 1963, pp. 219–46.

[23] Motley, Brian, 'A demand-for-money function for the household sector—some preliminary findings', *Journal of Finance*, December 1967, pp. 405–18.

[24] Radcliffe Report, *Committee on the Working of the Monetary System*, Cmnd. 827, August 1959, para. 392.
[25] Teigen, R. L., 'Demand and supply functions for money in the United States: some structural estimates', *Econometrica*, October 1964, pp. 476–509.
[26] Tobin, James, 'The monetary interpretation of history', *American Economic Review*, June 1965, pp. 464–85.

7

THE DEMAND FOR MONEY: SOME RESULTS FOR THE UNITED KINGDOM

The Bank of England*

Both in the main paper and in Appendix I [see Readings 1 and 6] a number of issues were raised about the nature of the demand function for money,[1] which are crucially important in assessing the role of money in the economy, and which are subject to empirical testing. These were:

(i) the basic predictability of the function;
(ii) the role of interest rates in the function; and
(iii) the relative importance of long-term and short-term interest rates.

This appendix reports a number of statistical tests of the demand function for money, using quarterly U.K. data over the period from 1955 to 1969.[2] It begins by considering a very simple model, and examines the empirical implications of modifying it to take account of theoretical refinements.

* Extract reprinted from 'The importance of money' (Appendix II), *Bank of England Quarterly Bulletin*, vol. 10, no. 3, June 1970, pp. 191–7, by permission of the publisher. The article was prepared in the Bank of England's Economic Section, being largely the work of C. A. E. Goodhart assisted, particularly in the preparation of the appendices, by A. D. Crockett. Both Goodhart and Crockett are currently members of the Bank's research staff.

[1] It is largely optional whether the function is cast in demand-for-money or in velocity form. In fact, if income is included as a determinant of velocity, the two functions would be equivalent when cast in logarithmic form.

[2] [The results reported in the tables printed here differ slightly from those given in the original, being based on revised calculations made available by the Bank of England.]

Perhaps the simplest model of the demand for money is

$$M = a_0 + a_1 Y + a_2 r + u \qquad (1)$$

where

M = money stock;
Y = income;
r = some interest rate; and
u = an error term demonstrating the relationship to be a behavioural one.

This single-equation model was estimated using the technique of ordinary least squares. Three definitions of the money stock, and two kinds of interest rate were considered. The results are given in Table B. The precise variables used are:[3]

M_1: Currency and net current account deposits of the London clearing banks[4] (quarterly average of monthly observations), seasonally adjusted, £ millions.

M_2: Currency and net deposits of London clearing banks[4] (quarterly average of monthly observations), seasonally adjusted, £ millions.

M_3: Currency and net deposits of U.K. residents with the U.K. banking sector (end-quarter figures), seasonally adjusted, £ millions.[5]

Y: Average of the three official estimates of gross domestic product at factor cost, separately derived from output data, expenditure data and income data, seasonally adjusted, £ millions. (Before 1958 it was only possible to take the average of income and expenditure-based estimates.)

[3] The data used in the equations reported in this appendix may be obtained on application to the Economic Section, Bank of England, London, E.C.2.

[4] London clearing bank data were chosen primarily because of limitations in other series. However, it can also be argued that the liabilities of the 'other' banks are significantly less liquid than those of the L.C.B.s, so that their omission would be justified on theoretical grounds. In 1955, almost 90 per cent of U.K. residents' deposits with the U.K. banking sector were with the L.C.B.s; in 1969, some 65 per cent.

[5] Data for M_3 were also adjusted for day-of-the-week variations. M_3 is only available on an end-quarter basis, so that observations of this variable are not properly in phase with those of the independent variables in the equation. A half-quarter lag is thus built into the adjustment process. (It was not thought appropriate to average adjacent observations, since this would introduce serial dependence.)

r_S: The ratio of 100 plus the interest rate on 3-month local authority debt[6] to 100.

r_L: The ratio of 100 plus the yield on 2½ per cent Consolidated Stock to 100.

Functions for M_1 and M_2 are estimated for the period including the third quarter of 1955 to the third quarter of 1969; and M_3 for the period including the second quarter of 1963 to the third quarter of 1969.

All the variables have been expressed in logarithmic form. The only departure from usual practice is that the interest rate variable has been taken as the ratio of future to present value so that an interest rate of 4 per cent is expressed as 104/100 = 1·04.[7] This means that a percentage point change in interest rates is assumed to have much the same effect on the demand for money whether the level of rates is high or low; and so differs from the more conventional formulation, where the logarithm of the interest rate itself is used. A disadvantage of this latter approach is that it implicitly regards the conceptual floor to interest rates as being zero, and so cannot admit negative rates of return. However, to simplify comparison with other published work, elasticities have also been calculated on the conventional basis.[8]

Clearly the estimates shown in Table A suggest that the simplest formulation of the demand-for-money function is inadequate. It is true that the coefficients of determination are high and the income-elasticity of demand for money—though a little low for M_1 and M_2

[6] The yield on three-month local authority deposits was chosen in preference to the Treasury bill rate, on the grounds that in recent years the local authority market has attracted a wider range of active participants and has been less dominated by the direct influence of the authorities than has the Treasury bill market. The local authority rate is also somewhat suspect, however, because of the 'thinness' of the market in the early part of the estimation period. (Indeed the first two observations in the series are not directly available, and have been estimated from changes in other short-term rates.)

[7] The logic of this approach may be seen more easily by considering interest as a measure of the future value of present assets. If the interest rate is 4 per cent, today's £1 will be worth £1·04 a year hence. If the interest rate rises to 5 per cent, the future value of today's £1 has increased by 1/104 (or very nearly 1 per cent) not by 25 per cent.

[8] The equations reported in this appendix were also estimated using logarithms of the interest rates, i.e. $\log r$ rather than $\log(1 + r)$. The elasticities computed on this basis were very similar to those reported in Table C, and there was little change in the fit of the equations or in the significance of the estimated interest rate coefficients.

TABLE A

Estimated forms of equation (1)

Dependent variable	Estimated coefficients of:				Coefficient of determination [a]	Standard error of estimate [b]	Durbin–Watson statistic [c]
	Constant	Nominal income	Interest rate				
			Short	Long			
M_1 (nominal)	4·57	0·47 (0·02)	0·28 (0·32)		0·959	0·0244	0·30
	4·40	0·50 (0·03)		−0·36 (0·79)	0·959	0·0245	0·28
M_2 (nominal)	3·34	0·66 (0·01)	0·78 (0·26)		0·987	0·0196	0·35
	3·50	0·64 (0·03)		1·31 (0·66)	0·986	0·0204	0·26
M_3 (nominal)	−1·68	1·24 (0·06)	−0·44 (0·51)		0·980	0·0184	0·84
	−0·87	1·14 (0·08)		0·70 (1·04)	0·980	0·0186	0·76

Note: Standard errors of the estimated coefficients are shown in brackets.

[a] $\bar{R}^2$, the coefficient of determination adjusted for degrees of freedom.

[b] The standard error of the observed value of the dependent variable from its estimated value.

[c] This is a measure of serial correlation in the residuals [see footnote 4 on p. 126]. In general, the closer the statistic is to a value of 2, the greater the confidence with which the hypothesis of serial correlation can be rejected.

in comparison with other studies—is not altogether implausible[9] but these results can be accounted for by common trends in the variables. More disturbing are the perverse signs on the interest rate variables, and the strong evidence of first order serial correlation in the residuals as indicated by the very low values of the Durbin–Watson statistic. It seems likely, therefore, that this simple model mis-specifies the demand-for-money function in one or more important ways.

Lagged adjustment

One possible source of specification error is the implicit assumption in this simple model that adjustment to equilibrium is achieved within a single time period (in this case, one quarter). This seems unduly restrictive, for it may take time for money holders to become aware of changed external circumstances, and accordingly to rearrange their asset portfolios. A lagged process of adjustment to equilibrium suggests a two-equation model, defining not only the equilibrium relationship, but also the adjustment mechanism. One such model is:

$$M_t^* = a_0 + a_1 Y_t + a_2 r_t + u_t \tag{2}$$

$$M_t = M_{t-1} + b(M_t^* - M_{t-1}) + v_t \tag{3}$$

where M^* = desired (or equilibrium) money balances—all the other variables being defined as before—and b is a constant representing the average proportion of the discrepancy between actual and equilibrium money balances eliminated during a quarter. Combining equations (2) and (3) the following reduced form is obtained:

$$M_t = ba_0 + ba_1 Y_t + ba_2 r_t + (1 - b) M_{t-1} + w_t \tag{4}$$

where $w_t = bu_t + v_t$, a composite error term. This equation was estimated using the earlier definitions of money stock and interest rates, and the results are presented in Table B.

The properties of these estimated equations are considerably better than those shown in Table A. The coefficients on interest rates have the right sign, the fit of the function is better, and the standard error is reduced. Although the Durbin–Watson statistc has a different distribution where an equation contains a lagged

[9] Most studies using U.S. data have found the income-elasticity of demand for money to be in the range 1·0–1·5.

TABLE B

Estimated forms of equation (4)

Dependent variable	Estimated coefficients of: Constant	Nominal income	Interest rate: Short	Interest rate: Long	Lagged dependent variable	Coefficient of determination	Standard error of estimate	Durbin–Watson statistic
M_1 (nominal)	−0·05	0·05 (0·02)	−0·77 (0·14)		0·96 (0·05)	0·994	0·0093	1·75
	0·03	0·12 (0·03)		−1·61 (0·32)	0·89 (0·05)	0·994	0·0097	1·76
M_2 (nominal)	0·29	0·10 (0·03)	−0·20 (0·10)		0·87 (0·04)	0·998	0·0067	1·31
	0·11	0·12 (0·02)		−0·73 (0·22)	0·89 (0·04)	0·999	0·0063	1·60
M_3 (nominal)	−0·63	0·23 (0·13)	−0·63 (0·27)		0·85 (0·11)	0·995	0·0096	2·03
	−0·57	0·17 (0·14)		−1·01 (0·61)	0·91 (0·12)	0·994	0·0101	2·15

Note: Standard errors of the estimated coefficients are shown in brackets.

dependent variable, it is possible to adjust for this. When this is done, it is clear that in all cases serial correlation has been markedly reduced (though it is still present).[10]

The implied long and short-run interest-elasticities using the conventional definition of elasticity[11] are given below.

TABLE C

Interest-elasticities

	r_S		r_L	
	Short-run	Long-run	Short-run	Long-run
M_1	−0·04	−1·05	−0·09	−0·80
M_2	−0·01	−0·09	−0·04	−0·35
M_3 [a]	−0·03	−0·21	−0·06	−0·51

Note: Since the interest-elasticity, under this definition, is not constant in equation (4), its value has been calculated at the mean value of the interest rate.

[a] As data for M_3 are end-quarter, the 'short' run refers to a slightly different period than for M_1 and M_2.

These elasticities are well within the range of values reported in the survey of empirical evidence in Appendix I [Reading 6], and they suggest that the experience of the United Kingdom has not been markedly different from that of the United States in this respect.

Standard errors of estimate (expressed as percentages) are lowest for the broader definition of money, M_2, although the absolute size of the error is not much different because, of course, M_2 is larger than M_1. There is little to choose between the explanatory power of short and long rates; but whichever is used, its

[10] See Durbin, J., 'Testing for serial correlation in least squares regressions when some of the regressors are lagged dependent variables', *Econometrica*, May 1970. The Durbin two-stage test was also applied, and produced results very favourable to the hypothesis of partial adjustment rather than serial correlation.

[11] See p. 140.

statistical significance is usually much the same as that of the income variable.

Although the equations in Table B gave quite satisfactory results,[12] the lagged adjustment model embodies a number of theoretical assumptions which can be questioned. Changes in income are implicitly assumed to have the same effect on the demand for money whether they result from changes in real output or in prices. As mentioned in the main paper,[13] there are plausible reasons for expecting real money balances to increase either faster than real incomes, if money is considered a 'luxury good', or slower than incomes, if there are economies of scale in cash management; but there is no sound reason for expecting a change in the price level or a change in population size to have an effect on the equilibrium money/income ratio. This line of reasoning suggests that the appropriate formulation of the demand-for-money equation is one which explains real *per capita* money balances in terms of real *per capita* incomes. It is quite a simple matter to adapt the variables in equation 4 to take account of this. Thus, money and incomes are each divided by np, where n is the adult population of the United Kingdom (obtained by interpolation of annual population estimates)[14] and p is the price level (the G.D.P. deflator).[15] The results of the equations run in real *per capita* terms are given in Table D.

[12] As noted in Appendix I *[Reading 6]* a more searching test of the strength of a relationship where trends are present is its explanatory power when the variables are transformed into first differences. The equations presented in Tables B and C were therefore estimated in first difference form. None of the results of these tests could be taken as contradicting the results obtained using levels of the data, but neither do they provide strong confirmation. Coefficients of determination were uniformly low, with a maximum of $R^2 = 0{\cdot}22$. The short-term interest rate was always more significant than the long-term rate, giving some support to the hypothesis that money is more substitutable for short-term than for other assets.

[13] *[Reading 1, p. 9]*.

[14] The population over fifteen years of age was chosen as the series which most closely approximated the number of potential independent money-holding units. Total population includes children, who will in general not hold money, and working population excludes pensioners, who probably are significant money holders. A more appropriate series might have been the numbers of households, but data are not available.

[15] The choice of this deflator follows immediately from the fact that we have been working with G.D.P. as our income estimate. As there is no separate deflator for income-based G.D.P., nor a quarterly deflator for output-based G.D.P., it follows that p is derived from the G.D.P. estimates made from the expenditure side.

TABLE D

Estimated forms of equation (4) in real per capita *terms*

Dependent variable	Estimated coefficients of: Constant	Real *per capita* income	Interest rate: Short	Interest rate: Long	Lagged dependent variable	Coefficient of determination	Standard error of estimate	Durbin–Watson statistic
$\frac{M_1}{np}$	0·30	0·06 (0·03)	−0·80 (0·16)		0·89 (0·04)	0·940	0·0116	1·78
	0·27	0·14 (0·04)		−1·82 (0·35)	0·83 (0·04)	0·941	0·0115	1·73
$\frac{M_2}{np}$	0·65	0·09 (0·02)	−0·21 (0·14)		0·80 (0·05)	0·908	0·0096	1·60
	0·45	0·14 (0·03)		−0·76 (0·28)	0·79 (0·04)	0·915	0·0092	1·69
$\frac{M_3}{np}$	−0·96	0·29 (0·22)	−0·66 (0·33)		0·91 (0·13)	0·967	0·0113	2·15
	−0·60	0·19 (0·22)		−0·74 (0·74)	0·94 (0·15)	0·963	0·0120	2·07

Note: Standard errors of the estimated coefficients are shown in brackets.

TABLE E

Estimated forms of equation 5

Dependent variable	Estimated coefficients of: Constant	Real *per capita* income	Price	Interest rate: Short	Interest rate: Long	Lagged dependent variable	Coefficient of determination	Standard error of estimate	Durbin–Watson statistic
$\frac{M_1}{n}$	0·11	−0·02	0·07	−0·82		1·02	0·990	0·0096	1·78
		(0·09)	(0·04)	(0·16)		(0·07)			
	0·11	0·07	0·14		−1·74	0·93	0·990	0·0099	1·82
		(0·09)	(0·05)		(0·36)	(0·07)			
$\frac{M_2}{n}$	0·26	0·07	0·10	−0·21		0·90	0·998	0·0070	1·26
		(0·05)	(0·04)	(0·11)		(0·05)			
	0·22	0·06	0·13		−0·87	0·92	0·998	0·0064	1·62
		(0·05)	(0·04)		(0·24)	(0·04)			
$\frac{M_3}{n}$	0·45	0·10	0·35	−0·55		0·84	0·994	0·0095	1·96
		(0·23)	(0·19)	(0·28)		(0·11)			
	0·97	−0·04	0·37		−0·92	0·87	0·994	0·0098	2·11
		(0·22)	(0·20)		(0·60)	(0·12)			

Note: Standard errors of the estimated coefficients are shown in brackets.

Somewhat surprisingly, these estimates are rather worse[16] than those presented in Table B, but the reason is not far to seek. Deflating both money and income by prices implies not only that the demand for money is homogeneous in prices in the long run, but also in the short run. In other words, this last set of estimated equations implies that the demand for money will adjust almost immediately to an increase in aggregate money incomes due to a rise in population or in the price level, but only after a long time-lag will it adjust to a rise in real *per capita* incomes. The fact that the estimated equations in Table D have higher standard errors of estimate than those of Table B suggests that this assumption is unjustified.

It therefore seems appropriate to allow for a gradual adjustment to price changes. Since it was argued earlier that the effect of a change in real incomes may be different from the effect of a change in prices, the price level was included as a separate explanatory variable. The estimated equations when this is done are set out in Table E. In principle, population might also be included as an additional independent variable, but there is little theoretical justification for expecting lagged adjustment in the case of the population variable.[17] Thus in Table E, money and income are expressed in *per capita* terms, viz.:

$$\left(\frac{M}{n}\right)_t = ba_0 + ba_1\left(\frac{Y}{np}\right)_t + ba_2 r_t + ba_3 p_t + (1-b)\left(\frac{M}{n}\right)_{t-1} + w_t \quad (5)$$

For the first two definitions of the money stock, Table E shows rather less satisfactory results than Table B; standard errors of estimate are greater. This is a little surprising, for the only changes introduced that would have any effect on the standard errors are the separate specification of price and real income as explanatory variables and the specification of income and money holdings in *per capita* terms. The first change would if anything tend to reduce the standard errors if the effects of prices and real incomes differ; indeed, it is evident from new estimates of equation 5 with money and real incomes no longer expressed in *per capita* terms that it is the latter adjustment which has caused most of the deterioration. This result casts doubt on the assumption that the demand for money is homogeneous in population, but it is also possible that

[16] Not only are the coefficients of determination lower (this could be explained by the lower initial variance in the dependent variable), but the standard errors of estimate are larger.

[17] Additions to the population will not affect the behaviour of existing money holders; nor are they likely to 'adjust gradually to their own existence'.

the population series used is inappropriate.[18] Failing a more appropriate series, it seems preferable to use totals of money and of incomes, at least with regard to the relatively short time-series we are using.

The estimated coefficient of the real income variable in equation 5 is never statistically significant,[19] though for the price variable it is significant, or nearly so, and has the expected positive sign. But there is some degree of collinearity between the price and real income variables (the simple correlation coefficient is 0·972) so that not much can be read into these results. Furthermore, the implied long-run price elasticity is in some cases implausibly high, suggesting that the estimates are attributing to the price variable some of the effect on money holdings that should properly be accounted for by real incomes.

Models which included interest rate differentials and the annual rates of change in prices of goods and services as explanatory variables were also tested. The interest rate differential employed was the interest rate on three months' local authority deposits minus Bank rate.[20] The estimated coefficient of this variable was statistically significant and of the expected negative sign when it was the only interest rate variable appearing in the equation; but when included with the level of the local authority rate, multi-collinearity was encountered, and implausible results were obtained. The rate of change of prices was included as a measure of the relative return on real as against financial assets.[21] The estimated coefficients attaching to this variable were rarely significant and the results obtained are not presented here.

All the results presented so far have indicated the importance of time-lags, but little attention has been paid to the precise nature of

[18] The sharp post-war rise in births led to a rapid increase in the adult population in the early 1960s—a period not included in the data used to estimate the equations for M_3. It seems plausible to suppose that this rapidly increasing younger proportion of the population held less money than the average for the adult population as a whole.

[19] As throughout this work, 'statistically significant' is intended to imply that the estimated coefficient is significantly different from zero at the 5 per cent probability level. In other words the estimated value is not attributable to sampling fluctuations.

[20] Bank rate was used as a proxy for the interest rate paid on deposit accounts.

[21] Inflation would tend to make real assets more attractive than financial, and thus cause a switch out of money; though it could also be argued that rising prices would generate expectations of rising interest rates and thus cause a switch into money.

the lag. An exponential adjustment mechanism has been used, but, while computationally easy, it is not necessarily the correct specification. It implies that a constant proportion of any disequilibrium will be eliminated in a given time period, irrespective of:

(i) the source of the disequilibrium; and
(ii) the size of the disequilibrium.

If the reason for time-lags is the existence of transactions costs associated with compositional changes in a portfolio, there is no reason to expect the speed of adjustment to be influenced by the *source* of the initial disequilibrium. But the speed of adjustment might well be influenced by the *size* of the disequilibrium.

It is not necessary, however, to attribute the presence of time-lags wholly to transactions costs. Indeed, it would seem more likely that transactions costs were relatively low in financial markets. A more plausible explanation might be that people take time to become aware that changes in incomes and interest rates made revisions in their money holding habits appropriate.[22] If these 'awareness' or 'inertia' lags are important, then it is not clear that the speed of adjustment can be regarded as invariant to the source of the disequilibrium. In other words, people may become aware of changes in their real income faster, or slower, than they become aware of changes in the price level or in interest rates.

All this implies a much more complex model incorporating a separate pattern of adjustment for each independent variable; but the estimation of such a model raises a number of problems. Unlike a common exponential adjustment lag, which can be simply estimated by taking into account lagged values of the dependent variables, a variety of lags would make the equation over-identified unless restrictions were placed on the values of the coefficients of the variables. Using exponential lags, different speeds of adjustment could be assumed to apply to different explanatory variables in the hope of finding some unique combination of lags which gave the best results. Alternatively, the Almon technique[23] could be employed, and a finite lag structure estimated for each variable. Work is in hand using both these techniques of estimation.

[22] It should be remembered that three-quarters of clearing bank deposits are held by the personal sector, and 'persons' may well be slow to adapt to changes in interest rates.

[23] Almon, Shirley, 'The distributed lag between capital appropriations and expenditures', *Econometrica*, January 1965.

8

THE DEMAND FOR MONEY IN THE UNITED KINGDOM, 1877–1961[1]: PRELIMINARY FINDINGS

N. J. Kavanagh *and* A. A. Walters*

Introduction

The revival of interest in monetary policy in recent years has produced a spate of studies of monetary phenomena. The general result of these studies is 'that money is important' as an explanatory variable in macro-economic models. The most interesting group of studies is concerned with the demand for money and the reaction of changes in the demand for goods to changes in the quantity of money. There is fairly wide agreement that reasonably stable demand curves for money emerge from the data. The shape and quantitative characteristics are, however, not at all clear. For the United States, Selden has argued that money is a luxury like mink coats—that the demand for money increases proportionately more than income. He finds that the long term rate of interest has little effect in determining the demand for money to hold. On the other hand, Meltzer shows that the demand for money increases roughly proportionately to the quantity of wealth and that the rate of interest significantly affects the demand for money.

Many of the differences in these results are due to variations in definitions—particularly in the definition of the stock of money. But it is of some concern that most of these results have been derived

* Reprinted from the *Bulletin of the Oxford University Institute of Economics and Statistics*, vol. 28, no. 2, May 1966, pp. 93–116, by permission of the authors and publishers. N. J. Kavanagh is at the University of Birmingham and A. A. Walters is Cassel Professor of Economics at the London School of Economics.

[1] This paper is adapted from Discussion Paper No. 48 (July 1964) of the Faculty of Commerce and Social Science, University of Birmingham.

for the United States. The basic data have been the same in each case. It seems important to see what the results would be with data from other developed countries. In this paper we examine some of the hypotheses about the demand for money in the light of evidence from the United Kingdom for the period 1877–1961. Broadly speaking the results suggest that over the long run money increased proportionately to income, but short run variations in income were much sharper than those in money. The rate of interest cannot be dismissed as an insignificant determinant of the demand for money. There are, however, many methodological problems which cast some doubt on the validity of these conclusions.

I. Some aspects of theory

It is possible to be brief in setting out the theory of the demand for money because excellent accounts have already been presented by Friedman, Tobin, Baumol, Meltzer, Burstein and others.[2] Money is viewed as one among many forms in which an individual can hold his assets. But money has a peculiar significance since the government can, directly or indirectly, control the quantity of nominal money whereas government regulation of the quantity of other assets is not normally practised in capitalist countries. One element in the *aggregate* balance sheet of the economy is under the government's control. But though the government controls the total quantity of nominal money it does not regulate the amount of money which each individual maintains in his accounts. Each of us decides on his stock of money according to his particular circumstances. The sum of the individual demands for money may differ from the amount of money made available by the government. If demands exceed supply (and the supply of nominal money does not change), people will attempt to add to their stocks of money by selling or reducing purchases of other assets. The demand for goods will be reduced and this will result in either a fall in the level of prices or a reduction in the output of goods or a combination of both.

[2] Friedman, M., 'The Quantity Theory of Money—A Restatement' in Friedman, M. (ed.), *Studies in the Quantity Theory of Money* (Chicago 1956); Tobin, J., 'Money, Capital and Other Stores of Value', *American Economic Review*, vol. 51, no. 2, Papers and Proceedings, May 1961, pp. 26–37; Baumol, W., 'The Transactions Demand for Cash...', *Quarterly Journal of Economics*, vol. 66, no. 4, November 1952, pp. 544–56; Meltzer, A. H., 'The Demand for Money: the Evidence from the Time Series', *Journal of Political Economy*, vol. 71, no. 3, June 1963, pp. 219–46; Burstein, M., *Money* (Cambridge 1963).

Correspondingly if the sum of individual demands is less than the total amount of nominal money available, the attempts by individuals to reduce their money balances and increase their stocks of other assets will drive up the price of goods and will tend to increase employment and output.

This simplified version of the quantity theory throws all the burden of adjustment on the price of goods or on output and employment changes. But it is likely that part of the adjustment will be reflected in the price paid for holding money. Keynesian theory concentrates attention on the adjustment through the price paid for holding money—the rate of interest. A supply of money in excess of the aggregate of individual demands will lead to persons trying to reduce their stocks of money. The typical adjustment according to Keynesians is, however not the purchase of capital goods but the purchase of bonds and other monetary obligations. The effect is to drive up the price of bonds and so to reduce the interest rate. Then the fall in the rate of interest will encourage entrepreneurs and consumers to add to their inventories and stocks of capital equipment. The demand for goods will increase and so drive up the price of goods and increase output.

The two theories have qualitatively similar end-results. The essential difference is quantitative. Keynesians argue that there are important slips 'twixt cup and lip. For example many economists would suggest that changes in the rate of interest have little effect on the level of investment. But the most important objection lies in the postulated functional form and shape of the demand for money. In most macro-models the demand for money is written as a function of the rate of interest. Owing to speculative expectations, it is argued that the elasticity of demand with respect to the rate of interest is very high at low interest rates. Because of this 'liquidity trap' an increase in money may be absorbed into portfolios without any marked reduction in the rate of interest.

The theoretical rationalizations for writing the demand for money as a function of the interest rate are well known and need not be repeated. There are, however, one or two subtleties which have emerged in the recent literature which ought to be taken into account. The work of Baumol and Tobin has demonstrated that there are good theoretical grounds for supposing that *transactions* balances depend on the rate of interest. Using a simple inventory model they showed that there were economies of scale in cash requirements and that the elasticity of demand for transactions money with respect to the rate of interest was, theoretically, –0·5. But the Baumol–Tobin theory was couched in terms of *certain* cash requirements for transactions purposes in known periods. No account was taken of the chance variations in transactions demands, nor was there an option of borrowing to finance expenditure. On general grounds it has long been argued that an increase in the rate of interest has a two-fold effect: it increases the cost of existing money balances; it raises the cost of borrowing. The former will induce the transactor to hold a smaller stock of money, the latter will encourage him to keep a larger amount of cash to avoid the high cost of borrowing. The more or less offsetting forces of these two motives suggest that the rate of interest will, as Keynes suggested, have little or no effect on transactions balances. This conjecture has been supported by using a stochastic inventory theory which involves both lending and borrowing. The theory suggests, albeit tentatively, that provided that the lending and borrowing rates change proportionately, there will be no change in the demand for money.[3]

This leads us back more or less to the model of the *General Theory* where transactions balances are a function of income only and are not influenced by the rate of interest. But there is a small residual result. If the interest rate *does* influence transactions balances then it is likely to be the *short run* rate which has this effect. The inventory model in its stochastic formulation considers the distribution of spending power between money and near money so that the cost of financing transactions is as low as possible. The essential element for *transactions* balances is that there be no chance of capital loss. This means that alternatives to holding cash for transactions purposes are short term paper, time deposits or similar monetary obligations. The appropriate return on these loans, then, is the *short term* rate of interest.

This contrasts with the long rate which is appropriate for explaining speculative balances. Money is held for speculative purposes because of the chance of changes in the long term rate of interest. The likelihood of a fall in the price of bonds will induce transactors to hold money; but they may also hold short term obligations, savings deposits, etc., according to their expectation of the length of the interval before the fall takes place. This implies

[3] See Walters, A. A., 'Two Papers on the Demand for Money', First Paper Discussion Paper A 34, University of Birmingham, 1963. (The second paper contains a serious error.)

that, apart from statistical difficulties, we cannot use the short term and long term rates to distinguish transactions balances from speculative money. It also makes it important to use broad definitions of money—i.e. definitions which include savings deposits, etc.

The variables which should be included in the demand for money emerge naturally from this analysis. For transactions balances, it is clear that income or expenditure is an important variable. For speculative balances the hypothesis is that they depend on the rate of interest and expectations of future rates. But it is surely true that the amount of speculative balances held by an individual will depend on his total wealth. If a transactor is perfectly certain that interest rates are going to fall he will borrow all he can in order to finance purchases of bonds. The maximum is set by his borrowing powers. It is not unreasonable to suppose that the total amount of borrowing of a transactor is limited by his collateral and income expectations. Conversely if he expects with certainty that the price of bonds will fall he will convert all his bonds into cash. This suggests that the balances held for speculative motives will be a function of the total wealth—both human and non-human forms of wealth. The larger the wealth of a transactor the larger are likely to be the balances which respond speculatively to expectations about changes in the rate of interest.

In Friedman's recent account of the sophisticated quantity theory of money, several other variables are included in the demand function for money. The nominal rate of return on equities is included since it is possible to hold one's wealth in ordinary shares. The expected rate of change in the price level will also affect the conversion of nominal rates of interest into real rates; this too should be included as a variable determining the demand for money. (If one wished to retain the Keynesian dichotomy between transactions and speculative balances it is clear that these rates would determine the latter.) The final way in which one may hold wealth is in the form of human capital; instead of holding a quantity of money (or bonds, etc.), one may invest in education either for oneself or for some other person. Switches from money or bonds into investment in human beings cannot be made quickly; nor can one easily measure the rate of return on such investment. As Friedman has suggested it is possible to treat the distribution between human and other forms of capital as given at a point of time. The ratio of human to non-human capital and not the rate of return on education, etc., is the variable to be included in the demand for money.

The demand for money considered so far has been that of an individual transactor. The concept useful for monetary analysis is, however, the aggregate of the individual demands. The obvious first approximation is to assume that the aggregate demand for money is of the same form as that of the individual function. For transactions balances this is not an unreasonable approximation. Much depends on the form of the function and the rule of aggregation used.[4] But with only slight twinges of conscience we shall ignore these problems.

For speculative balances the effects of aggregation are much more serious because of the diversity of expectations. Indeed it is clear from the discussion in the *General Theory* that it is the difference in views about expected future interest rates which accounts for the existing rate being what it is. A liquidity function is defined for given expectations. The aggregate demand must then clearly be a function of the distribution of expectations. Apart from the problem of measurement, there seems to be no obviously satisfactory way of representing such a distribution as an aggregate function.

In studies of the demand for money the closed economy is such a convenient abstraction that international complications are rarely mentioned. But in applications to the United Kingdom it seems a necessary exercise to set out at least some of the complications. Foreigners hold sterling and U.K. residents hold stocks of foreign currency. The proximate causes of these demands are simple to specify. Foreigners hold sterling because they wish to buy British goods (or goods from some other sources for which sterling is normally accepted in payment). This is a natural extension of a transactions demand—the greater the volume of British exports the larger the balance of sterling held. Since exports are included in the national income variable this effect has already been reflected in the demand function. But analogously there is also a speculative demand for sterling. Foreigners (and U.K. residents) will tend to extend or reduce their balances of sterling according to their views of the likelihood of price changes and changes in the managed

[4] The common form of the demand function for money is double logarithmic. This suggests that one should use geometric means rather than arithmetic averages for the aggregation relationships. One conjectures that no serious distortions are introduced by using arithmetic methods but, so far as we know, no experimental evidence is available.

exchange rate. In order to earn a return on their money, probably a large part of these funds would be held as short term paper, call loans or in deposit accounts. These all affect indirectly or directly (in the case of deposit accounts) the demand for sterling.[5]

The upshot of this discussion is that one may expect some instability in the demand for money owing to speculative shifts of funds brought about by the expectations of foreigners. But as a first and rather extreme approximation it is simplest to regard foreign market sentiment as being similar to domestic market expectations. 'Opening' the economy merely magnifies the domestic effect. There is, however, one notable consequence in 'opening up' the economy. The stock of nominal bonds held by residents can be very quickly changed. The aggregate nominal stock of bonds instead of being fixed, as in the closed model of Keynes, becomes a variable which is determined by the aggregate of decisions of individuals. Foreign bonds are another form in which a person may hold his wealth and the substitutability of foreign bonds for domestic bonds, money and real capital plays a role in determining the elasticities of demand for money. As far as *demand* studies are concerned, the availability of foreign substitutes is analogous to similar problems in the study of the demand for commodities. Studies of demand have made good progress by ignoring these problems; it seems likely that no great harm will be done if they are ignored in this preliminary study of the demand for money.

We can now set out algebraically the demand functions for money. First with the individual demand function, the quantity of nominal money (M_i) is the dependent variable. We propose the function for the ith transactor:

$$M_i = f_i\left(r_{b_i}, r^e_{b_i}, r_{s_i}, Y_i, P, \left(\frac{\mathrm{d}P}{P}\right)^e_i, W_i\right) \qquad \text{I.1}$$

where r_b is the rate of interest on bonds, r^e_b is the 'expected' rate of interest on bonds, r_s is the short term rate of interest, P is the price level, W_i is the level of wealth, and $(\mathrm{d}P/P)^e_i$ the 'expected' change in prices, and where we define the flow magnitude Y_i as personal income after tax at current prices.

We have supposed that the rate r_b is suitable also for reflecting movements in the rate of return on equities and real capital. (We

[5] The demand for sterling as a reserve to purchase long term securities is likely to be small. We ignore it.

do not at this stage wish to examine the different degrees of substitution of money for these other assets.) As a further simplification one may suppose that the function is homogeneous in prices, i.e.

$$\frac{M_i}{P} = f_i\left(r_{b_i}, r_{b_i}^e, r_s, \frac{Y_i}{P}, \frac{W_i}{P}, \left(\frac{\mathrm{d}P}{P}\right)_i^e\right) \qquad \text{I.2}$$

It is also obviously useful to eliminate either the income or the wealth term since they are closely related. Recalling that our supposition was that an individual can borrow against his income expectations as well as against his collateral, we defined wealth to exclude money. But if the rate of return on human and non-human wealth were equal to the rate of bonds (and ignoring short term debt) we would have:

$$W_i = Y_i / r_{b_i} \qquad \text{I.3}$$

The function then reduces to:

$$\frac{M_i}{P} = f_i\left(r_{b_i}, r_{b_i}^e, r_{s_i}, \frac{Y_i}{P}\left(\frac{\mathrm{d}P}{P}\right)_i^e\right) \qquad \text{I.4}$$

(There is much more to the choice between wealth and income than implied here; discussion is pursued below.)

One critical issue is the representation of expected values—in other words the expectations hypothesis which is used. The obvious candidates in ascending order of difficulty are:

(a) Extrapolation of present values
(b) Extrapolation of the trend of immediate past values
(c) Some version of the rational expectations hypothesis
(d) Some probability distribution of expectations based on (a) to (c) above.

There are many clear and straightforward objections to using (a); for example if $r_b = r_e^b$, etc., then there will be no speculative demand for money. It is ruled out *a priori*. However, it is useful as an exploratory device to examine how much of actual behaviour can be explained with hypotheses of this kind. Writing $(\mathrm{d}P/P)_i^e$ as zero we have:

$$\frac{M_i}{P} = f_i\left(r_{b_i}, r_{s_i}, \frac{Y_i}{P}\right) \qquad \text{I.5}$$

To reduce the function further we may subsume the short term rate of interest in the long rate or, as argued above, one may suppose the short term lending rewards are nicely offset by the increased borrowing cost. We also assume that the bond rate is the same for all individuals so that $r_{b_i} = r_b$. The form then reduces to:

$$\frac{M_i}{P} = f_i\left(r_b, \frac{Y_i}{P}\right) \qquad \text{I.6}$$

This is almost the simplest form possible for the liquidity function; and, of course, much of this simplicity is due to the rudimentary state of the expectations hypothesis. An alternative hypothesis (b) is that the trend of the rate of interest and the rate of change of prices will continue as they have been doing in the recent past. Extrapolation, except in certain trend situations which are obviously expected to continue, does not seem to be a good hypothesis where cyclical phenomena are dominant. Probably the best workable hypothesis is to suppose that views about the expected rate are formed by current government operations, forecasts by market leaders or, in Britain, the reported foreign trade statistics. This is, however, extraordinarily difficult to formalize, and we have no workable model on these lines.

On aggregating the micro-relationships of the form I.6 one meets the problem of identifying which is the dependent (or more correctly), endogenous variable(s). Clearly in the micro-function there was no doubt; r_b and P are given by the market, Y_i/P by productive resources: the transactor decides on the quantity of money he retains in his portfolio. But the aggregate variable $M = \sum_i M_i$ is clearly not the endogenous variable. This is determined by the government.[6] On the other hand P, Y (aggregate income) and r_b are now all candidates to be considered as endogenous variables. Ignoring P, for it is already a component of Y, we may consider Y as the endogenous variable and M as exogenous. This simple version of the monetary multiplier suffers from the fact that the rate of interest (r_b) is still endogenous and yet must appear among the 'independent' variables, i.e.

$$Y = f(r_b, M) \qquad \text{I.7}$$

Alternatively one may write:

$$r_b = g(Y, M) \qquad \text{I.8}$$

[6] One can rephrase this in terms of the government creating reserves and the various financial institutions determining the quantity of money.

Stock of money and National Income, U.K. 1877–1961

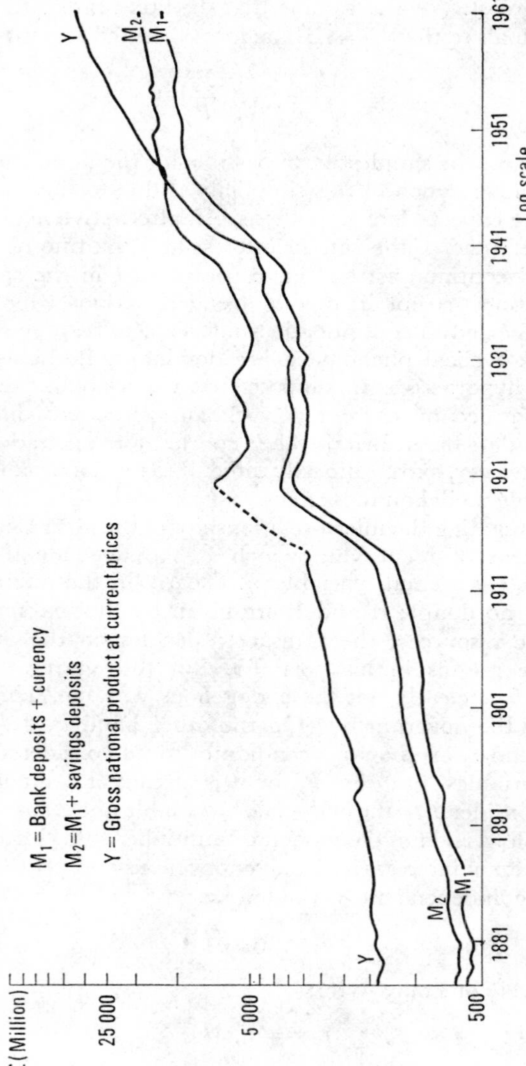

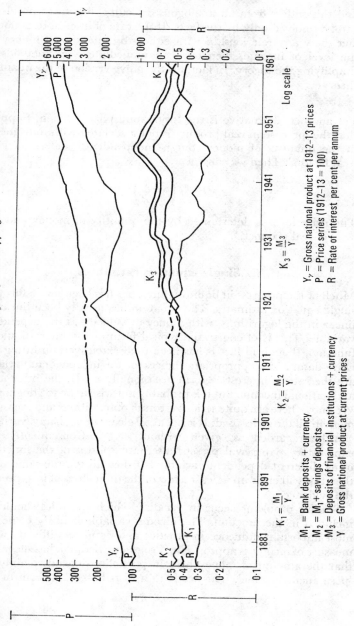

Stock of money, income and prices, U.K. 1877–1961

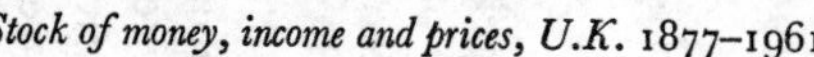

$K_1 = \frac{M_1}{Y}$ $K_2 = \frac{M_2}{Y}$ $K_3 = \frac{M_3}{Y}$

M_1 = Bank deposits + currency
M_2 = M_1 + savings deposits
M_3 = Deposits of financial institutions + currency
Y = Gross national product at current prices

Y_γ = Gross national product at 1912–13 prices
P = Price series (1912–13 = 100)
R = Rate of interest per cent per annum

and this suffers from an analogous difficulty. But these problems can be resolved only by the facts. If the rate of interest does not in fact show any relationship with either the quantity of money or the level of income, then one can immediately see methods of simplifying the theory. In fact it is the naïve version of the quantity theory:

$$Y = f(M) \tag{I.9}$$

Yet another alternative is the 'price multiplier' version. Suppose that the increase in real product is not associated with movements in the quantity of money, but is independently determined by 'real factors'. Then we can write:

$$P = f\left(M, \frac{Y}{P}\right) \tag{I.10}$$

The price level is determined by the quantity of money and the level of real product.

II. Single equation estimates

Much of the progress in liquidity functions has been made through single equation estimates. The equation has usually been linear or linear in the logarithms, with money or velocity as the dependent variable. This is of course the typical form of the micro-liquidity function, though in fact it has been used extensively in fitting the *macro*-data. More appropriate choices for the independent variable are the rate of interest (a form occasionally used), the price level and national income. But it is probably not wise to be too dogmatic. We know there are quite serious errors of observations and measurement in all the series used. It is not at all clear which, if any, variable can be regarded as 'given without error'. Consequently this exploratory paper will present alternative forms of the function, using different dependent variables. If they all tell the same story then this will clear up at least a few of the difficulties of interpreting the evidence.

Similar problems occur in deciding which variables should be included in the function. The income variable is likely to be the most important influence in practice and opinions differ on what measure of income is appropriate. Professor Friedman has suggested that the amount of money held in portfolios depends mainly on 'permanent income'. This leads to a distributed lag form of the demand function. The problems of dealing with this demand function have been discussed by one of us elsewhere.[7] In this paper we use a particular form of the permanent income hypothesis as one alternative formulation of the demand for money.

In recent papers Meltzer has presented strong arguments in favour of using wealth as the independent variable in the regression. Wealth, it is argued, is the constraint which is taken into account when individuals decide on their holdings of money.[8] But there are many concepts of wealth and, in order to see the implications of the various measures, one may profitably simplify discussion. Suppose that all non-human wealth is held either in bonds or in money, i.e. in an obvious notation:

$$W_t = M_t + \frac{B_t}{r_t} \qquad \text{II.1}$$

Since M_t is a substantial fraction of W_t it is sensible to subtract it from wealth to get the reduced form of the micro-function.[9] The wealth variable left consists of the number of obligations to pay £1 per annum in perpetuity divided by the rate of interest.

If we use a log-linear function we get:

$$M_t = kr_t^{\gamma_1}\left(\frac{B_t}{r_t}\right)^{\gamma_2} \qquad \text{II.2}$$

where we would expect $\gamma_1 < 0$ and $\gamma_2 > 0$.

Holding the number of bond obligations constant (a useful approximation in the short run) we see that the effect of an increase in the rate of interest is magnified through the wealth effect. Money demand is reduced not only because of the substitution effect (γ_1) but also because of the reduction in wealth due to the fall in the price of bonds (γ_2). In principle there is a perfect negative correlation between the rate of interest and the measured value of wealth.

But there are several obvious objections which one may make, on intuitive grounds alone, to this formulation. The aggregate demand for money is the sum of individual demands, and these may in turn

[7] Walters, A. A., 'Professor Friedman on the Demand for Money', *Journal of Political Economy*, 1965, vol. 73, pp. 545–51.

[8] Notice that in principle one should reverse the relations when dealing with aggregate data. The quantity of money determines the value of wealth.

[9] Meltzer did not subtract M_t and he argues that from the statistical evidence it makes little difference.

depend on the *gross* value of assets and not on the net balance. A transactor who borrows £1 million and lends or spends £1 million would have a demand for cash the same as the millionaire. The demand for money is a function of the degree of inter-indebtedness of the economy.[10] Secondly, one might reasonably argue that the transactor will hold a quantity of money consistent with his *permanent* wealth; he will discount most of the swings in the price of bonds as temporary. Aside from speculative demands, portfolio equilibrium will take into account the long run expectations about the value of bonds. These two criticisms suggest that the appropriate wealth concept is the level of 'permanent' gross wealth.[11] For Britain, unfortunately, this discussion is academic. There are no useful wealth statistics for the United Kingdom.

From the graphs[12] it is clear that there are dominant trends in both money and income series. Over the whole statistical record from 1877 to 1961 the quantity of money and the national income have increased at roughly the same average annual percentage rate. Ignoring changes in the cost of holding money, it is tempting to interpret these movements as evidence of a unitary elasticity of demand for money with respect to income. It seems then that money is a 'neutral good'—neither a necessity nor a luxury. (This contrasts with Professor Friedman's results for the U.S.A. over roughly the same period. The American data suggest a long run demand elasticity of 1·8; money is a luxury in the United States. If, however, time deposits are excluded from the definition of money the evidence is not then dramatically inconsistent with our data for the United Kingdom.)

With any other commodity which showed a marked trend over as long a period as 80 to 100 years, most demand analysts would be

[10] This argument is analogous to the old discussion of the use of transactions rather than income and the effect of integration in the classical quantity theory.

[11] The permanent wealth seems to be a concept closely analogous to the concepts measured by Goldsmith. Tangible assets are assessed at written down values in the perpetual inventory method. With suitable 'grossing', this seems to be the concept favoured by Meltzer, op. cit., though he does not use the permanent wealth idea as such. Meltzer shows that empirical results are closer to theoretical expectations when the gross concept rather than consolidated wealth is used in his equations. It should be added that he also reports a relatively low (−0·47) correlation between real wealth and the rate of interest. This suggests that using the concept of permanent wealth, etc. has met the objections advanced above.

[12] For statistical series and notes on sources see Walters, A. A., and Kavanagh, N. J., 'Demand for money in the U.K.', University of Birmingham Discussion Paper No. 48, July 1964.

tempted to conclude that 'tastes' had been changing systematically over time. The analogues of 'tastes' in the demand for money are changes in the structure of debts, assets and other transactions and in the extent of the monetization of the economy, changes in 'tastes' for precautionary security etc., and any increases in the credit opportunities as 'technical' progress takes place in the credit business. The long trends in the data probably reflect these movements rather than the demand curve for money with respect to the level of income or wealth.[13] The past trends may, of course, be quite good predictors of the future values. As a long run predictor the trend may be better than any alternative. The evidence for the U.K. suggests some long run stability combined with very large variations in the short run. But it would obviously be misleading to incorporate the derived 'trend' elasticity as a characteristic of a static demand function in any further studies of demand.

Some additional evidence of the long run relationship between income, wealth and the demand for money can be derived from cross-section studies. The Lydall cross-section study of households is the only one at present available for Britain.[14] These results show that there is a *low* elasticity of demand for money with respect to income (about 0·16) and a rather higher elasticity with respect to net worth (about 0·62). There are good reasons for supposing that these results have serious shortcomings.[15] But it is difficult to believe that there are not effective economics of scale in cash balances with respect to the level of income. Lydall's results apply only to households, but we know that a sizeable fraction of the total quantity of cash is held by firms. A cross-section study of the demand for cash for a sample of British firms has been carried out by one of us.[16] Again the evidence is not consistent with the Baumol–Tobin hypothesis. There are no marked economies of scale in the cash balances of firms.[17] It must be observed, however, that these results

[13] One way of checking certain aspects of this conjecture is to use cross-section data; see below.

[14] Lydall, H. F., 'Income, Assets and the Demand for Money', *Review of Economics and Statistics*, vol. 40, no. 1, February 1958, p. 1. See also Pesek, Boris P., 'Determinants of the Demand for Money', *Review of Economics and Statistics*, vol. 45, no. 4, November 1963, p. 419.

[15] See Pesek, op. cit., p. 422. The data would probably best be interpreted in terms of the permanent income hypothesis.

[16] Kavanagh, N. J., in an unpublished paper.

[17] This effect has also been observed by Heston in a Cowles Commission Discussion Paper.

pertain to variations in the size of *firm*. To be rendered consistent with the time series studies one must convert the independent variable to the 'average sales' of the economy. If the large firms grow at a more rapid rate than the small firms, the time series will give a mongrel result: the relative growth of large firms will reduce relatively the money balances required by the growth of national income.

For many purposes one is mainly interested in the short run relationship between money and income. This suggests that one should try and filter out the trend term by moving average or variate difference techniques. The simplest transformation is to take first differences. The equation in differences then shows the reaction of changes in income to changes in the quantity of money. As well as filtering out the trend, the difference method does measure the relationship which is required for any attempts at short-run management of the economy by monetary means.[18] Stability in this relationship would constitute some evidence in support of the effectiveness of short-term monetary control. In this study we have primarily relied on first differences, and mainly on first differences in the logarithms. This probably corresponds most closely to the concept used in policy discussions. Moving average techniques have not been applied to the annual data.[19]

Velocity—some results

The first group of results is for the traditional velocity relationships—or more accurately the dependent variable is the Cambridge 'k'. This tests the strong hypothesis that the demand for money is homogeneous with respect to income. We begin with the usual form of velocity equation, i.e.

$$\frac{M_t}{Y_t} = a_0 + a_1 R_t + a_2 \left(\frac{Y_t}{P_t}\right) \qquad \text{IIB.1}$$

or in a logarithmic version

$$m_t - y_t = \alpha_1 r_t + \alpha_2 (y_t - p_t) - \alpha_0$$

where the lower case letters are the logarithms.

[18] It is, however, well known that filtering techniques generate statistical problems of their own.

[19] Moving averages have been used on the monthly and quarterly data in order to eliminate seasonal variation. These results will be reported in a later paper.

The results for the logarithmic form broadly confirm the impressions obtained from the graphs.

$$m - y = -1{\cdot}2052 - \underset{(0{\cdot}0815)}{0{\cdot}2024}\, r + \underset{(0{\cdot}0407)}{0{\cdot}2914}\, (y - p) \qquad \text{IIB.2}$$

$$N = 84 \qquad 1877\text{–}1961 \qquad \bar{R}^2 = 0{\cdot}395$$

$y - p$ = logarithm of national income at 1912–13 prices
r = logarithm of consol rate
m = logarithms of quantity of nominal money.[20]

The $\bar{R}^2$ suggests that 40 per cent of the variations in $\log M/Y$ is due to the rate of interest and real income. The coefficients have the expected signs. The rate of interest coefficient is negative and a little over twice the standard error, and real income coefficient is positive and about seven times its standard error.

On the 'demand' interpretation the effect of an increase in real income is to increase the amount of money held. It is clear from the graphs that most of this effect is brought about by the large movements in velocity during the war and post-war years, and during the slump of the 1930s.

Are the results (and the real income coefficients in particular) simply a consequence of the trend in real income and the war-time increase in M/Y? The easiest way to check this is to omit the series before 1922 so that the dominant group of observations with low money stock and low real income disappears. (An incidental advantage is that the data are much more reliable for the later period.) For 1923 to 1961 we get the following results:

$$m - y = 0{\cdot}55609 - \underset{(0{\cdot}06275)}{0{\cdot}55276}\, r - \underset{(0{\cdot}05697)}{0{\cdot}13518}\, (y - p) \qquad \text{IIB.3}$$

$$N = 38 \qquad 1923\text{–}61 \qquad \bar{R}^2 = 0{\cdot}695$$

This is different from the previous results. The rate of interest coefficient has increased almost three-fold, but it is still of the expected sign. The coefficient of real income has changed sign and is now *negative*. Here the results suggest that money is something of a *necessity* and not a luxury, and that the elasticity of money with

[20] The money stock used here included Bankers' Deposits at the Bank of England. The income series in the velocity analysis is usually net national income; although on occasion gross national product has been adopted. The different definitions do not produce any substantial difference in the results.

respect to the interest rate is about 0·5. These results are not markedly inconsistent with the Baumol–Tobin hypothesis. One probably puts most trust in the post-1922 results. The data are more reliable and the sample is more homogeneous.

Many questions are still left open: probably the most important are whether we get the same sort of results with other definitions of 'money', and whether small changes in the period of investigation give the same sort of results. Experiments with other time series suggest that the results are not drastically modified—though these experiments have not been pushed very far. To check how critical the definition of money is in this context we used the most expanded concept of money employed in this paper for a regression covering roughly the same period. Money is defined to include not only savings bank deposits but also building society deposits and money held on deposit in other financial non-bank institutions (we call this M_3).

The results are produced in the following equation:

$$m_3 - y = -0{\cdot}1494 - \underset{(0{\cdot}0814)}{0{\cdot}6799}\, r + \underset{(0{\cdot}0713)}{0{\cdot}1189}\, (y - p) \qquad \text{IIB.4}$$

$$N = 38 \qquad 1923\text{–}61 \qquad \bar{R}^2 = 0{\cdot}6565$$

The coefficient of the rate of interest is *increased* by the inclusion of savings bank deposits, etc., in the money variable, and the sign is still significantly negative as predicted by the theory. The coefficient of the real income variable has changed sign and is now positive. This is explained by the growth of 'near money', especially building society deposits, savings bank deposits, and similar funds, over the years 1923–60. There is no powerful case for regarding money as a luxury, however, since the difference between the coefficient and zero can be readily explained by sampling variation.[21]

The long run results from these equations are of limited use. They may serve as indicators of trends and as a general background within which short-term movements take place. For most policy purposes the short-run results are the important ones. Consequently we have calculated the regressions using first differences. The logarithmic form used is

$$\Delta(m_t - y_t) = \alpha_1 \Delta r_t + \alpha_2 \Delta(y_t - p_t) + \alpha_3$$

where the lower case letters represent logarithms.

[21] We had to omit the year 1961 as complete data were not available when series was being compiled.

One or two examples of the results with this relationship are:

1878–1914

$$\Delta(m-y) = \underset{(0{\cdot}254)}{-0{\cdot}524}\,\Delta r - \underset{(0{\cdot}242)}{0{\cdot}554}\,\Delta(y-p) + 0{\cdot}00625$$

$N = 36$ 1878–1914 $\bar{R}^2 = 0{\cdot}155$

1878–1961

$$\Delta(m-y) = \underset{(0{\cdot}073)}{-0{\cdot}437}\,\Delta r - \underset{(0{\cdot}104)}{0{\cdot}880}\,\Delta(y-p) + 0{\cdot}00854$$

$N = 83$ 1878–1961 $\bar{R}^2 = 0{\cdot}535$

1951–61

$$\Delta(m-y) = \underset{(0{\cdot}140)}{-0{\cdot}224}\,\Delta r + \underset{(0{\cdot}573)}{0{\cdot}284}\,\Delta(y-p) - 0{\cdot}01721$$

$N = 10$ 1951–61 $\bar{R}^2 = 0{\cdot}144$

1878–1961 (excluding war years)

$$\Delta(m-y) = \underset{(0{\cdot}092)}{-0{\cdot}447}\,\Delta r - \underset{(0{\cdot}224)}{0{\cdot}670}\,\Delta(y-p) + 0{\cdot}00491$$

$N = 63$ 1878–1914 $\bar{R}^2 = 0{\cdot}327$
1923–38
1951–61

1920–51

$$\Delta(m-y) = \underset{(0{\cdot}200)}{-0{\cdot}200}\,\Delta r - \underset{(0{\cdot}142)}{0{\cdot}854}\,\Delta(y-p) + 0{\cdot}00781$$

$N = 31$ 1920–51 $\bar{R}^2 = 0{\cdot}591$

(Approximately the same results are obtained if 1941–46 is excluded.)

The first striking result is the very low values of $\bar{R}^2$, especially when they are compared with the values for the non-differenced data. But one must expect this since it is much more difficult to 'explain' the variance of a difference than that of an absolute value. One interesting result is that all the coefficients of the rate of interest have the expected negative sign. The ratio of money to national income varies inversely with the rate of interest. For what they are worth, significance tests suggest that at conventional 5 and 1 per cent levels, the coefficients for both versions of the long series are significantly different from zero. One's best guess at this 'interest elasticity' is about –0·4. It is not possible to interpret any of the subtle variations in the coefficient between the various periods since the sampling variations effectively preclude this.

All the coefficients of real income (except for the period 1951–61) are negative. The results conform to the cyclical pattern observed by Professor Friedman in the U.S.A. Relative increases in real income give rise to a relative fall in the Cambridge 'k' (or a rise in the income velocity of circulation). With the United States data we get almost precisely the same results for the income coefficient.[22]

The real income coefficient is not significantly different from unity in all the series so that, for the short run relationship, the homogeneity hypothesis is not discredited. But clearly one might also argue that the Baumol–Tabin hypothesis also cannot be *confidently* dismissed. The simple non-stochastic inventory model predicts that the elasticity of money demand with respect to income is +0·5—and some of the results are not inconsistent with this value.

More general formulations

The velocity concept or its reciprocal the Cambridge 'k' is a traditional variable in monetary economics. For this reason our empirical work first concentrated on these magnitudes. From the results, however, it is clear that the ratio of money to income is not the most satisfactory variable to use. The money demand equation is not clearly homogeneous in nominal income. For this reason it is best to pursue the analysis by using simpler linear (and log linear) forms of hypothesis where the level of nominal balances is the dependent variable. Income will appear only among the independent variables.

We have argued that it would be more consistent with theory to take the rate of interest or the level of income as the dependent variable and the quantity of money as the independent variable. Here we shall pursue only the models with the rate of interest as

[22] These results, and particularly the interest coefficients, contrast with those which have been found in the United States. There an expanded definition of money (currency plus time and checking deposits) produced a very marked 'luxury' effect; Professor Friedman found that the elasticity is about 1·8 which corresponds roughly to a regression coefficient of about 0·8. With the narrow definition of money there appears to be no evidence that money is either a luxury or a necessity. With a broad definition of money in the United States the rate of interest seems to have little relationship with velocity. But with the narrow definition the American interest elasticity is large and significant.

the dependent variable. Monetary multipliers, with the level of income as dependent variable, will be presented in another paper.

The forms of the equations used fall naturally into the following categories:

I. *Nominal Money as the dependent variable* with consol rate, money national income, past incomes, prices and rates of change of prices as independent variables.

II. *Rate of Interest as the dependent variable* with money national income, prices, past rates of change of prices as independent variables.

III. *Real Money as the dependent variable* with consol rate, real national income, rate of change of prices as independent variables.

The data were also split up into various time periods so that separate regressions were calculated for different time periods. Money was defined: M_1 as currency *plus* bank deposits, M_2 as M_1 *plus* savings bank deposits and M_3 (1923–60 only) as M_2 *plus* deposits of other non-bank financial institutions. Y_t is defined throughout this subsection as gross national product, P_t is price level and R_t consol rate.

We have fitted both arithmetic and logarithmic linear regressions to all the formulations discussed above. Many investigators of demand function, however, prefer to fit logarithmic functions directly. The advantages (*inter alia*) are that homoskedasticity is more likely to be true for the logarithmic series than for the arithmetic data, and that the regression coefficients can be immediately interpreted as elasticities. The real issue, however, is whether a log-linear surface is a 'best-fit' or at least a better fit than any other simple function. From three-dimensional figures constructed for the various series from 1880–1961, one cannot see any obvious advantage in either linear or log-linear form. The regression results more or less confirm this judgement. We shall therefore report only the logarithmic results.

Table IIC 1 sets out the estimates for the whole period 1880–1961.

The general pattern of the coefficients is consistent with expectations. The income coefficient is positive and a little over unity. This indicates that, as we saw in the graphical description of the series, the proportionate trend in the quantity of money was matched by a slightly less steep trend in the value of gross national product. Formal significance tests (taking account of the high

TABLE IIC 1

Money, income and the rate of interest 1880–1961 (*logarithms*)

Dependent variable	Independent variables					$\bar{R}^2$	d
$m_1(t)$	1·149 $y(t)$ (0·021)	−0·306 $r(t)$ (0·086)				0·98	0·114
$m_1(t)$	1·191 $y(t)$ (0·080)	−0·280 $r(t)$ (0·099)	−0·081 $p(t)$ (0·149)			0·98	0·115
$m_1(t)$	1·203 $y(t)$ (0·076)	−0·303 $r(t)$ (0·095)	−0·782 $p(t)$ (0·284)	0·708 $p(t-1)$ (0·248)		0·98	0·134
$r(t)$	−0·455 $m_1(t)$ (0·127)	0·661 $y(t)$ (0·141)				0·48	0·118
$r(t)$	−0·387 $m_1(t)$ (0·121)	0·243 $y(t)$ (0·175)	0·149 $p(t)$ (0·336)	0·471 $p(t-1)$ (0·290)		0·59	0·158
$m_1(t)$	0·621 $y(t)$ (0·275)	0·011 $y(t-1)$ (0·485)	0·542 $y(t-2)$ (0·277)	−0·333 $r(t)$ (0·079)		0·99	0·093
$r(t)$	−0·431 $m_1(t)$ (0·125)	−0·121 $y(t)$ (0·341)	0·127 $y(t-1)$ (0·573)	0·296 $y(t-2)$ (0·334)	0·609 $p(t)$ (0·143)	0·59	0·159
$m_2(t)$	1·272 $y(t)$ (0·072)	−0·461 $r(t)$ (0·090)	−0·112 $p(t)$ (0·135)			0·99	0·152
$r(t)$	−0·609 $m_2(t)$ (0·107)	0·604 $y(t)$ (0·168)	−0·124 $p(t)$ (0·304)	0·579 $p(t-1)$ (0·258)		0·67	0·191

TABLE IIC 2

Money, income and the rate of interest 1926–1960 (*logarithms*)

Dependent variable	Independent variables					$\bar{R}^2$	d
$m_1(t)$	0·9644 $y(t)$	−0·4987 $r(t)$				0·968	0·240
	(0·0303)	(0·0890)					
$m_1(t)$	0·1066 $y(t)$	−0·7543 $r(t)$	1·331 $p(t)$			0·980	0·630
	(0·1968)	(0·0918)	(0·303)				
$m_1(t)$	0·1593 $y(t)$	−0·8357 $r(t)$	0·4804 $p(t)$	0·8216 $p(t-1)$		0·982	0·671
	(0·1880)	(0·0950)	(0·4914)	(0·3854)			
$r(t)$	−0·9927 $m_1(t)$	1·010 $y(t)$				0·513	0·265
	(0·1772)	(0·167)					
$r(t)$	−0·9085 $m_1(t)$	−0·3078 $y(t)$	1·867 $p(t)$			0·813	0·878
	(0·1106)	(0·2098)	(0·259)				
$m_1(t)$	0·4553 $y(t)$	−0·4324 $y(t-1)$	1·008 $y(t-2)$	−0·6164 $r(t)$		0·979	0·380
	(0·3829)	(0·6850)	(0·394)	(0·0782)			
$r(t)$	−0·9873 $m_1(t)$	−0·3641 $y(t)$	−0·3982 $y(t-1)$	0·8455 $y(t-2)$	1·454 $p(t)$	0·859	0·957
$m_3(t)$	0·1879 $y(t)$	−0·9054 $r(t)$	1·353 $p(t)$			0·978	0·666
	(0·2261)	(0·1055)	(0·348)				
$r(t)$	−0·7773 $m_3(t)$	−0·2348 $y(t)$	1·671 $p(t)$			0·824	0·923
	(0·0906)	(0·2076)	(0·254)				
$r(t)$	−7·323 $m_3(t)$	−0·1040 $y(t)$	0·4519 $p(t)$	1·001 $p(t-1)$		0·854	0·932
	(0·0841)	(0·1951)	(0·5049)	(0·368)			

autocorrelation of residuals) show that the coefficient is not significantly different from one. We cannot therefore say with any confidence that money is a luxury. The other finding which is not discredited by these figures is that there is a negative relationship between money and the rate of interest. The relatively high standard errors give one some qualms about making categorical statements about the actual value of the elasticity—but –0·2 to –0·5 would be the likely range of values.

In equations which have the logarithm of the rate of interest as the dependent variable one can see the relationship between income (or strictly gross national product) and the rate of interest is positive as predicted by extended Keynesian theory. A 1 per cent rise in gross national product is matched by a 0·6–0·7 per cent rise in the rate of interest. And it seems that 'price' effects on the rate of interest are more important than 'real income' effects. Again one suspects that these results relating to price effects, both here and for the arithmetic equations, are statistical illusions due to the association of high interest rates and high prices in the last decade of the period. The graphical and three-dimensional figures suggest that this may be the explanation, but it requires more investigation.

One result on the logarithmic transformation is quite different from the arithmetic regression. In the arithmetic regression the addition of price to the independent variables changed drastically the income coefficient and in fact made it quite insignificant. On the other hand, the inclusion of the price level in the logarithmic version for 1880–1961 made virtually no difference to any of the coefficients. It is difficult to find any obvious explanation of this phenomenon. Partly it must be due to the record before the 1920s, since if one examines the logarithmic regression for the period 1926–60 one finds that the behaviour of the coefficients, when price is introduced as an 'independent' variable, is not unlike the arithmetic results.

Table IIC 2 displays the logarithmic coefficients for the period 1926–60. The results for this short period gave high $\bar{R}^2$, and the Durbin–Watson statistics are not quite so unsatisfactory as those for the period 1880–1961. The coefficients are roughly similar to those which were obtained for the whole period 1880–1961. There are, however, some important changes in magnitude. Generally the rate of interest coefficient is increased. The elasticity of demand for money with respect to the rate of interest seems to be between about –0·5 and –1·2. The coefficient when all types of deposits are included in the definition of money changes in a now predictable way. The interest elasticity rises to between −0·6 and −1·4. And the income coefficient is increased slightly.

One important limitation on these results is the very high autocorrelation in the residuals. There is a distinct pattern with long runs of negative signs (where money is the dependent variable) followed by a long string of positive residuals; finally there is another run of deviations less than zero. This confirms the impression one gets from a graphical representation of the series. At the formal level high autocorrelation of residuals affects only the estimate of the standard errors of the regression coefficient. But the important aspect is, that it emphasizes the heterogeneity of the data. The regression plane cuts through the long cyclical swings in the monetary behaviour of the economy. One way of getting round this heterogeneity is to analyse the data for sub-periods. Unfortunately one foregoes degrees of freedom in the process, but we shall do this in a later paper.

Relationships between changes in variables

The high autocorrelation in the residuals of the regressions reviewed in the previous paragraphs is reason enough for considering a suitable transformation. The very high positive value of the autocorrelation coefficient clearly indicates that a full first differencing would be not inappropriate.[23] The trend is to a large extent eliminated by the differencing procedure. In addition this is often the relationship which is of most interest for policy decisions.

Table IID 1 sets out the results for the period 1880–1961. The $\bar{R}^2$s are, as one would expect, considerably lower than those derived from the ordinary observations (but higher than those for arithmetic differences). Between 30 per cent to 65 per cent of the dependent variable is explained by moments in the independent variables. The improvement in the Durbin–Watson statistic is marked in all the equations—but there is still some evidence of autocorrelated residuals in all the specifications.

The behaviour of the variables about the trend is, predictably, similar to the trend results. The income coefficient is, however,

[23] In retrospect it would probably have been better to use some other transformation for certain equations. In some of the equations where the rate of interest is the independent variable, for example, the first difference transformation introduced some *negative* autocorrelation in the differences. But such effects are quantitatively not serious.

TABLE IID 1

Money, income and the rate of interest 1881–1961 (*differences of logarithms*)

Dependent variable	Independent variables				$\bar{R}^2$	d
$\Delta m_1(t)$	$0{\cdot}655\ \Delta y(t)$ (0·074)	$-0{\cdot}223\ \Delta r(t)$ (0·068)			0·49	0·816
$\Delta m_1(t)$	$0{\cdot}164\ \Delta y(t)$ (0·137)	$-0{\cdot}257\ \Delta r(t)$ (0·062)	$0{\cdot}566\ \Delta p(t)$ (0·138)		0·58	1·007
$\Delta m_1(t)$	$0{\cdot}140\ \Delta y(t)$ (0·125)	$-0{\cdot}260\ \Delta r(t)$ (0·057)	$0{\cdot}426\ \Delta p(t)$ (0·130)	$0{\cdot}277\ \Delta p(t-1)$ (0·067)	0·65	0·940
$\Delta r(t)$	$-0{\cdot}548\ \Delta m_1(t)$ (0·166)	$0{\cdot}800\ \Delta y(t)$ (0·137)			0·29	1·403
$\Delta r(t)$	$-0{\cdot}706\ \Delta m_1(t)$ (0·171)	$0{\cdot}306\ \Delta y(t)$ (0·227)	$0{\cdot}646\ \Delta p(t)$ (0·241)		0·34	1·457
$\Delta r(t)$	$-0{\cdot}834\ \Delta m_1(t)$ (0·182)	$0{\cdot}298\ \Delta y(t)$ (0·223)	$0{\cdot}586\ \Delta p(t)$ (0·240)	$0{\cdot}241\ \Delta p(t-1)$ (0·130)	0·36	1·458
$\Delta m_1(t)$	$0{\cdot}480\ \Delta y(t)$ (0·075)	$0{\cdot}220\ \Delta y(t-1)$ (0·081)	$0{\cdot}172\ \Delta y(t-2)$ (0·068)	$-0{\cdot}240\ \Delta r(t)$ (0·059)	0·62	0·737
$\Delta m_2(t)$	$0{\cdot}619\ \Delta y(t)$ (0·073)	$-0{\cdot}259\ \Delta r(t)$ (0·067)			0·46	0·787
$\Delta r(t)$	$-0{\cdot}736\ \Delta m_2(t)$ (0·161)	$0{\cdot}322\ \Delta y(t)$ (0·222)	$0{\cdot}602\ \Delta p(t)$ (0·232)		0·37	1·476

TABLE IIID 2

Money, income and the rate of interest 1926–61 (differences in logarithms)

Dependent variable	Independent variables				R^2	d
$\Delta m_1(t)$	0·3796 $\Delta y(t)$ (0·1440)	−0·2469 $\Delta r(t)$ (0·0856)			0·23	0·558
$\Delta m_1(t)$	−0·0306 $\Delta y(t)$ (0·2330)	−0·2469 $\Delta r(t)$ (0·0809)	0·5551 $\Delta p(t)$ (0·2559)		0·31	0·770
$\Delta m_1(t)$	−0·2913 $\Delta y(t)$ (0·2394)	−0·2626 $\Delta r(t)$ (0·0750)	0·4748 $\Delta p(t)$ (0·2386)	0·4905 $\Delta p(t-1)$ (0·1974)	0·41	0·874
$\Delta r(t)$	−0·8570 $\Delta m(t)$ (0·2972)	0·6979 $\Delta y(t)$ (0·2692)			0·23	1·424
$\Delta r(t)$	−0·9596 $\Delta m_1(t)$ (0·3145)	0·3312 $\Delta y(t)$ (0·4556)	0·5326 $\Delta p(t)$ (0·5339)		0·23	1·535
$\Delta r(t)$	−1·132 $\Delta m_1(t)$ (0·323)	−0·0829 $\Delta y(t)$ (0·5094)	0·5119 $\Delta p(t)$ (0·5195)	0·7112 $\Delta p(t-1)$ (0·4316)	0·27	1·659
$\Delta m_1(t)$	0·1881 $\Delta y(t)$ (0·1744)	0·1065 $\Delta y(t-1)$ (0·1968)	0·3040 $\Delta y(t-2)$ (0·1664)	−0·2790 $\Delta r(t)$ (0·0813)	0·33	0·781
$\Delta m_3(t)$	0·3439 $\Delta y(t)$ (0·1567)	−0·2590 $\Delta r(t)$ (0·0931)			0·19	0·441
$\Delta r(t)$	−0·8390 $\Delta m_3(t)$ (0·2907)	0·3364 $\Delta y(t)$ (0·4614)	0·4357 $\Delta p(t)$ (0·5329)		0·21	1·524

7

reduced considerably to between a half or two-thirds the trend value. An increase of 1 per cent in the gross national product is associated with a 0·65 per cent increase in the quantity of money. In the results for the period 1926–61, however (Table IID 2), we see that the income effect is considerably muted. An increase of one per cent in income is associated with a 0·38 per cent increase in the quantity of money.

The coefficients of the rate of interest and money relationship are all negative as predicted in the theory—though hardly significant in some cases. There is no marked change in the interest elasticity of demand for money from the long period to the post-World War I period. On the other hand, there is a considerable difference between the measured elasticity when money is the dependent variable, and that when the rate of interest is the dependent variable. The elasticity is about −0·25 with money as the dependent variable, whereas with the rate of interest as dependent we get an elasticity ranging between −0·8 and −2·0 (in 1880–1961). The direction of causation in the specification is critically important in determining the numerical value of the elasticity coefficient. For the demand interpretation where the rate of interest is the dependent variable which is, in turn, determined by the government controlling the quantity of money, the interest elasticity is very high—indicating that the liquidity trap is no illusion. It is interesting that, in the major studies in the United States, such as that of Selden, low elasticities were obtained by regressing money or velocity on the rate of interest. On this evidence Friedman, for example, has regarded the rate of interest effect as of little importance. But the effects of interest rates clearly cannot be dismissed if, as we have argued, the equation is properly specified.

The curious effect of introducing a price variable was the most surprising result of the trend regressions. One suspects that the high coefficient of the price variable may be due to trend effects. This suspicion is discredited by the results of this section. Indeed where the price effect was small for the trend results (as for the logarithmic results in the period 1880–1961) we find in the corresponding first difference figures a marked price effect. A 1 per cent change in price is associated with about a 0·5 per cent change in the quantity of money. The addition of lagged values of price changes does not appear materially to affect the results. This suggests that in Britain the monetary multiplier has a classical price effect; money affects price changes but not the annual variation in the rate of growth of real income. This tentative result will have to be examined with specific formulations of the monetary multipliers.

Another interesting feature of these results is that the distributed-lag version of the relation between the per cent change in money and past percentage changes in income is not inconsistent with the predictions of the permanent income hypothesis. Looking at the 1880–1961 results, for example, one finds that the coefficients of past percentage changes in incomes are all positive and decay in the predicted manner. The sum of these coefficients is rather higher than one would expect (i.e. 0·87), but it is clearly not so far away that one can, for example, reject the hypothesis of a sum of 0·5 to 0·6. For the period 1926–61 the sum of the coefficients is nearer to expectation (i.e. 0·58). The point estimates of the coefficients however do not have the expected 'decaying' property.

A general review of these results shows that there is no startling difference between using the narrow and broad definition of money; indeed the two sets of results are remarkably alike. With money as the dependent variable the coefficients are increased (absolutely) when the broader definition is used. With the rate of interest as dependent variable the coefficient of the money stock is reduced. No changes in sign are introduced by the changed definition and even the magnitudes are remarkably near those which we would expect from the expanded concept of money.

The issue, much debated in the United States, of which is the most useful definition of money, does not seem to be so vitally important in the monetary climate of the United Kingdom. Professor Friedman's claim that a different definition of money will merely change the numbers but not the substance of monetary relationships is supported by the data for the United Kingdom, at least as far as the long run relationship is concerned.

Concluding remarks

In this exploratory study of money in the United Kingdom we have examined only certain limited aspects of monetary theory. The concentration of research on the demand for money and the fact that we have largely ignored the problems of determining the supply of money means that the results have little use for direct policy purposes. But they have some value in discussing the framework of monetary and counter cyclical policy generally.

We summarize briefly the main results:

(a) the long run 'trend' figures suggest that money is neither a luxury nor a necessity;
(b) the short run (difference) results show that variations in money are associated with larger percentage changes in money income;
(c) both long run and short run results show that the rate of interest is negatively associated with the quantity of money;
(d) when the rate of interest-money stock aggregate relationship is 'properly' specified, the implied elasticity of aggregate demand for money is in the region of −0·8 to less than −2·0;
(e) different specifications of the demand function do not seem drastically to change the general results though, as in (d) above, by taking different variables as dependent one does considerably change the numerical values of the parameters;
(f) variations in the definition of money do not have very serious effects on the estimates of the parameters; contrary to American data, the effect of an expanded definition of money is to increase the interest elasticity of demand.

There is a large number of areas which are left for investigation. The first one is the behaviour of money, prices and real income. The detailed statistical relationship between these series has received little attention even in the United States. The effects we have uncovered lead one to suspect that this should be a priority for further research. The evidence at present suggests that the changes in import prices may be a major explanation of these effects. The second main area is the behaviour of the series for quarterly and monthly periods. We have already got many results for the quarterly data. These show no marked disagreement with the annual results—but much more work remains to be done. The third job for future attention is to split the series according to trade cycle phases. We have already made a start on this analysis. The simultaneous equations system for the monetary sphere needs more detailed and extensive investigation. Finally we have found that there is some evidence of a fairly strong monetary multiplier—although it is not a high one compared with those which have been estimated for the United States; we shall elaborate on this elsewhere.

9

THE DEMAND FOR MONEY IN THE UNITED KINGDOM, 1955–1967: PRELIMINARY ESTIMATES[1]

D. LAIDLER *and* J. M. PARKIN*

I

MEASURING the parameters and assessing the stability of various formulations of the demand for money function have attracted a great deal of attention and effort over the last ten years. Most of this work has been carried out using data generated by the United States economy, and, though there have been studies of the United Kingdom, we still know a good deal less about that economy than we do about the United States. In particular the work carried

* Reprinted with revisions from *The Manchester School*, vol. 38, no. 3, September 1970, pp. 187–208, by permission of the authors and publishers. David Laidler and Michael Parkin are both Professors of Economics at the University of Manchester.

[1] This is a substantially revised version of the original paper. In particular the time period covered by the data used is a little longer, while some minor errors have been removed from the money supply series utilized. Even now there is some doubt about the accuracy of the data for the 1960–2 period and all the computations reported in this paper have also been carried out on data from which these years are omitted in order to ensure that none of the reported results depends critically upon the use of data for these years. The results in question have survived this test. We are grateful to Rodney Barrett, Antoinette Dowden, and Lorne Ellingson for research assistance and to Robyn Kemmis and Jonathon Stewart for programming help. Edgar Feige, Douglas Fisher, Milton Friedman, Charles Goodhart, Harry Johnson, Michael Kennedy, Rainer Masera, Marcus Miller, E. Victor Morgan, Anna Schwartz, and Alan Walters have all contributed helpful suggestions at various stages in this paper's preparation. They are of course to be exonerated of blame for any errors that might remain in the paper. David Laidler gratefully acknowledges the financial support of the Houblon–Norman Fund, and Michael Parkin that of the Social Science Research Council.

out by A. A. Walters and his collaborators [11] shows that the behaviour of the monetary mechanism in the 1950s and the 1960s is difficult to interpret in the light of simple money multiplier models that appear to work quite satisfactorily for earlier periods. However, a study of the demand for money function over the years 1951–67 carried out by Douglas Fisher [4] strongly suggests that a stable demand relationship, of the same type that has worked well for the United States economy, is capable of dealing with the British experience over the very years that Walters found so troublesome.

Though these sets of results do not contradict each other outright, because a stable demand for money function, though necessary, is far from being sufficient to guarantee a stable money multiplier, the problem of the stability of monetary relationships over the last ten years still seems to warrant further investigation.[2] This study presents the results of further work on the period, and the main conclusions that may be drawn from these results are as follows: Fisher seems to overstate the stability of simple formulations of the demand for money function as far as post-war Britain is concerned, largely as a result of his failure to employ in his tests money and income data cast in *per capita* real terms. Nevertheless, provided that care is taken with the specification of the lag structure of the demand for money function, it does appear that the data may be interpreted in terms of a model which makes the demand for money depend upon permanent income. Such a model has, of course, been widely and successfully used in dealing with United States data. The role of the rate of interest in the demand for money function is left obscure by our results. The main conclusion to be drawn in this respect is that much more work is required on assessing which variables best represent the opportunity cost of holding money. In particular, careful attention should probably be paid to the expected rate of inflation. We cannot be more specific about our results without explicit reference to our tests and to the model of the demand for money in terms of which they were carried out. It is to the task of setting out this model that we will turn first of all.

[2] For the money multiplier to be stable in the absence of a direct wealth effect, it is necessary for there to exist a stable relationship between interest rates and aggregate demand in addition to there existing a stable demand for money function. Thus, there is nothing to be inferred solely from the existence of a stable demand for money function about the existence or otherwise of a stable money multiplier.

II

The model of the demand for money which generated our results is conventional enough. It may be expressed in the following three equations, where all variables are in natural logarithms.[3] If m^* is desired real money balances, m is actual money balances, y^e is expected (permanent) real income, y is actual income, r is the rate of interest, β is the elasticity of demand for money with respect to permanent income, γ is the elasticity of demand for money with respect to the interest rate, λ is the elasticity of expected income with respect to actual income, and θ is the elasticity of actual money balances with respect to desired money balances, and the subscript $_{-i}$ $(i = 1, 2)$ refers to lags in quarters, we have:

$$m^* = \alpha + \beta y^e + \gamma r \tag{1}$$

$$y^e = \lambda y + (1 - \lambda) y^e_{-1} \tag{2}$$

$$m = \theta m^* + (1 - \theta) m_{-1} + u \tag{3}$$

From these three equations, it follows that

$$m = b_0 + b_1 y + b_2 r + b_3 r_{-1} + b_4 m_{-1} + b_5 m_{-2} + v \tag{4}$$

The coefficients of equation 4 are related to the parameters of the original model in the following way.[4]

[3] The model is, as the reader will notice, very similar to that used by Feige [3] in dealing with American data. We do, however, have some doubts about Feige's conception of the role of the 'expected' interest rate in the demand for money function and have not followed him in this regard. Feige uses an exponentially weighted average of past and present values of the interest rate to measure the opportunity cost of holding money. If the rate of interest on an asset is expected to differ in the future from its current value then the return to be earned by holding that asset is, as the Keynesian theory of the speculative demand for money teaches us, the average rate of interest on that asset over whatever the relevant holding period might be, plus the expected rate of capital gain (or loss) that arises from changes in that rate of return.

To postulate that the 'expected' rate of interest differs importantly from the actual rate of interest, and then simply to use the 'expected' rate as a measure of the opportunity cost of holding money fails to capture the mechanism involved here. In this study we treat the three-month Treasury bill rate, rather than its 'expected' value, as an indicator of the opportunity cost of holding money.

[4] Equation 4 is derived as follows. Ignoring the error term for the sake of simplicity, substitute equations 1 and 2 into equation 3 to yield

$$m = \theta\alpha + \theta\beta\lambda y + \theta\beta(1 - \lambda) y^e_{-1} + \theta\gamma r + (1 - \theta) m_{-1}.$$

Then lag equations (1) and (3) one period, and substitute the former into the latter and multiply the result by $(1 - \lambda)$ to get

$$(1 - \lambda) m_{-1} = \theta\alpha(1 - \lambda) + \theta\beta(1 - \lambda) y^e_{-1} + \theta\gamma(1 - \lambda) r_{-1} + (1 - \theta)(1 - \lambda) m_{-2}$$

This, subtracted from the foregoing expression yields equation 4.

$$b_0 = \alpha\theta\lambda \tag{5}$$

$$b_1 = \beta\theta\lambda \tag{6}$$

$$b_2 = \gamma\theta \tag{7}$$

$$b_3 = -\gamma\theta(1 - \lambda) \tag{8}$$

$$b_4 = 2 - \theta - \lambda \tag{9}$$

$$b_5 = -(1 - \theta)(1 - \lambda) \tag{10}$$

Furthermore, the disturbance term v is related to u, and may, for example, if the original disturbances are serially independent, follow a first order autoregressive pattern. For most of our work we have assumed that the original disturbances follow whatever pattern is required to guarantee serial independence of the residuals of any equation we fit, and work not reported here suggests that to modify the assumption and explicitly allow for first order autocorrelation in the residuals of equation 4 does not substantially alter any results.

Our basic model is one in which the demand for money depends upon permanent income and the rate of interest, and in which actual cash balances approach equilibrium with an exponentially distributed lag. It also contains, as special cases of itself, a number of models which are normally regarded as providing competing explanations of the demand for money. For example, if we assume that λ is equal to unity, we have a model in which the demand for money depends upon measured rather than permanent income, but in which actual cash balances approach equilibrium with a lag.[5] In this case equation 4 reduces to

$$m = b'_0 + b'_1 y + b'_2 r + b'_4 m_{-1} + v \tag{4a}$$

and its coefficients become

$$b'_0 = \alpha\theta \tag{5a}$$

$$b'_1 = \beta\theta \tag{6a}$$

$$b'_2 = \gamma\theta \tag{7a}$$

$$b'_4 = (1 - \theta) \tag{9a}$$

If, instead, we set θ equal to unity but permit λ to be less than unity, we have the conventional permanent income hypothesis of

[5] This model has been used for the United States by Teigen [**10**] and Bronfenbrenner and Mayer [**2**] among others.

the demand for money in which cash balances are always assumed to be in equilibrium.[6]

We have

$$m = b''_0 + b''_1 y + b''_2 r + b''_3 r_{-1} + b''_4 m_{-1} + v \quad (4b)$$

and

$$b''_0 = \alpha\lambda \quad (5b)$$
$$b''_1 = \beta\lambda \quad (6a)$$
$$b''_2 = \gamma \quad (7b)$$
$$b''_3 = -\gamma(1 - \lambda) \quad (8b)$$
$$b''_4 = (1 - \lambda) \quad (9b)$$

Finally, if λ and θ are both equal to unity, we get a straightforward measured income formulation of the demand for money function[7]

$$m = b'''_0 + b'''_1 y + b'''_2 r + v \quad (4c)$$

where $b'''_0 = \alpha$, $b'''_1 = \beta$, $b'''_2 = \gamma$ and $v = u$.

Our general model thus contains several important alternative hypotheses about the nature of the demand for money function. There is clearly a great deal to be learned from estimating equation 4 subject to the constraints upon the values of its coefficients implied by equations 5–10. By doing so we could test simultaneously these alternative hypotheses about the demand for money function. For example, if lagged adjustment to equilibrium is an important phenomenon, then this procedure would reveal that the parameter θ was less than unity, while if adjustment was more or less instantaneous the estimate of θ ought not to differ significantly from unity. The value taken by the parameter λ would yield information about the importance of the permanent income hypothesis for explaining the demand for money in the United Kingdom. At the same time it should go without saying that both β and γ should conform to certain *a priori* expectations both as to sign and order of magnitude.

Even so, it would be wrong to rely solely on equation 4. The simpler special cases derived above can provide important insights in their own right. Consider the simplest of them, equation 4c. Even if, in fact, both θ and λ were to turn out to be significantly

[6] This model, with the addition of the interest rate is that utilized by Friedman [5].

[7] Heller [7] is one of those who has claimed that such a model is appropriate for dealing with United States data.

smaller than one in an estimate based on equation 4, it is still worth asking how well one can do with a function that nevertheless ignores the existence of lags. To begin with, this is the kind of demand for money function that is widely used in teaching macroeconomics, and in any event it is not the case in any science that it is always worth buying greater explanatory power for an hypothesis at the price of greater complexity. Equation 4c is a good deal simpler and easier to manipulate than equation 4 and the information that it was a useful rather than a misleading approximation to a more general formulation of the demand for money function would be welcomed by anyone concerned with the interpretation of monetary data and the prediction of monetary phenomena.

There are similar arguments in favour of testing equations 4a and 4b in their own right. It is worth knowing whether it is of critical importance to distinguish between the operation of a lag in the formation of income expectations on the one hand and a slow adjustment of real balances towards equilibrium on the other. Were the rate of interest a variable of no importance, were γ equal to zero, the empirical formulations of these hypotheses would, after all, be identical and it is by no means clear *a priori* how sharp a difference between their explanatory powers is made by the presence of the rate of interest in the demand for money function.[8] Thus, the test procedure followed in this study involved starting with the simpler 'special case' formulations, equations 4a, 4b and 4c, and looking at their empirical relevance for the United Kingdom economy. Having done that, we went on to face the special problems involved in dealing with functions of the complexity of equation 4.

III

All our tests were carried out with seasonally adjusted quarterly data for the United Kingdom covering the period 1955(3) to 1967(4). The money supply is expressed in *per capita* real terms and is based on the series published by the IMF; deposit accounts (time deposits) at commercial banks are included in it. The income variable is *per capita* real gross domestic product, and the implicit deflator for that series was the price index used for deflating the money stock. The interest rate is the three month treasury bill rate.

[8] That the models are identical when the rate of interest does not belong in the demand for money function may be shown by substituting the value zero for γ in equations 4–10.

The population series used to put the data on a *per capita* basis is total United Kingdom home population.[9]

As we have already indicated, the first tests we carried out were of the simpler special cases of our model embodied in equations 4a, 4b and 4c. The results of these tests are given in Table 1, and as the reader will see at a glance, none of the equations is very satisfactory. The simple measured income function—equation 4c—produces quite anomalous results:—a statistically significant positive sign on the interest rate, an income elasticity of demand for money that is rather too low to be entirely plausible, as well as a coefficient of determination that indicates an unusually low degree of explanatory power for a time series test of this type.[10] The simple textbook version of the demand for money function embodied in equation 4c fails to provide a satisfactory account of the data being dealt with here.

The introduction of the lagged value of the dependent variable into the function—equation 4a—improves matters somewhat. The interest rate now at least enters with a negative sign, although the relevant coefficient does not differ from zero at any conventionally accepted level of statistical significance. The coefficient of determination rises considerably, but the lag implicit in the coefficient of m_{-1} is rather long. Taken at face value this coefficient tells us that, at the end of three months, 16·4 per cent of any initial discrepancy between desired and actual cash balances will have been made good. The results, in short, are not plausible enough to bear the weight

[9] The income and price level data are taken from issues of *Economic Trends* for October 1966, 1967, and 1968. The interest rate series is an average of the monthly observations given in the *Annual Abstract of Statistics* 1961 and 1968. The annual population observations between which the quarterly ones were interpolated also come from the 1968 *Annual Abstract of Statistics*. The money supply series is based on data taken from *International Financial Statistics*, vols. 18 (1965, supplement and no. 4), 19 (July 1966), 20 (April 1967), and 21 (February and November 1968). Three slightly different series are available for overlapping time periods and these were spliced into a single series by the simple ratio method. The data given are end of quarter values. They were centred on the middle of the quarter by taking simple averages of two end quarter observations. Detailed descriptions of the series involved are to be found in *International Financial Statistics*, vol. 18, no. 5, 1965, p. 325 and vol. 21, no. 3, 1968, p. 325.

[10] By 'plausible' we mean here compatible with *a priori* expectations based in part upon economic theory, which has never suggested a likely value for the income elasticity of demand for money lower than 0·5 (cf. Baumol [1]), and in part upon United States evidence to the effect that this parameter seems to have been in the region of 1·0 most of the time, though perhaps a little less post-war.

TABLE I

Demand for money functions, per capita *real terms*, *United Kingdom quarterly data* (1955(3)–1967(4))

Equation	b_0	Y	r	r_{-1}	m_{-1}	R^2	ESS	β	γ	λ	θ
4a	−0·050 (0·386)	0·097 (4·081)	−0·004 (0·328)		0·836 (12·475)	0·856	0·008	0·591	−0·024	1†	0·164
4b	0·050 (0·382)	0·099 (4·014)	−0·005 (0·322)	0·002 (0·141)	0·837 (12·314)	0·856	0·008	0·607	−0·031*	0·163*	1†
4c	−1·45 (11·227)	0·146 (2·911)	0·052 (2·539)			0·368	0·034	0·146	0·052	1†	1†

† *A priori* fixed value. * Not based on the coefficient of r_{-1}.

Figures in parentheses are t-statistics. ESS is error sum of squares.

of any firm conclusions as to the nature of the demand for money function. Much the same account may be given of the results obtained with our permanent income formulation of the demand for money function, equation 4b. The addition of the lagged value of the interest rate to the regression equation adds nothing of significance to its explanatory power and leaves the coefficients of the other variables virtually unchanged. The lagged interest rate variable takes the predicted sign, but that is about all that can be said.[11]

The results reported in Table 1 tell us that the simple measured income hypothesis is not a good explanation of the demand for money; they also suggest most strongly that lag effects are very important in the demand for money function; so important, in fact, that if predicting as opposed to explaining the demand for money was the object, a first order autoregressive equation would probably perform as well as many more sophisticated models. The results in question, however, give no clue as to whether the lags involved are more likely to be adjustment lags than lags in the formation of income expectations, although the lags implied are so long that it is difficult plausibly to interpret them as being exclusively adjustment lags.

Now these conclusions are at some variance with those reported by Fisher [**4**], who, using only marginally different data, fitted functions closely akin to equations 4a, 4b and 4c.[12] His results imply an income (or permanent income) elasticity of demand for money that is closer to one than our estimate. He also presents

[11] Since the effect of the interest rate on the demand for money is so weak, it is hardly surprising that the results of equations 4a and 4b tell much the same story. If γ were equal to zero, they would be equivalent expressions. Cf. footnote 8.

[12] Fisher's period is 1951–1967, and his data are not quite the same as ours. His money supply series contains deposits at London clearing banks only and when using permanent income, he used series constructed using *a priori* fixed weights. Indeed, he appears to have used, on *quarterly* data, the weights that Friedman originally applied to *annual* data, but he gives no justification for this. Cf. Fisher [**4**], p. 133 for his description of the data. It should also be noted that Fisher used linear as opposed to log. linear regression for most of his work. The results that are most comparable with ours, being based on log. linear regressions, are given in Fisher [**4**], Table III, p. 337.

His version of equation 4a using the Treasury bill rate for r, and a broad definition of money, will suffice to illustrate the difference between his results and ours. It is, with t values in parentheses,

$$\underset{}{m = \alpha + \underset{(4{\cdot}10)}{0{\cdot}24y} - \underset{(0{\cdot}08)}{0{\cdot}001r} + \underset{(7{\cdot}23)}{0{\cdot}66m_{-1}}}$$

a value for θ that suggests that as much as 33 per cent of any adjustment of actual to desired cash balances takes place within three months. The major difference between our procedure and Fisher's is that his data are deflated by neither the price level nor the population. His income variable, therefore, picks up the joint effects of population changes, price level changes, and income changes on the aggregate demand for money. His estimates of time lag lengths confuse speeds of adjustment of aggregate nominal balances to changes in the price level, changes in the population and changes in the level of real income. Our results may be reconciled with Fisher's by postulating that the aggregate demand for nominal money is more stably related to the former two variables, and responds more rapidly to changes in them, than to changes in real income. Implicit in this reconciliation is the suggestion that, for post-war United Kingdom, Fisher's results overstate the explanatory power of simple demand for money functions of the type embodied in equations 4a, 4b, and 4c.[13]

[13] In order to see the kind of problems to which failure to deflate data by population and the price level can lead, consider the following simple example. Let the ith individual's demand for money function, written in logarithmic terms, be given by

$$m_i = \alpha + \beta y_i + \gamma r$$

where m is real money balances, y is income and r the rate of interest. If the distribution of income is uniform and is held constant over all observations so that we have no aggregation problems arising from this source, then, where π is the logarithm of population, the aggregate demand for real balances may be written as

$$m_i + \pi = \alpha + \beta y_i + \pi + \gamma r$$

Moreover, if the demand for real balances is independent of the price level, then, where p is the logarithm of the price level, the aggregate demand for nominal balances is given by:

$$m_i + \pi + p = \alpha + \beta y_i + \pi + p + \gamma r$$

This is *not* the function fitted when nominal income and nominal money are used in a demand for money function. The latter procedure involves fitting:

$$m_i + \pi + p = \alpha + \beta(y_i + \pi + p) + \gamma r$$

It should be quite clear that the effect of this is to overstate the importance of income as an explanatory variable as well as to bias the estimate of β towards unity because of the inevitable correlation between $(\pi + p)$ on both sides of the equation.

Though expressions derived from equation 4 are not quite as simple as the one dealt with in this example (for one thing we completely ignore the aggregation problems that arise from inequality in the distribution of income), we nevertheless have results that show how much 'better' equations 4a, 4b and 4c appear to

As we shall now see, results obtained from the more complex equation 4 go some way towards clearing up the difficulties we have just noted and, perhaps even more important, point clearly to the issues upon which further work is required. Equation 4 contains six coefficients, though the model from which it is derived has only five parameters. The model is over-identified and consistent estimates of its parameters can only be obtained by using a technique to estimate equation 4 that constrains its coefficients to bear to one another the relationships implicit in equations 5–10. An appropriate estimation technique was employed. The technique involves specifying values for the parameters of the model *a priori* and then follows an iterative procedure which continues to change the values of the parameters so long as doing so increases the explanatory power of the model. Since it is far from clear that using a technique of this type finds anything more than a locally optimal set of parameter values, we took the precaution of starting off the search procedure from a number of different initial points. As it turns out, there are two locally optimal sets of parameter values, between which there is nothing to choose on the basis of explanatory power, but one of which is more satisfactory from the point of view of economic interpretation.

The two sets of estimates are presented in Table 2, and the key difference between them is in the estimated values of θ and λ.[14] The data and the technique employed do not enable us to discriminate between an explanation of the behaviour of the demand for money that relies on a relatively long lag in the formation of income expectations (a small value of λ) and a rapid adjustment of cash balances to equilibrium (a large value of θ), and an alternative explanation that reverses the length of these lags. However, if orthodox statistical criteria do not help here, we may nevertheless make a tentative selection on the basis of economic plausibility.

perform when the data are not deflated by population, and we also have results showing a close proportional relationship between the aggregate demand for nominal balances and the price level. These results are given, and discussed briefly, in the Appendix.

[14] The reader will note that the ratios of parameter estimates to their standard errors given here are not comparable with the *t*-statistics presented in Table 1. The latter appertain to the coefficients of reduced form expressions, while the statistics presented in Tables 2 and 3 appertain to the structural parameters of the model from which the reduced form expression is derived. It should also be noted that the statistics in Tables 2 and 3 are based on estimates of the 'asymptotic standard errors' of the parameter values.

There is nothing to choose between the two alternative sets of estimates as far as β and γ are concerned. However, a value of 0·203 for θ is a little too small to be convincing. The notion that only just over 20 per cent of any disequilibrium in the money market is cleared up in a period of three months is rather counter-intuitive. The alternative estimate of θ implies that 80 per cent of any discrepancy would have vanished and this is much more reasonable; it is also, incidentally, compatible with Feige's **[3]** conclusion that, as far as the United States is concerned, the money market adjusts fully to a new equilibrium within a year. At the same time, the

TABLE 2

Parameters of demand for money model, per capita *real terms, United Kingdom quarterly data* 1955(3)–1967(4) *estimated by non-linear constrained least squares*

Equation	α	β	γ	θ	λ	ESS
4	−0·074	0·543	−0·016	0·203	0·803	0·0075
		(2·14)	(0·25)	(2·03)	(4·25)	
4	−0·077	0·539	−0·008	0·794	0·204	0·0075
		(2·47)	(0·40)	(4·26)	(2·16)	

Figures in parentheses are ratios of parameter estimates to their standard errors.

ESS is error sum of squares.

idea that any deviation of actual from expected income starts expected income changing at a rate of about 20 per cent of the discrepancy per quarter is more appealing than the much more rapid rate of adjustment implied in accepting a value of 0·803 for λ.[15]

[15] It is tempting to compare directly our results with those obtained by Feige **[3]** for the United States. However to do so would be misleading and not only because the two sets of results deal with different economies; we have used quarterly data, and Feige used annual data. As Mundlak **[9]** has pointed out, the specification of the period over which decisions are made is a fundamental matter in the use of distributed lag models, and choice of the wrong period involves a misspecification of the model. Consider the following simple example. If, on a quarterly basis, it were true that

$$y_t = b\lambda x_t + (1 - \lambda)y_{t-1}$$

The root cause of our inability to distinguish between adjustment and expectation lags on statistical criteria is of course the poorly determined relationship between the demand for money and the rate of interest which runs right through our results. As the reader will see from inspecting equations 4–10, the coefficients of the interest rate variables are the only ones into which λ and θ do not enter in a symmetrical manner. Indeed, if the interest elasticity of demand for money, γ, were to be equal to zero, equation 4 would become

$$m = b_0'''' + b_1'''' y + b_4'''' m_{-1} + b_5'''' m_{-2} \tag{4d}$$

and its parameters would be equal to

$$b_0'''' = \alpha\theta\lambda \tag{5d}$$

$$b_1'''' = \beta\theta\lambda \tag{6d}$$

$$b_4'''' = 2 - \theta - \lambda \tag{9d}$$

$$b_5'''' = -(1-\theta)(1-\lambda) \tag{10d}$$

Though α and β would still be identified it would be impossible to distinguish between λ and θ. This point is easily illustrated: when fitted to our data equation 4d produces the following results (with t-values in parentheses)

$$\begin{aligned} m = -0{\cdot}096 &+ 0{\cdot}086\, y + 0{\cdot}988\, m_{-1} - 0{\cdot}158\, m_{-2} \\ (0{\cdot}97) &\quad (3{\cdot}53) \quad\;\; (6{\cdot}47) \qquad\quad (1{\cdot}15) \end{aligned}$$

This equation implies that $\alpha = -0{\cdot}565$, $\beta = 0{\cdot}506$, and that λ and θ equal either 0·212 or 0·800. These results in no way contradict any conclusion that may be drawn from equation 4 but it is worth drawing the reader's attention to the fact that they could be read

then, using annual aggregate data, this implies

$$\sum_{t}^{t+3} y_t = b\lambda \sum_{t}^{t+3} x_t + (1-\lambda) \sum_{t-1}^{t+2} y_t$$

The procedure normally used in fitting such distributed lag models to annual data involves the use of the expression

$$\sum_{t}^{t+3} y_t = b\lambda \sum_{t}^{t+3} x_t + (1-\lambda) \sum_{t-4}^{t-1} y_t$$

which is clearly a misspecification of the true model. Perhaps our specification, or Feige's, is correct, but not both. In any event, the results they generate are not comparable. Our own specification is, of course, open to question, for Grossman and Dolde [6] make a strong case for treating aggregate adjustment processes as continuous.

to imply that the behaviour of the velocity of circulation in Britain is adequately explained by a model which, like the one dealt with by Friedman [5], rules out the interest rate as an important determinant of the demand for money. Though we believe this to be an arguable view, we would not take it ourselves, for we believe that there are sufficient problems with our study to provide adequate alibis for the interest rates' poor performance. We take these issues up in the next section of this paper.

IV

Any conclusions based on the results presented in this paper must be tentative indeed, for these results are not firmly enough grounded to bear the weight of much positive argument. They are, however, consistent with a view of the demand for money function that stresses the importance of time lags in interpreting behaviour and which finds the source of those lags mainly to lie in the way in which income expectations respond to changes in current income. This interpretation of the lag effects seems to us to be more satisfactory than putting them down to long delays in the public's adjustment of its money balances towards new equilibrium levels. Our results also imply that the income elasticity of demand for real balances in post-war Britain has probably been less than one, and that variations in the Treasury bill rate have had little, if any, systematic effect on the velocity of circulation.

However, the firmest conclusions that our work yields are the negative ones. In the light of the results presented here, it is impossible to argue that the behaviour of the British monetary sector can sensibly be interpreted, even as a useful approximation, in terms of a simple textbook model of the demand for money that ignores time lags. Moreover, though our interpretation of the data is somewhat similar to that of Fisher [4], we are somewhat less confident that we have the right explanation. Be that as it may, we have presented our results and an interpretation of them. It is reasonable for us to indicate what further work ought to be carried out in order to see whether our interpretation is a sensible one. First and foremost, it would make sense to replicate our tests, but over a much longer time period. The post-war years are difficult ones to analyse with available statistical techniques, since the dominant pattern in the relevant time series has been a smooth upward trend. United States data betray similar characteristics over the period in question, though to a somewhat lesser extent, and these data too have proved more difficult to analyse than those generated in earlier time periods. If the model implied by our explanation of the post-war data can be shown to produce well determined and stable statistical results over a longer time period, we can have a great deal more confidence in it than would be justified at present.

Second, it should be noted that we have said little in presenting our results about the poor performance of the interest rate variable. The interest rate is included in the demand for money function as a measure of the opportunity cost of holding money. Its poor performance may be the result either of money holders being insensitive to rates of return on alternative assets, or of the particular rate chosen being a bad measure of the cost of holding money. We tend to favour the latter interpretation.

Though Treasury bills are a highly liquid asset, and clearly an alternative to money, we are doubtful that the rate of return on them measures the opportunity cost of holding money with any degree of accuracy. We reached this conclusion after, rather than before, looking at the evidence presented earlier, for the interest rate's poor performance surprised us. One of the striking characteristics of American work on the demand for money has been the consistency with which it has turned up the result that the demand for money is stably related to the rate of interest regardless of the particular variable chosen to represent it, and regardless of the time period over which the test was carried out. As far as post-war Britain and the Treasury bill rate is concerned, this does not seem to be the case.

Ex post we can think of two reasons for this. First, it should be noted that our definition of money includes time deposits with commercial banks, and that the latter assets bear interest. This fact has never caused trouble when broader money definitions have been used in the course of analysing the United States economy, but the conventions which govern the fixing of the rate on time deposits differ in the two countries. In the United States the Federal Reserve fixes a maximum value for the rate on time deposits, and the actual rate paid does not vary much over time. In Britain the rate is fixed in relation to Bank rate and moves with it. Variations in the Treasury bill rate, then, are probably a very poor measure of variations in the *difference* between the rate of return on time deposits and that on other assets, particularly since the Treasury bill rate's level is by no means independent of bank rate. This matter is certainly worth more investigation and future workers on the demand for money in post-war Britain might do well to include the rate of interest on time deposits in any regression equations fitted. In this context, it is worth noting that Fisher also had trouble in establishing a relationship between broadly defined money and the interest rate, but did not run into similar difficulties when time deposits were excluded from the money concept he used.[16]

Our second reason for doubting that the Treasury bill rate is an appropriate one to use stems from the manner in which monetary policy is managed in Britain and from the fact that the period covered by our analysis has seen continuously rising prices. The expected rate of inflation is a component of the opportunity cost of holding money, but one would normally expect variations in this anticipated rate to be reflected in fluctuations in the rate of return on a nominal asset such as a Treasury bill. In Britain, however, the monetary authorities avowedly attempt to fix interest rates on assets such as Treasury bills, rather than attempting to control the quantity of money. If the authorities would permit interest rates to fluctuate freely, then a rise in the expected rate of inflation would normally lead to attempts to exchange Treasury bills for real assets which would drive up the relative rate of return on the former by an appropriate amount. However, given the authorities' practices, a rise in the expected rate of inflation is more likely to result in an increase in the Bank of England's purchases of Treasury bills. Now this is not to say that, if inflationary expectations increase, the Bank will continue indefinitely to buy Treasury bills, or any other securities, from the public at an increased rate. Eventually it is likely to permit the price at which it is willing to enter the market to fall. However, until it does so, the level of the Treasury bill rate will mis-state the opportunity cost of holding money.

The way that we have utilized the Treasury bill rate in our tests requires that quarter to quarter variations in it measure quarter to quarter shifts in the opportunity cost of holding money, and the foregoing argument provides good reasons for doubting that it does so. Thus, any future work on the demand for money in post-

[16] Cf. Fisher [4], Table III, p. 337. Note that even with narrow money, Fisher did not get universally good results with the interest rate variable, as inspection of his Tables II, p. 334, and IV, p. 343, will reveal. Note also that the use of a broad money definition was often blamed for Friedman's [5] inability to find a close relationship between the demand for money and the rate of interest in the United States, but that this explanation has been shown to be false in Laidler [8].

war Britain must pay closer attention than have we to measuring the opportunity cost of holding money. In particular, we suspect that the role of the expected rate of inflation as a determinant of the demand for money would repay careful investigation.[17]

To sum up then, though our work has by no means settled the nature of the demand for money function in post-war Britain, it has provided evidence that rules out certain simple formulations of the function as being empirically helpful. That same evidence has enabled us to make certain tentative suggestions as to what the function may look like, and hence provides a guide as to what further work is likely to prove particularly fruitful. For these reasons, we believe that it has generated useful results which are worth taking into serious account when planning further research.

APPENDIX

In the course of discussing the results set out in Table 1, we remarked that to fail to deflate the money supply and income data by population and the price level would produce misleading results which would tend to overstate the usefulness of equations 4a, 4b and 4c, as explanations of the demand for money in post-war United Kingdom.

Table A.1 presents estimates of these equations using data cast in real terms, but not put on a *per capita* basis. Comparing these results with those given in Table 1, we may note that, though equation 4c still produces the 'wrong' sign for the rate of interest, the size of the income coefficient increases, as does its statistical significance. At the same time, equations 4a and 4b both produce more stable relationships, as measured by *t*-statistics, between income and the demand for money than they do when based on *per capita* data. The implied income (or permanent income) elasticities of demand for money are also a little closer to one.

Table A.2 presents the results of an experiment in which the log of the real money stock is replaced as dependent variable by the log of the nominal money stock, and the log of the price level is added as an extra independent variable. These results speak for themselves, providing strong evidence for the existence of a proportional relationship between the demand for nominal balances and the

[17] This is, of course, much easier said than done. This matter is discussed in some detail by Walters [**12**], who makes a very strong case for the proposition that the role of inflation expectations in the demand for money function is the area of monetary economics most badly in need of further empirical work.

TABLE A.1

Demand for money functions, real terms, United Kingdom quarterly data 1955(3)–1967(4)

Equation	b_0	Y	r	r_{-1}	m_{-1}	R^2	ESS	β	γ	λ	θ
4a	0·573	0·117	−0·004		0·828	0·938	0·008	0·680	−0·023	1*	0·172
	(1·183)	(4·498)	(0·339)		(12·204)						
4b	0·570	0·116	−0·006	0·002	0·829	0·938	0·008	0·678	−0·035†	0·171†	1*
	(1·164)	(4·417)	(0·344)	(0·161)	(12·066)						
4c	6·174	0·339	0·048			0·739	0·032	0·339	0·048	1*	1*
	(19·703)	(9·006)	(2·419)								

* *A priori* fixed value. † Not based on the coefficients of r_{-1}.

Figures in parentheses are t-statistics. ESS is error sum of squares.

TABLE A.2

Demand for money functions, nominal terms, United Kingdom quarterly data 1955(3)–1967(4)

Equation	b_0	Y	r	r_{-1}	m_{-1}	P	R^2	ESS	β	γ	λ	θ
4a	0·703	0·094	−0·004		0·835	1·023	0·993	0·008	0·570	−0·024	1*	0·165
	(1·107)	(1·257)	(0·335)		(11·622)	(14·346)						
4b	0·693	0·096	−0·005	0·002	0·835	1·020	0·993	0·008	0·582	−0·030†	0·165†	1*
	(1·067)	(1·245)	(0·296)	(0·101)	(11·492)	(13·910)						
4c	4·43	0·544	0·044			0·774	0·970	0·030	0·544	0·044	1*	1*
	(4·077)	(4·268)	(2·239)			(5·755)						

* *A priori* fixed value. † Not based on the coefficient of r_{-1}.

Figures in parentheses are *t*-statistics. ESS is error sum of squares.

price level. This result not only confirms a fundamental proposition of monetary theory, too often taken for granted, that the underlying relationship on the demand side of the money market is a demand for real balances, but also confirms our suspicion that to use a nominal income variable in a demand for nominal balances equation would result in the influence of the price level on the demand for nominal money being attributed to income, and hence in the overstatement of the latter variable's importance and to a biasing of the parameter on nominal income towards unity.

REFERENCES

[1] Baumol, W. J., 'The Transactions Demand for Cash—An Inventory Theoretic Approach', *Quarterly Journal of Economics*, vol. 66, no. 4, November 1952, pp. 545–56.

[2] Bronfenbrenner, M., and Mayer, T., 'Liquidity Functions in the American Economy', *Econometrica*, vol. 28, October 1960, pp. 810–34.

[3] Feige, E. L., 'Expectations and Adjustments in the Monetary Sector', *American Economic Review*, vol. 57, no. 2 (Papers and Proceedings, May 1967), pp. 462–73.

[4] Fisher, D., 'The Demand for Money in Britain: Quarterly Results 1951 to 1967', *Manchester School*, vol. 36, no. 4, December 1968, pp. 329–44.

[5] Friedman, Milton, 'The Demand for Money—Some Theoretical and Empirical Results', *Journal of Political Economy*, vol. 67, no. 4, June 1959, pp. 327–51.

[6] Grossman, H. I., and Dolde, W. C., 'The Appropriate Timing of Monetary Policy', Mimeo, Brown University, 1969.

[7] Heller, H. R., 'The Demand for Money—The Evidence from the Short-Run Data', *Quarterly Journal of Economics*, vol. 79 (June 1963), pp. 219–46.

[8] Laidler, David, 'The Rate of Interest and the Demand for Money—Some Empirical Evidence', *Journal of Political Economy*, vol. 74, no. 6, December 1966, pp. 545–55.

[9] Mundlak, Y., 'Aggregation over Time in Distributed Lag Models', *International Economic Review*, vol. 2, no. 2, April 1961, pp. 154–63.

[10] Teigen, R., 'Demand and Supply Functions for Money in the United States', *Econometrica*, vol. 32, no. 4, October 1964, pp. 477–509.

[11] Walters, A. A., *Money in Boom and Slump* (Hobart Paper 44), London, Institute of Economic Affairs, 1969.

[12] Walters, A. A., 'The Radcliffe Report—Ten Years After: A Survey of Empirical Evidence', in Croome, David (ed.), *Money in Britain 1959–69* (London, 1970).

III

THE SUPPLY OF MONEY

III

THE SUPPLY OF MONEY

EDITED BY
J. M. PARKIN

Introduction

WHAT determines the supply of money? How may the Bank of England act to influence that supply? These are the questions dealt with in the five readings in this chapter.

The question of what has determined the supply of money in the U.K. has generated a good deal of controversy in the past two decades. The traditional textbook analysis emphasizes the relationship between the level of cash reserves and the volume of bank deposits. Both the banks and the rest of the economy are viewed as holding a stable fraction of total deposits in the form of cash: the Central Bank determines the supply of cash; hence, the volume of deposits is determined as some stable multiple of the amount of cash made available. The chapter from Professor Newlyn's book, [reprinted here as Reading 10], sets out the basis of this model.

The application of this model to the determination of the U.K. money supply has been objected to on several grounds.

The first objection is this. Because the banks have access to call loans with the Discount Houses and because the Discount Houses have access as an automatic right to last resort loans, the level of total cash reserves cannot be controlled by the Bank of England. The first paper by Crouch (reprinted here as Reading 11), shows, however, that the Discount Houses and their access to last resort loans do not affect the outcome provided the authorities do not offset their open market operations in the pursuit of interest rate stabilization.

The second objection to the cash base model is that the authorities are concerned with interest rate stabilization and hence choose not to control the cash base. This objection gave rise to the contributions from Mr. Manning-Dacey and Professor Sayers during the late 1950s. They set out two different versions of what came to be known as the 'new orthodoxy'. The 'new orthodoxy' is, broadly speaking, the proposition that changes in the volume of bank deposits are determined by changes in the outstanding stock of Treasury bills. Rather than reprint the original contributions in this debate, we have chosen to print the paper by Professors Coppock and Gibson, which gives a compact, readable, and, in our view, accurate account of both the Dacey and Sayers versions of the 'new orthodoxy'. To supplement Coppock and Gibson on the relevance of 'new orthodoxy', we also reprint some empirical results from a section of Professor Crouch's 'The Inadequacy of "New Orthodox" Methods of Monetary Control'.

The main conclusion of these papers is that if the authorities wish to control the money supply, they would do better to control the cash base than the Treasury bill stock. The relation between the cash base and total money is very stable compared with that between the Treasury bill stock and total money.

The present state of knowledge in this field is summarized in a clear—if tightly written—summary by John Karaken in Reading 14.

This present position may be summarized thus. If the Central Bank wants to control interest rates, then the money supply will be perfectly elastic at the chosen rates. If the Central Bank wants to control the money supply:

(a) it must abandon interest rate stabilization; and

(b) it has a variety of techniques for control at hand.

It could operate on cash, Treasury bills, or any other nominal quantity it chooses. The *precision* of the control and the size of the multiplier linking the money stock to the magnitude controlled will depend on the predictability and interest elasticity of the demand functions for those assets. In the present state of knowledge, control of the cash base would give the surest control.

FURTHER READING

Bain, A. D., *The Control of the Money Supply* (Harmondsworth, 1970).

Manning-Dacey, W., 'Floating Debt Problem', *Lloyds Bank Review*, no. 40, April 1956, pp. 24–38.

Manning-Dacey, W., 'Treasury Bills and the Money Supply', *Lloyds Bank Review*, no. 55, January 1960, pp. 1–16.

Sayers, R. S., 'The Determination of Bank Deposits in England 1955–6', *Quarterly Review* of the Banca Nazionale del Lavoro, no. 35, December 1965, pp. 179–88, reprinted in *Central Banking after Bagehot* (Oxford, 1957).

Cramp, A. B., 'Control of the Money Supply', *Economic Journal*, vol. 76, no. 302, June 1966, pp. 278–87.

10

MONEY AS THE CREDIT BASE

W. T. Newlyn*

The purpose of this chapter is to investigate the basic relationships between the different levels of money and credit by means of a general model. This will be illustrated by reference to the United Kingdom monetary system.

We define as primary money those assets which constitute the ultimate means of payment as distinct from secondary money which is a claim to primary money. Generally primary money is the liability of the monetary authority which is normally a Central Bank. In the United Kingdom primary money consists of coin, Bank of England notes and the balances which the banks keep with the Bank of England. With the exception of coin (which can be disregarded for the purpose of monetary analysis in developed economies) primary money therefore consists of liabilities of the Bank of England in the form of notes and deposits. The former are held by the public and by the banks while the latter are held exclusively by the banks.

These liabilities, which are the primary money of our general model, we shall call *cash*. The secondary money of the model comprises, in the United Kingdom, the deposit liabilities of those institutions which the official statistics now include in the *banking sector* and which are here referred to as banks. These deposits are claims to cash which the public can exercise at its discretion.

Since primary and secondary money are interchangeable at the option of the public, a bank must always hold a stock of cash with which to meet an excess of encashments over cash deposits by its customers. We shall refer to the difference between these two items

* Reprinted from Newlyn, W. T., *Theory of Money* (Oxford, 2nd edn. 1971), Chap. II, pp. 19–41, by permission of the author and publisher. W. T. Newlyn is Professor of Economics at the University of Leeds.

as the *encashment balance*. In addition, in a multi-bank system, it must hold a stock of cash out of which to meet any excess of claims by other banks over claims against them; that is to say an excess of cheque payments by its own customers over their cheque receipts. This balance is established daily by a process of offsetting cheques at the Bankers' Clearing Houses and is then settled by drawing on the debtor banker's balance at the Bank of England; we shall refer to this as the *clearing balance*.

The effect of a negative encashment balance is a fall in the notes and coins held in the tills and vaults of the bank; the effect of a negative clearing balance is a fall in the bank's balance with the Bank of England. Since banks in this country regard balances at the Bank of England as equivalent to coin and notes (into which they are always instantly convertible), the problem of adjusting the relative magnitudes of the two elements in banks' cash reduces to an administrative problem without monetary significance. For our purpose it is only the total which matters, and we conclude therefore that the banker must hold cash in one or other of these forms to provide for the possibility of the clearing and encashment balances, taken together, being negative.

We next come to the question of how much he must hold. This may be determined by experience, convention, or law. In the United Kingdom it is an amalgam of the first two, but with the nationalization of the Bank of England in 1946, the specific request made by the Bank in this regard, backed by the powers of the 1946 Bank Act, must be regarded as tantamount to a legal requirement. This requirement is that the commercial banks shall keep in hand or at the Bank of England an amount of cash equal to 8 per cent of their deposits. We shall refer to the ratio of banks' cash to deposits as the *banks' cash ratio*.

Once it is established that the banker must not allow his cash to fall below a fixed proportion of his deposits, it will be evident that a limit is set to his ability to create money by buying assets or making advances. The fixed cash ratio imposes on him the constraint of arranging his lending so that the following equation is satisfied:

$$D = \frac{1}{\beta} C_b \qquad (1)$$

where β is the bank's cash ratio, D is deposits and C_b is the bank's cash. We shall first make the simplifying assumption that an increase in deposits will not lead to any increase in the amount of cash required by the public. This means that the banker can increase deposits, by buying securities and making advances, without any permanent loss of cash through the encashment balance. On this assumption, the banker passively receiving an additional cash deposit can actively increase deposits by an amount equal to the increase in cash multiplied by the reciprocal of the cash ratio. Using Δ to indicate increments of deposits and cash we may, therefore, write:

$$\Delta D = \frac{1}{\beta} \Delta C_b \tag{2}$$

That this equation holds for the system comprising only one bank is obvious, since a single bank cannot lose cash through the clearing balance (there is none), and we are assuming, for the moment, that it does not lose cash through the encashment balance. On receiving additional cash, a monopoly banker can increase his loans (and therefore his deposits) by an amount bearing the same ratio to the additional cash as his existing deposits bear to his existing cash.

On the same assumption regarding encashments, the equation holds equally for the multi-bank system as a whole, but in that case the final result is achieved as the product of a series of steps. Each individual step corresponds with the description of his business which is contained in the banker's argument that he does not 'create' deposits but simply lends money which has been deposited with him. Indeed, in view of the necessity of keeping a constant ratio between cash and deposits, he is able to lend only $1 - \beta$ times any additional cash he obtains. What the banker's argument does not recognize is that, even if it is assumed that the whole of any additional loans are lost at the clearing (the assumption made here), the cash lost would simply be transferred to another bank, where it would again constitute the basis for expansion. This process will go on until the drain of cash into bank tills resulting from the necessity to keep back part of any cash gain has exhausted the whole of the initial increase in cash. At each stage of expansion total deposits increase by a gradually diminishing amount until the limiting value is reached. The expansion thus takes the form:

$$\Delta D = \Delta C_b + (1 - \beta)\, \Delta C_b + (1 - \beta)^2\, \Delta C_b \ldots + (1 - \beta)^n\, \Delta C_b$$

which approaches the limit $\Delta C_b/\beta$ as in equation (2) above.

Thus, as in the case of the single bank system, the volume of deposits which any number of banks create on the basis of an initial increase in their cash is a multiple of that increase in cash, and the multiplier is given by the reciprocal of the cash ratio. We shall call this the *bank multiplier*.

So far we have assumed that the public keeps its holding of cash constant while its deposits are increasing and that, as a result, there is no loss of cash by encashment. This assumption is unrealistic and must now be removed. We approach nearer to reality if we assume that in normal circumstances the members of the public, like the banks, arrange their assets so that cash bears some fairly constant ratio to deposits. We shall call this the *public's cash ratio*. Since it is the result of rough adjustments to an imprecise concept of mere convenience, it is not, of course, nearly so rigid as the banks' cash ratio, but for the moment it will be assumed to be constant. We shall write this ratio as α.

From this relation it follows that there must be a drain of cash out of the banks as deposits increase, since the public seeks to keep the ratio of cash to deposits constant. This encashment drain must therefore be added to the drain into the tills of the banks which we have already examined. At each step in the process of expansion the amount of banks' cash which is surplus to the requirement of the cash ratio becomes reduced, not simply by β times the increase in deposits but by $\alpha+\beta$ times this increase. Thus, when we take this factor into consideration, equation (2) must be replaced by:

$$\Delta D = \frac{1}{\alpha+\beta}\Delta C.$$

We shall call this factor $1/(\alpha+\beta)$ relating changes in primary money (cash) to changes in secondary money (deposits), the *marginal coefficient of expansion*. Alternatively we can express the same relationship in terms of total money (M) which equals $D+C_p$ thus:

$$\Delta M = \left(\frac{1+\alpha}{\alpha+\beta}\right)\Delta C.$$

The marginal and average coefficients may differ, and in that case, although the marginal coefficient may be constant, the average coefficient will change as the volume of money changes. Moreover these coefficients show the relationship which must necessarily exist between primary money and secondary money, and are nothing more than convenient arrangements of the data. They do not imply anything concerning the direction of causation and they are consistent either with cash being adjusted to deposits or with deposits being adjusted to cash.

We now turn to a consideration of the actual magnitudes of these variables as revealed in the United Kingdom statistics. It has been stated above that the commercial banks in this country treat their balances at the Bank of England as cash. Thus, what is loosely described as banks' cash actually consists of three elements: coin, Bank of England notes, and balances at the Bank of England. The public's cash consists of coin and Bank of England notes and the notes issued by commercial banks in Scotland and Northern Ireland. These latter are an interesting historical survival but have no monetary significance because they can now only be issued against a one-for-one reserve of Bank of England notes. To calculate the total effective cash we can ignore the Scottish and Northern Irish commercial note issue and count instead the Bank of England notes which they represent. Thus primary money in the United Kingdom consists of the coin issued by the Royal Mint and the liabilities of the Bank of England to the commercial banks (in the form of notes and deposits) and to the public (in the form of notes). We shall call this the *cash base* of the system. In June 1969 it was made up and distributed as shown in Table 1.

The official statistics of bank deposits for the United Kingdom were, until 1959, confined to the figures of the London clearing banks, that is to say the eleven joint-stock banks which were members of the London Clearing House. Thanks to the great improvement in financial statistical data brought about by the recommendations of the Radcliffe Committee it is now possible to get figures for total deposits of all banks in what the Central Statistical Office defines as the *banking sector*. This includes all the United Kingdom deposit banks, overseas banks, accepting houses, the discount market, and (since 1968) the National Giro.[1]

It is a nice theoretical point which types of deposits should be included in the money supply; the official statisticians include all institutional types but exclude deposits not owned by United Kingdom residents. The inclusion of acceptance houses and the discount market might be rationalized in terms of theoretical

[1] Bell, G. L., and Berman, L. S., 'Changes in the Money Supply in the U.K. 1954 to 1964', *Economica*, N.S., vol. 33, no. 130, May 1966, pp. 148–65. See also Newlyn, W. T., *Theory of Money* (Oxford, 2nd edn., 1971), Appendix I.

analysis by the fact that it is an institutional peculiarity that their functions have developed separately. From the point of view of overall monetary analysis they can be regarded as integrated with the deposit banks. The theoretical justification for deducting foreign

TABLE I

The cash base (June 1969)

Composition	£m	Distribution	£m
Banks of England Notes	3,237	Currency held by banks	556
Coin	273	Banks' balances at Bank of England	304
Currency	3,510	Banks' cash = C_b	860
Banks' balances at Bank of England	304	Currency held by the public = C_p	2,954
Cash Base	3,814	Cash = C	3,814

Notes: (i) Scottish and Northern Irish notes are excluded because they are issued one-for-one against Bank of England notes except for an insignificant authorized fiduciary issue.
(ii) Bank of England notes held in the Bank of England's reserve have been deducted from the total outstanding.
(iii) to correspond with (i) Bank of England notes held by the Scottish and Northern Irish banks have been deducted from total currency held by U.K. banks.

Source: Central Statistical Office, *Financial Statistics*, No. 92, December 1969, Tables 33, 50, and 52.

owned deposits is not acceptable; nationality of ownership is irrelevant to monetary effects. But since these deposits equal those in acceptance houses the dubious inclusion of the latter offsets the wrongful exclusion of the former. It is worth noting at this point, however, that in June 1969 they amounted to £11,846 million as compared with £12,510 million owned by residents.

Using this figure of deposits, which is net (after deducting items which constitute double counting), and the data in Table I we can set out the relationships discussed above which are as follows:

$$\alpha = \frac{C_p}{D} = \frac{2{,}954}{12{,}510} = 0{\cdot}2334$$

$$\beta = \frac{C_b}{D} = \frac{860}{12{,}510} = 0{\cdot}0715$$

$$D = \frac{1}{\alpha + \beta} C = 3{\cdot}28C = 12{,}510$$

The coefficient of expansion of the banking system, $1/(\alpha + \beta)$, is 3·28, and this relationship between total deposits of residents and cash is shown in Fig. 1 in which α and $\alpha + \beta$ are reflected in the two vectors. For a given cash base the level of deposits is determined by α and β, and if these ratios were constant over time it would be possible to deduce the total of deposits for any value of the cash base by applying a constant coefficient of expansion. In fact this is not the case. In the first place there are large seasonal variations in the public's holdings of cash.

The extreme deviations from the mean are in July and December, and if these changes in the public's cash holdings were not compensated by the deliberate policy of the monetary authorities, the loss of cash by the banks would occasion a monetary contraction and expansion of considerable magnitude each year. For over a century the Bank of England, by expanding and contracting the cash base, has provided the seasonal elasticity in the currency necessary to avoid such secondary fluctuations. These seasonal variations can thus be regarded as having no significance for monetary policy and, by taking averages of quarterly figures, they can be eliminated from the statistics.

There have also been large swings in the long term—from 0·175 in 1933 to 0·269 at the war-time peak in 1945. The circumstances causing the rise in currency holdings during the war are not hard to find: the accumulation of emergency reserves; the physical destruction by air raids; the disruption of normal cash flows; the use of U.K. currency outside the country, and the large volume of black-market transactions.

During the 1960s the value of α has fallen (amost continuously) from 0·277 in 1960 to 0·233 in 1969—a reversal of the upward trend of the previous decade following the sharp fall at the end of the war.

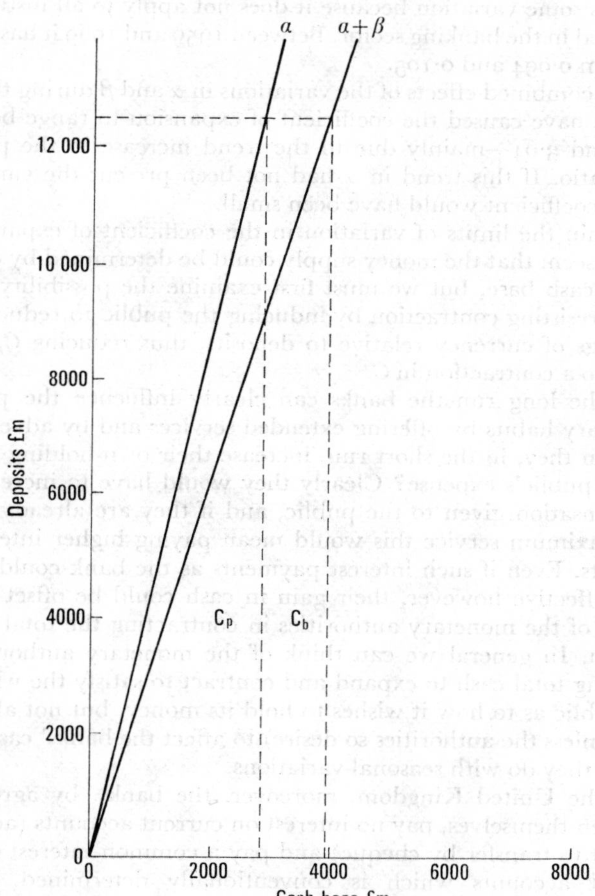

FIG. 1. *Relationship between Cash and deposits: June 1969*

This trend is almost certainly the result of technical progress in the financial system operating against the tendency for currency holdings (relative to deposits) to rise with income.

The value of β has varied very little since the rigid application of the 8 per cent minimum cash ratio was applied in 1946, though there is some variation because it does not apply to all institutions included in the banking sector. Between 1959 and 1969 it has varied between 0·094 and 0·105.

The combined effects of the variations in α and β during the past decade have caused the coefficient of expansion to range between 2·56 and 3·04—mainly due to the trend increase in the public's cash ratio. If this trend in α had not been present the variations in the coefficient would have been small.

Within the limits of variation in the coefficient of expansion it would seem that the money supply could be determined by control of the cash base, but we must first examine the possibility of the banks resisting contraction by inducing the public to reduce their holdings of currency relative to deposits, thus reducing C_p as an offset to a contraction in C.

In the long run the banks can clearly influence the public's monetary habits by offering extended services and by advertising. But can they, in the short run, increase their own holding of cash at the public's expense? Clearly they would have to increase the compensation given to the public, and if they are already giving the maximum service this would mean paying higher interest on deposits. Even if such interest payments as the bank could afford were effective however, their gain in cash could be offset by the action of the monetary authorities in contracting the total supply of cash. In general we can think of the monetary authorities as allowing total cash to expand and contract to satisfy the whims of the public as to how it wishes to hold its money, but not allowing this (unless the authorities so desire) to affect the banks' cash base, just as they do with seasonal variations.

In the United Kingdom, moreover, the banks, by agreement between themselves, pay no interest on current accounts (accounts subject to transfer by cheque) and pay a common interest rate on deposit accounts which is conventionally determined by the authorities. So long as this arrangement persists the distribution of cash between the public and banks is independent of the banks' control. Moreover, the evidence from United Kingdom statistics is that there is no significant correlation between the deposit interest rate and the public's cash ratio. In the short run therefore we conclude that the banks are obliged to accept their cash as being determined by the monetary authorities.

The major conclusion derived from the above analysis is that there is a definite, though not rigid, multiple relationship between the stock of money as a whole and the liabilities of the central bank. So long, therefore, as the central bank can control its own liabilities it can control, broadly, the total stock of money, and we must now examine how this is done.

In general a central bank which has sole issue of primary money varies its liabilities by buying and selling financial assets in the open market. Since it uses primary money for these transactions, the cash base changes by an equal amount. Thus the sale of an asset by the central bank must reduce primary money by a like amount, no matter who buys the asset. If the sale is made to a member of the public, he will pay by drawing on a commercial bank in favour of the central bank; if the sale is to a commercial bank, that bank will draw on its balance with the central bank in favour of the central bank. The result, in both cases, is that the commercial banks' balances at the central bank are reduced. As we have seen, these balances are regarded by the banks as cash and are therefore part of the cash base.

Such sales and purchases undertaken by the central bank at its own initiative are known as *open-market operations* and there can be no doubt that any central bank can perform such transactions so long as there is a ready market in which to operate and it is willing to take the consequences. Before we can conclude, however, that this gives the central bank control of the cash base, we must inquire whether there is any way in which market operations undertaken by the financial system can cause the total assets and liabilities of the central bank to alter. To answer this question with regard to the United Kingdom requires some analysis of the financial structure.

Since the banks in the United Kingdom are obliged to keep a minimum cash ratio, they must provide for variations in their cash requirements either by holding excess cash or by holding part of their remaining assets in such a form that they can be converted into cash at will. In fact, in the United Kingdom the banks rely upon their holdings of *money market assets* and do not find it necessary to hold excess cash.

Money market assets consist of trade bills and Treasury bills together with short-term loans to the discount market. The bill portfolio is so arranged that a proportion of bills will be falling due every day, and, to that extent, represents a constant flow from which cash can be replenished.

The character of loans to the discount market is more complex.

A large part of these loans is in the form of call money which can be recalled by the banks without notice, and it is through this element in the banks' assets that the relationship with the discount market is most clearly seen. If a bank is short of cash to satisfy the cash ratio requirements, we can represent it as calling loans from the discount market, since the other alternative of allowing bills to run off without renewing them will have exactly the same effect in the market, namely that of increasing the demands on the funds available. If only one bank is calling funds from the market, it is likely that this will be the result of an adverse clearing balance which will have provided other banks with surplus cash. This they will put into the market on call, thus providing the funds required to satisfy the demands of the bank which was short. Thus, unless there is a general shortage of cash, the market simply acts as a reservoir into which the banks put their surplus cash and from which they replenish their cash as required. Thus the market provides a means of economizing the holding of cash by offsetting complementary movements.

But the situation is different where there is a general shortage of cash such as would result, for example, from a general adverse encashment balance. In this situation there will be a net shortage of cash in the market which, if it is unrelieved, will prevent the discount houses from carrying out their obligations to meet the call by the banks. Such shortage can only be relieved by the creation of more cash, and this can only come about as the result of an expansion of the assets and liabilities of the Bank of England.

By tradition going back more than a hundred years, the Bank of England is always prepared to relieve such a situation by acting as *lender of last resort*. Thus the Bank of England is always prepared to lend to the discount houses on the security of first-class bills, or to re-discount such bills for the discount houses, at a rate not less than its published *Bank Rate*. It is this fact which gives to call money its special characteristic of being convertible into cash whenever the banks need to replenish their cash holdings.

Thus far it would appear that the Bank of England is deprived of control over the cash base because of its traditional obligation as lender of last resort. This is not so; control can be retained by means of Bank Rate. Along with the tradition of lender of last resort goes the tradition of the penal rate; although the Bank always stands ready to lend to the market it can choose its own rate and this rate can always be kept above market rate. By long-established tradition Bank Rate is always above market rate.

From the fact that Bank Rate is always higher than market rate it follows that the discount houses must bear losses on such part of their activities as is financed by borrowing from the Bank of England at Bank Rate. It follows therefore that such borrowing will never be a permanent part of the market's resources, and Bank of England liabilities resulting from such borrowing cannot be a permanent part of the cash base. Such borrowing must be regarded as a temporary expedient adopted because of a miscalculation by the discount market as to the volume of funds available, and to be terminated as soon as possible.

The consequence of the market's efforts to terminate its debt to the Bank are crucial to an understanding of the subject. In order to examine these consequences we shall, at this stage, make an assumption which will allow us to consider two quite separate issues without confusing them. In the present discussion of the obligations of the Bank as lender of last resort to the private sector of the economy, it is most desirable to avoid the complications arising from the Bank's obligations as lender of last resort to the Government. For our present purpose we shall assume that the variable element in money market assets consists of commercial bills.

Let us now suppose an initial position in which the banks find their cash deficient. Thus, in relation to the initial level of the cash base, deposits are over-expanded. The banks call from the market and, since there is an over-all shortage of cash, the discount houses are 'forced into the Bank' which, as lender of last resort, is obliged to expand the cash base. At this point the marginal cost of bill financing exceeds its marginal revenue. In this situation the discount houses will seek a solution which must consist of some combination of two elements: (i) raising prices (that is to say raising the market rate of discount, thus causing a contraction in the volume of bills held) and (ii) reducing marginal cost (that is to say finding loans which, although dearer than the initial market rate, will be cheaper than Bank Rate). Both (i) and (ii) imply a rise in market rate but are alternatives; to the extent that one operates the other need not. We must now show the consequences of each of these alternatives.

In order that (ii) should operate the discount market would have to attract funds not previously available. By hypothesis, the banks have no spare cash, but if the change were made sufficiently attractive they would sell other assets in order to increase call money. Such assets would have to be bought by the public and this would give the same result as direct loans from the public to the discount houses. It is possible therefore to concentrate on the case in which the discount houses induce non-bank lenders to increase their short loans by raising the rate of interest on such loans. As a result of this, payments would be made from the accounts of customers of the commercial banks to the discount houses, whence they would pass to the Bank of England in settlement of the temporary borrowing. The net effect would be a reduction in bank deposits and an equivalent reduction in bankers' deposits at the Bank of England. Thus the banks would once again be short of cash, but the deficiency would be less than initially because the deposits would be lower. Once again the banks would have to call money from the market, forcing the discount houses 'into the Bank' with the same results as before. Other things being the same, this process would go on until the level of deposits had been reduced to the correct multiple of the cash base without recourse to the Bank of England. At this point the discount market would be able to support its bill holding without loss and the commercial banks would have the cash required to satisfy the cash ratio.

To the extent that the above alternative failed to eliminate the excess of marginal cost over marginal revenue, the scale of lending would have to be reduced. Since the discount market is so nearly perfect, we may assume that the result will be achieved by an increase in price. The result of this net contraction of bills held by the market is that payment would be made from accounts of customers of the commercial banks to the discount houses (in settlement of mature bills) which would be used to pay off the temporary borrowing from the Bank of England. Once again deposits would be reduced without any gain in cash, and the process would continue until deposits had been reduced to a level at which they could be supported by the initial cash base without penalized borrowing from the Bank of England.

Thus, however these elements are combined in the solution, the final result is the same: a reduction in deposits, as implied by the coefficient of expansion, and higher interest rates. This result is inevitable, in spite of the automatic operations of the Bank of England as lender of last resort to the private sector of the economy. We can thus conclude that, by reason of the penal rate, the obligation to act as lender of last resort to the private sector is no bar to control of the cash base. Furthermore, since it is only through this obligation that the total assets and liabilities of the Bank can be affected at the initiative of the private sector, we can conclude that control of the cash base cannot be frustrated by the operations of the private sector of the economy.

We have now to consider whether the same is true regarding the operations of the Government. The first point which must be clearly made is that although transfers to the Treasury's account (for example, in respect of taxation) reduce the cash base, and payments expand it, we can ignore this factor entirely, for the simple reason that this account remains virtually constant at a minimum working level. It is not through variations in its bank balance that the Treasury affects the system.

By virtue of its function as banker to the Government the central bank accepts an obligation to ensure that the Government is always provided with the funds necessary to cover any excess of expenditure over revenue from day to day. To the extent that the arrangements made to this end rely upon money creation, the authorities thereby deprive themselves of independent control of the money supply. Clearly any direct lending by the central bank to the Government has this characteristic, but in the United Kingdom there is a very strong prejudice against direct central bank lending to the Treasury except 'overnight'. It is necessary therefore to analyse the conventions and relationships to see how the Treasury's requirements are ensured.

We define the Treasury's *residual requirements* as the amount which, after taking into account all other receipts, it finds it necessary to borrow from the market at the weekly Treasury bill tender. It is measured over time therefore by changes in the amount of market Treasury bills outstanding. These bills are tendered for by the discount market syndicate (which puts in a single bid on behalf of the discount houses) and by various other institutions which we shall refer to as the *outside tenderers*. By a convention which has operated since 1939 the discount market syndicate undertakes to 'cover the tender', that is to say it bids for the total issue. In fact it is allotted the residual amount after all bids at higher prices from outside tenderers have been satisfied. Now this undertaking could not be given were it not that the market has access to the Bank of England in the event of being unable to balance its books. But we have already shown that borrowing from the Bank at Bank Rate will only be temporary, since it involves losses; if cash were only to be had at Bank Rate the result would be the same as that already shown in the case which did not involve Treasury borrowing. That is to say the discount houses would offer higher rates to lenders in order to replenish their funds and would reduce their syndicated bid at the next tender in order to reduce the scale of their lending. Thus the provision of the Treasury's requirements by means of the syndicated bid and the obligation to cover the tender, even though it is backed by the obligation of the Bank as lender of last resort, does not deprive the authorities of control of supply of money via the cash base, provided that the Bank performs its function at the penal rate.

Having regard to the characteristics of the monetary system, it has been shown that control of the supply of money lies within the power of the monetary authorities if they elect to use it; indeed it would be surprising if the conclusion were otherwise. But having regard to the consequences of such action the authorities may decide not to use their power; this is a policy matter which will be discussed in the final chapter.

The relationship we have set out above in respect of the money stock and the banking system which creates it are not unique, they are reproduced in essentials in respect of the non-bank financial intermediaries which form the next 'layer' in the financial system. They too create credit and thus finance deficit expenditure on the part of the ultimate borrower; they too need to keep reserves in the form of assets into which their liabilities are convertible; they too can be regarded as generating a multiple expansion of credit the limiting factor in which is (as with the banks) the quantity of *reserve assets* they can get hold of. But in this case, the reserve assets are the deposits of the banking sector; they are secondary money, not primary.

The equation showing the significant relationships is as follows:

$$F = \frac{1}{\gamma + \delta}\left(\frac{C}{\alpha + \beta}\right)$$

where F is assets of non-bank intermediaries; γ the desired ratio D_p/F; δ the desired ratio D_f/F; D_f the intermediaries' reserve bank balances; D_p the public's deposits in banks. Since $C/(\alpha + \beta) = D$, we have $1/(\gamma + \delta)$ as the multiplier based on a change in deposits, assuming both ratios constant.

Alternatively, if we suppose that bank deposits remain unchanged but that there is a once and for all shift in bank deposits to financial intermediaries with the marginal ratio remaining constant, the effect of such a shift in deposits is given by

$$\Delta F = \frac{1}{\delta} \Delta D_f.$$

Finally, suppose that there is a fall in the ratio D_f/F from δ to δ'. Assuming that $\alpha + \beta$ remains unchanged, this will give rise to an initial transfer of bank deposits from the public to non-bank intermediaries; this (except for money reserves retained by the latter) will be lent out thus starting the normal multiplier sequence, the increment in assets of intermediaries being given by

$$\Delta F = \frac{\delta - \delta'}{(\gamma + \delta')(\gamma + \delta)} D.$$

In no case does the volume of money alter as a result of the activities of intermediaries—its velocity increases as debt increases. Moreover, financial intermediaries are not peculiar in sharing with banks this credit-creating expansionary characteristic; on similar assumptions the same analysis could be applied to all institutions or individuals creating debt, but the values of the multipliers would only be meaningful if the ratios were constant.

In this wider version of the 'inverted pyramid' of credit the model presents too rigid a picture of the relationships. Nevertheless it does bring out the essential point that the whole pyramid, to which we could add a further layer of trade credit, is based on money which is the base of the whole credit system because it is the ultimate reserve asset by virtue of its unique function as a means of payment.

Identification of this unique asset has long been the subject of controversy and we must now deal with the extreme view on this matter as revealed in a well known proposition advanced by Professor R. S. Sayers that '. . . there is no single asset or group of assets that uniquely possesses a uniform monetary quality that is totally absent from all other assets'.[2] It will be contended that this proposition neglects the essential characteristic of money and that when this characteristic is given its correct significance the proposition is not true.

As Professor Sayers himself says, 'the difficulty of identification

[2] Sayers, R. S., 'Monetary Thought and Monetary Policy in England', *Economic Journal*, vol. 70, no. 280, December 1960, pp. 710–24. [Reprinted here as Reading 27.]

has derived from the two-fold nature of money as a medium of exchange and as a store of value'. It is the present contention that Sayers's failure to identify money results from his failure correctly to apply the criteria relating to the former function. If we look at the status of assets as a store of value from the point of view of the owner, the monetary quality consists in the ability to exercise the purchasing power which the assets represent, by right, without penalty or delay. It is this criterion which has been the basis of most of the 'perennial questions of controversy' and which involves the hair-splitting, which Sayers finds so unsatisfactory in distinguishing between money and non-money. On the basis of the foregoing criteria we should include as money: current accounts but not deposit accounts; Post Office Savings Bank accounts up to the 'on demand' limit but not the rest; demand deposits in Building Societies but not time deposits; indeed, any form of call loan but not any period loan. It will be generally agreed that such distinctions are of negligible significance in monetary analysis; but if they are abandoned where do we stop? The answer surely is that we cannot stop. Financial assets, looked at from this point of view, constitute a class within which the individual components are differentiated only by the point in time at which they possess the characteristic of entitling the owner to means of payment.

This being so, we draw the line according to the purpose which we have in mind, and no class of assets which we choose to distinguish will possess a uniform monetary quality that is totally absent from all other assets. It is to the exchange function that we must turn if we are to identify this quality.

Sayers dismisses the medium of exchange criterion as follows: 'The usual answer is that we should include as money only those assets which are commonly used as media of exchange. Resort to the adverb "commonly" at once emphasizes the absence of any sharp line of distinction.' It is the basis of the present argument that this is not the case if the line of distinction is correctly specified in terms of operational effects in the economy rather than according to asset status from the point of view of the owner.

The analytical distinction we wish to draw in the money/non-money classification is clearly exemplified in the distinction between currency and bonds. Currency (being commonly used as a medium of exchange) changes hands physically in making a payment, and this involves no repercussions in the economy whatever. Bonds, on the other hand, not being commonly used as a medium of exchange, can only be drawn upon to finance a payment by recourse to the bond market.

We have now to generalize this distinction. An asset can only be regarded as a means of payment if the effect of drawing upon it to make a payment is identical with the effect of a physical transfer of currency. That is to say, the effects outside the banking sector must be confined to the change in the indebtedness between payer and payee. This will be the case only if the consequential adjustments in the banking sector have a zero sum. When this is so the payment will not involve any change in the asset/liability complex of the public other than that between the payer and the payee; such a payment will be termed *neutral*.

When this neutrality condition is not satisfied the non-zero sum of the consequential financial transactions must involve an effect in the market for loans which could not attach to the transfer of a medium of exchange *simpliciter*. This effect may take either of two forms: (i) the sale of an asset by the person making the payment; or (ii) a draft on the payers' claims by a financial intermediary, involving a reduction in the aggregate of such claims and a consequential sale of an asset by the intermediary. The nature of the first case is obvious; we shall be concerned with the second case.

Bank deposits subject to transfer by cheque have long been treated as means of payment, in spite of the fact that their use does not involve a simple transfer between payer and payee. In fact, payment by cheque involves at least three elements:

1. a reduction in the payer's deposit;
2. a transfer of cash from the payer's bank to the payee's bank;
3. an increase in the payee's deposit.

The treatment of this process as equivalent to a transfer *simpliciter* is justified on the neutrality criterion by the well-established fact that in a developed banking system the consequential financial transactions have a zero sum either because the banks have homogeneous reserve conventions or they have an internal market in bank funds.

But there has always been a class of assets (generally known as *quasi-money*) whose classification has been ambiguous. This ambiguity is due to the fact that the question as to which assets are properly classed as money has been dominated by consideration of the status of assets as a store of value from the point of view of the owner, to the neglect of the functional criterion. Consider the following questions: can a line be drawn between current accounts and deposit accounts? Are balances in the Post Office Savings Bank money? Are demand deposits in a Building Society any different from clearing-bank deposits? What about unused overdraft facilities? If we answer these questions with reference to the store of value status of the asset from the owner's point of view we shall split hairs which are of no real significance in monetary analysis and ignore the really significant distinction which is revealed by the neutrality criterion. Let us apply this criterion to the above questions.

On this basis the first question is an easy one. The answer is that deposit accounts should be classified with current accounts in the United Kingdom because the banks do not distinguish between them in their liquidity conventions. A payment made with a cheque on a deposit account and credited to a current account leaves the total of deposits in equilibrium at an unchanged level, and thus has no repercussions in the market for loans. Although the status of the asset acquired is not identical with that given up, the practical distinction in the United Kingdom is insignificant in monetary analysis.

In banking systems where the banks differentiate in their liquidity conventions between deposit accounts and current accounts (using the English terms for convenience) the classification of the former as money would render analysis inaccurate to the extent that payments made from them would not be neutral. Correct analysis would require that the operation should be decomposed into its two elements: (i) the conversion of the deposit account into current account (involving a repercussion in the loan market); and (ii) the transfer of the current account deposit (which is neutral in its effects) to the payee.

The question about Post Office Savings Bank deposits is somewhat more difficult. If the status of deposit accounts is not significantly different from that of current accounts, then neither is that of P.O.S.B. deposits. It is not surprising therefore that on this criterion Professor Sayers concludes: 'I find it impossible on the evidence of recent practice, to find any watertight reasons for so distinguishing.' This reference to recent practice might suggest that this conclusion is based not on status but upon operational characteristics; in the sense of the preceding analysis this is not the case. The recent practice to which Sayers refers is presumably that revealed in the evidence given to the Radcliffe Committee, which is summarized in the following extracts from the P.O.S.B. Memorandum:[3]

The tendency for depositors to use their accounts as current banking accounts has increased to some extent in recent years although it affects only a small proportion of the total number of accounts.

The number of accounts which are operated as current banking accounts, in many cases with the account being replenished at the beginning of the month and most of the balance withdrawn by the end, is estimated at about half a million [out of 40 million].

It is clear that this evidence does not touch upon the operational effects of using P.O.S.B. accounts, and is only relevant to the status of this type of asset from the point of view of its owners. To the extent that such accounts are used as a source from which cash is obtained for making payments, the deposits themselves are definitely not functioning as a medium of exchange, even though they are used as current banking accounts in the sense defined in the above quotation. In applying our operational criterion we can disregard all cash withdrawals (amounting to 65 per cent of the total in 1956) and concentrate on the effects of making payments by means of crossed warrants—these being the nearest equivalent to cheques. Their magnitude (£144 million in 1956) can clearly not be dismissed as insignificant, but before we conclude that this fact justifies classifying P.O.S.B. deposits as money, we must ask what happens to these warrants. The answer is implicit in the memorandum already quoted, which states:

The P.O.S.B. has very little in the way of business relations with the Clearing Banks or other financial institutions except that the Clearing Banks clear the crossed warrants issued by the Savings Bank. In 1956 there were about 1,173,000 such warrants of an aggregate value of £144 millions.

From the fact that this statement is made in respect of the total figure, without qualifications, it is inferred (as might be expected) that the extent to which such warrants are cleared *within* the P.O.S.B. is insignificant. This means that payment by warrant on a P.O.S.B. deposit results in the payee acquiring a clearing-bank deposit; were the two banks homogeneous in the operational sense distinguished above, the equilibrium levels of the class of asset to which both belong would be unchanged and there would be no

[3] *Radcliffe Committee Memoranda*, part IV, no. 9, Appendix A.

repercussions in the market for loans; but this is not so. The difficulty in dealing with this particular question is that P.O.S.B. deposits are indirectly a government liability, and the outcome will therefore depend on the debt-management policy being followed. The most reasonable assumption (that is to say that which leaves debt policy independent of the operations considered) is that where a unit of non-market debt is redeemed at maturity it is replaced by the sale of a unit of market debt. From this it follows that the National Debt Commissioners will sell government securities in the open market to meet withdrawals from P.O.S.B. deposits. The net result of the whole operation will be that clearing-bank deposits remain in equilibrium at an unchanged level, while P.O.S.B. deposits are reduced by the amount of the payments. The operation is thus not neutral, since the aggregate of the assets in question is reduced, the reduction being reflected in the sale of securities in the market.

By similar reasoning deposits in a Building Society cannot be classified as money. Cheques (or their equivalent) drawn on such deposits will be credited to clearing-bank accounts; the Building Society (*ceteris paribus*) will need to restore its working balances, and must therefore either sell securities or reduce its loans. The net effect will be unchanged clearing-bank deposits but reduced Building Society balance-sheet totals (a reduction in the total of the class of assets considered), reflecting the repercussion in the market for loans, which is inconsistent with neutrality.

The currently accepted answer to the question about unused overdraft facilities follows Keynes's *Treatise*[4] in including them in money. Once again, however, this is the result of looking at the status of the asset from the point of view of the owner; on the functional criterion such facilities cannot be regarded as money, for the simple reason that any net use made of them could not be neutral. Given the banks' liquidity conventions, net increase in the use of overdraft facilities must necessitate a reduction in some other asset (e.g. securities), and thus involve a repercussion in the market for loans and a net reduction in the class of assets which includes both deposits and unused overdraft facilities.

This approach does seem to give watertight reasons for distinguishing between money (assets which operate like a medium of exchange in making payments) and quasi-money (assets which have virtually the same characteristics as money as a store of value but do not operate like a medium of exchange). It is not claimed

[4] Keynes, J. M., *Treatise on Money*, vol. 2, London 1933, pp. 42–3.

that this analysis entirely disposes of the problem of identification but that the problem which remains is trivial in the context of any particular piece of analysis. There may be actual instances where P.O.S.B. or Building Society deposits are transferred in making payment, just as there may be instances where bonds are so transferred, but for purposes of analysis these instances are insignificant.

It has been argued that this criterion is not valid because when bonds are drawn on to make a payment the person receiving the payment may buy bonds, and the effect would then be the same as if bonds had changed hands. It is true that this could happen but it is not the *necessary* consequence of the payment. Moreover the set of transactions which is necessary to make the payment terminates with the receipt of money by the payee but includes the sale of bonds. Only if the set of transactions effecting the payment is exactly equivalent to a hand-to-hand transfer of currency can the asset which was drawn upon to finance the payment be regarded as money.

In general equilibrium terms we define money as consisting of those assets the use of which to finance an excess demand in the market for commodities or factors of production, necessarily has zero effect in the market for loans. In terms of our previous analysis of deficit finance, money is the only asset the possession of which enables spending units to finance deficits without recourse to a market or intermediation. Its unique character is further delineated by the following:

1. Its possession is necessary for making any payment.
2. In particular it is exclusively used in payment for services of factors of production.
3. As a corollary it is the asset in which all incomes are received.
4. As a further corollary it is the asset the holding of which automatically rises and falls with receipts and expenditure and is thus the asset in which surpluses are embodied in the absence of purchase of another financial asset.

11

A RE-EXAMINATION OF OPEN-MARKET OPERATIONS[1]

R. L. Crouch*

Since the publication of a celebrated series of articles by highly regarded students of monetary affairs in the late 1950s, it has become increasingly accepted that open-market operations are ineffective as a method of controlling the commercial banks' cash reserves and, consequently, their deposit liabilities.[2] This situation has arisen, it is variously asserted, because the banks can always replenish any cash reserve deficiency brought about by an open-market sale by recalling loans to the discount houses, who have automatic access to cash through their borrowing privilege at the Bank of England, or by running off Treasury bills—the villain of the piece. Thus the cash-assets ratio type of analysis is outmoded. In its place has emerged the liquid-assets ratio doctrine with its

* Reprinted from *Oxford Economic Papers*, N.S., vol. 15, no. 2, June 1963, pp. 81–94, by permission of the author and publisher. R. L. Crouch is now Associate Professor of Economics, University of California at Santa Barbara.

[1] I have benefited from extended discussion of this topic with my colleague, Professor M. L. Burstein.

[2] The seminal references are: Manning Dacey, W., 'The Floating debt problem', *Lloyds Bank Review*, no. 40, April 1956, pp. 24–38; King, W. T. C., 'Should liquidity ratios be prescribed?', *The Banker*, vol. 106, no. 363, April 1956, pp. 186–97; Jasay, A. E., 'Liquidity ratios and funding in monetary control', *Oxford Economic Papers*, N.S., vol. 8, no. 3, September 1956, pp. 245–52; Sayers, R. S., 'The determination of the volume of bank deposits; England 1955–6', *Quarterly Review* of the Banca Nazionale del Lavoro, vol. 8, no. 35, December 1955, pp. 179–88, reprinted in Sayers, R. S., *Central Banking after Bagehot* (Oxford, 1957). Excellent summaries of the 'new orthodoxy' are provided by Smith, W. L., and Mikesell, R. F., 'The effectiveness of monetary policy: recent British experience', *Journal of Political Economy*, vol. 65, no. 1, February 1957, pp. 18–39, and Kenen, P. B., *British monetary policy and the balance of payments* (Cambridge, Mass., 1961), especially Chaps. II, VII, and VIII.

emphasis on funding as the only effective method of controlling bank deposits.

Those who have been critical of these developments[3] must acknowledge at least temporary defeat since the 'new orthodoxy' has been written into the *Radcliffe Report* and the control of liquid assets as the *sine qua non* to control deposits became so entrenched that the authorities, in defiance of their traditional distaste for monetary gimmicry, unbent so far as to embrace the Special Deposit procedure. This is striking testimony indeed to the influence of those who have advocated the liquid-assets ratio approach and the necessity of funding. Nonetheless, I assert that open-market operations can still be made effective notwithstanding a liquid debt structure and the Bank's obligation to act as lender of the last resort. In the following section a crude process analysis is developed to demonstrate this. In the light of this analysis, issue is joined with the advocates of the new orthodoxy in section II. Finally, in section III, some of the more immediate policy implications of effective open-market operations are examined.

I

Consider the consolidated balance-sheets on pp. 230–31 representing, in a stylized form, the Bank of England, the discount houses, and the commercial banks. For the most part, the asset and liability subdivisions of these institutions are familiar and self-explanatory. However, three points are worth drawing attention to. First, the banks' cash assets are assumed to consist solely of deposits at the Bank. Second, special deposits, as an asset of the banks and a liability of the Bank are omitted—on the grounds of irrelevance. Third, the banks are assumed to observe a 10 per cent cash-ratio—merely to avoid the arithmetic involving five places of decimals which arises if the actual 8 per cent cash-ratio is used. None of these simplifying assumptions have any substantive implications. Referring now to the column headings in these balance sheets:

1. Shows the initial equilibrium position of the three institutions (in unspecified units). Full equilibrium has two implications; the

[3] Foremost among whom must be mentioned W. T. Newlyn, T. Wilson, and J. R. Sargent. See Newlyn, W. T., *Theory of Money* (Oxford, 1962), Chap. III; Wilson, T., 'The Rate of Interest and Monetary Policy', *Oxford Economic Papers*, N.S., vol. 9, no. 3, October 1957, pp. 235–60; and Sargent, J. R., Letter to the Editor, *The Economist*, 19 May 1956, p. 687.

discount houses have no outstanding 'discounts and advances' at the Bank and the banks have the required cash reserve. When only one of these conditions holds, there is partial equilibrium; equilibrium for that institution—whether discount houses or banks—but not for the system.

2. The Bank of England sells 50 securities (any securities, long or short). As the discount houses and banks are in equilibrium, these will be bought by the public. When the payees' cheques are cleared, bank deposits, bank cash, and the Bank's security portfolio will all be down by 50. This is a position of partial equilibrium; the

Bank of England

Liabilities	1	2	3	4	5	6	n
Bankers' deposits	1,000	950	995	950	990·5	950	950
Other liabilities	2,000	2,000	2,000	2,000	2,000	2,000	2,000
	3,000	2,950	2,995	2,950	2,990·5	2,950	2,950

Assets	1	2	3	4	5	6	n
Securities	3,000	2,950	2,950	2,950	2,950	2,950	2,950
Discounts and advances	0	0	45	0	40·5	0	0
	3,000	2,950	2,995	2,950	2,990·5	2,950	2,950

Discount Houses

Liabilities	1	2	3	4	5	6	n
Call money	1,000	1,000	955	955	914·5	914·5	550
Discounts and advances	0	0	45	0	40·5	0	0
	1,000	1,000	1,000	955	955	914·5	550

Assets	1	2	3	4	5	6	n
Securities	1,000	1,000	1,000	955	955	914·5	550
	1,000	1,000	1,000	955	955	914·5	550

Clearing Banks

Liabilities	1	2	3	4	5	6	*n*
Deposits	10,000	9,950	9,950	9,905	9,905	9,864·5	9,500
	10,000	9,950	9,950	9,905	9,905	9,864·5	9,500
Assets	**1**	**2**	**3**	**4**	**5**	**6**	***n***
Cash	1,000	950	995	950	990·5	950	950
Call money	1,000	1,000	955	955	914·5	914·5	550
Treasury bills	1,000	1,000	1,000	1,000	1,000	1,000	1,000
Investments	2,000	2,000	2,000	2,000	2,000	2,000	2,000
Loans and advances	5,000	5,000	5,000	5,000	5,000	5,000	5,000
	10,000	9,950	9,950	9,905	9,905	9,864·5	9,500
Cash ratio (%)	10		10		10		10
Liquid ratio (%)	30		29·65		29·33		26·32

discount houses are in equilibrium but the banks are not since their cash reserves are less than 10 per cent of their deposits.

3. The banks withdraw 45 in call loans to the discount houses to rebuild their cash ratio to 995 (10 per cent of 9,950).[4] This forces the discount houses into the Bank for 45. Thus, bank cash and discounts and advances increase by 45 and the discount houses' call money decreases by the same amount. Again we have partial equilibrium; equilibrium for the banks but not the discount houses since they have discounts and advances outstanding at the Bank. The penal rate on such accommodation ensures that discounts and advances cannot be positive in equilibrium. The discount houses' marginal costs now exceed their marginal revenue. As profit maximizing enterprises, the discount houses will be disposed to reduce the scale of their operations.

4. Assume that the discount houses sell 45 securities to obtain the funds to repay their panel borrowing.[5] Since the banks are in equilibrium and the Bank is engaged in an open-market selling

[4] Other possibilities are open to the banks. These are taken up below.

[5] Other possibilities are open to the discount houses. These, too, are investigated below.

policy, these will be bought by the public. So, the discount houses' security portfolio and discounts and advances are reduced by 45 rapidly followed by a similar sized decrease in bank deposits and bank cash. Partial equilibrium again; equilibrium for the discount houses but not the banks. In fact, throughout this process the even-numbered columns show the banks out of, and the discount houses in, equilibrium while the odd-numbered columns show the banks in, and the discount houses out of, equilibrium. To this observation there are two exceptions; columns 1 and *n* are positions of full equilibrium.

5. Having less than a 10 per cent cash reserve, the banks act to rebuild it up to 990·5 (10 per cent of 9,905—their present level of deposits). Consequently, they withdraw 40·5 of their call loans to the discount houses. Thus, bank cash increases, and their call loans decrease, by 40·5. This again forces the discount houses into the Bank so discounts and advances also increase by 40·5.

6. With marginal cost exceeding marginal revenue, the discount houses sell 40·5 of their securities, which will be bought by the public. Thus, the discount houses' securities and discounts and advances decrease by 40·5 and, simultaneously, bank deposits and bank cash decrease by the same amount. The banks respond to this reduction in their cash ratio by withdrawing call loans to the discount houses—and so on.

Attention is drawn now to the behaviour of deposits during this process. Under the initial impact of the open-market sale, they decreased by 50 in the first 'round'. Then, as the discount houses sell securities, they decrease by a further 45 in the second 'round' and 40·5 in the third 'round'. Arithmetically, after three 'rounds', deposits have decreased by,

$$50 + 45 + 40{\cdot}5 = 50[1 + \tfrac{9}{10} + (\tfrac{9}{10})^2]. \qquad (1)$$

Clearly a geometric series is being generated. By well-known properties of such series, the total decrease in deposits after an infinite number of 'rounds' *n* will be

$$50\left[\frac{1}{1-\frac{9}{10}}\right] = 500. \qquad (2)$$

Examine also the behaviour of bank cash throughout the process outlined above at each moment when the banks are in equilibrium (positions 1, 3, 5, &c.). In the first 'round' bank cash decreases by 5 and in the second 'round' by 4·5. In the third 'round' (not shown) it would decrease by 4·05. The total decrease in the bank cash after three 'rounds' is

$$5 + 4{\cdot}5 + 4{\cdot}05 = 5[1 + \tfrac{9}{10} + (\tfrac{9}{10})^2], \qquad (3)$$

and the total decrease after *n* 'rounds' will thus equal

$$5\left[\frac{1}{1 - \frac{9}{10}}\right] = 50. \qquad (4)$$

Similarly, it can be shown that the total decrease in call money to the discount houses will be 450. And as the discount houses can only permanently finance their security portfolio with non-penal borrowings, this security portfolio will also ultimately decrease by 450.

The final full equilibrium position is shown in the column headed *n*. The initial open-market sale of 50 has, then, eventually resulted in a contraction in deposits of 500 and a contraction in bank cash of 50. Notice, however, the causality-emphasis which emerged. In each 'round' the public's deposits were decreasing and the banks were adjusting their cash to fit the new, now lower, level of deposits. This is rather different from the standard (i.e. pre-new orthodoxy) expositions where the open-market sale was frequently held to irremedially reduce bank cash which forced the banks to retire assets in order to lower their deposits to fit their new cash position. Such standard expositions were never truly descriptive of the British situation; at best they were applicable to systems with ill-developed money markets where the banks did not own highly liquid assets which could be turned into cash immediately. The fact is that, in Britain, the *permanent* cash in the system is irremedially reduced. However, the Bank—acting as lender of last resort—provides *temporary* cash which smooths the adjustment process. My feeling is that the new orthodoxy advocates do not distinguish sharply enough between permanent and temporary cash. The discount houses' penal-borrowing privilege is, truly, a safety-valve in the system and not a leak. It serves to smooth, by extending over time, the adjustment process without interfering with the final outcome.

There are five basic variations to the adjustment mechanism outlined above in response to an open-market sale by the Bank which require consideration. All, however, lead to a multiple contraction in deposits provided two conditions—which will emerge from the discussion—are met.

1. After the initial open-market sale reduced bank cash, the banks could have responded by allowing some of their Treasury bills or other government securities to run-off instead of calling loans from the discount houses. If the authorities are not to allow the work of their open-market sale to be stopped in its tracks, they must respond in one of two ways. The Treasury must either re-issue an equivalent amount of securities (long or short) or, failing this, the Bank must sell additional securities equal in amount to those run-off by the banks. Whether issued by the Treasury or sold by the Bank, these securities will be purchased by the public thus reducing the public's deposits and bank cash. As the banks replenish their cash to the required amount by allowing more securities to run-off, the Treasury must again respond by re-issuing an equivalent amount or, in default of Treasury action, the Bank must again sell securities equal in amount to the securities run-off if the effects of the initial open-market sale are to run their full course.[6] Let the authorities jointly pursue this policy which, for want of a better phrase, may be described a a policy of 'netting' the open-market operation. *All such a policy amounts to is that the non-authority sector (discount houses, banks, and public) are forced (induced) to permanently increase their joint holdings of government securities by the amount of the open-market sale.* This can clearly be achieved by the Treasury re-issuing any securities that the non-authority sector tries to run-off, or the Bank selling an equal amount. This 'netting' requirement has been laboured. The post-war situation, with the relatively high proportion of short-term debt in the total government debt, makes it necessary. However, the 'netting' requirement is nothing new. Open-market operation analyses have always (though usually implicitly) been based on the assumption that the operation is 'netted'. Lack of specific reference to the fact was frequently justified because the opportunity of the non-authority sector to undo the open-market sale by running-off maturing securities was circumscribed by their limited supply. The present high proportion of near-to-maturity securities merely means that the authorities have to be more active, and more agile, in fulfilling the 'netting' requirement.

Referring back to the process analysis given above, if the banks allow Treasury bills to run-off to rebuild their cash, the outcome—as far as the total reduction in deposits is concerned—resulting from an initial open-market sale of 50 will still be 500 as long as the

[6] For an interesting alternative approach along these general lines compare Burstein, M. L., *Money* (Cambridge, Mass., 1963), Chap. V B.

sale is 'netted'. The banks' balance-sheet would merely show a decline in Treasury bills of 450 instead of, as before, a decline in call money of 450 (in a process analysis along these lines the discount market would, of course, be by-passed).

It might be objected that the obligation to 'net' its sale would necessitate continuous security sales by the Bank in order for it to maintain its pressure. However, the Treasury only keeps the smallest of cash balances so its freedom *not to re-issue* securities as they are run-off by the banks is narrowly circumscribed.[7] If the Treasury's cash balance is always held at a minimum—and the smallness of both its size and fluctuations would indicate that it is—the Treasury *must* re-issue securities equal to the amount run-off by the banks. Thus, in all probability, the need for the Bank to intervene again after its initial open-market sale will be slight. Nonetheless, the fact should be recognized that the cash shortage brought about by the open-market sale could be relieved by the transfer of deposits at the Bank from the Treasury's to the banks' account if the Treasury does not re-issue other securities to replace the Treasury bills run-off by the banks.

2. The banks could both withdraw call loans to the discount houses and allow Treasury bills to run-off. However, this only complicates the arithmetic. As long as the open-market operation is 'netted', a reduction in deposits of 500 will result from an open-market sale of 50.

3. The banks could accept the reduction in cash brought about by the open-market sale and, instead of reducing their call loans or Treasury bill holdings, take other measures such as selling their investments or recalling loans and advances to bring down their deposits to match their lower level of cash. Obviously, a multiple contraction in deposits must ensue if the banks adopt this policy.

It is appropriate to point out here that the multiple contraction in bank deposits which occurred in the above process analysis did so notwithstanding that the banks liquid assets/ratio fell to just over 26·3 per cent; their observance of a minimum liquid assets/ratio was not a necessary condition for the contraction. However, as the banks have *desired* asset allocation ratios, they would hardly let one class of assets take the whole strain. Actually, they will react to an open-market sale by distributing the burden over all their

[7] Here we are abstracting from the seasonal pattern of tax and expenditure flows.

assets; withdrawing call loans, running-off Treasury bills, selling investments and recalling loans in such a way as to maintain the desired ratios between these various asset classes. This more realistic adjustment is examined in greater detail in the final section. For the moment, matters of essential principle will be pursued.

4. The discount houses need not sell securities but may reduce the scale of their operations by allowing securities—of which they hold three classes—to run-off. If these securities which are allowed to mature are 'commercial and other bills', no further action need be taken by the authorities. Bank cash and deposits will be reduced and the contractionary process will continue. If, however, the securities which are allowed to mature are Government securities—Treasury bills or longer term—the authorities' response must be the same as their response when the banks adopt this procedure, if the full effects of the initial open-market sale are to be enforced. That is to say, the open-market operation must be 'netted' by the Treasury re-issuing, or the Bank selling, an additional, equivalent amount. These will be purchased by the public, reducing deposits and bank cash; and the contractionary process will continue as outlined above when the banks were allowing government securities to mature as long as the authorities 'net' their sale.

5. The discount houses may be able to avoid being forced into the Bank when they are faced with demands to repay call money to the banks if they can generate call money from the non-clearing bank sector. But, again, this can only be at the expense of bank deposits and bank cash, thus forcing the banks to renew their demands for the repayment of call loans. So, the eventual outcome will still be a multiple contraction in bank deposits if the discount houses pursue this practice.

Thus, it would seem that whatever action is taken by the banking system in response to an open-market sale by the Bank, that sale can be made to enforce a multiple contraction in bank deposits if the authorities fulfil two conditions. First, they must only act as lender of last resort to the discount houses. That is to say, they must only lend penal assistance at the discount window and should not make themselves available at the 'back-door'. If they assist the market at the 'back-door', the discount houses will disgorge their securities into the Bank, which immediately relieves the pressure imposed by the initial open-market sale. Second, the authorities must make the sale 'net'. If they fail to do this, the effects of the open-market sale will be attenuated to the extent that government securities run-off by the discount houses and banks are not re-issued by the Treasury or replaced by further sales by the Bank.

One final point should be made in this section. The process analysis given above assumed that the securities sold by the Bank were purchased immediately by the public. If the securities were Treasury bills, this is an unrealistic assumption since, as is well known, the public *market* in Treasury bills is weak or non-existent. More likely, they would have been initially purchased by the discount houses—because of their attractive price. This does not, however, affect the outcome. In this case, the discount houses would be forced to finance their enlarged portfolio by borrowing 50 on penal terms. But this is merely an interim, disequilibrium position for the discount houses and they will be disposed to contract the scale of their operations or generate additional non-penal finance. Success in either direction will still result in a multiple contraction of deposits so long as the authorities adhere to the 'penal relief only' and 'netted sale' conditions.

II

Those responsible for the development of the new orthodoxy can, I think, be criticized on two grounds. First, they misunderstand the impact of the Bank's actions as lender of last resort. Second, the particular assumptions on which they base their analysis automatically entail the ineffectiveness of open-market operations. Individually, they are not all guilty of both errors; some err in the first direction, others in the second.

W. T. C. King has stated that, 'it is through it [the liquidity principle] alone that the total volume of credit can be regulated, so long as the Bank of England performs . . . as lender of last resort'.[8] This observation is in marked contrast to the process analysis presented in the previous section. There, the liquidity principle was grossly violated (the banks liquid assets ratio is a mere 26·3 per cent in column *n*) and, moreover, throughout the process of adjustment from full-equilibrium to full-equilibrium the Bank was prepared to, and did, operate continuously as lender of last resort. Notwithstanding, a 5 per cent reduction in deposits was obtained. Nowhere in his article does King explain why the automatic right of the discount houses to borrow on penal terms should prevent a contraction. One must assume, since it is implicit in his assertions, that he

[8] King, op. cit., p. 188.

believes the discount houses will operate continuously where their marginal costs exceed their marginal revenue. T. Balogh has also stated that the Bank's perpetual readiness to act as lender of last resort will lead to 'the *continuous* use by the discount market of the Bank of England as a source of funds'.[9] And, without stating why this should occur, consequently sees a 'need to restrict rediscount facilities' which is to be accomplished by re-establishing 'the old convention that the discount market must not borrow from the Bank of England continuously'.[10]

The authorities quoted above make no attempt to economically justify why the discount houses should continuously operate in an apparently non-optimal position where their marginal costs exceed their marginal revenue. It remains true, however, as the most casual examination of the Bank Return will reveal, that the discount houses do, in fact, borrow continuously from the Bank. Is there an economic explanation for this practice? A. E. Jasay has suggested one. He states that, 'the margin between the regular [call] money rate and the bill rate . . . can . . . best be understood as a subsidy paid by the clearing banks to the discount market, in return for which the latter broadly adjusts its policy of tendering for Treasury bills to the needs of the banks, and shoulders the burden of borrowing from the Bank'.[11] By inference, I understand this to mean that the discount houses' 'true' revenue exceeds their observable revenue by an amount equal to Jasay's non-pecuniary 'subsidy'; and the discount houses are actually equating their marginal 'true' revenue and marginal costs which leads them to be willing to borrow continuously from the Bank. Jasay's argument is certainly very subtle.[12] But I remain unconvinced.

My own explanation of the discount houses' continued willingness to borrow on 'penal' terms is more straightforward. The discount houses hold three types of asset; Treasury bills, short bonds, and other bills. Of these, Treasury bills are an intra-marginal asset to

[9] Balogh, T., 'Dangers of the New Orthodoxy', *The Banker*, vol. 106, no. 365, June 1956, p. 350, Balogh's emphasis. In all fairness it should be mentioned that Balogh is no advocate of the new orthodoxy. He does, however, accept certain of their premisses.

[10] Balogh, op. cit., p. 352.

[11] Jasay, op. cit., p. 249. See also, for an expanded development, Jasay, A. E., 'The Technique of Quantitative Monetary Control', *Committee on the Working of the Monetary System, Memoranda of Evidence*, vol. 3, London, 1960, pp. 129–31.

[12] Possibly, my paraphrase does not do justice to its complexity; consequently, the reader should refer to the original sources.

the discount houses. This conclusion is derived from two considerations. First, because the discount houses are obligated to cover the tender and, second, because they are the sole source of bills for the banks whose thirst for stale bills must continuously be assuaged. Clearly, the banks' non-participation in the tender rests on the fact that the discount houses continue to supply them with an adequate bill portfolio. These factors are, I suggest, sufficient to specify that Treasury bills are an intra-marginal asset for the discount houses. Thus, bonds and other bills are their marginal assets. What is the nature of the return on these two asset classes? Examination of the statistics reveals that the yield on 'fine trade' bills, for example (one component of 'other bills'), is almost invariably above bank rate while the yield on short bonds frequently is, too. Is it not possible, then, that the discount houses are, in fact rationally-acting, profit-maximizing enterprises who are permanently financing part of their portfolio by borrowing continuously from the Bank since, in doing so, their marginal revenue still exceeds their marginal costs? In short, they are not borrowing on penal terms at all. The solution to this problem lies in making the discount houses' Bank-borrowing 'penal in fact'—and not merely 'penal in appearance'. This can be accomplished by the Bank only providing such accommodation on terms equal to no less than the yield of the discount houses' most profitable assets. Accommodation of the discount houses at rates in excess of bank rate is not new; ample past precedents exist.[13]

Examine, now, the particular assumptions on which the advocates of the new orthodoxy base their analysis. W. Manning Dacey's process analysis keeps 'going round in circles' without any reduction in deposits occurring as a result of an open-market sale by the Bank just so long as he assumes that any Treasury bills which the discount houses or the banks are allowing to run-off 'are paid off with the proceeds of fresh bills sold to the central bank'.[14] In this situation, one is hardly justified in describing the Bank as engaged in an open-market selling operation at all. It is an open-market sale with the left hand and an open-market purchase with the right. As soon as Dacey drops this assumption, and has the maturing bills 'paid off by means of funds withdrawn from the public', at once 'things begin to happen . . .'.[15] Even so, he links the contractionary process

[13] This paper was completed before the January 1963 reduction in bank rate. On that occasion the Bank of England did, in fact, announce that it reserved the right to render assistance to the discount houses at rates in excess of bank rate.

[14] Dacey, p. 28. [15] ibid., p. 30.

to the banks' observance of a 30 per cent liquidity ratio. This, it has been shown, is not a necessary condition. H. Johnson has also observed that the Bank no longer controls the cash situation since 'the banking system can offset the effects of open-market operations on its cash reserve position by disposing of bills to the central bank'.[16] Again, this amounts to saying that an open-market sale is not effective because the Bank is obliged to follow it up with an open-market purchase.

The new orthodoxy appears, then, to be based on two misconceptions and one unusual assumption. The misconceptions (1) that the ability of the banks to turn their secondary reserves into cash, and (2) the Bank's operations as lender of last resort (on truly penal terms), have divested the authorities of their power to independently determine the quantity of *permanent* cash in the system; the unusual assumption that an open-market sale must be followed by an open-market purchase. The misconceptions are, I believe, logical errors. However, the unusual assumption is a policy arrangement and it is certainly true that the Bank has frequently relieved the money market through the back-door in pursuit of orderly market conditions and in an attempt to minimize the Treasury's interest burden. This being so, the Bank can be described as having relinquished its power to independently determine the quantity of cash in the system and the new orthodox type of analysis—as presented by Dacey, for example—becomes relevant. It must be stressed, however, that this only means that the authorities have chosen not to conduct effective open-market operations; not that open-market operations would be intrinsically ineffective in the present environment. Assume, now, that the Bank makes no attempt to maintain orderly conditions or minimize the Treasury's interest burden. In short, they conduct themselves in accordance with the rules established earlier—'netting' the sale and lending only at penal rates—so that their open-market operations are effective. What are the probable consequences?

III

Between 1954 and 1955 the gross deposits of the London clearing banks were reduced by £329 million (from £6,941 million to £6,612 million)—or 4·7 per cent. This was a sizeable reduction—

[16] Johnson, H. G., 'The Revival of Monetary Policy in Britain', *Three Banks Review*, no. 30, June 1956, pp. 3–20.

by far the largest annual reduction of deposits in the post-war period. However, to be dramatic, assume that sometime in 1963 the authorities demand a 5 per cent reduction in deposits. At this hypothetical date in 1963 the banks' consolidated balance-sheet is as shown in column 1 of Account I.

ACCOUNT I

London Clearing Banks, 1963

Liabilities	1 (£m)	2 (£m)	3 (£m)
Deposits	8,000	7,600	7,600
	8,000	7,600	7,600

	1		2		3	
Assets	(£m)	(%)	(£m)	(%)	(£m)	(%)
Cash	640	8	608	8	608	8
Call money	880	11	696	9·16	836	11
Treasury bills	880	11	696	9·16	836	11
Investments	1,600	20	1,600	21·05	1,520	20
Loans and advances	4,000	50	4,000	52·63	3,800	50
	8,000		7,600		7,600	
Liquid assets ratio		30		26·32		30

The banks' deposits have reached £8,000 million and their assets are allocated as shown. (Special deposits are zero or, hopefully, have been discarded.) Moreover, the banks are required to maintain only one asset ratio—namely, an 8 per cent cash ratio.

The authorities wish to reduce deposits by 5 per cent (from £8,000 million to £7,600 million or £400 million). To accomplish this, they must reduce the permanent cash in the system by £32 million.[17] Consequently, the Bank sells £32 million securities

[17] If deposits are to be reduced to £7,600 million and the banks maintain an 8 per cent cash ratio, then the banks' cash must be reduced to £608 million. More generally, with an 8 per cent cash ratio,

$$\Delta D = \Delta S\left[\frac{1}{1-\frac{23}{25}}\right],$$

(Treasury bills) and the authorities jointly 'net' the sale. If it is assumed that the banks allow the whole burden of contraction to fall on their call money and Treasury bill holdings, full equilibrium will be reached, after a process analysis similar to that of section I, when the banks' assets are as shown in column 2. The discount houses will have reduced their assets by £184 million (Treasury bills) and the banks have also reduced their Treasury bills by a similar amount. Under these conditions, then, the process of 'netting' the sale has required that the public purchase £400 million Treasury bills.[18] This is a considerable amount. But recall the restrictive assumptions (1) a 5 per cent reduction in deposits was demanded—surely enough to appease the most hard-money advocate, (2) the banks let all the burden fall on their liquid assets thus causing their liquid assets ratio to fall to about 26 per cent, (3) the asset reduction forced on the discount houses was all in the form of Treasury bills, i.e. they did not reduce their bond or commercial bill holdings at all, and (4) the Bank's open-market sale was in Treasury bills.

However, retain all these assumptions except (2). In its place, assume instead that the banks have desired asset allocation ratios which conform to the percentage figures of column 1. In other words, they desire that, in full equilibrium, their asset-classes always bear those relations to deposits. To reduce deposits to £7,600 million the Bank must again sell, and 'net' the sale of, £32 million (Treasury bills). Throughout the contraction process, the banks now reduce all their asset classes to maintain the desired ratios and full equilibrium will be reached when they appear as in column 3. How many Treasury bills have the public been required to take up? A mere £120 million—of which £32 million were previously held by the Bank, £44 million by the discount houses, and £44 million by the banks. Are the public capable of this? It would certainly seem so considering the fact that the public's Treasury bill holdings varied between 1951 and 1961 from a minimum of £999 million to a maximum of £1,820 million. What is equally certain, however, is

where ΔD is the desired change in deposits and ΔS is the necessary open-market operation ('netted'). This formula, corresponding to (2), emerges from a process analysis of the type presented in section I when an 8 per cent cash ratio is used. In the present example, substituting £400 million for ΔD yields £32 million for ΔS.

[18] £32 million from the Bank (after having been momentarily held by the discount houses), £184 million previously held by the discount houses, and £184 million previously held by the banks.

that the interest rate on Treasury bills would have to rise to provide the necessary inducement. This, of course, will not cause surprise. You cannot decrease bank deposits by 5 per cent without raising interest rates whether the reduction is made through open-market operations or through funding. The only difference arises between which type of securities bear the major brunt; Treasury bills or longer term securities. For reasons which need not be gone into here, my own preference is to see short term rates take most of the impact. Note also that this figure of £120 million is, in some sense, a maximum since it might reasonably be reduced even further. For example, the Bank's open-market sale could be in the form of long-term securities and the discount houses might reduce their other assets besides Treasury bills. The discount houses' assets are approximately allocated fifty-fifty between Treasury bills and other assets. If the discount houses desire to maintain this asset-allocation structure, in the last example they would have reduced their Treasury bill portfolio by £22 million. Taking account of these two factors then, to engineer a 5 per cent reduction in deposits, the public might only be required to take up £66 million Treasury bills—£44 million previously held by the banks and £22 million previously held by the discount houses. Notwithstanding that the authorities 'have considered the market in Treasury bills as narrowly limited . . .',[19] it is almost inconceivable that the public could not be induced to absorb this sum.[20]

In conclusion, a practical matter of money-market management is worth drawing attention to—should the authorities adopt the practice of operating effectively in the open market. The currency circulation shows a marked seasonal pattern of variation which, in the absence of offsetting action by the Bank, would—at Christmas, for example—generate undesirable tightness in the money market. Offsetting action can take the form of back-door relief. However, it has been established that one of the necessary conditions for effective open-market operations is that back-door relief be terminated. This is essential. Consequently, it is, perhaps, unwise to permit any

[19] *Radcliffe Report*, para. 583.

[20] This is merely opinion, but I submit that the public would absorb this quantity (on a one-shot basis) without any rise in Treasury bill rates if the Treasury reduced the minimum acceptable tender from the current astronomical £50,000. At present, one feels about as much sympathy with the authorities when they complain about lack of 'strength, breadth, and resiliency' in the public Treasury bill market as one would were the proprietors of Claridge's to complain about a low occupancy rate.

exceptions to a cardinal operating procedure even for the relatively blameless purpose of accommodating seasonal variations. How else could seasonal accommodation be provided? One alternative worth attention is through the negotiation of repurchase agreements (at market rates) between the Bank and the money market institutions. Such arrangements are particularly well suited to provide cash on a strictly temporary basis. Repurchase agreements provide 'cash with strings'—as the saying goes in the United States where such transactions are used with some skill.

12

THE VOLUME OF DEPOSITS AND THE CASH AND LIQUID ASSETS RATIOS

D. J. Coppock *and* N. J. Gibson*

In recent discussions of British monetary policy the liquid assets ratio and the supply of Treasury bills have tended to displace the traditional cash ratio and the supply of cash as the major determinants of the volume of clearing bank deposits. A number of eminent economists have had a part in propagating various versions of this theory. Professor R. S. Sayers seems to have been first in the field with an article in the *Quarterly Review* of the Banca Nazionale del Lavoro, December 1955, in which he argued that: 'In current conditions it is (the) 30 per cent rule and not the conventional cash-ratio that appears the limiting factor in the creation of bank deposits.'[1] Other notable economists, including Professor H. G. Johnson, Mr. W. Manning Dacey, and Mr. W. T. C. King, were early supporters of the theory which later received the additional authority of the Radcliffe Committee.[2]

* Reprinted from *The Manchester School*, vol. 21, no. 3, September 1963, pp. 203–22, by permission of the authors and publishers. D. J. Coppock is Professor of Economics at the University of Manchester and N. J. Gibson is Professor of Economics at the New University of Ulster.

[1] Op. cit., 'The Determination of the Volume of Bank Deposits: England 1955–6', p. 101. The page reference is to a reprint of the article in Sayers, R. S., *Central Banking after Bagehot* (Oxford, 1957), pp. 92–107.

[2] Johnson, H. G., 'The Revival of Monetary Policy in Britain', *The Three Banks Review*, June 1956, pp. 3–20. Dacey, W. Manning, 'The Floating Debt Problem', *Lloyds Bank Review*, no. 40, April 1956, pp. 24–38; 'Treasury Bills and the Money Supply', *Lloyds Bank Review*, no. 55, January 1960, pp. 1–16; *Money Under Review* (London, 1960). King, W. T. C., 'Should Liquidity Ratios be Prescribed?', *The Banker*, vol. 106, 1956, pp. 186–97. Committee on the Working of the Monetary System. *Report*, particularly para. 376 and paras. 583–90.

We propose to concentrate on the contributions of Mr. Dacey and the Radcliffe Committee. Dacey's model helps to throw light on the whole question and he is undoubtedly the most forceful exponent of the theory. It will be remembered that he claimed on behalf of the Committee that they 'should finally have disposed of the notion that has done perhaps more than any other to confuse monetary discussion. This is the concept, given an extra thirty years' lease of life by the Macmillan Report, that the effective basis of credit resides in the cash reserves of the banks.'[3] The views of the Committee are of such obvious importance that their discussion requires no justification.

To the best of our knowledge only one economist, Mr. W. T. Newlyn, has publicly taken strong exception to the new theory. In a letter to the *Economist* (14 December 1957, p. 951) he suggested that the liquid assets ratio might be developing into 'the popular fallacy of the decade'. Mr. Newlyn has continued to protest[4] but seems to have been largely ignored. We further refer to his position below.

It is a truism that if logically correct theories conflict, then their basic premises must be different; the present controversy is in part an illustration of this rule. The substance of our argument is that the liquid assets theory of deposit determination can be made formally valid in at least two different ways. The Dacey version involves extremely restrictive assumptions about the market for Treasury bills and the nature of the money market, assumptions that do not seem to be empirically correct. The Radcliffe version depends on the assumption that the authorities want to stabilize the Treasury bill rate and therefore prefer 'to deal very freely between cash and Treasury bills'.[5] We accept that if the authorities opt for a given structure of rates this validates the liquid assets theory, but that a willingness to allow necessary departures from rate stability where a given change in deposits is a policy aim casts doubt on its usefulness, since its final implications may be indistinguishable from those of the cash ratio approach.

[3] 'Treasury Bills and the Money Supply', op. cit., p. 1.

[4] See, e.g., '*Radcliffe Report*: A Socratic Scrutiny', *The Bankers Magazine*, January 1960. [Reading 28.] His *Theory of Money* (Oxford, 1962) gives a rigorous exposition of his views on the subject of deposit regulation.

[5] *Report*, para. 376.

I

The traditional theory of credit creation rested on the basic principle that the cash base of the banking system was determined at the discretion of the central bank. A single bank in a closed economy could gain or lose cash from the rest of the system but, subject to any cash movements between banks and hand-to-hand circulation, which the central bank could allow for in setting the cash base, a gain by any one bank meant a loss to the rest. Any attempt to set up the volume of liquid assets or Treasury bills as the credit base must establish a similar conservation principle. It is easy to construct a model in which this principle applies. Mr. Dacey provides an example in his discussion of the problem.[6]

Let us recall the main points of Dacey's 'simplified model' of the British monetary system. His banking system consists of the clearing banks, the Discount Market and the Bank of England. In the background are the Government and the public. The economy is closed. The clearing banks observe a 30 per cent liquid assets ratio and an 8 per cent cash ratio. The cash is all held at the Bank of England—notes are ignored throughout the discussion. Liquid assets consist of cash, money at call to the discount market and Treasury bills. The other assets are advances and investments. The Discount Market holds only Treasury bills and gets all its money at call from the clearing banks. The Bank of England also holds only Treasury bills except for advances to the Discount Market when acting as lender of last resort. The public demand for advances from the banks is completely inelastic in relation to the rate of interest. All Treasury bills are held within the banking system.

Dacey sets his model to work by postulating that the Bank sells Treasury bills to the Discount Market which finances them with additional call money from the clearing banks. (It is not clear why the banks, which are in equilibrium as far as their cash and liquid assets ratios are concerned, should extend additional call money, but perhaps it can be accepted for the sake of the discussion.) But this reduces the cash ratio of the banks which replenish it by calling funds from the Discount Market which is driven into the Bank which must act as lender of last resort. This restores the banks' ratios but leaves the Discount Market with an advance to repay to the Bank. Fortunately for the Discount Market, the Treasury

[6] *Lloyds Bank Review*, no. 40, April 1956, pp. 26–31. *Money Under Review*, pp. 68–73.

bills pledged against the advance mature and so it is the authorities that have to find the funds. If they try to raise them by replacing the maturing bills with a new issue to the Discount Market then the merry-go-round will just be repeated without any effect on the banks' deposits. If the Bank of England buys the Bills, we will be back to where we started. But if the Treasury raises the funds from the public, things begin to happen. The banks' deposits and cash will drop by equal amounts and so liquid assets will also be reduced. According to Dacey there will now be only sufficient liquid assets in the system to support deposits reduced by $3\frac{1}{3}$ times the reduction in liquid assets that has taken place. The banks will have to sell investments and/or reduce advances and adjust their cash, to the correct proportion of the new level of deposits, by selling Treasury bills to the Bank. If the Bank tried to resist this adjustment, then the system would travel round in circles once again.

It is obvious that, in this model, the level of deposits is limited by the market supply of Treasury bills since this supply can accrue to the banking system only from the monetary authorities. The model requires that, in equilibrium, $D = 3\frac{1}{3}T$ and $D = 12\frac{1}{2}C$, where $D =$ deposits, T is the market supply of Treasury bills determined by the authorities and C is the supply of cash which must be made equal to $\frac{4}{15}T$. Expansion or contraction of the money supply is impossible without a corresponding increase or decrease in the market supply of Bills as long as the liquid assets ratio is maintained at the conventional minimum level. The conservation principle applies to the Treasury bill supply, since an increase in holdings by one bank must imply a reduction in holdings by other banks unless the central bank takes action to raise the aggregate supply of Bills in the market. It is equally obvious that the supply of cash must be a passive element in this model since the level of deposits cannot be consistent with two separate ratios unless these imply compatible volumes of cash and secondary reserves. A change in the supply of Treasury bills must be followed by a passive adaptation of the supply of cash.[7]

Dacey rightly concludes on the basis of his model 'that defla-

[7] In this discussion, for the most part, we abstract from the problem of seasonal variation. One of the oddities of the liquid assets theory is the complete vagueness about the size of the seasonal variation. This makes it extremely difficult to test the theory except for the seasonal minimum month of March. In the period 1955 to 1963 the March ratio fell within the range of 30 to 31 per cent only on three occasions and on four occasions was well above the 30 per cent level.

tionary pressure does not begin when the market is forced into the Bank but only when the supply of liquid assets in the system is reduced'. He also correctly concludes that high short-term rates of interest do not 'play an indispensable part in the disinflationary process'.[8] This is a striking conclusion but perhaps not surprising as interest rates do not explicitly enter into the model. And as he subsequently puts it, 'it would be pointless for the authorities to raise Bank Rate as an indication to themselves that the floating debt should be reduced.'[9] Glancing at the larger world he concedes that Bank Rate may at times have to be raised, particularly to keep short rates from getting too far out of line with other financial centres. But by and large he feels that 'the yield on Treasury bills and short bonds (should) remain as far below long-term yields as possible, so as to provide the maximum encouragement to the locking up of liquid funds in long-term form.'[10] In other words, funding is an essential weapon of monetary policy in reducing the liquidity of the banks. Moreover, whilst admitting that funding may be difficult at times, he believes that it is generally possible and that the authorities were much too passive in their funding policies in the early 1950s.[11]

Dacey admits that his model rests on a number of unrealistic assumptions but argues that in the main they simply carry 'to their logical extreme tendencies which are acknowledged to be prominent features of our actual situation'.[12] He suggests that the only important departure from reality is the assumption that all Treasury bills are held within the banking system. This assumption is crucial for his theory since the existence of an outside demand for Treasury bills destroys the logical necessity of his formulation of the liquid assets theory. If the banks or Discount Market can acquire Bills from outside holders or dispose of bills to them, the banks secondary reserves are no longer determined exclusively by the activities of the authorities.[13] If the banks can vary their secondary reserves at their own discretion the controlling factors determining the level of deposits become the cash ratio and the supply of cash which is

[8] *Lloyds Bank Review*, April 1956, p. 31, et seq.

[9] *Money Under Review*, p. 114.

[10] ibid.

[11] *Money Under Review*, Chap. VI.

[12] ibid., p. 73.

[13] The model also breaks down if the banks have money at call to others besides the Discount Market, if the latter holds bonds as well as Treasury bills and gets call money from others besides the banks. These points are elaborated below.

at the discretion of the Bank.[14] Mr. Dacey seems to deny the empirical relevance of this argument rather than its logical validity. We shall discuss this argument at a later stage.

II

It is reasonable to infer that the arguments expressed on the subject of deposit control in the *Radcliffe Report* were strongly influenced by the evidence given to the Committee by the Bank of England. Neither the Bank nor the Committee put forward a formal model of the liquid assets theory of deposit determination and their views tend to be scattered throughout the Report and the voluminous memoranda and evidence.[15] Perhaps the most clear cut presentation of the position of the Bank is to be found in its twelfth memorandum to the Committee. They tell us that the most important factor in the banks' liquid assets is the Treasury bill and that 'To control the volume of these Bills in the market is a first and necessary step to exerting influence on the actions of the banks.' A rise in the Treasury bill issue 'is most likely to lead to an increase in the . . . holdings of the banks . . . This causes a rise in the banks' liquidity.' The corresponding increase 'in bank deposits will make the existing cash resources of the banks insufficient to maintain their normal 8 per cent proportion. But the banks will rectify this by calling funds from the Discount Market who in turn have access to the Bank of England for whatever additional cash they may need in order to be able to take up the amount of Treasury bills allotted at the tender. Thus the system requires that, if the Exchequer cannot meet its outgoings in any other way, the Bank of England must in

[14] It may be objected that the central bank may easily offset any change in the banks' holdings of Treasury bills (or other non-cash liquid assets) by suitable open market operations just as it would offset movements of cash between banks and hand-to-hand circulation in setting the cash base. The rejoinder is that such a policy would be logically indistinguishable from a refusal to supply cash passively to the banks and in this case there would be no basis for distinguishing between the cash and liquid assets theories. A given level of deposits may be viewed as either a $3\frac{1}{3}$ multiple of the liquid assets base or a $12\frac{1}{2}$ multiple of the cash base. A similar argument will be used later with reference to the Radcliffe version of the liquid assets theory.

[15] *Report*, ibid., *Principal Memoranda of Evidence*, vol. 1, Memoranda of Evidence submitted by the Bank of England, especially nos. 4, 12, and 13, and *Minutes of Evidence*, pp. 40–89, 2256–75, 2616–798. See also 'Bank Liquidity in the United Kingdom', *Bank of England Quarterly Bulletin*, vol. 2, no. 4, December 1962, pp. 248–55.

the last resort ensure that the Discount Market and the banking system are not prevented by a cash shortage from taking up the full amount of Treasury bills on offer.'[16]

The Radcliffe Committee throws additional light on these statements. They make it clear that a major policy aim of the monetary authorities is stability of the Treasury bill rate which is desired because 'the authorities have feared that irregularities in bill rates would spread through to the short end and then to the long end of the bond market, with undesirable repercussions on confidence in the bond market impeding the authorities' funding programme.'[16] Instability of the bill rate could arise because the authorities 'have considered the market in Treasury bills as narrowly limited, so that relatively higher rates would not attract additional buyers'.[17] Because of this they argue that:

> the Bank prefers to deal very freely between cash and Treasury bills. It readily varies its own holdings of Treasury bills . . . in order to secure reasonable stability of the Treasury bill rate. Treasury bills can therefore always be turned into cash without much disturbance of the market rates of discount on them. It follows that the bank cannot restrain the lending operations of the clearing banks by limiting the creation of cash without losing its assurance of stability of the rate on Treasury bills. It is because of this circumstance that the effective base of bank credit has become the liquid assets (based on the availability of Treasury bills) instead of the supply of cash.[18]

It is clear from the above that the Radcliffe theory of the liquid assets ratio control is different from that of Mr. Dacey. In Dacey's formal theory the level of deposits must be an exact $3\frac{1}{3}$ multiple of the volume of liquid assets, since these consist exclusively of Treasury bills which are held only by the clearing banks, directly and indirectly.[19] In the Radcliffe version this simple relationship no longer holds because of the existence of outside holdings of Treasury bills. The banks can, in principle at least, vary their direct and indirect holdings of Treasury bills independently of the initiative

[16] op. cit., paras. 5–7.

[17] *Report*, para. 583.

[18] *Report*, para. 376. In a later section of its *Report* (para. 583) the Committee goes a stage further and argues that 'the supply of Treasury bills and not the supply of cash has come to be the effective regulatory base of the domestic banking system'.

[19] Assuming the operation of the 30 per cent ratio and ignoring seasonal variations. Indirect holdings are, of course, Bills held by the Discount Market on the basis of call money from the banks.

of the Bank of England by sales to,[20] or purchase from, outside holders. Thus the volume of deposits may be determined strictly by the cash base and the cash ratio since the necessary level of secondary reserves may be attained through the routine operations of the banks in acquiring earning assets.

If, however, the Bank of England operates to stabilize the level of the Treasury bill rate the aggregate of cash and secondary reserves is conserved and the liquid assets base and ratio become the controlling factors. If the banks find themselves with surplus cash and seek to acquire Treasury bills from outside holders to support an expansion of deposits the Treasury bill rate will fall, and assuming a narrow market for bills it will fall sharply. An equivalent sale of Treasury bills by the Bank will prevent the fall in bill rates and will simultaneously deplete the cash base by an amount equal to the volume of bills purchased by the banks. Thus the volume of liquid assets is conserved as automatically and effectively as if there were no outside holdings of Treasury bills.

The conservation argument applies only to dealings in Treasury bills at the initiative of the clearing banks. If there is an autonomous increase in the demand for Treasury bills by outside holders the supply of liquid assets to the banks will be reduced *ceteris paribus*. A sale of Treasury bills by the Bank to prevent the implied fall in the Bill rate will at the same time deplete the cash base and therefore the liquid assets base. In this case the prevention of instability in the Bill rate will threaten a reduction in the level of deposits unless the Bank offsets its Bill sales by bond purchases.[21]

To Mr. Dacey the Radcliffe version of the liquid assets theory is unsatisfactory. His comments on their argument of para. 376 is particularly illuminating for our present discussion. Dealing with the Radcliffe argument that 'the Bank cannot restrain the lending

[20] For brevity we use this form of words to mean that the banks allow Bills to mature without replacing them, thus forcing the authorities to place them with outside holders at the cost of an increase in the Bill rate. The variation in the liquid assets of the banks can, of course, take place by other measures, e.g., by variation in the holdings of short bonds by the Discount Market on the basis of call money from the banks.

[21] If the autonomous increase in demand for Bills reflected a shift out of bonds such offsetting transactions by the Bank would be consistent with the general aim of stabilizing the rate structure and would, at the same time, conserve the liquid assets base. Such offsetting actions by the Bank appear to be the logical equivalent of those involved in stabilizing a given cash base against movements of cash between banks and hand-to-hand circulation in the traditional cash ratio theory. The order of magnitude of the latter problem may be much smaller.

operations of the clearing banks by limiting the creation of cash without losing its assurance of the stability of the rate on Treasury bills' he writes:

The unequivocal implication is that if only the Bank of England were prepared to raise Bank Rate drastically it would be able to prevent the exchange of Treasury bills for cash. *And if that were so it follows that cash, and not the liquid assets as a whole, would have remained the true basis of credit.* The truth is surely the opposite: even wide fluctuations in rates . . . will not necessarily induce any contraction in the supply of market bills, and this is why Treasury bills have become convertible into cash, regardless of the policies and actions of the central bank. In attributing this circumstance to a policy of stabilization of the Treasury bill rate, the Committee really undermine the logical foundations of the 'liquid assets' approach, which is so welcome a feature of their Report.[22]

We believe that this quotation contains the key to the solution of the controversy between the cash and the Dacey and Radcliffe liquid assets approaches. Mr. Dacey appears to be reverting implicitly to his simplified model in which all Treasury bills are held within the banking system. If this is *not* the case the liquid assets of the banks can be reduced even if the supply of market bills is wholly inelastic to changes in Bank Rate and the Bill rate provided that the rise in Bill rate induces outside holders of Bills to substitute these for other short term assets.[23] In which case the banks collectively are powerless to increase the cash base of the system. In these circumstances an excess of liquid assets held by the banks is quite incapable of serving as a basis for deposit expansion unless the Bank of England is prepared to create the necessary increase in the cash base.

The practical problem is, therefore, a question of fact regarding the elasticity of demand for Treasury bills on the part of outside

[22] *Money Under Review*, pp. 83–4. (Our italics.)

[23] cf. Johnson, op. cit., p. 7. Both Johnson and Sayers make the point that the induced demand for Bills by outside holders, when the Bill rate increases, depends on the fact that the clearing banks retain a maximum deposit rate (Johnson, op. cit., p. 6; Sayers, *Central Banking after Begehot*, p. 104). The same point is also raised in the *Radcliffe Report* (para. 587). It is difficult to foresee the exact implications of the removal of this condition, but we take it in our argument as a given fact of the system. We disregard a possible increase in demand for Treasury bills arising from an inflow of short term funds from abroad following an increase in Bank Rate, since this will usually be met by an increased supply of tap Bills. (Cf. Newlyn, op. cit., pp. 137–8). But this demand could be utilized given offsetting bond sales by the Bank.

holders. If this is high enough to allow significant transfers of Bill holdings between the banks and outside holders it would seem, following the first part of Dacey's argument, that cash and not liquid assets is the true basis of the supply of bank deposits.[24] If significant transfers of Bill holdings between banks and outside holders are possible but only at the cost of what the Bank of England would regard as unacceptably high variations in Bill rates, Mr. Dacey's criticism of the Radcliffe Committee is invalid. In these circumstances a policy of stabilizing the Bill rate by dealing freely between cash and Bills in effect insulates the banks' Bill holdings from those of the outside holders and conserves a given liquid assets base. It, therefore, effectively validates their version of the liquid assets theory and replaces control via the cash base by control via the liquid assets base.[25] It will be argued later, however, that the stability of interest rates which is the aim of this policy may be illusory in the context of attempts to achieve a given change in the level of bank deposits.

The Radcliffe Committee clearly held the view that the substantial holdings of Treasury bills by outside holders were not inelastic with respect to either the Treasury bill rate or the margin between the Bill rate and the bank deposit rate,[26] and it would seem reasonable to extend the argument to cover the differential between the Bill rate and rates of return on other very short dated investments. Mr. Dacey is compelled, at one point, to admit that: 'On general principles it is no doubt safe to conclude that the interest in Treasury bills of domestic non-bank holders will be slight if the return on Treasury bills shows no differential over deposit rate, and will be greater if the Treasury bill rate itself is very close to Bank rate'[27] but immediately qualifies his admission by the remark that: 'this influence can easily be overshadowed by others.' This is doubtless true but beside the point unless it can be

[24] The meaning of the word *significant* has to be determined by the quantitative nature of a specific problem of expansion or contraction of deposits. We admit that there will, in practice, be limits to the size of the transfers which are possible and at these limits the banks' holdings of liquid assets may become an independent controlling factor. It must be remembered that Treasury bills are not the only non-cash liquid asset.

[25] Subject to the qualification noted earlier regarding autonomous changes in demand by outside holders and appropriate modifications in respect of other types of clearing bank liquid assets.

[26] *Report*, paras. 585–7.

[27] op. cit., p. 88.

shown that the other influences, whatever they may be, inevitably offset the former.

Dacey attempts to bolster his argument by an appeal to the 'facts'. Strictly speaking his 'simplified model' requires that the liquid assets of the banks and the supply of market Treasury bills should be identical which, of course, they are not. His thesis, however, might still be plausible, even with outside holdings of Treasury bills, if changes in the supply of bills were, by and large, absorbed by the banking system, with corresponding changes in the liquid assets of the banks. Using graphical analysis Mr. Dacey compares the behaviour of bank and discount market holdings of Treasury bills and clearing bank liquid assets for the period 1953–58 and notes that 'the virtual identity both of trend and of seasonal pattern is unmistakable'. He also compares the behaviour of clearing bank liquid assets with the over-all supply of market Treasury bills and concludes that 'the similarity of trend and of seasonal variation is remarkable'.[28] We do not deny that there is a strong seasonal correlation between the market supply of Treasury bills and the liquid assets of the banks but this is completely irrelevant to the general problem. A high correlation is, for instance, consistent with a strict cash ratio approach to deposit determination and merely reflects the fact that the liquid assets ratio is allowed to vary to support the seasonal variation in the market issue of Treasury bills. The alleged similarity in trend is relevant but appears to have no foundation in fact insofar as it refers to a relation between market bills and liquid assets. In the table (p. 256) we present figures for the market supply of Bills, the liquid assets of the clearing banks and the holdings of Treasury bills by the clearing banks and Discount Market for the period 1953–62 inclusive.[29] It is obvious that there are both substantial year to year variations in the ratios of liquid assets to market Bills, and bank and discount market holdings of Bills to liquid assets, and drastic changes in these ratios over the 10-year-period. The former ratio increased from 74 to 95 per cent whilst the latter fell from 80 to 50 per cent over the

[28] op. cit., pp. 84–8. He excludes from diagrams 7 and 8 (p. 87) market Treasury bills held by the Bank though his model strictly requires their inclusion. We have followed his convention in our table (p. 256).

[29] Data represent the averages of quarter-end figures 1953–8 and averages of 30 June and 31 December, for 1959–62. This limited coverage is dictated by the availability of data on the supply of market Treasury bills. However, comparisons with annual averages for outstanding tender bills and bank assets suggest that the figures give a satisfactory impression of the main trends.

period. It is true that these ratios exhibit substantial offsetting movements so that the bank and Discount Market share of market Bills is relatively stable, the only severe changes being a fall from 59·3 per cent in 1953 to 47·0 per cent in 1955 and a fall from 50·3 per cent in 1959 to 44·3 per cent in 1960. But it is clear that this relative stability in their share does not imply that the volume of liquid assets of the clearing banks was closely determined by the market supply of Treasury bills, and Dacey's suggestion that there

Market Treasury bills (excluding Bank of England holdings), liquid assets of clearing banks and clearing bank and discount market holdings of Treasury bills. Average of values held at selected dates (£ million).

Year	Market bills (1)	Liquid assets (2)	Bank and discount market holdings of Treasury bills (3)	Col. (2) as % Col. (1)	Col. (3) as % Col. (2)
1953	3,050	2,253	1,809	73·9	80·3
1954	3,126	2,199	1,636	70·3	74·4
1955	3,223	2,119	1,511	65·7	71·3
1956	3,285	2,232	1,603	67·9	71·9
1957	2,947	2,279	1,516	77·3	66·5
1958	3,173	2,266	1,603	71·4	70·7
1959	3,211	2,449	1,617	76·3	66·0
1960	3,392	2,421	1,503	71·4	62·1
1961	3,255	2,631	1,458	80·8	55·4
1962	2,897	2,741	1,370	94·6	50·0

Source: Financial Statistics, *Monthly Digest of Statistics*, Radcliffe Report.

is a 'very close' relationship between these aggregates is manifestly untrue.[30] When we observe that between 1953 and 1962 the market supply of Treasury bills fell by £153 million, whilst the volume of liquid assets rose by £488 million and the volume of gross deposits (on the same basis) rose by £1,661 million we are inclined to

[30] op. cit., p. 84. In fairness to Mr. Dacey we must note that his discussion of pp. 84–9 recognizes some substantial variations for the period 1953–8 in the ratios of liquid assets to market Bills and bank and Discount Market Bills to liquid assets. However, we believe that he draws the wrong conclusions from his own analysis largely because he is influenced by the undeniable seasonal relationship between these aggregates.

suggest that whatever else may regulate the volume of bank deposits it is not the supply of market Treasury bills.

It is clear that during the period 1953 to 1962 there was a wholesale substitution of other assets for direct and indirect holdings of Treasury bills in the liquid assets of the clearing banks. These other assets have consisted of commercial bills held directly and indirectly, short bonds held indirectly and call money placed outside the Discount Market. In Dacey's 'simplified model' the banks and the Discount Market are not permitted to hold commercial bills and the latter holds no bonds. These possibilities were also not greatly emphasized by Radcliffe. Dacey later refers to them but only to dismiss them as relatively unimportant. He implies that their existence is 'no reason for doubting that a contraction in the Treasury bill issue *as a deliberate act of policy* would almost certainly bring downward pressure to bear on the liquid assets of the banking system, and therefore on the supply of money'.[31] We believe that this is false both on *a priori* grounds and on the basis of the empirical evidence we have already examined. To the extent that the banks and the Discount Market can substitute commercial bills for a loss of Treasury bills there will be no effect on the banks' liquid assets; the same is true to the degree that the Discount Market is willing to replace Treasury bills by short bonds. It is also relevant in this context that the banks supply call money to other borrowers as well as to the Discount Market. And it is of particular significance that, over the past two years, the former have increased substantially their borrowing from the clearing banks, whilst the Treasury bill supply has fallen.

Both Dacey and Radcliffe seem also to have ignored the fact that the Discount Market borrows call money from other sources than the clearing banks. Once again a change in the supply of market Treasury bills may have no effect on the liquid assets of the banks or the volume of deposits; an increase in the supply of Bills, for example, may be bought by the Discount Market on the basis of call money that was formerly on deposit with the clearing banks.

In the light of the above discussion it seems beyond question that the extreme view that the volume of liquid assets of the banking system is regulated by the supply of market Treasury bills is invalid and that there is nothing in the system which prevents the commercial banks from carrying the volume of their liquid assets at their own discretion in the ways discussed above. It may be objected

[31] op. cit., p. 91.

that such action by the banks can only take place with the consent of the Bank of England but this invites the reply that the Bank can prevent an increase in the liquid assets base at the discretion of the banks by operating rigorously to restrict the cash base, which suggests that the traditional analysis remains valid.[32] As long as it is committed to convert Treasury bills into cash without penalty or without offsetting bond sales it is abdicating control over the money supply. It is impossible, without detailed econometric study, to say to what extent such variation of the liquid assets base at the discretion of the banks would involve instability of the Treasury bill rate, though the size of the money and bond markets and the large range of near substitutes at the short end of the markets makes this doubtful on general theoretical grounds. But we do not wish to deny that such operations by the banks will involve some variations in short term interest rates. If it is the view of the monetary authorities that such operations threaten the stability of the Treasury bill rate and therefore must be offset by Bank of England operations an effective conservation of the liquid assets of the banks may result and the liquid assets theory of deposit regulation will be formally valid.

It is arguable, however, that the implied stability of the Treasury bill rate which is gained by the Banks' policy of dealing freely between cash and Bills may be entirely spurious in the context of an attempt to change the level of bank deposits by a specific quantity. To illustrate this point we shall take the case of a decision by the monetary authorities to reduce the level of bank deposits by 1,250 units. If the theory of cash ratio control is applied, such a reduction in deposits would be achieved by open market sales to the value of 100 units. We shall assume that the Bank sells Treasury bills.[33] Assuming that the cash and liquid assets ratios are at equilibrium levels of 8 and 30 per cent respectively, these open market sales must be absorbed by non-bank holders with a primary increase in

[32] The operations described above may not increase the liquid assets of the banks if the Bank of England follows its policy of stabilizing the Bill rate. Thus if the Discount Market buys extra short bonds using additional call money from the banks this will raise liquid assets if the sellers of the short bonds move into assets other than Treasury bills. If they move into Bills the Bank of England must offset their Bill purchases by Bill sales, thus reducing the liquid assets base to its original level.

[33] It may, of course, sell bonds or may choose not to offset an equivalent net transfer of balances at the Bank of England from Bankers' Deposits to Public Deposits. To economize discussion we ignore the latter case.

Bill rates. In the final equilibrium position the banks must have reduced their liquid assets by a total of 375 units of which 100 units is the original reduction in the cash base. If we assume that the banks shift Treasury bills to outside holders the latter must, in total, absorb 375 units of Bills with implied primary and secondary increases in the Treasury bill rate.

If we now adopt the Radcliffe approach and assume that the Bank of England is not prepared to tolerate instability of the Treasury bill rate, it must be prepared to absorb the defensive Bill sales by the banks in exchange for cash balances which are non-temporary. On this basis the liquid assets of the banking system are reduced by the 100 units of the original open market sale, the effects of which cannot be offset without negating the whole process. The banks are allowed to decide the allocation of their reduction in the liquid assets base to make this consistent with the cash and liquid assets ratios and in the final equilibrium deposits will have been reduced by 333 units. Since the banks have been compelled to reduce deposits and assets some increase in bond rates is inevitable through the liquidation of bank Investments, but the increase in the Treasury bill rate will be mainly confined to the primary increase due to the open market sale. The Bank has achieved stability of the Bill rate but only at the cost of reducing the deposit multiplier from 12·5 to 3·3. If the original target reduction in bank deposits is to be achieved it is now necessary to revise the volume of the original open market sales of Treasury bills to 375 units. But if the liquid assets base is permanently reduced by this amount the implied final increase in the Treasury bill rate will, *ceteris paribus*, be the same as that which follows from the cash ratio theory. The alleged stability of the Bill rate gained by dealing freely between cash and Bills is an illusion.

Obviously it is possible to eliminate any increase in Bill rates by switching the original open market sale from Treasury bills to bonds and offsetting any Central Bank Bill purchases by equivalent bond sales. But this merely replaces a rise in Bill rates by a rise in bond rates. Since the rationale of the Bank of England policy is that instability of the Bill rate leads to instability of bond rates, the substitution hardly makes sense. Given the target reduction of 1,250 units of deposits it is inescapable that a total of 375 units of Bills and/or bonds has to be absorbed by outside holders on account of the reduction in the liquid assets base. The Bank of England can choose where the impact shall fall but it cannot escape the increase in interest rates unless it sacrifices its policy aim of reducing deposits by a fixed amount. Given such a policy aim it seems to be completely unimportant whether one approaches it in terms of the cash ratio or liquid assets theory; the final practical implications are indistinguishable, given the same bill/bond sales, as one would expect from the basic consistency of the numerical relationships. This general point seems to us to be so obvious that we find it odd that it has not been stressed in discussions of the problem. From the point of view of the monetary authorities the explanation may be that the concept of changing the overall level of deposits by a final amount is 'armchair analysis' by the theoretical economist. They are more likely to work vaguely in terms of a practical policy of 'tightening' or 'easing' the existing monetary situation. It is difficult, however, to restrain the view that their excessive concern with rate stability may stem from a desire to minimize the cost of managing the National Debt and that this has led to some loss of control over the money supply which is rationalized in terms of the liquid assets theory.[34] In this connection it may be interesting to quote from one of the supporters of the liquid assets theory. Professor Johnson, writing in 1956, said:

> The shift of emphasis from 8 to 30 per cent has been interpreted by some authorities, notably Professor R. S. Sayers, as a radical change in the orthodox technique of central bank control of credit; but it could also be interpreted as evidence that monetary policy is still strongly conditioned by the Treasury's interest in keeping interest rates low.[35]

In their evidence to the Radcliffe Committee, the Bank of England denied that their desired stability of interest rates was due to an attempt to hold down the cost of Government borrowing and stated that, though obviously concerned about the cost of the National Debt, this had never inhibited them if general economic policy required higher interest rates.[36] And, since Johnson wrote the general level of interest rates has increased. But this may only make his argument more cogent since it could be held to increase the importance to the Treasury of avoiding further increases in

[34] We believe that Mr. Newlyn would agree broadly with this conclusion. See his *Theory of Money*, pp. 31–7 [first edition].

[35] op. cit., p. 9. We believe that Johnson may not do justice to Professor Sayers in view, especially, of the latter's comments on choosing between a level of deposits and a structure of interest rates (Sayers, op. cit., p. 103). See also *Radcliffe Report*, para. 378.

[36] *Minutes of Evidence*, Q. 1762, Q. 1797, and Q. 2324.

rates and an even higher cost of servicing the National Debt. Given the major policy aim of the Government that inflation should be checked, the substantial increase in the money supply, and particularly in bank advances, since 1956 is prima facie evidence that interest rates should have increased to even higher levels than they in fact attained. Certainly the impression gained from the Radcliffe Report of the attitude of the Bank of England to active monetary policy is somewhat disturbing. Instability of Bill rates is feared because it might make funding more difficult through its effects on the bond market.[37] Apparently the authorities take the view that a fall in bond prices leads to an expectation of further falls and therefore causes buyers to hold off the market.[38] The Radcliffe Committee found this argument hard to accept, as well they might, since it implies logically that the bond market is completely unstable. Obviously it is possible, and indeed probable, that open market sales of bonds on a substantial scale would cause an adjustment in the state of expectations regarding future rates. Such an adjustment may involve a momentary sharp fall in bond prices but the further this fall goes the more likely is a re-emergence of stabilizing speculation. There is nothing to prevent the adjustment being limited and guided by the authorities, as the Committee hints (para. 565). If the official view is taken literally we are forced to a curious conclusion. Open market sales of Treasury bills are impossible because this would disturb (i.e. raise unduly) the Treasury bill rate whilst open market sales of bonds are impossible because this would produce unacceptably high fluctuations in bond rates. In other words all active open market policy is impossible and quantitative control of the money supply is ruled out. Even the liquid assets theory will not work in these circumstances since, granting an original reduction in the liquid assets base, the implied reduction of bank deposits via sale of bank Investments would destabilize the bond market.

III

If the preceding analysis is correct the following inferences and conclusions seem to be justified.

(1) The liquid assets theories of Mr. Dacey and the Radcliffe Report are both formally valid in the context of their assumed

[37] *Report*, para. 583.

[38] *Report*, para. 563.

policy and behaviour relationships, in particular the willingness of the Bank of England to deal freely between cash and Treasury bills. An increase in the liquid assets base is a necessary and sufficient condition for an increase in deposits only if the Bank of England is willing to meet, passively, the cash requirements of the banking system.

(2) In either version of the theory it is possible to postulate conditions under which the clearing banks can alter their volume of liquid assets at their own discretion. The Bank of England can offset such actions by appropriate open market operations and thus conserve the liquid assets base, but such action may involve some disturbance in the structure of interest rates which may or may not be acceptable to the central bank. In any case the willingness to use such offsetting action can easily be used to validate the traditional cash ratio theory of deposit control, e.g., the Bank can freely convert Treasury bills into cash whilst selling an equivalent volume of bonds.

(3) The lower deposit multiplier which is implied by the liquid assets theory is illusory from the standpoint of active open market policy, since the achievement of a given change in the level of deposits requires a proportionately greater initial change in the liquid assets base. Given the same complex of bill/bond sales between the banking system (including the Bank of England) and the non-bank public, the final implications for interest rates are the same for the cash ratio and liquid assets ratio theories.

(4) The existence of a minimum liquid assets ratio in addition to the conventional cash ratio means that there may be circumstances where an increase in the cash base may not be a necessary and sufficient condition for an increase in deposits because there are insufficient potential liquid assets to support the new level of deposits. This is scarcely an important constraint, since if the central bank really desired an increase in the money supply, it could easily adjust the structure of the National Debt to make the necessary liquid assets available.

Taking these factors into account, there seems to be little justification for rejecting the traditional cash ratio theory and substituting the liquid assets theory of deposit regulation. Without doubt, the latter theory can be a useful description of actual processes as long as the full implications and structural requirements are understood. If, however, it is allowed to capture the elementary text books as a dogmatic truth, which is somehow believed to be incompatible with traditional cash ratio theory, it may cause a great deal of confusion to students, particularly if the policy relationships on which it depends are subject to change. Bearing in mind the ambiguity caused by seasonal variations in the minimum liquid assets ratio, and the complete absence of quantitative information on this variation, it would seem to be sensible to retain the traditional cash ratio theory with modifications to allow for a possibly changing Bank of England Bill rate stabilization policy.

13

THE INADEQUACY OF 'NEW ORTHODOX' METHODS OF MONETARY CONTROL

[EXTRACT]

R. L. CROUCH*

WE may now state our hypotheses. *When the supply of bills is reduced*, (1) short-term rates of interest will fall relative to long-term rates of interest. As a result, (2) the 'outside tenderers'' bill portfolio will decline, (3) the banks' liquid assets ratio may decline if it is above the required minimum and (4) the discount houses' bond and commercial bill portfolios will increase relative to their bill portfolio. (5) *There will be no reduction in bank deposits.* These are empirically testable propositions—a matter to which we shortly turn our attention. However, first, we briefly draw attention to one horrendous feature of these hypotheses should it transpire that they are corroborated. A policy which a proponent of 'new-orthodox' methods could only describe as contractionary, viz., a reduction in the supply of bills, turns out to have a net expansionary impact—the supply of deposits is unchanged but interest rates decline.

Time series for seven selected magnitudes from the beginning of 1955 to the middle of 1963 have been plotted in Fig. 1.[1] Casual inspection of series 2 (bills issued by tender) immediately reveals that the outstanding stock was significantly reduced on three occasions. These periods of bill contraction have been shaded in the

* Extract reprinted from the full article of the same title which appeared in the *Economic Journal*, vol. 74, no. 296, December 1964, pp. 916–34, by permission of the author and publisher. (The extract covers pp. 929–32 of the original.) R. L. Crouch is Associate Professor of Economics, University of California at Santa Barbara.

[1] The nature and sources of the data plotted in Fig. 1 will be found in notes to Table 1.

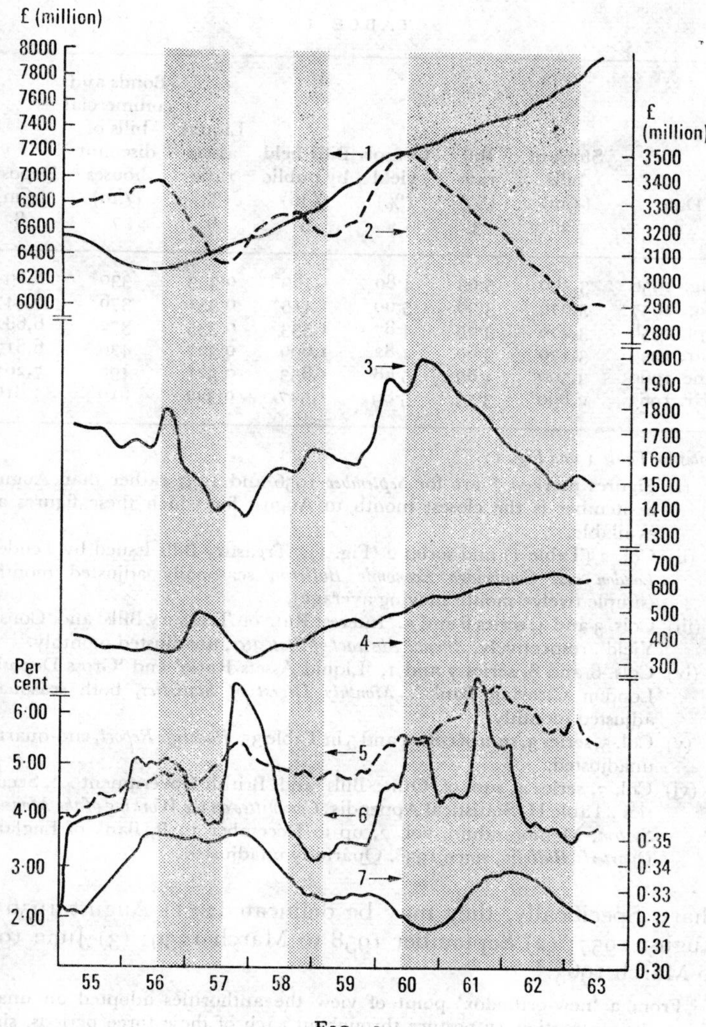

FIG. 1

1. *Deposits.* 2. *Bills issued by tender.* 3. *Bills held by public.* 4. *Commercial bills and bonds of discount houses.* 5. *Consol yield.* 6. *Treasury bill rate.* 7. *Liquid assets ratio.*

TABLE I

Date	Stock of bills (£m)	Bill rate (%)	Consols yield (%)	Bills held by public (£m)	Liquid assets ratio (%)	Bonds and commercial bills of discount houses (£m)	Deposits (£m)
1	2	3	4	5	6	7	8
Aug. 1956	3,390	5·03	4·80	1,789*	0·353	330*	6,294
Aug. 1957	3,070	3·98	5·09	1,415*	0·351	376*	6,447
Sept. 1958	3,270	3·65	4·87	1,533	0·335	372	6,682
Mar. 1959	3,170	3·60	4·82	1,609	0·327	430	6,817
June 1960	3,500	4·89	5·68	1,853	0·321	490	7,207
Mar. 1963	2,890	3·55	5·89	1,527	0·322	610	7,818

Notes to Table 1 *and Fig.* 1:

(i) Figures marked * are for *September* 1956 and 1957 rather than August. September is the closest month to August for which these figures are available.

(ii) Col. 2 (Table 1) and series 2 (Fig. 1), 'Treasury Bills Issued by Tender', *London and Cambridge Economic Bulletin*, seasonally adjusted monthly (simple twelve-month moving average).

(iii) Cols. 3 and 4, series 6 and 5, 'Interest Rate on Treasury Bills' and 'Consols Yield', respectively, *Annual Abstract of Statistics*, unadjusted monthly.

(iv) Cols. 6 and 8, series 7 and 1, 'Liquid Assets Ratio' and 'Gross Deposits, London Clearing Banks', *Monthly Digest of Statistics*, both seasonally adjusted monthly.

(v) Col. 5, series 3, sum of cols. 4 and 5 in Table 35, *Radcliffe Report*, end-quarter, unadjusted.

(vi) Col. 7, series 4, sum of 'Other Bills' and 'British Government . . . Securities', Table II, Statistical Appendix, *Committee on the Working of the Monetary System*, Memorandum, vol. 2, up to December 1958, Bank of England, *Quarterly Bulletin*, since 1958. Quarterly unadjusted.

chart. Specifically, they may be delineated: (1) August 1956 to August 1957; (2) September 1958 to March 1959; (3) June 1960 to March 1963.[2]

[2] From a 'new-orthodox' point of view the authorities adopted an unambiguously contractionary posture throughout each of these three periods, since the supply of bills decreased uninterruptedly on each occasion. However, it must be mentioned that the authorities' own intentions were somewhat different and varied between, and within, these periods. In the first period the authorities' announced intentions were contractionary (see *Radcliffe*, Memorandum, vol. 1, pp. 30–1), while, in the second, their intentions were expansionary (see, *Radcliffe*,

Between August 1956 and August 1957 the outstanding stock of bills was reduced by £320 million (from £3,390 million to £3,070 million, see Table 1). Multiplying this decrease by ten-thirds, deposits should, according to 'new-orthodox' doctrine, have decreased by more than £1,000 million—or almost 17 per cent of their August 1956 level. Inspection of series 1 (deposits) reveals that this did not occur. In fact, between these dates deposits actually increased by £153 million or 2·4 per cent.

Hypotheses which attempt to establish a direct and proportional relationship between deposits and the stock of bills fare no better when the other two occasions on which a significant reduction in the stock of bills was achieved are examined. Between September 1958 and March 1959 the stock of bills was reduced by £100 million, deposits increased by £153 million; between June 1960 and March 1963 the stock of bills was reduced by no less than £610 million, deposits increased by £611 million. This latter increase is to be contrasted with the decrease in deposits of more than £2,000 million (i.e., £610 × $\frac{10}{3}$) predicted by 'new-orthodox'-type hypotheses in these circumstances. Since it takes only one exception to *dis*prove a rule, the evidence presented thus far would already seem to have decisively refuted hypotheses implying a strong, positive, proportional relationship between deposits and the stock of bills. The *coup de grâce*, however, is contained in the following simple regression result.[3]

$$D = \underset{(475{\cdot}687)}{11{,}326{\cdot}137} - \underset{(0{\cdot}545)}{1{\cdot}361}\,T, \qquad R = 0{\cdot}404$$

Apparently, deposits and bills are *inversely* related. The sign of the coefficient of T is not only negative, by common criteria its size is

Minutes, p. 969). In the third period the authorities' economic intentions varied. Up to December 1960 they were mildly contractionary. From this date until July 1961 they were neutral or slightly expansionary. In July 1961 extremely contractionary measures were invoked. These were retained until September 1961, when mild relaxation occurred. Further steps towards relaxation were taken up to April 1962, after which date the emphasis became cautiously expansionary. From September 1962 very expansionary actions were taken which were still in force in March 1963. (This brief synopsis of the authorities' own intentions is derived from Bank of England, *Quarterly Bulletin*, *passim.*)

[3] Where D represents deposits and T represents the stock of bills. The sources of the data used are given in Notes to Table 1. The regression result was derived from seasonally adjusted quarterly data from January 1955 to February 1963. The figures in parentheses are standard errors, and R is the correlation coefficient.

significant, too.[4] Bills have been described as the modern equivalent of the printing press; the more appropriate analogy, it would seem, is a mulching machine.

We now confront the hypotheses we have presented with the observed facts. Inspection of series 5 and 6 in Fig. 1 reveals that on each of the three occasions when the supply of bills was reduced the Treasury bill rate did, in fact, fall relative to long-term interest rates. In the first period (see Table 1), the Consol–Treasury bill gap increased by 1·33 per cent (from –0·23 to 1·11 per cent); in the second period by 0·30 per cent (from 1·22 to 1·52 per cent); and by 1·55 per cent (from 0·79 to 2·34 per cent) in the third period.

The increase in the relative price of bills which occurred when their supply was reduced had the predicted effect on the discount houses' asset portfolios, i.e., substitution occurred. In the first, second and third periods, respectively, the discount houses increased their holdings of commercial bills and bonds by £46 million, £58 million and £120 million. Faced with a similar increase in their relative price, the quantity of bills demanded by the public declined in two of the three periods; by £374 million in the first and £326 million in the third. In the second period, however, the public's demand for bills increased by £76 million. Clearly, a shift in the public's demand occurred. This shift makes the period from September 1958 to March 1959 particularly interesting. Not only was the supply of bills reduced but the public's demand for bills increased, too. According to 'new-orthodox' doctrine, both forces should operate to reduce the banks' liquid assets and, thereby, bank deposits. In fact, the decline in (seasonally adjusted) liquid assets was imperceptible while bank deposits increased uninterruptedly. The reasons for this were, of course, that the discount houses increased the commercial bills and bonds in their portfolios while the banks increased the proportion of the now relatively more attractive investments and advances in theirs, i.e., reduced their liquid assets ratio.

Most proponents of the 'new-orthodoxy' recognize that deposits would decline when the supply of bills is reduced *if* (1) the public does not reduce its bill portfolio, and *if* (2) the discount houses do not substitute commercial bills and bonds for bills in their portfolios, and *if* (3) the banks do not reduce their liquid assets ratio. But

[4] Our hypothesis denies a causal relationship between bills and deposits. In our opinion they are unrelated variables. Thus, for us, the above result only demonstrates the existence of negative spurious correlation.

conditions (1)–(3) are most unlikely to obtain if, as appears to be inevitable when the supply of bills is reduced, bill rates fall relative to long rates. Examination of the evidence shows that this sequence of conditions has been breached in one way or another on every occasion that the supply of bills was reduced. Table 1 shows that in the first period (1), (2) and (3) all failed to hold; (2) and (3) failed in the second period; and (1) and (3) failed in the third. In each period, too, the extent of the failures was sufficient to allow deposits to increase. Examine, now, the following simple regression result, where T_p refers to bills held by the public.[5]

$$T_p = -905{\cdot}043 + 0{\cdot}788\ T, \qquad R = 0{\cdot}749$$
$$(107{\cdot}677)\ (0{\cdot}123)$$

On the face of it, this indicates that a £1 decrease (increase) in the stock of bills issued by tender is, in general, associated with a decrease (increase) in the public's bill holdings of 15*s*. 9*d*. (= 0·788 of £1, approximately). However, the coefficient of T is statistically indistinguishable from unity at the 95 per cent level. Thus, at this level of confidence the relationship between T and T_p could be one for one. This is most destructive for the proponents of the 'new-orthodoxy'. But from our point of view it is singularly gratifying.[6]

We feel that the evidence we have presented shows conclusively that control of the supply of bills is not sufficient to provide control of bank deposits. The author has redemonstrated elsewhere the orthodox proposition that it is not necessary.[7] In diametric opposition to 'new-orthodox' doctrine we conclude, therefore, that control of the supply of bills is neither necessary nor sufficient to provide control of bank deposits. In the paper last cited the orthodox proposition that, with minor technical adjustments, control of the supply of cash is sufficient to provide control of bank deposits was also redemonstrated. The present paper may be regarded as evidence that such control is also necessary. We especially wish to point out that the fall in the bill rate which always occurs when the

[5] The period was again from January 1955 to February 1963. For T, see note 3 on p. 267; for the source of T_p, which is quarterly unadjusted, see notes to Table 1.

[6] [The results confirmed what Crouch calls the '*in vacuo* simulations' which he presented earlier in his article.]

[7] Crouch, R. L., 'A Re-Examination of Open-Market Operations', *Oxford Economic Papers*, N.S., vol. 15, no. 2, August 1963, pp. 81–94 [Reading 11].

authorities attempt to reduce deposits by reducing the supply of bills (a fall which has seen to be *the* weak link in the 'new-orthodox' chain) can be prevented only by the Bank engaging in an open-market selling operation, that is to say, reducing the supply of cash in the system. Hence we conclude that control of the supply of cash is both necessary and sufficient to provide control of bank deposits.

14

TREASURY BILL SALES AND THE STOCK OF MONEY

John Kareken*

Can the Bank of England, by selling Treasury bills, effect a decrease in bank deposits and loans? Although the question may seem naïve, it has been debated for more than a decade.

Actually, there can be no disputing the Bank's ability to decrease the money stock. It can always call for special deposits; and if it does not provide the cash to meet the call, bank deposits must decrease. Moreover, the Bank can decrease the money stock by selling Treasury bonds. Other than a poorly considered debt management objective, there is nothing to prevent its changing the money stock by changing the private sector's portfolio of bonds. What has interested British monetary experts, however, is whether bank deposits and loans decrease when the Bank sells Treasury bills. The Bank, in its Radcliffe testimony, said 'no', and thereby challenged the orthodoxy of the 1931 *Report* of the Committee on Finance and Industry (Macmillan Committee).

The Bank is of the opinion that it has to serve as lender of last resort to discount houses, or, as is sometimes said, to the discount market.[1] When the market asks for a loan, it cannot be turned away,

* Extract reprinted from Kareken, J., 'Monetary policy', Chap. II, *in* Caves, R. E. (ed.), *Britain's Economic Prospects* (London, 1968), pp. 97–103, by permission of the author and publisher. J. Kareken is Professor of Economics at the University of Minnesota.

[1] The discount market is made up of firms which deal—for their own accounts, but presumably for customers as well—in Treasury and commercial bills and short-dated Government stocks, as Government coupon issues of near and intermediate maturity are called. To finance their holdings of assets, they borrow from bank and non-bank sources and on occasion from the Bank of England. See Bank of England, 'The London Discount Market', in *Principal Memoranda of Evidence*, vol. 1, pp. 10–12; and also 'The London Discount Market: Some

except for lack of proper collateral, which it always possesses. The Chancellor of the Exchequer willing, the Bank may charge what it wants on loans to the discount market, or in other words set Bank rate where it wants. But if the market has the collateral and is willing to pay the going rate, the Bank cannot send it away empty-handed. If the Bank were to refuse to serve as lender of last resort, it might be forced to lend directly to the government—make large Ways and Means Advances, as direct loans from the Bank to the government are known, or buy Treasury bills which had not even passed through some private portfolio. This the Bank for reasons of its own would avoid at all costs.

As things stand presently, the government will have such bills as it wants to sell taken up, if not by the public, then by the discount market.

> . . . the Discount Houses . . . have come to accept as an informal responsibility that their combined tenders should be sufficient in total to cover the amount of Treasury bills on offer. This is a point of great importance to H.M. Government since it means that they can rely upon their weekly need to borrow on Treasury bills being satisfied.[2]

The market has agreed to cover the bill tender, though, only because the Bank has agreed to lend it such sums as it may need. Again, if the Bank were to refuse to serve as lender of last resort to the discount market, it might find itself having to lend directly to the government, since whatever its flow of tax receipts the government must have the money it needs to meet commitments.

Lord Cobbold, then Governor of the Bank, told the Radcliffe Committee: 'If I were not sure the tender were going to be covered next Friday, I should be in a continual state of anxiety as to how the Government's requirements for finance for the following week were going to be met.'[3] Had he been given to using the language of economists, he would have told the Committee that, in the judgement of the Bank, the public's demand for bills does not increase steadily as the bill rate increases. If it did, there would be no obligation. The market would always take the weekly offering of bills, if at an average price of its own choosing.[4]

Historical Notes', *Bank of England Quarterly Bulletin*, vol. 7, no. 2 (June 1967), pp. 144–56.

[2] Bank of England, 'The London Discount Market', p. 11, para. 5.

[3] Radcliffe Committee, *Minutes of Evidence*, p. 201, para. 2621.

[4] The Bank has never explained how it came to its judgement about the public or outside demand for bills. I would hope not, but possibly it resulted from reading

According to the Bank, because it serves as lender of last resort, it can find itself unwillingly supplying cash or reserves to the banking system, or unable to reduce the banking system's cash, except temporarily. British banks have long made it a practice to lend money at call to the discount houses, and so are able, at a moment's notice as it were, to raise large sums of cash. The discount houses may not like having loans called, but by going to the Bank they can always get enough cash to meet any calls. The Bank increases the banking system's cash or reserves, however, by lending to the discount houses or paying off called loans for them.

British clearing banks, like most U.S. banks, must hold a certain cash reserve. Since the end of World War II they have been required to hold cash equal to 8 per cent of their total deposits. Clearing banks, unlike the U.S. banks, must also hold a certain amount of liquid assets in the form of cash, call loans to the money market, Treasury bills, and commercial bills acceptable for discount at the Bank of England. For a while they were required to hold liquid assets equal to 30 per cent of their total deposits, but in October 1963 the liquid assets requirement was reduced to 28 per cent. Therefore the clearing banks have two reserve requirements. As the Bank would have it, however, if banks are able to satisfy their liquid asset requirement, they are able to satisfy their cash requirement. With the Bank serving as lender of last resort, the exchange of call loans for cash is assured. What this means, in the Bank's opinion, is that 'a loss of cash need not in itself . . . bring (the banks) under pressure to reduce their deposits.'[5] To quote the Bank again:

> The point has been made . . . that under present arrangements monetary control cannot be achieved solely by operations on the cash reserves of the banking system. This, in the first instance, is because the discount houses are able, at will and without specific limit, to turn certain liquid

outside bids for the weekly offering of bills. In a recent paper, 'The Treasury Bill', *Bank of England Quarterly Bulletin*, vol. 4, no. 3 (September 1964), pp. 186–93, the Bank acknowledged that outsiders do bid for bills, but then went on to say (p. 188) that outside bids have only rarely been sufficient to cover the total issue. The point would seem to be that the outsiders are perfectly well aware of the discount houses' practice of tendering for the whole bill issue at an agreed price and so do not bid for bills at prices less than that which, they suspect, the discount houses are going to agree upon. (Apparently it is not that the outsiders are very vague about the discount market's bid price.) It may be that the true tail of the outside demand for bills is not revealed in the weekly auction.

[5] Bank of England, 'The Control of Bank Credit in the United Kingdom', p. 9, para. 8.

assets into cash by borrowing from (or discounting at) the Bank of England.[6]

In the opinion of the Bank monetary control can only be achieved by operations in the liquid asset reserves of the banking system. Only a loss of cash, which is also a loss of liquid assets, puts the banks under pressure to reduce their deposits.

Putting the Bank's point differently, it cannot reduce bank deposits and loans by selling bills: 'If bankers' balances at the Bank are increased by open market operations (in bills), the banks have a strong inducement to increase their earning assets and thus their deposits; but if they are reduced, the banks can adjust their position by calling upon their most liquid assets other than cash.'[7] Thus bills sold are taken up by the discount market, which finances its purchase with call loans from the banking system. With the bills being taken up in the market, the banks suffer a loss of cash, but no loss of deposits and consequently no loss of liquid assets. They are able therefore to adjust their cash positions, so in the end there is no reduction in deposits.

It may be (as the Bank seemed to assume in its Radcliffe evidence) that when it sells more bills, discount houses take them up, using call loans from the banking system. It may also be that these loans are subsequently called and that even the discount houses go into the Bank. As the Bank's critics would have it, however, this is not the end.[8] The discount houses' borrowing costs having gone up, they sell previously issued bills to the public or lower their bid at the next auction, thereby giving a larger share of the new issue of bills to the public. Or they increase their indebtedness to the public.[9]

[6] Bank of England, 'Some Possible Modifications in Technique', p. 40, para. 24.

[7] Bank of England, 'Some Possible Modifications in Technique', p. 38, para. 1. The words in parentheses were added.

[8] See Morgan, E. Victor, *Monetary Policy for Stable Growth*, pp. 33–5, 54. In footnote 1, p. 54, Morgan cites several authors who, whether explicitly or implicitly, have taken the Bank to task.

[9] As Dr. Goodhart has called to my attention, the discount houses have agreed with the clearing banks not to compete for the deposits of firms and households. It would not be 'fair' for them to borrow from the banks at a rate which changes only when Bank rate changes, and at the same time take deposits away by offering a higher rate. H. F. Goodson has given the following example of a rate structure: '. . . Bank rate is 6 per cent and the clearing banks' deposit rate is fixed at 4 per cent for money at seven days' notice . . . the discount houses also adopt the same deposit rate, but in their case they can take deposits on a day-to-day basis at 4 per cent. For deposits at seven days' notice their rate is 4½ per cent, and these

In any event, deposits of the banking system decline; however the discount houses get command of additional deposits, they use them to pay off Bank loans.

Apparently the Bank can reduce banks' cash and thereby their deposits and loans or advances by selling bills; it is only required that it lend to the discount houses at a penalty rate, or that Bank rate be a penalty rate. As will be clear, however, the Bank's critics have assumed what the Bank denied, that the public's demand for bills increases steadily as the bill rate increases. Had they taken the Bank's assumption, they would not have been able to portray the discount houses as in one way or another selling bills to the public.[10] Possibly therefore the Bank's critics have been disputing, not its analysis, but its empirical judgements.[11] The Bank's critics might call attention to recent empirical studies which, in showing households and firms to be influenced by interest rates, would seem to contradict the Bank's judgement. Admittedly, most of these studies used U.S. rather than U.K. data. They are suggestive, however, and to dismiss them one would have to argue that Anglo-Saxons are not all alike.

In the Bank's Radcliffe evidence, it set out yet another proposition, that it is able by selling bills to increase short-term interest rates.

It should be noted that the creation of a cash shortage is not without effect. For, particularly if it is such as to compel borrowing from the Bank of England, which is relatively expensive to the Discount Houses, they will try to reduce such borrowing as far as possible by raising their bids for money in the money market, thus causing short-term interest rates to rise. Further, if the authorities allow the Discount Market to be subjected to any substantial pressure for cash, it is likely to be taken by the banks and

are the maximum rates which they can pay to anybody or any commercial concern that is outside the banking community.'

See 'The Functioning of the London Discount Houses', in *The London Discount Market Today* (London: The Institute of Bankers, 1962), p. 23. But the discount houses are free to bid for deposits owned by, for example, overseas banks, or by accepting houses. The Bank, in its Radcliffe evidence, wrote of the discount houses' 'raising their bids for money from the money market'. ('The Control of Bank Credit in the United Kingdom', p. 10, para. 11.) The discount houses can, then, increase their indebtedness to the public, if only indirectly.

[10] They would still have been able to portray them as borrowing more from the public. For an official sale of bills to result in a reduction in banks' cash, it is not necessary that the discount houses' bill portfolios decrease.

[11] Maynard, Geoffrey, 'The Futility of Funding: A Comment', *The Bankers' Magazine*, September 1965, pp. 143–6.

the market as an indication that the authorities desire to exert pressure on the supply of bank credit.[12]

Having claimed that it can increase short-term interest rates by selling bills and long-term rates by altering expectations,[13] the Bank should have made plain its belief that the public's demand for bank deposits is unaffected by changes in interest rates. If the public's demand for deposits is affected by changes in interest rates, then an official sale of bills which increases interest rates must at the same time reduce deposits. Again, the evidence has been accumulating that interest rates indeed appear among the determinants of the public's demand for bank deposits.

There would seem nothing to do but conclude, if hesitantly, that the Bank is able, by selling bills, to reduce banks' cash and deposits and advances.[14] If the Bank had provided evidence in support of

[12] Bank of England, 'The Control of Bank Credit in the United Kingdom', p. 10, para. 11. The discount houses 'try to reduce their . . . borrowing[s] . . . by raising bids for money in the money market', but they do not succeed.

[13] As the Radcliffe Committee complained (*Report*, p. 215, para. 583), the Bank was of two minds about whether long-term rates change when short-term rates do. In the last sentence of the passage quoted immediately above, the Bank would appear to be suggesting that a cash shortage changes expectations about tomorrow's interest rates and thereby today's long-term rates.

[14] I should acknowledge here having been taken to task by several of those who read a preliminary draft of this chapter for not having pointed out that the British financial scene has changed. Local authorities, which once borrowed from the non-bank public (if at all) only at long term, have for some years now been borrowing large sums at short term, and thus there is today in London a highly developed local authority money market, a 'parallel' market, as it has been called. But I cannot see that the emergence of local authorities as short-term borrowers, or of a parallel market for short-term local authority claims, has made the Bank of England any less able than it was to decrease bank deposits by selling Treasury bills. Admittedly, Treasury bills have, in the words of one expert in the Treasury, 'been replaced in non-bank portfolios by short-term local authority deposits'. It is surely wrong to conclude from this, however, as apparently my critics have, that the non-bank public has entirely lost interest in Treasury bills, or that it has come to prefer short-term local authority claims to Treasury bills, whatever the rate spread. (If this is not what they have concluded, how can they suggest, as they seem to have, that the Bank is today unable to decrease bank deposits by selling Treasury bills?) Assuming that Treasury bills and short-term claims on local authorities are substitutes, whether perfect or imperfect, one can still account for the observed change in the non-bank public's holdings. There has been a sharp increase in short-term local authority debt outstanding and a decrease in the bill indebtedness of the government. Also, Treasury bills count as liquid assets for the clearing banks, whereas short-term local authority claims do not. But if Treasury bills and short-term local authority claims are substitutes, the conclusion holds: the Bank can, by selling bills, decrease bank deposits.

its judgement about the public's demands for bills, its rejection of orthodoxy would have seemed more convincing.

To all appearances, the Radcliffe Committee was not persuaded by the Bank. Nowhere in its report did it deny that the Bank is able to reduce banks' cash, deposits, and loans by selling bills and then lending to the discount houses at a penalty rate. It did insist, as the Bank had, that to limit banks' deposits and investments and advances, the Bank has to limit not the supply of cash but the supply of liquid assets—or, what for the committee was the same, the availability of Treasury bills.[15] The Bank, however, had traced this to its role as lender of last resort to the discount houses, whereas the committee traced it to 'the desire of the authorities for a high degree of stability in the Treasury bill rate'[16] or the Bank's willingness 'to deal very freely between cash and Treasury bills'.[17]

The committee saw the Bank as pegging the bill rate, or at the very least as allowing only minor day-to-day changes in the rate, and as therefore unable to deal in bills, except at the invitation of the market. It thus concluded that to limit banks' deposits and investments and advances the Bank must limit their liquid assets, or in other words sell Treasury bonds to the public.

It is not difficult to see why the committee thought it might on occasion be appropriate for the Bank to sell bonds, even while pegging the bill rate at the level deemed appropriate. Except in times of crisis, the Bank has apparently aimed to keep the rate on U.K. bills equal to the highest of other international money market rates. But with the bill rate determined this way, it is possible to want a higher Treasury bond rate, or a smaller quantity of bank deposits.

As I have suggested, the Bank's argument against orthodoxy is not convincing. It must be assumed that bank deposits decrease when the Bank sells Treasury bills. Not that it necessarily should sell bills, or bonds either, with the objective of ensuring some particular money stock. It is doubtful that the money stock should be *the* target variable of monetary policy, although as *one* it might be acceptable. The point is simply that both a desired total of output and a desired composition of output cannot be realized by ensuring any particular money stock.

[15] *Radcliffe Report*, p. 128, para. 376; p. 215, para. 583.
[16] ibid., p. 215, para. 583.
[17] ibid., p. 128, para. 376.

IV

EFFICIENCY

IV

EFFICIENCY

EDITED BY

M. J. Artis

Introduction

Until comparatively recently, the traditional concerns of the monetary economist in Britain have in the main been with descriptions of the functioning of the financial system and the *modus operandi* of monetary policy within a given, if developing, institutional framework. The last few years have witnessed a considerable change in this respect, and alongside the growing volume of econometric work touching areas crucial to the design of monetary policy, there has also been a development of welfare analysis, applied to monetary systems, a development which has taken place not only at a theoretical but also at the institutional level.

This development has been marked by the publication of two important reports—that of the National Board for Prices and Incomes (the PIB) on Bank charges[1] and the *Monopolies Commission Report* on the proposed bank mergers[2] both of which viewed the banking system as an industry, and were led to ask of it the kinds of questions which economists investigating an industry would normally ask. Whilst this was in itself a comparatively novel departure, the conclusions drawn in both Reports were sharply critical of existing institutional arrangements and so gave rise to considerable controversy. The practical upshot, by the Spring of 1971, had been limited but important: the banks were by then no longer taking advantage of the provisions allowing them less than full disclosure of profits, a merger of two large banks (Barclays and Lloyds) had been prevented, and most important of all perhaps, it

[1] National Board for Prices and Incomes, *Report No.* 34, 'Bank charges'.

[2] Monopolies Commission, *Barclays Bank Ltd., Lloyds Bank Ltd., and Martins Bank Ltd.*; *Report on the proposed merger* (H.M.S.O., 1968).

seemed that the monetary authorities were more conscious than before of the need to take account of the requirements for an efficient and fully competitive banking sector (compare Reading 32 below).

The prevailing institutional arrangements in the banking sector cannot simply be divorced from the proximate objectives assigned to monetary policy, and the techniques of control adopted by the policy-makers. This consideration underlies much of the controversy engendered by proposals for reform. One view of the existing system sees the collection of monetary controls and restraints on competition as constituting between them a more or less indivisible package of *quid pro quo*s on both sides. Thus, the banks cannot be expected to compete for deposits while their advances remain subject to direct controls; and their apparent ability to generate quasi-monopoly profits can be viewed as a counterpart to the special form of taxation to which they are subject as a result of the imposition of cash and liquidity controls, calls for special deposits, and the like. The pace at which competitive pressures can be sharpened, then, depends among other things, on the authorities' ability to devise alternative forms of monetary control. In this connection it may be noted that the Prices and Incomes Board *Report* favoured a second-best solution, suggesting the spread of liquidity controls, or their analogue, to non-bank financial institutions, as a means of securing an equitable basis for competition (Reading 16, page 316).[3]

A less cumbersome alternative is available if it is assumed that there are no (or should not be any) constraints on the monetary authorities' ability to practise open-market operations (some of the considerations relevant here are covered in Chapter VI), and that control of the money supply is the correct proximate objective of monetary policy. The constraint on a completely free and openly competitive banking and financial system is then virtually removed.[4]

Quite aside from the question of its relationship to the efficacy of

[3] But this was objected to by H. G. Johnson in his review of the *Report* (see Reading 17, p. 326).

[4] It might still be argued that the monetary authorities' knowledge of the portfolio behaviour of the system would be sufficiently imprecise and their requirements sufficiently exacting as to justify retention of some control, for example a cash ratio, set at a level which was not on average a significant penalty. Its purpose would be, not to subsidize the issue of government debt, but to increase the predictability of response.

monetary control, the application of the competitive nostrum to the banking industry is rich in the issues it raises, some no doubt more significant than others. There is, for example, the question of the right mix of cash (notes and coin) and bank deposit money in the total money supply and how that mix should and could be affected; there is the question of the side-effects on equity of any change in the existing arrangements, covering the interests of shareholders, depositors, and borrowers, and the question how far the restraints on price competition lead to 'excessive' service competition and how far they serve to produce, not monopoly profits, but inefficiency.

The first of the readings included in this Chapter, a paper by H. G. Johnson, ranges widely over the area covered by 'efficiency' in monetary affairs including not only an analysis of structural efficiency of the banking system *qua* industry, but also an examination of efficiency needs in the conduct of policy. The next selection, Reading 16, is an extract from the PIB's *Report on Bank charges*, which is followed by a review, again by H. G. Johnson, of that *Report*. His review gives the *Report* some additional theoretical clothing, and in particular clarifies the complementary roles of public policy and the banking industry's interests. One of the PIB *Report*'s conclusions was that the cartelized system of interest rate control in the banking industry had produced a situation in which an expensive form of competition flourished in the proliferation of bank branches. The *Report* suggested that some consolidation of units could rationalize this position. This recommendation, rather ironically in view of the *Report*'s emphasis elsewhere on competition, led to a phase of merger activity culminating in a proposal that Barclays and Lloyds Banks might be allowed to amalgamate. This proposal was the subject of a Monopolies Commission inquiry. The Commission's report found a majority against the merger, and a minority in favour of it.

According to M. J. Artis's review of this *Report* (Reading 18), the division of opinion which emerged may well have had as much to do with a difference of approach to the terms of reference—which effectively excluded the existing cartel agreement from the agenda—as with the issues on which the sides nominally joined argument in their respective statements.

The suggestions for further reading include a recent detailed plan of reform of the banking system by Brian Griffiths and an article by Paish, more critical of the general thrust of those reprinted here.

FURTHER READING

Symposium on Bank Charges, *The Bankers' Magazine*, vol. 204, no. 1481, August 1967, pp. 61–74.

Monopolies Commission, *Barclays Bank Ltd., Lloyds Bank Ltd., and Martins Bank Ltd.: Report on the proposed merger* (H.M.S.O., 1968).

Griffiths, Brian, *Competition in Banking*, Hobart Paper No. 51 (Institute of Economic Affairs, 1970).

Paish, F. W., 'Deposit rates after Mr. Jones', *The Banker*, vol. 117, no. 500, October 1967, pp. 845–9.

POSTSCRIPT

Events were to move rapidly in the direction of a more competitive banking system in 1971, after the above Introduction was written. In May, the Bank of England set out proposals involving *inter alia*, the abolition of the clearing bank 'cartel', the abolition of the cash and liquidity ratios and their replacement by a uniform reserve ratio to be applied to all banks (and subsequently in modified form to finance houses), together with the removal of direct controls over bank lending. These changes, the rationale and background to which are in effect outlined in the Readings included in this Section, are too recent to have provided material for thorough assessment; some initial appraisals were, however, published *inter alia*, in issues of the *Bankers' Magazine* for August and September 1971 and the Bank of England's proposals were published in the *Quarterly Bulletin of the Bank of England*, June 1971, under the title 'Competition and credit control'.

15

PROBLEMS OF EFFICIENCY IN MONETARY MANAGEMENT

HARRY G. JOHNSON*

I. Introduction

MONETARY management as generally understood means the management of the money supply and monetary and credit-market conditions by the monetary authority (the central bank) in the pursuit of certain general social objectives. These objectives may either by assigned to the central bank by the national government or be left to the central bank to establish for itself, depending on whether the central bank is a subordinate instrumentality of national economic policy or is allowed a substantial measure of independence. In the past, economists specializing in the study of monetary management have been predominantly either institutionalists concerned with the detailed structure of the financial system and the precise institutional ways in which the central bank operates on that system in pursuit of its objectives, or economic historians concerned with the evolution of the financial organization of a particular country or countries, the theories of monetary management advocated by historically influential personages, and the influence of these theories on legislation affecting the structure of the financial system and the central bank's concept of its role and functions. (There have, of course, always been non-specialist critics of financial organization and monetary management, some of whom have in due course achieved the status of historically influential personages.) With the professionalization of economics,

* Reprinted from the *Journal of Political Economy*, vol. 76, no. 5, September/October 1968, pp. 971–90, by permission of the author and publisher. H. G. Johnson is Professor of Economics at the University of Chicago and the London School of Economics.

the accompanying increase in confidence in the scientific approach to economic problems, and the resulting tendency to apply the scientific approach increasingly to problems of economic policy—problems in normative rather than positive economic science—that has occurred since the 1930s and especially since the Second World War, economists concerned with monetary management have become decreasingly concerned with institutional and historical questions per se and increasingly concerned with normative problems—that is, with problems of efficiency in monetary management. This approach requires the application of economic theory—and in some cases of econometrics—more intensively to the processes and practices of monetary management than has generally been the case in the past.

The purpose of this paper is to survey some of the problems of efficiency in monetary management, as they have emerged from recent theorizing and research. For this purpose, three aspects of the problem of efficiency are distinguished: (1) structural efficiency, by which is meant efficiency in the ordinary economic sense of the banking system considered as an industry whose primary function from the monetary point of view is to provide the means of payment (currency and deposits subject to check) for the economy, though from a broader point of view it also plays an important part in the capital market as a medium for saving and an allocator of capital among competing borrowers; (2) efficiency in stabilization policy, that is, policy directed at keeping the economy on a desired course and correcting deviations from that course; and (3) efficiency in secular economic policy, that is, efficiency with respect to the choice of the desired level and trend over time of the major macro-economic variables that reflect the economy's performance. It should be emphasized that these last two problems are, generally speaking, not problems of monetary management alone, if monetary management is identified with central bank policy, but are rather problems in the joint use of monetary, fiscal, and possibly exchange rate policy for the purpose of economic stabilization and the fulfilment of the general objectives of full employment, price stability, economic growth and balance-of-payments equilibrium. In some cases, it is possible to indicate theoretical solutions to the problems of efficiency; in other cases, it is only possible to indicate the considerations that must enter into an efficient solution. Where the analysis depends upon assumptions about institutional practices, it should be understood that the reference is to the monetary and banking institutions of the United States, United Kingdom, and other countries in the British tradition of banking, so that the conclusions may not be directly applicable to other countries, particularly those of Continental Europe.

II. Problems of structural efficiency

As already mentioned, the banking system can be regarded as an industry that, on the one hand, provides a payments mechanism for the economy and, on the other hand, through its payments-mechanism operations and the acceptance of interest-bearing non-checkable deposits, assembles capital for investment in various forms of assets, thereby playing an important part in the capital market.

There is at the foundation of normative (welfare) economics a presumption that free competition will promote the efficient performance of economic activities; and this presumption would seem to apply to the banking industry, with important qualifications deriving from the special characteristics of money to be noted below. Free competition in the banking industry would lead banks to compete for checkable deposits by offering interest and charging competitive rates related to costs for the provision of the services of the payments mechanism, in order to obtain funds for investment. It would also lead banks in their lending operations to provide those loan facilities and invest in those marketable assets that the banks could manage with an efficiency superior to that of other financial institutions. The result, assuming that the banking system remained competitive, would be to maximize efficiency in the provision of a payments mechanism and in the allocation of capital, with one potentially important qualification.

Efficiency in the allocation of capital would follow from the usual arguments for free competition among rival business firms; the achievement of efficiency in the provision of the payments mechanism, however, requires some explanation since it involves an application of monetary theory. Briefly, the payment of competitive interest rates on checkable deposits means that holding assets in monetary form would entail no alternative opportunity cost for wealth-owners other than the real social costs—operating expenses and a normal rate of return on the capital employed—of maintaining the system of checking accounts, so that the public would be encouraged to satiate its desire for liquidity. At the abstract level of pure theory, the costs of maintaining a system of bank accounts—as distinct from the costs of using these accounts to make payments—can be regarded as negligible: in theoretical terms, money can be provided at zero social cost. Maximization of welfare requires that a good that can be provided at zero marginal social cost should be provided in the quantity that yields zero marginal utility, that is that satiates demand, and this result would be insured by the payment of competitive interest rates on checkable deposits. Similarly, the charging of competitive costs for the use of the services of the payments mechanism would induce the deposit-holding public to make optimal use of that mechanism: in other words, to arrange its monetary transactions so as to use the bank account payments mechanism only for transactions that are privately worth their social cost. In short, a competitive banking system would encourage the public to hold the socially optimum quantity of money and make socially optimum use of the payments mechanism.

This conclusion, however, is subject to a qualification that arises from the availability of currency—coin, but especially notes—as an alternative means of making payments. This alternative medium of exchange is non-interest-bearing, and it would be extremely difficult, though not necessarily impossible, to arrange for the issue of an interest-bearing currency. On the other hand, the issuing authority (the treasury or the central bank) bears the real resource cost of providing currency. In the case of the coinage, the direct costs are the capital cost of the metal and the running costs of coining and recoining and the loss of metal through abrasion. In the case of paper money, there is the cost of the special paper and of design, printing and reprinting. In addition, in both cases there is the additional direct cost of security precautions and the indirect cost of policing against forgery. The coinage is known to be directly profitable, as a general rule: when it ceases to be so because of a rise in the value of the metal used, steps are taken fairly quickly to restore its profitability by substitution of cheaper metals. The issue of paper money also is generally assumed to be directly profitable, in the sense that the interest earned by the issuing authority on assets bought with paper money exceeds the running cost of providing the paper money; though there are limits to the validity of this assumption, as evidenced by the fact that the Bank of England some years ago found it necessary to curb a vogue for making payments in newly printed money by requesting the customers of banks to make do with already-used Bank of England notes. Whether coinage and the issue of paper money are socially profitable when the indirect costs of policing against forgery are taken into account is an unresolved question. But on the assumption that the issue of notes and coin is socially profitable, in the sense of yielding a surplus above the cost of production and policing, it follows that the private cost of holding currency exceeds the social cost, or that the private return from holding currency falls short of the social return. On the other hand, the private cost of using currency for making payments falls short of the social cost, insofar as the circulation of currency leads to its deterioration; but this aspect of the use of currency can probably be safely disregarded as of trivial importance, since the social cost of individual exchanges of currency, in the form of physical depreciation of the medium of exchange, must be negligible. The substantive point therefore is that, because the private cost of holding currency (the interest foregone) substantially exceeds the social cost (raw material, value added, and policing), free competition in banking, by making the private and social cost of deposit-holding coincide, would tend to produce a socially non-optimum overallocation of resources to the provision of deposit money and underallocation of resources to the provision of currency for holding. The charging of full cost for the use of the deposit payments mechanism would similarly promote overuse of currency and underuse of deposits in making payments, though this source of inefficiency can be regarded as negligible for the reasons already given. The social loss resulting from the stimulus to excessive deposit-holding relative to currency-holding would depend on the elasticity of substitution between the two forms of money in the demand of users of money. On the assumption that currency cannot be issued other than as a non-interest-bearing asset, achievement of the 'second-best' welfare optimum would require a tax on the holding of deposit money at a rate somewhere between zero and the competitive interest rate on deposits, the precise tax rate depending on the relative strength of the effects of the tax in discouraging the holding of checkable bank deposits as compared with untaxed non-monetary assets and encouraging the holding of currency as compared with checkable bank deposits. This qualification of the argument for free competition in banking is disregarded in the remainder of the analysis.

The case just presented for free competition in commercial banking depends crucially on the assumption that a banking system in which competition among banks was unregulated by legislation or central bank supervision would remain competitive. Historical experience strongly suggests, however, that unrestricted competition among banks tends to lead to concentration of the industry through expansion of the larger units and through mergers. The reason presumably is that there are significant economies of scale—both in the operation of the deposit payments mechanism and in the operation of the lending and investment side of the banking business—which give a profit incentive to concentration and, on the payments side at least, may indicate the social desirability of operating the banking business as a public utility. In the United States, the tendency to concentration has been held in check at a relatively early stage of concentration by public fears of a banking monopoly given expression through banking legislation, which falls to the responsibility of the individual states in the federal system of American government; but the trend to concentration has nevertheless been persistent. The U.S. banking system therefore can probably be fairly described as competitive and efficient within the framework of legislation governing it, but possibly socially inefficient in providing a payments mechanism in the sense that a national 'giro' system of some sort might reduce substantially the cost of making payments. In the United Kingdom, control over bank mergers of an 'informal' but nevertheless effective sort, designed to prevent bank mergers in restraint of competition, was introduced after the wave of mergers that occurred toward the end of the First World War. The result has been to consolidate and perpetuate a situation of oligopolistic competition in British banking, which appears socially inefficient from a variety of points of view, but which has been tolerated and even encouraged by the monetary authorities since it lends itself readily to control by persuasion and directive in subservience to the objectives of economic policy. Britain, incidentally, to improve the efficiency of her payments mechanism, is in the process of introducing a 'giro' system with which the banks will have to compete.

In general, the presence of economies of scale in the banking business forces social policy concerned with efficiency to contemplate the familiar choice between (a) designing a regulatory system that will enable private competitive organizations to obtain the economies of scale while preventing them from exercising monopoly power, and (b) replacing private enterprise by a public utility that will obtain the efficiency of a monopoly while operating in the public interest. With the rapid development of the electronic computer as an instrument of efficient large-scale bookkeeping, the feasibility of a single national, or even international, credit payments system that would be less expensive than traditional commercial bank payments operations is more likely; and it is possible that in the long run such systems will replace the checking facilities provided at present by the commercial banks, which would presumably revert to institutions primarily occupied in lending out savings deposits entrusted to them. In the meantime, however, to the extent that society values the preservation of a private enterprise, non-monopolized commercial banking system, the case for free competition remains relevant.

The analysis thus far has been concerned with the efficiency of the banking system, considered as an industry like any other industry. The banking system cannot, however, in strict logic, be so treated, because of the special characteristics that distinguish its product—money, the means of payment—from the products of other private enterprises—real goods and services. The crucial difference between the banking industry and other industries is that whereas other industries provide real goods and services that the public demands, so that a stable equilibrium of demand and supply will be attained under competition, the banking industry provides nominal money—money denominated in marks, pounds, dollars, or other monetary units of account—while the public demands real balances—stocks of purchasing power. The public can adjust the real value of any given quantity of nominal money balances supplied by the banking system to that quantity of real balances it desires to hold by changing the price level through its efforts to substitute goods for real balances when real balances are excessive at the current price level, and to substitute real balances for goods when real balances are insufficient at the current price level. In the alternative Keynesian framework of analysis, excess real balances lower the rate of interest, increase investment and possibly consumption demand, and so raise prices—and conversely for deficient real balances. Thus, in terms of static theory, the quantity of nominal balances supplied will be in neutral equilibrium; any other quantity could be made the equilibrium quantity through appropriate changes in the price level. Less abstractly, a competitive banking system would be under constant incentive to expand the nominal money supply and thereby initiate price inflation. With random economic variations, uncertainty, and 'money illusion' on the part of the banks (defined as confidence in the stability of the value of money), the price level would be inherently unstable; variations in it would produce changes in bank lending and the quantity of money that would reinforce the initial change.

Stability in the trend of prices (a special case of which is price stability) and in the trend of expectations about the future course of prices—which are generally agreed to be important to the social welfare—requires social control over the total quantity of money supplied by the banking system. By tradition, this control is exercised by the central bank. According to the general equilibrium theory of a monetary economy, central bank control presupposes the power to determine one nominal monetary magnitude in the system and one interest rate. In traditional central banking practice, this requirement is fulfilled by the central bank's control over the quantity of cash reserves available to the commercial banking system, its reserves being its own note and deposit liabilities (less currency in circulation among the public), and by the convention that its notes and deposits bear zero interest for the holder.

For the same reasons that economic efficiency requires the payment of interest on deposit money held by the public, optimal resource allocation requires the payment of interest by the central bank on its liabilities held as reserves by the commercial banks, at a rate determined by the yield on its assets less operating costs. This principle by itself is somewhat ambiguous, since as a government-sponsored monopoly the central bank is under no pressure to practice efficiency in its staffing and other management policies and is under considerable pressure to use its resources to lend to government at subsidized rates; and it should be extended by a stipulation of central bank efficiency in both office and portfolio management. The principle also raises the practical problem of implementation with respect to commercial bank holdings of reserves of currency, which as already mentioned conventionally bears no interest. Payment of interest on commercial bank holdings of central bank deposits but not on their holdings of currency would create an incentive for the banks to hold an excessive ratio of deposits to currency in their reserves. This incentive could possibly be removed by the central bank paying interest on the reported average currency holdings of the commercial banks. The convention of non-payment of interest by the central bank on commercial bank reserves constitutes in effect a tax on the creation and use of deposit money, which militates against the efficient provision of a payments mechanism. The incidence of this tax falls entirely on the deposit-holding public if the banking system is competitive and banking services can be provided at constant cost; it is shared between the public and the banks if the banking industry is subject to rising costs as scale increases or if the banking industry is monopolized or oligopolistic.

As just mentioned, the central bank can control the price level if it fixes the yield on its liabilities and controls the quantity thereof through open-market operations, quite consistently with free competition in the banking industry. It will, of course, have to acquire from experience an accurate knowledge of the factors determining the ratios of reserves to deposits the commercial banks will choose in their own self-interest to hold under varying circumstances; but this is a legitimate part of the task of central bank management. In the actual practice of central banking, however, reliance is placed on additional instruments and techniques of control over the commercial banks. From the point of view of the theory of monetary control, these additional controls are unnecessary, if not positively mischievous; and their effect for the most part is to impose taxation on the commercial banks and ultimately on the users of deposit money, additional to what is imposed by the non-payment of interest on bank reserves, to the detriment of efficiency in the long-run allocation of the economy's resources between the provision of the payments mechanism and other uses.

In the grand tradition of central banking, and especially in the practice of the Bank of England, great emphasis is placed on the use of rediscount policy, especially changes in the rediscount rate, as an instrument of monetary policy—in British practice, the primary instrument. The availability of the rediscount facility in fact, however, constitutes a breach in the central bank's control of the volume of its liabilities, permitting the commercial banks to offset the central bank's open-market operations by temporary or renewed borrowing; and this breach has to be plugged by the establishment of conventions against continued or 'excessive' use of the facility, supported ultimately by the threat of central bank denial of the facility to a transgressor, a situation undesirable because it entrusts the central bank with the exercise of arbitrary and ill-defined authority. At least in the presence of a well-developed capital market, and on the assumption of intelligent and responsible monetary management by the central bank, the commercial banks should be able to manage their reserve positions without the need for the central bank to function as 'lender of last resort'. Apart from this consideration, it is questionable whether changes in the rediscount rate perform very efficiently as signals of the central bank's intentions with respect to monetary policy—if communication of this kind is desirable, there are other ways of providing it. And at a deeper level of analysis it is questionable whether the central bank is well advised to aim at exercising monetary control through the fixing of the level of short-term interest rates rather than through the determination of the reserve base of the monetary system. Finally, the fact that in British practice changes in bank rate derive much of their leverage from the conventional fixing of interest rates on clearing bank deposits, advances, and other accounts by a percentage margin below or above bank rate raises the question whether a cartelized pricing policy of this type serves the interests of economic efficiency.

As already mentioned, the conventional non-payment of interest on commercial bank reserve holdings of central bank liabilities constitutes an implicit tax on the provision of deposit money through the commercial banking system. The burden of this tax is increased by the stipulation of minimum or average cash reserve ratios, to the extent that such stipulation obliges the banks to hold a larger volume of non-interest-earning reserves than they would voluntarily choose to hold for the efficient conduct of their business. By comparison with conventional average reserve ratio requirements, legal minimum requirements impose an additional burden, since the banks must guard against violation of the requirement by holding excess cash reserves or by keeping their non-cash assets sufficiently liquid to be able to meet unexpected reserve drains. In addition to this implicit tax imposed through the central bank's monopoly of the provision of cash reserves and the government's power to impose reserve requirements, the commercial banks, and ultimately the deposit-holding public, are taxed indirectly in a variety of other ways through regulations adopted either to control the banks' commercial operations, to facilitate central bank control, or to cushion the market for government debt against the impact of monetary policy. Thus, prohibiting the banks from undertaking certain kinds of lending or restricting the amount of such lending they can undertake, either permanently or in times of restrictive monetary policy, reduces the commercial profitability of banking; so does the fixing of liquid asset ratios, which obliges the banks to hold a larger proportion of lower-yielding assets than they would voluntarily choose and may also reduce the yield on these assets below what it would otherwise be. In similar fashion, the fixing of maximum interest rates on certain kinds of bank lending, such as consumer loans and mortgage lending, acts as an implicit tax by confining banks to those loans in these categories for which the credit risk is low enough to justify lending at the permitted rate.

The rule or convention against the payment of interest on checking accounts which exists in some countries is a special kind of tax, since it is levied on the depositors for the benefit of the banks rather than the government. The main argument for not paying interest on checking accounts, that it prevents reckless competition for deposits among banks, has been shown to be unsupported by the empirical evidence in the country where the argument is most fashionable (the United States) and is inconsistent also with the broad range of historical evidence. In any case the rule is impossible to enforce, since banks can get around it in part by crediting notional interest earnings against charges for deposit operation until charges are reduced to zero (as in England), or by offering free checking and other services proportioned to the size of the customer's account, and by competing via other attractions, such as gifts of merchandise (in the United States) or a plethora of conveniently located branches (as in England). To the extent that the ban on paying interest is effective, the result is a socially inefficient restriction on the holding of checking deposits; to the extent that interest can only be received by making free use of the payments mechanism, the result is the encouragement of socially excessive use of that mechanism; and to the extent that implicit interest earnings are returned to the customer in banking services and convenience that he would not freely choose if offered the alternative of cash payments, the result is a partial waste of resources.

From the point of view of the monetary authority, the various interferences with the commercial banks' freedom to choose the composition of their asset portfolios to maximize profits, discussed above, have the advantages (apparent or real) of increasing the predictability of commercial bank response to monetary policy action and of improving the short-run effectiveness of monetary control of economic activity. The latter is particularly the case where directives can strike at borrowers who have no other source of credit than the commercial banks (such as many consumers and small businesses), or where maximum lending rates imposed on certain types of bank-lending lead the banks to discontinue such lending when interest rates rise. Even from the point of view of effectiveness of control, however, such selectivity has corresponding disadvantages: Credit discrimination against particular classes of borrower or of loan-financed activity may involve short-run disruption of established financial relations and in the longer run distort the growth of the economy and reduce its efficiency. From the point of view of structural efficiency considered here, the most relevant consideration is that by imposing an implicit tax on commercial banking, these techniques of control restrict the scale of the check-payment system provided by the commercial banks to something below the social optimum. They also encourage the growth, in competition with the commercial banks, of rival financial institutions which offer money substitutes to asset holders and conduct lending operations similar to those of the banks, more or less free of the burden of implicit taxation imposed by monetary management proximately on the banks and ultimately on their depositors.

Furthermore, in this connection it is important to note that the burden of implicit taxation on the commercial banking system and its depositors is in general an increasing function of the level of interest rates. This is obviously so with respect to the taxation implicit in the compulsory holding of non-interest-bearing reserves, and also with respect to interest ceilings on particular categories of bank lending. As regards depositors, the burden of the ban on interest payments for checking deposits obviously increases as the general level of interest rates increases—with a consequent tendency for depositors to shift out of such deposits into substitutes bearing a more flexible rate of interest. The banks, by contrast, derive from this ban in the short run additional earnings which may compensate or more than compensate them for the greater loss of interest on their reserve holdings; but in the longer run, the effect must be to reduce the relative scale of the banking industry by reducing the relative attractiveness of its product.

The general effect of these various implicit taxes on commercial banking, in the context of the general trend toward rising interest rates since the Second World War, has undoubtedly been to contribute to the development of competing financial intermediaries and a relative loss of business to them by the banks. The spokesmen for the banking community have generally reacted to this development by arguing for the application to their competitors of the same sort of reserve requirements and control by directives as those to which the banks are subjected. This is an argument, however, for what is technically known as a 'second-best' solution, which might or might not produce an improvement from the social point of view. That is, while the equalization of conditions of competition between banks and rival financial intermediaries would improve the allocation of a given amount of resources between the two types of institutions, the imposition of comparable taxation on all intermediaries would involve a socially non-optimal restriction of all financial intermediation as compared with alternative economic activities, and the social loss on this account might outweigh the gain from improved allocation of resources among financial intermediaries. Improvement from the social point of view is far more likely to be attained by mitigation of the special implicit tax burden which existing techniques of monetary control impose on the commercial banking system.

III. Problems of efficiency in stabilization policy

Stabilization policy, as defined above, comprises the use of the government's instruments of economic control—monetary policy, fiscal policy, and possibly exchange rate policy as well as more direct and selective controls—to keep the economy on a desired path of evolution in the face of spontaneous destabilizing developments in the economic system. The general nature of the corrective actions that may need to be taken is familiar from the Keynesian theory of income determination and the associated theories of fiscal and monetary policy. These theories are, however, couched in terms of static equilibrium analysis, whereas the stabilization problem in practice requires the use of policy instruments which operate with a varying ('distributed') lag on an economic system that responds to both spontaneous and policy-induced changes according to its own distributed lag pattern. This fact creates a problem of efficiency in the design and operation of stabilization policy, quite apart from the problem of efficiency in the selection of the desired path of evolution of the economy, to be considered in the next section.

Ideally, those responsible for stabilization policy should be armed both with full knowledge of the distributed lag structures according to which the economy reacts to spontaneous and policy-induced changes, and with the means of forecasting accurately the spontaneous changes that it is the responsibility of stabilization policy to offset. Near-perfect or perfect stabilization would then be possible.

In practice, however, forecasting ability is limited, and the authorities have to rely to a large extent on responding in their policy actions to deviations of the current or immediately past performance of the economy from the desired path of evolution. Moreover, knowledge of the pattern and time distribution of lags in the response of the economy to spontaneous and policy-induced changes is also limited. This situation raises problems of efficiency in the design of policy responses to deviations in actual from desired performance; questions about the efficiency of stabilization policies as traditionally practiced, especially by central banks, in achieving a significant improvement in the stability of the economy; and the general problem of improving the stabilization operations of the central banks by founding them more securely on economic analysis of and empirical research on the stabilization problem.

The problem of efficient policy-response design in a system in which policy responds to deviations of actual from desired performance ('errors') is very similar to the engineering problem of designing efficient automatic control mechanisms and has been explored most thoroughly by electrical engineers interested in economic policy problems, notably by A. W. Phillips. An obvious point that emerges from this exploration is the importance of rapid reaction of policy to the observation of errors: The longer the lag in policy response, the lower the degree of improvement in stability that can be achieved, and the more likely is a policy response of a given magnitude to destabilize rather than stabilize the system. Less obvious, but in some respects more important, is the fact that an efficient system of economic control (stabilization) requires some mixture of three types of control reaction—the mixture and magnitudes of the control reactions depending on the general characteristics of the economic system being controlled, the lengths of the time lags in the reaction of the system to change, and the structures or time profiles of the various lags.

The three types of control reaction can be characterized as different ways of formulating the error in the performance of the system for the purposes of taking corrective policy action. Control may be based on three mathematical expressions of the error—its current level (*proportional control*), its cumulative value (*integral control*), and its rate of change (*derivative control*). Each has its advantages and disadvantages from the viewpoint of efficient stabilization. Proportional control has the advantage of pulling the economy in the right direction so long as it is off-target, but for that very reason it must fall short of the goal of stabilization; in addition, a sufficiently strong control response operating with a sufficiently long lag will introduce fluctuations. Integral control will keep the economy on target if it is already there and will tend to return it to the desired path in case of errors, but it involves a strong tendency toward overshooting especially if it operates with a long lag. Derivative control tends to stabilize the economy at its current level of operation—whatever that level may be—and may also induce fluctuations about that level if applied forcefully but with a long lag. Thus, for efficient stabilization, the three must be used in combination, both the relative and the absolute dependence on each having to be determined from the characteristics of the economy mentioned above.

The engineering approach to the requirements of an efficient stabilization policy leaves something to be desired from the economic point of view, since it formulates the problem in mechanical terms of achieving approximation to a desired stable path without reference either to the social costs of deviating from that path, or to the economy's reactions to the control operation itself. Further, this approach assumes somewhat inconsistently that disturbances cannot be forecast and that lags in policy response to errors cannot be altered, but that the requisite information on the lag structures of the economy's response to changes can be obtained. Nevertheless, the analysis does raise questions about the likely efficiency in stabilization policy of traditional central bank policy formation procedures, and it points to the need for scientific study of lag structures in the economy and in policy responses to change and for the use of the results of such study in the design of appropriate policy responses.

The prevalence of lags in the response of the policy-makers to changes in the economy, and in the response of the economy to changes in economic policy, together with the variability of these lags, has led a number of monetary experts to question whether traditional central banking operations can contribute much to the stabilization of the economy. Some—notably Milton Friedman—have become convinced by theoretical and empirical analysis that efforts at short-run stabilization given the present state of knowledge and with present institutional practices are likely to do more harm than good, and they have consequently argued that such efforts should be abandoned in favour of a 'monetary rule' according to which the monetary authority would be obliged to expand the money supply at a steady rate proportional to the normal rate of growth of the demand for money as the economy expands with stable prices. The argument for this proposal is partly that while a rule of this kind would not do as well as an ideal stabilization policy, it would produce better results than stabilization policy as actually practiced. More fundamentally, the proposal rests on the belief that arbitrary changes in monetary policy have been a more important source of economic disturbance than spontaneous changes arising in the private sector of the economy and that the primary problem of stabilization policy is to create a stable monetary environment within which the private sector can calculate rationally.

A number of economists have been concerned recently with the alternative possibility of improving the central bank's methods of management of stabilization policy to make it more effective in achieving its objectives. Formally, the central bank (and, more generally, the economic policy authorities) can be conceived of as making policy decisions on the basis of certain 'indicator' variables, which are taken to reflect the current state and direction of the economy and adjusting the 'instrument' variables of policy to alter the levels of 'target' variables which are assumed to govern the operations of the economy. (The same variable may serve in more than one capacity.) The problem of maximizing effectiveness then becomes a series of subproblems in the choice of the most reliable indicator variable or variables, and the choice of target variables at once amenable to control by the central bank by use of its policy instruments and potent in governing the economy, these choices requiring an empirically validated knowledge of the structure of the economy and the time lags of its responses. One of the chief issues in this area is whether the central bank should seek to control the economy by controlling the level of interest rates, or the level of some monetary magnitude such as total money supply, bank cash reserves, the 'free' reserves of the banking system, or the cash base of the entire monetary system. There is a theoretical presumption in favor of control of a monetary magnitude rather than interest rates (and, among the monetary magnitudes, in favour of the cash base) on the grounds of directness of control and clarity of theoretical significance of what is being controlled, but the issue can only be resolved by empirical exploration.

Like the application of control-system engineering to the design of monetary policy responses, work on these lines has tended to suffer somewhat from taking stabilization per se as the objective of policy and the measure of success. Even on this mechanical basis, a generally acceptable measure of performance with respect to stabilization of the economy is not easy to devise. In the broader context of economic theory, however, the purpose of short-run stabilization is to increase the economic welfare of the community, and an economic measure of the success of stabilization policy would have to specify what welfare is presumed to be in this context and how it is affected by stabilization policy operations. A major implication of the concept of 'stability' as an objective of policy is that stability will improve the accuracy of the calculations and predictions on the basis of which resources are allocated among current uses and between current consumption and investment for the satisfaction of future needs. This suggests that both the formulation of policy and the evaluation of its success require a formal definition of the economic costs of instability more sophisticated than some mechanical measure of the deviations of indicator variables from a trend or norm. It also suggests that there may arise internal contradictions between the objective of stabilization policy and the means employed to implement it, in the sense that stabilization operations, by disturbing public expectations derived from previous experience, may cause more distortions of private economic calculations than they prevent. The proponents of a 'monetary rule' believe that stability would be improved by removing the possibility of arbitrary discretionary policy changes by the central bank. Whether that belief is justified or not, it is clear that knowledge of the mechanisms by which the expectations of the public are formed, and the influence on these expectations of policy actions, is of great importance to the design of short-run stabilization policy, and these mechanisms cannot be fully satisfactorily dealt with by compressing them into the distributed lag structure of the economy.

IV. Problems of efficiency in secular economic policy

Short-run stabilization policy is concerned with minimizing deviations of the economy from its desired trend path of evolution. Secular economic policy is concerned with the selection of the desired trend path of evolution itself. While the objectives relevant to this social choice comprise at least the standard four of full employment, price stability, economic growth at a satisfactory rate, and balance-of-payments equilibrium, with possibly the addition of a fifth in the form of an equitable distribution of income, the analysis of the choice as it affects the use of the macroeconomic instruments of stabilization policy (monetary and fiscal policy) has concentrated on the first two, and specifically on the conflict or possible trade-off between full employment and price stability.

The possibility of a conflict between the objectives of full employment and price stability was discerned by writers on economic policy very soon after Keynes's *General Theory* had demonstrated that full employment was legitimately an objective of economic policy. (Previously, when the concern of policy was limited to the achievement of price stability, a similar conflict had been discerned between internal and external stability in a fixed exchange rate system, a conflict which is still urgent but lies outside the scope of this paper.) Analysis of this conflict and the social choice it made necessary was, however, confined to elaboration of the problem and exploration of the possibility of mitigating it by institutional reforms designed to increase the perfection of competition in the goods and labour markets of the economy, until the nature of the choice involved was formalized in the concept of the 'Phillips curve'.

The Phillips curve in its simplest form hypothesizes a relation between the percentage of unemployment in the economy and the rate of increase in wages or prices (the rate of price increase being lower than the rate of wage increase by the rate of increase of productivity), such that the rate of inflation increases more than proportionately as the percentage of unemployment falls and decreases less than proportionately as the percentage of unemployment increases. (In idealized geometrical textbook representations, the rate of inflation asymptotically approaches infinity as the unemployment percentage approaches zero; as the percentage of unemployment increases, inflation turns into deflation, and the rate of deflation asymptotically approaches a constant as unemployment increases.) This hypothesis derived great appeal from the fact that early empirical work, based on British data, appeared to confirm the presence of a surprisingly stable econometric relationship of this type; subsequent research, however, has called into question both the theoretical foundations and the statistical reliability of the curve.

Assuming the reality of the Phillips curve, society can be envisaged as choosing the socially optimum combination of unemployment and inflation available to it on its Phillips curve as the target which fiscal and monetary policy should be directed toward achieving.

Additionally, society would seek to use its control over the institutions of competition to shift the Phillips curve as far as possible in the favorable direction of less inflation with a given rate of unemployment and vice versa. The choice of position on a given Phillips curve can be formalized in the notion of a social preference system, attributing greater social welfare to less unemployment and less inflation, the optimal choice being represented by the tangency of an indifference curve of the preference system with the Phillips curve.

This formalization, while popular, is unfortunately rather empty of economic content, since it simply postulates that society is able to weigh more unemployed against more inflation in some unspecified manner to arrive at a preferred position. Yet the rate of inflation and the rate of unemployment, unlike the nuts and apples of conventional individual preference theory, are not strictly comparable objects of choice which can be rationally evaluated according to this theoretical schema. From one important point of view, indeed, the avoidance of inflation and the maintenance of full employment can be most usefully regarded as conflicting class interests of the bourgeoisie and the proletariat, respectively, the conflict being resolvable only by the test of relative political power in the society and its resolution involving no reference to an overriding concept of the social welfare.

If some concept of the general welfare is to be applied, it would seem necessary to go beyond the mere postulation of a social preference function comprising inflation and unemployment rates as arguments, into an analysis of the relative social costs of inflation and unemployment. The formulation of these costs turns out to be more difficult than may appear at first sight.

With respect to unemployment, it would seem natural to measure the social cost by the loss of potential output it causes; and this method has in fact been followed by the U.S. Council of Economic Advisers, among others. But this measure tends to overstate the social cost, for several reasons. One of the most important is that an expansion of employment is secured partly by a reduction in unemployment and partly by an expansion of the labour force through increased participation in it by housewives, older people, and youths, and by the working of more hours by the existing labour force. To the extent that the people or hours added to the labour supply are drawn from activities that contribute to economic welfare but are not included in the conventional measures of national income or output—such as the services of housewives in the home, or merely the enjoyment of leisure—the apparent expansion of output associated with increased employment is largely fictitious. Conversely, the reduction of output associated with an increased unemployment rate will be largely fictitious, to the extent that those who retire from the active labour force, or cut down their working hours, have been on the margin of indifference between paid employment and other, unpaid activities. The problem becomes even more serious when the activities which are close substitutes for paid employment are of the nature of an investment in increasing future earning power, as when the state of demand for labour influences the choices of youth between taking immediate employment or remaining in school for a longer period, or when overtime hours compete with self-education. Another relevant consideration is that, where workers become unemployed, the idle time is usually of some value to the unemployed individual, either as leisure time, or as time for self-employment in the improvement of the individual's housing facilities, or as time to be used for searching the labour market for better employment opportunities. The value of these uses of 'idle' time should be subtracted from the value of the output lost by unemployment to arrive at the true social cost of the latter.

With respect to inflation, the appropriate formulation of the social cost depends on the assumption made about whether the inflation is expected by the public or not. If inflation is assumed not to be expected, in the sense that in spite of actual inflation people continue to make their economic decisions on the basis of an assumed stability in the value of money, inflation entails no true social cost (waste of real resources) but only a redistribution of resources from the holders of assets whose value is fixed in terms of money to those whose liabilities are fixed in terms of money. It might, however, be possible to assign a social cost—or possibly a social benefit—to such redistributions according to whether the redistribution were judged to be undesirable or desirable. If on the other hand inflation is assumed to be expected, in the sense that the calculations underlying people's decisions incorporate the rate of increase in prices that is actually occurring, market rates of interest on securities and loans fixed in monetary terms will rise to include compensation for the rate of fall in the value of money, and there will be no redistribution of resources from creditors to debtors in the market for debt instruments contracted in monetary terms. There will, however, be a redistribution of real resources from creditors to debtors on monetary assets the rate of return on which is not fixed in a competitive market; specifically, if by convention or law, currency (and possibly bank deposits subject to check) bears no interest, holders of money will suffer a loss of real resources to the issuers of money (the monetary authority, and possibly the commercial banks). Since this loss will by assumption be expected, it will create a tendency for the holders of money to economize on their holdings of it by using real resources in various ways to substitute for it (for example, by increasing the frequency of income receipts or planning a closer matching of current receipts and payments); and this substitution will involve a waste of resources which, together with whatever social cost or value is attached to the redistribution of resources from holders to issuers of money, will constitute the social cost of inflation in this case.

The formulation of the costs and benefits of different combinations of inflation and unemployment in this way, and the determination of the optimum position on the Phillips curve by a cost-minimization criterion of social choice, rests however on the crucial assumption that the position of the Phillips curve is given independently of the expected rate of inflation, so that society can choose to move along the Phillips curve by an appropriate choice of fiscal and monetary policy. It has recently been argued by Friedman and Phelps that this assumption does not make economic sense and, consequently, that the Phillips curve cannot be used as a basis for secular policy-making. Their contention is that the statistical Phillips curve is derived from historical experience characterized by considerable variability of price movements and by consequent uncertainty about what rate of inflation or deflation to expect, and so incorporates the average expectation about prospective price movements during the period (which may be assumed to be an average expectation of price stability). If the monetary authority, instead of allowing variability of unemployment and inflation rates, attempted to pin the economy down to a particular position on the Phillips curve which involved a non-zero rate of price change, the public would come to expect this rate of price change and attempt to incorporate it in wage bargains and price-determination decisions. Consequently, in diagrammatic terms, the Phillips curve would shift upward. The unemployment rate initially associated with price stability would gradually come to require the rate of inflation the authorities had selected as their target, so that the benefit of lower unemployment would gradually disappear leaving no offset to the costs of inflation; or, conversely, unemployment could only be held at a level lower than that consistent with price stability by ever accelerating inflation and the associated rising social cost.

On this analysis, society does not in fact face a choice between alternative combinations of rates of inflation and rates of unemployment. Instead, the choices facing it involve securing transitional benefits from less unemployment currently and in the near future, at the expense of greater costs of inflation in the more remote future. The socially optimal choice will depend on the time lag in the adjustment of the economy's expectations to experience, and on the social rate of time preference used to discount the present benefits from increased employment and the future cost of more rapid inflation.

If the social rate of time preference is assumed to be zero or attention is focused on the long-run equilibrium growth path of the economy, the problem of efficient economic policy becomes that of choosing the optimal rate of price inflation or deflation. This problem raises some extremely complex theoretical issues if the influence of monetary policy on growth, as mediated by the target rate of price change, is assumed to be the only instrument for affecting economic growth available to the policy makers, and if (as is customary in contemporary models of growth in a monetary economy) the rate of saving is assumed to be influenced by the rate of inflation. If, on the other hand, the policy makers are assumed to have sufficient other policy instruments at their disposal for the analyst to be able to isolate the influence of the chosen price trend on monetary behaviour from its influence on the 'real' side of the economic system, the solution becomes much simpler. If the distinguishing characteristic of money, as contrasted with other assets, is taken to be the non-payment of explicit interest on it, it follows from welfare-maximizing principles of the type analysed in the second section of this paper that the optimal monetary policy entails deflation of prices at a rate equal to the rate of return on non-monetary assets. This would provide an implicit rate of return on money sufficient to encourage optimal holdings of it, that is, to reduce the marginal private cost of money-holding to equality with its (approximately zero) marginal social cost. If, on the other hand, the system of provision of money were made to conform to the requirements of the social optimum, on the lines suggested in that section, the public's holdings of money would be optimal regardless of the rate of inflation or deflation chosen by the authorities, since the real rate of return on money holdings would be the same as the real rate of return on alternative assets, and the chosen rate of price change would be neutral with respect to the social welfare achieved. That being the case, it could be argued that the authorities should aim at the achievement of price stability rather than at any non-zero rate of price change, inflationary or deflationary, on the consideration not so far introduced into the analysis that the costs of rational economic calculations will be less with price stability than when prices are expected to change at some rate, even though those expectations are held with certainty.

SELECTED BIBLIOGRAPHY

Part I:

Friedman, Milton, *A Program for Monetary Stability* (New York, 1959).

Johnson, Harry G., 'Monetary Theory and Policy', *American Economic Review*, vol. 52, no. 3, June 1962, pp. 335–84. Reprinted in Johnson, H. G., *Essays in Monetary Economics* (London, 1967).

Johnson, Harry G., *Alternative Guiding Principles for the Use of Monetary Policy in Canada* (Princeton International Finance Series No. 44), November 1963. Reprinted in Johnson, H. G., *Essays in Monetary Economics.*

Part II:

Johnson, Harry G., 'The Report on Bank Charges', *Banker's Magazine*, vol. 204, no. 1481, August 1967, pp. 64–8.

Meltzer, Allan, 'Major Issues in the Regulation of Financial Institutions', *Journal of Political Economy* (Supplement), vol. 75, no. 4, Pt. II, August 1967, pp. 482–501; and comments by Adelman, M. A., Marty, A. L., Tobin, James, and Walker, Charles E.

Part III:

Phillips, A. W., 'Stabilization Policy in a Closed Economy', *Economic Journal*, vol. 59, no. 254, June 1954, pp. 290–323.

Saving, T. R., 'Monetary-Policy Targets and Indicators', *Journal of Political Economy* (Supplement), vol. 75, no. 4, Pt. II, August 1967, pp. 446–56; and comments by Horwich, George, and Hood, William C.

Part IV:

Johnson, Harry G., 'Money in a Neo-Classical One-Sector Growth Model', in Johnson, H. G., *Essays in Monetary Economics.*

Phelps, E. S., 'Phillips Curves, Expectations of Inflation and Optimal Unemployment over Time', *Economica*, vol. 34, no. 135, August 1967, pp. 254–81.

Phillips, A. W., 'The Relation between Unemployment and the Rate of Change of Money Wages in the United Kingdom, 1862–1957', *Economica*, vol. 25, no. 100, November 1958, pp. 283–99.

Reuber, G. L., 'The Objectives of Canadian Monetary Policy, 1949–61: Empirical "Trade-Offs" and the Reaction Function of the Authorities', *Journal of Political Economy*, vol. 72, no. 2, August 1964, pp. 109–32.

16

BORROWING AND LENDING

[Extract from the National Board for Prices and Incomes *Report on Bank Charges**]

IN this Chapter we direct our attention to the general terms on which the banks borrow and lend, while in the succeeding Chapters we comment on the specific lending rates and charges of the banks under the present system.

The banks are only one part, though an important part, of the whole financial system, and no recommendations about possible changes in their activities can be made without regard to this fact. Indeed, what can be said about such changes must flow from a view of what are the desirable characteristics of a financial system.

For our part we think the financial system should be so organized that it adapts flexibly to the evolution of the requirements upon it of borrowers and lenders, that it meets these requirements adequately and equitably so that individual groups of borrowers and lenders are not arbitrarily disadvantaged, and that all the possible economies in administrative and other costs are realized. At the same time, the solvency and liquidity of financial institutions must be assisted and adequate monetary control ensured.

In relation to the banking sector of the financial system, these desiderata particularly call into question the banks' collective agreements about their deposit and certain of their lending rates, as well as their tendency to segregate some of their newer activities into specialized institutions.

As to the general nature of their activities, the banks still continue to regard their basic function as borrowing short to lend short, undertaking what are known as 'self-liquidating' loans. The loans that banks make are normally on an overdraft basis, which for the

* Reprinted from National Board for Prices and Incomes, Report no. 34, *Bank charges*, Cmnd. 3292 (London, 1967), Chapter 4, by permission of the publisher.

borrower has a distinct advantage of convenience in that interest is payable at any time on only the net amount by which his current account is in debit. This is in contrast to the system of term loans characteristic of certain overseas banking systems and practised by the British banks in the case of some of their personal loans, where interest is payable on the original amount of the loan, with agreed repayment instalments. The banks' advances are nominally recallable on demand, but this is a power which for obvious reasons they quite rightly rarely exercise. Indeed there is some tendency for short-term loans to change imperceptibly into long-term loans by a process of renewal or continuation, thus losing their nominally self-liquidating purpose.

Be that as it may, the concept of lending short derives from the short nature of the banks' borrowings. About the terms on which this borrowing is conducted the banks have made certain collective agreements. A convention exists not to pay interest on current or demand deposits—i.e., deposits subject to instant withdrawal. The non-payment of interest on demand deposits is indeed common form throughout the western world. In this country, however, the charges levied on customers for the handling of their current accounts are generally abated by reference to an offsetting allowance for credit balances. The convention not to pay interest on current accounts is sustained in the sense that the abatement of charges does not proceed to the point where holders of demand deposits may receive a positive payment on their deposits.

As far as concerns deposits open to withdrawal subject to notice rather than on demand, i.e. time deposits, the London clearing banks offer only one such kind of deposit: that withdrawable at seven days' notice. There is an agreement between the clearing banks that the interest payable on this one class of time deposits shall be at two points below Bank Rate. The practices of the Scottish and Northern Irish banks are somewhat, though not materially, different. The Scottish banks offer deposits which can be cashed on demand, but earn interest only if maintained for a minimum of one month; the rate offered on these somewhat longer time deposits is ½ per cent below the clearing banks' rate, i.e. 2½ points below Bank Rate. The Northern Ireland banks offer rates for two classes of time deposits, both at 7 days' notice: for balances of £25,000 and over they pay the clearing bank deposit rate (2 points below Bank Rate), and for other balances they currently pay a rate 3 points below Bank Rate.

Before the war there would appear to have been two agreed deposit rates for the clearing banks, one for the country and one for London. It is doubtful whether this distinction could have continued to hold good. In any case during the war both rates became merged in a single agreed deposit rate. Historically, a case can be made out for an agreement between the banks on the rate of interest to be paid on time deposits so long as the banks remained the predominant financial intermediaries, for competitive bidding on deposit rates would have raised costs for all banks while not necessary substantially improving the position of one bank vis-à-vis another.

We would question, however, whether such a justification any longer holds good. Other financial intermediaries of a wide variety have appeared and developed, issuing liabilities which, in the eyes of the investor, are closely competitive with bank deposits. At the same time investors themselves, and not least the treasurers of corporate bodies, have become increasingly discriminating in their selection of institutions with which to place short-term funds. Against the background of developments such as these, the banks have suffered a relative diminution in importance.

We have already seen [in Chap. 2 of the *Report*] that the quantity of assets which may be considered most closely competitive with bank deposits is significantly large, and that the rate of growth of bank deposits has not kept up either with the expansion of these competitive assets, or with the growth in the Gross National Product. The question arises whether any initiatives on the banks' part can help to stem this decline in their relative importance.

We consider that the banks can in fact successfully take such initiatives, and that the contrary view implicitly rests upon an assumption that the volume of bank deposits is arbitrarily determined at some level by the monetary authorities. It is of course true that the actions of the monetary authorities play a crucial role in determining the volume of bank deposits, but they do so in the context provided by the preferences of the public (including financial institutions) about the kind of assets it wishes to hold and the ways in which it wishes to borrow. The actions taken by the monetary authorities—for example in buying and selling bonds or in making calls for, or releases from, Special Deposits—will be taken with the ultimate aim of securing the stability of the economy, and are directed at such variables as the level (and pattern) of interest rates, the flow of lending and the general state of liquidity. That being so, it seems to us that the volume of bank deposits can be greater—consistently with the monetary authorities realizing their aims—the more attractive are bank deposits and the less inclined is the public to shift funds into other liquid claims.

It may be said that, because bank deposits are accepted as money, the banks as a group cannot 'lose' deposits to other financial institutions, that if, for instance, someone transfers a deposit in a bank to, say, a building society, then a deposit in that person's name at his bank will be transferred to the building society's bank account and the building society will eventually again transfer the deposit to the name of some borrower and hence to the seller of a house, that, in short, what is involved is merely a transfer in the ownership of bank deposits. Further, it may be said that if the banks remain the cheapest lenders then they cannot directly lose any lending business to other financial institutions. The logical corollary of this line of argument would be that the payment of any deposit rate is a needless cost for the banks.

The financial institutions to which deposits can be transferred from a clearing bank are of two kinds. First, there are the financial institutions that belong to the public sector—e.g. the Post Office Savings Bank and the Trustee Savings Banks. These public sector institutions lend largely to the Government; deposits transferred to them will result in an increase in their lending to the Government; cheques will be drawn on the clearing banks with a resultant fall in the latter's reserves with the central bank and therefore in its ability to maintain deposits. Secondly, there are the private sector financial institutions—e.g. hire purchase companies. Deposits transferred to them from a clearing bank will enable them to increase their lending, thus driving down interest rates and tending to raise the level of spending and income, with possible adverse effects on the balance of payments. In such a case the monetary authorities would need to take offsetting action, e.g., the sale of bonds, so as to reduce the lending power of the clearing banks themselves. Either way, whether deposits are transferred to a public sector non-bank or to a private sector non-bank, the reserves and deposits of the clearing banks suffer in the last analysis a decline. We consider, therefore, that the banks, consistently with the broad economic aims of the monetary authorities, can maintain a larger volume of deposits, the more attractive these are for the public to hold, and we think that a freeing of the deposit rate from collective agreements would produce this result.

It could be claimed that at present the banks have no need to secure for themselves a greater volume of deposits in order to meet the demands of their traditional business. But in the long run they could experience a shortage of funds even for their traditional business. More important, insufficiently attractive deposit rates are likely to inhibit the banks from experimenting with more diversified lending. We view the abandonment of the banks' present cartel agreement on deposit rates as a necessary step towards the creation of a system in which the banks could play a greater role than they do at present by developing a more diversified pattern of lending.

Historically, the British banks have stood aside from the main development of mortgage loans and instalment credit. These fields have been taken over by building societies and finance houses. Nor have the British banks diversified their liabilities. In other countries it has not been so. There is nothing in the nature of banking as such which prevents the British banks from following the example of, say, the American banks in these respects. Banks in the United States issue a wide variety of time deposits, including negotiable certificates of deposit which may be traded in the money market. And they are prominent in the field of instalment credit and in making mortgage loans. Nor are the American banks the only examples of a banking system with a more widely diversified structure of liabilities and types of lending.

To all intents and purposes it could indeed fairly be said that the present agreement between the banks on the rate for time deposits has already broken down. It has broken down in the sense that the clearing banks have established or acquired in whole or in part interests in hire purchase and other companies which are operated as quite distinct entities—their activities, that is, are divorced from those of the clearing bank. Customers offering time deposits to the clearing bank can however be, and are, diverted to these institutions where higher and differential rates of interest can be obtained. To this extent the agreed deposit rate offered at the clearing bank counter is unreal.

Various arguments are adduced in favour of the decision to run newer financial activities separately from traditional banking activities. First, it is said that an activity such as hire purchase requires special expertise and therefore special personnel. Secondly, it is contended that to keep clearing banking separate from newer banking activities makes possible the continued attraction of deposits at low rates of interest and thus low bank costs. Thirdly, there seems to be an inclination to adhere to the traditional conception of confining clearing bank activity to nominally short-term lending.

Equally weighty arguments can, however, be adduced on the other side and perhaps are all the more deserving of attention in the light of the fact that British clearing banks are almost alone in Anglo-Saxon countries in separating their new activities such as hire purchase from their clearing bank activities; in Canada and the United States and to some extent in Australia the activities are merged together. A merging should obviate some duplication of premises and personnel and should facilitate some reduction in unit costs; the great natural advantage of the banks branching system could be placed at the service of new activities. More important to our mind is the thought that segregation implies that hire purchase or instalment credit is just one new activity which the banks might develop alongside their traditional activities, whereas we envisage it rather as part of an entire spectrum of new activities, each part of the spectrum being related to another and the whole therefore being pursued more effectively together. For example, as regards the personal customer, instalment credit, in giving greater knowledge of an individual's credit-worthiness, could lead to an extension of personal loans; as regards the industrial customer, instalment credit could lead to the leasing of industrial equipment. This extension of activities could be facilitated by joint operation, but impeded by segregated operation.

A similar segregation exists between the activities of the clearing banks in London, and the activities in the same city of their overseas affiliates. A foreign institution, for instance, wishing to leave money in London can receive only the agreed deposit rate if it leaves it at the clearing bank. It can receive more than the agreed deposit rate if it leaves money at the overseas affiliate in London. Money lodged at the overseas affiliate is not, however, subject to any guarantee by the clearing bank itself. The amounts of money left there tend therefore to be limited and further amounts are placed elsewhere, even with industrial companies.

We have said that the argument adduced for the segregation of ordinary clearing bank business from new activities is that it enables the practice of discrimination between depositors to be carried on. While, that is, the customer with a large deposit is guided to the subsidiary institution, where a higher deposit rate is obtainable, small deposits are accepted at the clearing bank cartel rate. In fact, there seems to be no reason why this discrimination could not, if desirable, be conducted quite as effectively by the clearing banks if the present cartel arrangement were abandoned. Instead of the single type of 7-days' notice time deposit, the banks could experiment with offers of various maturities and differing rates for balances of specified minimum amounts offered openly over the counter.

Clearly, it cannot be 'proved' that the degree of specialization of financial activities by the clearing banks is less economic than their amalgamation, for the only comparison possible is with conditions overseas and international comparisons are notoriously difficult. Clearly also a balance has to be struck between the advantages of specialization, on the one hand, and those of amalgamation on the other. It is, however, pertinent to question the case for the relatively high degree of specialization and the segregation of activity that has occurred in the British banks in the light of overseas experience. There is also a presumption that the amalgamation of new and old business has been inhibited both by the existence of the cartel agreement on deposit rates and by the nature of the requirements by way of monetary regulation. For instance, it is clear in the case of at least one bank[1] that the more stringent requirements by way of monetary control on the traditional as distinct from the newer banking activities would have been regarded as sufficient reason in itself for that bank to take its interest in hire purchase by way of equity participation in a separate finance house. As things now stand, the basis upon which the gains of specialization are assessed is distorted to the extent that deposits received at the clearing bank counter require the holding of a liquid assets ratio of 28 per cent, including a reserve of cash equal to 8 per cent of total deposits,

[1] '. . . It is common knowledge that the authorities have wished to exercise more effective control over hire purchase lending in inflationary conditions, and that they have not hitherto found a means of doing so. It is also well known that official control over bank lendings is much more effective; even though it is normally exercised on a basis of voluntary agreement, there is a sanction which could be operated if necessary within certain well-defined limits. In so far as hire purchase business becomes a function of the banks, it becomes susceptible to control through the banking machinery. This would have been a sufficient reason, if none other had existed, to make us wish to avoid taking a direct part in this field of business, even through a subsidiary company whose actions we should have the power, and therefore perhaps the duty, to bring under formal control. It would be much better that the Authorities should find means of applying any control considered necessary directly to the hire purchase companies themselves.'

Extract from a Statement by the Chairman of Barclays Bank at the Annual General Meeting held on 4 February 1959.

whereas no similar requirements are made of the deposit liabilities of many of a wide range of financial institutions, including those which are subsidiaries of (or in which substantial participation has been taken by) the clearing banks. This unequal basis of competition between institutions must have the effect of tipping the scales against an amalgamation by the banks of their newer activities with their established ones.

The Radcliffe Committee, reporting in 1959 and faced with the question of the growing competition between traditional banks and 'near-banks', concluded in favour of maintaining the restrictions on the clearing banks while claiming impracticable any extension of control over the newer institutions. In fact controls over the volume of lendings undertaken by the newer institutions have subsequently been introduced. The placing of older banks and newer institutions on a more equal basis of competition could be brought about in one of three ways: either the restrictions on the clearing banks could be removed or mitigated, or restrictions could be further extended over the newer institutions, or some combination of the two courses could be sought. We would judge the first course—complete removal of restrictions over the clearing banks—to be unacceptable to the monetary authorities.

An appropriate solution to the problem could be found by way of requiring of deposit-taking financial institutions an appropriate ratio of liquid assets to deposit obligations, together with the maintenance of a specified ratio of capital and reserves to total borrowed funds, or total assets. Such requirements could be combined, if need be, with a reduction of the cash and liquidity ratios to which the clearing banks are currently asked to work. There is evidence that the required cash ratio of 8 per cent is greater than the banks require for clearing purposes, while the required liquidity ratio of 28 per cent is higher than the clearing banks consider necessary for commercial purposes. Just as the liquidity ratio has already come down from 30 to 28 per cent, we judge that the commercial pressures of the clearing banks for further reductions in the ratios will continue.

The purpose of requiring appropriate liquidity and reserve ratios of non-bank institutions would be three-fold. First, they would be designed in the light of recent events to help ensure the liquidity and solvency of non-bank deposit-taking institutions. The illiquidity and failure of some of them from time to time creates indiscriminate hardship for depositors and shareholders and can threaten the stability of other parts of the financial system. Secondly, the requirements suggested would place competition between banks and near-banks on a more equitable basis. Thirdly, the newer requirements which we suggest could in their turn be used as instruments of monetary control if and when this was thought necessary. It is obvious that new requirements could not be introduced overnight; their introduction would need to be phased in the light of the monetary situation as seen by the Bank of England.

We are conscious that there are other inequities between essentially competing institutions besides those which we have described. The tax system provides for the offsetting of interest payments on loans against taxable income in most cases, but there are differences of treatment as between traders and private individuals and as between different types of loan. The most generally recognized difference of treatment is the fact that private individuals cannot offset any part of their hire purchase payments against their taxable income, whereas traders can, while interest on bank loans can be offset against their taxable income by both private individuals and traders. This means among other things that an individual can enjoy tax relief of interest payments on a bank loan entered into for the purchase of a car, whereas an individual who buys on a hire purchase contract gets no relief. We do not pronounce on this problem, but draw attention to it as meriting a wider investigation.

We have advocated in this Chapter the abandonment of the agreement between the clearing banks on the rate offered on time deposits. We have also implicitly suggested that the banks should feel free to offer a range of time deposits of varying maturity dates carrying different rates of interest. These rates could also vary with the size of the deposit. For the banks to advance further into the field of long-term lending to meet the requirements of modern technology could well involve them in the necessity of issuing deposits at very long periods of notice, and thus following the example which other financial institutions are presently setting in the issue of debenture stock. We see no reason in principle why the banks should be inhibited from further diversifying their borrowing practices in this fashion if they want to.

The purpose of the recommendations we have made so far in this Chapter is to ensure that the terms upon which the banks decide to limit and specialize or extend and amalgamate their activities should not be arbitrarily distorted. The commercial judgements of the individual banks should then result in the striking of a better balance between the economies of limitation and specialization, on the one hand, and those of extension and amalgamation, on the other. This requires that the banks should be free to compete for deposits as against other institutions. If the agreed deposit rate is dissolved, it follows that there should also be a dissolution of the collective agreements maintained by the banks on lending rates.

Freedom for both deposit and lending rates would imply release from the traditional fixed relationship between both and Bank Rate. Two important questions then arise: what would be the implications of such a release for monetary policy and would more competitive deposit rates necessarily result in higher lending rates? We address ourselves in the remainder of this Chapter to these two questions.

First, the implications for monetary policy. At first sight the breaking of the traditional relationships between certain borrowing and lending rates and Bank Rate might appear to impair monetary control. We consider, on the contrary, that for a number of reasons the efficiency of monetary control need not be decreased and indeed could ultimately be increased as a result of our suggestions. In the first place, the central bank affects the lending policies of the clearing banks by the purchase and sale of bonds, such purchases or sales bringing about an increase or decrease in the banks' cash reserves and liquidity ratios, and thus increasing or decreasing their ability to lend; these open market operations of the central bank can be reinforced by a requirement that the banks shall lodge Special Deposits with the central bank from time to time which immobilize part of their reserves and decrease their ability to lend, these Special Deposits being released again when an expansion of lending is desired. These two essential instruments of open market operations and Special Deposits together with requirements with regard to reserve ratios would remain unaffected by our recommendations.

Secondly, continued use by the central bank of open market operations combined with more flexible requirements with regard to Special Deposits could mean that, in place of the immediate link between Bank Rate and certain rates of the clearing banks, which means that clearing bank rates change quickly while other rates lag behind, the effects of a given change in Bank Rate accompanied by appropriate operations in the market might spread rather more evenly throughout the entire financial system. In place of a tight link between Bank Rate and a narrow set of bank lending and borrowing rates there would in effect be a looser control, but over a wider set of rates.

Thirdly, the net effect of our suggestions should be to enlarge the scope of activity of the clearing banks and these are more susceptible than the newer financial institutions to the operations of the central bank.

Fourthly, as we indicated earlier, liquidity reserve requirements, such as we propose might be imposed upon non-bank financial institutions, could be bent to suit the purposes of monetary control if the authorities found it so desirable.

Finally, we should add that if the monetary authorities form the view that some other control of deposit rates may be required, a reserve power could be taken over the maximum deposit rates offered for specific types of deposit.

We now turn to the question whether our suggestions, and particularly the proposal that the banks should offer more competitive deposit rates, must necessarily lead to higher lending rates. In the absence of quantitative research in the monetary field which might indicate the extent of likely responses to changes in rates, no certain answer can be given to this question. We consider, however, that our suggestions would have greater implications for the relative lending rates of different intermediaries than for the general level of lending rates. We should regard the latter as more closely determined by the activities of the monetary authorities than by the influence of recommendations such as we have made. We have proposed that the banks should give up their agreements on deposit and advances rates, so that both sets of rates would be determined by more vigorous competition for business of different kinds. Competition in advance rates for advances for particular purposes would tend to drive them down; on the other hand competition for deposits would tend to raise the level of lending rates at which the banks could do profitable business. We have also proposed that banks and other deposit-taking institutions should be put on a more equal footing by imposing certain liquidity and reserve requirements upon the latter and perhaps reducing existing requirements on the former. We should expect that competition by the banks for deposits would lead to an increase in their relative importance and to some extension of their range of lending. This should enable them to achieve lower unit costs, thus making it possible to maintain profit margins without necessarily a corresponding increase in lending rates. We would also expect some diversion of borrowers from higher cost sources to the banks, so that even if a rise in bank lending rates occurred, the overall average of lending rates could remain unaffected. In any case the most successful institutions in competition would be those offering the most favourable mix of lending and deposit rates (and services), and this would be a desirable result from the point of view of the efficient use of resources.

We indicated in our report on building societies (Cmnd. 3136) [2] that, pending our investigations into the agreements between banks on deposit and lending rates, the arrangement by which the Building Societies Association recommends to its members changes in deposit rate and lending rate should stand. We did this because prima facie there seemed to be a close parallel between the two sets of arrangements. We have concluded that there is no case for agreement among the clearing banks on their deposit rate and certain other lending rates. We are forced logically to conclude also that there is no case for the continued recommendation by the Building Societies Association of appropriate deposit and lending rates for its members. It does not follow that no uniform deposit and lending rate would emerge. Uniformity would not, however, necessarily be the result of collusion and we would expect the rates to be determined more by the more competitive societies as against the weaker. The purport of this Chapter has been in part that the clearing banks should compete more aggressively with the building societies in the finance of house purchase. It follows that building societies should also compete more aggressively among themselves. We do not consider that in either case more aggressive competition would have any untoward implication for the efficacy of monetary policy.

[2] National Board for Prices and Incomes Report No. 22, Rate of Interest on Building Society Mortgages (Cmnd. 3136).

17

THE *REPORT ON BANK CHARGES*

H. G. Johnson*

The PIB's *Report on Bank Charges* brings a welcome draught of fresh air into the economic analysis of the British banking system. In place of the traditional assumption that the commercial banking system is the chosen instrument of the Bank of England's monetary policy, and that its practices, whatever their economic effects may be, are sanctified by that high destiny, the *Report* takes the more sensible and rational view that the banks are commercial institutions on which the Bank operates to implement its monetary policy, and raises the question whether the banks' practices are conducive to the satisfactory continuation of that rôle and appropriate to the maximization of the efficiency of the British financial system. It concludes that the elements of monopolistic price-fixing on which the banking system's practices are built are an important source of inefficiency which inhibits the long-run growth of the banks relative to competing financial intermediaries, recommends the replacement of price-fixing by price competition on both sides of the banks' balance-sheets, and takes the position that the techniques of monetary policy should be adjusted to the evolution of a more competitive banking and financial system. In proceeding so audaciously to challenge the conventional wisdom that has dominated the discussion of British banking practices heretofore, the *Report* opens up for discussion issues that have been debated for many years in North America and elsewhere, and that should have been discussed in this country for as long but have not been.

I am strongly in agreement with the general line of analysis and the recommendations of the *Report*, which is indeed an exceptionally imaginative and subtly reasoned document for a report of this type.

* Reprinted from the *Bankers' Magazine*, vol. 204, no. 1481, August 1967, pp. 64–8, by permission of the author and publisher. H. G. Johnson is Professor of Economics at the University of Chicago and the London School of Economics.

My major criticisms of it are that it does not delve deep enough into the fundamental issues involved in the existing regulation of commercial banking in this country, that consequently its analysis falters at various points, and that occasionally it is bemused by its central assumption—which, however, is the source of its main strength—that banking is after all a business like any other. For these defects, however, the *Report* has two valid excuses. The first concerns its terms of reference, which gave it the difficult problem of deciding how far it could legitimately venture into the area of intersection of bank charging practices and monetary policy, but, more important, implicitly limited it to the excessively narrow conception that excessive profits in banking, as in other businesses, should be remedied by reducing charges to customers. The *Report* in fact is to be congratulated on going well beyond its terms of reference rather than censured for not going as far as an unrestricted investigator should have gone. The second excuse is that, thanks to the pusillanimity of British monetary economists in accepting and indeed improving on the banking community's defences of the *status quo*, the *Report* has frequently had to break what is for this country new theoretical ground, and to do so subject to severe resource and time constraints.

Since space is limited, I shall begin my comments by outlining a more comprehensive position on the problem of bank charges than the *Report* has adopted, and using it to discuss the general analysis and recommendations of the *Report*. I shall then comment on details of the *Report* with which I disagree or alternatively would like to record agreement, for convenience taking these in the order in which they appear in the *Report*.

Banking subject to special taxes and monopoly charges

From the fundamental point of view of effects on the efficiency of the economic system, the central fact about the relationship between a central bank and the commercial banks it controls, under present arrangements in most countries, is that this relationship implicitly imposes a special tax on the banking business which is not imposed on competing financial intermediaries. That tax takes the form of the obligation to hold as cash reserves non-interest-bearing obligations of the central bank,[1] the implicit tax being the interest foregone

[1] For simplicity, the problems posed by holdings of till money are ignored at this point.

on these assets and accruing to the state in the form of the central bank's earnings on the assets it holds against these non-interest-bearing liabilities. By convention rather than by economic logic bankers are generally aware of this tax only to the extent that they are obliged by custom or law to hold more non-interest-bearing cash than they would voluntarily choose to hold. For any given level of bank assets, this tax is higher the higher the general level of interest rates, and the same applies to its effects in imposing a disadvantage on the banks in competition with rival financial intermediaries.

In addition to the taxation implicit in obligatory cash reserve ratios, banks in Britain are subject to two other forms of implicit taxation: first, the minimum liquid assets ratio and the Special Deposits requirements impose a tax by forcing the banks to hold lower-yielding assets than they otherwise would, and probably also by making the yields of those assets lower than they otherwise would be; second, directives imposing constraints on the magnitude and composition of Advances impose a tax by preventing banks from choosing the most profitable portfolio of assets. The burden of the second implicit tax, but not of the first, probably increases as interest rates rise; the discriminatory effect of the former tax on bank competitiveness with other financial intermediaries has been mitigated somewhat in recent years by the extension of similar controls to the latter institutions.

In addition to the discriminatory taxation imposed on the banks by the techniques of monetary control, additional taxation—more accurately, a tax-and-subsidy system—on financial intermediation by the banks is imposed by the banks' own charging practices, with the sanction of the alleged usefulness of these practices to monetary control; the difference from the taxes previously discussed is that the proceeds accrue to the banks as a sort of monopoly profit margin. The taxation is implicit, with respect to current accounts, in the agreement not to pay positive interest on such accounts, and the possibility (not adequately explored by the *Report*) that the interest offset on the average balance is lower than bank earnings on the corresponding assets would justify; with respect to deposit accounts, it is implicit in the wide margin below Bank rate offered on such accounts and the absence of interest-rate competition for the variety of such funds. On the assets side of the balance-sheet, there are elements of both taxation and subsidization in the fixing of advances rates in relation to Bank rate and the narrow spread of such rates, taxation being exemplified by the case of the local authority rate to which the *Report* takes objection (paras. 90–92) and subsidization by the fact that the narrowness of the rate spread precludes competition for bank credit from the less credit-worthy borrowers and so favours the credit-worthy (para. 84).[2] Owing to the composition of bank assets on the one hand and bank liabilities on the other, the rate of the charging-practices tax or the monopoly profit margin rises with the general level of interest rates, as documented in the *Report* (paras. 40 ff.).

The general effect of a special tax on financial intermediation by banks, and especially of a tax whose rate rises with the general level of interest rates applying during a period when interest rates are rising, must be to divert financial intermediation away from banks towards their competitors, and, as the *Report* demonstrates, to induce the banks themselves to expand their intermediary activities through subsidiaries rather than through their traditional branch-banking network. This effect is contrary to the objective of efficiency in financial intermediation, and in the long run militates against the effectiveness of monetary policy on the traditional lines of general banking operations directed primarily at the commercial banks—as has been recognized by the extension of direct control methods beyond the banks to other financial institutions.

Direct controls and the banks' monopoly charging practices should both be ended

On grounds of economic efficiency (subject to one theoretical difficulty to be discussed below), what is required is to eliminate the special taxes on financial intermediation by banks, whether imposed by monetary regulation or by private monopolistic charging practices. In principle this would require not only the

[2] It may be remarked in passing that, like many other elements in the British (and other countries') financial system, the banks' charging practices tend to have a regressive effect on the distribution of income, both because wealthier and better-established borrowers are favoured with eligibility for bank advances and because the wealthier asset-holders will be shrewd enough—and will even be advised by their bankers—to seek higher-yielding assets than the current and deposit accounts that are frequently the most obvious available forms of asset-holding for the small man. It is one of the paradoxes of public opinion and policy on banking, which the *Report* attempts to dispel by reasoned argument (para. 80), that it is widely believed that low interest rates on bank loans and deposits serve equalitarian purposes, rather than the reverse.

introduction of competition among the banks (eliminating private monopoly taxation), but also, and perhaps with much more significant quantitative effect, the termination of direct controls on bank assets, minimum liquid assets ratios, Special Deposits and cash reserve ratios, and the payment of a market rate of interest on Bankers' Deposits at the Bank of England. None of these changes would be inconsistent in principle with the maintenance of effective powers of monetary control, since open market operations alone could perform the tasks of monetary management. What would be required on the part of the authorities would be, first, the scrapping of a whole series of regulations and market-rigging arrangements whose purpose, though not necessarily whose effect (compare para. 96 on practices in the Treasury bill market), is to ease the Treasury's debt-placement problems and reduce the cost to the Treasury of interest on the public debt, an endeavour which should not be the central objective of Bank of England policy and is not self-evidently in the public interest properly defined; and, second, the exercise of somewhat more effort in developing techniques of monetary control appropriate to a more competitive, efficient, and dynamic system of financial organization.

The theoretical qualification to the general principle stated above is recognized and well stated in the *Report* (para. 123). It arises from the fact that while banks compete with other institutions as financial intermediaries, bank deposits compete with currency as a means of payment; and that whereas bank depositors pay charges for using the deposit payments mechanism, and receive some interest offset for the capital they have invested in it, users of the currency payments mechanism neither pay the costs of supplying currency nor receive interest on their currency holdings. Removal of the taxes imposed on the banks, while it would remove the distortion of competition between banks and other financial intermediaries, would increase the attraction of using deposits rather than currency for payments, and so would increase or reduce distortions of competition at this margin, depending on whether the cost of supplying the deposit payments mechanism is greater or less than the cost of supplying the currency payments mechanism. Unfortunately there is no evidence on the relative magnitudes of these costs; but it could be reasonably argued that the issue is relatively unimportant by comparison with the financial intermediation issue, as the *Report* in effect assumes.

It is with respect to the fundamental principle stated above that the *Report* fails to push its analysis to its logical conclusion, and also vacillates somewhat. Initially, in response to its terms of reference, it considers the possibility of correcting the 'endowment' element in bank profits (the variation of the profit margin with the Bank rate) by a tax-subsidy scheme for bank profits geared to Bank rate; and while it recommends deferring action on this proposal until the results of increased competition have been seen, it does not make clear enough the objection that this solution, while perhaps equitable in the circumstances envisaged, would merely consolidate the taxation of bank intermediation associated with present charging practices, doing nothing to promote efficiency.[3] Later, when it comes to discuss the distorting effects of publicly-imposed implicit taxation of banks on their ability to compete with other intermediaries (paras. 67–70), the *Report* fails to ask whether this taxation may not be more inhibitory than the private taxation imposed by the charging practices that are its main concern, dodges the argument for substantially mitigating or removing them by a judgement that complete removal would be unacceptable to the monetary authorities, and proposes an alternative combining a mild reduction in the cash and liquidity ratios required of banks with the imposition of liquidity ratios and required ratios of capital to total assets on competing financial institutions. This proposal is objectionable for three main reasons. First, it ignores the tax on banks implicit in the required cash ratio, and, since it proposes no such cash reserve requirement for the banks' competitors, would not in fact secure equity of competitive status.[4] Second, it is by no means self-evident that extending the competitive disadvantages now imposed on banks to competing institutions would increase rather than reduce the efficiency of resource allocation in the British economy as a whole. Third, in arguing for the proposal the *Report* perpetrates the usual fallacy of confounding regulations imposed for purposes of monetary control with regulations designed to improve the management of the business, overlooking the simple point that

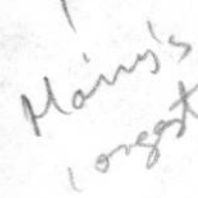

[3] In para. 54, the *Report* slips inconsistently into siding with the monopolistic justification of bank charging, by accepting the argument that 'competitive bidding on deposit rates would have raised costs for all banks while not necessarily substantially improving the position of one bank *vis-à-vis* another'; for the phrase 'raised costs for all banks', read 'turned monopoly profits for bank shareholders into competitive interest receipts for bank deposit-holders'.

[4] This oversight may be associated with the fact that the *Report* confusingly uses the terms 'reserves' and 'reserve ratio' to refer both to cash reserves and to capital reserves.

liquid assets held to conform to a monetary regulation are by that very fact not available for use in emergencies, which emergencies have to be provided for out of additional 'free' liquidity. Finally, it is unfortunate that the *Report* should have qualified its general enthusiasm for competition by conceding a possible need for the authorities to assume reserve powers to set maximum deposit interest rates against the chance of 'destabilizing rate competition', thus lending its authority to the hoary myth that bank managements are irresponsible speculators, and the fallacious view that if they are they can be frustrated by preventing them from using their own judgement with respect to one small aspect only of their business.

Turning to the details of the *Report*, I find the discussion of bank profits somewhat unsatisfactory, at least as regards the concept of the 'endowment' element in profits. In the middle of the chapter, the *Report* switches from the rate of profit on shareholder capital, which is the appropriate concept for evaluating excess profits, to the profit margin on total assets, which is relevant to efficiency but not necessarily to the excessiveness of profits. In a period of restraint and high Bank rate the margin rises for the reason given, but the effects on total profits and the rate of profit will depend on what happens to aggregate assets, as well as on associated shifts between current and deposit accounts and elsewhere in the balance sheet. While all three profit magnitudes appear from the data given to have been positively associated with Bank rate since 1956, the evidence presented for the earlier period 1951–56 seems to show, on rough examination, an inverse correlation between actual profits and Bank rate, and thus to pose the question whether total profits and the rate of profit can be expected always to rise with Bank rate. I would suggest that the 'endowment' concept needs to be separated from the profit margin, and subjected to rather more careful study than it receives in the *Report*.

I agree with the main point made in Chapter 4 of the *Report*, that the amount of deposits the banks can be allowed to have at any point of time, consistently with monetary stability, depends on the relative attractiveness of deposits and competing assets, and the questions raised about the degree of specialization of the banks on traditional banking activities as distinct from new types of business. I also agree with the general argument (paras. 75–79) that more competition in banking would not impair monetary control, though I would question the importance attached by the *Report* to the Special Deposits technique; and I would go farther than the *Report* does (para. 80) in regarding the effects of competition on bank lending rates as an irrelevant question. I also agree with the argument of Chapter 5, on specific lending rates, except that I do not consider that the fact that the agreement on export credit rates was mediated by the Bank of England to be an automatic point in its favour, nor do I find it easy to translate the *Report*'s argument on this subject (para. 93) into plain English.

Chapter 6, On Charges and Commissions, seems to me rather weak. Given the dual nature of the usual charging system—a charge for entries or turnover and an interest offset based on the average balance of the account—a proper evaluation of charges should have looked at each element separately, rather than merely pass judgement on whether the net outcome seemed 'reasonable'. In addition, the *Report* consistently regards an entry-charge and a turnover-charge system as equally acceptable, though one or the other must be discriminating between depositors, depending on whether costs are proportional to number of transactions or to size of individual transaction. However, I welcome the *Report*'s recommendation of publication of schedules of bank charges, since individual haggling with the branch manager about charges has always seemed to me an inefficient and degrading procedure. Chapter 7 in my judgement makes a powerful point in its recommendation of greater flexibility of opening hours; there is no obvious reason why cheque-cashing and depositing facilities should be provided only during the hours in which banks conduct their lending and investment operations.

As regards the chapter on Disclosure of Profits, I am entirely on the side of the *Report*. More absolute drivel and sheer nonsense has been passed off as superior wisdom and arcane understanding on this subject than on almost any other connected with British banking that one can think of. It is high time that the banks were divested of the special privileges of secrecy they enjoy, in the national interest which they annexed to themselves on the basis of their success in avoiding bankruptcy after the failures of the Austrian and German banks in 1931.

Present monetary controls hinder banks' efficiency

In conclusion, the chief argument that will undoubtedly be brought against the *Report* is that all of the inefficiencies promoted by present methods both of monetary control and of bank charging are essential to effective monetary control in Britain. The *Report* indeed offers almost unlimited scope for the pompous assertion of the mysterious rectitude of the *status quo* that has become virtually the hallmark of British monetary scholarship. But it also challenges the defenders of the *status quo* to produce reasoned economic argument and statistical evidence in support of their position; this will be not only a novel exercise for many, but one rather more exacting than they may expect. They may possibly be right after all; but at least the *Report* will force a public debate on issues that so far have been kept closed by gentlemen's agreement.

18

THE *MONOPOLIES COMMISSION REPORT*

M. J. Artis*

The most important feature of the *Monopolies Commission Report* on the proposed bank merger is its indictment of the lack of competition within the banking system. The *Report* provides a second opinion which in essentials confirms the diagnosis and prescription made by the Prices and Incomes Board last year.

There are, of course, some differences of emphasis between the Monopolies Commission's analysis of the banking system and that of the PIB *Report*. The Commission's analysis is in the main concerned with the effects of the banks' cartel agreements and the special provisions for the non-disclosure of profits, upon the level of efficiency of the banks, their cost-consciousness and the degree and nature of competition between them. The Commission argues that the banks' agreements on maximum deposit and minimum advance rates lead to heavy expenditure on the provision and maintenance of extensive branch networks; but that this form of competition, although expensive, fails to operate very effectively in transmitting pressure from the more to the less efficient banks. In this way, the agreements on rates of interest help perpetuate inefficiency and encourage a lax attitude towards costs. Bad has been made worse by the provision for the non-disclosure of profits, which serves to prevent inter-bank comparisons, and by the fact that there has been a rising trend of interest rates. In the context of the agreements, this trend of increasing interest rates has automatically provided rising revenues and helped the banks to absorb

* Reprinted from the *Bankers' Magazine*, vol. 206, no. 1494, September 1968, pp. 128–35, by permission of the author and publisher. M. J. Artis is at the National Institute of Economic and Social Research and is editor of its *Economic Review*.

rising costs whilst maintaining satisfactory profits. Finally, official policy has quite severely limited the possible scope of mergers for half a century, and this too has played its part in tempering competitive pressures.

With all this, there seems little reason to quarrel. In the attitudes of the bankers, their failure to provide yardsticks of efficiency, and their inability to compare their respective performances, the Commission found evidence of a state of inefficiency in the banking system which is only too readily explained in the conditions which govern banking operations. The surprising thing is the vehemence with which the discoveries are reported.[1]

A contention in favour of maintaining the protective provisions which govern the banking system must be powerful indeed if it is to carry conviction in the face of the testimony which the *Report* bears to the damage these provisions have done. At least up until recently, however (the matter now being open to review), the main force behind the maintenance of the agreements has been the Treasury;[2] and a fragment of the Treasury's argument is recorded in the *Report*. 'The Treasury representatives', the *Report* notes, 'said that they would wish the present arrangements to survive because they believed that they enabled the major part of the credit requirements of the country's industry and commerce to be satisfied at lower rates than would otherwise be the case' (para. 206). This seems to mean that the interest rate agreements can be regarded as a mechanism by which a subsidy is transferred from other sectors to the favoured areas of commerce and industry, with bank lending rates being held at a lower level *relative to the general level* of interest rates than would otherwise be the case, and perhaps (it is not clear) with a lower general level of rates too. (For the latter to be the case would seem to involve denying that the monetary authorities either can or do control this level as an objective of policy—which is not necessarily ridiculous.) In either event it would be wrong to infer the size of the subsidy crudely from the low enforced maximum

[1] Thus the *Report* at one point describes the banks' rate agreements as having 'such a soporific effect . . . that, so long as they exist, no foreseeable change in the structure of the clearing bank system could greatly increase the degree of competition in it' (para. 230), and at another the bald statement appears that . . . '. . . the bankers when questioned by us made no satisfactory suggestions for measuring their own efficiency let alone for comparing it with that of their rivals' (para. 219).

[2] The Bank of England, on the evidence of the *Report*, apparently holds a less entrenched view.

deposit rates; for not only are the deposit rate agreements accompanied by agreements on minimum advance rates, but allowance must also be made for the excess expenditure on branches and services generated by the agreements. But even if the system operates to provide a subsidy in the way described, it does not follow that it should be supported on this account. To reach such a favourable conclusion would involve not only justifying the giving of a subsidy of this kind at all, and the consequences for equity of doing so, but also a demonstration that the costs of this particular means of subsidy do not outweigh the benefits expected of it and are not greater than those involved in alternative methods. These costs include not only the internal operating inefficiencies to which the Monopolies Commission has drawn attention, but the wider loss of economic efficiency to which the PIB *Report* pointed. On the face of it, the burden of proof on the Treasury case looks heavy; and the Commission for one was apparently not convinced by it.[3] However, the case can hardly be properly judged on the basis of the short summary given in the *Report* and quoted above. It is to be hoped that, in the course of the re-examination now promised by the Government, a way can be found to give the Treasury argument full ventilation.

It is appropriate to ask how far the Commission's analysis of the effects of the rate agreements and provisions for non-disclosure of profits could be relevant to its weighing of the pros and cons of the mergers proposed. Its direct relevance could, in the circumstances, only be very small. Since there was no sign that the merged bank would break away from the agreements or set an example on disclosure, and since the authorities' views were not sympathetic to such developments, the merger *per se* had to be judged essentially on the assumption that the prevailing rules of the game continued to hold. What is more difficult to say is how far the Commission's analysis and evidently strongly-held views on the question of the rate agreements and other provisions may have had an indirect bearing on its recommendations; how far, that is, the division of opinion within it may have been guided by unstated differences in

[3] Strictly, it is the four Dissenters only who explicitly state that they were not convinced by the Treasury argument (para. 292); but it seems fair to say that the Majority share their view. The language used in the *Report* to describe the effects of the rate agreements is, as explained, very strong, and the Majority evidently did not feel that the Treasury case was a sufficiently conclusive argument against it to prevent them from considering the abolition of the rate agreements as a condition of permitting the merger to go through (para. 277).

assessment of the relative likelihood of a dissolution of the agreements in a merged and in an unmerged situation. Perhaps significantly, it is possible to find the division of argument between Majority and Dissenters a somewhat strained one, and to find the Majority case not wholly convincing; and one can also reflect on the fact that the Government's response to the 6–4 verdict has indeed included a promise to review the case for perpetuating restrictions on bank competition. These facts are no proof that there was more to the Commission's recommendations and the split vote than meets the eye. But they are consistent with that contention.

The stated differences in opinion between the Majority and the Dissenters concern two major issues: the savings to be made from a rationalization of branches and in other ways; and the impact of the merger on the degree of competition. On other aspects of the merger—for example, the benefits supposed to accrue to the overseas business of the banks—the two sides appear to be in agreement.

The difference between the two sides on the savings issue is expressed in terms which are difficult to comprehend. Both the Majority and the Dissenters seem to be prepared to accept as an estimate of the eventual order of magnitude of the annual rate of savings in question a figure of £10 million (although the Majority also go on to argue that £10 million represents in effect an outside estimate dependent on there being no weakening of competitive pressures);[4] the two sides appear then to differ over whether this sum is 'significant' and whether if, as the banks suggested, these savings made them better able 'to hold bank charges steady' this would be a significant benefit (or indeed a benefit at all) to the consumer.[5] There is a tendency in the argument to use relative or comparative terms without clearly defining what comparisons it is proper to make; and where a comparison is suggested, which involves the future trend of bank charges, there is an unresolved disagreement about what this trend is. This is not very satisfactory; if estimates of the future trend of bank charges were in question, some figures should have been prepared. It is difficult to believe that they could have shown a flat or falling trend, if the reasonable assumption were made that the upward trend of interest rates has

[4] In para. 251. The Dissenters for their part do not trouble to make out a case for a significantly higher figure on the assumption—which is the one they make—of the merger resulting in a greater pressure of competition.

[5] Compare paras. 249 and 250 with para. 281.

now come to a stop. The prospect of steady or falling rates over the next few years, together with increased competition from outside institutions, surely promises a squeeze—perhaps a formidable one—on bank profit margins and a tendency for charges to rise. There seems in any event no necessary reason to link the savings specifically with lower bank commission charges. Perhaps it is only that these changes are the sole ones determined independently by individual banks.[6]

The second point on which the two sides take issue is over the effects the merger is likely to have on competitive pressures in the banking system. Indeed it is highly arguable that the difference of view is greater than can readily be reconciled with those agreed statements in the *Report* which deal with the prevailing arrangements and their effect on competition. It would appear from these statements that there could hardly be any change in the structure of the system which could materially affect competition while the rate agreements and other provisions hold,[7] yet the two sides are able to discover sufficient potential for change in the degree of competition to make it the main bone of contention between them. The Majority go so far as to conclude that a removal of the rate agreements, in a system with three banks, would not increase competitive pressures above existing levels.

The Dissenters think that within the existing rules, the merger would produce more competition: for the large bank would be a vulnerable target and the Midland Bank in particular would be forced to adopt a more aggressive role in a three-bank system where it would initially be the smallest unit. The Majority thinks that the dominance assumed by the merged bank would take the heart out of competition by other banks, that the merged bank would not want to be too aggressive, for fear of provoking either a duopoly or a nationalization situation. Both agree that in the short term, management energies would be absorbed by the merger; neither side supposes that the merger would bring about a breakaway from the rate agreements. (The Dissenters suggest that abolition of the

[6] The banks, when asked how the savings would be used, significantly omitted to mention interest charges in a statement which must appear otherwise empty of real content. (Para. 93 states that '. . . They would use the savings in costs that would result from the mergers in four ways: to maintain charges to customers at a reasonable level, to remunerate the staff at a level which would attract the best quality, to ensure a fair return to the stockholder, and for research and development.')

[7] This is as good as said to be so in para. 220 of the *Report*.

rate agreements would be necessary to get full benefit from the merger, but do not make it an explicit condition.) For the rest, the Majority point to a reduction in the number of sources for finance for medium and small business, which the Dissenters (surely, correctly) regard as being exaggerated in view of the growth in alternative forms of finance. All in all, this discussion is not particularly satisfactory: an assertion that the merged bank would be on its mettle to protect its market share is met by another to the effect that the other banks would be disheartened at the merged bank's dominance. Assertion is met with counter-assertion. The differences seem strained. It seems clear enough from the Commission's own analysis that the merger *per se* would make little or no difference to the state of competition and it is sustainable that the change that would have ensued would be small relative to the impact of competitive pressure from outside institutions. This is a matter which receives some, but not much, attention from the Commission.[8] But it is pertinent to the competition debate, both to the extent that more powerful outside pressures must bring discipline to bear on the banking system, merger or no merger, and also to the extent they reduce the amount of difference the merger could make.

The Commission had cause to consider the extent of the challenge posed by the American banks in London, because their growth was cited by the banks under reference as a reason for merging. This, in any event, it may not be; but the Commission is content to show that the extent of the American banks' challenge had been exaggerated in the banks' submission.

But whilst it correctly denies that figures of the growth in their *total* deposits are a relevant indicator of the American banks' competitive potential (most of this growth being due to Euro-currency deals in which the clearing banks are little interested), the Commission probably overstates its position, first by concentrating entirely on the present and past position of the American banks, and second, by citing figures of the level of (appropriately defined) overall deposits and advances of American banks in relation to those of the clearing banks. Thus the Commission cite as relevant figures the volume of U.K. resident sterling-dominated deposits of the U.S. banks as a proportion of those of the clearing banks—1 per cent at the end of 1964 and 2 per cent at the end of 1967. But an alternative way of looking at the problem is to compare the change in

[8] The Note of Dissent explicitly considers Giro (paras. 286–7) and predicts a further growth in sources of finance for small business (para. 284).

deposits and advances over a period; the increment in American banks' sterling advances to U.K. residents over the period 1964–67 was in fact about 15 per cent of that of the clearing banks; in deposits the corresponding share was over 9 per cent. Thus, taken at the margin of advance of clearing bank portfolios, the competition provided by the American banks looks rather more intense than suggested in the *Report*. Moreover, what has happened in the recent past is not necessarily a very good guide; there is certainly gossip about the plans of the American banks to expand further into clearing bank territory. The Commission did submit a questionnaire to the American banks in London which inquired, among other things, how actively they sought domestic business; while this is some check on the gossip and as far as it goes a negative one, it is not clear how far the questionnaire was designed to cover future plans and intentions or referred mainly to current practice. One might wish then to vary somewhat the Commission's conclusions on the threat posed by American banks, though without necessarily accepting that this threat constitutes a case or argument for merger. More important is it to stress that so far as the competition of other financial institutions like the American banks can be foreseen to increase, so will the pressures on the banks and probably on their rate agreements grow. It is in this perspective (which is one that effectively makes much current criticism of the banks an attempt to have them save themselves before it is too late) and in the light of the Commission's own analysis of the effect of the rate agreements, that the Majority case as it stands appears not wholly convincing. Within the existing rules of the game, if this framework were accepted, there seems on the evidence more to be said—but not much, in any event—for the mergers proposed. Compared with a different proposition—abolition of the rate agreements—the merger looks much less attractive: and it is this which perhaps the Majority decision will bring about if the Treasury's review of its policy on the banks' agreements results in its reversal.

There are many more aspects of the merger dealt with in the *Report* which there is not space to review here: there is a thoroughgoing examination of the question of branch rationalization; consideration of the economies and selling points associated with size in international business; and discussion of the argument that bank size should grow as the average of loan-size demanded grows with the industrial merger movement. There is not much reason for dissenting from the Commission's arguments on these issues.[9]

A more controversial point is the Commission's consideration of the possibility that the mergers, if allowed, would lead to a duopoly situation.

The threat of duopoly is probably of rather greater significance in the final outcome than appears from the actual argument of either the Majority or the Dissenters. It was certainly an explicit element in the Government's statement disallowing the merger, and duopoly had been envisaged in the Treasury's representations as a likely eventual outcome of the mergers if they were permitted. The Bank of England seems to stand alone in regarding such an outcome without necessary dismay; and both Majority and Dissenters regard it as clearly inimical to the public interest. Yet this is not clearly argued; all depends on the circumstances which would bring about the movement to a duopoly situation. Should it prove, contrary to the expectations entertained in the *Report*, that economies of scale were the driving force, then there would be a case for considering duopoly or even monopoly as a proper system of organization (in either case probably incorporating some element of public ownership). Nor are the circumstances of outside competition in which duopoly could occur at all clearly delineated. Duopoly in 50 years' time would be, conceivably, quite a different proposition from duopoly today. But it is the latter hypothetical situation that one is in effect invited to consider because no clear time dimension is given to the discussion. As a result, the duopoly threat tends to operate in the *Report* as a kind of bogeyman. A banking dupoly might in truth be a fearsome monster, but that is not properly established in the Report.[10]

Finally, it should not pass without mention that this *Report* is

[9] There are one or two minor points where the i's remain to be dotted or the t's crossed, perhaps. For example, the *Report* does not point out that although the problem of large loans can be resolved by consortia-lending, such consortia are non-competitive devices. It also seems odd to expect consumers to give a revealing answer when asked whether there are too many bank branches and it is not revealing when they object on grounds of loss of convenience (cf. para. 224). The Commission's use of questionnaires is not always reassuring: at least, it does not make clear the difference between questions designed to give evidence of attitudes and questions designed to produce judgements which could be accepted as in some way informed or reasoned views.

[10] All that is established is that bank customers believe they would not like a duopoly, that a duopoly may in certain conditions operate like a monopoly, and that both Majority and Dissenters would dislike the idea.

replete with nuggets of fascinating information. It tells how the Bank of England made it clear that Martins Bank could not be absorbed by a non-British bank (compare Aubrey Jones' suggestion made in this Journal a year ago that a Commonwealth bank be permitted to take over a small clearing bank and opt out of the agreements); and how the channels of communication between the Bank and the clearing banks became so confused that Barclays and Lloyds still believed there was a ban on mergers of the Big Five at a time when the National Provincial and Westminster were planning theirs. It discloses that one of the banks would not mind bidding direct for Treasury bills on its own behalf, and that Barclays would be willing to disclose their true profits; and it criticizes the constitution of the bankers' clearing house.

The Monopolies Commission Report on the bank mergers is an important document. Its analysis complements that produced by the PIB a year ago, and in so doing has compelled the Treasury to review its case for restraining competition in the banking system. Its examination of the banks' case for a merger is thorough and severe, but it is hard to point to more than the occasional misplaced emphasis. The concluding section of the *Report*, containing the division of recommendations, appears the least satisfactory part of it. This may be only the reflection of a delicate balance of argument; but perhaps it is also partly due to the play of unstated considerations more intimately connected with the Commission's basic underlying analysis than could be the direct arguments for and against the merger.

V

FINANCIAL INTERMEDIARIES

V

FINANCIAL INTERMEDIARIES

EDITED BY

N. J. GIBSON

Introduction

IN terms of the growth of their assets, insurance companies, building societies, and the savings banks—the major non-bank financial intermediaries—have on average expanded faster than the deposit banks for at least ninety years. Hire purchase finance, though of ancient origin, began to be used extensively for the purchase of consumer durables only from about the First World War. Investment trusts and unit trusts seem to have experienced their period of greatest growth since the Second World War. Trade credit, one must presume, is as old as trade itself and was certainly a significant feature in the economy of the nineteenth century. There is thus nothing new about the existence of non-bank financial intermediaries and financial intermediation, but it was not until the second half of the 1950s in the United Kingdom, with the advent of the *Radcliffe Report*, that non-bank financial intermediaries came to be considered as a threat to the effectiveness of monetary and credit policy.

The flavour of the Radcliffe approach to the whole question of financial intermediaries, together with some early cogent comments on that approach, will be found in the first article by M. J. Artis, reprinted in this chapter.

Since the publication of the *Radcliffe Report* there has been a great deal of research into the role of financial intermediaries and their significance for monetary policy. The theoretical writings of Tobin and Brainard indicate that, so long as non-bank financial assets and forms of credit are *imperfect* substitutes for bank money and credit, the activities of non-bank financial intermediaries will not be a complete offset to monetary policy, though that policy may be somewhat weakened.[1] Furthermore, Tobin and Brainard point out that it cannot be concluded that the weakening of the effectiveness of particular policy instruments is necessarily undesirable since it may mean that the economy is less vulnerable to all kinds of shocks.

On the empirical level there is now persuasive evidence that it is possible to identify and estimate reasonably stable demand for money functions, which also suggests that the *Radcliffe Report* may have exaggerated the importance of financial intermediaries as an offset to monetary policy.[2] The question remains, however, what conjunction of circumstances gave rise to the view in the 1950s that non-bank financial intermediaries were a threat to the effectiveness of monetary policy? First, it seems odd that non-bank financial intermediation had apparently either not posed a threat to monetary policy in the past or, if it had, that it had not been noticed. Rather than accept either of these interpretations it seems much more plausible to suppose that the explanation is indeed to be found in the economic and financial circumstances and intellectual climate following the Second World War.

It is well known that the United Kingdom emerged from the Second World War with a vastly inflated stock of privately held financial assets and a greatly increased national debt, relative to national income or the stock of real assets. As rationing and physical restrictions were removed it was to be expected that people would attempt to substitute financial assets for real goods and services and so get their balance sheets and income flows into a more desired position. But at the same time, and perhaps in part as a consequence of the Keynesian revolution and in part because of a social milieu that held unrestrained market processes in distaste, together with the powerful vested interest of successive governments in trying to keep down the cost of servicing the national debt, there was a determined desire, at first, to keep market interest rates on government debt as low as possible, and later, as stable as possible.

This conjunction of circumstances, large surplus holdings of financial assets on the one hand and a determination to keep

[1] Tobin, J., and Brainard, W. C., 'Financial Intermediaries and the Effectiveness of Monetary Control', *American Economic Review, Papers and Proceedings*, May 1963.

[2] To the extent that it holds, the same point of course applies to the interpretation of the *Radcliffe Report*'s approach given in the Artis paper, as its author has conceded to the present writer.

interest rates low and/or stable on the other, with the authorities necessarily exercising monetary and credit policy through the attempted control of the availability of credit, may provide a clue to the emergence of the view that non-bank financial intermediaries were a serious handicap to this policy. For the policy hinges crucially upon specific controls that try to contain particular sources of credit, whereas a principal function of financial intermediation is to broaden and make more efficient the markets for credit, a possibility that is clearly open in a regime of partial controls. Thus the view of non-bank financial intermediaries that emerged in the 1950s may be peculiarly related to the immediate experience of the period.

The contributions which follow the Artis article also help to throw light on a number of important aspects of the financial intermediaries debate. The Brechling and Lipsey article is a pioneering and perhaps controversial study of trade credit; the Ball and Drake paper is a sophisticated study of the impact of credit controls on consumer durables expenditure; and finally, the Revell paper is an invaluable source of information on that interesting phenomenon of the 1960s, the growth of a secondary banking system alongside the more traditional deposit banks.

FURTHER READING

Bank of England, 'The Financial Institutions', *Quarterly Bulletin of the Bank of England*, vol. 10, no. 4, December 1970, pp. 419–31 (part II); vol. 11, no. 41, March 1971, pp. 48–71 (part II); vol. 11, no. 2, June 1971, pp. 199–217 (part III).

Brainard, W. C., 'Financial Intermediaries and a Theory of Monetary Control', *Yale Economic Essays*, vol. 4, no. 1 (Fall 1964). Reprinted in Hester, D. D., and Tobin, J. (eds.), *Financial Markets and Economic Activity*, Cowles Foundation Monograph 21 (New York, 1967).

Clayton, G., 'British Financial Intermediaries in Theory and Practice', *Economic Journal*, vol. 72, no. 288, December 1962, pp. 869–886.

Gibson, N. J., *Financial Intermediaries and Monetary Policy*, Hobart Paper no. 39 (Institute of Economic Affairs, 2nd edn. 1970).

Tobin, J., and Brainard, W. C., 'Financial Intermediaries and the Effectiveness of Monetary Policy', *American Economic Review*, vol. 53, no. 2 (Papers and Proceedings), May 1963, pp. 383–400.

19

LIQUIDITY AND THE ATTACK ON QUANTITY THEORY

M. J. ARTIS*

ALTHOUGH the *Radcliffe Report*[1] was well received on all sides for its description of the financial institutions of the U.K., its analysis of the theory and practice of monetary policy has been greeted with something less than enthusiasm by academic economists.

The specific complaint has been that the *Report*'s attack on 'quantity theory' approaches to monetary policy was not complemented by a positive attempt to construct a new (and comprehensible) alternative. It is certainly true that the committee's effort to construct a new theoretical approach is characterized as much by woolliness as by novelty, that not even the central concept in this new approach—'the whole liquidity position'—is clearly defined, and that the new insights promised by the concept are not worked out in clear detail. In the circumstances it is not surprising that among economists the result has been confusion and dissension, hostility and misunderstanding: as one witness reminded the committee,[2] academic economists 'all quarrel amongst themselves so that one does not know what to believe'.

Now that the dust has begun to settle it should be possible to discern more clearly what the committee thought they were saying, and to assess some of the implications of their analysis; this task is the easier, now that we can benefit from the ex-post rationalizations

* Reprinted from *The Bulletin of the Oxford University Institute of Statistics*, vol. 23, November 1961, pp. 343–66, by permission of the author and publisher. M. J. Artis is at the National Institute of Economic and Social Research and is editor of its *Economic Review*.

[1] *Report of the Committee on the Working of the Monetary System*, Cmnd. 827. (It may be noted that where particular paragraphs of the *Report* are referred to in this article the number of the paragraph is indicated in parentheses.)

[2] *Min. of Evidence*, Qn. 13235. The witness was Mr. Tuke.

of the two academic economists on the committee,[3] as well as from the numerous contributions by other experts. Accordingly, this article aims to examine some of the arguments used by the committee in its rejection of what might be called 'quantity theory policies', and to assess, in the light of these arguments, what it meant by 'liquidity', and what insights into the modus operandi of monetary policy are suggested by this concept. In addition, statistical material has been used to illustrate and test some of the committee's conclusions on crucial issues.

Naive quantity theory

Lamentably enough, the committee had to deal first with the crudest and most simple form of quantity theory, such as enjoyed a resurgence of favour under the chancellorship of Mr. Thorneycroft. On this view increases in money supply and price levels are 'magically' linked together (i.e. in terms of the Fisher equation of exchange $MV = PT$, T and V are to be treated as constants). The committee was in no doubt that variations in money supply could be offset, in their effect on price levels, by variations in the velocity of circulation, adding moreover, that 'we . . . cannot find any reason for supposing . . . that there is any limit to the velocity of circulation' (391). Although the committee mentioned that it was statistically possible to demonstrate that rises in velocity during the past few years had financed a continuous expansion in expenditure, they did not in fact produce any such demonstration.

A. E. Holmans had subsequently tested the relationships between money supply, expenditure and price levels, using annual data for 12 countries, concluding that a close connection between changes in money supply, expenditure and price levels had yet to be proven.[4] A similar test of 'naive' quantity theory using quarterly data for the U.K. has been made here, from which the conclusion is once again, 'unproven'. Table 1 sets out the figures, the sources and definitions of which are set out at the bottom of the table. The correlation coefficient between excess money supply increase and price levels

[3] Professor Sayers's address to the British Association, 'Monetary Thought and Monetary Policy in England', reprinted in *The Banker*, vol. 110, no. 416, October 1960, pp. 671–83, and *Economic Journal*, vol. 70, no. 280, December 1960, pp. 710–24. Professor Cairncross, 'Monetary Policy in a Mixed Economy', *Wicksell Lectures* (1960).

[4] In an article 'The Quantity of Money, Gross National Product and the Price Level', *The Scottish Journal of Political Economy* (February 1961).

TABLE I

Year and quarter		(1) Real G.D.P. (seasonally adj.) (£m)	(2) Total money supply (seasonally adj.) (£m)	(3) Excess money supply increase (qr. to qr.) (%)	(4) Price increases (qr. to qr.) (%)
1956	I	4081	7897·0	—	—
	II	4089	7882·8	−0·376	0·7
	III	4085	7919·3	0·561	0·40
	IV	4100	7940·2	−0·103	2·57
1957	I	4177	7964·3	−1·574	−0·19
	II	4201	8030·7	0·259	0·48
	III	4209	8135·9	1·120	2·60
	IV	4181	8135·9	−0·665	1·12
1958	I	4193	8200·7	0·509	2·32
	II	4177	8261·7	1·126	0·72
	III	4177	8311·3	0·600	−1·08
	IV	4237	8383·2	−0·571	1·82
1959	I	4259	8480·5	0·642	1·53
	II	4358	8573·0	−1·233	−0·53
	III	4437	8692·7	−0·417	−0·98
	IV	4551	8860·7	−0·636	0·18
1960	I	4606	8945·6	−0·251	0·72
	II	4646	8981·0	−0·472	1·52
	III	4638	8938·2	−0·305	−0·18

Sources: *London and Cambridge Economic Bulletin. National Institute Economic Review, Economic Trends*, Statistical Appendix to the *Memorandum of Evidence to the Committee on the Working of the Monetary System* (vol. 2), and the *Quarterly Bulletin of the Bank of England.*

Column:

1. Derived from the *London and Cambridge Economic Bulletin* and *N.I.E.S.R. Economic Review.*
2. Money supply is defined as total net deposits with London Clearing Banks, and Scottish Banks plus cash in circulation, seasonally adjusted by the method of moving averages.
3. Excess money supply increase is defined as the excess of quarterly increase in money supply (col. 2) over the increase in real G.D.P. (col. 1).
4. Quarterly price increases derived from the deflation used in calculating constant price G.D.P. from current price G.D.P. estimates as they appear in *Economic Trends.*

(unlagged) is only 0·35; when prices are lagged 1 quarter on money, the coefficient reduces to 0·1, and with a lag of two quarters 0·09.[5] These calculations confirm that the committee was correct in condemning outright the crude form of quantity theory. The committee's views on more sophisticated forms of quantity theory are dealt with later.

The whole liquidity position

The committee did not conclude, from its rejection of naive quantity theory as a suitable approach to the theory and practice of monetary policy, that it should examine the determinants of velocity, arguing that velocity 'is a statistical concept which tells us nothing directly of the motivation that influences the level of demand.' (391) This is a reasonable conclusion from the fact that in practice velocity has to be deduced by deflating PT of the Fisher equation by M, both terms being arbitrarily defined; V is nothing but a residual. (Per contra, an independent definition and calculation of V devalues M or PT to the status of residual.)

At this point then, the committee introduced the concept of 'liquidity', analysis of which, it promised, would 'direct attention to the behaviour and decisions that do directly influence the level of demand'.

It is not easy to assure oneself that the promises made of the concept of liquidity are fulfilled. Indeed, there is no precise definition of this concept anywhere in the *Report*, and to some economists this in itself has seemed too ungracious a gesture to be ignored.[6] It does not, however, follow that because the *Report* offers no precise definition of 'the whole liquidity position' that it is suggesting something quite meaningless or suggesting nothing at all. Nor does the fact that the concept is used to mean apparently different things on different occasions rule out the possibility that these 'different things' are actually different aspects of the same thing. New concepts, moreover, characteristically involve—if they are fruitful concepts—new ways of looking at problems, and thus may appear to resist definition in terms of the old familiar concepts. It has, at any rate, now been recognized that the term 'liquidity' cannot be

[5] The correlations obtained by using seasonally *un*adjusted data are even lower.

[6] Thus Sir Roy Harrod, reviewing the *Report* in the *Westminster Bank Review*, November 1959: 'One would expect it [the *Report*] to offer a definition of great precision.' Harrod's own definition of the concept is dealt with later in the article.

ruled out if it refers to both stock and flow aspects,[7] or because it may refer to both a quantity and a quality.[8]

In distilling the meaning of the 'whole liquidity position', the aim must be to see what is involved in 'looking at the whole liquidity position', and this should be borne in mind in the following section, where an attempt has been made to arrive at a view of what 'liquidity' means, by matching the various interpretations offered against the uses of the concept in the *Report* itself.

In his early review of the *Report*,[9] Harrod suggested a definition of the concept of liquidity, which is based on Keynes' use of the term 'amount of liquidity available', by which he evidently meant something synonymous, or virtually so, with the supply of money.[10] The only concession to novelty that Harrod is prepared to make, is to consider the possibility of including unused overdraft limits along with the quantity of money, to supply the reason for using a new label for an old concept. Even this concession is qualified as worthless, as Harrod assumes that overdraft limits move with the supply of money; and for the same reason no other financial asset will qualify for inclusion,[11] so that, in Harrod's hands, the 'new' concept of liquidity turns out to be no advance on the old concept of money supply, as 'the foundation stone of British monetary theory'.

If this is the definition of liquidity, then it clearly follows, as Harrod says, that the *Report*'s 'belittling references to the significance of the quantity of money must be wrong'; it is certainly clear that the committee thought they meant something different from the supply of money by talking about liquidity, although the two are not separate. For instance, in para. 478 where the committee set out to discuss the prospective liquidity position of the economy

[7] Gaskin, 'Liquidity and the Monetary Mechanism', *Oxford Economic Papers*, October 1960.

[8] Jasay, in a generally unsympathetic review, 'The Working of the Radcliffe Monetary System', *Oxford Economic Papers*, June 1960.

[9] 'Is the money supply important?', *Westminster Bank Review*, November 1959, pp. 3–7.

[10] As Professor Sayers has subsequently pointed out in his article in *The Banker* (loc. cit.), 'Keynes was thoroughly traditional in drawing a sharp line between money and other assets.' For this reason he characterizes the Radcliffe Committee's views as 'a departure from Keynesianism'.

[11] Professor Cairncross in his contribution 'Monetary Policy in a Mixed Economy' (*Wicksell Lectures* 1960), p. 14, specifically denies that liquid deposits with non-bank institutions must move in the same direction as bank deposits. Unfortunately U.K. statistics are not comprehensive enough to give full empirical support to this statement, but some main series are shown in Table 3.

in the 1960s, they begin by observing the fall in the supply of money relative to GNP, interpreting this as an augury of decreased liquidity. But even here the committee are regarding the supply of money only as a prominent constituent of liquidity, for they move on to discuss the size and growth of deposits with banks and financial institutions outside the London Clearing Banks.

Harrod would presumably deny that these institutions constitute a source of liquidity to anyone, and argue that they are only channels of lending; but this view ignores the liabilities of the institutions in question. The fact is that money deposited in a financial intermediary is nearly as good as cash to many individuals and firms, and such deposits therefore can be held for much the same reasons as cash is held; accordingly, the need to hold actual cash balances at a given level is much reduced—it is possible to 'get by' on a smaller quantity of money.

The second view of liquidity which has to be discussed also involves the assumption—as does Harrod's view—that liquidity is a quantifiable concept, that one might speak, in one and the same breath, of 'the amount of liquidity available' and 'the whole liquidity position'. Some support, indeed, can be marshalled from sections of the *Report* in favour of the notion that liquidity is measurable; in this case, 'liquidity' will differ from the supply of money by the amount of other financial assets included in the aggregation. The argument that the current controversy over liquidity and the supply of money is strictly analogous with the Banking and Currency School controversies[12] of the last century is perhaps suggestive of such an interpretation. In addition, paras. 389, 393, 507 and 981 of the *Report* might be read as suggesting that liquidity should be construed as a quantitative concept. Again, Table 22 of the *Report* and the accompanying text (esp. para. 478) would reinforce this view, were it not for the fact that the *Report* explicitly states (478) that there is no way of aggregating the deposits held in different kinds of financial institutions in such a manner as to take account of the varying degree of liquidity of these deposits. Moreover, not only does the degree of liquidity vary between various kinds of deposit; it also varies through time.[13] Nevertheless, it is clearly implied that

[12] This analogy has been suggested by Cramp, A. B., 'Radcliffe's Victorian Forebears', *The Banker*, September 1960, and Sayers, 'Monetary Thought and Monetary Policy in England' (loc. cit.).

[13] e.g. (478) 'Building society shares, for instance, are certainly regarded as more liquid than they used to be.'

a study of such figures as are presented in Table 22[14] of the *Report* constitutes part of what is meant by looking at the whole liquidity position.

Although the use of the concept in the *Report* clearly resists it, this interpretation has undoubtedly gained a following among economists and some of its implications will be examined below. It is noteworthy that the proponents of this view do not agree with Harrod that the quantity of liquidity is no more important than the quantity of money, or that the growth of non-bank intermediaries makes *no* difference to the effectiveness of orthodox monetary policies. Even the most orthodox theorizing in this line would not deny that the creation of near-money (one of the products of financial intermediaries) makes a difference. Thus Gurley and Shaw, in their book *Money in a Theory of Finance*, whilst assuming that the banking system is the sole administrator of the payments mechanism (which allows them to theorize with a fixed definition of money), argue that non-bank financial intermediaries, 'may reduce the effectiveness of monetary policy in that a given change in nominal money has less effect on the interest rate and on the price level than it otherwise would have'. Notwithstanding which, on their analysis, the desired aims of monetary policy (control over prices and interest rates) can still be achieved by using orthodox monetary policy (controlling the supply of money)—but only by using this kind of policy with much greater severity.

To avoid such a conclusion it would not be illogical to advocate 'liquidity controls' over the non-bank sector, in order to make monetary policy effective with a minimum risk of inducing panic. The *Radcliffe Report* rejected this idea as impracticable (394) 'not mainly because of its administrative burdens, but because the further growth of new financial institutions would allow the situation continually to slip from under the grip of the authorities.'

Paish, in an early statement of views[15] on the *Report*, expressed the quantitative view of liquidity succinctly, when he said that 'an increase in non-monetary liquidity therefore has the same effect as an increase in the quantity of money, since the money set free by the increase in non-monetary liquidity is available for additional

[14] This table (p. 171 of the *Report*) shows net personal deposits with the London Clearing Banks, Building Societies, Post Office, and Trustee Savings Banks under the heading 'Liquid Assets of the Personal Sector'.

[15] 'What *is* this liquidity?', *The Banker*, vol. 109, no. 404, October 1959, pp. 590–7.

expenditure on assets'. The mechanism by which this works is presumably like that described above in discussing Harrod's interpretation.

One of the objections to this kind of (quantitative) definition of liquidity has already been mentioned—the liquidity of assets varies both relatively and through time in such a way as to defy quantification. But the committee could be expected, in any case, to reject a quantitative definition of liquidity for precisely one of the reasons for which it rejects quantity theory (by the implication of its derogatory remarks)—namely, that it would be no easier to define the limits of liquidity than to define money; this argument, if acceptable, need not deny that changes in the stock of near-money can—on certain assumptions—act like changes in the supply of money. But it is evident that something more is meant.

For its views on the quantity theory of money the Committee lent heavily on the evidence submitted to it by R. F. Kahn,[16] on the basis of which it was led to dismiss, as invalid, monetary policies of which the centrepiece of action was held to be the quantity of money. Kahn pointed out that the physical limitation of the supply of money could not in itself affect spending or prices; any such effects will flow from the level of interest rates. Demands for money to spend will be affected by interest rates, and the consequent movement in velocity will therefore be a consequence of this process. Changes in money supply, as well as changes in other factors, are necessary to achieve a given desired level and structure of interest rates. Some experts have considered that the *Report* garbled Kahn's evidence, but part (*g*) of para. 397 seems quite a fair representation: 'The Authorities thus have to regard the structure of interest rates rather than the supply of money as the centrepiece of the monetary mechanism. This does not mean that the supply of money is unimportant, but that its control is incidental to interest rate policy'. The quantitative view of liquidity can uphold the committee's position in devaluing monetary policies which take the supply of money as the centrepiece of action. For the quantitative view recognizes that the existence of a stock of near money will loosen the connection between variations in money supply, interest rates and price levels. But this is not the whole basis for the committee's shift of emphasis from the supply of money to the level and structure of interest rates, for factors other than the existence of a stock of near-money intervene to distort the connection between

[16] *Memo. of Evidence*, vol. 3, pp. 138–46 and *Min. of Evidence*, Qn. 10938–11024.

money supply and interest rates;[17] moreover the problem of drawing a line between the liquid and the non-liquid is insoluble.

Thus neither of the foregoing interpretations of liquidity meets the requirements of consistency with the use of the concept in the *Report*, or of providing insights into the monetary mechanism which cannot be manufactured from existing orthodoxy. Further interpretations have been offered, suggesting that liquidity is a qualitative concept—(803) 'the liquidity is greater the closer the assets approximate to money'. As we have shown that the committee do not regard liquidity as an independent attribute unchanged through time and comparable between assets as a quality, we must ask, what does it depend on? At the farthest extreme, liquidity may appear to be as great as people desire, since 'it is the whole liquidity position that is relevant to spending decisions' (389) and spending 'is related to the amount of money people think they can get hold of'. More concretely, the amount of money people think they can get hold of will depend on the size and composition of their assets, their borrowing power, their expectations of future income flows and the 'methods, moods and resources of financial institutions and other firms which are prepared (on terms) to finance other people's spending.' (389). The market position of a borrower thus influences his liquidity, as does the market structure of the financial sector, which influences the terms on which money can be raised.

Impressed by the ease with which would-be borrowers, frustrated in their attempts to obtain bank accommodation, found finance elsewhere, the Committee described all financial institutions as 'competing in a single market for credit' (981). It did, however, qualify this statement ('there are at some points structural faults in that market') and in its suggestion of using the 'liquidity' (or locking-in) effect of a rise in the rate of interest, certainly relies in part on the exploitation of institutional rigidities, and market imperfections. The liquidity of would-be spenders thus depends on an institutional framework which confers liquidity on assets in various ways.

What is more, in the not-so-long run, this institutional framework

[17] Nor does the committee, as we have seen, seek to suggest that the paramountcy of quantity theory policies can be restored by the eradication of the influence of near-money substitutes, either through imposing 'liquidity controls' over the entire financial sector, or by indulging quantity theory policies more severely.

shows itself to be extremely flexible in meeting liquidity requirements. The response to pressures of demand—and pressures of directional monetary controls—is the creation of new institutions and the formation of wide markets in formerly illiquid assets. Whether or not it is true that such innovations would take place so quickly as to make administrative controls over the non-bank sector permanently obsolescent is not clear, but it is certainly obvious that the committee regarded the pressure of demand as responsible for its own satisfaction, eventually, through processes of innovation.

It should also be obvious that the distribution of financial assets and other sources of liquidity is as important as the total stock. The accumulation of undistributed profits in the hands of Mrs. Robin son's[18] 'sleepy monopolies' will have different consequences for monetary policy than if the same quantity of assets were to be held by fast growing firms—notwithstanding the powerful redistribution function exercised by an efficient financial system (480, 481).

It should now be possible to see more clearly what 'looking at the whole liquidity position' entails. It certainly involves looking at the supply of money in relation to the size of the national income (388, 389, 478), and at total deposits held in a range of institutions outside the London Clearing Banks (478). The amount of trade credit in existence, the quantity and distribution of undistributed profits and the company holdings of tax reserve certificates are also important (479, 480), as is their distribution among fast and slow growers (481). In addition, some assessment of the potential for further innovation in the financial sector (or of developments in industry with similar consequences) is called for: although the *Report* tends to suggest that the forces of innovation in this field are inexorable, it could hardly hold that there are no limitations in the short run, or that such limitations cannot be manufactured (e.g. by a ban on capital issues by financial intermediaries, etc.).

In view of what has been said it should be clear that there are strong limitations to the interpretation of 'liquidity' as a (definable) stock of liquid assets, exercising a predictable effect on quantity theory policies as a stock of money-substitutes, although this is no doubt part of the import of the introduction of the concept.

[18] See Joan Robinson's article 'Radcliffe's General Liquidity', *The Banker*, vol. 110, no. 418, December 1960, pp. 790–5. There is no straightforward recognition of this point in the *Report*.

The attack on sophisticated quantity theory

The attack on naive quantity theory, which simply involves an assault on the assumption that the velocity of circulation is a constant, can of course be accepted by those quantity theorists who hold a more sophisticated position. Friedman[19] holds that the sophisticated quantity theorist can be distinguished by his beliefs on three issues—the stability of the demand function for money, the independence of factors affecting the supply of, and the demand for money, and the form of the function itself. A frequent reaction to the attack on naive quantity theory is to claim that a rise in velocity is not a neutral offset to a fall in money supply, as—other things being equal—this rise in velocity will take place in the context of higher interest rates. One of the proponents of this view—L. S. Ritter[20]—even goes so far as to claim that the accommodating response of velocity to variations in money supply is a positive benefit, since this kind of policy can thus be used 'without continuous fear that a sudden financial crisis will occur'. At the same time he maintains that monetary policy *is* effective in controlling inflation, though a gradual moderation of inflationary pressures requires a sharp change in monetary policy.

In the Keynesian tradition it has been usual to maintain that the demand function for money is of a peculiar shape (the liquidity trap thesis) and that it is, in any case, not particularly stable. The 'longer' the interest rate under consideration, the less useful will a simple form of demand function be; and most unpredictable of all, is the influence of expectations.

The *Radcliffe Report*, whilst basing a part of its theory of interest rate determination on questions of expectations, and being particularly anxious that a suitable *structure* of interest rates should be the aim of the authorities, added a new weapon to the armoury of anti-quantity theory conceptual equipment. As this form of attack has a good deal to do with the 'whole liquidity position' it seems important to examine and test it.

It has already been shown that the concept of liquidity is nowhere firmly nailed down in the *Report*; even less adequately dealt with is the process by which 'liquidity' affects the monetary system. The

19 'The Quantity Theory of Money—a Restatement' *in* Friedman, M. (ed.), '*Studies in the Quantity Theory of Money*' (Chicago, Ill., 1956).

20 In an article entitled 'Income Velocity and anti-inflationary monetary policy', *American Economic Review*, vol. 49, no. 1, March 1959, pp. 120–9.

most obvious exception to this generalization occurs in para. 392, where the impact of financial intermediaries on the relationship between velocity and interest rates is outlined. This paragraph has been hailed as an 'admirable account of the determination of the level of interest rates', by one prominent critic, John Gurley, in his very valuable and exhaustive review in the *American Economic Review* for September 1960. Substantially similar explanations of the working of a Radcliffe monetary system have been put forward by Gaskin (*O.E.P.*, October 1960) and H. B. Rose (*Banker*, March 1960), among others. It should not be surprising that Gurley finds para. 392 'an admirable account', for it bears a close resemblance to the statement of the impact of financial intermediaries on monetary policy by Gurley and Shaw.[21] The conclusion of their analysis is the advocacy of heavier doses of traditional monetary policy; the same could presumably follow for the Radcliffe Committee's analysis, were it not for the fact (deplored by Gurley) that they go out of their way to raise other factors of crucial importance in the determination of the interest rate, elsewhere in the *Report*.[22] Nonetheless para. 392 has been widely held to be the content of the *Radcliffe Report*'s 'theory'.

It will be worth stating the relevant part of the para. 392 in full; it reads: 'If there is less money to go round in relation to other assets (both physical and financial) it will be held only by people willing to make a greater sacrifice in order to hold it: that is to say, rates of interest will rise. But they will not, unaided, rise by much because in a highly developed financial system . . . there are many highly liquid assets which are close substitutes for money, as good to hold and only inferior when the actual moment for a payment arrives.' A footnote states the position even more clearly: 'i.e. the more efficient the financial structure the more can the velocity of circulation be stretched without serious inconvenience being caused.'

It had formerly been assumed[23] that the velocity of circulation is an increasing function of the short-term rate of interest; that given increases in velocity require larger and larger increases in the

[21] In their book *Money in a Theory of Finance* (Brookings Institution, 1960).

[22] In addition, as will be suggested at a later stage, the committee may hold a certain view on the creation of near money which would make the pursuance of quantity theory policies in 'heavier doses' a *non sequitur*.

[23] For instance, by Kalecki, *The Theory of Economic Dynamics*: *an essay on cyclical and long-run changes in a capitalist economy* (reprinted: London, 1965), pp. 73–9.

interest rate. Testing this hypothesis with pre-war data, Kalecki obtained encouraging results.[24] The *Radcliffe Report* seems to be suggesting that under post-war conditions such a reliable relationship will not be found to hold.

The thesis advanced in para. 392 is not dissimilar to an idea put forward by Minsky,[25] and subsequently tested with U.S. data by S. W. Rousseas[26] and Bernstein.[27] The basis of Minsky's thesis was that the process of innovation in financial institutions would result in a continuous rightward shift in the velocity-interest schedule, since financial innovation means precisely the devising of ways and means of supporting the same turnover on smaller cash balances, and minimizing the inconvenience in doing so.

The diagram (p. 357) summarizes this proposition; each k curve represents a Kalecki-type velocity-interest schedule; through time the schedule shifts to the right, so that the observed schedule is much flatter than the individual k-curves. All kinds of innovation in institutions can have the required effect—industrial integration, the creation of new institutions whose liabilities are considered to be nearly as good as money, the widening of formerly narrow markets, so that the price of an asset liquidated on those markets becomes more predictable, and so on.

An appropriate analogy as far as the statistical methodology is concerned, is with the analysis of statistical demand curves: data collected over time will not provide a suitable basis for drawing up 'the' demand curve, since the ceteris paribus conditions are almost certainly violated. An important source of disturbance to these conditions will, of course, be the relative availability of substitutes. What Minsky has suggested is that the provision of money-substitutes is systematically connected with movements along the velocity-interest schedule, since high interest régimes give the incentive to innovate in constructing new financial institutions and creating new financial arrangements; in other words, the shift of the curve is not an autonomous, quasi-accidential, or once-for-all occurrence, but a consequence of the fact that high interest rates themselves destroy

[24] op. cit., p. 77.

[25] In his article 'Central Banking and Money Market Changes', *Quarterly Journal of Economics*, vol. 71, no. 2, May 1957, pp. 171–87.

[26] 'Velocity change and the effectiveness of monetary policy, 1951–57' and 'A Rejoinder', in the *Review of Economics and Statistics*, vol. 42, no. 1, February 1960, pp. 27–35, and no. 4, November 1960, pp. 455–7.

[27] 'The response of income velocity to interest rate changes: a comment' in the *Review of Economics and Statistics*, vol. 42, no. 4, November 1960, pp. 453–5.

the ceteris paribus assumptions, by increasing the incentive to innovate.

In the articles mentioned above, Rousseas and Bernstein, working with American data, certainly demonstrate that over a comparatively short period of time (1951–9), higher velocities come to be associated with a given level of the interest rate. The precise explanation for this, and its consequences for monetary policy are not so obvious: if the potentialities for further innovation in financial

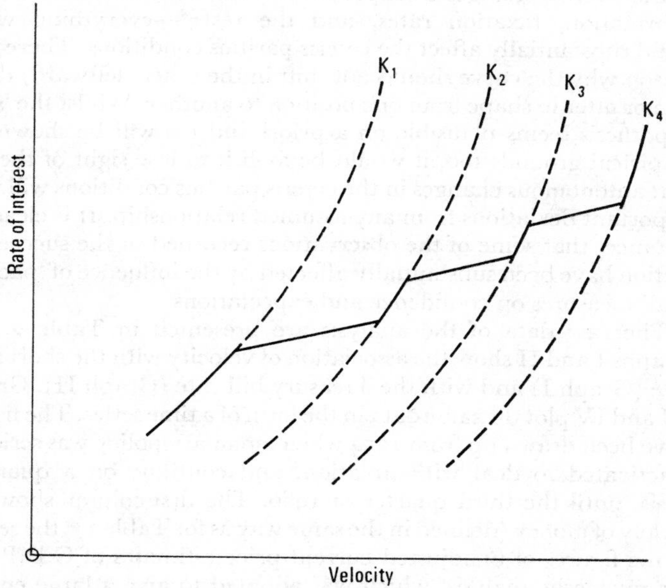

arrangements could be shown to have been exhausted, then one might view the rightward 'shift' with equanimity, and begin to talk of the existence of an asymptote to velocity. Such an assumption, however, does not seem to be warranted, at least not if the *Radcliffe Report*'s evident respect for the flexibility of the financial system is justified.

The analysis of velocity and interest rates undertaken here with U.K. data from 1954 to the third quarter of 1960 raises similar questions. It is certainly true, once again, that during this period the velocity associated with a given interest rate rises substantially.

It is tempting to interpret this as the resultant of a shift (or series of shifts) in the velocity-interest relationship of which an important cause could well be the growth of financial intermediaries—especially as the most obvious 'shift' from the statistical point of view coincides with what one could plausibly expect on economic grounds. Other interpretations readily present themselves, however: a change in any other parameter of the velocity-interest relationship could induce a similar shift, or alteration in the shape of the curve—changes in expectations, the distribution of wealth, information, taxation rates, and the rest[28]—everything which could substantially affect the ceteris paribus conditions. There is no reason why the curve should not shift in the other (leftward) direction or alter in shape from one position to another. Whilst the 'shift' hypothesis seems plausible on a priori and (as will be shown) on empirical grounds too, it would be foolish to lose sight of the fact that autonomous changes in the ceteris paribus conditions will yield important deviations from any assumed relationship. It is clear, for instance, that some of the observations recorded in the succeeding section have been substantially affected by the influence of 'package deal' measures on confidence and expectations.

The raw data of the analysis are presented in Table 2, and Graphs I and II show the association of velocity with the short bond rate (Graph I) and with the Treasury bill rate (Graph II). Graphs III and IV plot the same data in the form of a time series. The figures have been drawn up from 1954 when monetary policy was seriously reactivated to deal with inflation, and continue on a quarterly basis, until the third quarter of 1960. The first column shows the supply of money (defined in the same way as for Table 1); the second shows figures of unadjusted current price estimates of G.D.P.; for the quarterly analysis, which was adopted to give a large enough number of observations, only G.D.P. figures are available, not those for G.N.P.[29] The third column then gives the income velocity

[28] Including of course the increased exploitation of existing financial arrangements and institutions, such as would occur, for instance, after the removal of restrictions on bank advances.

[29] This excuse for using G.D.P. figures seems to be quite sufficient in the circumstances; the measurement of income velocities has always been bedevilled by controversies over the suitable definition of 'money supply' and 'income'; G.D.P. has never been, so far as I know, considered as a candidate for the latter. However, even the principles of choice between G.N.P., N.N.P., personal, and disposable income are not very clear and since G.D.P. does not move in a way too different from G.N.P. and N.N.P., honour can be maintained and expediency satisfied without resort to insistence on essentially arbitrary definitions.

TABLE 2

Year and quarter		Money supply (unadjusted) (£m)	G.D.P. (current prices) (£m)	Income velocity (v)	Treasury bill rate (r')	Short bond rate (r'')
1954	I	7815·3	3712	0·475	2·096	2·91
	II	7915·8	3848	0·486	1·848	2·59
	III	8104·8	4068	0·502	1·599	2·22
	IV	8239·1	4043	0·491	1·666	2·29
1955	I	8073·4	3985	0·494	2·909	2·66
	II	7968·1	4132	0·519	3·890	3·66
	III	8056·6	4205	0·522	4·017	4·43
	IV	8014·9	4440	0·554	4·086	4·47
1956	I	7839·4	4271	0·545	4·685	4·74
	II	7759·0	4579	0·590	5·041	4·60
	III	7958·9	4510	0·567	5·047	4·54
	IV	8083·1	4763	0·589	4·996	4·83
1957	I	7906·2	4590	0·581	4·337	4·84
	II	7904·6	4782	0·605	3·906	4·82
	III	8176·6	4775	0·584	4·415	4·98
	IV	8282·3	5035	0·608	6·527	6·04
1958	I	8140·8	4811	0·591	6·042	5·38
	II	8132·0	4947	0·608	4·921	4·69
	III	8352·9	4994	0·598	3·857	4·51
	IV	8534·1	5230	0·613	3·445	4·32
1959	I	8418·6	4793	0·569	3·174	4·11
	II	8438·4	5191	0·615	3·345	4·10
	III	8736·2	5159	0·591	3·474	4·22
	IV	9020·2	5489	0·609	3·479	4·23
1960	I	8880·3	5233	0·589	4·376	4·78
	II	8840·0	5568	0·630	5·707	5·29
	III	8982·9	5435	0·605	5·564	6·10

Sources: *Economic Trends. Monthly Digest of Statistics*, the *Economist*, and Statistical Appendix to the *Memorandum of Evidence to the Committee on the Working of the Monetary System*, vol. 2.

derived by dividing the G.D.P. figure by the money supply figure; in the fourth column is the Treasury bill rate, calculated as the weighted average of the weekly rates at the tender, and in the fifth, the short bond rate as shown in the *Monthly Digest*.

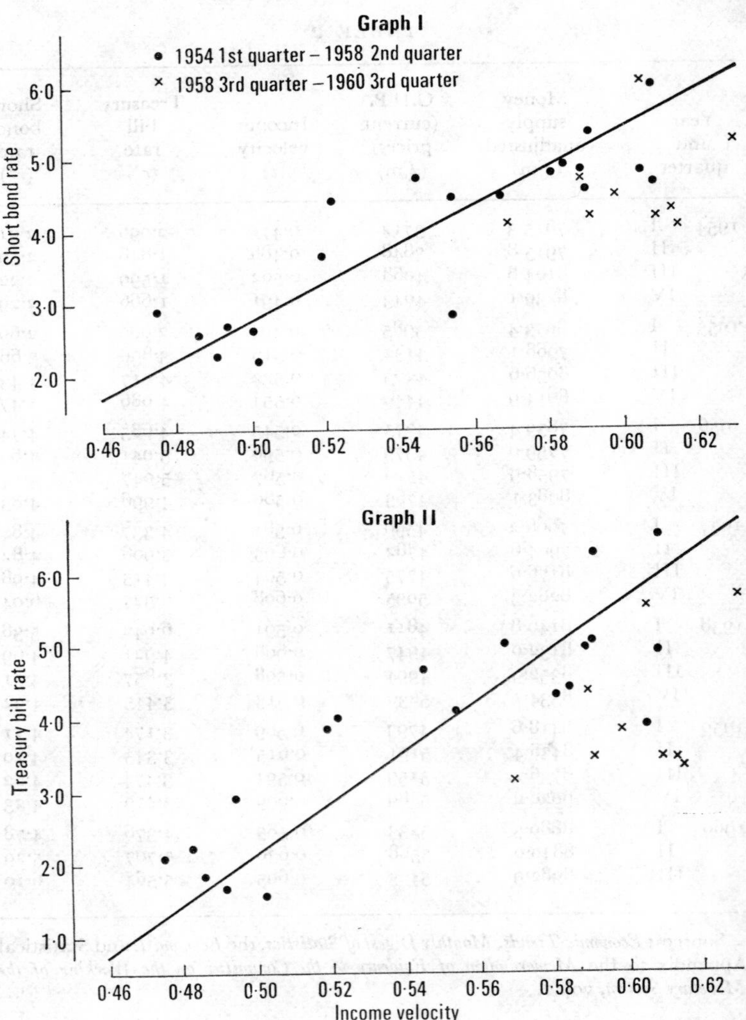

The use of the Treasury bill rate as an indicator of 'the short rate' is subject to the difficulties associated with the fact that the discount market is at one and the same time under the quasi-monopolistic control of the Discount House syndicate and the influence of the Authorities' operations. Similar kinds of objection apply to using other short term interest rates such as the rate on call money. In consideration of these difficulties the yield on short bonds has been used as an alternative indicator; whilst it would not be expected that identically similar results would be obtained, the results of using one index of the short-term rate of interest should not differ too much from those obtained in using the other.

We have already observed that towards the end of the period much higher velocities are associated with a given level of the interest rate; this is true whichever interest rate is used. In the case of the Treasury bill rate, for example, 1959 velocities of 0·569 to 0·615 are associated with a range of Treasury bill rates between 3·174 and 3·479, whilst in 1955 lower velocities, between 0·494 and 0·554, occur in a Treasury bill rate range of 2·909 to 4·086. This drift to higher velocities at given interest rates can best be seen from the two time series graphs (III and IV).

It is not clear how continuous Minsky—or the *Radcliffe Report*—supposes shifts in the velocity-interest curve to be; but if it is plausible to assume that major bursts of innovation have a long gestation period, and that tight money policies (especially policies which concentrate control directionally on a few recognized banks) provide the necessary stimulus, then it would be logical to look to the period when de-control begins for evidence of any shift that may have occurred. It is clear that, with the exception of part of 1954, the whole period up to 1958 can be regarded as a régime of restrictive monetary policies, whilst in 1958 itself the dismantling of the controls began. Nevertheless, as can be ascertained from Table 2, control over the supply of money was not significantly relaxed (indeed, the income velocity of circulation continued to increase during 1959). Table 3, which shows the growth, from year to year, in deposits with a range of financial institutions whose liabilities can be thought of as liquid, demonstrates the great increase in non-money financial assets during 1959 after the de-control in 1958 had taken place.

The economic evidence, then, would suggest that if a 'shift' occurred it would be most likely to have done so during 1958. This judgement is supported by the statistical evidence (Table 2 and Graphs I and II). For the purpose of demonstrating the extent of the shift more effectively a precise dating for the shift has been assumed in the third quarter of 1958, although it must be borne in

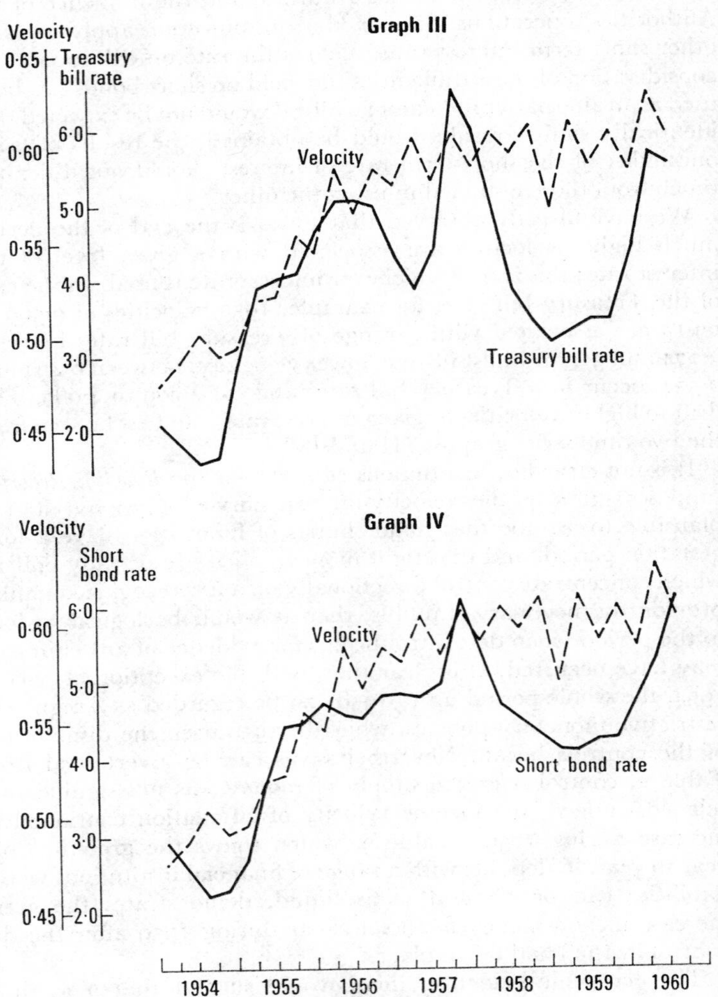

mind that the selection of this particular quarter of 1958 rather than another is essentially arbitrary. The regression lines shown in the two Graphs I and II, then, have been drawn up, in each case, for the observations of the period 1954–1958 II; observations for this period are shown as dots, and those for the succeeding period (1958 III–1960 III) as crosses. The correlation coefficients relating to the periods for which the regression lines have been drawn up

TABLE 3

Increases from year to year in supply of money, and deposits with other financial institutions in percentage form

	(1) Money supply	(2) Deposits with other banks	(3) Deposits with finance houses
Dec. 1953	—	—	—
1954	+1·9	+0·7	—
1955	−2·4	−1·3	+67·5
1956	+1·0	−1·6	−5·5
1957	+3·1	+1·7	+61·0
1958	+2·7	+0·6	+35·5
1959	+5·0	+6·4	+56·5
1960	−6·1	+6·5	+38·3

Definitions:

(1) Money supply is defined as in Table 1. End-year figures are used.

(2) Deposits with other banks include balance outstanding at year end in the Post Office Bank and Ord. Dept. of the Trustee Savings Bank, the deposits of United Kingdom residents with U.S. banks in London, British Overseas Banks, Accepting Houses, and other foreign banks and the funds of the Disc. Market borrowed from 'other sources' (i.e. excluding banks). As far as possible end-year figures have been used; discrepancies should not be too large.

(3) Current and deposit accounts with members of the Finance House Association.

The figures are mainly those from *Memoranda of Evidence to Radcliffe Committee*, vol. 2, supplemented by continuation of the series in the *Quarterly Bulletins of the Bank of England.* Figures for finance house deposits here have been drawn from the *Monthly Digest* and also those for the Post Office and Trustee Savings Banks.

are both very high; in the case of the Treasury bill rate it is 0·858, and in the case of the short bond rate 0·898. The number of observations in the period following 1958 II is too small to allow the position and slope of a new curve to be ascertained.

The sophisticated quantity theorists can still accommodate the phenomenon of a shift in the velocity-interest curve, if the rationale of the shift process can be explained in a certain way. If, for instance, the shift can be ascribed simply to the growth of a stock of near-money (i.e. the growth of a stock of money substitutes), which is not systematically connected with the implementation of tight money policies, and if the shift is thus a once-for-all or occasional occurrence, then the quantity theorist can continue to theorise on the assumption of a dependable relationship, and to advocate the same kind of policy (if necessary, in heavier doses). If the *Radcliffe Report*'s 'liquidity' concept is interpreted in the quantitative manner (and given that para. 392 of the *Report* purports to be a demonstration of the effect of liquidity on a certain monetary relationship) then it might be logical to conclude that all that is necessary in these circumstances is to implement quantity theory policies more energetically. There are reasons for thinking, however, that this is not a correct piece of reasoning: first of all, as we have already seen, liquidity is not readily definable as some given stock of financial assets; secondly, the *Radcliffe Report* has a good deal to say on the determination of interest rates in addition to the comments in para. 392; thirdly, the wording of para. 392 is not detailed enough to warrant the conclusion, on the basis of that paragraph alone, that the 'Radcliffe theory' on the effect of liquidity on the velocity-interest rate relationship is one which can be accommodated to a quantity-theory position. The general tenor of the *Report*—in particular the accent on the effect of changing expectations on monetary relationships and the emphasis on the flexibility of the financial system—suggests that the model for para. 392, is not an advanced quantity theory model but the Minsky model. In this model, as we have already seen, there is no question of 'assuming other things to be equal', since the very existence of high interest rates and tight money policies is sufficient to increase the incentive to innovate in the financial sector, and thus to infringe the cet. par. conditions.

It is in fact fairly clear that the *Radcliffe Report* does not suggest that the determination of interest rates is, or need be, left to the interaction of a stable demand function for money (modified only by occasional autonomous shifts) and the supply of money relative to the level of the national income. Since, in some cases, a rise in velocity occurs along with a rise in interest rates, and in other cases not (as in Graphs I and II), a good deal must be attributed to the influence of the 'package deal', both on psychology and on the physical framework of the financial sector. The increase in velocity which occurred between the third and fourth quarters of 1957 is no greater than that which occurred between the first and second quarters of 1959. It would be absurd to ascribe the startling difference between the movements of the rate of interest in these two periods to a shift in the curve, where all other things remain the same. The authorities in the Summer and Autumn of 1957 were very eager that other things should not remain the same.

In the *Report* itself the committee clearly state that they regard the Authorities as having power over interest rates other than their power over the quantity of money. In para. 504, policies operating on the supply of money as 'the centrepiece of monetary policy' are distinguished from those that have interest rates as the centrepiece of action. In para. 397 it is asserted that control over the supply of money is 'only incidental to interest policy'—which is a more reasonable thesis. It is not correct to extract para. 392 as the 'Radcliffe Report Theory', and particularly not if the interpretation of the theory suggested in para. 392 is of a type which automatically accommodates it to a quantity theory viewpoint. In fact, as some critics have noted, the *Radcliffe Report* is inclined to view expectations as the prime mover in interest rate determination.[30] To those who believe it is possible to salvage the essentials of quantity theory by making concessions to liquidity as a stock of near-money, this is an unpalatable conclusion, and they are thus driven to deride it, ignore it, or maintain that it is inconsistent with the para. 392 doctrine. But, as we have seen, it is not at all clear whether the doctrine expressed in para. 392 can be assimilated to a quantity theory viewpoint, or is more akin to the Minsky thesis; whilst an emphasis on expectational influences would certainly not be incompatible with the latter interpretation, it consorts less comfortably with the former.

The economic effects of the rate of interest

As we have seen, the *Radcliffe Report*, in addition to denying the 'magical' effects of crude quantity theory, also denies to variations

[30] A view characterized by Gurley, in his review article 'The *Radcliffe Report* and Evidence', *American Economic Review*, vol. 50, no. 4, September 1960, pp. 672–700, as 'the theory that interest rates are determined by words and faces' (ibid. p. 679).

in the supply of money an all-important role in the determination of interest rates. In so far as the *Report* is thus maintaining that the demand function is neither simple nor stable, and in so far as it suggests that the authorities have some control, not only of the supply of money but also over the demand for it (through the creation of certain states of expectation), the *Report* effectively denies the assumptions on which the sophisticated quantity theorist works. The circle is closed with the further denial that interest rates have a substantial effect in influencing decisions to borrow and spend, and hence on price levels.

An examination of the *Report*'s analysis of the effects of interest rates sheds further light on the concept of liquidity, and the following discussion is carried on under the headings of 'interest-incentive' and 'liquidity' effects, categories suggested by the *Report* itself.

The interest incentive effect

The Committee concluded that the effective 'bite' of interest rates—both short and long—on the body of spending and borrowing decisions is small, directional and delayed (see especially paras. 386–440).

In making these claims the Committee was not saying anything very new, and it should be said that the evidence of questionnaires submitted to it on this subject would not alone have been sufficient to support a scepticism about the interest incentive effect.[31] The fact remains, however, that ever since the well-known enquiry by Oxford economists in 1938,[32] theorists have been engaged in suggesting reasons why the direct effect of interest rates may not be very great; these contributions are probably more important than the evidence of subsequent questionnaire surveys, which may all be suspect for the reason that businessmen are expected to rationalize complex decisions in retrospect, and may well choose to omit the more minor factors influencing such decisions, which does not, of course, mean that those factors are totally

[31] Gurley, in his review in the *American Economic Review* (loc. cit.) makes it quite clear that he regards the committee as having gone *against* the trend of the evidence on this matter. This is too strong; an equally impressive case can be made out for the alternative view and the motivation ascribed by Gurley to the committee is necessarily based on circumstantial evidence alone.

[32] Wilson, T., and Andrews, P. W. S., *Oxford Studies in the Price Mechanism* (Oxford, 1951).

insignificant.[33] The factors which suggest that the committee was right in its comments on the interest incentive effect can be summarily set out as follows:[34]

(1) Risk and the length of life: where the risk of obolescence is high and the prospective life of capital equipment short, depreciation payments will swamp interest payments and the prospective rate of return is likely to dwarf the borrowing rate. The direct influence of interest rates is thus immediately concentrated on the non-risky, long-life investment.[35]

(2) Taxation System: The fact that interest payments are deductible for tax purposes means that a given change in the rate of interest has a lessened effect on the demand for investment goods if it is the absolute changes in percentage rewards that is important.[36]

(3) The extension of the public sector: The extension of the public sector has brought a large part of the interest-sensitive investment sector under direct public control. The use of the rate of interest in this case is thus either redundant (since investment plans can be modified by political decision) or wasteful (in that if no modifications are made to the investment plans, the effect is to raise the cost).

(4) The extension of the full-cost pricing sector: It is open to oligopolistic industries (and, a fortiori, monopolies) to pass on increased interest charges in the form of higher prices. The evidence furnished to the Committee by the National Union of Manufacturers[37] was explicit on this point: 'the increased cost of borrowing has been regarded, in a period of general and continuing inflation,

[33] A comprehensive bibliography of the interest-rate controversy is given in a series of footnotes by Dow, *Memorandum of Evidence to the Committee on the working of the Monetary System*, vol. 3 (especially pp. 86–7).

[34] It will be obvious to the reader that the author has derived great benefit, in preparing this section, from Balogh and Streeten's article 'A Reconsideration of Monetary Policy', *Bulletin of the Oxford University Institute of Statistics*, vol. 19, no. 4, November 1957, pp. 331–9.

[35] Shackle, G. L. S., 'Interest rates and the pace of investment', *Economic Journal*, vol. 56, no. 221, 1946, pp. 1–17; and Henderson (*Oxford Studies in Price Mechanism*), have provided the theoretical justification for this; Klein and Goldberger in their *An Econometric Model of the United States* 1929–1952 (Amsterdam, 1955)—among others—have furnished empirical evidence.

[36] This is worked out more fully in Balogh and Streeten, op. cit. See also the *Radcliffe Report*, para. 451, '. . . we were told also how taxation in effect halves the interest cost; this belief has evidently bitten so deeply into business consciousness that it may well weaken the force of interest rate changes even when it is not strictly applicable.'

[37] *Memo. of Evidence*, vol. 2, p. 137.

merely as one among many increased costs, to be passed on as far as possible in higher prices.'[38]

(5) The bias against the small firm: the difference between borrowing and lending rates removes from the margin of decision all those firms which typically rely upon reserves of undistributed profits for their investment finance. On the other hand the smaller firm, or the fast-grower, which soon exhausts its reserves, is forced to borrow from outside at the going borrowing rate: but, in addition to meeting the cost of extra interest charges on what is borrowed, the small firm is likely to find itself faced with the problem of providing adequate security for a loan, or of risking a possible loss of control by going into the new issues market. Even where the problems of providing security or maintaining control are not to the fore, the small firm may find itself forced to pay more than the large firm for the privilege of borrowing money.[39]

(6) The lagged effect of interest charges: The *Radcliffe Report* also suggested (456) that the effect of interest rates could be lagged by a year or more, since firms were sometimes induced, by the prospects of increasing interest rates, to postpone altogether work on projects which had barely been conceived, rather than to postpone work on projects actually under way. (This phenomenon was confined largely to small and medium-sized firms, and perhaps as much reflects the bias against firms of this size as the effectiveness of interest charges themselves.)

There is therefore good reason to support the *Radcliffe Report*'s view that the interest incentive effect is of minimal importance as a weapon of control, and that, in so far as it works, it does so directionally.

The committee was equally sceptical of the effectiveness of short term rates of interest, and the view that variations in the short rate can affect production via stock-building for 'we have found that stocks of commodities are extremely insensitive to interest rates' (486). It is not so clear that the committee had, in their evidence, a warrant for making so firm a claim as this, nor is the body of evidence on this subject by any means as extensive as that relating to the effectiveness of long rates. In fact, the debate initiated by Keynes

[38] In addition, oligopolistic conditions typically lead to increased profits and investment reserves, immunizing the industry from 'outside' monetary conditions: Steindl, J., *Maturity and Stagnation in American Capitalism* (Oxford, 1952).

[39] See Steindl, op. cit. and *Small and Big Business* (Monograph No. 1, Oxford 1945), also Kalecki, M., *Essays in the Theory of Economic Fluctuations* (London, 1939)

and Hawtrey on this question several years before the war, has hardly been advanced at all.

In his written evidence to the committee,[40] Sir Ralph Hawtrey laid renewed emphasis on his familiar theory that 'borrowing for the purchase of materials for sale or for the purchase of materials for use in production is bound to be sensitive to the terms of lending';[41] but no discussion of this view took place when Hawtrey gave oral evidence to the committee. Of the other witnesses who gave evidence, most of the industrialists were sceptical of the effectiveness of short term rates on stock-building, although there were some important exceptions—witnesses from the Multiple Shops Federation disagreed completely on this question,[42] those for the Scottish Chambers of Commerce[43] claimed to have heard that retailers had responded to the credit squeeze by making smaller and more frequent orders, whilst witnesses for the Federation of Wholesale Organizations[44] were almost vehement in asserting that interest charges made a significant impact on stocks.

Impressionistic evidence of this type, which the committee gained by questioning witnesses was, on the whole, biased against the view expounded by Hawtrey. Further evidence, based upon questionnaires and surveys carried out at the committee's request, was more mixed. The questionnaire carried out by the Association of British Chambers of Commerce in March 1958[45] showed that 4 per cent of those respondents who had reduced their stocks, or cut their expenditure on investment, named higher costs of borrowing as the principal consideration. The special survey carried out in Birmingham,[46] which showed that 40 per cent of those firms which had cancelled or postponed their plans since 1955, did so because of increased costs of borrowing, did not single out stocks for special consideration.

A further survey was presented to the committee, by the Federation of British Industry,[47] and this showed that 178 out of the 1595 respondents had reduced stocks during 1957 as a result of 'difficulty in borrowing'; 184 had refrained from stock-building in that period

[40] *Memo. of Evidence*, vol. 3, pp. 117–23.
[41] op. cit., para. 26.
[42] *Memo. of Evidence*, vol. 2, pp. 138 f., and *Min. of Evidence*, Qn. 8143–8210.
[43] *Memo. of Evidence*, vol. 2, pp. 97 ff., and *Min. of Evidence*, Qn. 8857–8992.
[44] *Memo. of Evidence*, vol. 2, pp. 150 ff., and *Min. of Evidence*, Qn. 6686–6750.
[45] *Memo. of Evidence*, vol. 2, pp. 85 ff., and *Min. of Evidence*, Qn. 11114–11180.
[46] See above.
[47] *Memo. of Evidence*, vol. 2, pp. 114 ff., and *Min. of Evidence*, Qn. 5525–5767.

for the same reason. In evidence, the results of these questionnaires were qualified by the witnesses, partly because of the high non-response rate common to them all, and partly because it was felt that business men could not be expected to rationalize in retrospect their reasons for reducing stocks or postponing investment; in particular it was felt that a good deal of the reduction in stocks and postponement of plans must have been due to a recession in activity, and was not directly due to the effect of interest charges.

The evidence presented to the committee on this question, was, therefore, somewhat mixed in character, but it became clear, both from the evidence of academic economists,[48] and from the responses of other witnesses, that there are strong a priori objections to the unmodified view that stocks are sensitive primarily to interest rates. Most commercial witnesses took the view that the risk of being caught 'out of stock' was worth insuring against, however high the premium (in the form of interest charges) might be. The benefits of bulk-buying, the maintenance of constant production flows, coupled with the influence of views on the likely course of prices and demand, also severely restrict the scope for interest rates in varying stock levels, especially when such a large proportion of stocks is not in fact carried on short term finance at all.

Hawtrey, in his written evidence, agreed that in those cases where costs of storage, insurance and handling were relatively large, stocks would not be interest-sensitive, but he maintained that the other 'technical' factors cited above were important only in so far as they set maximum and minimum tolerable levels of stocks, the rate of interest being responsible for determining the actual stock level between these limits. In reviewing its policy of raising Bank Rate in June 1960,[49] the Bank of England also professed the view that increased interest charges would have beneficial effects in reducing stocks, both through the increase in the cost of holding stocks, and by moderating expectations of a price rise. (Evidently, neither of these assumptions was a reliable datum.)

The fact of the matter is that it is not known to what degree stocks are interest-sensitive; the balance of a priori judgements does not accord with the Hawtrey thesis, but it remains possible that stocks of *some* goods (where costs of storage, handling, etc., are not high), and stocks held in *some* sectors of the market (especially, perhaps,

[48] See particularly, the evidence submitted by Dow, J. C. R., *Memo. of Evidence*, vol. 3, paras. 94–100.

[49] *Quarterly Bulletin of the Bank of England*, vol. 1, no. 4, December 1960.

the wholesaling sector, where short term finance is widely used) would prove to be interest-sensitive if there were adequate data outstanding on which to perform tests. In fact, present official figures, though recently much improved in coverage, do not afford a sufficiently long and consistently based time series or a sufficiently fine breakdown by type of holder or character of commodity stocked to make a thorough statistical analysis possible. In view of the allegedly crucial nature of stock-building for the balance of payments it is to be hoped that some further empirical work based on wider information can at some stage be carried out.[50] It might be added that if this digression has indicated the possibility that stocks held in the wholesale sector might be interest-sensitive, then for policy purposes, this would have to be balanced against the probability that manufacturers' stocks may counter-adjust to variations in wholesalers' stocks. Although from 1957–1960 III, wholesalers' stocks formed, on average, 11·95 per cent of total stocks the variations in this proportion were quite marked. Witnesses before the committee certainly made it clear that when wholesalers run down stocks for reasons connected with a fall in demand, manufacturers take up the slack, maintaining output and building up their own stock.[51] Before reducing output manufacturers would even grant credit on 'cut-price' terms.[52]

Thus it can be seen that, both in the case of capital equipment and in the case of stocks, investment is unlikely to be significantly affected by movements in the rate of interest, at least not by movements in the normal percentage range. The committee's support for this contention, however, seems the stranger in the case of capital equipment than with stocks, but even in the latter case there is little doubt that interest effects will be severely qualified by other factors.

The liquidity effect

Although the *Radcliffe Report* regards the interest incentive effect (the effect on borrowers) as unreliable,[53] its enthusiasm for the

[50] In his evidence to the committee (*Memo. of Evidence*, vol. 3, p. 98, para. 158), J. C. R. Dow suggested that firms seeking bank credit for stock-building should submit returns on their stocks, so that fluctuations could be quickly detected, and methods of control devised.

[51] *Min. of Evidence*, Qn. 6695.

[52] *Min. of Evidence*, Qn. 6693.

[53] Thus, para. 386, 'we have sought, without much success, for convincing evidence of its presence in recent years.'

'liquidity effect' (effect on lenders) is boundless. It argued that a 'movement of interest rates implies significant changes in the capital values of many assets held by financial institutions' (393), and that a rise in interest rates will thus make financial institutions less willing to lend—in some cases because capital values have fallen, in others because the interest rates on which the institutions operate are sticky.

This view of the effective modus operandi of interest rates has long been current in the United States as the 'locking-in effect', and was discussed, à propos of the U.K., by Nevin,[54] as the 'quantitative', aspect of the rate of interest as a policy weapon. Despite all this, several observers[55] have claimed that the liquidity effect is no different from the interest-incentive effect, so that the *Radcliffe Report* is committing a logical howler in arguing that the one is reliable, and the other unreliable.

The case for arguing that the two effects are the same rests simply on the assumption that a financial institution, whose asset values have been hit by a rise in the rate of interest, will continue to finance direct lending by liquidating its securities, and charging a higher rate of interest on its new loans, to recoup the capital loss. This is not, of course, how financial institutions do at present react to a change in interest rates, other than a change in Bank Rate; lending rates are typically tied to some institutional rate (like Bank Rate)—which may or may not allow recoupment, or, in some cases (e.g., the building societies) lending rates are adjusted only with a lag to the movement of interest rates, whether institutional or not. Some of these rigidities would no doubt vanish if the authorities were actually to pursue an active monetary policy based on liquidity effects, but it is important to notice that the liquidity effect does not rely exclusively on the exploitation of institutional rigidities and market imperfections of which adjustment with reference to 'key rates, such as Bank Rate, is a symptom.

The *Report* points out (487, 488) that the argument for using interest rates as an economic weapon is an argument for widely fluctuating rates. It is an argument, in other words, for inducing different kinds of expectation and various degrees of uncertainty

[54] *The Mechanism of Cheap Money: a study of British monetary policy 1931–39* (Cardiff, 1955), pp. 312–31.

[55] See, for instance, Jasay, 'The Working of the Radcliffe Monetary System', *O.E.P.*, June 1960, and Gaskin, 'Liquidity and the Monetary Mechanism', *O.E.P.*, October 1960.

into the environment in which financial institutions operate. The liquidity effect will not operate if a rise in the interest rate is construed as permanent; in such a case, as Mrs. Robinson has pointed out,[56] there is no distinction to be made between real and book losses and it would be unrealistic to expect financial institutions to behave as if there were.

If, on the other hand, financial institutions are uncertain about the future level of the rate of interest, they are likely to be cautious about liquidating their securities *en bloc* to finance new lending (unless of course they expect even higher interest rates to ensue and to hold for a long time); if they do make loans it is as likely that they will raise their demands for proofs of creditworthiness from their customers, as require higher interest payment from them.[57] The pessimistic atmosphere would induce a greater degree of credit-evaluation—'banks can and do, vary their concept of a satisfactory borrower, as well as the rate of interest which they propose to charge him'.[58] In these conditions some would-be borrowers will be frustrated altogether, for although they may be willing to pay more for a loan they will be unable to provide the security for it.

That the *Radcliffe Report*'s emphasis, in dealing with the liquidity effect, is actually on uncertainty, rather than on questions of lagged interest rates, has been confirmed by Professor Cairncross.[59]

Conclusion

This analysis of the *Radcliffe Report*'s attack on quantity theory, and its introduction of 'the whole liquidity position' as the conceptual basis for a theory of monetary policy shows that the stable—if not precise—relationships which characterize the quantity theorists' approach cannot be relied upon. The basis of an effective monetary policy is not, as it turns out, the fine adjustment of the supply of money (or of money substitutes), and the rate of interest, nicely calculated to reduce expenditure on the margin of profitability, but the inducement of certain kinds of expectations, the production (in emergency) of shocks, and the exploitation of uncertainty and market imperfections. Desired levels of the rate of interest are to

[56] In her article 'General Liquidity' in *The Banker* (loc. cit.).

[57] Indeed the two go together—in the most elementary sense that to accept a loan at a high interest rate arouses the suspicion that default is more likely to ensue.

[58] Nevin, op. cit., p. 315.

[59] 'Monetary Policy in a Mixed Economy', *Wicksell Lectures* (1960), pp. 37–8.

be achieved by manipulating expectations, desired levels of demand by exploiting institutional rigidities, and bruising business confidence.

Yet the attractiveness of monetary policy has always been held to reside in the fact (or rather, the supposition) that it regulates levels of demand in an optimal manner; it has been contrasted favourably with direct controls which intervene 'arbitrarily' in the market. The interest rate mechanism, on the other hand, was supposed to be capable of affecting total demand by inducing the advancement or postponement of projects on the marginal of profitability—interest entering as a cost of borrowing for all borrowers, as foregone income for those who finance their expenditure out of their own funds. Now it appears that higher interest rates are not only ineffective over large areas of industry but actually discriminate in terms other than profitability, against certain sectors of industry, so much so, that the diminution of expenditure by small firms may be counter-balanced by increased investment in the insulated oligopolistic sectors.

If the 'shock' effect of monetary policy is to be relied upon to achieve a generalized and equable effect, three limitations are immediately apparent. First of all, whilst shock tactics may achieve an overall reduction in demand, they cannot achieve it in the equable way in which interest rates are supposed to work, for the simple reason that the reaction to psychological shock depends on the psychology of the subject, and it cannot be supposed that the psychology of entrepreneurs is uniformly similar. Secondly, shock effects are not capable of the fine adjustments of which the supply of money or interest rates are; and as a consequence of this the Authorities will constantly find themselves in a difficult position, knowing that if they underestimate the shock required they will have a more difficult job on the next occasion to make their tactics effective, whilst at the same time, if the shock is overdone, it will not be easy to rectify the situation. Thirdly, as the *Radcliffe Report* makes clear, the production of shock effects of one kind—the inculcation of business pessimism—is severely limited when the government stands committed to full employment policies.

Once it is recognized that the *Radcliffe Report* did not introduce 'the whole liquidity position' as a proxy for the supply of money writ large—and that the *Report*'s emphasis is on expectations and psychological atmosphere, the case for monetary policy as an optimal weapon disintegrates. This fact, plus the regrettable woolliness of the *Report*'s own conceptual contributions, must largely explain why this recognition is not forthcoming.

20

TRADE CREDIT AND MONETARY POLICY[1]

F. P. R. Brechling *and* R. G. Lipsey*

Although the history of trade credit and its potential ability to act as an inflationary agent dates back to J. S. Mill, it has received special attention in the recent past from R. F. Henderson, the Radcliffe Committee, H. B. Rose, and R. S. Sayers.[2] Their aim was to obtain an assessment of the importance of trade credit as an institutional mechanism through which the periodic restrictive monetary policies were evaded in the 1950s. The aim of the present paper is the same: we wish, first, to reconsider the theory which predicts that trade credit may frustrate the attempts made by the

* Reprinted from the *Economic Journal*, vol. 73, no. 292, December 1963, pp. 618–41, by permission of the authors and publisher. F. P. R. Brechling is Professor of Economics at Northwestern University and R. G. Lipsey is Sir Edward Peacock Professor of Economics at Queen's University, Kingston, Ontario.

[1] The authors have given earlier versions of this paper to the L.S.E. Staff Seminar on Methodology, Measurement, and Testing, the Post-Graduate Seminar at Nuffield College, and the Staff Seminar at University College, London. We are grateful for the ideas and suggestions received at these meetings. We also wish to acknowledge valuable comments which we have had from R. Alford, G. C. Archibald, N. J. Cunningham, W. M. Gorman, R. F. Henderson, R. L. Klein, D. Laidler, H. B. Rose, R. S. Sayers, M. D. Steuer, and R. Turvey. Our special thanks are due to Mrs. June Wickins and Miss J. Roberts for research assistance. The present paper is part of a wider research project financed by the Ford Foundation.

[2] Mill, J. S., *Principles of Political Economy*, vol. 2, 4th edn., Chapter XI. R. F. Henderson, 'Trade Credit', Chap. VII, *in* Tew, Brian, and Henderson, R. F. (eds.), *Studies in Company Finance* (Cambridge, 1959). *Committee on the Working of the Monetary System*: *Report*, Cmnd. 827 (H.M.S.O., 1959), pp. 102–6. Rose, H. B., 'Domestic Trade Credit and Economic Policy' in *Principal Memoranda of Evidence* (of the *Radcliffe Report*), vol. 3, pp. 219–27. Sayers, R. S., 'Monetary Thought and Monetary Policy in England', *Economic Journal*, vol. 70, no. 280, pp. 710–24, December 1960, p. 713.

monetary authorities to reduce the private sector's expenditures and, second, to make an empirical estimate of the extent to which trade credit actually did frustrate the efforts of the monetary authorities in the 1950s.

I. Aspects of monetary policy

Consider the outcome of a restrictive monetary policy which attempts to influence national income by preventing firms from obtaining the cash balances that they require for transactions purposes. Firms may be expected to react to this policy in an attempt to restore their desired ratios between stocks of cash and flows of receipts and disbursements. Broadly speaking, there are two main ways in which this can be done: firms may alter their *income-creating payments*, or they may attempt to turn other *assets* into transactions balances. In the former case the policy has a direct influence on income, and we shall refer to this as the *quantity effect* of monetary policy. In the latter case the policy will affect income only if asset transactions cause changes in interest rates which, in turn, cause firms to revise their plans for income-creating expenditure; in this case we shall speak of the *interest effect* of monetary policy.

The maximum quantity effect occurs if all firms wish to keep rigidly to a policy of holding a stock of cash equal to k times the value of their transactions, and if all firms attempt to restore this ratio by varying income-creating payments. In this case keeping the actual stock of cash below its desired level by an amount ΔM has the effect of reducing income, initially, by ΔM, and, in final equilibrium, by $(1/k)\Delta M$.

The existence of a quantity effect of monetary policy requires either: (1) that firms readjust their actual cash ratios to their desired ones by voluntarily varying income payments, or (2) that firms are unable to adjust actual cash ratios to desired ones by asset transactions, and so are forced to reduce income payments. To the extent that (1) is expected to hold there can be no question of the quantity effect of monetary policy being frustrated by institutional mechanisms; to the extent that (2) is expected to hold, the quantity effect may be frustrated by the existence of institutional mechanisms which make cash or cash substitutes available to firms.

We may now outline the ways in which an expected quantity effect can be frustrated. We shall consider a policy which is designed to effect a once-and-for-all reduction in the price level or the level of activity by reducing actual balances below their desired level[3] (e.g., by limiting increases in the volume of bank balances). Broadly speaking, we may distinguish three ways by which firms can evade the quantity effect: (1) they may use their own idle (M_2) balances for transactions (M_1) purposes;[4] (2) they may obtain other people's idle balances; or (3) they may use their existing M_1 balances more intensively, possibly by employing money substitutes, thus raising the velocity of circulation.[5] It has often been argued that trade credit can be used to produce cases (2) and (3) either by passing idle balances, from firms which have access to them, to firms which are in need of them (case 2) or by providing a money substitute enabling firms to fulfil their plans by purchasing from each other on trade credit in spite of a reduction in bank credit.

The present paper is devoted to a study of the extent to which trade credit can and does frustrate a potential quantity effect of monetary policy. In the first half of the paper we analyse the theory of trade credit and build up a picture of the possible ways in which trade credit could frustrate the quantity effect either by increasing the stock of M_1 balances or by allowing an increase in V_1, the velocity of circulation of existing M_1 balances. In the second half of the paper we consider the evidence to see if it is consistent with the theory that trade credit has operated to frustrate monetary policy.[6]

[3] The analysis extends *mutatis mutandis* to a policy which attempts to effect a permanent change in the rate of change of prices or the level of activity.

[4] We use, as a convenient expository device, the familiar distinction between M_1 (transactions and precautionary) balances and M_2 (speculative) balances, and the corresponding concept of the velocity of circulation of M_1 balances, V_1. In doing this we do not wish to imply that firms keep such balances physically separated. It may be simplest to think of the demand for money as an additive function of transactions and interest rates: $M_D = f_1(T) + f_2(r)$. This is not necessary, however, and all that we require for our purposes is that at any one time, at given levels of T and r, there exist balances which are not circulating in the income stream but which could be used for income payments.

[5] It has several times been argued to us that there is another method by which the quantity effect can be avoided: by financing expenditure out of undistributed profits. This is indeed possible if these profits would have been added to idle balances. This is, of course, equivalent to method (1) in the text. If, however, the undistributed profits would have been spent in any case, then they cannot be used to frustrate the quantity effect of monetary policy.

[6] As is well known, there is no quantity effect in the simple textbook Keynesian model. The present study thus has important implications for the Keynesian model, since evidence that the system was working hard, with varying degrees of success, to avoid an effect which is absent from the model would clearly be

II. The theory of trade credit

i. *The individual firm*

Trade credit is defined as the sum of outstanding bills and accounts which arise out of transactions among firms or between firms and households. Trade credit given is the amount of money which is owed to a particular firm by its customers and trade credit taken is the amount the firm owes to its suppliers. The credit period is defined to be the time, measured in weeks, between delivery of goods and payment for these goods. The total amount of credit which a firm gives to its customers can then be defined as the product of its sales (averaged over the credit period) and the credit period. For instance, if the firm has weekly sales of £4,000 on five weeks' credit, then the total credit given will be £20,000. If both the credit period and the level of sales remain constant the stock of credit will remain constant as well: each week £4,000 worth of new credit will be created, but £4,000 worth of credit extended five weeks previously will be paid off. These relationships may be expressed as follows:

$$G_i \equiv c_g S_i \tag{1}$$

$$T_i \equiv c_t P_i \tag{2}$$

where G_i is the stock of gross credit given, T_i is the stock of gross credit taken, S_i and P_i are the average levels of sales and purchases of materials, respectively, c is the credit period with the subscripts g (for given) and t (for taken), and the subscript i refers to the firm.[7] In addition, we require the following definitions. The quantity $G-T$ is called the firm's net credit given if $G-T>0$, or net credit taken if $G-T<0$. The amount of credit that the firm 'passes on' is G if $G<T$ or T if $G>T$.

Our identities (1) and (2) imply that trade credit can change because of a change in the credit period and/or a change in sales or purchases. We are especially interested in *changes* in G and T.

interesting. Indeed, we believe that our evidence sheds light on the whole problem of whether or not quantity constraints are important limitations to variations in the circular flow of income of the magnitude which we normally seek to control.

[7] We here assume that all transactions are on credit. This is generally true inside the business sector; for transactions involving consumers one might wish to adjust the formulae for the proportion of transactions which are on credit, and write $T = c_t' P.p$ for the amount of gross credit taken by consumers, where p is the proportion of purchases made on credit. Since it makes little difference whether people change c' or p, we have decided to define c to include changes in p.

An increase in gross credit given (G) must be offset by an equal increase in the firm's liabilities or an equal fall in some asset (other than G). There may, of course, also be a rise in T, so that ΔG is offset, wholly or partially, by ΔT. This would require offsetting changes in the other items of the firms' balance sheet only to the extent of the change in net credit ($\Delta G - \Delta T$).

Let us list the possible changes which might occur in the balance sheet of our firm and discuss their consequences. On the asset side $\Delta G - \Delta T$ may be offset by: (a) money; (b) financial securities; (c) stocks; (d) capital equipment; and on the liabilities side by (e) borrowing.

If the firm's increase in net credit given is financed by a reduction in its money balances it exerts an inflationary impact upon the economy because an amount of money equal to $\Delta G - \Delta T$ is put into circulation. The manner in which a firm might reduce its money balances and raise its ($G - T$) may be illustrated by the following example: if $S = £4{,}000$ per week, $P = £2{,}000$ and both credit periods are five weeks, then $G = £20{,}000$ and $T = £10{,}000$. If the firm's customers now lengthen the credit period to six weeks they will suspend their payments for one week and, hence, $\Delta G =$ £4,000, and the firm does not receive the £4,000 which it would have received had the credit period remained at five weeks. Our firm might pass on part of the pressure by suspending its own money outflows for, say, one week, so that $\Delta T = £2{,}000$. Consequently, the loss in money will be equal to $\Delta G - \Delta T = £2{,}000$.

Should the firm be unwilling (or unable) to suffer the loss of £2,000 in money, it may, by methods (b) or (e), attempt to sell financial assets or incur financial liabilities by borrowing ((b) and (e) above). To say anything about the inflationary or deflationary impacts of these two methods we require knowledge of what would otherwise have happened to the money thus raised.

Should (a), (b) and (e) be out of the question, the firm must reduce its real assets (stock or equipment). Such action would be deflationary. In the above example our firm may finance $\Delta G - \Delta T = £2{,}000$ out of stocks. It might, therefore, reduce its purchases of materials by £1,000 and refrain from hiring £1,000 worth of factor services for one week. It would, thereby, reduce its current cash outflow immediately by £1,000 (being the payment for factor services) and, in six weeks' time, by another £1,000 (when current purchases of materials will have to be paid for). As a consequence of this reduction of income-creating expenditure, the firm will not replace its stocks at the previously established rate, and hence, stocks (valued at cost) will fall by £2,000.

The firm's capital accumulation may be reduced if, for instance, undistributed profits or depreciation charges, which would otherwise have been used for capital expenditure, are now used to pay for the net credit given. This reduction in income-creating expenditures has a deflationary impact upon the economy.

So far we have dealt only with net credit givers (i.e., firms for which $\Delta G - \Delta T > 0$). Let us now consider a net credit taker. Should the firm offset its net credit taken by raising its money holdings, its impact on the economy would be deflationary. On the other hand, a rise in stocks and/or capital equipment would be inflationary. Finally, increases in financial securities or decreases in borrowing may be either inflationary or deflationary.

To sum up: changes in a firm's gross credit given (taken) may be brought about by changes in the credit period and/or in sales (purchases). Any ΔG must be offset by other balance-sheet items. If $\Delta G - \Delta T \neq 0$, we can classify the ensuing changes in balance-sheet items according to whether they have an inflationary or deflationary impact upon the economy. Clearly, if $\Delta G = \Delta T$ no other balance-sheet changes are required.

ii. *Gross credit theories*

We consider the ways in which trade credit can frustrate the workings of monetary policy by raising either M_1 or V_1. We divide trade credit theories into *gross theories* and *net theories*. Gross credit theories hold that it is possible to frustrate monetary policy through equal increases in G and T for each firm so that gross credit increases while net credit does not change.[8] Net credit theories hold that trade credit can effect an increase in M_1 or V_1 only if there is an increase in net credit.

Gross theories may be divided into two types: those which require trade credit to be transferable and those which do not. By transferable trade credit we mean any form of trade credit whereby A can use his evidence of B's indebtedness to A to clear a debt which A owes to C. Examples of this type of credit are generally

[8] It is important to distinguish between the interesting case in which $\Delta G_i = \Delta T_i$ for some or all of the n units comprising a closed economic system and the definitional identity that

$$\sum_{i=1}^{n} \Delta G_i \equiv \sum_{i=1}^{n} \Delta T_i.$$

acceptable bills of exchange and also book-entry credit, provided that there exists a clearing-house arrangement whereby B's debt to A can be crossed off A's books and transferred to C's books. Transferable trade credit is a money substitute in the areas in which it is acceptable. An example of non-transferable credit is book-entry credit which can be cleared only between the original contracting units. A firm that is a net credit giver can be driven bankrupt under a system of non-transferable trade credit if it is forced to pay its creditors before it can collect from its debtors. Thus non-transferable credit is not a substitute for money.

The first gross credit theory which we need to mention is based on the existence of transferable trade credit. If the I.O.U.s of firms were universally accepted by households and by firms, then trade credit would be money, and a fall in legal tender could be offset by a rise in trade credit.

A second gross credit theory occurs if trade credit I.O.U.s are only transferable amongst firms but not households. These I.O.U.s can be used as transactions balances on inter-firm sales. Thus an *increase* in trade credit may free money balances which were formerly used in inter-firm trade; these balances may now be used for making income payments to households. In this case trade credit could be used to raise the velocity of circulation of the existing supply of M_1 balances.[9]

These two versions of the gross credit theory may be rejected as being inapplicable to Britain (and indeed to most advanced capitalist countries in the twentieth century) because, in fact, the great bulk of trade credit is non-transferable.

The third gross credit theory assumes that trade credit is non-transferable but points to the fact that extra demand can be created directly through the media of gross credit. Such a theory might be suggested by the following quotation from Professor Sayers:

If, for example, a statistical measure is sought, it is supposed that only the excess of a firm's claims over its debts to others should be counted. This is a position that cannot be sustained. We are thinking of the power to exercise demand for goods and services, and for this purpose the gross total of trade credit is relevant. An entire closed circle of firms in manufacturing industry may begin giving credit more freely, and all of them proceed to place large orders with each other; there is no doubt about the increase in effective demand although the increase in credit granted by

[9] J. S. Mill appears to have adhered to this version of the gross credit theory, see *Principles*, op. cit., pp. 314–17.

all the firms together is balanced by the increase in credit taken by all the firms together.[10]

Of course, if firms agree to sell goods to each other without demanding payment in money, V_1 can be raised as more transactions occur with the same stock of M_1. But sooner or later payment must be made in cash. If we assume fixed credit periods, a rise in sales occasions a rise in money flows after the elapse of this credit period, which is typically about four to six weeks on transactions between firms, but typically only one or two weeks on the sale of services by households to firms. If there were no trade credit a rise in production and sales would entail an immediate rise in money flows; with trade credit the rise in money flows is postponed for the period of the credit, but it then rises just as if there had been no trade credit, so that the problem of financing the increased money flows with an unchanged stock of cash asserts itself in exactly the same way as if there had been no credit. The increased money flows between firms consequent on the increased goods flows can be postponed for as long as the period of credit can be increased on inter-firm transactions It is a fact, however, that the period of credit on sales of factor services by households to firms is inflexible, and it follows that money flows between firms and households must rise within a week or so of a rise in production. We must conclude that the existence of gross trade credit does nothing to allow increases in M_1 or V_1 in the face of an unexpanded total supply of money, except for a temporary rise in V_1 during the period over which a rise in sales and purchases has not yet resulted in a corresponding rise in money flows.[11]

A fourth and final gross credit theory can be obtained even though trade credit is non-transferable and households will not vary the period over which they give credit to firms; the theory holds as

[10] Sayers, R. S., op. cit., p. 713. See our footnote 8, p. 380. The last phrase in the quotation states a definitional identity. Presumably, since he refers immediately above to net credit, Professor Sayers is thinking of the case in which $G_i = T_i$ for each $i = 1, 2, \ldots, n$. Professor Sayers also refers to orders rather than to sales. As soon, however, as increased orders lead to increased prices and/or increased production (i.e., the demand becomes effective), then increased income payments follow with a very short time lag, so that the analysis in the text applies without serious amendment.

[11] We chose the passage quoted above because it seemed to us to provide one of the clearest statements of Professor Sayers's gross-credit view. Professor Sayers, however, has stated in correspondence that the passage we have quoted from his writings is not intended to imply the theory that we have criticized.

long as firms are willing to vary the credit period on trade with each other, and as long as desired cash balances are a function of current *cash* flows and not the current level of *goods* flows.[12] Say that, in a period of monetary squeeze, all firms run up extra trade credit by not paying some of their bills to each other after the customary credit period has elapsed. Thus, for each firm, credit given and credit taken will rise, and cash flows between firms will be reduced. Individual firms still have to make income payments to the households from which they buy factor services. They do not obtain anyone else's cash to make these payments, nor do they economize on transactions balances which are actively circulating between themselves; but if precautionary balances are held as security against random fluctuations in receipts and disbursements and if the demand for these balances is a function of current *cash* inflows and outflows their own cash may be set free to make these payments to households. This effects an increase in V_1. Once the transitional period is over and the outflows and inflows of cash are resumed between firms, then the M_1 balances must be restored and, unless other ways of economizing on cash can be found, payments will have to be reduced in order to rebuild these balances; payments will, in fact, have to be reduced below their original level. At this stage the deflationary impact of reduced expenditure will exactly balance the inflationary impact of the original extra expenditure and, after this has occurred, payments can return to their original level. The main point about this theory is that cash is released for only as long as the cash flows between firms are reduced. This reduction of cash flows in the face of unchanged transactions requires that the stock of credit outstanding be increasing week by week. Once the stock of credit is stabilized (say at four weeks' sales instead of three weeks'), then cash flows are resumed and the problem of how to maintain planned flows in the face of an unexpanded supply of money recurs.

The maximum amount of cash that can be made available through this means depends on the proportion of weekly sales held as a precautionary balance. The time for which the cash is made available depends on the amount of cash which is obtained and the number of weeks that the average period of credit taken, c_t, can be extended. For example, if Δc_t is three weeks, then an amount of money equal to transactions balances held against one week's

[12] We are indebted to Mr. David Laidler for pointing out this gross credit theory to us.

purchases can be made available for three weeks by postponing payment on all accounts for that period of time. On the other hand, an amount of money equal to the balances held against one-half the week's sales could be made available for six weeks' time by delaying the payment of accounts covering one-half of one's purchases for one period of three weeks and then delaying payment of accounts covering the other half of purchases for another period of three weeks. In general, if it is required to finance a single expenditure of cash to be made in week one, then the time for which this cash can be made available is

$$t = \frac{\alpha}{d} \Delta c_t \tag{3}$$

where t is the time measured in weeks for which cash is to be available, α is the proportion of weekly purchases covered by precautionary balances, d is the required cash payment expressed as a proportion of weekly purchases $(0 < d \leqslant 1)$ and Δc_t is the increase in the credit period measured in weeks.[13]

A more interesting case arises when it is desired to finance an increased weekly flow of expenditure by this method. Unfortunately, a full analysis of this situation would require a treatment of article length, and we can only hint at the results in a footnote.[14] The

[13] The total cash made available is $\alpha P \Delta c_t$, where α and Δc_t are defined in the text and P is the value of weekly purchases. Since the most that can be done is to postpone payment on all accounts, the maximum amount of money that can be made available is αP and the time for which this cash is made available is Δc_t. Writing $X = \alpha P \Delta c_t$ and letting D be the amount of money made available for expenditure in the first week, $D = X/t$, we get $Dt = \alpha P \Delta c_t$. Defining $d = D/_P$, i.e., the cash made available as a proportion of weekly purchases we get

$$t = \frac{\alpha}{d} \Delta c_t.$$

[14] Assume that c_t can be extended indefinitely and let D be the increased weekly flow of expenditure to be financed out of balances. Total speculative balances that can be made available is αP and the total spent by time t is tD, so that $t = \alpha P/D = \alpha/d$. Now assume that there is a limit, Δc_t to the possible extension of c_t. It is possible that the increased flow of expenditure will be brought to a halt because credit periods will have been fully extended before balances have been used up. The credit-period limit is reached when

$$\sum_{1}^{t} = \frac{\alpha}{d} \Delta c_t.$$

(This is analogous to equation (3) in the text except that we now have the sum from 1 to t, since an extra D is spent each period.) Our empirical observations

general idea, however, is the same as that already analysed: an increased flow of expenditure on factor services can be financed out of precautionary balances by reducing cash payments between firms (raising c_t), thus *temporarily* freeing balances for other uses.

This is a perfectly tenable gross credit theory, but we have not been able to subject it to rigorous testing.[15] In the absence of such tests we may be able to gain some idea of the potential of the mechanism described, by considering some plausible values for the relevant parameters. Assume that we wish to make a single expenditure equal to 5 per cent of annual purchases so that $d = 1{\cdot}11$, take α as $1{\cdot}66$, and Δc_t as four.[16] Substituting these values into equation (3) gives $t = 6$ weeks, indicating that sufficient cash could be made available to finance this single increment of expenditure for a period of six weeks through an increase of four weeks in the credit period.

Now consider the case of a continuing flow of extra expenditure. Substituting the values[17] $d = 0{\cdot}0214$, $\alpha = 1{\cdot}66$ and $\Delta c_t = 4$ into the second equation in footnote 14, p. 384, gives a value of t of just over 24 weeks.[18] This indicates that, assuming the behavioural

suggest that Δc_t seldom exceeds four weeks. Since

$$\sum_{1}^{t} = 4t$$

when $t = 7$, it follows that the credit period, rather than the fund of precautionary balances, will set the limit to t as long as balances are sufficient to finance the extra flow of expenditure for more than seven weeks.

[15] This is mainly because we did not see the full implications of the theory until Professor Gorman pointed out a serious error in the analysis of this theory which we presented in the penultimate version of this paper.

[16] Data presented in Part III suggest that total purchases are divided into 30 per cent income payments and 70 per cent purchases from other firms (our P). Since extra purchases only require money for new income payments (purchases from firms can be made on credit), a rise in production of 5 per cent gives an annual d of $1{\cdot}5/70 = 0{\cdot}0214$, which is $1{\cdot}11$ times weekly P.

The total money supply is roughly $0{\cdot}3$ times income, and thus $0{\cdot}13$ times our P ($P = 7/3Y$). Assuming the total money stock to be divided equally between transactions, precautionary and speculative balances, and assuming that 70 per cent of precautionary balances are held against P, this gives the available balances as $0{\cdot}0302$ times annual P or $1{\cdot}66$ times weekly P.

Our empirical studies suggest a maximum value of Δc_t of four weeks.

[17] This is the d appropriate to a continuous flow of expenditure equal to 5 per cent of weekly purchases.

[18] Substituting 24 weeks into the first expression of the footnotes indicates that about 35 per cent of the available precautionary balances would have been spent by week 24 when the credit-period limit is reached.

assumptions on which the theory rests to be true, and taking the most favourable values of the parameters, the theory could account for a frustration of a monetary policy designed to cut expenditure by 5 per cent for a period of up to one-half a year.[19] The major uncertainty in this very rough estimate of order of magnitude is in the estimate of the proportion of the total stock of money that is held as precautionary balances against inter-firm transactions.

iii. *Net credit theories*

The second major set of theories require as a necessary condition for their working that there are some net givers and, hence, some net takers of credit in the economy. However, as we pointed out in Section II, i, changes in net credit are not a sufficient condition for an inflationary impact upon the economy. We require also that: (a) the net credit givers finance additional net credit by reductions in money holdings, and (b) the net credit takers use it for the accumulation of currently produced real assets. In order to study the theoretical possibility of the frustration of monetary policy by net credit we shall assume that conditions (a) and (b) are satisfied.

A single firm can frustrate monetary policy by taking net credit which enables it to maintain its real assets at a level which would not have been possible with an efficient restrictive monetary policy. Suppose that the firm was considering expansion of its real assets but that, owing to the credit squeeze, it is now unable to raise the necessary funds from the financial sector. Hence its plans might have to be revised. If, however, the firm decides to lengthen its c_t by, say, one week (whilst leaving its c_g unchanged), then it suspends its money payments for one week and these funds can be used for the purchase of materials, machines, labour and other services.

When we look at the economy as a whole the net credit taken by our particular firm must be accounted for by some other firm's net credit given. By assumption, the net givers of credit offset it in their balance sheets by reductions in their cash holdings.

The relationship between net credit givers and net credit takers need not be a direct one. There may be intermediate firms which pass on the pressure from taker to giver. Assume, for example, that

[19] The theory has other implications which, given time and appropriate detailed observations, could be tested. The most obvious one is that c_t must be observed to rise steadily, and at an increasing rate, for the whole of the period for which the restrictive monetary policy is being frustrated.

firm A is initially squeezed and delays paying bills to B. Firm B, however, offsets this pressure, not by reducing money holdings or stocks, etc., but by delaying payment to firm C so that its $\Delta G = \Delta T$. Firm C, on the other hand, may absorb the pressure by reductions in its money holdings. In these circumstances firm B merely passes on the pressure; yet this function is an important one if A and C do not trade with one another.

It may be useful to distinguish three types of net credit theories. The first one assumes that some firms have idle balances which they are prepared to let run down. One motive for holding this type of idle money may be to ensure that trade can be carried on in spite of unexpected increases in the demand for credit. Firms with such idle balances will let their net credit given increase by allowing c_g to rise without trying to increase c_t. In this case trade credit is a mechanism which is equivalent to the transfer of idle balances from those firms which have them (net credit givers) to those firms which need them (net credit takers).

The second theory is based on the assumption that there are some weak firms in the economy which are unable to refuse a rise in gross credit given, yet too weak to pass the pressure on by taking more gross credit. For such firms any ΔG cannot be offset by a corresponding ΔT. Under this constraint the firm may decide that it is preferable to reduce money holdings rather than other assets; whilst in the absence of the constraint the firm would have preferred to raise T.

The third theory assumes that no firm has idle balances which it will voluntarily let run down; thus everyone reacts to a rise in their credit given by raising their credit taken; but this reaction takes place only after a significant time-lag. Thus, if firm A finds itself pressed for funds because of a credit squeeze it does not pay its bills to B for an extra week. B absorbs the pressure by reducing money holdings and, after a lag, it reacts by delaying payment to C, thus restoring its cash position at the expense of C. After a lag C does the same thing by not paying its accounts. Say that C buys from A so that C restores its cash position at the expense of A. Now all firms have suffered an increase in gross credit. If A again tries to obtain extra cash from B, then the process repeats itself. In this theory as long as firms form a sub-circuit, as do A, B and C in the above example, then the disequilibrium is passed around from one to another and cash is obtained, but only for so long as credit periods are extended. Once the process comes to an end, then no cash will have been extracted and the inflationary effects, which are dependent on someone being a *net* giver of credit, will no longer exist.

All three net-credit theories predict that in periods of restrictive monetary policies there will be net givers and net takers of credit whose actions tend to frustrate the squeeze. With the available data we shall be able to observe the inflationary and deflationary net credit changes in which we are interested, but we shall be unable to discern which of the three theories provides the correct explanation of these changes.

iv. *Conclusion*

We have rejected three versions of gross-credit theories, two because they require transferable credit and the third because it does not account for any increase in purchasing power not backed by cash except for a very short period of time (a few weeks at most). A fourth gross-credit version cannot be so easily rejected. This version depends on a freeing of precautionary balances for other uses during the time over which money payments are being reduced because the credit period is being increased. Insertion of plausible values of the relevant parameters into the expressions derived shows that this theory can account for a postponement of the effects of a restrictive monetary policy for something up to six months as a maximum.

The most important theory of how trade credit can frustrate monetary policy is the net-credit theory, whereby movements in net credit can be used to redistribute money balances from those firms which have access to them to those firms which are in need of them. This theory can account for a frustration of monetary policy of indefinite length. As long as some firms are prepared to extend an increased supply of trade credit the cash which was formerly idle can remain in active circulation.

The remainder of this paper is directed to a study of empirical evidence relevant to these trade-credit theories. There are several questions for which answers are required: (1) Does trade credit respond to monetary policy? The absence of such a response would be sufficient to refute all theories that trade credit frustrates monetary policy. (2) To what extent do the changes in trade credit that we observe indicate changes in net credit or in passing on? (3) To what extent have the net credit changes which we observe been inflationary or deflationary in their impact on the economy?

III. The empirical analysis

i. *The determinants of trade credit*

When we come to study the relationship between monetary policy and trade credit we cannot, unfortunately, confine our attention to these two series. As we pointed out earlier, a firm's trade credit given may be thought of as the product of its average sales and its credit period ($G \equiv c_g S$). Both the credit period and the level of sales may be influenced by the activities of the monetary authorities. However, if we assume that the credit period is determined primarily by monetary policy and by institutional factors (which remain constant in the short-run) and that the level of sales is only partially determined by monetary policy then our behavioural equations may be written as:

$$G_i = G_i(S_i, M, \epsilon_i) \tag{4}$$

$$T_i = T_i(P_i, M, \mu_i) \tag{5}$$

where G_i, T_i, S_i and P_i refer to credit given by, credit taken by, sales of and purchases of the ith firm; M refers to the strength of monetary policy in the economy as a whole, while ϵ_i and μ_i are error terms for each firm. We must allow for the fact that this relation differs between firms, not only because the normal credit periods may differ between firms but also because firms' reactions to a monetary squeeze may differ.

In order to study the reaction of trade credit to monetary policy, there are two possible approaches. The first would entail a multiple regression for each firm using a linear form of equations (4) and (5). We rejected this approach for two main reasons. (a) Although there is some general agreement of a qualitative sort about the years of easy and tight money, it is not easy to get a good *quantitative* estimate of the relative strength of monetary policy for a ten-year period. (b) We did not wish to commit ourselves to the theory that an individual firm would react in the same fashion to successive credit squeezes. The theory that net credit changes frustrate monetary policy predicts that in periods of credit squeeze we will see a number of firms increasing their net credit taken; it does not say (as would be implied by multiple regression) that it must be the same firms in each period of squeeze.

For these reasons we decided to adopt the second possible approach, which consists of removing the effects of sales and purchases on credit given and taken and then to study the behaviour of the residual credit movements.[20]

ii. *The nature of the sample*

One of the pre-requisites of the empirical work suggested in the last section is the availability of turnover data for individual firms. Companies in the United Kingdom are not required by law to publish their sales figures. However, some do so voluntarily, and we have used their figures. In addition, we approached a substantial number of companies with the request to supply their sales figures, and some complied. Balance-sheet data were used for figures for credit given and taken, cash, and stocks.[21]

The final sample consists of 75 firms, some of which are very large. Fig. 1 contains a frequency distribution of our firms according to the level of sales in 1959.

In 1959 the sales of our 75 firms amounted to well over £4,000 million. In a later section we shall estimate the income–sales ratio to be approximately 27 per cent. Hence our firms may have contributed £1,080 million, or 5·4 per cent, to national income. Another method of assessing the size of our sample involves looking at the total level of credit given and taken. A comparison of our totals with those obtained by the Board of Trade for 3,000 United Kingdom public companies shows that our sample amounts to 2·5 per cent of their total number of firms, but that the gross credit given by our sample came to 19·0 per cent and the gross credit taken to 17·7 per cent of their total in 1958. These figures show that our sample includes a higher proportion of large firms than the Board of Trade one.

Our data cover the ten years from 1950 to 1959. Variations in trade credit lasting less than one year will not be picked up in our figures. Since, however, monetary policy in the 1950s has tended to fluctuate in a two- or three-year cycle, and since major changes have occurred at different times throughout the year, annual

[20] A third possible method consists of estimating that part of G and T which is due to deviations of the credit period from its normal value. A large part of our calculations were repeated with this method, for which the normal credit period was taken to be the ten-year mean of the actual credit periods. The results were almost identical to those of our simple regression technique.

[21] We are much indebted to Moodies Services Ltd. for permitting us to use their facilities for this purpose.

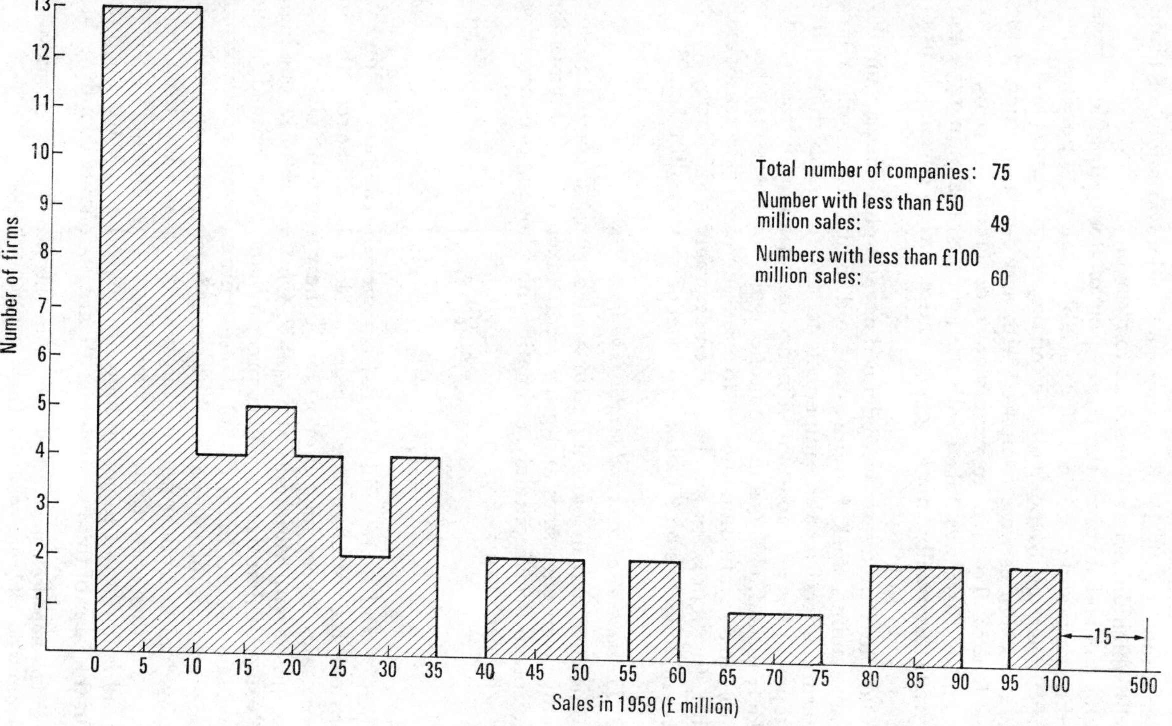

FIG. 1. *Size distribution of firms in sample*

observations are likely to register any major variations of trade credit which did occur in response to monetary policy.

Our method involves the correlation of stock variables (trade credit, stocks and cash) with flow variables (sales and purchases)—the first referring to a point of time and the second to a period of time. The stock figures were compared with a two-year average of the flow figures. To give an example: trade credit referring to 31 December 1950, was linked with the average of sales in 1950 and 1951. Conceptually, therefore, the entire period covered is from July 1950 to June 1959.

Our purchase figures were defined as sales plus stock accumulations or minus stock decumulations and minus gross profits. This measure suffers from three imperfections: first, we imply that capital equipment has no important influence on variations of trade credit taken; second, changes in the money value of stocks may be due simply to a revaluation and not to a real increase or decrease; and, third, the figures for purchases include wages and salaries which have no influence on the observed level of gross credit taken.[22]

iii. *The influence of sales and purchases on trade credit*

The first step in our empirical analysis was to correlate gross credit given with sales and gross credit taken with purchases for each of our firms separately, estimating the following two regression lines for each firm:

$$G_i = a_i + b_i S_i + g_i \qquad (6)$$

$$T_i = c_i + d_i P_i + t_i \qquad (7)$$

where g_i and t_i are residuals. A frequency distribution of the r^2's for these 150 correlations is given in Table 1. It will be seen that in most cases a very high proportion of the variance in G and T is associated with variations in S and P. On the face of it, our high r^2's suggest that trade credit is predominantly determined by the level of turnover. In the case of about 50 firms there is a fairly strong time trend in turnover as well as credit levels. An examination of individual firms does not suggest, however, that a low time trend goes together with a low r^2; some r^2's are low although the time trend is high, and some are high although the time trend is low. On the basis of this examination, we are reasonably confident that

[22] This imperfection will present difficulties only in so far as wage and salary payments do not bear a constant relation to total purchases.

TABLE I

Distribution of r²'s *for correlations between credit given and sales and between credit taken and purchases*

r^2's	G	T
0·00–0·19	5	9
0·20–0·39	2	5
0·40–0·59	7	7
0·60–0·79	2	15
0·80–1·00	59	39
Mean r^2	0·81	0·69

our regressions reveal a real causal relation between credit and turnover.

iv. *Fluctuations in abnormal credit*

We now calculated two series for each firm: the residuals of credit given from regression equation (6) g_i, and the residuals of credit taken from regression equation (7) t_i. These series show the behaviour of *that part of trade credit which cannot be explained on the basis of the sales and purchases of the firm.* In order to see whether or not trade credit tends to react to monetary policy we merely aggregated this abnormal trade credit across firms for each year. Thus,

$$g = \sum_{i=1}^{75} g_i \tag{8}$$

$$t = \sum_{i=1}^{75} t_i \tag{9}$$

where g_i is the abnormal credit given by the ith firm and t_i the abnormal credit taken. The time series of g and t are presented in Figs. 2 and 3. Fig. 4 contains four alternative indicators of the strength of monetary policy (consol yield, bill rate, ratio of money to G.N.P., ratio of advances to G.N.P., all of which are adjusted for their time trends). Clearly during periods of tight money there was a considerable increase both in the abnormal credit given and

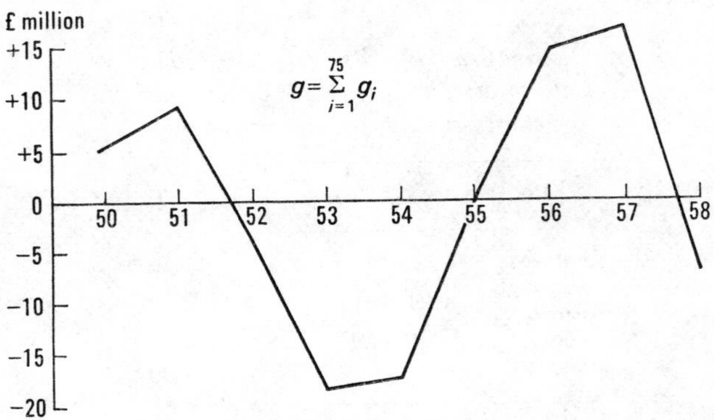

FIG. 2. *Abnormal trade credit given*

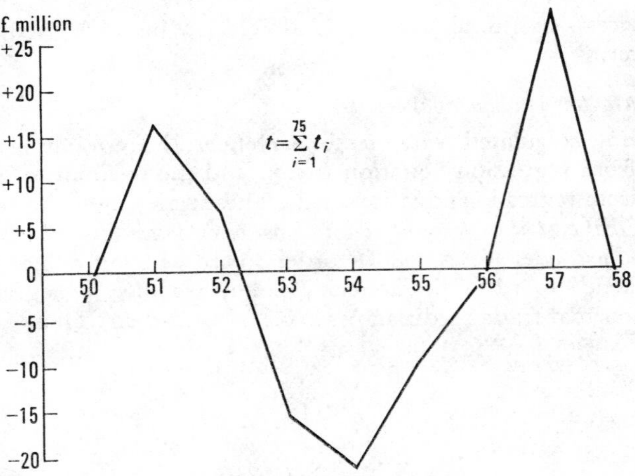

FIG. 3. *Abnormal trade credit taken*

taken. Thus, in periods of tight money, credit periods tended to become longer than normal, while, in periods of easy money, credit periods tended to become shorter than normal.[23]

[23] Both g and t are composed of positive and negative elements; a positive g_i means that the firm is giving abnormally much credit, while a negative g_i means the firm is giving abnormally little credit. When monetary policy is strict the sum

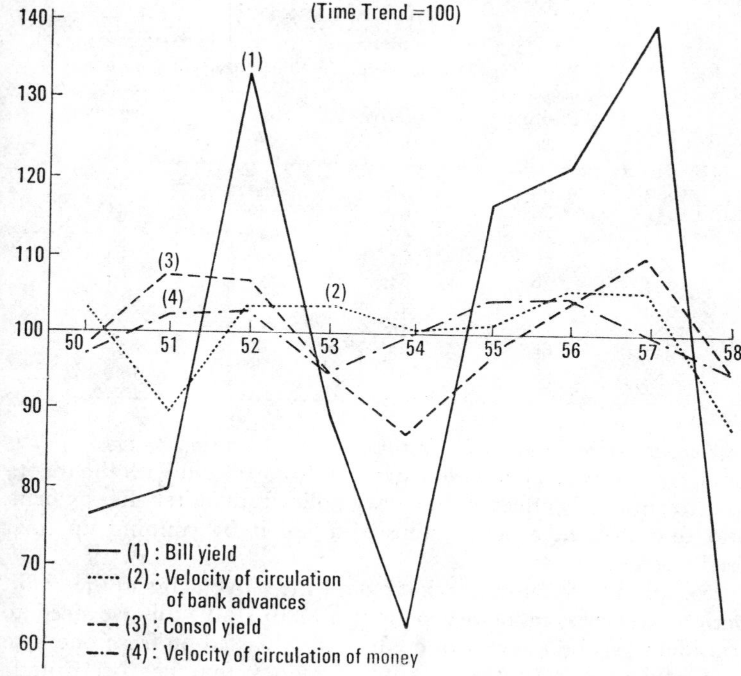

FIG. 4. *Indicators of monetary policy*

It is possible that the fluctuations in Figs. 2 and 3 were caused by a small number of dominant firms. Hence we looked also at the *number* of firms that have positive or negative residuals in various years. They are presented in percentage terms in Table 2. These figures show that in periods of monetary pressure (1951–52 and 1955–57) there are a relatively large number of positive residuals, whilst in periods of monetary ease (1953–54 and 1958) negative residuals predominate.

Thus, we have reached our first major conclusion of the empirical analysis: *trade credit shows definite signs of reacting to monetary policy*;

of both the positive and negative g_i's tends to rise (i.e., the sum of the negative g_i's approaches zero). Thus, all firms (both those who are granting abnormally much and those who are granting abnormally little credit) tend to lengthen the credit period. A similar result is observable for the behaviour of the series for abnormal credit taken.

TABLE 2

	Percentage of firms with		Percentage of firms with	
	Positive g_i	Negative g_i	Positive t_i	Negative t_i
1950	63	37	52	48
1951	69	31	59	41
1952	48	52	41	59
1953	36	64	36	64
1954	36	64	36	64
1955	57	43	44	56
1956	55	45	52	48
1957	65	35	80	20
1958	36	64	41	59

both credit periods tend to rise in times of monetary squeeze and to fall in times of easy money. This evidence is clearly consistent with the theory that the quantity effect of monetary policy is definitely felt by firms and that they take active steps to avoid it by running up their credit taken.

We still do not know to what extent the movements in the credit periods frustrate monetary policy; and to study this we need to consider: (a) the amount of credit that is passed on from one firm to another, and (b) the amount of money that has been made available by one set of firms to another through the medium of net credit.

Having established in this section that trade credit *does* fluctuate with monetary policy, we shall argue from now on as though all *abnormal* trade credit was caused by monetary policy.

v. *Gross credit, passing-on and net credit*

In an earlier section we defined gross credit, passing-on and net credit in terms of absolute levels of G and T. These definitions must now be amended, since we wish to deal with g and t, that is with *abnormal* trade credit.

(i) For an individual firm, gross credit given (taken) is the gross amount of credit made available by (taken from) the firm without reference to how much credit it takes (gives). Expressed in symbols:

$$\text{Gross credit given} = g_i^+ + |t_i^-| = g_i^+ - t_i^-$$
$$\text{Gross credit taken} = |g_i^-| + t_i^+ = t_i^+ - g_i^-$$

where the superscripts refer to the signs of the residuals. A particular firm has, of course, only two residuals (one g and one t) and, hence, the other two in the above formula must assume the value of zero. Thus, gross credit given is the sum of the abnormally high credit given and the abnormally low credit taken. (Clearly gross credit is made available both by giving abnormally much and by taking abnormally little.)

(ii) Net credit, in terms of abnormal trade credit, is simply the difference between abnormal credit given and abnormal credit taken:

$$n_i = g_i - t_i$$

If $n_i > 0$ the firm is a giver and if $n_i < 0$ it is a taker of abnormal net credit.

(iii) Passing-on is defined as follows: if g_i and t_i have the same sign then the figure which has the smaller absolute value measures the amount of credit passed on. If g_i and t_i have opposite signs, then passing-on is zero. For example, if a firm's abnormal credit given amounts to £500 and it manages to take abnormal credit to the extent of £300, then £300 is said to have been passed on. If it takes abnormally *little* credit, on the other hand, then no part of the £500 is passed on.

The sum of net credit and passing-on must be equal to gross credit, since that part of gross credit that is not absorbed by the firm must be passed on to some other firm.

Definitions of aggregate gross credit, net credit and passing-on can be derived easily from the above formulae:

$$\text{Aggregate gross credit given} = \sum g_i^+ + \sum |t_i^-|$$
$$\text{Aggregate gross credit taken} = \sum t_i^+ + \sum |g_i^-|$$
$$\text{Aggregate net credit given} = n^+ = \sum n_i^+ = \sum (g_i - t_i)^+$$
$$\text{Aggregate net credit taken} = n^- = \sum n_i^- = \sum (g_i - t_i)^-$$

Aggregate passing-on is the difference between gross and net credit.

We calculated gross credit, passing-on and net credit in order to obtain some idea of the extent to which attempts by firms to ease the monetary pressure result in passing-on rather than in movements in net credit. Net credit is expressed as a percentage of gross credit in Table 3.

These figures show that, on average, passing-on amounts to about 40 per cent of gross-credit movements. To this extent, then, our firm's attempts to escape the squeeze by generating abnormal net-credit movements were unsuccessful.

TABLE 3

	Net credit given as % of gross credit given	Net credit taken as % of gross credit taken
1950	73	62
1951	62	70
1952	65	77
1953	47	54
1954	53	48
1955	70	58
1956	77	60
1957	37	56
1958	50	56

TABLE 4

In £000

	Abnormal net credit given n^+	Abnormal net credit taken n^-
1950	19,282	11,541
1951	16,617	23,679
1952	12,248	22,359
1953	12,037	15,621
1954	18,349	14,907
1955	24,389	14,715
1956	28,340	13,051
1957	9,769	21,222
1958	13,740	17,659

Net-credit figures are presented in Table 4.[24] The difference between n^+ and n^- is the amount of abnormal trade credit made available by our sample of firms to other firms and households.

24 Firms which during the squeeze were net credit givers became net credit takers in periods of monetary ease. Hence, an aggregate figure of net credit cannot be expected to correlate in a simple linear fashion with monetary policy.

vi. *Inflationary and deflationary net credit*

Having established the size of abnormal net credit that was given and taken by our sample of firms, we must now attempt to estimate the proportion of net credit that was inflationary in the sense that it was offset by cash reductions in the givers' balance sheets and by accumulations of real assets in the takers' balance sheets. Since we are concerned only with abnormal net credit, we must confine our attention to abnormal changes in other balance-sheet items.

We considered only two types of assets which may be used to offset abnormal net credit: (a) money balances and financial securities, and (b) stocks. Abnormal stocks and money (including financial securities) are defined as the residuals from the regressions of these two series upon our firms' sales; they are thus those parts of stocks and money which cannot be accounted for by sales.

The net credit givers' influence was assumed to be inflationary to the extent that his $(g - t)$ was *not* observed to be offset by abnormal decreases in stocks. The net credit takers' influence was assumed to be inflationary to the extent that $(t - g)$ was *not* offset by increases in money.

These estimates of inflationary and deflationary net credit were obtained for all net givers and all net takers. They were then aggregated and expressed as a percentage of net credit given and taken. For instance, in a particular year 40 per cent of all abnormal net credit given may have been observed to be offset by abnormal stock decumulations. At the same time 30 per cent of abnormal net credit taken may have been observed to be offset by a change in cash holdings. Hence, 60 per cent of net credit given is said to be inflationary, whilst 30 per cent of net credit taken is said to be deflationary; the total impact of net credit will therefore be inflationary to the extent of 30 per cent (60 per cent − 30 per cent).

Table 5 contains our estimates of the proportions of abnormal net credit that is inflationary in the sense that it facilitated a rise in expenditures by the redistribution of money balances. We suspect that there is a fairly large margin of error in these figures owing to our method of estimating them.[25]

[25] Our cash figures are extremely volatile, the ratio of *cash/sales* varying considerably from year to year for most firms. If cash also varies considerably from month to month our estimates of the normal *cash/sales* ratio based on *year end cash/annual sales* will be subject to considerable error. Similarly, our estimate of the firm's typical abnormal cash position for the year is liable to error, since it is based on the difference between the *observed year end cash/sales* ratio and the

TABLE 5

	Inflationary net credit as per cent of total net credit
1950	31
1951	68
1952	78
1953	0
1954	−29
1955	9
1956	63
1957	64
1958	33

vii. *The importance of trade credit as an inflationary agent*

In order to assess the amount of expenditure that trade credit actually facilitated in periods of monetary restraint, we must obtain from Table 4 a single measure of net credit.

In a completely closed system of firms, households and foreigners abnormal net credit given must be identical to net credit taken ($n^+ = n^-$). Our figures in Table 4, however, indicate that, for our sample, $n^+ \neq n^-$. As a group, the firms in our sample become strong takers of net credit in 1951–52 and 1957.[26] This observation[27] might have arisen for two quite different reasons: first, since households are excluded from our investigation, our estimates may reflect the true behaviour of the business sector, so that differences between n^+ and n^- represented flows of abnormal net credit between households and firms. Second, this difference may have arisen because of sampling fluctuations.

We are inclined to think that the differences arose primarily for the second reason, because consumer credit is financed mainly by

estimated typical ratio. The total net credit movements show the *potential* inflationary effect, and we are inclined to believe that the majority of the potential effect is in fact inflationary. Here is an uncertainty which subsequent more detailed study might be able to resolve.

[26] In comparing these figures with other published statistics, say the Board of Trade figures on trade credit, we must remember that the figures in Table 4 refer to *abnormal* net credit, i.e., trade credit after adjustment for turnover.

[27] The same is true though not as marked as in Table 4 when we look at the *number* of firms that are net credit givers or takers.

hire-purchase finance companies and not by the firms themselves. Thus, changes in abnormal net credit taken by households would cause asset changes in households and hire-purchase finance institutions, but not in firms.[28]

If our argument is correct, then our best estimate of the actual amount of abnormal trade credit would be the mean of n^+ and n^-, since, owing to sampling errors, one is an overestimate and the other an underestimate of the true amount of net credit. Consequently, a series of the mean abnormal net credit can be derived from n^+ and n^- in Table 4 which can then be adjusted by the ratios in Table 5 to give our estimate of inflationary net credit.[29]

The final stage of our procedure is to compare net credit with certain other financial flows in order to gain some impression of its relative importance. Having obtained net credit figures, we now require estimates for the volume of income generated by our sample in order to assess the percentage impact effect of trade credit on income.

We do have data on our firms' sales. They have to be multiplied by an income–sales ratio in order to get the level of income generated by our sample. Out of a total of 75 firms 30 do publish income sales ratios (or data from which the latter can be ascertained). They are distributed as follows:

Income–sales ratio, %	No. of firms
10–15	3
15–20	4
20–25	4
25–30	8
30–35	8
35–40	1
Over 40	2

[28] A third possible reason is the existence of import and export credit. The ratio of exports to G.N.P. is about 20 per cent. The ratio of exports to sales will therefore be about 7–8 per cent. This means that only a small proportion of total trade credit is accounted for by dealings with foreigners. It is unlikely that such a small amount is responsible for the considerable differences between n^- and n^+

[29] Should the differences between n^+ and n^- arise because our sample leaves households out of account, then the larger of the two figures should be taken as the correct estimate of net credit.

The mean income–sales ratio is 26·8 per cent.[30]

Applying this ratio to our sales figures, we obtained estimates of income generated by our sample of firms. They were used to calculate the figures presented in Table 6, which measure the percentage impact effect that trade credit is estimated to have had on income. Table 6 also contains certain other financial flows which may help to increase M_1 balances. They are: (a) new capital issues of United Kingdom companies; (b) changes in commercial banks' advances; (c) changes in building society advances; (d) changes in public borrowing.[31]

TABLE 6

	Abnormal net credit as % of income	Inflationary net credit as % of income	New capital issues as % of income	Changes in commercial banks advances as % of income	Changes in building societies' advances as % of income	Changes in public borrowing as % of income
1950	2·9	0·9	1·5	2·2	—	—
1951	3·3	2·2	1·4	0·1	0·8	2·1
1952	2·6	2·0	1·0	0·9	0·8	4·4
1953	1·9	0·0	0·9	0·7	1·0	6·4
1954	2·0	−0·6	1·4	1·5	1·2	1·3
1955	2·1	0·2	1·6	−1·0	1·2	2·7
1956	2·0	1·3	1·4	0·3	0·8	3·5
1957	1·4	0·9	1·5	0·3	0·9	3·0
1958	1·3	0·4	1·1	3·7	0·8	1·2

A comparison of the trade credit percentages with other flows must rest on the assumption that our sample is representative. If this is true, then the trade credit figures are quite substantial

[30] The input–output tables for the United Kingdom can be used to calculate an income–sales ratio of about 28 per cent. See Table A of 'Input–Output Tables for the United Kingdom, 1954', *Studies in Official Statistics*, no. 8 (H.M.S.O., 1961). According to this table, turnover in 1954 amounted to £51,000 million, whilst net national income came to about £14,500 million. The Census of Production, 1958, yields a net value added to sales ratio of 35·8 per cent for manufacturing industry.

[31] Data for changes in consumer hire-purchase credit are available only for 1955–58. As percentage of income the highest figure was 0·5 per cent in 1958. In other years it was much smaller and sometimes negative.

compared with the other flows. If we look at column (1) of the table we find that net trade credit was larger than most of the other sources of potentially inflationary finance in the economy. Even if we accept that all the other movements were 100 per cent inflationary,[32] while trade credit was only inflationary to the extent estimated in column (2), then trade credit still remains a major source of inflationary finance which can be utilized to frustrate the quantity effect of monetary policy.

viii. *Conclusions*

The empirical results of our study may be summarized as follows:

1. There is substantial evidence that firms do feel the quantity effect of monetary squeezes and that they react to them by (on the whole) lengthening their credit periods.
2. Of the gross credit changes thus generated, about 40 per cent consist of passing-on, the remaining 60 per cent represent movements of net credit.
3. The net credit changes are substantial (as percentage of income). This would indicate that net credit is at least a very strong potential frustrator of monetary policy. We have considerable confidence in this estimate.
4. We attempted to separate the inflationary from the non-inflationary parts of net credit, but we do not have a high degree of confidence in the results. However, Table 6 shows that, even after eliminating its estimated non-inflationary part, net credit is likely to have had a significant inflationary impact on the economy.[33]

[32] None of the four other series in Table 6 have been adjusted for their deflationary content and, hence, they should be compared with unadjusted net credit in the first column.

[33] In our analysis abnormal trade credit was measured by g and t. Should factors other than monetary policy have had a systematic influence upon G and T, they may have caused a significant auto-correlation in ϵ and μ (equations (4) and (5)). In this case, it would be more appropriate to measure abnormal trade credit by the first differences over time of g and t. To check on this possibility, all our calculations were repeated in terms of first differences of g and t. The results of this experiment are almost identical with the ones presented in the paper; the only difference being that the figures corresponding to columns (1) and (2) of Table 6 are higher than those reported here. Thus our conclusions are, in substance, unaffected.

THE IMPACT OF CREDIT CONTROL ON CONSUMER DURABLE SPENDING IN THE UNITED KINGDOM, 1957–1961

R. J. BALL *and* PAMELA S. DRAKE*

I. Introduction

ONE of the ultimate ends of econometric analysis is to uncover structural relationships with a high degree of autonomy. For a variety of familiar reasons, the use of time series data to estimate such relationships is sometimes fraught with such difficulties that this end cannot be realized. Nevertheless even in such cases the application of standard statistical techniques to the data can still be revealing, for while the results lack the required degree of autonomy, they may still provide a picture of the relative magnitudes of forces at work during the sample period.

In this paper we examine the impact of variations in consumer credit control on consumer durable spending as exercised through the minimum deposit rate and maximum length of life related to hire purchase contracts. We are not entirely satisfied that our results possess the desirable degree of autonomy in all respects as referred to in the above paragraph. However our analysis indicates that variations in hire purchase business governed by credit controls have been a major factor explaining consumer durable goods spending over the period 1957–61.

The statistical analysis presented below is based on a relatively small sample of data by quarters from 1957 III to 1961 IV. The lack of adequate data prevented the use of a larger sample. This

* Reprinted from the *Review of Economic Studies*, vol. 30, no. 4, October 1963, pp. 181–94, by permission of the authors and publisher. R. J. Ball is Professor of Economics at the London Business School and Pamela S. Drake is at the Department of Trade and Industry.

relatively small number of observations (18) added to the necessity of including 'seasonal' variables in the regression analysis as described in Klein *et al.* (1961) meant that the number of degrees of freedom was nearly always reduced to 11, which imposes obvious limitations on the statistical results. Nevertheless it was considered worth laying a foundation of analysis of the data concerned at this time, which can be improved on as new data become available.

The procedure followed below is to begin with some analysis of consumer durable spending ignoring credit effects entirely. We then examine the results of introducing 'credit' variables in a number of alternative formulations. The analysis is extended to consider a simple two equation model in which we attempt to offer some explanation of the joint determination of new credits issued and their effect on demand for durable goods. Finally we advance some tentative conclusions that suggest themselves to us in the light of the statistical results.

II. The consumption function for durable goods

Putting credit effects on one side for the moment, the basic model of consumer durable spending we have employed is derived from the assumption that individuals maximize a utility function depending on their stock of non-physical (i.e. 'financial') assets, the flow of services from their current stock of durable goods, and their current consumption of non-durable goods, where the concept of consumption is taken in accordance with the published figures in the quarterly National Income accounts. Since the flow of services from durable goods is not directly measurable, they are assumed to depend on the current stock of durable goods which is introduced into the utility function in their stead.

Under fairly weak restrictions on the utility function we derive a basic durable goods demand function of the form

$$(C_d)_t = \alpha_0 + \alpha_1 Y_t + \alpha_2 (K_d)_{t-1} + u_{1t} \qquad (2.1)$$

where C_d is current consumption of durable goods in constant prices, Y is the current value of disposable income deflated by the price of durable goods and K_d is the stock of durable goods. Functions of the form (2.1) and variants of it have been derived by others including Stone and Rowe (1957) essentially from the stock-adjustment principle. We prefer the utility formulation which leads to a unified treatment of durable goods, non-durable goods and personal savings which we hope to describe in a subsequent paper.

In practice we have found great difficulty in obtaining a reliable estimate of the stock of durable goods. It was therefore decided to replace the stock of durable goods in (2.1) by a cumulated sum of durable goods spending from a specific reference point. In view of the linearity of (2.1) this would be satisfactory provided that the cumulated sum was made up of net purchases. Since this was not possible the alternative formulation is only wholly adequate provided that net spending in any period is a given constant proportion of gross spending. Since this is unlikely to be a constant relationship, as shown in another context by Domar (1953), the function

$$(C_d)_t = \alpha_0' + \alpha_1' Y_t + \alpha_2' \sum_{i=1954}^{t-1} (C_d)_i + u_{1t} \tag{2.2}$$

can only be regarded as an approximation whose justification rests largely on its predictive and explanatory performance.

We have preferred to introduce the effects of hire purchase in a two stage formulation. One approach is to introduce explicit 'control' variables such as the minimum deposit rate on contracts and the maximum length of contract into (2.2). A second approach is to replace the concept of income in (2.2) by that of disposable resources where income is augmented by the net inflow of purchasing power from sources of hire purchase finance. In each period new credits are received and repayments out of income are made, so that net resources consist of current income plus new credits less repayments. This approach is implicit in some official publications such as *Economic Trends* (1961) and the *Economic Survey* (1962). A third and final procedure is to select new credits granted as the critical variable, to be introduced as an additional variable in (2.2). The two latter possibilities appealed to us more than the former, for initially we were persuaded that while it might be possible to establish a fairly close relation between the volume of hire purchase business and consumer durable spending, it might be rather more difficult to explain the volume of hire purchase business. Since the basic control variables presumably directly affect the volume of (or demand for) hire purchase facilities it seemed more informative to 'disaggregate' the problem so that the difficulties might be more clearly visible. For even if it had not been possible to pin down the effects of the control variable on the volume of hire purchase business, it would still have been an important result to have established the effects of changes in the volume of hire purchase business on consumer durable spending for their own sake.

The second of the above approaches raises an additional problem, namely that of explaining repayments. This subject was given lengthy consideration but ran into the repeated difficulty that the models analysed required a larger number of lagged observations than the sample size would permit. Very simple rule of thumb formulations were ruled out at an early stage, so that while some analysis was pursued with a 'resources' variable, the complete model including the generation of new credits and repayments was never realized. This did not turn out to be a great loss, since in the event the approach did not yield satisfactory results from an empirical point of view when used to explain consumer durable spending.

We were left then with the third approach in which durable goods spending was taken to depend directly amongst other things on the flow of new credits, while new credits were explained by a separate equation. Our initial approach to the explanation of new credits was based on the idea that they depended on current income, the terms of hire purchase contracts and the existing burden of hire purchase debt. Subsequently a more simultaneous model was considered in which the demand for durable goods was taken to be related to new credits both as cause and effect.

Statistical estimates of the majority of the relationships presented below were obtained initially by classical least squares. The most interesting relationships obtained in this way were re-estimated using the method of two stage least squares described in Klein *et al.* (1961). The single stage least squares estimates are of course biased, but the initial screening was conveniently carried out in this form.

III. Statistical estimates of demand for durable goods

Equation (2.2) was fitted to the data available on a quarterly basis from 1957 III–1961 IV. The data are described in the Appendix below. For comparative purposes a variety of other consumer durable functions were fitted, excluding credit variables, and we include some of these to gain perspective. The following results are of interest.

$$(C_d)_t = 471{\cdot}55 - 35{\cdot}16\,Q_{1t} + 1{\cdot}04\,Q_{2t} - 42{\cdot}65\,Q_{3t}$$
$$\quad (399{\cdot}5) \quad (41{\cdot}82) \quad (18{\cdot}97) \quad (28{\cdot}08)$$

$$+ 0{\cdot}077\,Y_t - 0{\cdot}044 \sum_{i=1954}^{t-1} (C_d)_i \qquad (3{\cdot}1)$$
$$(0{\cdot}117) \quad (0{\cdot}023)$$

$$\bar{R}^2 = 0{\cdot}71 \qquad \delta^2/S^2 = 1{\cdot}06$$

$$(C_d)_t = -303{\cdot}97 + 42{\cdot}70\,Q_{1t} + 11{\cdot}72\,Q_{2t} + 2{\cdot}10\,Q_{3t}$$
$$\quad (202{\cdot}45) \quad (44{\cdot}06) \quad (22{\cdot}41) \quad (30{\cdot}43)$$

$$+ 0{\cdot}165\,Y_t - 0{\cdot}249\,\frac{1}{8}\sum_{i=1}^{8} (C_d)_{t-i} \qquad (3{\cdot}2)$$
$$(0{\cdot}106) \quad (0{\cdot}891)$$

$$\bar{R}^2 = 0{\cdot}64 \qquad \delta^2/S^2 = 0{\cdot}72$$

$$(C_d)_t = 91{\cdot}25 - 36{\cdot}90\,Q_{1t} - 22{\cdot}90\,Q_{2t} - 6{\cdot}3\,Q_{3t}$$
$$\quad (99{\cdot}98) \quad (24{\cdot}41) \quad (23{\cdot}82) \quad (26{\cdot}71)$$

$$+ 0{\cdot}054\,Y_t \qquad (3{\cdot}3)$$
$$(0{\cdot}024)$$

$$\bar{R}^2 = 0{\cdot}25 \qquad \delta^2/S^2 = 0{\cdot}77$$

The first of these equations is the standard form of (2.2). The second, with no distinction between wage and non-wage income, is similar to the form of durable goods function used in the United Kingdom quarterly statistical model presented in Klein *et al.* (1961). Neither of these relationships is satisfactory. Disposable income does not appear to have been a significant variable, and the degree of serial correlation as measured by the Neumann Ratio is relatively high. Equation (3.3) considers the gross influence of disposable income in isolation, and the decline in the goodness of fit statistic is marked, with a continued high degree of serial correlation. The residuals from these equations all show pronounced peaks occurring in the periods of most rapid expansion of durable good spending, particularly in the last quarter of 1958. This it will be remembered is the period most affected by the sharp relaxation of hire purchase controls that took place in September of that year.

Other forms of distributed lag, with some inclusive of the rate of interest (a time weighted average of Bank Rate) all yielded a similar residual pattern, and there appeared to be a strong *a priori* case for ascribing part of the pattern to the omission of explicit hire purchase variables.

The question may be raised as to the apparent contradiction between the result (3.2) together with the inference we have drawn from it, and the result reported in Klein *et al.* (1961, pp. 59–60) that they examined the 'possibility of an influence of hire purchase conditions on durables expenditure but could find no empirical evidence for a stable relationship'. It should be pointed out that the sources of hire purchase data on which the present paper is based were not available at the time the study by Klein *et al.* was undertaken. This restriction in data availability explains the sample size we have utilized here. The only data that were utilized to test for hire purchase influence in the study by Klein *et al.* was based on statistics made available privately by a national motor manufacturer, and as such were scarcely adequate.[1] It follows that it is not possible to test directly with a consistent set of adequate data any hypotheses with regard to the possibilities of structural change with regard to credit effects over the period 1948–61. It is, however, possible to examine the consumer durables function used in Klein *et al.*[2] by extending it to cover the period 1957–61. Such an examination based on estimates over the sample period 1948–56, the 'forecast' period 1957–61 and the whole period suggests that the sample and 'forecast' period cannot be regarded as homogeneous with regard to structure if the identical set of explanatory variables is relied on.

Disposable income was therefore replaced in (3.1) by a resources variable, R as defined above. The least squares estimate obtained was

$$\begin{aligned}(C_d)_t = {} & \underset{(405{\cdot}3)}{-1132{\cdot}3} + \underset{(28{\cdot}31)}{29{\cdot}61}\, Q_{1t} - \underset{(17{\cdot}90)}{18{\cdot}92}\, Q_{2t} + \underset{(43{\cdot}90)}{113{\cdot}80}\, Q_{3t} \\ & + \underset{(0{\cdot}120)}{0{\cdot}419}\, R_t - \underset{(0{\cdot}026)}{0{\cdot}079} \sum_{i=1954}^{t-1} (C_d)_{t-i} \qquad (3{\cdot}4) \\ & \bar{R}^2 = 0{\cdot}57 \qquad \delta^2/S^2 = 0{\cdot}80\end{aligned}$$

Somewhat surprisingly perhaps this result was even worse than the relation including disposable income. The double peak in the residual pattern persisted and the particular peak for 1960 accentuated. Other variants including the resources variable led to un-

[1] The data referred only to H.P. contracts based on a standard 'family' car.

[2] Such an examination has been carried out by M. Mohan. Exact tests for structural change are complicated by the fact that this function was originally estimated by limited information maximum likelihood methods.

acceptable results, in certain cases the sign of the coefficient on this variable going negative.

The introduction of new credits N into (2.2) resulted in a marked improvement in the goodness of fit achieved. Estimates by least squares were obtained.

$$
\begin{aligned}
(C_d)_t = & -395{\cdot}60 + 1{\cdot}11\, Q_{1t} - 10{\cdot}90\, Q_{2t} + 40{\cdot}35\, Q_{3t} \\
& \quad (234{\cdot}8) \quad (15{\cdot}20) \qquad (9{\cdot}71) \qquad (24{\cdot}63) \\
& + 0{\cdot}165\, Y_t + 0{\cdot}936\, N_t - 0{\cdot}031 \sum_{i=1954}^{t-1} (C_d)_i \qquad (3{\cdot}5) \\
& \quad (0{\cdot}071) \qquad (0{\cdot}117) \qquad (0{\cdot}015) \\
& \bar{R}^2 = 0{\cdot}88 \qquad \delta^2/S^2 = 1{\cdot}13
\end{aligned}
$$

and from two-stage least squares

$$
\begin{aligned}
(C_d)_t = & -683{\cdot}10 + 15{\cdot}00\, Q_{1t} - 11{\cdot}51\, Q_{2t} + 67{\cdot}80\, Q_{3t} \\
& \quad (333{\cdot}61) \quad (18{\cdot}62) \qquad (10{\cdot}41) \qquad (31{\cdot}31) \\
& + 0{\cdot}253\, Y_t + 0{\cdot}907\, N_t - 0{\cdot}051 \sum_{i=1954}^{t-1} (C_d)_i \qquad (3{\cdot}6) \\
& \quad (0{\cdot}092) \qquad (0{\cdot}133) \qquad (0{\cdot}021) \\
& \bar{R}^2 = 0{\cdot}86 \qquad \delta^2/S^2 = 1{\cdot}25
\end{aligned}
$$

In both cases the coefficients of all the main variables are at least twice their standard errors, and the new credits variable is very highly significant indeed. This can be seen visually from an inspection of the panel diagram Fig. 1, which depicts the contribution of each variable separately to the computed value of durable consumption, obtained from the two stage least squares version (3.6). The degree of serial correlation is still high for a sample of this size, but the residual pattern has been 'broken' up, in particular the double peak has been removed and the computed value brought very close to the actual value of durable goods spending during the relaxation period of late 1958 and early 1959. However there still remains a discrepancy for the 1960 period, where the residuals are markedly positive. The explanation of the persistence of this peak may be due to the omission of bank advances as a source of finance for durable goods purchasers. This period saw an extremely rapid rise in bank advances and it is possible that many people preferred to finance their durable spending, particularly for cars, in this way. We have not found it possible to break down bank advances from published data in any meaningful way to test this hypothesis, so that such analysis must await more adequate statistical data.

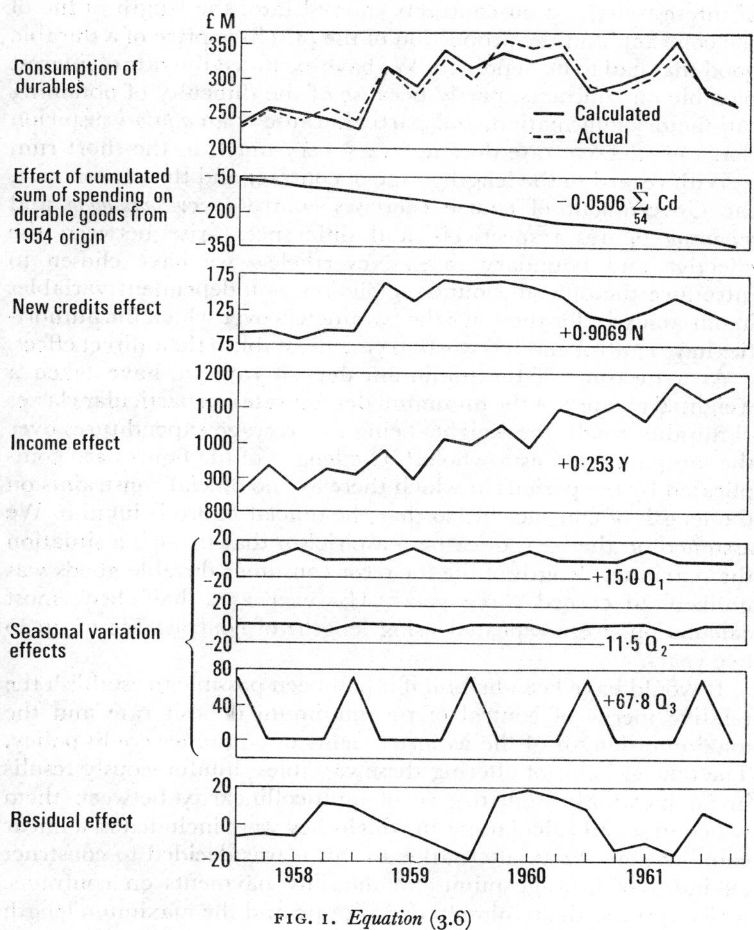

FIG. 1. *Equation* (3.6)

IV. Statistical estimates of the demand for new credits

As stated in 2.6 above, the initial approach to the determination of the volume of new credits led to the hypothesis that disposable income, the burden of the debt and the terms of hire purchase contracts are the main explanatory variables involved. The terms on which credit is offered were taken to embrace the effective rate of interest charged on contracts entered into, the length of life of the contract, and the proportion of the purchase price of a durable good that had to be deposited. We have excluded the rate of interest payable on contracts, partly because of the difficulty of obtaining satisfactory information, and partly because of an *a priori* suspicion that the effective rate does not vary very much in the short run.

With regard to the length of life of contract and the deposit rate, the Government of course exercises control over *maximum* and *minimum* figures respectively and differences arise between the effective and boundary rates. Nevertheless we have chosen to introduce the official 'boundary' figures as independent variables in our analysis, for these are the parameters over which the authorities have control and it is worth trying to establish their direct effect.

As a measure of the minimum deposit rate we have taken a weighted average of the minimum deposit rates on particular classes of durable goods, the weights being the average expenditures over the sample period as a whole.[3] The length of life figures are complicated by the periods in which there are no official constraints on the length of contract life so that the official figure is infinite. We assumed on the basis of casual empiricism that in such a situation the maximum length of life for most consumer durable goods was unlikely to exceed three years. However as a half-check most calculations were repeated using lengths of contract life of up to five years.

It would have been helpful if it had been possible to establish the relative merits of control of the minimum deposit rate and the maximum length of life as instruments of consumer credit policy. The official habit of altering these variables simultaneously results in an inevitably high degree of multicollinearity between them which upset all calculations in which they were included in a linear combination. As an alternative to this it was decided to construct an index of average minimum monthly payments on contracts, which utilized the minimum deposit rate and the maximum length of contract life,[4] and to include this with the minimum deposit rate as a separate variable.

[3] We run here into the familiar problem of correlation between the deposit rates and the weights. In this particular case there is a sufficient broad uniformity of movement in the rates that serves in mitigation. The general problem is analogous to the construction of an index of tariff rates.

[4] The measure used as an index of the real burden of payments was one minus the minimum deposit rate divided by the maximum contract length. This is not identical with a measure of cost per period for no account is taken of interest

In all calculations, disposable income over the sample period did not appear to play a significant role in explaining the demand for new credits. It is arguable that not only is the demand for durable goods dependent on willingness to take on new credits, but *vice versa* the demand for durables will affect the demand for credit. Following this line of approach, disposable income was omitted and the level of durable good spending included. The effects of this move may be seen by comparing two results that include only the minimum deposit rate as a measure of the terms on which credit was available.

$$\underset{}{N_t} = \underset{(100{\cdot}06)}{130{\cdot}30} - \underset{(12{\cdot}07)}{7{\cdot}19}\, Q_{1t} - \underset{(10{\cdot}0)}{10{\cdot}37}\, Q_{2t} - \underset{(15{\cdot}60)}{12{\cdot}99}\, Q_{3t}$$

$$+ \underset{(0{\cdot}033)}{0{\cdot}025}\, Y_t - \underset{(0{\cdot}079)}{0{\cdot}082}\, D_{t-1} - \underset{(0{\cdot}36)}{2{\cdot}56}\, d_t \qquad (4.1)$$

$$\bar{R}^2 = 0{\cdot}79 \qquad \delta^2/S^2 = 2{\cdot}15$$

$$N_t = \underset{(26{\cdot}9)}{33{\cdot}99} + \underset{(5{\cdot}60)}{9{\cdot}37}\, Q_{1t} + \underset{(4{\cdot}86)}{0{\cdot}96}\, Q_{2t} - \underset{(5{\cdot}50)}{4{\cdot}40}\, Q_{3t}$$

$$+ \underset{(0{\cdot}082)}{0{\cdot}548}\, (C_d)_t - \underset{(0{\cdot}013)}{0{\cdot}062}\, D_{t-1} - \underset{(0{\cdot}22)}{1{\cdot}44}\, d_t \qquad (4.2)$$

$$\bar{R}^2 = 0{\cdot}96 \qquad \delta^2/S^2 = 1{\cdot}75$$

In equations (4.1) and (4.2) D is the hire purchase debt deflated by the price of durable goods and d the minimum average deposit rate. They are single equation least squares estimates.

From a crude statistical point of view it is apparent that (4.2) is considerably superior to (4.1). In both cases the signs on the lagged stock of debt and the deposit rate are negative as required. In the second case however the fit and standard errors are superior overall. It does not unfortunately follow immediately that (4.2) is to be accepted as superior without further consideration. If disposable income could be treated as a variable properly exogenous to the

cost. If the deposit rate falls with a given length of contract life and purchase price the interest cost for a given rate will rise. Thus the deposit rate effect will be correlated with the interest effect on overall cost per period. The index used does not, however, mirror the effects of changes in cost due to changes in the rate of interest itself which for cases already given has been excluded as an explanatory variable.

markets for credit and durable goods, then the use of (4.2) introduces an element of simultaneity into the model represented by (4.2) and the durable goods equation (3.6). Treating disposable income as exogenous, the model consisting of (4.1) and (3.6) is recursive. Consequently a better choice between (4.1) and (4.2) is made in principle by comparing the sum of squares of residuals obtained from the reduced form for N with the sum of squares of residuals from (4.1). In this case the reduced forms would be derived from the structural parameters estimated for the individual equations (3.6) and (4.2).

Treating disposable income as exogenous to the model, the appropriate sums of squares were computed and it appeared that on this criterion the model consisting of (3.6) and (4.2) was superior. However the result was marginally in favour of (3.6) and (4.1) when two-stage least squares was applied to the individual equations. The two-stage least squares estimates were as follows:

$$\begin{aligned} N_t = \underset{(124{\cdot}9)}{161{\cdot}98} - \underset{(12{\cdot}20)}{9{\cdot}32}\, Q_{1t} - \underset{(10{\cdot}05)}{10{\cdot}25}\, Q_{2t} - \underset{(15{\cdot}93)}{16{\cdot}70}\, Q_{3t} \\ + \underset{(0{\cdot}034)}{0{\cdot}015}\, Y_t - \underset{(0{\cdot}081)}{0{\cdot}058}\, D_{t-1} - \underset{(0{\cdot}36)}{2{\cdot}52}\, d_t \end{aligned} \tag{4.3}$$

$$\bar{R}^2 = 0{\cdot}79 \qquad \delta^2/S^2 = 2{\cdot}23$$

$$\begin{aligned} N_t = \underset{(40{\cdot}20)}{80{\cdot}07} + \underset{(7{\cdot}31)}{3{\cdot}55}\, Q_{1t} - \underset{(5{\cdot}82)}{2{\cdot}02}\, Q_{2t} - \underset{(6{\cdot}86)}{9{\cdot}07}\, Q_{3t} \\ + \underset{(0{\cdot}130)}{0{\cdot}400}\, (C_d)_t - \underset{(0{\cdot}016)}{0{\cdot}052}\, D_{t-1} - \underset{(0{\cdot}304)}{1{\cdot}717}\, d_t \end{aligned} \tag{4.4}$$

$$\bar{R}^2 = 0{\cdot}94 \qquad \delta^2/S^2 = 2{\cdot}24$$

It appears that this criterion does not enable us to make a conclusive choice between the two relationships, and in any event in the last analysis an adequate decision can only be taken in the context of a wider model in which disposable income appears as an endogenous variable.

To complete the analysis of the demand for new credits, the average monthly payment as defined above was introduced as an additional explanatory variable. In this case both the two-stage and single stage least squares estimates produced a negative coefficient on the level of disposable income where it was included. The inclusion of the consumption of durable goods in place of disposable income, led to results that were superficially more satisfactory. Two-stage least squares estimates are given below for three measures of the minimum average monthly payment involving maximum contract lengths of five (M_5), four (M_4) and three (M_3) years respectively.

$$\underset{}{N_t} = \underset{(39{\cdot}1)}{100{\cdot}6} - \underset{(5{\cdot}19)}{7{\cdot}35}\, Q_{1t} + \underset{(5{\cdot}62)}{3{\cdot}51}\, Q_{2t} + \underset{(5{\cdot}40)}{3{\cdot}67}\, Q_{3t}$$
$$+ \underset{(0{\cdot}129)}{0{\cdot}337}\, (C_d)_t - \underset{(0{\cdot}284)}{1{\cdot}425}\, d_t - \underset{(0{\cdot}022)}{0{\cdot}024}\, D_{t-1} - \underset{(4{\cdot}83)}{9{\cdot}20}\, (M_5)_t \tag{4.5}$$
$$\bar{R}^2 = 0{\cdot}96 \qquad \delta^2/S^2 = 1{\cdot}00$$

$$N_t = \underset{(36{\cdot}2)}{104{\cdot}5} - \underset{(4{\cdot}86)}{7{\cdot}23}\, Q_{1t} + \underset{(5{\cdot}23)}{3{\cdot}27}\, Q_{2t} + \underset{(4{\cdot}97)}{4{\cdot}23}\, Q_{3t}$$
$$+ \underset{(0{\cdot}114)}{0{\cdot}356}\, (C_d)_t - \underset{(0{\cdot}256)}{1{\cdot}517}\, d_t - \underset{(0{\cdot}018)}{0{\cdot}031}\, D_{t-1} - \underset{(4{\cdot}76)}{10{\cdot}40}\, (M_4)_t \tag{4.6}$$
$$\bar{R}^2 = 0{\cdot}97 \qquad \delta^2/S^2 = 1{\cdot}00$$

$$N_t = \underset{(32{\cdot}0)}{106{\cdot}6} - \underset{(4{\cdot}30)}{6{\cdot}88}\, Q_{1t} + \underset{(4{\cdot}55)}{2{\cdot}05}\, Q_{2t} + \underset{(4{\cdot}30)}{5{\cdot}75}\, Q_{3t}$$
$$+ \underset{(0{\cdot}093)}{0{\cdot}410}\, (C_d)_t - \underset{(0{\cdot}230)}{1{\cdot}727}\, d_t - \underset{(0{\cdot}012)}{0{\cdot}049}\, D_{t-1} - \underset{(4{\cdot}35)}{11{\cdot}20}\, (M_3)_t \tag{4.7}$$
$$\bar{R}^2 = 0{\cdot}97 \qquad \delta^2/S^2 = 1{\cdot}00$$

Judging by the relation of coefficients to their standard errors, the results indicate that a choice of maximum contract life of three years is most satisfactory. In equation (4.7) the coefficients of the main explanatory variable are all at least twice their standard errors, and the signs are all as expected. The contributions of the main variables to the computed values are depicted graphically in Fig. 2.

V. The impact of policy instruments

The analysis employed in this paper has depicted the minimum deposit rate and maximum length of contract life as the chief

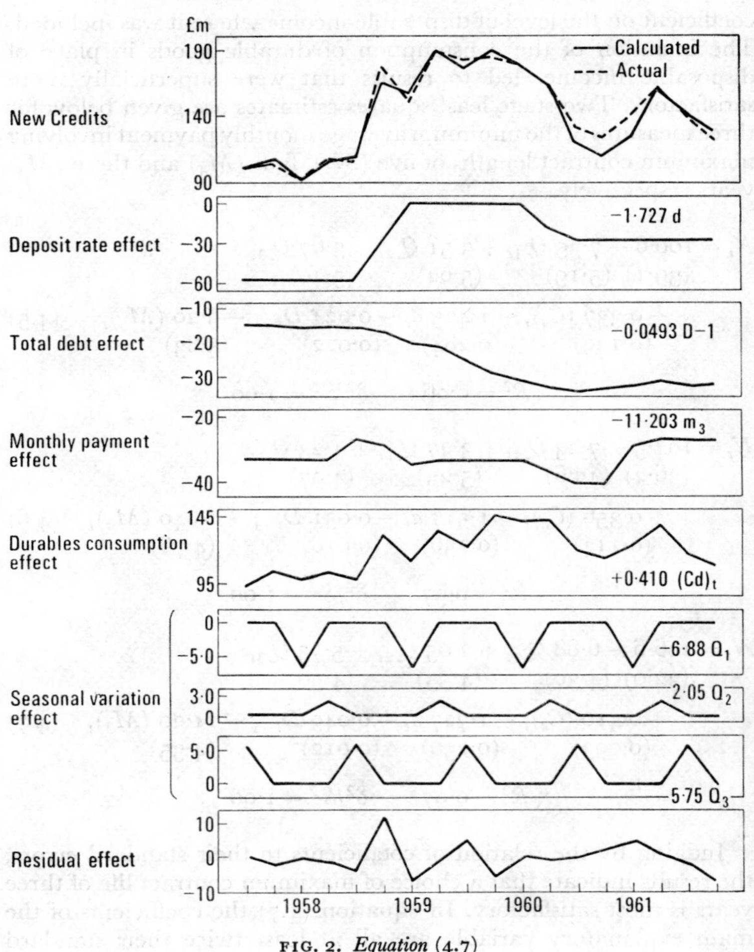

FIG. 2. *Equation* (4.7)

policy instruments affecting consumer credit and its relation to durable goods spending. A complete model of the economy is required to estimate the total effects of changes in these variables which would be computed from the reduced forms of such a model. We confine ourselves here to a partial analysis that holds the level of disposable income constant in terms of durable goods.

To carry out this analysis we solve the equations (3.6) and (4.7) for the jointly dependent variables of the sector model, C_d and N. This gives the equation for durable goods

$$(C_d)_t = \text{constant} + \text{seasonals} + 0{\cdot}403\ Y_t - 0{\cdot}081 \sum_{i=1954}^{1} (C_d)_{t-i} - 0{\cdot}071\ D_{t-1} - 2{\cdot}493\ d_t - 16{\cdot}20\ (M_3)_t \qquad (5{\cdot}1)$$

The minimum average deposit rate was introduced for the purposes of estimation as a set of integers indicating percentages. Over the sample period the rate varied from a low point of zero to a maximum of 33 per cent. Hence the contribution of this term to the computed level of real spending can be seen from (5.1) to have varied from zero to a negative figure of just over £80 million in 1954 prices. To put this figure in perspective the mean value of durable goods spending on a quarterly basis over the sample period was £291 million in 1954 prices. Equation (5.1) implies that a change in the minimum deposit rate from (say) 30 to 15 per cent taken at the point of sample means would result in a change in consumer durable spending of about 13 per cent (taking the estimates at their face value) provided that the length of contract life was extended to maintain a constant average monthly payment. In general the total effect of a change in the rate is less if the length of contract is held constant, for if for example the deposit rate is reduced, other things being equal, the average monthly payment is thereby increased. To continue the present illustration, setting the length of life (with a maximum of 36 months) equal to its sample mean, the net effect in the current example would be to reduce the change in durable good spending from roughly 13 to about 10 per cent.[5]

In a similar manner we can also consider the effect on durable good spending of a change in the length of contract life, holding constant the remainder of the variables appearing in (5.1). Taking the minimum average deposit rate at its mean value of 6 per cent, equation (5.1) implies that a reduction in the maximum length of contract life from three years (36 months) to two years (24 months) would lead *ceteris paribus* to a fall in spending on consumer durable

[5] The average monthly payment series was scaled to produce a set of numbers around 3·0 which were obtained by subtracting the deposit percentage as an integer from 100 and dividing by the maximum length of contract in terms of months.

goods of something over 6 per cent. This interval covers the range of variation of the maximum contract length over the sample period, assuming a three year maximum in the absence of any restriction by the authorities.

Considering the range of operation of the minimum deposit rate and the maximum length of contract life over the sample period, the statistical results suggest that the observed variation in the deposit rate has been on average roughly twice as important absolutely as the length of contract life in determining consumer spending on durable goods. Taking the statistical results at their face value this is a statement of fact and does not entail in itself any conclusion as to which may be considered the most effective instrument of consumer credit control with regard to hire purchase debt.[6] Given that within the formal framework of the above equations there is an infinite number of pairs of values of the deposit rate and the contract life that will produce a given level of spending on consumer durable goods the choice of an optimal combination will be in part at least governed by *a priori* notions of feasibility that it is not our purpose to discuss here. Even apart from this, decisions as to the optimal combination, in a broader context of general influence on demand must take into account the net effect of changes in control variables on other components of total consumer spending. For example it is important to know whether a rise in the deposit rate on durable goods is met partially at least by realizing other asset holdings or whether it is met primarily by a reduction in the rate of consumer spending on non-durable goods. Such questions can only be answered with the use of a complex simultaneous model that is outside the scope of this paper.[7]

VI. Summary

In this paper we began by showing that simple models of consumer durable spending excluding credit variables, fail to explain ade-

[6] The tentative character of the statistical results limit the degree of confidence that we might attach to any *general* conclusions about the impact of credit controls. We see little reason to suppose however that the technical difficulties that make us cautious in drawing such conclusions, severely distort the relative importance of the individual variables we have studied over the sample period actually utilized, as evident in the regression analysis.

[7] For some theoretical analysis cf. Chiang (1959).

quately such spending over the period 1957–61. The introduction of new credits issued resulted in marked improvement in our ability to account for the movement of the consumption of durable goods over the period.

The flow of new credits was accounted for by the level of spending on consumer durable goods, the minimum average deposit rate on new contracts, the minimum average monthly payment and lagged stock of consumer hire purchase debt. All these variables contributed significantly towards an explanation of new credits.

Combining our equations for consumer durable goods and new credits, we obtained an equation for consumer durable goods which depended directly amongst other things on the control variables, i.e. the minimum average deposit rate and the minimum average monthly payment. Holding the level of real disposable income constant, calculations based on this equation suggested that variations in the control variables over the sample period have played a substantial role in determining the movement of consumer durable goods spending. Taking the results at their face value, we conclude therefore that variations in these controls by the authorities constituted an effective weapon in their armoury for working on the level of consumer demand over the sample period studied.

Our results are clearly limited in a number of ways. From a statistical point the sample size employed has been small and the reliability of our results affected accordingly. Serial correlation has persisted in some of the estimates and this too must be taken into account in judging the reliability of our estimates. From an economic point of view we have confined our attention to the effects of variations in credit and credit conditions relating to hire purchase finance houses and household goods shops. No account has been taken of additional sources of consumer finance such as bank credit which we suspect may have been significant at some points during the sample period. Finally it must be re-emphasized that a full analysis of the impact of consumer credit policy can only be carried out in the context of a more complete model that has been beyond the scope of the present enquiry. Our picture is only a partial one, but it is suggestive that a larger scale analysis might produce more fruitful results as a guide to the quantitative impact of consumer credit policies.

APPENDIX

*Data used in estimation**

		(1)	(2)	(3)	(4)	(5)	(6)	(7)	(8)	(9)	(10)
		Y	Cd	N	$\sum_{t=1954}^{t} (Cd)_t$	R	D_{-1}	d	M_5	M_4	M_3
1957	III	3458	228	101	1274	3464	297	33	2·98	2·98	2·98
	IV	3698	253	103	1527	3702	302	33	2·96	2·96	2·96
1958	I	3421	240	93	1767	3424	307	33	2·98	2·98	2·98
	II	3668	253	106	2020	3680	307	33	2·98	2·98	2·98
	III	3603	237	105	2257	3613	320	33	1·72	1·99	2·46
	IV	3876	319	177	2576	3942	333	16	1·52	1·90	2·54
1959	I	3552	273	151	2849	3591	403	0	1·84	2·30	3·07
	II	4001	327	187	3176	4068	437	0	1·80	2·25	3·00
	III	3930	297	181	3473	3992	514	0	1·79	2·23	2·97
	IV	4177	354	184	3827	4233	580	0	1·79	2·23	2·97
1960	I	3913	346	177	4173	3953	636	0	1·79	2·23	2·98
	II	4338	351	163	4524	4359	675	11	2·59	2·91	3·31
	III	4243	292	130	4816	4231	694	16	3·61	3·61	3·61
	IV	4475	280	123	5096	4451	683	16	3·60	3·60	3·60
1961	I	4234	301	139	5397	4222	661	16	2·66	2·66	2·66
	II	4660	338	162	5735	4671	646	16	2·45	2·45	2·45
	III	4445	285	140	6020	4448	655	16	2·47	2·47	2·47
	IV	4613	266	121	6286	4597	652	16	2·48	2·48	2·48

* Columns (1)–(6) measured in 1954 constant prices. Column (7) to be read as 'per cent'. Columns (8)–(10) to be read as (average minimum) monthly payment as per cent of average purchase price.

SOURCES

1. Columns (1), (2), and (4): *Economic Trends* and *Monthly Digest of Statistics.*
2. Column (3): 1958–61 *Economic Trends.* 1957 III and IV estimated from data available in *Board of Trade Journal.* (a) New credits issued by household goods shops obtained by applying average deposit rate to credit sales by household goods shops. (b) New credits to consumers from finance houses obtained by taking total new credits issued by finance houses and subtracting new credits issued by finance houses via household goods shops and industrial new credits. Figures in Column (7) for 1957 III and IV obtained by adding (a) and (b).
3. Column (5): obtained as the sum of Column (1) and Column (3) minus repayments obtained from *Economic Trends.*

4. Column (6): total consumer hire purchase debt from *Economic Trends*.

5. Column (7): *Midland Bank Review*. Weighted average of minimum deposits for durable sub-groups. Weights from 1957 Census of Distribution.

6. Columns (8)–(10): 100—Column (7) divided by maximum contract length in months. Maximum contract length is a weighted average of maximum lengths for durable sub-groups from *Midland Bank Review*. Weights as for Column (7). In the absence of legal maximum, 60 months, 48 months and 36 months were assumed in the construction of Columns (8)–(10) respectively.

REFERENCES

[1] Chiang, A. C., 'Instalment Credit Control; A Theoretical Analysis', *The Journal of Political Economy*, vol. 67, no. 4, August 1959, pp. 363–76.

[2] Domar, E., 'Depreciation, Replacement and Growth', *Economic Journal*, March 1953.

[3] Klein, L. R., Ball, R. J., Hazlewood, A., and Vendome, P., *An Econometric Model of the United Kingdom* (Oxford, 1961).

[4] Stone, J. R. N., and Rowe, D. A., 'The Market Demand for Durable Goods', *Econometrica*, vol. 25, no. 3, July 1957, pp. 423–43.

22

A SECONDARY BANKING SYSTEM

JACK REVELL*

IT is now more than nine years since the *Report* of the Radcliffe Committee analysed the structure and operation of the British banking system, but it is not always appreciated how striking have been the changes in the banking system in that short space of time. Some of these changes have been pointed out in financial journals over the years, but these have tended to concern themselves mainly with the deposit banks (London clearing banks, Scottish banks and Northern Ireland banks). The changes here have been in the structures of their balance sheets (the greatly increased proportion of advances and the swing towards holdings of commercial bills, for instance), in the services that they offer, and in the moves towards larger groupings of banks, usually including other kinds of financial institutions under a banking umbrella. The changes among the other banks have been equally great, but they have not been documented nearly so well. What has happened is that the non-deposit banks, which used to have somewhat specialized functions, have become knit together into what may be called a secondary banking system. The banks in this system have grown much faster than the deposit banks, and they have all begun to participate in a new form of banking, which differs considerably from that described in the textbooks.

The banks in the secondary system are distinguished from deposit banks by the fact that they take very little part in transferring payments from one organization to another, which is the main

* Reprinted from *The Banker*, vol. 118, no. 500, September 1968, pp. 798–804, by permission of the author and publisher. The article was based on an earlier paper written by the author and published by Hill, Samuel and Co. Ltd., 100 Wood Street, London E.C.2, as Hill, Samuel Occasional Paper, no. 3, under the title of 'Changes in British banking; the growth of a secondary banking system'. Jack Revell is Professor of Economics at the University of Wales at Bangor.

function of deposit banks. For the most part the banks that comprise the secondary system have been established in London for many years—accepting houses, other merchant banks, overseas banks and foreign banks. But the growth of this new banking system has also been accompanied by the influx of a large number of foreign banks, particularly from the U.S.A., which were not previously represented by an office in London, and by the participation in the last few years of the deposit banks themselves, operating through special subsidiary banks such as Westminster Foreign, Lloyds Bank (Europe), Midland and International and so on.

On any reckoning the rate of growth of the deposits of the banks that comprise the secondary banking system has been most impressive and in contrast with the sluggishness displayed by the deposit banks. From 1951 to 1966 the deposits of deposit banks grew only about 1½ times, while over the same period secondary bank deposits grew around eight times. In 1951 deposit bank deposits were nearly nine times as great as the total deposits of banks in the secondary system, but only 1·6 times as large in 1966. Even if we exclude from the deposits of secondary banks those elements which are internal to the banking system (deposits of branches to head offices overseas and inter-bank deposits), the growth is equally striking: on this basis the deposit bank deposits were 14 or 15 times those of the secondary system in 1951 compared with around three times in 1966.

There are two types of secondary bank whose deposits have grown faster than even these figures indicate. The first of these groups consists of the American banks in London, whose deposits have grown 24 times from 1951 to 1966, whichever measure of their deposit we use. American banks have come over to London in increasing numbers over the past few years, and once here they have grown fast for two main reasons. The first is the desire to provide services to U.S. companies which have branches or subsidiaries in this country, and probably about three-quarters of the London sterling business of American banks is accounted for by British subsidiaries of U.S. companies. The second factor has been the continuing deficit on the U.S. balance of payments, which has resulted in the American bank branches in London having to find their own resources by aggressive tapping of the Euro-dollar market, in which the American banks are now by far the biggest operators in London. In the past two or three years a very large part of the Euro-dollar deposits secured by American banks in London has been lent on to the head offices in New York, where they have been employed to increase the domestic resources of those U.S. banks which have London branches. In effect U.S. domestic banking competition has been transferred to the international arena, where American banks are not bound by the restrictions on interest rates and the periods for which they may be paid which are imposed by Regulation Q.

The second group of secondary banks with an exceptionally fast growth rate consists of the new affiliates of the deposit banks mentioned above. No overall statistics are published, but we can estimate that by the end of 1966, after little more than one year's operation by most of them, the total deposits of these nine banks were around £600 millions.

Deposits and advances

As soon as we look at the nature of the deposits and advances of secondary banks, we can see the complete contrast with the type of business undertaken by deposit banks. In this country deposit banking business is overwhelmingly domestic in character and conducted in sterling; more than half of all deposits consists of current accounts, and the greater part of advances is in the form of overdrafts; although some deposits and advances are very large, these are counterbalanced by great numbers of relatively small accounts. The deposits and advances of banks in the secondary system differ from those of deposit banks in all these respects.

Of the total deposits of the secondary banking system at the end of 1966 over 60 per cent came from overseas residents, and 56 per cent of total deposits was in currencies other than sterling. Of total advances over 70 per cent was to overseas residents, and roughly the same proportion was in currencies other than sterling. Within these overall proportions there is considerable diversity between the different types of banks and between individual banks of the same type. In general, the foreign-owned banks do a higher proportion of business with overseas residents and in non-sterling currencies than the predominantly British-owned banks, accepting houses and overseas banks; the American banks have the highest proportions of all.

Although international business thus accounts for more than half of all the assets and liabilities of secondary banks, their domestic business is by no means negligible, but it differs markedly from that of deposit banks. Over 60 per cent of their deposits of non-bank U.K. residents at the end of 1966 came from non-financial companies, and about 75 per cent of their advances went to non-financial companies. Nearly all the deposits of non-bank U.K. residents are in sterling, and of these sterling deposits perhaps one-quarter consists of current accounts, so that current accounts work out at less than 5 per cent of the total deposits of the banks in the secondary system. The remaining deposits are all interest-bearing, and the bulk of them is fixed for a definite period. The maturities of these term deposits vary considerably, from overnight up to one year or more, and in most cases the rate of interest is fixed for the whole period.

Of the advances, both in sterling and in other currencies, only a small part is of the overdraft type common to deposit banking in this country. The remaining loans take a variety of forms because secondary bankers pride themselves on being able to find a 'tailor-made' solution to each financing problem. One common feature is that the loans are nearly all for a definite period, with or without provision for repayment by instalments, and we shall lump them all together under the generic description of 'term loans'. With advances it is much more common than with deposits to have a variable interest rate, usually geared to Bank rate.

It is worth pausing to enquire why term loans should have become so popular in this country, which pioneered the overdraft and still relies so heavily on it. The first reason is that term loans, especially when they are repayable by instalments, are made on the security of the flow of income rather than on the security of assets in the balance sheet. Term loans extend the limits of credit-worthiness, so that even first-class companies can borrow more from the banking system than they could on overdraft alone. This ties in with two other features of the economic climate in this decade. The liquidity which companies had built up during the war was not finally exhausted until about 1960, and since then non-financial companies have leant heavily on the banking system to finance capital investment because new issues could not grow fast enough to compensate for the decreased availability of finance derived from internal sources—the cash flow. Alongside this there has been a tendency to move away from the generalized finance which the overdraft represents towards the tying of borrowing to particular capital projects.

The other main features of both deposits and advances is that the units are large. For many banks in the secondary system the minimum unit for a sterling deposit is £50,000, and the minimum tends to be larger for other currency deposits. Hardly any of the banks would look at the offer of a deposit of less than £10,000. For advances the unit is typically larger still, and £500,000 would be regarded as the norm by many banks, with advances occasionally running into millions of pounds. The Americans would describe the business of the banks in the secondary system as 'wholesale banking', contrasting it with the 'retail banking' undertaken by deposit banks.

Such large deposits and advances are very cheap to process. Secondary bankers can conduct their business with few of the expensive clerical procedures that face the deposit banker, there is no need for a widespread branch network and the number of staff is small, consisting largely of specialists. An equally important factor is that the secondary banker is not forced to keep 8 per cent of his assets in the barren form of cash, with a further minimum of 20 per cent as liquid assets earning far less than advances. For all these reasons the banks in the secondary system are low-cost institutions, operating with narrow margins between borrowing and lending rates. There are no agreements as to the rates to be paid and charged, and the system is highly competitive.

The rates paid to customers on deposits fluctuate according to market conditions, but they are normally lower than the rates paid by local authorities for deposits of the same maturity; the normal range lies between Bank rate and 1 per cent below Bank rate. The rates charged for loans cover a much wider range than for deposit banks. On occasion secondary banks actually undercut deposit banks, but in general their loans are more expensive than deposit banks overdrafts; a fair average would probably be ½ per cent over the rate charged by deposit banks, with a minimum of 1 per cent over Bank rate. With these wide fluctuations and ranges of rates it is difficult to generalize about the extent of the margin, but it is safe to say that the average margin is considerably less than the 3–3½ per cent which is the effective average for deposit banks. For deposits passed on to other banks the margin between taking and placing rates is usually only about $\frac{1}{16}$ per cent.

The matching principle

The contrast between the type of business that we have just described and deposit banking is almost complete. The large deposit banker has millions of separate accounts, some of them quite large but most of them relatively small, and virtually all of them are in sterling. Usually no more than half of his deposits is fixed at all, and of the fixed deposits the overwhelming part is at seven-days' notice. With his overdrafts he cannot always tell when credit limits will be used, and he cannot tell for certain when the overdrafts will be repaid, although they are formally repayable on demand. But because the bulk of the deposits is for small amounts and represents mainly working balances, he can treat his deposits as a revolving fund and rely on the law of large numbers as his main protection. As a second line of defence he keeps at least 50 per cent of his assets in a form which sacrifices yield for liquidity—cash, money at call, bills and investments.

The secondary banker has a small number of large accounts on both sides of his balance sheet, and a very large proportion is expressed in currencies other than sterling. The bulk of his deposits is fixed for a definite term, and he knows when repayment of his advances is due in full or in part. The secondary banker can thus control his balance sheet in two dimensions that are not under the control of a deposit banker, maturity and currency. If he does not attempt to control the structure of his balance sheet in these two dimensions, he is at considerable risk because of the large units of his accounts. He needs liquidity in the conventional sense for two reasons. First, a fair proportion of his deposits is for short periods, and these must be covered by assets of a fairly short maturity. Secondly, his published balance sheet and his returns to the Bank of England are cast in a conventional form, and they will be judged on the conventional basis of adequate liquidity. But the secondary banker would be very loath to obtain his liquidity by investing mainly in the normal 'discount market' assets because of the sacrifice of yield entailed. Instead he goes very largely to the new parallel markets for local authority loans, hire-purchase finance house deposits and inter-bank deposits. Although the maturity of some of these parallel market assets is often several months, they normally yield far more than Treasury bills, commercial bills or money at call, and they have the considerable advantage that they all appear fairly liquid when they are listed in balance sheets.

The controlling of the maturity and currency structure of a banker's balance sheet is known as 'matching'. It is, of course, an age-old principle of banking, but it is only in the last few years that it has come into play in British banking with the advent of large deposits and advances, fixed for definite periods and expressed in a number of different currencies. A completely matched balance sheet is one in which for every deposit of a certain amount and in a certain currency maturing on a certain day there is an asset of the same amount and in the same currency maturing on the same day. Provided nobody defaults, it is a self-liquidating balance sheet. In practice few secondary bankers have a completely matched position. Because of the narrow margins in this kind of banking, there is very little profit in just 'putting business through', and most secondary bankers aim to increase their profits by having assets somewhat longer than deposits because yields rise with maturity. Nearly all secondary bankers also take a view on future interest rates and exchange rates, although some do so far more than others.

Just as liquidity is the basic principle of deposit banking, so matching is the basic principle of secondary banking. We must not overstate the case, however. There is such diversity among banks in the secondary system that no universal principle can be made to apply to all of them without qualification. We have already mentioned that some banks will be more closely matched than others, but equally some banks in the secondary system are rather scornful of the principle of matching, describing it as 'broking' (as opposed to banking) or as 'dollar banking' (since it was first used for the Euro-dollar business and is still more widespread here than with deposits and advances in sterling, at least for British banks). Some of the banks have a fair amount of current account business and often lend on overdraft; it is only natural that such banks should behave more like deposit banks and rely largely on conventional liquidity. Some of the larger banks in the secondary system can begin to count on the fact that a high proportion of short-term deposits remains beyond the maturity date; they, too, can behave more like deposit banks. Even when these qualifications have been made, however, the original statement still stands, since it applies to some of the business of nearly all the banks in the system and to all the business of some of the banks.

Parallel money markets

The growth of the secondary banking system which we have been describing is closely bound up with the development of the London market for deposits and loans in currencies other than sterling—the 'Euro-dollar market'. It has also been dependent on the newer parallel money markets in sterling. These started first with the demand from local authorities for deposits with a maturity of less than one year, and they soon extended to cover a similar demand from hire purchase finance houses. Although the secondary banks have not completely forsaken the conventional discount market, with its money at call, Treasury bills and commercial bills, they have increasingly depended on the parallel markets for a large part of their liquidity. These markets have provided assets with a much wider range of maturity than those of the discount market and with a higher level of yields. The parallel market which has played a crucial rôle in the development of secondary banking, however, is the market for inter-bank deposits; this dealt at first only in deposits denominated in currencies other than sterling, but has extended to sterling in the past few years.

It is an unbreakable convention of English deposit banking that no bank may be seen to borrow from another, whether it is the Bank of England or another deposit bank. The realities of the operation of the discount market are such, of course, that banks lend to each other through the advancing of money at call and borrow from each other by the withdrawal of money at call, but the appearances are maintained. With this background it is a little strange that such a flourishing and open market for inter-bank deposits should have grown up in London. Although they are called 'deposits', the fact is that secondary banks actively solicit these deposits through brokers, and they are really loans from one bank to another. The explanation is that secondary banking as we have described it could not exist without an active inter-bank market.

As we have seen, the secondary banker typically has a small number of large deposits and a small number of even larger advances, the bulk of both deposits and advances being fixed for definite periods, with many different currencies involved on both sides of the balance sheet. The essence of secondary banking is that the banker should be able to provide a 'made-to-measure' solution to any financing problem presented to him by a customer, and he will be very loath to turn away any lending business that offers. A deposit banker can normally meet the needs of his customers for advances without trouble out of the proceeds of maturing assets because loans tend to be small relative to the balance sheet total, and he also maintains a 'cushion' of quoted investments that can be liquidated without great loss in normal circumstances. The secondary banker can behave differently: he can arrange the loan first and then cast around for additional deposits to finance it. If he has arranged to make a loan of £1 million for one year, it is most unlikely that his customers will of their own accord come forward with the offer of deposits to that amount and with a maturity that he can accept as matching the loan—at least he cannot rely on this happening within the next two or three days. Instead the secondary banker turns to the inter-bank market for the deposits he needs to support the loan. His chances of success are many times greater than if he relied on his own customers because all that is required is that somewhere in the secondary banking system deposits shall have been placed with banks that have no immediate lending business in prospect. For these banks the inter-bank market is in competition with local authorities and finance houses as an outlet, and they also have the possibility of switching from one currency to another within the limits allowed by exchange control to find a profitable use for the deposit that they have taken.

If there were no inter-bank markets, both in sterling and in other currencies, the secondary banker would have to behave in the same way as the deposit banker: he would have to secure his deposits first and then seek ways of employing them. To some extent he does this because he will never turn away a deposit that is offered to him. The existence of the various parallel markets ensures that he can employ the deposit with an adequate return, even when no customer is seeking an advance that would match it. But the inter-bank market ensures that he also has the possibility of making loans before he has secured his deposits. He needs no 'cushion' of assets with an inferior yield to meet the possible demand for loans. The main function of inter-bank deposits is thus that of filling in gaps in the maturity structure on both sides of the balance sheet.

Monetary implications

The picture that we have been presenting in this article is that of the growth of an entirely new banking system, with a method of operation quite different from that of the deposit banks as described in the textbooks. This is 'wholesale banking', in which the accounts on both sides of the balance sheet are in very large units and have a fixed maturity. Most of the banks still retain specialist functions, but nearly all the non-deposit banks enter into this secondary banking system to some extent, and many of them do nothing else but this type of banking. The individual banks are tied together into the secondary banking system by the network of inter-bank deposits, both in sterling and currencies, which has grown up.

The development of this secondary banking system has many implications. Two may be mentioned. First is it sensible to continue to speak of *the* banking system? Would it not be better to split these secondary banks off from the deposit banks, and to cease to count their deposits as part of the money supply? In many ways the functions of secondary banks are more analogous to those of a finance house than to those of a deposit bank, and they need to be considered separately. The second implication arises from the first. It is that any attempt to control the operations of these secondary banks by the imposition of liquidity controls or by requiring deposits with the Bank of England will be very difficult. Not only do the liquidity ratios of these banks differ very widely one from another, but the need for overall liquidity is replaced by the need for a reasonable matching of the maturities and currencies of assets and liabilities.

VI

DEBT MANAGEMENT

VI

DEBT MANAGEMENT

EDITED BY
M. H. MILLER

Introduction

THE scope of debt management is as wide as the definition of government debt. If, as in the *Radcliffe Report*, the latter is defined to include notes and coin—the monetary base—then 'monetary policy' comes under the heading of debt management; and it is this wider concept which is relevant to the readings which follow.

A specification of the authorities' policies of debt management can be regarded as a description of the conditions of supply of the various instruments by which they borrow. The determination of the *total* supply of all such instruments falls, however, largely within the realm of fiscal policy whose deficits and surpluses, together with transactions in existing assets, mark the contraction or expansion of this total. If the stocks of all outstanding instruments are fixed, the supply functions are perfectly inelastic with respect to interest rates. If the latter are 'pegged', then the supply functions are perfectly elastic with respect to own rates. Clearly these are two special cases, and more generally elasticities will lie between such limits. The question of whether the money supply is exogenous or endogenous, however, is closely related to the question of which of the above caricatures is closer to the truth. If rates are pegged, for example, the quantity of money, and so of the monetary base, will be determined by demand and not by (the perfectly elastic) supply.

As is apparent from the Bank of England article included below, and the discussion of this by Goodhart, these supply functions cannot be considered without reference to the dynamic structure of the demand functions for the debt instruments. While, for example, a higher bond rate may raise the demand for bonds, a *rising* rate may damage bond sales. This is because speculators may project such rising rates into the future and, anticipating capital losses, stay out or get out of bonds until rates are expected to stabilize. A simple appreciation of the significance of such dynamic elements in the market for bonds may be given by the following three-equation model:

$$D(t) = a_0 + a_1 r(t) + a_2(r(t) - r(t-1)) \tag{1}$$

$$S(t) = b_0 + b_1 r(t) + b_2(r(t) - r(t-1)) \tag{2}$$

$$D(t) = S(t) \tag{3}$$

where D is the demand for the stock of government bonds ('gilt-edged') by the private sector, S is the supply of bonds by the government, r is the bond rate, and t indicates time.

The downward slope of the demand for money function would lead us to expect that the demand for bonds would be increasing in its own rate ($a_1 > 0$), while the speculative behaviour discussed above implies that rising rates reduce demand ($a_2 < 0$). In equilibrium, when rates have settled down (i.e. $r(t) = r(t-1) = r^e$), equality between demand and supply will ensure an equilibrium rate (r^e) characterized as follows:

$$r^e = \frac{b_0 - a_0}{a_1 - b_1} \tag{4}$$

But whether such an equilibrium will be reached is in part determined by the nature of the supply function. Substitution of (1) and (2) into (3) yields a first order difference equation in r, that is where $r(t)$ depends on $r(t-1)$, *inter alia*. The condition for stability is that the coefficient on lagged r is less than one in absolute value, i.e.

$$\left| 1 \Big/ \left(\frac{a_1 - b_1}{a_2 - b_2} + 1 \right) \right| < 1 \tag{5}$$

Even if b_2 is equal to zero, high negative values for b_1 will help to increase the denominator and ensure stability. A negative value for b_1 means that the authorities must place less debt on the market the higher the interest rate, a fairly natural assumption for a cost-conscious borrower. For a given value of b_1, however, a higher negative value of b_2 will help to satisfy the stability condition. A negative value for b_2 implies counter-speculating by the authorities, a readiness to take stocks off the market as rates are rising, and so to absorb the stocks which speculators are selling, and the capital losses which they are avoiding. The idea of the authorities 'leaning into the wind' can be thought of in terms of the size and signs of b_1 and b_2. The papers by Goodhart and Norton reprinted in this chapter emphasize the dynamic aspects of the demand for gilt-edged and the fact that it would appear to be unstable in the absence of authorities' stabilizing behaviour if $b_1, b_2 = 0 < a_1 + a_2$. This would appear to justify the authorities' policy of leaning into the wind as above described. However, Norton suggests that the speculation in demand only exists precisely because the speculators know that the authorities will act to damp interest movements. But the argument that speculators only speculate because they know that the authorities will ensure gentle trends in rates, has as its complement the proposition that many gilt-edged holders only put their funds into government stocks because they can be taken out at reasonably predictable prices. Hence the authorities fear that a change in their policy of stabilization would reduce the demand for gilts at any given rate of interest, or, alternatively, increase the interest cost of placing the existing amount of bonds.

This raises the important question of what authorities are trying to do in managing the debt. Some would advocate using debt management to control the money supply, others the bond rate, and others the required rate of return on the stock of privately held physical capital, which may be only indirectly related to both the other targets (cf. Dow, in Reading 5 of the present volume). The Bank of England article (Reading 23) stresses 'sales maximization' as an objective, which implies a reduction of short debt and so, indirectly, the money supply. But this is a long-run objective conditioned by the need to stabilize the market in the short-run, and, presumably by the need to limit debt interest costs at all times. There is, however, little explicit discussion of whether this is the best possible long-run strategy.

The rather alarming implication of the policy just described is that when the balance of payments is weak and rises in Bank Rate are anticipated, expectations of capital losses on gilt-edged lead to sales of gilts by the private sector and a consequent increase of liquid debt. This is of course the contrary of the classical gold standard recipe. There is, however, the question of whether tight money will work in an economy set in a world of increasingly perfect capital markets, for such a tight-money policy would pull in reserves but not act on the current account as the gold standard would require. Despite these considerations, the authorities have, since the devaluation of 1967, been trying to use debt management to affect the money supply more than before, as is explained in the article reprinted from the *Midland Bank Review* (Reading 26).

It is probably because managing the gilt-edged market is so beset with problems that the authorities have preferred trying to affect aggregate demand by striking directly at the lending by banks.

FURTHER READING

DEBT MANAGEMENT

Committee on the Working of the Monetary System (*Radcliffe Report*), Cmnd. 827, H.M.S.O. 1959, Chap. 7.

Musgrave, Richard A., *The Theory of Public Finance* (Maidenhead, 1969), Chap. 6.

Tobin, J., 'An Essay on the Principles of Debt Management', *Fiscal and Debt Management Policies*, Commission on Money and Credit (Englewood Cliffs, 1963).

TERM STRUCTURE

Meiselman, D., *The Term Structure of Interest Rates* (Englewood Cliffs, 1962).

Grant, J. A. G., 'Meiselman on the Structure of Interest Rates', *Economica*, vol. 31, 1964.

Rowan, D. C., and O'Brien, R. J., 'Expectations, the Interest Rate Structure and Debt Policy' in Hilton, K., and Heathfield, D. F. (eds.), *Econometric Studies of the U.K.* (London, 1970).

23

OFFICIAL TRANSACTIONS IN THE GILT-EDGED MARKET

BANK OF ENGLAND*

THE management of the national debt is a central part of monetary management and at the same time a branch of Exchequer financing; as the Radcliffe Committee observed, it now consists of much more than a search for the cheapest way of dealing with a nuisance. The reconciliation of the diverse and often conflicting aims involved, and the methods and tactics adopted in pursuing them, are as much issues of monetary policy as of good housekeeping for the Government, though clearly they are not the whole of either.

This article is not a comprehensive review of the management of public sector debt in all its forms. It deals only with the nature of the market for gilt-edged stocks (government stocks and stocks of the nationalized industries carrying government guarantees), and with the purposes, tactics, and limitations of stock issues and official transactions in this market.

Debt management as an instrument of policy

First, management of the gilt-edged market and Bank rate are together the principal means of executing interest rate policy. Almost all fixed rates for government borrowing and lending, such as the rates for national savings certificates, national development bonds, tax reserve certificates, and Exchequer loans to the nationalized industries, are fixed from time to time by reference to the current yields on gilt-edged stocks. The structure of these yields therefore has a strong influence on the structure of prime rates generally; and the authorities can pursue their aims for interest

* Reprinted from the *Bank of England Quarterly Bulletin*, vol. 6, no. 2, June 1966, pp. 141–8, by permission of the publisher.

rates throughout the economy by seeking to influence the behaviour of prices and yields in the gilt-edged market. Secondly, management of the gilt-edged market, and the outcome in terms both of prices and of the net amounts of stock sold or bought in official dealings, have a considerable bearing on credit policy and the liquidity of the banks and others, creating conditions that may help or hinder policy in this field. Neither interest rate policy nor credit policy, however, is the dominant long-term consideration in debt management; this is rather to ensure so far as possible that suitable finance for the Exchequer is available, and will continue to be available in the future, so that there need be no excessive recourse to short-term borrowing from the banks on Treasury bills and accompanying increase in the money supply.

The Government's need for long-term finance

The total of British government and government guaranteed marketable stocks outstanding is about £19,500 million (nominal); of this total £16,000 million is in stocks which have to be redeemed by fixed dates, and some £3,500 million in stocks, such as 3½ per cent War Loan, with no final redemption dates. The fact that the dated stocks, of which about £11,500 million is currently in the hands of the general public, will have to be repaid by the final date given in the prospectus is one certain element in the Government's future need for finance. Moreover, about a third of the total amount of dated stocks falls due for repayment over the next five years, with an average amount of more than £1,000 million reaching its final date each year; these magnitudes are likely to be at least maintained while the patterns of demand in the gilt-edged market continue as they are.

The certain need to provide for debt redemption year after year on such a scale is a suitable point from which to begin a statement of purposes in debt management. This, however, is not the only need for finance to be borne in mind; it is almost as certain that the Government will also need to raise new funds each year for capital requirements, and will thereby also add to the redemption problem in the future. It is not that the central government's own capital expenditure requires financing in this way; on the contrary, their revenue has been more than enough, over recent years, to provide for all their expenditure, both on capital and on current account. But the central government also provide substantial sums for the capital programmes of the nationalized industries and, through the Public Works Loan Board, for those of the local authorities. In the five years from March 1960 to March 1965 the central government have financed capital investment other than their own to the extent of nearly £3,000 million.

The need to refinance maturing debt together with the need to borrow to finance new capital investment, and the certain prospect for many years to come that these pressing needs will both persist, enable the chief purpose of debt management to be stated simply; it is to maintain market conditions that will maximize, both now and in the future, the desire of investors at home and abroad to hold British government debt.

Demand for gilt-edged stocks

The turnover of stocks in the gilt-edged market is large and varies quite considerably from time to time; the figures published by the London stock exchange for 1965, a year in which activity was somewhat below the recent average, show that, including official dealings, the amount of stock passing from one investor to another during the year was about half the total of £19,500 million outstanding.[1] Much the greater part (in money terms) represents the business of the large financial institutions, sometimes investing new funds, more often switching between stocks. These institutions—the banks, discount houses, insurance companies and pension funds—and the large industrial and commercial companies with substantial sums which they need to invest in highly marketable securities hold between them something like half of the gilt-edged stocks in the hands of the general public. The banks and discount houses hold mainly the shorter-dated stocks; the insurance companies and pension funds mainly the medium and longer-dated. Most of them have large individual holdings and expect to be able to buy or sell, or to switch between stocks, in amounts of several million pounds at a time. This ability to deal freely at all times is highly important for them; although an institution may not often wish to deal in such amounts, yet if it thought that there was a risk of its not being able to do so at any time that it wished, it would feel that its liquidity and its freedom of manoeuvre were becoming impaired and would become increasingly reluctant to maintain its investment in gilt-edged stocks.

[1] Table 15 of the statistical annex, *Bank of England Quarterly Bulletin*, vol. 6, no. 2, June 1966, p. 186.

Alternative investments for the financial institutions are the stocks of local authorities and industrial debentures, many of which offer unquestionable security with a somewhat higher yield than is to be had on gilt-edged stocks. But these alternatives are not so readily marketable in large amounts that the institutions can feel sure of being able to sell at once whenever they choose; it is the assured and, for practical purposes, limitless marketability of gilt-edged stocks that gives them their chief advantage over the best alternatives, and their greatest appeal for the institutions.

The institutions have for many years taken the unrestricted marketability of gilt-edged stocks for granted. Their investment decisions in the gilt-edged market have in consequence come to be governed principally by their expectations of future movements in prices; not surprisingly there is often a substantial consensus of view among such investors, and there is therefore likely to be, at any one time, a preponderance either of buyers, or of sellers, in the market.

The aggregate of the resources that the jobbers in gilt-edged stocks are able to commit, however, is small in relation to the volume of trading; unsupported, they might not be able, even with the help of wide swings in prices, to absorb the kind of pressures that build up when sentiment in the market veers sharply one way or the other. It has therefore become a prime consideration in official dealings to keep the pressures on the jobbers within supportable limits, and so contain the risk that a holder of government debt might find it impossible to deal either way in the market for whatever amount of stock he wished—subject only, if he is a buyer, to the particular stock he wants being available.

Official dealings

Official dealings in the gilt-edged market comprise those of the National Debt Commissioners and those of the Issue Department of the Bank of England. The National Debt Commissioners are responsible for the management of the National Insurance Funds, the funds of the Post Office Savings Bank and the trustee savings banks, and many smaller funds of an official nature. The timing and extent of their operations are matters in the first instance for the National Debt Office to decide in the light of the needs of those funds; and, except when the National Debt Office are buying or selling large amounts of stock, the Government Broker will usually be able to deal for them in the market on normal terms. If, however, any of their operations is likely to have a significant effect on prices inimical to debt management policy at the time, it may be preferable to keep the transaction wholly within the official group; the deal will then be done between the National Debt Office and the Bank, at current market prices but without effect in the market. In this way the National Debt Office are at all normal times able to manage the funds for which they are responsible without subordinating their decisions to tactical considerations of debt management. But they also stand ready to vary holdings in the interests of debt management policy, where to do so is not prejudical to their other interests.

The Issue Department has resources of nearly £3,000 million invested in government securities, a large part of which is invested in marketable gilt-edged stocks; this provides the means for dealing in the market in whatever way seems most likely to help achieve the current aims of debt management. With such a *masse de manoeuvre* in their hands, it would be possible for the Bank to intervene vigorously in the market, taking the initiative in dealing and instructing the Government Broker to sell or buy specific amounts of stocks at the best prices he could get. In normal official dealings, however, the Bank leave it to the jobbers in the market to take the initiative; the Bank offer stock—when they have it to offer—in response to bids made by the jobbers to the Government Broker, and bid for stock, if conditions justify doing so, when it is offered by the jobbers through the Government Broker. In this way they stand behind the jobbers in the gilt-edged market—acting as the jobbers' jobber, or a jobber of last resort. Though the Bank give no formal commitment to buy or sell when asked, they are in fact normally willing to do so at prices of their own choosing. They thereby give the market a very much greater capacity to meet the needs of investors than the jobbers' own books would provide. The choice of this method of dealing rests on a judgement that it broadens the market, increases its activity, enhances its appeal to institutions with large sums to invest, and in the long run increases their desire to hold government stocks, and that the alternative method would strike investors as being more arbitrary and capricious and would therefore make them reluctant to commit themselves to the same extent in the gilt-edged market.

The Bank's role in these dealings is nevertheless not a passive one. Although they deal in the market only in response to offers originating there, they pursue an active policy in the great majority of cases through their choice of the prices at which they are prepared to respond. Moreover, the Bank's continuous presence in the market, not seeking business but normally willing to deal at prices reflecting official policy, and in practice dealing almost every day and often in substantial quantities, provides ample opportunity for seeking to influence prices, even on the minority of days when supply of stock is roughly in balance with demand. This close involvement in the daily turnover of an active market both enables the Bank to pursue their aims continuously and without undue attention being drawn to individual transactions and gives the Bank a useful degree of flexibility when they are seeking occasions for implementing a shift of policy on prices. It is worth mentioning that not only is the identity of the Government Broker well known throughout the market, but all official bargains are done by him and there is seldom any doubt as to whether or not he is dealing for one or other of the official funds. The prices he bids in response to an offer are therefore seen as the expression of the Bank's current policy, and are closely watched by the jobbers for any sign of a change of emphasis in the policy, such as might lead the market to expect new movements in prices.

New issues

Because the gilt-edged market is so largely made by the financial institutions, and because these institutions fall into fairly homogeneous groups with broadly similar investment preferences, new issues do not need to be made in great variety. There are at present just under fifty gilt-edged stocks for investors to choose from; new interest in the market and increased demand from the institutions can usually be encouraged, and can then be satisfied, by making a small number of relatively large new issues, which in each case will probably be sufficient to meet the demand from investors for some months to come. These are the 'tap' stocks which the Issue Department, having taken up the unsubscribed balance at the time of issue, gradually sells as public demand develops. When a new stock is issued, and becomes available on tap, many investors who have had their funds invested in other stocks will decide, because the price is attractive or for some other reason, that the new stock is more suitable for their portfolios, and they will therefore wish to switch out of other stocks into the new one. The jobbers will probably be able to faciliate many of the switches, by taking the stocks offered on to their own books until they are able to resell them. Where these are shorter-dated than the tap stock for which they are being exchanged, the Bank will generally be willing to facilitate the switch by themselves taking the shorter-dated stocks from the jobbers, if the jobbers so wish, in exchange for the tap stock; in this way the Bank may ease the pressure on the jobbers' stock holdings that is caused when large-scale switching is taking place into a stock available through the tap.

Redemptions

The redemption of maturing stocks, if they were always firmly held by investors to the last, would be likely to cause considerable disturbance, both in the money market—as most of the cash paid out sought employment—and in particular in the gilt-edged market as the investors receiving the money took steps to reinvest it. Fortunately, not all investors are equally attracted by the prospect of being repaid in cash on the redemption date. The Bank therefore stand ready, as a stock approaches maturity, to buy it in when it is offered, usually at a price that gives, over the remaining life of the stock, the current rate on Treasury bills. This is a widely known practice; and many large investors find it convenient to sell their holdings on these terms, so that they can reinvest at times of their own choosing, rather than wait for the redemption proceeds at a time when many others may be moving in the same direction. It is quite usual for the Bank to acquire in this way three-quarters or more of the maturing stock; and most of these purchases will be matched one way or another by sales of other stocks by the Bank. The investor who sells the maturing stock may reinvest his money in a stock which the Bank do not at that time hold; but his purchase will bring a seller into the market and may initiate a sequence of switches, perhaps involving a number of investors and jobbers, and leading eventually to a purchase of a stock that can be met by a sale by the Bank. This is a very common form of switching which both appeals to the investors and suits the Bank.

Switching

Between these two special kinds of switching—into the new tap stocks or out of the next maturing stock—which together may amount to several hundred million pounds of stock over a period of a few months, there will be a variety of individually matched purchases and sales attractive to particular investors. An institutional holder of gilt-edged stocks, except where the lives of his assets are already closely matched to his liabilities, is likely to pursue a regular policy of exchanging shorter-dated for longer-dated stocks in order to push on the average life of his portfolio and offset the continual shortening that occurs with time. This alone gives rise to many substantial switches; and the Bank can often help this process along, with advantage to their own position, by being prepared to sell the longer-dated stocks, when the Issue Department has them to sell, against purchases of shorter-dated.

There are occasions, of course, when some investors are switching, not into longer-dated stocks, but into shorter-dated. This may be because a new stock with a shorter life than the one already held is seen by the investor to have greater attractions for him, such as, perhaps, a higher coupon, giving a higher running yield, or because he expects prices to move in a way that would make it advantageous to be invested for a time in shorter-dated stocks. Such switches are seldom much help to the Bank in managing the debt; on the contrary, if the counterpart is provided by the Bank, they would—unless later reversed—increase the weight of maturities for which refinance would have to be provided sooner rather than later. The Bank therefore normally do little or nothing to facilitate them; but if the pressure from investors is more than the jobbers between them can well support, so that there is a real risk of dealings becoming difficult, or if it appears likely that intervention will rapidly restore conditions more favourable to the execution of current policy, then the Bank may step in, but normally only at prices fully reflecting the disadvantage for the authorities of switches of this type.

Other switches are made attractive to particular investors by the differences in their liability to tax and the different effects of the tax laws as between one stock and another. A recent and particularly striking example of this has been the extensive switching provoked by the provision in the Finance Act 1965 that, as regards gilt-edged stocks issued before the Budget in 1965, capital gains taxes would not apply to gains or losses caused by price movements within the range between the lowest issue price and the redemption price.[2] Some gilt-edged stocks now outstanding were issued at or near par, and others were issued well below par; under the new provision this difference brings a new and quite significant factor into the calculation of yields.

Normally the Bank will provide a counterpart to switches of any

[2] *Bank of England Quarterly Bulletin*, vol. 5, no. 1, September 1965, p. 221.

of the kinds described where the investor is moving into longer-dated stocks than he already holds. These transactions will ordinarily be done at current market prices and will leave those prices unaffected. As already mentioned, the price at which the Bank will buy the next maturity is usually kept in line, in terms of yield, with the average price of Treasury bills at the tender. A new stock is issued at a price that is closely in line with market prices of other stocks; when it is put on sale by the Bank on the first day of dealings it is generally offered at a price fractionally above the issue price, so as not to undermine the position of those who applied for the stock at the time of issue. As demand for the stock grows and sales through the tap increase, and provided that other prices in the market are firm, the price of the tap stock can be moved upwards in steps; the steps are typically $\frac{1}{32}$ per cent in a short-dated stock and $\frac{1}{8}$ per cent in a medium or long-dated stock. But, if the market suffers a general weakening and prices of other stocks fall so far that the Bank's price for the tap stock becomes out of line with other prices, the tap price will not ordinarily be lowered immediately lest to do so should depress the market further. It is allowed to remain out of line until it seems that demand is capable of being restimulated, and is then reduced in a single step to bring it back into line with other prices.

The aims of debt management

The chief purpose of management of the gilt-edged market was stated above to be to strengthen the demand for government stocks. It is not immediately concerned with the day to day finance of the Exchequer's payments: as an earlier article has explained,[3] the machinery of the money market ensures that enough government debt is always taken up to provide for residual needs, and the Bank's techniques for managing that market smooth out the day to day irregularities. In the gilt-edged market the principal concern is to encourage the widest possible variety of investors, other than the banks, to increase their holdings, and to hold longer- rather than shorter-dated stocks. These are essentially long-term aims; in the long run success will depend on investors' confidence in the market and this in turn will rest decisively on their experience of dealing in it.

[3] 'The management of money day by day', *Bank of England Quarterly Bulletin*, vol. 3, no. 3, March 1963, p. 15.

The tactics used to attract and hold the interest of investors have already been described: to issue new stocks that are tailored to the current demands of large investors; to ensure that dealings do not become seriously inhibited by the absence of buyers to match sellers, or that the market does not become too volatile due to a preponderance of buyers unable to satisfy their demands for stock; to spread the impact of the issue and redemption of large blocks of securities, and in particular to minimize the fortuitous disturbances, always less than welcome, that these give rise to in the market and in the banking system; and generally to slow down and moderate violent movements in the market unless there is likely to be a particular advantage in a rapid adjustment, as in the case of a change in Bank rate.

Other aims of debt management become important from time to time; and to keep down the cost of the Government's borrowing is important at all times. Of these additional aims the principal ones are, in normal times:

(i) to assist economic policy by promoting or sustaining the most appropriate pattern of interest rates; and

(ii) to assist credit policy, usually by increasing sales of government debt, so that the Government's needs can be met with less recourse to the banks, less addition to their liquid assets, and less scope, in consequence, for them to increase their lending.

These short-term aims are not, of course, alternatives but usually present themselves in combination. The actions on prices that they suggest can at times conflict, either between themselves or with actions that seem necessary to preserve the attractions of government stocks in the long run; and they cannot be pursued without regard to the danger of causing damage in the long run to the health and capacity of the market—a limitation that may sometimes preclude all but a fairly narrow choice of policies in the short term.

This can well be illustrated by the problems which arise when policy is judged to require interest rates to move upwards. Circumstances may sometimes allow an adjustment to be easily and smoothly achieved. A number of investors may read the economic scene as pointing towards higher interest rates. They may therefore enter the market as sellers and an insufficiency of buyers then leads to offerings of stock to the Bank which allow the Bank, by bidding at successively lower levels, to secure a drop in market prices of broadly the dimensions thought desirable. This drop may then prove sufficient to discourage other investors from selling, so that the market stabilizes itself naturally at the new level.

At other times the process may be more difficult to achieve smoothly. The economic scene may not be read in such a way that a preponderance of sellers appears. Or, while there may be sellers, a first small downward movement in prices may be enough to cause them to hold off and the selling movement to come to an early end. In different circumstances a downward movement, once started, may feed upon itself and threaten to go much further than the authorities would desire, perhaps even to the extent of risking serious demoralization of the market. Another possiblity is that, perhaps because of outside circumstances or because investors take alarm at the pace of the adjustment, signs of demoralization may appear at an early stage. In all these circumstances the Bank may, because of their overriding concern for the long-term health of the market, have to modify their tactics.

It is sometimes argued that in such circumstances the desired results could more often or more nearly be attained if the Bank regularly adopted a more positive line in their market dealings. For instance, they could take steps to initiate a downward movement in prices by themselves entering the market as determined sellers; or, if there were sellers already in the market, an adjustment to a desired new level of prices could be made more quickly, and so with the prospect of quicker recovery and an earlier reappearance of buyers in the market, if the Bank were to decline to buy stock until the level of prices was reached at which they hoped to see it settle.

One of the problems of applying such techniques is that of judging where this new level should be established. This can seldom, if ever, be clearly discerned at the outset, not least because it depends in substantial part on the reactions of investors as the market movement gets under way and on other changing circumstances and expectations. By remaining in the market the Bank can better judge, from market reactions to their offers, when a stabilizing move should be developed. Another important consideration is that the pace of a decline in prices can build up very rapidly once expectations that it will continue have taken hold; if such expectations are further strengthened by the visible withdrawal of the Bank from the market, to arrest or retard the fall may in the end require a disproportionate amount of official support. Not only will additional liquidity then accrue to the banks, despite the probable desire at the time to restrain credit, but the authorities may also be led, in order to get the movement under control, to adopt so definite a stand as will seriously restrict their freedom of manoeuvre in the period ahead. Finally, a market in which downward movements of prices is too abruptly initiated by selling by the Bank or, if originating elsewhere, is generally left unmoderated and then as abruptly halted by official intervention at some predetermined level, may come to be viewed by investors as arbitrary and unpredictable in its behaviour; there is then a danger that they would be seriously discouraged from investing their funds in it. The likely consequence would be that the capacity of the market would be permanently reduced and with it the ability of the Government to borrow at long term.

A change in Bank rate might at first sight appear to be in contradiction to this approach. But even here the change to a new basis of gilt-edged yields is substantially influenced both by the guidance given by the Bank in announcing the new Bank rate and by the new prices that the Bank subsequently quote for the tap stocks, or bid for any stock that may be offered to them.

The opposite case, in which policy aims to encourage a rise in prices and a fall in interest rates, can present almost as many problems. It is more obviously true in this case that an attempt by the Bank to induce a movement is unlikely to succeed, without inordinate expenditure on the purchase of stock, unless investors generally hold the view that the movement is justified by the state of the economy, or by some development such as a substantial reduction in the amount of borrowing in prospect for the Exchequer. But it is also true that the Bank can, when conditions are right, stimulate the market's appetite for stock by selling at gently rising prices; and once the market has come to expect an upward movement, it may absorb very considerable quantities of stock and yet bid prices further upward in the market. In this case, too, it is important that the movement should not gather too much momentum or go too far, because once a rise is judged to have become excessive the reaction of the market is likely to be abrupt and damaging to investors' portfolios, and in the end is probably harmful to their confidence in the gilt-edged market. But if the Bank are to moderate a rise in prices which the market is convinced, at least for the moment, will go further, they must sell stock to meet the demand, whatever level it may reach; and these heavy sales could be as little in tune with credit policy at the time as the purchase of stock is at times of credit restriction.

Conclusion

The examples given above by no means exhaust the possible variations, in policy and in market behaviour, with which debt management may be faced. The market is dominated for most of the time by its own expectations of future movements in prices, or occasionally by its uncertainty and nervousness about the future. The market's expectations about the prices that the Bank will quote in future official dealings are an important factor in its assessment, but not one that in the end carries greater weight than the balance of supply and demand among the holders of the £14,500 million of stock in the hands of the general public. This is a market in which, however, total supply is highly elastic and responsive even in the short run, both because there are normally tap stocks available for purchase by the market, and because the Bank are normally willing bidders, even if only at prices that discourage the sellers, when stock is offered. Variations in demand in the market are therefore likely to lead to variations in supply at unchanged or only slowly changing prices, rather than to immediate variations in prices big enough to bring demand back into balance at nearly the same level of supply. Policy on interest rates can, and in all the circumstances must, concentrate largely on fostering demand, in the future as well as in the present.

With the demand for gilt-edged stocks so fully satisfied, a shift in the holders' expectations can quickly give rise to a strong tide in dealings that may owe nothing to any stimulus from the Bank, for there are many other factors contributing to the market's views and expectations, or causing it to be uncertain. It is hardly surprising therefore that the business of debt management is less often a matter of stimulating a movement than of retarding one that is gathering momentum, or moderating the more exaggerated day to day fluctuations that occur when markets are thin or nervous. And even in this limited field of action, the fundamental forces of the market are usually too strong to be contained or diverted for long. Thus the daily concern of debt management is usually to steady the market without opposing it too rigidly, but always within the context of its aims for interest rate and credit policy and for the maximization of demand for British government debt.

24

THE GILT-EDGED MARKET

C. A. E. GOODHART*

THE main burden, which bears down upon the Bank of England domestically, derives from the continuing need to place the Public Debt[1] with firm holders, a requirement which precedes the desirable objectives of managing or controlling the Debt. The extent of this task should be recognized in terms of the problems involved not only in ensuring the continued placement of the existing stock of Debt at all times, but also the need to find holders for the additional flow of issues which the authorities must sell every year.

The current state (31 March 1966) of the Public Sector Debt (excluding identified holdings within the Public Sector) can be seen in Table 1. The first, and most important point, is that the size of the Public Sector Debt in relation both to the total supply of financial liabilities and to net worth is much higher in the U.K. than in the U.S.A. The differences are owing to the fact both that the public sector in the U.K. has built up a proportionately larger

* Reprinted from Goodhart, C. A. E., 'British monetary policy', in Holbik, K. (ed.), *Monetary policy in the Atlantic Community* (forthcoming) by permission of the author. C. A. E. Goodhart is on the research staff of the Bank of England.

[1] The National Savings Movement, the Post Office, and the Trustee Savings banks have the direct executive responsibility for encouraging small savings, although even here the authorities (i.e. the Bank and the Treasury) have the over-riding power and responsibility for seeing that the terms on which the savings are borrowed are in line with monetary policy. For the rest the central authorities (the Bank and the Treasury) have direct responsibility for the management of all the debt, with the important exception of the Local Authority Loan Debt. The relationship between the local authorities and the central authorities will be considered at greater length in Section 3b */not reprinted here/*. The Government guaranteed marketable stocks of the nationalized industries are treated by everyone as indistinguishable from other Government marketable securities. Ever since 1956 the nationalized industries have borrowed directly from the Government (at the going rate on similar Government securities) and the latter, when necessary, refinances itself by borrowing in turn from the market.

TABLE I

*Public Sector Debt**

Nominal amount outstanding 31 March 1966, excluding identified holdings of Public Sector Debt within the Public Sector:

National debt	£ million		£ million
Marketable securities	12,330†	Accrued Interest on National Savings	600
Market Treasury bills	2,310	Amounts invested	
National Savings securities	3,660	in Post Office	1,840
Tax Reserve certificates	190	in Trustee Savings banks	1,070
Other	4,060	Notes and Coin in circulation	3,080
		Local Authority Loan Debt	6,800
		Government guaranteed marketable securities	1,770
		Other debt	940
Total	22,550	Total	16,100
	Total Public Sector Debt 38,600		

* Sources: *Annual Abstract of Statistics*, no. 103, 1966, Tables 323 and 345: *Bank of England Quarterly Bulletin*, vol. 7, no. 1, March 1967, pp. 43–7: For estimate of Local Authority Temporary Debt held by Overseas Residents, see [2] pp. 412–13 and [3].

† Assumes all holdings of Marketable Government and Government Guaranteed Securities are of Marketable Government Securities. In practice Government securities and Nationalized Industries' stocks guaranteed by H.M.G. are indistinguishable.

Elements of Public Sector Debt

	Holders				
Asset and maturity	Banking sector	Other financial institutions	Overseas residents	Other holders	Total
Total marketable securities guaranteed by HMG	2,210	4,200	1,930	5,730	14,100
0–5 years maturity	1,260	510	820	1,710	4,300
5–over 5 years maturity	950	3,680	1,120	4,020	9,800
Market Treasury bills	1,150	10	1,000	150	2,300
Local Authority 31 March 1965					
Temporary debt	Neg.	N.A.	350–450 (Est.)	N.A.	1,825
Securities, bonds, and other longer-term debt:	N.A.	N.A.	N.A.	N.A.	4,000
of which up to 1 year					750
1–5 years maturity					1,330

share of physical assets—the acquisition of which had, and has, to be financed—and also to the remaining heritage of the costs of war and defence. A direct comparison of the percentage shares of the public sectors in the U.K. and the U.S.A. for the year 1958 has been made by J. Revell [1].

	Percentage share of Public Sector in Country's				
	Total assets	Physical assets	Financial assets	Liabilities	Net worth
U.K. Public Sector	19	27	13	43	−10
U.S. Public Sector	8	13	4	24	−2

Of this very large volume of debt, some £38,500 million, only about £3,000 million consist of currency, notes, and coin, and another £1,200 million of Treasury bills held as liquid reserves within the banking sector. The proportion of the debt forming a basis for the money supply is in the U.K. a relatively small proportion of the total debt. Any tendency, even of relatively minor proportions, by non-bank holders of the Debt to shift out of Public Sector Debt could, unless contained, potentially result in an excessive enlargement of the monetary base. Furthermore, of course, any desire by overseas residents to transfer their holdings abroad would have serious effects upon the U.K.'s reserve position.[2]

Moreover, the passage of time uneluctably shortens the maturity of the marketable securities held by the general public. In the five years 1968–72 some £6,500 million of these gilt-edged securities are due for redemption, cf. [4], an average of approximately £1,300 million per year.

[2] Since, however, the sales of sterling to the Exchange Equalization Account by foreigners repatriating their funds provides the Government with additional funds, and enables them to finance a deficit with equivalently less recourse to borrowing, it follows that reductions in the debt held by foreigners will not have, in general, any expansionary effect upon the monetary base. For a detailed account of the effects of purchases/sales of Public Sector Debt by foreigners, see the *Bank of England Quarterly Bulletin*, vol. 2, no. 2, June 1962, 'Inflows and Outflows of Foreign Funds', pp. 93–103. The analysis is slightly hard to follow, until it is realized that it is being assumed that all transactions in the market are being made with the Government broker as one of the two parties to the deal. Thus the treatment in this article of a sale of a bond by an overseas resident to a U.K. resident would be in two parts, first the effect of a sale by the foreigner to the Government broker, followed by a sale by the broker to a U.K. resident.

The net increase in financial liabilities of the Public Sector over the last five years 1962–6 averaged about £800 million per annum. The local authorities during these years, however, regularly increased their market debt outstanding by some £400–600 million per annum, by so doing reducing the net balance of financial requirements which the central government had to meet. In the last six years the Central Government had to raise the following sums to finance its deficit[3]

Net Balance (£ million)

1961	1962	1963	1964	1965	1966
220	−79	148	423	597	531

A small contribution on average towards the financing of this total is made by small savings, being increased holdings of National Savings Certificates, Premium Bonds, Tax Reserve Certificates,[4] deposits in Post Office Savings Banks, etc. In recent years this has amounted to the following totals:[4]

£ million

1961	1962	1963	1964	1965	1966
172	99	151	210	−104	−76

It is unlikely that the contribution to be expected from small savings will expand significantly in future. A sizeable part of the small savings movement is devoted to providing satisfactory repositories for the savings of the poor, who on the achievement of greater affluence tend to turn more towards private sector intermediaries. In any case the National Savings movement has not on the whole been aggressively competitive in attempting to

[3] Source: CSO, *Financial Statistics*, no. 63, July 1967, Tables 4 and 16.

[4] These certificates which carry a small, but tax-free, rate of interest are not negotiable, but can be surrendered to the Treasury in payment for tax due. They are available on tap. Their use helps to even out the inflow of tax receipts to the Treasury over the fiscal year.

attract funds by offering more attractive terms, preferring to accentuate in its public relations the ethical to the financial advantages of thrift.[5] Furthermore, possibly owing to bureaucratic delays, there is believed to be a pronounced tendency for changes in their interest rates to lag behind rates offered by competing intermediaries in the private sector. When interest rates are generally cyclically low or declining, usually in a slump or when the government wishes to encourage business, this lag may well cause small savings to flow in faster, and thus act to transfer funds to the public sector reducing the monetary base, and conversely slower in times of stringency, when the authorities would find such an inflow more welcome.[6]

Unfortunately in recent years too large a proportion of the financial needs of the Central Government have been met by direct borrowing abroad and running down our gold and currency

[5] The issue of Premium Bonds, which have attached to their terms of issue the possibility of obtaining a large capital gain by lottery, was an exception to this rule. Not surprisingly in this context they were widely condemned as immoral.

[6] For example, Professor E. V. Morgan writes [5], 'For administrative reasons, changes in rates on National Savings securities are infrequent so that, when interest rates are rising, the flow of National Savings tends to diminish, and vice versa.' Although there is evidence of outflows of National Savings in 1955, late 1957, and 1965–6 when interest rates were felt to be high, I am not entirely convinced of the validity of this view. I regressed the inflow of non-marketable debt, ΔD, (small savings and tax reserve certificates) first against the interest yield (end quarter) on $2\frac{1}{2}$ per cent Consols (i) and the increase in personal total income before tax (ΔY), and then again substituting the first differences in the Consol rate (Δi) in place of (i), all data seasonally adjusted, for the period 1955 (2nd quarter)–1966 (4th quarter).

The results were

$$\text{(I)}\quad \Delta D = 133{\cdot}4 + \underset{(0{\cdot}089)}{0{\cdot}0006\,\Delta Y} - \underset{(10{\cdot}01)}{19{\cdot}75\,i}$$

$$R^2 = 0{\cdot}08 \qquad \text{SE} = 44 \qquad \text{D.W.} = 0{\cdot}86$$

$$\text{(II)}\quad \Delta D = 26{\cdot}3 - \underset{(0{\cdot}09)}{0{\cdot}03\,\Delta Y} + \underset{(39{\cdot}1)}{9{\cdot}22\,\Delta i}$$

$$R^2 = 0{\cdot}004 \qquad \text{SE} = 52{\cdot}1 \qquad \text{D.W.} = 0{\cdot}78$$

There is only a tenuous suggestion that high—but not rising—interest rates may reduce the inflow of small savings.

It may be that $2\frac{1}{2}$ per cent Consols was a bad choice. The occasional sharp changes made by the authorities in the rates on, and the form of, small savings might have obscured the underlying relationship; for the views set out above are certainly widely accepted, by the authorities as well as by most financial commentators.

reserves. The figures show that this source has in recent years provided the following amounts:

£ million

1961	1962	1963	1964	1965	1966
277	−239	13	515	203	244

The intention of the Government is to achieve a sufficient balance of payments surplus in the next few years to pay off the debts incurred over the last few years and, if possible, to bolster our own reserves. If this aim is achieved, it will follow that this will involve a very large use of funds every year, say in the region of £200 million.

If account is taken of the payments of cash out by the Central Government on the redemption of maturing, gilt edged, say £1,300 million p.a., and to provide funds to finance the provision of social capital and investment in the nationalized industries, say £500 million p.a., less the £100 million that small savings may be expected to bring in, but adding £200 million in respect of the repayment of overseas debt and the building up of reserves, it suggests that there remains the large annual average sum of £1,900 million to be found each year, either by the sale of gilt-edged marketable securities or through the expansion of the currency supply and the volume of Treasury bills. Since the present outstanding volume of cash, plus Treasury bills held by the banking sector, amounts to little over £4,200 million, any inability to place a large proportion of this sum with purchasers of gilt-edged securities would lead to a calamitous rise in the monetary base.

Although this situation has been analysed in terms of current statistics and prospects, exactly the same train of thought has been exercising the minds of the monetary authorities over the years. Mr. L. K. O'Brien, when Deputy Governor of the Bank, said in a lecture in July 1964 that,

> We have been faced with the problem of financing growing official borrowing needs . . . and of providing for the re-finance of large tranches of maturing debt. The total amount involved in both types of operation can approach £1,500 million a year, and in the inflationary climate of the mid-1950s it was often difficult to persuade the gilt-edged market to absorb

as much long-term debt as we would have wished. The consequent necessity for large-scale short-term borrowing created a situation in which the traditional market methods of controlling bank liquidity proved inadequate to the task of restraining the growth of bank credit [**6**].

So far it has been established that the U.K. Public Sector Debt is relatively large, that any large-scale shift out of holding the Debt would be very embarrassing to the authorities, and that the authorities have a continuing need to sell additional gilt-edged stock to the public if they are to prevent an excessive increase in the monetary base. Where, however, the economist will ask himself, is the particular problem in that? If the supply of gilt edged onto the market has to be relatively rather larger, than, say, in the U.S., then the price of the bonds must be lowered to induce the public to demand just sufficient marketable securities to bring about that monetary base, or level of interest rates, which the authorities desire.

It is precisely the fact that financial markets do *not* work in this rather *simpliste* fashion, in the opinion at any rate both of the Bank, the Treasury and all market commentators, that makes monetary policy in the U.K. difficult to execute and confusing to the outsider. Essentially the view of the Bank may be construed as follows. The market is dominated by investors with short planning periods.[7] This not only relates to the private, but also to the institutional investor. In the latter case the institution may prefer assets of a maturity related to that of its liabilities, and also may have at any time a concept of the long-run optimal portfolio shape. In the short run, however, it will choose to invest proportionately among the various assets of roughly equivalent maturity depending upon the likelihood in the short run of achieving the maximum expected gain. Thus a life insurance company may hold a portfolio consisting of long-term government debt, industrial debentures, equities, and property, and may have some views about the long-run desirable composition of that portfolio. In the short run, however, its investment policy will be decisively influenced by the expectation of the relative short-term capital gain, or loss, to be expected over the coming year on each asset.[8]

[7] For a reasoned academic view in support of this hypothesis in the case of the U.S.A., see B. G. Malkiel's study of the *Term Structure of Interest Rates* (Princeton University Press, Princeton, New Jersey, 1966), esp. p. 74.

[8] For example in 1962, a year in which there was a general expectation that gilt-edged prices would rise both absolutely, and relatively to the gain on most

For investors with short planning periods the essential element, in order to enable them to decide what portfolio holding will maximize their expected return, is the forecast of future short-term price changes. As the Governor of the Bank (Mr., later Lord, Cobbold) said in evidence to the Radcliffe Committee [7], 'What influences demand in this [the gilt-edged market], as in other markets, is not so much the price of the day as the public's view of the likely movements [in price] in following weeks, months, and years.' This appraisal of the determinants of demand in the market has not been subjected to any rigorous, quantitative analysis, and there are those who might doubt its validity.[9] In the main, however, general financial comment suggests that most of those close to the market are convinced that the Bank's appreciation of the situation is correct. For example, here are two quotations culled from the financial press:

> For if the yield on undated gilt-edged falls below 6 per cent . . . then the institutions which have bought so much stock in the last six months will turn their attention elsewhere. It is only the expectation that rates would fall further that keeps them buying at the long end. *The Economist*, 15 April 1967, 'What about gilt-edged', p. 263.

> Our gilt-edged market may still find support from the actuaries of the life offices who do their calculations as to what a long term interest of around 6¾ per cent will bring to their policy holders over the next 20, 30, or 40 years. For the rest it is a place for buying like mad, when the going is obviously good, and selling, PDQ [pretty damn quick], when you've got a profit (like the bad wartime sardines which weren't for eating but for buying

other assets, the insurance companies bought £149 million of gilt-edged, purchasing £280 million of stocks with a maturity of over 15 years. In the same year they purchased £99 million of company debentures and £86 million of shares. In 1964 the respective figures for these three uses of funds was £88 million (£158 million with a maturity of over 15 years), £189 million and £156 million, and in 1965 the figures were respectively £48 million (45 with a maturity over 15 years), £205 million and £86 million respectively. In 1966 the purchase of long bonds, over 15 years to run, by the insurance companies quarterly, was respectively in £ million 16, 19, 36, and 98, which reflects accurately, *not* the level of rates, but the view of the market about the likely short term change in prices on such stock. Source: CSO, *Financial Statistics*, e.g. no. 63, July 1967, Table 61.

[9] See for example the comment made in *The Banker*'s Commentary, on 'Managing Gilt-Edged', p. 435, July 1966, that 'These . . . objections [to a more positive approach to debt management] rest on the fundamental proposition, which the Bank does not seek to justify, that "the market is dominated for most of the time by its own expectations of future movements in prices".'

and selling). Harold Wincott, 'Thoughts on "borrowing" £1,842,000,000', *Financial Times*, 20 June 1967.[10]

The economist may possibly accept that in this market demand is not a function of price, but of the future expected short term change in price, $D = f(P^e_{t+n} - P_t)$, where P^e_{t+n} is the price expected to rule in *n* quarters.[11] This assumption, if true, should not, however, by itself complicate debt management. All that is necessary for debt management to be traditionally simple is that sales of debt by the authorities should have at all times a significantly more depressing effect upon actual prices than upon expected future prices. If this were so, it would still be possible to undertake open market operations in the gilt-edged market in order to achieve the desired monetary base, or interest rate. The only difference would be that the swings in interest rates would have to be somewhat larger. It is absolutely crucial to a proper understanding of the Bank's actions to realize that they do not believe that the demand for bonds is well behaved in the above sense. On the contrary they argue that intervention by the authorities in the market sufficient to lower prices could so affect confidence in the future level of prices that sales would be lessened rather than improved. Thus in an article on 'Official Transactions in the Gilt-Edged Market' in the *Bank of England Quarterly Bulletin*[12] it was stated that,

Another important consideration [on the subject of a more positive approach to debt management] is that the pace of a decline in prices can build up very rapidly once expectations that it will continue have taken hold; if

[10] Cf. also the evidence of the Government broker, Mr. Mullens, to the Committee on the Working of the Monetary System in answer to Qn. 11,967 *Minutes of Evidence*, 'The majority of people who are in charge of investing money, whether it be on behalf of banks, insurance companies, or pension funds, do not only look at the stock at the price it is on sale that day. They look to see what they think it is going to be in two or three months' time, and if they see the market falling nobody will buy.'

[11] For what it is worth, it is my belief that this is probably valid.

[12] Vol. 6, no. 2, June 1966, pp. 141–9. Since an understanding of the Bank's view of this market is an absolute precondition to comprehension of recent monetary policy in the U.K., this article should be treated as required reading. Also of great value is the article by J. Q. Hollom (Chief Cashier, Bank of England) on 'The Methods and Objectives of the Bank's Market Operations' from *The Bank of England Today* (The Institute of Bankers, London 1964), pp. 18–32, particularly on this subject pp. 23–8. For those wishing to explore rather more deeply, the Radcliffe Committee went over this issue at great length when taking evidence, see Qns. 11,919–12,065 (Evidence of Government broker), 634–86, 1018–27, 1762–1809, 1841–98, 2937–72.

such expectations are further strengthened by the visible withdrawal of the Bank from [support of] the market, to arrest or retard the fall may in the end require a disproportionate amount of official support. Not only will additional liquidity then accrue to the banks, despite the possible desire at the time to restrain credit, but the authorities may also be led, in order to get the movement under control, to adopt so definite a stand as will seriously restrict their freedom of manœuvre in the period ahead.

Equally 'it is also true that the Bank can, when conditions are right, stimulate the market's appetite for stock by selling at gently rising prices; and once the market has come to expect an upward movement, it may absorb very considerable quantities of stock and yet bid prices further upwards in the market.'[13] The qualification—when conditions are right—is important, because the market will not always be persuaded of the likelihood of a continuing rise in prices by the gentle upwards nudging of prices by the Government broker. Ultimately the market operators have got to be prepared to believe that broader considerations warrant such a move. Effectively, therefore, while the market's expectations may be very volatile over a certain range of prices, there are considerations, for example, a belief in a 'normal rate', views as to the underlying market forces arising from the demand and supply of capital, and the likely extent of inflation, etc., which must imply that at some level there will be checks to any movement whether upwards, or downwards, in expectations of future prices—in market terms 'support levels' will eventually be reached on any downwards movement from which a rebound can take place. Thus in view of the probability that movements of expectations will only vary over a limited range, while the Government broker, who can utilize the vast resources of bonds and cash available from the Issue Department on the market,[14] has the power to move current prices very sharply, it would seem that textbook debt management techniques could still be applied, as long as the authorities were prepared to envisage large swings in long term interest rates.

This the Bank is not prepared to do. The reasons which they give

[13] *Bank of England Quarterly Bulletin*, vol. 6, no. 2, June 1966, p. 147. And when the market became prone to panic and disorganization in May 1967, the Government broker checked the slide and ended the flood of sales by raising the price at which he would buy in gilts in the market, rather ostentatiously. See *The Times* report, 16 May 1967.

[14] Those who are unfamiliar with the technicalities of the working of this market—and do not understand the role of the Issue Department of the Bank—should read paras. 108–15 of the *Radcliffe Report*.

vary from time to time, but it is possible to distinguish four basic reasons.

(1) Large swings in interest rates would impose upon a numerous public considerable capital gains/losses over a short period of time at what would seem the arbitrary whim of the Government. This would be not only morally dubious, but would also be politically dangerous (a few widows and children, who still may hold gilts, would no doubt be paraded). Furthermore, the foreigner, who does not really understand us anyhow, might believe that a sharp fall on the gilt-edged market, presaged the collapse of the United Kingdom. This was argued very forcefully by the Governor of the Bank, Mr. Cobbold, in evidence to the Radcliffe Committee. Probably this argument would be given less emphasis now.

(2) It is pure supposition that the potential range of expectations of future price levels is bounded. Nobody in practice knows how far prices would have to be varied before a support level was reached. Even if it was discovered at one time that, say, a 10 per cent reduction in prices was sufficient to bring in buyers, the formation of expectations is such a complex matter that this would be little help for future guidance, particularly since such actions by the authorities—in moving prices sharply up or down—would in turn have incalculable effects upon the future formation of expectations. Thus the Bank would always be working in conditions of acute uncertainty. It is facile to reply that if the initial reduction in price did not achieve its effect, then simply continue putting down the price until success was achieved. The adverse psychological impact both upon the market operators and the authorities of a major forced change in price levels, which failed to achieve its purpose, would be considerable and could well prejudice the success of further efforts in the same direction.

(3) The extent of variation of long term interest rates, if such techniques were used, could well be considerably larger than at present. While, in general, movements in interest rates of the extent so far experienced in the U.K. have not had much impact—in the view of the authorities, as will be discussed later—upon expenditure, so that the general effect of wider movements of interest rates would not be expected to be too severe, there remain certain problems owing to the uneven impact of such measures upon certain particular sectors. Two may be distinguished. First not only may the demand for purchasing private housing be responsive to quite small variations in interest rates, but also, owing to imperfections in the

working of the market, Building Society lending and borrowing rates tend to be 'sticky', i.e. do not vary in line with other interest rates. As actually happened in 1965, the Building Societies (the U.K. equivalent of the Savings and Loan Associations) found themselves, therefore, unable to attract funds and, *a fortiori*, to lend. The result was a rapid and severe collapse of the housing market, at a time when the expenditure of industry generally did not seem significantly affected by the high level of rates.

Secondly the high yields on bonds available, and presumably the urgent demand for loans from businesses at the same time, could encourage financial intermediaries to pare their liquid reserves to the bone, in search of higher yields, at the same time as the capital values of their assets were being lowered. A situation could be created where intermediaries would at best be embarrassed and at worst the public might come to suspect their solvency or liquidity and withdraw their funds.[15] Variations in gilt-edged prices would, however, have to be very large before they would impair the stability of reputable financial institutions. It is doubtful whether under present conditions the Bank would feel constrained to refrain from a somewhat more positive policy on these grounds. Even so the Bank, in its role as sponsor[16] of the City, would not be desirous of any course that did seriously jeopardize the stability of major financial institutions.

(4) The argument which the Bank puts most forcefully is that the greater uncertainty, that would be engendered by the rapid  and considerable variations in price resulting from a more positive approach to debt management, would cause the long run demand for bonds to lessen. It was stated in the *Bank of England Quarterly Bulletin* article on 'Official transactions in the gilt-edged market'[17]

[15] The gibe is sometimes made that those who reject a tougher use of monetary policy are arguing inconsistently that present levels of interest rates are ineffective, but much higher levels would be disastrous. This taunt only shows that those who make it are unaware that monetary stringency has always taken effect, severely through the mechanism of the collapse of some financial intermediary. Such collapses by their nature occur when some unperceived threshold is passed.

[16] This term has a particular meaning within administrative circles in the U.K. It implies that the industry, or body, or whatever, will normally communicate with the Government through its sponsor Department, that the sponsor will be expected to appreciate and understand the views of those in authority in that industry, and to make the rest of Government aware of those views. It does not, however, imply that the sponsor must itself invariably, or even usually, suppor those views.

[17] Vol. 6, no. 2, June 1966, p. 142.

that, 'The chief purpose of management . . . is to maintain market conditions that will maximize, both now and in the future, the desire of investors at home and abroad to hold British government debt.'

Two comments should be made here. First, as Professor Sayers and others pointed out to the Treasury witnesses giving evidence to the Radcliffe Committee [**8**], the price of bonds has been slowly sagging in the U.K. for years and a miasma of distrust of gilt-edged has been instilled in the investing community. Have these conditions been any more likely to secure confidence in the future trend of prices than a policy of varying prices more rapidly in the short run to achieve certain effects which could well improve the overall management of the economy? To this point the Bank might well respond that as most investors had short planning periods it was uncertainty in the short, rather than the longer run, that was relevant, and that present methods clearly reduce potential losses over the next six months, even though losses over the next six years might be reduced by a firmer handling of debt management.

The second query might well be to ask exactly why the Bank should put maximizing the long term demand for its debt as its prime objective at all? In the past funding the debt has occasionally been regarded by the monetary authorities as a Good in itself, an ethical absolute. The serious answer to this, however, has already been outlined (cf. page 457 above), which is that the Public Debt is so large that any major shift away from holding it could well

involve the authorities in having to accede to a massive increase in the monetary base. It is possible to conceive of a situation, if confidence in the gilt-edged market ebbed away, in which there would exist simultaneously both a much larger volume of liquid assets *and* a much higher level of interest rates.

These matters have been discussed above from a point of view consciously sympathetic to the views of the Bank. It is worth doing so, precisely because these views may be unfamiliar and alien, but an appreciation of them is necessary to an understanding of British monetary policy. This is not intended to prejudice the wider question of whether it would have been wiser for the Bank to brave the shadowy dangers of a more positive policy of debt management than to constrain its own actions in the way it has done in recent years.

In any case the positive conclusion is that the Bank has as a matter of policy refrained from any tendency to lead the market, or to fix prices.[18] Instead the policy, which the Bank follows, may be characterized as one of continuously leaning into the wind: that is to say, if at the going price there is an excess demand from the public, the Bank will either meet that demand by sales, or will allow prices to rise (the choice between the two depending on policy considerations), but it will not, if the public is a net buyer, add to the excess demand by trying to purchase bonds as well, nor will it try to sell so much that prices are forced down. Equally if the public has, at the going price, an excess supply, the Bank will choose a policy between the limits of either sopping up all the excess supply at the going price by purchases, or allowing the excess supply to cause a fall in prices under its own weight by withdrawing entirely from the market.[19]

[18] This is not an immutable policy. If the market becomes disorganized, either through panic sales or (may we live to see the day!) an unhealthy speculative boom, the Bank would step in to correct the situation, as it did on 15 May 1967, for example. But even under more normal conditions, there are occasional conjunctions which will cause the Bank to adopt a more positive policy. For example, in the 3rd and 4th quarters of 1960 short term rates on Treasury bills were reduced, in order to limit the inflow of speculative funds and to lessen the pressure on the dollar, while at the same time a conscious pressure of sales in the gilt-edged market was maintained on grounds of domestic policy, a form of Operation Reverse Twist. Thus in the *Bank of England Quarterly Bulletin*, vol. 1, no. 1, December 1960, in the Commentary, p. 12, it was stated, 'In these circumstances it was decided that a reduction of ½ per cent in Bank Rate, desirable on international grounds, would not be inconsistent with the maintenance of adequate restraint at home. This move, which was made on the 27 October, was not intended to signal any change in the general policy of credit restraint. In the gilt-edged market the Government broker continued as a seller of certain medium and long term stocks at unchanged prices, indicating that a further fall in medium and long term interest rates was not being encouraged.'

Those interested in the subject of the extent to which the term structure of rates can be flexed by Government intervention should find the experience of this period valuable. Treasury bill rates fell from 5·582 per cent in August, to 5·53 per cent in September and then further to 4·46 per cent in December. Yields on 2½ per cent Consols fell from 5·60 per cent in August to 5·48 per cent in September, but then rose again to 5·63 per cent in December. This was achieved with the help of large scale net sales of gilt-edged by the authorities in the market, £243 million, 3rd quarter, and £162 million, 4th quarter, of 1960 (£216 million and £147 million respectively, seasonally adjusted).

[19] It is considerably easier to assess quantitatively how the authorities have in fact acted in the market, than it would be to establish whether their assessment of the form of the public's demand function was accurate. The basic hypothesis to be tested is that the authorities were continuously acting to moderate and offset shifts in demand, caused by exogenous factors influencing the public's expectations. The data are of net sales of marketable securities in £ million by the authorities (Source: Radcliffe, *Memoranda* of Evidence, Paper 1 submitted by H.M.

Treasury up till 1959, vol. 1, pp. 78–81, subsequently *Monthly Digest of Statistics*) and interest rates on $2\frac{1}{2}$ per cent Consols, end quarter (source: *Monthly Digest of Statistics*). The test was to see whether the quarterly net sales of marketable securities (S) were inversely related to the change in interest rates over the quarter (end quarter–end quarter) (di). Both series were seasonally adjusted by the simple method of adjusting for the difference between quarterly and overall means (there was no trend in either series). The observations ran from 1st quarter 1953 to 4th quarter 1966, 56 in number; the result was

$$S = 37{\cdot}73 - 390{\cdot}0\, di$$
$$(87{\cdot}1)$$

$$r^2 = 0{\cdot}2707 \qquad r = -0{\cdot}52 \qquad \text{SE} = 122 \qquad \text{D.W.} = 1{\cdot}69$$

This (r^2) is significant at the 1 per cent level. It suggests that if interest rates have risen by $\frac{1}{2}$ per cent in any quarter, the authorities will have been busy supporting the market by net purchases of approximately £155 million of marketable securities, while equivalently a market boom, involving a fall in rates of $\frac{1}{2}$ per cent, would bring out the authorities in selling some £235 million.

I should emphasize that in my view these results considerably understate the real strength of this inverse relationship. First there is the point that if the authorities' policy of sales of marketable securities were taken entirely without consideration of the state of the rest of the market one would expect the weight of their actions to cause interest rates to move directly with their sales. Thus even a zero correlation would have implied some degree of leaning into the wind.

Secondly a policy of leaning into the wind still allows the authorities considerable freedom of action. Assume that the authorities wish to impose a restrictive monetary policy, and that, as the authorities believe, expectations are volatile. Then within the quarter there will be periods of public excess supply, which the authorities will allow to depress prices with few supporting purchases, and periods of public excess demand, which the authorities will meet with large scale sales. Thus within a period of a quarter a policy of leaning into the wind can well involve an observation of the combination of large sales and rising interest rates. This possibility is of real interest because of the direct evidence from the Bank, in several cases of apparent positive relationship between sales and interest rates, that this is what happened. For example a combination of large net sales by the authorities and rising rates was seen in the Spring and Summer of 1955, and occurred in the manner suggested above, cf. Appendix to *Minutes of Evidence* to the Radcliffe Committee, note on Questions 2164–71. There has been a regular commentary on Bank actions in this market since publication of the Quarterly Bulletin began in 1960 (when in fact, see p. 465, policy seemed to change for a short time and the Government broker did take steps to keep prices down by large sales). Since then positive relationships between net official sales and interest rates appeared in the following quarters, 3rd 1961, 4th 1964, 1st 1965, 3rd 1965, 2nd, 3rd, 1966. For these periods see the Commentaries in the relevant *Quarterly Bulletins*, vol. 1, no. 5, December 1961, pp. 8–9; vol. 5, no. 1, March 1965, pp. 8–9; vol. 5, no. 2, June 1965, p. 112; vol. 6, no. 3, September 1966, p. 216; vol. 6, no. 4, December 1966, pp. 316–17. From these it is quite clear that the explanation of positive relationships is as given above. Indeed it is impossible to read the regular Commentaries on the gilt-edged market without coming to realize the consistency with which the Bank 'leans into the wind'.

Such a policy, however, does impose important limitations upon the actions of the authorities, for it implies that as long as the public continues to act on one side of the market, as buyers or sellers, the authorities are fully in command of neither the volume of sales of debt nor the level of interest rates. Only in periods during which the public alternates between moods of optimism and pessimism can the authorities, by coordinating their policy during selling waves with those during buying sprees, achieve either a planned volume of sales of debt, or a desired level of rates. Of course, the assumption that expectations are not stable, which underlies the rejection of more positive debt management by the authorities, would also suggest that a policy of 'leaning into the wind' would be more successful, since one would expect more rapid reversals of mood in the market.

Furthermore, the authorities are able to influence the state of the gilt-edged market by their positive actions leading to variations in rates in the Treasury bill market.[20] The influence on the gilt-edged market may occur purely as a result of arbitrage or the change in bill rates may also influence expectations of future bill rates (and bond prices). The view of the Bank as put forward to the Radcliffe Committee[21] was, 'that, generally speaking, a rise in the level of short term rates tends to work through, and to cause some rise in the level of long term rates but that this is by no means a regular rule and there is no time factor that you could ascribe to it'.

But the extent to which the authorities are free to control monetary conditions by altering the Treasury bill rate with a view to influencing conditions in the gilt-edged market, is strictly limited. As will be shown later, the authorities tend to vary bill rate in response to external conditions, principally the movements of the U.K.'s foreign exchange reserves. Indeed in view of the U.K.'s limited foreign exchange reserves and exposure to international capital movements, it would be hard to expect anything else. Reductions in our foreign exchange position are likely also to be associated with periods when the British economy is regarded as

[20] It is not easy to appreciate the rationale of the position of the Bank in accepting the necessity of price leadership in the bill market, but refraining from it in the Bond market. The attempt by the spokesmen of the Bank to justify their position in evidence before the Radcliffe committee was not a model of intellectual clarity, cf. *Minutes of Evidence*, cf. Qns. 1841–98.

[21] *Minutes of Evidence*, Qn. 1764 and subsequent.

being 'overloaded' and when foreigners are directly selling investments, so the gilt-edged market would be likely to be weak anyhow; increases in short term rates have tended to fall upon an already impressionable market. In short, not surprisingly, when conditions are such that monetary stringency is desirable, and desired, the gilt-edged market will fall. But under these conditions the authorities move in to support and to stabilize this market. Therefore the desired stringency is offset by an increase in liquidity. This can be restated another way. Under a fixed exchange rate system a fall in foreign exchange reserves should reduce the monetary base,[22] so that an automatic reduction in the money supply should ensue. This hardly happens in the U.K., since the outflow of reserves will be associated, via a fall in gilt-edged prices, with open market purchases by the authorities in the gilt-edged market.[23]

[22] In the U.K. a purchase of foreign currency spot will be bought from the Exchange Equalization Account for sterling. This receipt of sterling is lent to the Government (on tap Treasury bills), who are therefore able to reduce the volume of Treasury bills which they issue in the market.

[23] These assertions are also open to quantitative assessment. The hypotheses are that yields on gilt-edged will be positively associated with outward movements of reserves and that net sales of gilt-edged by the authorities will be negatively related to outward flows of reserves. The data for reserves used were quarterly changes in gold and convertible currency reserves + change in account with IMF (dG) in £ million (Source: Monthly Digest of Statistics, overseas finance, a positive value representing a decline in reserves and a negative value implying an increase), seasonally adjusted as before. The results run for the period 1st quarter 1953–4th quarter 1966 and were as follows:

$$di = 0{\cdot}04 + \underset{(0{\cdot}0002)}{0{\cdot}0008}\, dG$$

$$r^2 = 0{\cdot}198 \qquad SE = 0{\cdot}17 \qquad D.W. = 1{\cdot}41$$

$$S = 21{\cdot}2 - \underset{(0{\cdot}17)}{0{\cdot}24}\, dG$$

$$r^2 = 0{\cdot}035 \qquad SE = 140{\cdot}4 \qquad D.W. = 1{\cdot}70$$

Considering the large amount of random 'noise' in both the series di and dG, the first result gives much support to the first hypothesis above.

This latter result does not, however, provide support for the second hypothesis above. This is very largely owing to the fact that the data used does not adequately portray the true state of our reserve position, either because the run down of our reserves was felt by all to be a short term phenomenon as in the 4th quarter 1956 and 1st quarter 1957 (Suez), and/or because the data used above does not incorporate direct borrowing from other Central Banks under the Basle or other agreements, as for example in 3rd quarter 1961 when we repaid £295 million under our previous Basle borrowings, but the series used here shows a net fall in our reserves of £231 million (seasonally adjusted). After 1964 the series used here

SOURCES

[1] Revell, Jack, 'The Wealth of the Nation', *Moorgate and Wall Street Review*, Spring 1966, pp. 57–89, especially p. 72.

[2] Mendelsohn, M. S., 'London's many money markets', *The Banker*, May 1967.

[3] 'London's "new" markets for money', *Midland Bank Review*, August 1966.

[4] 'Gilt-edged market; the crowded years', *The Economist*, 5 August 1967, p. 524.

[5] Morgan, E. V., 'Gilt-edged—can the Budget help?', *The Banker*, August 1966, p. 534.

[6] O'Brien, L. K., 'Central Banking developments', from *Banking trends in Europe today*, lecture delivered at the 17th International Banking Summer School, the Institute of Bankers, London, July 1964, pp. 9–28; quotation from page 25.

[7] Mr. Cobbold, Governor of the Bank, Answer to Question 1762 *Minutes of Evidence to the Radcliffe Committee.*

[8] *Minutes of Evidence to the Radcliffe Committee*, Qns. 2956 and subsequent.

becomes even less accurate as an indicator of changes in our reserve position. After inspection I decided to reject seven observations, the three quarters mentioned, 4th 1964, 2nd 1965, 1st 1966 and 4th 1966 on the grounds that the reported change in the reserves did not reflect the change in the real position in these quarters. This is not a satisfactory procedure; it would be preferable to adjust the reserve figures by the amount of Aid. I have not yet been able to do this. Still, for what it is worth, the re-run equation, 49 observations, gave the following results:

$$S = 0{\cdot}17 - \underset{(0{\cdot}20)}{0{\cdot}845}\, dG$$

$$r^2 = 0{\cdot}267 \qquad \mathrm{SE} = 110{\cdot}2 \qquad \mathrm{D.W.} = 1{\cdot}70$$

This would suggest that if there was an outflow of foreign reserves of £200 million over a period, draining the monetary base by the same extent, that the authorities would simply pump £170 million approximately of that back into the system by their support of the gilt-edged market.

DEBT MANAGEMENT AND MONETARY POLICY IN THE UNITED KINGDOM[1]

W. E. NORTON*

I. Introduction

CURRENT monetary policy in the United Kingdom is markedly different from the orthodox monetary policy of text-books on money and banking. The authorities reject orthodox monetary policy, which traditionally relied on a combination of a change in Bank Rate and supporting open-market operations to alter the price and volume of money, because, as argued below, it is inconsistent with their debt-management policy. Instead they use other means in their attempts to influence the operations of the banks and the level of expenditure. These alternative measures include requests to restrict the level of advances (referred to hereafter as 'requests') and special deposits.[2]

This paper presents some regression results that may assist in an appraisal of the present debt management and monetary policies. In particular, estimates are made of the effects on non-official holdings of government securities of expectations about future interest rates on these securities and of the effects on the portfolios of the banks and the rest of the private sector of requests and special

* Reprinted from the *Economic Journal*, vol. 79, no. 315, September 1969, pp. 475–94, by permission of the author and publisher. W. E. Norton is on the research staff of the Reserve Bank of Australia.

[1] The author is very grateful to N. J. Gibson for supervision of the doctoral thesis on which this paper is based and for comments on earlier drafts of this paper. R. J. Ball, external examiner for the thesis, also suggested several useful improvements.

[2] The most recent instrument announced by the Bank of England, 'cash deposits', had not appeared when this study was in progress. See, 'Control of Bank Lending: the Cash Deposits Scheme', *Bank of England Quarterly Bulletin*, vol. 8, no. 2, June 1968, pp. 166–70.

deposits. But it is useful to begin by recalling the content of the authorities' debt-management and monetary policies.[3]

II. The authorities' debt management and monetary policies

The official view is that the chief purpose of debt management is neither credit policy nor interest-rate policy but the maintenance of market conditions that maximize the present and future demand for government debt. A broad stable market, one in which large amounts can be traded with little effect on prices, is necessary, it is claimed, to attract the large institutions and companies. Hence the authorities try to modify the extent and speed of short-term movements in the prices of government securities. It follows that they are unwilling to press open-market sales of these securities when prices are falling. Indeed, they argue that investors' expectations are such that a fall in the price of government securities may result in a decline rather than an increase in demand in the immediate future;[4] and *mutatis mutandis* for a rise. An attempted open-market selling operation may end in net purchases because 'when the authorities are endeavouring to exert pressure (on the banks' liquidity) by sales of securities to the non-bank public, the latter's appetite for securities may so wane that the authorities may in the end find themselves buying, rather than selling, such debt.'[5] Furthermore, sharp short-term movements in the prices of government securities due to official action would undermine confidence in the market and the Government's credit.[6] Finally, the cost of servicing the national debt may be substantially increased, for at

[3] These views have been outlined recently by the Bank of England in 'Official Transactions in the Gilt-edged Market', *Bank of England Quarterly Bulletin*, vol. 6, no. 2, June 1966, pp. 141–8.

[4] *Bank of England Quarterly Bulletin*, vol. 6, no. 2, June 1966, pp. 146–7; *Radcliffe Minutes*, Q 1612–14, 1631–9, 1762, 1798, 1804, 1896–7, 11967; *Radcliffe Report*, paras. 551, 563. It is convenient to refer to the Committee on the Working of the Monetary System, *Principal Memoranda of Evidence*, vols. 1, 2, and 3 (London: H.M.S.O., 1960), *Minutes of Oral Evidence* (London: H.M.S.O., 1960), and *Report*, Cmnd. 827 (London: H.M.S.O., 1959) as *Radcliffe Memoranda*, *Radcliffe Minutes*, and *Radcliffe Report* respectively.

[5] *Bank of England Quarterly Bulletin*, vol. 2, no. 2, December 1962, p. 254. There was an example of this particular situation in 1966. See *Bank of England Quarterly Bulletin*, vol. 6, no. 3, September 1966, p. 216.

[6] *Bank of England Quarterly Bulletin*, vol. 6, no. 2, June 1966, p. 147; *Radcliffe Minutes*, Q 1649, 1762, 1792, 1848, 1886–9, 2963; *Radcliffe Report*, para. 551.

least the immediate future, by a policy of pressing sales of government securities and 'to keep down the cost of the Government's borrowing is important at all times.'[7]

Many questions arise about this debt-management policy. It is, for instance, highly questionable whether maximization of future demand for debt is consistent with maximization of present demand. Similarly, it is doubtful whether the present policy is *necessary* to finance and refinance the national debt. An alternative policy might require higher interest rates, at least in the first instance, but this could prove to be a small price to pay for a reduction in inflationary pressure and the freedom to apply a flexible interest-rate policy. Again, the argument that a rise in interest rates may produce a fall in demand for government securities in the immediate future is not easy to accept. Some results relevant to this theory are given below. The view that rapid movements in interest rates would damage the Government's credit is also questionable but more difficult to test.[8]

But the most important question about the present debt-management policy concerns its effects on the content and effectiveness of monetary policy. A Director of the Bank of England sums up the situation as follows:

> at a time at which market expectations about the future of prices are unfavourable, we may well be unable to persuade the public to buy the securities in sufficient volume to produce the pressure on the banks which we would wish to see; and it is this consideration, of course, which has led in recent years to the development of such devices as 'requests' to the banks for moderation in the expansion of their advances and the use of special deposits.[9]

III. The basic model

The results reported in this paper are taken from a more detailed study of the monetary sector of the United Kingdom economy.[10] The focal point of that study is a thirty-nine-equation linear model, referred to in this paper as the basic model, that emphasizes the monetary sector and the role of monetary variables in the rest of

[7] *Bank of England Quarterly Bulletin*, vol. 6, no. 2, June 1966, p. 146; also *Radcliffe Minutes*, Q 1018, 1649.

[8] *Radcliffe Report*, para. 564.

[9] Hollom, J. Q., 'The Methods and Objectives of the Bank's Market Operations' in *The Bank of England Today* (London: Institute of Bankers, 1964), p. 26.

[10] Norton, W. E., 'An Econometric Study of the United Kingdom Monetary Sector, 1955–1966' (University of Manchester, unpublished Ph.D. thesis, 1967).

the economy. The basic model distinguishes four broad groups of transactors and eleven financial markets. The four transactors are the clearing banks, the discount houses, the authorities (Bank of England, Treasury, and other government departments, nationalized industries, and local authorities), and the public. The public is the rest of the domestic economy plus external residents holding the assets or liabilities of the other three sectors. The financial markets involve bank reserves, currency, demand deposits, time deposits, call-money deposits, Treasury bills, commercial bills, special deposits, national savings, bank advances and government securities. Markets for durable and non-durable consumption goods, fixed capital, inventories and imports are also included to permit an endogenous explanation of gross domestic product. Finally, a government budget identity and equations for income and expenditure taxes are added so that tax revenues and the domestic borrowing requirement are endogenous variables.[11]

The typical portfolio behavioural equation of the basic model is of the conventional stock adjustment form, modified to allow for short-term flow and stock constraints on 'desired' portfolio changes. The assumptions underlying this formulation are outlined in studies by de Leeuw and Goldfeld.[12] The modified stock-adjustment model explains the quarterly changes in a sector's holding of some asset (or liability), ΔA, by variables measuring the sector's wealth, the expected interest rate on asset A, the expected interest rates on other relevant assets, short-term constraints on the sector's portfolio adjustments and the stock of asset A held by the sector at the end of the last quarter.

IV. Expected interest rates

The first question for empirical study in this paper is the effect of expected interest rates on the public's holdings of government securities. The testing of hypotheses about the formation of expectations is notoriously difficult, but de Leeuw has suggested a way of

[11] The domestic borrowing requirement is defined as the net balance of the Central Government's capital account less external borrowing. See, for instance, Table 16 in *Financial Statistics*, no. 56 (London: H.M.S.O., 1966).

[12] de Leeuw, F., 'A Model of Financial Behaviour', Chap. 13, in J. S. Duesenberry *et al.*, *The Brookings Quarterly Econometric Model of the United States* (Chicago, 1965), pp. 467–72; Goldfeld, S. M., *Commercial Bank Behaviour and Economic Activity* (Amsterdam, 1966), pp. 24–7.

representing two common theories about the formation of expectations.[13]

The first, the Keynesian normal-rate hypothesis, assumes that investors have a normal level of interest rates in mind towards which they expect rates to move. When current rates are greater than the normal rate investors are said to expect interest rates to fall, and vice-versa. De Leeuw represents the normal rate by a weighted average of past interest rates on a government security and uses the difference between the current rate and the normal rate as a proxy for Keynesian-type expectations about future movements in rates. This proxy variable is expected to have a positive coefficient in demand functions for government securities.

The second hypothesis stems from Duesenberry's critical reaction to the Keynesian theory. He argues that

> on a priori grounds there is no reason why the (Keynesian) argument should not be turned just the other way. In many fields, trend projection seems to be the dominant influence on expectation. It would not, therefore, be surprising if it turned out that a rise in rates led to an expectation of a further rise in rates and vice-versa.[14]

De Leeuw represents this extrapolative hypothesis of expectations formation by the difference between the current government security rate and another weighted average of past rates, with the weights in this case giving greater importance to very recent rates. This second proxy variable is expected to produce a negative coefficient in demand functions for government securities, since if current rates are above recent rates they are expected to rise further, causing a fall in the price of fixed-interest securities.

Following de Leeuw, variables of the form

$$r_t - \frac{1-k}{1-k^{11}} \sum_{i=1}^{11} k^{i-1} r_{t-i} \qquad 0 < k < 1$$

are constructed.[15] This variable is assumed to represent the Keynesian normal theory for values of k of 0·85 and 0·75 and the extrapolative theory for values of 0·25 and 0·35. These variables,

[13] de Leeuw, op. cit., p. 500.

[14] Duesenberry, J. S., *Business Cycles and Economic Growth* (New York, 1958), p. 318.

[15] de Leeuw, loc. cit. The variable for $k = 0{\cdot}05$ is virtually a first difference; the variable for $k = 0{\cdot}95$ is the current value in relation to a much longer average.

$r^N(k)$ and $r^E(k)$ respectively, are used to gauge whether the formation of expectations about interest rates is closer to the Keynesian or extrapolative hypotheses. Simpler variables of the form

$$r(n) = r_t - \frac{1}{n}\sum_{i=1}^{n} r_{t-i}$$

are also constructed.[16] The variables $r(3)$ and $r(10)$ are used as alternative, simpler representations of the extrapolative and normal theories respectively.

Another way of allowing for the influence of expectations about government security rates is suggested by the authorities' view that sales of government securities by the banks may lead other holders to expect the prices of these securities to fall and therefore to shift out of government securities.[17] This argument suggests that the quarterly change in the banks' holdings of government securities should have a positive coefficient in the demand equation of the public for government securities.

V. Public's demand for government securities

The specification of the public's demand equation for government securities is based on the modified stock-adjustment model of portfolio behaviour. This model suggests that the public's holdings of government securities can be explained by a measure of this sector's wealth, a vector of interest rates representing substitution possibilities between government securities and other assets and a vector of short-term constraints on the public's portfolio allocation. There is no quarterly series for the wealth of the public. But recent empirical work makes considerable use of the concept proposed by Friedman as an index of wealth, permanent income.[18] A permanent income series was compiled for the present study by calculating a weighted average for current and past values of gross domestic product.

There are many potential substitutes for government securities in the public's portfolio. The interest rates on National Savings

[16] Goldfeld, op. cit., p. 56.

[17] *Bank of England Annual Report for the year ended 28th February 1959*, p. 8, *Radcliffe Minutes*, Q. 2742, 2745.

[18] Friedman, M., 'The Demand for Money: Some Theoretical and Empirical Results', *Journal of Political Economy*, vol. 67, no. 4, August 1959, p. 23.

Certificates, building society shares, Treasury bills and time deposits are tried. Moreover, official evidence to the Radcliffe Committee suggests that inflation reduces the public's appetite for government securities, so measures of the expected change in retail prices are also tested.[19] These measures are weighted averages of actual changes in retail prices in recent periods. Another argument put to the Radcliffe Committee was that official requests to the banks to restrict the level of their advances may result in the public seeking finance by selling government securities.[20] The Committee felt that the available evidence indicated that this was not a major factor but thought further research desirable.[21] A dummy variable (d^1), which is defined later in this paper, is introduced to allow for requests. Another dummy variable (d^2) is used to account for improvements in non-interest-rate terms on national savings. Changes in these terms vary in nature from the introduction of a new type of national savings, such as the Premium Savings Bond in 1956, to adjustments in the maximum holdings of particular issues of National Savings Certificates. Other variables tried as short-term constraints in this equation include disposable income, income tax and the quarterly change in sterling balances.

Several estimates of the public's demand function for government securities are given in Table 1. Quarterly seasonally unadjusted data for the period 1955(3) to 1966(2) are used for all the estimates reported in this paper.[22] Coefficients which are significant at the 5 per cent level are indicated by an asterisk. (Significance tests are not applied to the seasonal dummy variables.) Permanent income, the interest rate on national savings, income tax, and the lagged stock of government securities have significant coefficients. The coefficient of the latter variable suggests, subject to the usual qualifications, quite rapid adjustment of actual to desired stocks.[23]

Interest rates on other substitutes are insignificant, whereas

[19] *Radcliffe Memoranda Vol. 1*, Bank of England Memorandum 12, para. 16. Also, *Bank of England Annual Report for the year ended 28th February 1959* p. 8.

[20] Ibid., p. 3.

[21] *Radcliffe Report*, paras. 418, 545.

[22] The interest rates, measures of expectations about future interest rates on government securities and measures of the expected change in the price level are expressed in percentages; an interest rate of 5 per cent is 5·00. Other variables, except the dummy variables, are expressed in £ million. Stock variables are measured at the end of quarters. A data appendix is available from the author.

[23] See, for instance, Feige, E. L., 'Expectations and Adjustments in the Monetary Sector', *American Economic Review*, vol. 57, no. 2, Papers and Proceedings, May 1967, pp. 462–73.

TABLE I

Estimates of the public's demand equation for government securities

Equation number	Constant	Seasonal dummy variables 1	2	3	Permanent income	Yield on national savings	Yield on long-dated govt. securities	Expected yields on long govt. securities, i.e. $r_L^E(0{\cdot}25)$	Changes in banks' govt. securities	Changes in banks' govt. securities lagged one quarter	Income tax payments	Public's govt. securities lagged one quarter	Multiple coefficient of determination	Standard error of estimate	Von Neumann ratio
(1.1)	3536	464 (263)	−12 (39)	51 (41)	0·18* (0·07)	−76* (38)		−133* (48)	0·62* (0·23)	−0·56* (0·29)	0·33 (0·22)	−0·32* (0·11)	0·50	81	1·76
(1.2)	4561	694 (244)	22 (37)	81 (39)	0·26* (0·06)	−97* (38)		−115* (49)	0·41 (0·22)		−0·54* (0·20)	−0·42* (0·10)	0·45	85	1·45
(1.3)	3107	79 (41)	−26 (39)	21 (36)	0·09* (0·04)	−67 (39)		−133* (48)	0·66* (0·24)	−0·77* (0·25)		−0·27* (0·11)	0·47	83	1·79
(1.4)	4088	760 (249)	17 (37)	86 (39)	0·24* (0·06)	−129* (46)	58 (47)	−156* (59)	0·32 (0·23)		−0·61* (0·21)	−0·38* (0·11)	0·47	84	1·54
(1.5)	3249	534 (273)	−13 (39)	58 (41)	0·17* (0·07)	−102* (47)	45 (46)	−163* (57)	0·53* (0·25)	−0·52 (0·29)	−0·40 (0·23)	−0·30* (0·11)	0·52	82	1·79
(1.6)	3847	486 (277)	−16 (40)	63 (43)	0·17* (0·07)	−128* (55)	63 (55)	−151*† (59)	0·53* (0·26)	−0·56 (0·30)	−0·35 (0·24)	−0·35* (0·12)	0·50	83	1·73

† This variable is $r_L(3)$ not $r_L^E(0{\cdot}25)$.

disposable income, the quarterly change in sterling balances, measures of the expected change in retail prices and the two dummy variables yield coefficients of incorrect sign.

Greatest interest centres on the performance of measures of expectations about interest rates. The proxy variable for extrapolative expectations, $r_L^E(k)$, produces a significant negative coefficient, whereas the coefficient on the Keynesian normal rate variable is positive but very insignificant. Only estimates using a value of k of 0·25 for the variable representing extrapolative expectations are given in Table 1; little change occurs if $k = 0·35$ is substituted. A comparison of estimates (1.5) and (1.6) shows that the simpler variable $r(3)$ yields a poorer, but broadly similar, result.

The quarterly change in the banks' holdings of government securities (ΔG^B), the other variable used to represent expectations about interest rates, has its anticipated positive coefficient. This variable lagged one period is also tried to allow for delayed reactions by the public to the banks' actions in the market for government securities. It yields a negative coefficient and results in a substantial increase in the values of R^2 and the von Neumann ratio. A possible explanation of the apparently contradictory positive and negative coefficients on the variables ΔG^B and ΔG^B_{-1} is as follows. Sales of securities by the banks may depress prices and, in accord with the authorities' argument explained earlier, stimulate sales by the public in the same quarter. But by the next quarter the fall in gilt-edged prices may have created a level of interest rates which is high compared with the public's idea of a normal rate, so purchases of securities resume. If this interpretation is correct it is of the utmost importance, as it suggests that the short-run instability in the market for government securities, indicated by the significant coefficients on $r_L^E(k)$ and ΔG^B, does not extend beyond three months.

The positive coefficients yielded by the interest rate on long-dated government securities (r^{GL}) in estimates (1.4)–(1.6) are further evidence against the instability argument. Moreover, estimate (1.4) shows that the coefficient of r^{GL} increases when ΔG^B_{-1} is left out of the equation. This result supports the interpretation in the previous paragraph placed on the negative coefficient of ΔG^B_{-1}.

These results, however, give some support to the authorities' view of the gilt-edged market. But further study of the demand side of the market for government securities is obviously necessary. In estimate (1.1) there are six significant explanatory variables, apart from the seasonal dummy variables, yet the value of R^2 is only 0·50.

To obtain better results it may be necessary to use a less aggregative analysis and estimate separate demand functions for, say, life assurance and superannuation funds, other non-bank financial institutions, industrial and commercial companies, external residents and other domestic holders.[24] The use of non-linear expressions also may be helpful, particularly for representing the Keynesian-type expectations variable.

VI. Banks' demand for government securities

In initial attempts at estimating the banks' demand function the modified stock adjustment model was tried using as explanatory variables total deposits, a vector of interest rates related to each of the banks' major assets and liabilities, the quarterly flows of deposits, advances and special deposits and the banks' holdings of excess liquid assets and government securities at the start of the quarter.

But empirical and *a priori* considerations suggest that the stock-adjustment model should be rejected as the theoretical framework. Empirically, this model performs poorly in explaining changes in the banks' holdings of liquid assets.[25] Moreover, estimates of the stock-adjustment model for the banks' holdings of government securities suggest very slow adjustment between actual and desired stocks. This result is in agreement with the finding of Goldfeld with United States data, but is improbable on *a priori* grounds.[26] An alternative theoretical scheme seems to be at least as plausible as the stock-adjustment model. This *ad hoc* hypothesis assumes that the banks' holdings of government securities are dictated by their actions to satisfy the required cash, liquid assets and special deposits ratios and the public's demand for advances and deposits. Thus government securities are treated as a residual except for a modification to allow a choice between holdings of government securities and excess liquid assets, where the latter is the difference between actual and required liquid assets. This choice is assumed to be made on the basis of the banks' view as to their liquid-asset requirements in the near future and the actual and expected interest rates on liquid assets and government securities.[27] Support for this approach

[24] Such as Dr. W. R. White's unpublished University of Manchester Ph.D. thesis.

[25] Norton, op. cit., p. 142.

[26] Goldfeld, op. cit., pp. 57–8, 132.

[27] *Radcliffe Memoranda Vol. 2*, Committee of London Clearing Bankers Memorandum, para. 39.

in attempting to explain the banks' holdings of government securities is found in several official pronouncements. The Bank of England, for instance, comments:

The Clearing Banks' Liquidity Ratio, at 35·2 per cent, was unusually high on the 19th February 1958. The rate of return on liquid assets was falling relatively to that obtainable on gilt-edged securities and the outlook in the gilt-edged market had greatly improved since the previous autumn. In these circumstances the Clearing Banks continued to add to their investments, which rose by £97 million from 19th February to 30th June . . . (However in) . . . the five months to the 18th February 1959 . . . the Clearing Banks' advances . . . (rose) . . . by no less than £306 million . . . The rise in advances substantially exceeded the concurrent underlying rise in deposits . . . Considerations of liquidity . . . led them to reduce their investments and over the five months ending the 18th February 1959, these fell by £241 million. Their holdings of Treasury Bills fell by £178 million but the total of their liquid assets fell by only £81 million.[28]

and:

In the six months to March 1960, a diminishing growth in deposits with the Clearing and Scottish banks had been accompanied by a continuing rise in advances that led these banks to reduce their holdings of gilt-edged stocks. In the second quarter of 1960 . . . with deposits of the clearing banks tending to rise seasonally, broadly in line with the rise in advances, and with their liquidity ratio 31·5 per cent at the outset, the immediate need for them to sell gilt-edged stocks would have been small (compared with the succeeding quarter) had not the call for Special Deposits intervened . . . (and) obliged the banks to sell gilt-edged stocks on a larger scale than would otherwise have been necessary.[29]

Several interest rates were used in experiments with the banks' demand equation for government securities. These include the rates on short-dated and long-dated government securities, measures of expectations about these rates (i.e., $r^N(k)$ and $r^E(k)$) and interest rates on call money, Treasury bills and commercial bills.

The estimates in Table 2 show that the stock adjustment and *ad hoc* models produce very similar results. The total deposits variable was dropped because it yielded a negative coefficient; this may reflect the downward trend over the sample period in the banks' holdings of government securities, although the use of various sets of explanatory variables, including a time variable,

[28] *Bank of England Annual Report for the year ended 28th February 1959*, pp. 5–7.

[29] *Bank of England Quarterly Bulletin*, December 1960, pp. 12–13. See also *Radcliffe Minutes*, Q 168, 171, 3743–4, 3850–85.

TABLE 2

Estimates of the banks' demand equation for government securities

Equation number	Constant	Seasonal dummy variables 1	2	3	Deposits	Yield on short-dated govt. securities	Expected yields on short govt. securities, i.e. r_S^E(0·35)	Excess liquid assets, lagged one quarter	Change in advances	Change in deposits	Change in special deposits	Banks' govt. securities, lagged one quarter	Multiple coefficient of determination	Standard error of estimate	Von Neumann ratio
(2.1)	−113	96 (58)	73 (21)	85 (22)	−0·01 (0·01)	9 (14)	−20 (16)	0·35* (0·08)	−0·43* (0·10)	0·25* (0·08)	−0·67* (0·22)	−0·03 (0·03)	0·82	35	1·95
(2.2)	−148	96 (57)	73 (21)	84 (22)		6 (12)	−20 (15)	0·34* (0·08)	−0·45* (0·10)	0·24* (0·08)	−0·65* (0·22)	−0·02 (0·02)	0·82	35	1·95
(2.3)	−232	103 (57)	73 (21)	86 (22)		16* (8)	−25 (15)	0·32* (0·08)	−0·43* (0·10)	0·25* (0·08)	−0·70* (0·21)		0·81	35	1·95

does not change the result. The quarterly flows of advances, deposits and special deposits and the lagged stock of excess liquid assets are all significant. These results are consistent with the view of government securities as the banks' residual or buffer asset.

The results also have important policy implications. Payments into special deposits may be expected to generate substantial sales of government securities by the banks. On the other hand, a fall in advances due to, say, an official request to restrict their level may stimulate substantial purchases of government securities. These statements are supported by the coefficients of G^B with respect to SD and d^1 in the reduced form of the basic model.[30]

Only two interest-rate variables perform satisfactorily in this equation; the others produce coefficients which are either very insignificant or of the wrong sign. The proxy for extrapolative expectations about future interest rates on short-dated government securities, r_S^E (0·35), yields a negative coefficient. This result lends further support to the authorities' contention that market expectations are such that a fall in the price of government securities may result in a decline in demand for these securities in the immediate future. But the positive coefficient for the interest rate on short-dated government securities in the estimate of the *ad hoc* model suggests that this instability is limited.

VII. The supply of government securities

Further light is shed on the operation of the authorities' debt-management policy by a study of the supply side of the market for government securities. The interest rates on government debt are assumed to be policy instruments in the basic model, and therefore are taken as exogenous.[31] But it is unrealistic to assume that policy instruments will be unchanged in response to movements in endogenous variables.[32] It is of interest therefore to examine some estimates of the authorities' supply function for government securities.

The relationship is of the stock-adjustment form. The dependent

[30] Norton, op. cit., p. 268.

[31] Ibid.

[32] There is a substantial literature on behavioural relationships of governments. A recent contribution, which also contains a useful bibliography, is Havrilesky, T., 'A Test of Monetary Policy Action', *Journal of Political Economy*, vol. 75, no. 3, June 1967, pp. 299–304.

variable is the change in the interest rate on short-dated government securities. The determinants of the desired level of this interest rate are assumed to be Bank Rate (r^b), net official sales of government securities (ΔG) and the lagged change in the gold and convertible currency reserves (ΔRES^F_{-1}). The result of this regression is

$$\Delta r^{GS} = \underset{(0{\cdot}1282)}{-0{\cdot}0683\, s_1} + \underset{(0{\cdot}1271)}{0{\cdot}0279\, s_2} + \underset{(0{\cdot}1291)}{0{\cdot}1281\, s_3} - \underset{(0{\cdot}3331)}{0{\cdot}2326} + \underset{(0{\cdot}0609)}{0{\cdot}3016\, r^b}$$

$$- \underset{(0{\cdot}00033)}{0{\cdot}00059\, \Delta G} - \underset{(0{\cdot}00050)}{0{\cdot}00139\, \Delta RES^F_{-1}} - \underset{(0{\cdot}0772)}{0{\cdot}2487\, r^{GS}_{-1}}$$

$$R^2 = 0{\cdot}580 \qquad VN = 1{\cdot}783$$

The signs of the coefficients accord with *a priori* reasoning, and the values of R^2 and the von Neumann ratio are fairly satisfactory. The negative coefficient on ΔG may be taken to reflect the authorities' policy of adjusting prices in accord with market conditions.[33] In other words, when interest rates are declining stock is unloaded, and vice versa.

This result lends support to the use of ΔG^B as an explanatory variable in the public's demand equation for government securities. For sales of government securities by the banks may induce the authorities to make purchases, because of their policy of stabilizing interest rates in the short run. But the coefficients of ΔG and r^{GS}_{-1} in the foregoing equation indicate that the authorities, in accord with their statements, react to purchases (i.e., negative net sales) by *gradually* lowering the price of these securities, or alternatively, by raising interest rates. Anticipating this train of events, the public may respond to sales of securities by the banks by entering the market as sellers so as to avoid undue capital losses. This argument suggests that the behaviour of the authorities may be an important reason for the elements of short-run instability in the market for government securities.

VIII. Requests and the public's demand for advances

The authorities' debt-management policy has led to the rejection of open-market operations as a means of influencing the banks' operations. Instead, the authorities have used special deposits and requests to restrict the level of advances. Requests have been in

[33] *Bank of England Quarterly Bulletin*, vol. 6, no. 2, June 1966, p. 147; *Radcliffe Minutes*, Q 1762, 11919, 11965–6.

operation for more than half the period since their introduction in July 1955, but little is known about their effects.[34] Measurement of the effects of requests is not easy. This study uses a crude dummy variable technique to try to estimate some of them.

Requests have varied in severity. For example, the request made to the banks in July 1955 called for a 'positive and significant reduction in their advances over the next few months', whereas the request of July 1961 suggested that 'the rate in increase in advances should be greatly reduced.' The method used in this study to allow for these differences in severity is as follows: Two types of requests, types *A* and *B* are distinguished. The former refers to a request to the banks for a zero or negative rate of growth in advances (e.g., July 1955, September 1957, July 1966). A type *B* request refers to a call for a limited but positive rate of growth in advances (e.g., July 1961, May 1965, February 1966).[35] The dummy variable d^1 takes the values of two, one and zero when there is a type *A* request, type *B* request and no request respectively. A difficulty is that changes in other variables, such as hire-purchase controls, have often coincided with changes in the authorities' policy towards the level of advances. The dummy variable may therefore reflect several phenomena. This is an important qualification to the following results.

It is assumed that advances are essentially demand determined. The banks' supply of advances, or demand for private securities in exchange for advances, is treated as being completely elastic at the current interest rate on advances. As is well known, this rate is closely tied to Bank Rate. But the term 'demand determined' is being used in a special sense. The public's demand for advances is assumed to be modified by an official request to the banks to restrict the level of advances. This could occur in several ways. Some potential borrowers may decide not to approach the banks for a loan when a request is in operation. Other borrowers, under

[34] Requests about the composition of the total level of advances have existed for most of the sample period, but are ignored here. This omission reflects the aggregative nature of the present study and the difficulties of devising a measure of this type of request.

[35] The request of 1 February 1966, refers to the same 'one hundred and five per cent' ceiling as the previous request of 5 May 1965, but the level of advances at the mid-January call date was more than 2 per cent short of that ceiling, so a positive rate of growth was possible. The request of 12 July 1966, asked that the same ceiling be observed at least until March 1967. This request was more severe because the level of advances at the mid-June call date was close to the ceiling.

pressure from the banks, may negotiate reductions in their advances. Some support for these propositions can be found in *The Economist* in the early months of the 1955–58 credit squeeze.

> There has . . . been pressure . . . for acceleration of promised repayments wherever possible, or for a speedy search for alternative finance in cases where the loan has been made in anticipation of more permanent arrangements. . . .
>
> The real force of the squeeze, to the extent that it operates through advances is indeed being exerted more by its impact upon prospective borrowing than upon existing loans . . . the tests applied have been steadily tightened up and the public's knowledge of this has caused a notable contraction in the number of applications coming forward.[36]

Similarly, commenting on the 1961–62 credit squeeze the Bank of England says: 'There may also have been a big fall in demand for new advances brought about . . . by the known stricter attitude of the banks.'[37]

It is assumed that the demand function of the public for advances is of the modified stock-adjustment form. Several interest rates seem relevant on *a priori* grounds. An increase in Bank Rate should reduce the quantity of advances demanded by borrowers, *ceteris paribus*.[38] On the other hand, an increase in the interest rate on commercial bills should induce borrowers to seek finance from bank advances rather than by the issue of commercial bills. Similarly, increases in the interest rates on Treasury bills, government securities or other assets held by the public are expected to result in an increase in advances. Expectations of a fall in these interest rates in the near future, resulting in capital gains, should for two reasons also have a positive effect on advances. People will desire additional advances because of their reluctance to sacrifice expected capital gains by selling financial assets to meet current financing requirements arising from, say, previously arranged commitments to current expenditures; and they may seek additional advances so that they may increase their present stock of financial assets. Expenditure on inventories, consumer durables and fixed capital formation may be important factors generating a demand for bank accommodation,

[36] *Economist*, 3 December 1955, p. 862.

[37] *Bank of England Quarterly Bulletin*, vol. 1, no. 5, December 1961, pp.7–8. On the 1966 credit squeeze see H.M. Treasury, *Economic Report on 1966* (London: H.M.S.O., 1967), p. 28.

[38] *Radcliffe Memoranda Vol. 1*, Bank of England Memorandum 12, paras. 23–4.

whilst an increase in disposable income is likely to cause a decline in bank advances, *ceteris paribus*.

The stock-adjustment model performs well in the estimates of Table 3. Bank Rate seems to be a major determinant of demand for advances, but the other interest-rate variables produced insignificant coefficients. Inventory investment is also important, but fixed capital formation yielded a very insignificant coefficient. Disposable income produces its anticipated negative coefficient. Collinearity between this variable and income tax prevents their use together. Substitution of the latter for the former results in a lower value of R^2, so income tax is dropped from the equation. The coefficient of the lagged stock of advances suggests very slow adjustment of actual to desired stocks. This is highly plausible, as official intervention in the market has generally prevented rapid movements towards an equilibrium level of advances.

The dummy variable representing requests is highly significant. A comparison of estimates (3.1) and (3.2) shows that inclusion of the dummy variable causes a substantial rise in the values of R^2 and the von Neumann ratio. The von Neumann ratio for estimate (3.2) is close to the Theil-Nagar 1 per cent significance level. It seems likely that the hypothesis of no serial correlation in the residuals would be rejected for this estimate if one could allow for the bias in this statistic caused by the presence of the lagged value of the dependent variable among the explanatory variables. This evidence of mis-specification disappears when the dummy variable is included. Estimates (3.1) and (3.2) yield very different coefficients for spending on consumer durables; the coefficient in the latter equation is improbably high in view of the wide range of alternative avenues of finance available to the public in the form of current income, holdings of financial or real assets and other sources of external finance. The inclusion of the dummy variable produces a more plausible coefficient for spending on consumer durables.

Estimate (3.1) suggests a type A request can be expected to cause a fall in demand for advances of £112 million, *ceteris paribus*. This is the partial or structural effect.[39] The reduced form of the basic model shows that the total effect on advances of a type A request is slightly greater.[40] Estimates of the banks' demand equations for

[39] The distinction between partial and total analysis is clearly made in Goldberger, A. S., *Impact Multipliers and Dynamic Properties of the Klein–Goldberger Model* (Amsterdam, 1959), p. 2.

[40] Norton, op. cit., p. 268.

TABLE 3

Estimates of the public's demand equation for advances

Equation number	Constant	Seasonal dummy variables 1	2	3	Permanent income	Bank Rate	Inventory investment	Expenditure on consumer durables	Dummy variable for requests	Disposable income	Advances, lagged one quarter	Multiple coefficient of determination	Standard error of estimate	Von Neumann ratio
(3.1)	241	−326 (167)	−45 (36)	−96 (42)	0·28* (0·08)	−18 (10)	0·56* (0·19)	0·49 (0·29)	−56* (14)	−0·29* (0·10)	−0·09* (0·04)	0·85	48	1·91
(3.2)	205	−333 (200)	−85 (41)	−99 (51)	0·26* (0·10)	−37* (10)	0·66 (0·23)	1·08* (0·30)		−0·29* (0·12)	−0·09 (0·05)	0·78	58	1·58
(3.3)	244	−313 (171)	−27 (35)	−99 (43)	0·30* (0·08)	−18 (10)	0·56* (0·20)		−68* (12)	−0·28* (0·10)	−0·08 (0·05)	0·84	49	1·91

government securities (see Table 2 above) and Treasury bills show that the banks respond to a decline in their advances by holding more of these assets. A request therefore seems to be an effective weapon for reducing advances and inducing additional lending by the banks to the Government without a change in debt management policy.

IX. Requests and the public's demand for National Savings

But there are other results of a request which may offset these effects. Potential borrowers may substitute other methods of finance for advances. Evidence to the Radcliffe Committee suggests that requests may result in increased encashments of national savings.[41] To test this hypothesis the dummy variable, d^1, is introduced as a variable in the public's demand equation for national savings. Other explanatory variables in a modified stock-adjustment model for this equation include permanent income, the interest rate on National Savings Certificates and competing assets, income tax and the dummy variable for non-interest-rate terms on national savings.

Some results of these experiments are given in Table 4. Permanent income, Bank Rate, the interest rates on building society shares, long-dated and short-dated government securities and Treasury bills and measures of expectations about future rates on government securities produced coefficients which are either insignificant or of the wrong sign. But the interest rate on National Savings Certificates, a measure of the expected change in retail prices and the two dummy variables perform satisfactorily.

These estimates suggest that national savings can be expected to decline by about £70 million in response to a type *A* request. This will, first, offset the effects of the purchases of government debt by the banks on the Treasury bill issue and, secondly, offset the effects of a fall in banks' advances on the public's ability to finance new expenditure. The latter point suggests that imperfections in the capital market may not be as great as the authorities believe. It would be interesting to study the effects of requests to restrict the level of advances on other parts of the capital market, especially the markets for new issues of equities and debentures.

[41] *Radcliffe Memoranda Vol. 1*, Memorandum of National Savings Committee, para. 9, *Radcliffe Minutes*, Q 8001, 8004.

TABLE 4

Estimates of the public's demand equation for National Savings

Equation number	Constant	Seasonal dummy variables 1	2	3	Permanent income	Yield on National Savings	Expected change in retail prices (k=0·25)	Dummy variable for requests	Dummy variable for non-interest-rate terms on National Savings	Income tax payments	National Savings, lagged one quarter	Multiple coefficient of determination	Standard error of estimate	Von Neumann ratio
(4.1)	−27	−180 (76)	25 (11)	11 (15)	−0·04 (0·02)	37* (11)	−21* (8)	−33* (7)	21* (8)	0·01 (0·06)	0·03 (0·03)	0·96	23	1·92
(4.2)	46	−75 (45)	21 (11)	17 (15)		34* (12)	−20* (8)	−32* (8)	21* (8)	−0·08* (0·04)	−0·01 (0·02)	0·95	24	1·87
(4.3)	269	−168 (14)	17 (12)	10 (15)		28* (12)	−38* (9)	−38* (7)	20* (9)		−0·04* (0·01)	0·94	25	1·59

But this result needs some qualification. The value of R^2 for estimate (4.3) is satisfactory, but the von Neumann ratio suggests there is positive serial correlation in the residuals. The inclusion of income tax results in a better von Neumann ratio for estimate (4.2) but causes the coefficient of the lagged stock of national savings to be insignificant. This result, together with the small coefficient of the latter variable in estimate (4.3), suggests that the stock-adjustment model may be unsuited to some components of the aggregate labelled national savings in this study. Nevertheless, the foregoing estimates indicate that the effectiveness of requests as a policy instrument may be limited because of the way the system responds.

X. Special deposits

Special deposits are deposits that the banks must hold with the Bank of England in addition to those held as part of their cash reserves. Special deposits are intended to bring pressure on the banks' liquid assets with the aim of restricting advances.[42] But the quarterly change in special deposits yields an insignificant coefficient in the banks' demand equations for call money, Treasury bills and commercial bills in the basic model.[43] Moreover, this variable has a highly significant negative coefficient in the banks' demand equation for government securities, equation (2.3) above. Finally, equations (1.1)–(1.6) suggest that sales of these securities by the banks stimulate sales by the public. The authorities' preference for short-run stability in interest rates means that the public and the banks can effect sales at small cost. Thus on these arguments grave doubts are cast on the merits of special deposits as a policy instrument.[44]

The reduced form of the basic model yields estimates of the total effects of a change in special deposits which support the foregoing.[45] The coefficient of advances with respect to special deposits is zero, whereas the coefficient of non-official holdings of government securities with respect to special deposits is not significantly different

[42] *House of Commons Parliamentary Debates*, Fifth Series, vol. 590, Session 1957–8, cols. 1593–9.

[43] Norton, op. cit., p. 159.

[44] For the same conclusion see Gibson, N. J., 'Special Deposits as an Instrument of Monetary Policy', *The Manchester School*, vol. 32, no. 3, September 1964, pp. 239–59.

[45] Norton, op. cit., p. 268.

from minus one. Thus the chief effect of a change in special deposits would seem to be a movement of similar magnitude in the opposite direction in the outstanding stock of government securities. Government borrowing remains essentially the same except that it has a different label.

XI. Conclusions

The predilection of the authorities for short-run stability of interest rates and a managed gilt-edged market has led the authorities to rely on restriction of advances and special deposits in attempting to influence the activities of the banks and the level of expenditure.

There is little doubt, as was to be expected, that requests to restrict advances are effective and lead to their reduction and at the same time induce additional lending to the Government. But the process does not end there. Those experiencing the restriction will tend to substitute other forms of finance and, in particular, reduce their national savings. Thus the net effect of advances restriction may be limited.

The special deposits instrument on the basis of the evidence examined would seem to be largely ineffectual as a policy instrument.

It is tempting on the basis of the foregoing to argue that the authorities would be advised to abandon requests and special deposits and rely instead on more flexible interest rates and possibly a stricter control of the money supply. The official argument against more flexible rates has asserted amongst other things that the market is unstable. But the findings of this paper suggest that this is essentially a short-run phenomenon and may well be due to the way the authorities operate in the market. If this is correct, then a large part of the case for official policy disappears.

Appendix

Several variables in this paper require further definition.

Advances. Advances made by the clearing banks to customers and other accounts (excluding advances to the nationalized industries).

Disposable Income. Gross domestic product less income tax payments.

Dummy Variable d^1. Dummy variable for requests to restrict the level of advances:

$$d^1 = 2 \text{ for } 1955(3)\text{–}1958(2)$$
$$d^1 = 1 \text{ for } 1961(3)\text{–}1962(3);\ 1965(2)\text{–}1966(2)$$
$$d^1 = 0 \text{ for } 1958(3)\text{–}1961(2);\ 1962(4)\text{–}1965(1)$$

Dummy Variable d^2. Dummy variable for improved terms on National Savings in quarter t or the preceding quarter:

$$d^2 = 1 \text{ for } 1955(4)\text{–}1957(2);\ 1958(2)\text{–}1958(4)$$
$$1960(2)\text{–}1961(1);\ 1964(2)\text{–}1964(4)$$
$$d^2 = 0 \text{ for } 1955(3);\ 1957(3)\text{–}1958(1);\ 1959(1)\text{–}1960(1)$$
$$1961(2)\text{–}1964(1);\ 1965(1)\text{–}1966(2)$$

Expected Change in Retail Prices.

$$= \frac{1-k}{1-k^{11}} \sum_{i=1}^{11} k^{i-1} \Delta P_{t-i}$$

where ΔP is the quarterly change in the Retail Price Index and k is a constant.

Extrapolative Expectations about Yields on Long-dated Government Securities.

$$r_L^E(k) = r_t^{GL} - \frac{1-k}{1-k^{11}} \sum_{i=1}^{11} k^{i-1} r_{t-i}^{GL}$$

where r^{GL} is the yield on long-dated government securities and k is 0·25 or 0·35.

$$r_L(3) = r_t^{GL} - \frac{1}{3} \sum_{i=1}^{3} r_{t-i}^{GL}$$

Extrapolative Expectations about Yields on Short-dated Government Securities.

$$r_S^E(k) = r_t^{GS} - \frac{1-k}{1-k^{11}} \sum_{i=1}^{11} k^{i-1} r_{t-i}^{GS}$$

where r^{GS} is the yield on short-dated government securities and k is 0·25 or 0·35.

Income Tax. Income tax payments plus national insurance and national health contributions.

Inventory Investment. Value of the physical increase in stocks and works-in-progress.

National Savings. National Savings Certificates, National Development Bonds, Premium Savings Bonds, Tax Reserve Certificates and deposits with the ordinary departments of the Post Office Savings Bank and Trustee Savings Bank.

Permanent Income.

$$= \frac{1-k}{1-k^{11}} \sum_{i=0}^{10} k^i Y_{t-i}$$

where Y is gross domestic product at factor cost and k is 0·95.

26

MANAGING THE GILT-EDGED MARKET: A TEMPORARY CHANGE OF EMPHASIS?

MIDLAND BANK REVIEW*

ALMOST two-thirds of the national debt consists of the government and government-guaranteed stocks which are dealt in in the gilt-edged market. Since 1946, the nominal value of these marketable stocks has risen, from about £12,000 million to around £22,000 million, mainly because of the Government's need to borrow to meet the net overall deficits on its transactions. Of today's total, about £3,500 million is in stocks with no final date of redemption, and the remainder consists of stocks which must be repaid by the final date of redemption as given in the prospectus, which is moving steadily nearer all the time. The average remaining life to maturity of dated stocks in non-official hands is about 12½ years. However, about £7,000 million is due for redemption within the next five years, and about £1,100 million before the end of March next.

In their operations in the gilt-edged market, therefore, the authorities must take account not only of any need for finance to cover current requirements, but also of the continuing flow of maturities. Other considerations are the effects of operations on the structure of interest rates and monetary policy generally.

The relative importance attached by the authorities to the various factors in their market transactions has been clearly indicated on a number of occasions, notably in evidence given to the Radcliffe Committee ten years ago[1] and more recently in an article in the *Bank of England Quarterly Bulletin* for June 1966. The chief purpose

* Reprinted from the *Midland Bank Review*, May 1969, pp. 3–5, by permission of the publisher.

[1] Memoranda of Evidence, vol. I, Part II, Section 10, paras. 15–27.

of management of the gilt-edged market, according to the article, is 'to strengthen the demand for government stocks. . . . The principal concern is to encourage the widest possible variety of investors, other than the banks, to increase their holdings, and to hold longer- rather than shorter-dated stocks. These are essentially long-term aims; in the long run success will depend on investors' confidence in the market and this in turn will rest decisively on their experience of dealing in it'. Again, 'the dominant long-term consideration in debt management' is to 'ensure so far as possible that suitable finance for the Exchequer is available, and will continue to be available in the future . . .'.

Other aims are to influence the structure of interest rates, credit policy and the liquidity of the banks, but these were explicitly said to be subsidiary to the longer-term objectives. However, if the continued availability of suitable finance to the Government is ensured, then 'there need be no excessive recourse to short-term borrowing from the banks on Treasury bills and accompanying increase in the money supply'; while 'policy on interest rates can, and in all the circumstances must, concentrate largely on fostering demand, in the future as well as in the present'.

Steadying the market

The article explains how the Bank generally allows the broad level of prices to be determined by purchases and sales of investors, but intervenes to keep such movements steady and regular. 'The daily concern of debt management is usually to steady the market without opposing it too rigidly, but always within the context of its aims for interest rate and credit policy and for the maximization of demand for British government debt'. Thus it does not try to stop a downward movement, but bids on successively lower levels so as to secure a drop in market prices of 'broadly the dimensions thought desirable'. If 'signs of demoralization' appear the Bank may have to act more decisively, 'because of their overriding concern for the long-term health of the market'. Thus 'the market is dominated for most of the time by its own expectations of future movements in prices', including its expectations of the Bank's tactics, though this factor is 'not one that in the end carries greater weight than the balance of supply and demand' among the holders of the stock. However, because the Bank is able to intervene, either as buyer or seller, 'variations in demand in the market are . . . likely to lead to variations in supply at unchanged or only slowly changing prices, rather than to immediate variations in prices big enough to bring demand back into balance at nearly the same level of supply'.

In other words, the main concern of the authorities has been to ensure orderly marketing conditions with the overriding object of maximizing sales in the long run. On the tactical level, it was pointed out that 'a decline in prices can build up very rapidly once expectations that it will continue have taken hold', and if such expectations were strengthened by the withdrawal of the Bank from the market, 'to arrest or retard the fall may in the end require a disproportionate amount of official support'. More explicitly, a market in which selling 'is generally left unmoderated and then . . . abruptly halted by official intervention at some predetermined level, may come to be viewed by investors as arbitrary and unpredictable in its behaviour; there is then a danger that they would be seriously discouraged from investing their funds in it. The likely consequence would be that the capacity of the market would be permanently reduced and with it the ability of the Government to borrow at long-term'.

Recent movements

Nevertheless, the course of prices over the past twenty years or so may well have led investors at times to regard the market as 'arbitrary and unpredictable in its behaviour'. Prices of all gilt-edged securities have fallen substantially over the post-war period. Last autumn 2½ per cent Consols, for example, which at the end of 1964 were around par, stood at around 33 to show a yield of roughly 7½ per cent. During the past six months, /i.e. in the six months up to April, 1969/, gilt-edged prices have fallen to new low levels and yields have reached new heights. Early in April, almost all gilt-edged securities were showing gross redemption yields of between 8 and 9 per cent. Moreover, the movements over the past six months have perhaps been sharper and more rapid than in any other comparable period since the war.

It is stated in the latest issue—for March 1969—of the *Bank of England Quarterly Bulletin* that throughout the period November 1968 to February 1969 'the authorities were, as always, prepared to deal in response to market offers, at prices judged by them both to conform with the underlying trend of interest rates and to be consistent with the underlying long-term objective of preserving market conditions favourable to maximum official sales of Government debt—particularly sales to investors outside the banking sector'.

Thus the underlying strategy remained unchanged but the detailed description of official tactics during this period suggests, at the least, some modification of earlier practices. It is said that some selling of medium- and long-dated stocks occurred in the first half of November and 'the authorities readily allowed this to have its effects on yields'. At the time of the international currency crisis during that month the market became more unsettled and 'the authorities therefore modified their tactics in order to steady the market until the outlook was a little clearer'. Then the authorities 'reverted to a policy of allowing any weakness to be fully reflected in prices', for the reason that 'a rise in U.K. interest rates other than the very shortest was seen as an appropriate accompaniment to the measures which had been taken to restrain domestic demand . . .'. In December the market became very unsettled because of the rise in U.S. interest rates, and the authorities 'sought to exert a steadying influence by lowering relatively slowly the prices at which they were prepared to deal'. But they 'did little to resist' a burst of selling in mid-January, and again towards the end of January they 'did not resist a tendency for yields to rise'. The story is not taken beyond mid-February, when long rates had risen nearly 1 per cent above their October level, and signs of new buying appeared. Since then, however, Bank rate has been raised by 1 per cent—on 27 February—and prices for a time fell still further with little sign of official intervention.

A change of emphasis?

This change in tactics has naturally raised the question whether official policy in relation to the market also has changed. In the House of Commons in January a Government spokesman stated that it had not. Even so, according to the Bulletin 'changes in the surrounding circumstances led to adjustments in the authorities' tactics regarding the prices at which they were prepared to deal'. It would seem reasonable to expect that changed circumstances might also affect the weights given to the various policy objectives. Two developments may have a particular significance here. First may be noted the Letter of Intent sent to the IMF in connection with the application for a stand-by credit at the time of devaluation. This stated that the Exchequer's borrowing requirement for the financial year 1968–9 would be financed 'as far as possible by the sale of debt to the non-bank public', and that interest rate policy would be used to this end. The Letter also included an undertaking regarding the growth of the money supply, an aspect of policy to which the Fund gives considerable weight. Certainly if the authorities always stood ready to buy all securities on offer without allowing the price to fall to a level which might discourage sellers, this would give them no control over cash in the hands of the private sector and thus loosen the tight grip which the authorities are trying, with some success, to impose upon credit and liquidity generally. The second change in circumstances has been the swing into surplus of the Exchequer accounts on an annual basis. For 1968–9 a surplus of £287 million was achieved, and an even greater surplus is estimated for the current financial year.

As already indicated, at times of particular pressure in recent months—and notably during the international currency crisis in November—the authorities have acted to steady the market, but apparently on no more than a limited scale. According to the Bulletin, 'net purchases of medium- and long-dated stocks during the fourth calendar quarter totalled no more than £69 million. . . . By contrast, their purchases of short-dated stocks, at £336 million, were substantial—though the bulk of these reflected sales by the discount market and by holders outside the banking system of stocks maturing in 1969.' In unsettled conditions towards the end of January, 'once again the authorities did not resist a tendency for yields to rise and their purchases were largely confined to the 1969 maturities'.

The *Bulletin* articles referred to above, and the movements in prices of gilt-edged securities themselves, point to the conclusion that in recent months the authorities have been significantly less willing to intervene in the market as buyers than they would have been in similar circumstances previously. That there has been an adjustment of tactics in the operation of the gilt-edged market is acknowledged. Even if there has been no change in policy, it would seem that for a period at least there was a discernible shift of emphasis, with interest rate considerations in the context of the need to restrain domestic demand assuming more than their customary subsidiary role. In his recent Budget Statement, however, the Chancellor of the Exchequer expressed the view that the

prospects for the gilt-edged market were 'much better' than they had been a year before, 'primarily because the public sector as a whole will be repaying debt'. In addition, he thought that the abolition of long-term capital gains tax on government and govern-

ment-guaranteed marketable securities 'should make gilt-edged more attractive to investors and will encourage a more active market in gilts—a necessary condition for a successful selling policy'. So maximization of sales clearly remains the underlying objective, but doubtless subject to changes of emphasis and tactics from time to time.

VII

MONETARY POLICY

VII

MONETARY POLICY

EDITED BY

D. R. CROOME

Introduction

MONETARY policy is an area of stabilization policy comprising the use of a collection of instruments whose immediate impact is upon some financial variable believed to be relevant, directly or indirectly, to the control of aggregate demand and hence to the realization of the broad objectives of economic policy. The armoury of weapons available to the monetary authorities—the Bank of England and the Treasury—includes open market operations, adjustment of Bank rate, calls for special deposits, and 'requests' to financial institutions respecting the volume and allocation of their lending; the control of hire purchase deposit terms, too, is best accounted for as a monetary weapon, although the authority for changing them rests with the Department of Trade and Industry (formerly the Board of Trade) rather than with the two institutions usually styled, as above, as the 'monetary authorities'. In using this array of weapons, the authorities must effectively have in view some model of the economy which indicates to them the links between the use of a particular weapon of policy and the ultimate policy objective. This model may condition, too, the choice between fiscal and monetary policies as a means of achieving particular objectives, according, for example, to the speed of response required and the values attached to the side effects on equity and allocation of the alternatives.

The *Radcliffe Report*,[1] published in 1959, provided one such model. It left its mark on subsequent policy (and notably also on the

[1] *Report of the Committee on the working of the monetary system*, Cmnd. 827 (London, 1959).

collection and publication of financial data without which much recent work could not have been done), even though in some crucial respects the *Report*'s expectations were thwarted and its recommendations in detail often ignored. Perhaps the single most outstanding aspect of the *Report* is its emphasis on the 'non-uniqueness' of banks, and by implication of money. This emphasis is strikingly expressed, drawing on historical analogies with the disputes of the 'Banking' and 'Currency' Schools in the nineteenth century, by Professor Sayers, an influential member of the Radcliffe Committee itself, in the article reprinted here as Reading 27. Other important emphases appeared in the *Report*, too: the playing-down of the orthodox 'Keynesian' linkage between interest rates and expenditure on real assets (though the linkage is partly resuscitated through a more complicated mechanism involving the behaviour of financial institutions); the contention that the level of bank deposits depends on the volume of Treasury bills; and (somewhat ambiguously), the support given to the view that the demand for gilt-edged is governed by (perverse) expectations. All these emphases—some of them viewed with a good deal of entertaining scepticism by W. T. Newlyn in Reading 28—added up to the proposition that monetary policy should in general play a relatively minor role in economic policy. The *Report* also held a view about future prospects for the balance of payments which seems now (with the benefit of hindsight) unduly insouciant, and led it perhaps to a more negative conclusion than an alternative view might have produced. At any rate, it denounced the main measures of monetary control, bank advance requests, and allocations of hire purchase terms, except for situations of 'emergency' which it tended to associate with 'headlong inflation' or its imminence.

As events turned out, however, monetary policy was required to 'deliver' a good deal more than the *Radcliffe Report* had supposed, and one result was that the traditional style of advances controls and 'package deals' of measure was indulged in even more frequently in the latter half of the 1960s than it had been in the 1950s.[2] Yet in an important way, this was Radcliffean, even though conditions were hardly those of headlong inflation. It was Radcliffe 'in emergency'; it exploited availability effects and, most significant, the authorities spread the net of their 'requests' wider over the

[2] A comprehensive statement of policy post-Radcliffe is to be found in a recent paper by the Bank of England cited in the suggestions for further reading on p. 505–6.

financial institutions.[3] But it remained a good question just what were the real effects of these measures, and how they compared with alternative means of achieving similar deflation (or reflation) of demand. John Karaken raises several pertinent issues in this respect in his paper (Reading 29). The use of other kinds of measures is explored in an interesting fashion by Fisher in his paper (Reading 30), where an attempt is made to measure objectively the authorities' reaction functions and their trade-offs of alternative goals. Fisher's maxim is to explore these issues on the basis of what the authorities actually do, rather than what they say they do, although as his paper shows this is anything but an empty slogan. It is an injunction to undertake very difficult work if the proper distinctions are to be drawn between the reactions and the effects, between the authorities' 'model' (their view of how the economy works) and the 'real' model, and between their model and their preferences.

Towards the end of the 1960s, economic policy in general was subject to renewed questioning of a fundamental character partly because of (real or apparent) failures of orthodox policies, partly because of new developments (and similar failures) in the United States, and partly because of the interest of the International Monetary Fund in British economic problems. With the virtual exhaustion of other policies—fiscal policy, incomes policy, etc.—monetary policy was looked to for a new 'twist'. A by-product of this period was the formulation of monetary policy in terms of DCE, a financial quantity which provides links between changes in the domestic money stock and the financial flows across the exchanges. The paper by Artis and Nobay, however, takes a sceptical view of this departure.

A recent statement of official thinking on the problems of monetary policy, expressed with admirable lucidity, appears in the wide-ranging speech of the Governor of the Bank of England reprinted as Reading 32. It will be seen that this touches on many of the themes dealt with elsewhere in this book.

A chronology of the main monetary policy actions taken in the period 1960–1970 appears at the end of this chapter.

FURTHER READING

'The operation of monetary policy since Radcliffe', *Bank of England Quarterly Bulletin*, vol. 9, no. 4, December 1969, pp. 448–60, reprinted

[3] See the Chronology of main policy measures, Reading 33.

in Croome, D. R., and Johnson, H. G. (eds.), *Money in Britain* (Oxford, 1970).

'Money, banking and finance', Chap. 2 of Prest, A. R. (ed.), *The U.K. Economy—a manual of applied economics* (Weidenfeld and Nicholson, 1966, 2nd edn., 1968).

'Monetary survey', annually, in May issues of the *Midland Bank Review*.

MONETARY THOUGHT AND MONETARY POLICY IN ENGLAND[1]

R. S. SAYERS*

THE purpose of this paper is to review certain basic notions that have underlain English monetary policy during the nineteenth and twentieth centuries. I shall contend that the theoretical approach to the problems of policy needs redirecting in the light of changes in the institutional and political environment. I have nothing revolutionary to say and, restricting myself to the more elementary aspects, I shall throughout emphasize theory rather than the course of events.

In some of the more lively phases of monetary controversy during the last 160 years the front of the stage has been occupied by questions of the foreign exchanges and the balance of payments, but even in these phases discussions of practical policy have more or less explicitly assumed certain views on internal policy; indeed, the classical contribution of English thought was the insistence on the connection between the internal and external objectives of monetary policy. At other times, when attention has been focused on troubles common to many countries rather than disturbances in the monetary relations between countries, considerations most relevant to a closed system have naturally come to the forefront. It is with these internal aspects that I am directly concerned—remembering always, however, the sound tradition that we separate the internal from the external at our peril.

Throughout the period—we can date it from the Bullion Report

* Reprinted from the *Economic Journal*, vol. 70, no. 280, December 1960, pp. 710–24, by permission of the author and publisher. R. S. Sayers is Emeritus Professor of Economics at the London School of Economics.

[1] Presidential Address to Section F of the British Association for the Advancement of Science at Cardiff, 2 September 1960.

of 1810—the broad approach of every generation has been a Quantity Theory approach. I take this in the most general sense of a belief that the value of money is dependent, to an important extent, on its quantity, and that therefore some control of the supply of money is an essential prerequisite of any sensible monetary policy. The Quantity Theory, in all its simplicity, has great attraction. It is a supply-and-demand analysis, with a demand schedule whose peculiarity derives directly from the concept of money not as an object of exchange but as the medium of exchange. That this is only a small part of the truth is acknowledged even by those economists who rate it most highly, and I should be guilty of travesty if I were to accuse authoritative writers of allowing the Quantity Theory to monopolize their thoughts on monetary action. But I am going to suggest that we should all have a clearer view if we went back to the starting-point and looked afresh at the basic concepts. We must go back to the nature of money and the demand for it.

The word 'money' is used in two senses. Money is the standard by which we measure the exchange values of things and in which debts are denominated. This is the abstract sense in which we use the term; we know what pounds, shillings and pence are, in the sense that we know they are the units in which debts and prices are stated. We run into difficulties—the familiar index-number problem, on which I shall not comment—when we begin to generalize about 'the value of money', still using the word 'money' in this abstract sense, but at least there is no doubt about what is the 'money'. When we say that our economic system has acquired its present shape on the basis of a general assumption that the value of money is reasonably stable, it is of this abstract sense that we are thinking. Yet when we say that, in order to achieve this stability in the value of money, we must control the supply of money, we have switched away from the abstract sense of money to its other, concrete sense. For by 'control of the supply of money' we mean control of the availability of certain assets which are used as media of exchange and stores of value. We have switched from an unambiguous abstraction to a class of marketable objects whose boundary has neither sharpness nor certainty nor permanence. And we have arrived at one of the perennial questions of controversy: the question of what assets are, and what are not, included in the 'money' category. I suspect that, because money in the abstract sense is an unambiguous concept, people have subconsciously believed that there must also be a simple answer to the question of what is money in the concrete sense. They have been looking for a sharp line of distinction where only Marshallian shading has reality. This pursuit of a will o' the wisp has had its effects on discussions of policy, for people have been too ready to believe that there is an identifiable quantity the control of which is all-important.

The difficulty of identification has derived from the twofold nature of money (we are now speaking only of the concrete sense) as a medium of exchange and as a store of value. Money is both these. An asset which entirely ceases to be a store of value ceases to be used as a medium of exchange, as has been seen when a money is rejected in the final stage of hyper-inflation. There are articles which are stores of value but are clearly not money because they are *never* used as media of exchange. But are we to label as money all other stores of value, that is to say all those which are ever brought into use, whether commonly or occasionally or only rarely, as media of exchange? The usual answer is that we should include as money only those assets which are commonly used as media of exchange. Resort to the adverb 'commonly' at once emphasizes the absence of any sharp line of distinction. Are balances in a clearing bank to be labelled money while deposits in the Post Office Savings Bank are not? I find it impossible, on the evidence of recent practice, to find any watertight reasons for so distinguishing. It is sometimes supposed that the distinction can be made to turn on the simplicity of the procedure for transferring the asset. When I take a coin or a note out of my pocket, and hand it across the counter, I am using money to make a payment. When I draw a cheque on a current account at a bank, economists would certainly say that I am using money to make a payment. But if this act of writing an instruction to a bank is a use of money, why not also written instruction to the Post Office Savings Bank or a Building Society? And what could be more simple than the showing of a consumer's credit card? Nor is it altogether satisfactory to retreat to the fact that many Post Office and Building Society balances lie for long periods undisturbed, for this is also true of many balances in the Clearing Banks. Especially this is liable to be true of deposit account balances, yet most economists would regard them as money, equally with current account balances, and the procedure for paying them over to other people is scarcely less simple than drawing a cheque on a current account.

Nor is there conviction in the notion that the line can be drawn by reference to whether interest is earned. Present English practice is that interest is not paid on current accounts, but this has not always been so, nor does it universally apply in other countries where banking competition is more free. Even in present English conditions, large sums are held in current accounts as minimum balances, ordinarily undisturbed, as inducement to the banks to operate accounts without charge: interest is thus virtually paid and offset by turnover charges. Whether the question of what is money is made to turn upon what has been common usage among economists, or on whether the asset is commonly used as a medium of exchange, or on whether it yields interest, it is not possible to give an unambiguous answer.

A similar attempt to escape from the difficulties of identification of money is to be found in the distinction sometimes drawn between 'active money' and 'idle money'. The actual division of bank deposits into demand deposits and time deposits is often thought of as a statistically convenient approximation to an economically significant division into active money and idle money. But this distinction is at best misleading. No asset is in action as a medium of exchange except in the very moment of being transferred from one ownership to another, in settlement of some transaction, and no class of asset used in this way can logically be excluded from the class of active money. Between transactions all money is idle. Yet if activity is held to cover the state of being held in readiness against possible use in exchange, then all monetary assets are active all the time. It is not merely that we cannot easily earmark for statistical assessment the quantity that is active: there is no such quantity, except in the all-embracing sense of all those goods or claims regarded by their owners as potentially useful for settling market commitments. It is this wide concept of liquid assets that we must put, in the place conventionally occupied by 'the supply of money', as the monetary quantity influencing total effective demand for goods and services. And we must interpret it widely enough to include credit that can be brought into existence concurrently with a decision to exercise demand.

When all the assets included in this class are reviewed in detail we find that they include not only the deposit liabilities of banks but also the readily callable liabilities of a large and widening range of other financial intermediaries. The ease with which these intermediaries enlarge their balance-sheet totals is as relevant to the monetary situation as is the behaviour of those financial intermediaries we call 'banks'. Nor should we limit the range to firms ordinarily regarded as financial intermediaries. Among firms whose main activity is manufacturing or trading, most do a great deal of lending and borrowing: they extend 'trade credit' to their customers, and they take 'trade credit' from their suppliers. Many are active on both sides of the account, and nearly all are involved in credit transactions on one side or the other. The distinction between banks as creators of credit and other firms as users or intermediaries in the monetary field is if not completely false at least misleading. From the point of view of the pressure of effective demand, the crucial step is that which increases the power to acquire goods and services on the part of people inclined to exercise it immediately; and banks are by no means the only firms to place this power in the hands of others.

That trade credit, in the sense of credit granted by firms whose primary business is non-financial, is an effective element in the supply of purchasing power, is a view sometimes conceded but with the odd qualification that it is only 'net' credit that counts in this way. If, for example, a statistical measure is sought, it is supposed that only the excess of a firm's claims over its debts to others should be counted.[2] This is a position that cannot be sustained. We are thinking of the power to exercise demand for goods and services, and for this purpose the gross total of trade credit is relevant. An entire closed circle of firms in manufacturing industry may begin giving credit more freely, and all of them proceed to place large orders with each other; there is no doubt about the increase in effective demand, although the increase in credit granted by all the firms together is balanced by the increase in credit taken by all the firms together. No one would seriously suggest that bank credit should be 'netted out' by deducting the debts people owe to the banks, although one of the tables in the *Radcliffe Report* curiously errs in this way.[3]

We should pause here to notice that a distinction between 'credit' and 'capital' is no more helpful in monetary analysis than is the

[2] Cf. Viner, J., *Studies in the Theory of International Trade* (London, 1937). In the course of his review of the writings of the Banking School and the Currency School, Viner says (p. 247) that 'J. S. Mill went too far' in including trade credit in the stock of purchasing power. But Viner concedes the substantial point later in the same paragraph.

[3] Cmnd. 827 (1959), Table 22 (on p. 171). That in twelve months no one should, to my knowledge, have drawn attention to the oddity of column (1) in this table, is a sad commentary on the extent to which the arguments used in the *Report* have been understood.

distinction between banks and other creators of credit. This distinction between credit and capital was vigorously argued in the nineteenth-century literature of the subject, and there are echoes of it in those contemporary views that draw a distinction between the 'money market' (or 'credit market') where the central bank has its business and, on the other hand, the 'capital market', upon which the influence of the monetary authorities can only be indirect. It is better that we should think of a single market, or at least a single group of markets, in which immediate purchasing power is traded against claims whose variety, in maturity and in other respects, is infinite. In some countries this is a more imperfect, in others a less imperfect market; but the important likeness that links all parts of the market is the trading of more immediately for less immediately available purchasing power. All participants in the market are so trading; all are trading in capital in the sense of purchasing power, and none is trading in capital in the sense of goods. Each part of the market is as fundamentally a money market as any other, and each part of the market is just as much a capital market as any other. All are adding to the supply of credit when the claims against themselves are more immediately useful than the other claims which are the trading counterpart. This supply of credit, which can be immediately used for exercising demand, is no monopoly of the banks; the power of the banks to create credit (and it is credit, not money, that is relevant here) thus provides no justification for control of the banks while other credit agencies are left uncontrolled.

A presumption in favour of discriminatory control of the banks can, however, be established if it can be shown that there is a sufficiently firm proportionality between the volume of bank credit and the volume of other credit. If, when bank lending is curtailed, other lending must necessarily be curtailed in equal proportion, the control of banks becomes a useful technique, on the administrative principle that their heads are the easiest to hit. If every firm dealing in credit always held absolutely stable the proportionate distributions of its assets and its liabilities—that is to say, if balance sheets always had exactly the same structures—this proportionality of the supply of effective purchasing power to the supply of bank credit could be taken as the basis of policy. In fact, there are two important reasons why this strict proportionality cannot be assumed. The first is that in course of time people devise new financial intermediaries; the efficiency of the financial system increases, and this process tends to accelerate in a prolonged spell of business prosperity. The second—and in the short period relevant for most purposes of policy, this is the more weighty—the reliability of non-bank debtors varies according to the general trade prospect. This is, of course, our old friend 'the inherent instability of credit'; but it is important to recognize that in its modern form it refers not so much to bank credit as to the relation between bank credit and non-bank credit. At a time when, as an anti-inflation measure, the authorities are enforcing a restriction of bank credit, the apparently favourable position of other debtors makes the extension of non-bank credit peculiarly easy, as we saw in England in the middle 1950s.[4] The important practical question is how easily one source of credit can replace another, and whether such a disturbance sets up any corrective process which will act quickly enough to be useful for purposes of policy.

Before I turn to this fundamental question, I must refer to the use of another concept, deeply embedded in the literature of our subject. This is the velocity of circulation. I have hitherto been formulating monetary phenomena by referring to the supply of and the demand for various assets and liabilities; but many writers have thought it more convenient to refer to variations in demand as variations in the velocity of circulation of money. They think of people not as wanting more or less intensely to hold money but as being less or more quick to pass on money in exchange for goods and services. Put like this, the one concept is simply the reciprocal of the other, and it does not matter which we use. I myself prefer to think in terms of the demand for money balances, because the term 'velocity of circulation' implies closer analogy with a physical process than I can find in the working of the monetary system, and I notice that when economists seek to explain changes in the velocity of circulation they at once begin to talk about the intensity of the demand for money. Like houses and other assets, money is not going round steadily all the time. Instead—again like houses and

[4] No comprehensive statistics of trade credit exist, even for joint-stock companies. For companies quoted on the Stock Exchange and engaged in manufacturing, building, and distribution, however, some figures can be extracted from the investigations made by the National Institute of Economic and Social Research. For these companies, the balance sheets relating to late 1956 showed trade creditors £2,050 million, as compared with £444 million bank loans, and trade debtors £2,609 million, as compared with £649 million cash and bank balances. The swings in these figures for trade credit, from one year to another, also dwarf changes in the bank credit and bank balances employed by such companies (see *Radcliffe Report*, Cmnd. 827, paras. 297–311).

other assets—it is always resting in the ownership of one person or another, save for the isolated moments when it changes ownership. What people mean when they say that the velocity of circulation has increased is that the volume of transactions has increased relatively to the stock of money (in some sense), or that the national income has increased relatively to the stock of money (the ratio more specifically referred to as the 'income velocity of circulation'). As a label for the purely statistical phenomenon of the ratio of one quantity to another, the term velocity of circulation is harmless enough, and so well established in the literature that it would be foolish to refuse the convenience of using it. The trouble begins when we jump to the conclusion that a rise in the ratio of payments to bank deposits means only that firms have decided to put their bank deposits to faster use, whereas much of what has happened is that firms have decided to give more credit and people have shifted some of their savings into the hands of more nimble intermediaries. The artificiality of the concept lies, in short, in its reliance on a distinct and identifiable category of money; and one danger in using it lies in its encouraging us to overlook the relevance, to the pressure of total demand, of sources of credit outside this defined category. A further danger is that the definition normally used being either bank deposits or bank deposits plus notes, which (particularly the notes) come fully into action only late in productive processes, a rise in the velocity of circulation is a phenomenon that lags behind a rise in the disposition to spend. The existence of this lag should warn us against undue reliance on any corrective mechanism set up by 'a rise in the velocity of circulation'.

The basis of such a corrective mechanism is sometimes represented as the anchorage of the velocity of circulation in the peculiar demand for the medium of exchange. Our examination of the nature of money and of the demand for it has, however, warned us that there is no single asset or group of assets that uniquely possesses a uniform monetary quality that is totally absent from all other assets. Except for purely didactic purposes, it does not help to talk about a normal velocity of circulation any more than it helps to say (which is the same thing) that the elasticity of demand for money is unity. On the other hand, convenience in settling transactions is an important quality in a monetary asset; various monetary assets have this quality in varying degrees. If money income rises, or if the supply of some of these assets falls, people will feel some lack of this convenience in relation to the contingent needs against which they hold such assets, and this is the substance to which economists refer when they assume a certain normality in the velocity of circulation. But we must remember that many assets have the monetary quality in varying degrees; if, as the supply of some of them falls relatively to income or turnover, others can easily be increased, the sense of inconvenience is minimized, and we have to ask ourselves whether it remains effective enough to be interesting. We are in fact back at our major question of the relation between supplies of different classes of monetary assets, having merely reformulated, with the help of the concept of the velocity of circulation, the problems we had already traversed.

In our own time most attention has been given to a comparatively late link in the chain of argument: the question of how, as the supply of monetary assets becomes less adequate, increasing inconvenience manifest in rising interest rates provokes a fall in total demand. Although this part of the argument has always had some attention, the almost exclusive concentration upon it is something of a post-1920 novelty. In the great controversies of the nineteenth century the prior question of the relation between varied monetary assets was always well to the fore. In the early part of the nineteenth century one of the major questions related to the connection between the Bank of England's note issue and the issues of the country banks. Thornton, in his *Paper Credit* (1802), had developed the view that the issues by the country banks were substantially governed by the Bank of England's issue.[5] He may have been wrong in this opinion, but he certainly regarded it as important, because he regarded both kinds of notes as money, the supply of which was relevant to the price level. When the Bullion Committee (of which Thornton was a member) in 1810 investigated the depreciation of the pound they adopted this view in one of the more emphatic statements in their Report,[6] but only two pages later they carefully explained the power of country bank-notes permanently to displace Bank of England notes.[7] They also noted the importance of increasingly effective use of bank deposits in circumscribing the real demand for bank-notes. In the controversy which raged round the Report, and more especially in the controversies of the next three decades, the relation

[5] Thornton, H., *An Enquiry into the Nature and Effects of the Paper Credit of Great Britain*, pp. 211–41.

[6] In the opening of their Section IV.

[7] Cf. Thornton's Chap. IX, where qualifications are as abundant as in any modern survey.

between country notes and Bank of England notes continued to be hotly debated. There were no indisputable statistics that could be used to help settle the argument, just as in our own day there are not yet statistics to enable us to convince each other on the question whether or not the liabilities of the clearing banks are absolutely crucial to the behaviour of the wider structure of credit.

In the next generation the most hotly debated question was the regulation of the issue of bank-notes. In this phase—the Currency School and Banking School controversy—those who argued for strict regulation of the issue of Bank of England notes were no longer prepared to rely upon any automatic dependence of country issues upon Bank of England issues. They argued for—and obtained—strict and direct limitation of the country issues. But this relation of country to London issues of notes now scarcely held the centre of the stage. The main dispute now raged round the position of other claims—bank deposits, bills of exchange and trade credit generally. The Currency School argued for strict regulation of the issue of bank-notes. The Banking School, more diffuse in their remedies for economic instability, were united only in their negative view that the Currency School remedy was invalidated by the fact that bank-notes formed neither the only nor the governing part of the supply of purchasing power. The use of bank deposits, bills of exchange and other forms of credit as substitutes for bank-notes had long been acknowledged in the literature; on the historical order of events as we know them, it might rather have been argued that bank-notes were a substitute for bills of exchange. But now that a strong case was being made for strict control of the supply of money, the question which was money and which was not money became of high practical importance; moreover, the spectacular growth of banking was emphasizing the weight of bank deposits in the total circulation.

The simplest Currency School view was that only gold and notes were money, and that therefore the circulation of gold and notes together should be made to reflect the changes in the gold supply; this is the essence of the 1844 Bank Act. But this is doing the Currency School less than justice. Its protagonists did acknowledge the relevance of banking and other credit, but some took the line that while notes should be strictly controlled, deposit banking should be kept in order by some other measures; others argued that the velocity of circulation of banking and other instruments was comparatively so low that these were unimportant parts of the money supply; again others argued that, since gold or notes could be demanded in all final payments, the pressure of purchasing and economic activity could never for long get out of line with the supply of the basic monetary instruments. It was this last view that was destined to dominate many decades; it prevailed against the Banking School view that the components of the money supply were so many and varied, and such effective substitutes for each other, that any attempt to control their quantity was doomed to failure, and would probably aggravate economic crises.

The prevailing doctrine—which gave Britain its basic monetary laws for seventy years—depended on the fact that gold or Bank of England notes could be demanded in all final payments. This derived not merely from the law of 1833: it was deeply rooted in the country's practice for a long time before that. This singular quality of gold and notes became directly important as soon as a general breakdown of credit developed; at other times bank deposits and bills of exchange were generally good enough, but in a crisis a business-man had to be able to put his hands on notes or gold, or he risked bankruptcy. As long, therefore, as a financial crisis was thought a possibility, bankers and other granters of credit paid some regard, in the conduct of their lending business, to the state of the Bank of England's reserve. And just in these decades Bank Rate movements were beginning to be employed by the Bank of England as the method protecting the Reserve. A rise in Bank Rate became all important as an index—a warning that a breakdown of credit, followed by a disastrous spell of depressed markets, might be just round the corner.[8] The Banking School were right in emphasizing the variety and the importance of sources of credit, but the Currency School were right in arguing that the superstructure of credit could not for very long get out of line with the supply of the basic money, the gold and bank-notes. In this situation the broad line of argument developed in the first part of this paper was not important. But the economy was distressingly unstable.

It was also one in which some of the most relevant circumstances were changing. If it was right to assume that the superstructure of credit could not for very long get out of line with the supply of the basic money, experience very quickly showed that the possible

[8] This interpretation of the *modus operandi* of Bank Rate at this time is convincingly argued by A. B. Cramp in his article, 'Horsley Palmer on Bank Rate', *Economica*, N.S., vol. 26, no. 104, November 1959, pp. 341–55, and in his *Opinion on the Operation of Bank Rate, 1822–60* (London, 1962).

time-lag could be of devastating importance. Partly because the Bank of England was not using its warning signal promptly enough, and partly because the underlying causes of instability were very strong, crises of the first order of magnitude recurred in 1847, 1857 and 1866. This experience led the authorities to modify the Currency School policy to the extent of admitting that the Bank of England must act as lender of last resort to prevent breakdown of the system. The crisis of 1866 was the last of the old kind, and Bagehot's writings ensured the respectability of the new policy. Nevertheless, Bank Rate continued to retain something of its power as a warning signal internally; this was partly because memories of the old-fashioned crises lingered on, and partly because, although it ceased to portend a breakdown of credit, a high Bank Rate was still apt to portend a spell of trade depression. Not until the effective adoption of Full Employment policies was the warning power of Bank Rate reduced to a ghost of its old self.

The scene was also changing in that the internal effects of Bank Rate were becoming relatively unimportant. In the second half of the nineteenth century London's power as an international financial centre grew fast, and the Bank of England was enabled to perform its duty of keeping the pound on gold by operating principally on the international capital position.[9] (This had always been an element in the *modus operandi* of Bank Rate, but in the period 1860–1914 it became the principal element.) Some of its direct influence as a signal for business-men remained, as I have suggested above; more importantly, the disturbance of the international capital situation disturbed investment in the developing countries overseas, with severe repercussions on the trade of the home country. Just how much monetary conditions really affected the trade cycle it is impossible to say; if we are looking only at the last few decades before 1914 I find myself much in sympathy with Rostow's view of 'an essentially negative element',[10] for the rise in interest rates often waited until the boom was already cracking, and merely ensured that the depression should be severe. However, without going so far as this we must still admit that the quick power of Bank Rate on the international capital position was the dominant feature, and this change of emphasis was duly reflected in the dwindling literature

[9] For a contemporary exposition, see, e.g., Clare, G., *A Money Market Primer* (2nd edn., 1905), esp. pp. 103–7 (on effects on international movements) and 36 (for attitude that no disturbance of the internal economy is sought).

[10] Rostow, W. W., *British Economy of the Nineteenth Century*, p. 57.

on monetary questions. Bank Rate as the controller of international gold movements came to occupy a leading place in expositions of the monetary system; the Quantity Theory and the 1844 Act remained alongside the discussion of Bank Rate, but the old and the new were in this phase never really integrated. It was the literature of this phase that was more or less my introduction to the subject, and I well remember my first impression of confusion, whether a rise in Bank Rate increased the quantity of money (which seemed to be the result of attracting gold) or decreased the quantity of money (which seemed to be a necessary part of the deflation a rising Bank Rate was supposed to provoke). My teachers soon put this right, but when I look back at the pre-1920 literature I am not surprised at my early difficulties.

The main development of monetary thought in the course of the 1920s was the integration of these various elements into a single coherent body of theory. The development originated mainly, I believe, in the pre-1914 academic activity in the study of the trade cycle, though there was also powerful stimulus from the international monetary strains of the 'twenties themselves. Having regard to what we know Marshall to have been thinking at the turn of the century, it is not surprising that the reshaping of monetary thought in the next generation was largely the work of Marshall's successors, especially Lavington, Keynes and Robertson; and we must not forget that English economists were beginning to notice the work of Wicksell and his followers on the Continent.

As a survey of this kind must necessarily concertina many intricate episodes in the history of thought, I will summarize these developments of the 1920s simply by reference to the form in which they emerged, at the end of the decade, in Keynes's *Treatise on Money*. The *Treatise* has between its four covers many strands of thought, as those who were students in those days will remember too well; but for our present purpose we may confine our attention to two of them. The first is that the demand for money was refashioned by looking at money primarily as one among other stores of value, the preference for the peculiar convenience money possesses being weighed in the manner traditional in the ordinary theory of value, against the interest that could be obtained on the other stores of value. The second idea we must notice was, along Wicksellian lines, that the rate of interest influenced the balance between the demand for capital and the willingness to lend, thus providing a mechanism whereby the supply of money (and the demand for it) was linked with the pressure of total demand, and so with movements in the general level of prices.

The first of these developments—the liquidity preference theory of interest—represented a clean break from the Quantity Theory, in that money, ceasing to be a pure medium of exchange, ceased to have that freakish unit elasticity of demand and became something whose value was determined in a way we need not feel strange when we had just been learning a more universal Theory of Value.[11] But in his formulation Keynes preserved his links with tradition by notionally dividing money into 'active money', whose elasticity of demand was unity, and 'idle money', the utility of which behaved in the more ordinary way and had to be balanced against the interest that could be earned by holding bonds. For the purpose of establishing his main propositions Keynes need not have made this bow to his ancestors, but he did, and I suspect that life would be easier if we forgot about it; I have already noted the artificiality of the distinction. However, its use did facilitate demonstration of an equilibrating mechanism in the system. A rise in prices increased the amount of active money needed, the money available for idleness was thus reduced, the demand for bonds therefore fell, the rate of interest rose, demand for capital goods was checked—and so the rise in prices was stopped. This is the Keynesian system of 1930 in baldest form, and the précis omits many sources of friction continually emphasized by Keynes. In terms of practical policy, the analysis did point advantage in control of the supply of money; to Keynes this meant control of the supply of bank deposits, and his attention to such subjects as the cash ratio in banks and central bank operations is always related to this. He emphasized throughout—and this is a big step beyond the Currency School position—that there is a dangerously long time-lag between movements in 'bank-money' (i.e., bank deposits) and the corresponding movement in notes, 'so that a control over the volume of notes operates too late—after the evil has been done by a change in the volume of bank-money which may have taken place some months earlier'.[12] He went further and, emphasizing the crucial position of the rate of interest in the equilibrating mechanism, urged central bankers to

[11] Cf. Hicks, J. R., 'A Suggestion for Simplifying the Theory of Money', *Economica*, N.S. vol. 2, no. 5, February 1935, p. 3.

[12] Vol. 2, p. 264.

think more directly in terms of forcing the rate of interest to behave in the required way.[13]

This was, of course, not the end of the Keynes story, and in the *General Theory* (1936) Keynes developed ideas that drastically modified any notion of the economic system as a self-stabilizing system. Particularly, he argued certain consequences of the short-comings of the rate of interest as part of the equilibrating mechanism: the liquidity trap and the notion of an under-employment equilibrium came in. Like the *Treatise* before it, the *General Theory* bristled with ideas, many of which were hotly disputed; but both in his 1930 emphasis on the rate of interest as a crucial cog in the mechanism and in his subsequent relative loss of faith in its efficacy Keynes had wide following. In such investigations as they were able to make the Radcliffe Committee found a good deal of support for the later Keynesian view. In this sense the scepticism of Radcliffe is Keynesian, but in certain other respects—and here I am thinking of parts of the *Treatise* that Keynes did not revise—the Radcliffe view of the economic system is quite unlike that of Keynes.

The break from the Keynesian exposition may perhaps best be seen by exaggerating it, imputing to Keynes a simplicity that was never his. Keynes was thoroughly traditional in drawing a sharp line between money and other assets. To him money had changed from being coin and notes to being notes and bank deposits, notes being the small change of 'bank money'. In his model there are four major classes of assets: cash, bank money, bonds and others; there are central banks (whose liabilities are cash), there are banks (whose liabilities are bank money and who are holders of cash and bonds as well as other assets) and there are non-banks (i.e., corporations and individuals who are holders of cash, bank money, bonds and other assets, and who are also much concerned with spending on 'real' assets). A distinction between money and bonds is that the former is useful for payments and the latter are not; another distinction between them is that bonds do and money does not carry interest. With this classification and some reliance upon the interest rate as a balancer of savings and investment, we can make a coherent working model, useful for explaining how policy should be shaped.

But the world in which we live lacks these sharp distinctions. And, remembering that for purposes of policy we must get as close as we can to the points of business decision, the more we try to eliminate

[13] Ibid., pp. 369–74; cf. Report of the Committee on Finance and Industry (*Macmillan Report*), Cmnd. 3897, 1931, para. 359.

dangerous time-lags, the more blurred the distinctions become. There is no clear line between purchasing power that carries no interest and interest-earning assets that have no influence on purchasing power. 'Commercial banks' shade into industrial banks, savings banks and building societies, and these into a host of other financial intermediaries; the liabilities of these are close substitutes for each other, so that a clamping down on one group will not create such an abrupt scarcity of liquidity as will have a worthwhile impact on the pressure of total demand. This is, of course, the kind of argument that was being used by the Banking School a hundred years ago, when J. S. Mill and others pointed out that the substitutability of bank deposits for notes was high, whence they argued that a control of notes alone would be merely a nuisance. Time's answer to the Banking School was the recognition that bank deposits were as good as notes, coupled with institutional arrangements for making good a Currency School contention that the supply of bank deposits was proportional to the supply of notes. Having got so far, we then got into the habit of saying that bank deposits were the important quantity, that our central banks should regulate the bank deposits and that notes could be left to take care of themselves.

Can we now, as a latter-day Currency School, argue that, although other financial claims are good substitutes for money, we can rely upon the constancy of their ratio to the bank deposits we have learned to control? I doubt it. Or can we now, following those who taught us all about central banking, force the non-bank lenders into a pattern by imposing on them liquidity rules analogous to those whereby the clearing banks are controlled? The Radcliffe Committee looked at the question, and shuddered. Or can we try to check the development of financial institutions, by proclaiming that none but the clearing banks may create money? This is not just an idle fancy: our ancestors did something like this when they strangled the country note issue—but they did not stop the private creation of money. They could not stop it, because money is the creation of the public that chooses to impute certain qualities to certain claims.

I have referred repeatedly to the Currency School and Banking School controversy because I believe that the arguments of the last few years have very close parallels with that earlier controversy. The Currency School case depended on sharp lines of distinction and rigid proportionalities. The case was accepted as the basis for practical policy; we muddled through the next hundred years partly by modifying the policy, partly by imposing proportionalities and partly by enduring disadvantages we no longer find tolerable. In modification of the policy, we developed central banking to dull the terror of financial crises, and now we have gone much farther by insisting that there shall be no trade depression. The age-old tendency of financial institutions to become more numerous, more varied and more efficient flourishes in an economy that avoids major breakdowns; the process is accelerated, and a policy that depends on a stable relationship between institutions becomes less and less realistic.

This is a negative conclusion, and it is because they took this view of the nature of money and the monetary processes that the Radcliffe Committee's conclusions appeared to give such little positive guidance. But even negative conclusions have their importance: we sometimes need to search around for something quite different which will get results. And the conclusions to which our general discussion points do, after all, have highly practical implications. To take a major point, restriction of the supply of bank deposits, if long continued, can be expected to become increasingly ineffective as a curb on total demand, because the demand for liquidity can be so well satisfied from other sources. Worse than this, restriction of the banks will increase the opportunities for alternative lenders, so that the banks will lose ground to their competitors and the heads the Government can hit will become progressively less influential in the behaviour of the economy. Or to take another point, on which the Radcliffe Committee's recommendation was grossly misrepresented in some quarters, consider the channels for local-authority borrowing. The fact that Treasury bills are, and local authority mortgages are not, 'liquid assets' to the clearing banks has some very short-period relevance, in that the banks are outstandingly efficient lenders, but if the market for credit is fundamentally a single market, an addition of short government paper has much the same effect on the monetary situation wherever it is injected. Banks are not the only lenders sensitive to liquidity.

Our analysis has its uses for bankers as well as for policy-makers. The English clearing banks, acting as a cartel, fix the rate they pay on time deposits, and have only one class of such deposits: at seven days' notice. They are sometimes urged to compete for deposits now going to building societies or hire-purchase finance houses by offering higher rates for longer periods. Against this proposal, it has been argued that the total of deposits in the clearing banks is fixed by the supply of 'liquid assets', and that therefore the banks could get no more deposits by offering higher rates but would simply reduce their own profits. This over-simple argument can be made true only if we make certain assumptions about strictly rigid proportionality in the balance sheets of all sorts of firms and households, and insist that for one size of the national debt and one size of the national income there is only one possible size for the total of bank deposits. This is a particular manifestation of the old idea that there is only one kind of money (in this case bank deposits) and that the demand for it is rigidly related to the national income. But once we admit that the liabilities of other institutions may be quite good substitutes for the liabilities of the clearing banks, and that business attracted by non-bank intermediaries affects the non-bank demand for national debt, the consequences of non-competition by the clearing banks become expensive to them. By refusing to compete, they stand to lose a larger and larger proportion of the total lending business in the country. To put the point in an extreme way, if the banks always ignored competition on the principle to which I have referred, their place as creators of the chief monetary assets would gradually be lost to other more aggressive financial intermediaries. And no doubt there would be quantity theorists a century hence to point out that the then predominant money (claims on the aggressive intermediaries) had increased roughly in proportion to the national income: they might even find that clearing bank deposits had become the small change of the monetary system!

Or are we perhaps already there? If the crucial decisions to place orders for production depend 'upon the composition of the spender's assets and on his borrowing power and . . . upon the methods, moods and resources of financial institutions and other firms which are prepared (on terms) to finance other people's spending',[14] then in an important sense bank deposits have already become the small change of the system. This is no fad of a theorist's exposition, for its implications are surely lessons of the first importance to practical policy. For it means that there is no dependable monetary ceiling against which a boom will bump its head. As the boom rises, the sources of liquidity broaden, and the rising demand for the means of payment comes too late and is too easily satisfied. It follows that a policy of stabilizing bank deposits and waiting for the expanding volume of payments to force interest rates upward, while

[14] *Radcliffe Report* (Cmnd. 827), para. 389.

intuitive central bankers try to be nimble in 'following the market', is not enough; action would always be too late, as it was when strain on the note-issue was expected to set the corrective mechanism in motion. If monetary policy is to be used at all, we must make it operate on as broad a front as possible; action on the supply of bank money must be thought of as purely incidental to a positive, aggressive and far-reaching interest-rate policy. How far we can depend on this is, as the Radcliffe Committee emphasized,[15] a matter on which much more systematic investigation is required. If we want to catch up with events and accept the implications of the Full Employment policy we must urgently investigate the efficacy of a far more vigorous interest-rate policy than any we have yet seen, and, lest this should (as I expect) prove a non-starter, we must think again on how the flexibility of fiscal policy might be increased.

[15] Ibid., para. 474.

28

THE *RADCLIFFE REPORT*: A SOCRATIC SCRUTINY

W. T. NEWLYN*

After the style of Professor D. H. Robertson's Socratic dialogue in 'British Monetary Policy', *Lloyds Bank Review*, May 1939.

SOCRATES. I understand that there has recently been an authoritative report on the working of your monetary system?

ECONOMIST. That is indeed so Socrates—the *Report* of the Radcliffe Committee, composed of men of great ability and wisdom.

S. I have taken some interest in the past in the working of your monetary system; I should be most interested to hear what new light this report has thrown on the subject.

E. The report gives a great deal of very valuable factual data, but it also reflects significant changes in the theoretical analysis of domestic monetary policy.

S. Indeed? Then it may be that the ideas which I have obtained from reading your text books require some correction?

E. It may be so Socrates.

S. Pray expound the new doctrine.

E. I think the doctrine might be summarized in four propositions taken from the report, as follows:

(i) '. . . the supply of Treasury bills and not the supply of cash has come to be the effective regulatory base of the domestic banking system' (para. 583);

* Reprinted from the *Bankers' Magazine*, January 1960, by permission of the author and publisher. (The original has also been reprinted as Appendix 2 in Newlyn, W. T., *Theory of Money* (Oxford, 2nd edn., 1971).) W. T. Newlyn is Professor of Economics at the University of Leeds.

(ii) '. . . only very limited reliance can be placed on the interest incentive', as an influence on total demand. (para. 397);

(iii) '. . . it is the liquidity position as a whole upon which the authorities must act' (para. 312);

(iv) '. . . monetary action works upon total demand by altering the liquidity position of financial institutions and of firms and people desiring to spend on real resources; the supply of money itself is not the critical factor'.

S. From what I have learnt previously the second proposition does not surprise me, but I have difficulty in reconciling the other propositions with some of your text books. Kindly expound them.

E. Certainly Socrates. The first proposition is the result of the arrangements which have been made to ensure that the Government can always lay its hands on the funds necessary to discharge its day-to-day obligations.

S. Am I right in believing that this is one of the functions of the Bank of England as the Government's banker?

E. By no means Socrates. It is the view of the Bank of England that such provision would be inflationary because Treasury borrowing from the Bank of England expands the cash base thus allowing a multiple expansion of bank credit.

S. Indeed! This view, if I may say so, appears to be based on the text book account of these matters rather than on the version contained in your propositions.

E. So it would appear.

S. But if the Bank of England does not perform this function who does?

E. You must understand Socrates that it is one of the most important functions of the discount market to supply the Treasury with funds. The discount houses, acting together as a syndicate, are under an obligation to 'cover the tender'—that is to say the syndicate have to take up all bills which cannot be sold to 'outside' lenders at a better price.

S. This is certainly a great convenience for the Government, but have the discount houses always got sufficient funds?

E. No, not always. In such a situation the authorities must act to avoid a disturbance in the market.

S. What do you mean by a disturbance?

E. The excess demands for funds would force up the price.

S. I understand that to be the nature of a market.

E. Yes, but the short term money market has special significance in that it affects foreign confidence in sterling and the authorities regard it as important that there should be a stable short term rate.

S. I see. Now explain to me how the authorities act.

E. In order to maintain a stable short term rate the authorities make cash available in the market if the discount houses haven't enough.

S. By the authorities do you mean the Bank of England?

E. I suppose I do.

S. Then this cash which the Bank of England makes available to the discount market for loan to the Treasury is thought to be in some way less inflationary than if it were lent directly? Does the Committee approve these arrangements?

E. The Committee does not actually condemn them Socrates. The report says that the assumptions on which the need for this artificial short term market is based are open to question (para. 585) and expresses 'doubts whether a reversal of all this would now have any catastrophic results for the Treasury' (para. 587).

S. Indeed! I would have thought it pertinent to consider whether the arrangements themselves might not have catastrophic results for the economy. I understand you to say that it is a result of this stable rate arrangement that 'the supply of Treasury bills and not the supply of cash has come to be the effective regulatory base of the domestic banking system'. Pray how does that follow?

E. The banks are obliged to hold 30 per cent of their assets in liquid form; this means cash or bills or short term loans to the discount market. Since the banks can get cash by calling money from the market, thus forcing the Bank of England to create more cash, the cash ratio is of no significance; it is the liquid assets ratio which restricts bank lending. Hence bank-credit is based on total liquid assets not on cash.

S. But are not rather more than two-thirds of these liquid assets themselves bank credit?

E. They are indeed Socrates.

S. So that if we want to explain what it is that bank credit *as a whole* is based on, we must still say 'cash'?

E. I suppose we must. But since the authorities wish to have a stable short term market, cash is a passive element.

S. What this seems to me to amount to is that bank credit is still based (just as the older text books say) on cash, but the authorities have chosen to allow the cash base to be determined by requirements other than the requirements of monetary restriction.

E. That is a reasonable interpretation Socrates but there remains the ability of the authorities to control bank credit (I beg your pardon —I mean the *rest* of bank credit) by altering the supply of Treasury bills.

S. How is that done?

E. Simply this—if the banks are deprived of Treasury bills of an amount equal to x, their obligation regarding liquid assets forces them to contract credit by $\frac{10}{3}x$.

S. But how does the Treasury dispense with the need to issue x Treasury bills—do you mean that the government cuts its expenditure by that amount?

E. Certainly not Socrates—the budgetary requirements must be taken as a datum. The Treasury dispenses with the bills by *funding*. That is to say the issue of long term securities in their place.

S. Who buys the securities?

E. The public.

S. So that this is not simply 'funding' but a switch from borrowing from the banks to borrowing from the public?

E. That is so. The net effect is to reduce deposits and the banks' Treasury bill holdings by x, as a result of which they will have to contract credit by $\frac{10}{3}x$.

S. Wait—I am a little perplexed. The operation so far has not affected the banks' cash, since the borrowing on bonds is exactly offset by the repayment of bills, but the sale of bonds will reduce deposits by x, thus leaving the banks with $x/12$ surplus cash. Rather than contract will the banks not try to get a larger *share* of the outstanding Treasury bills? Or lend to the discount houses on short bonds? Or even lend to their customers by way of bills? And will this not cause a re-expansion of x, leaving the volume of bank credit as it was before the funding? Indeed it would appear to me that the only result would be a fall in the short term rate of interest.

E. There is something in what you say Socrates—I must have left something out.

S. Could it be cash?

E. Ah, yes of course: obviously the authorities would need to take the $x/12$ surplus cash out of the market at the same time as contracting Treasury bills.

S. If I may say so that is not at all obvious from the statements you have quoted from the Committee. It seems that for a contraction of x in bank money it is still a *necessary* condition that cash should be contracted by $x/12$—just as the older text books tell us?

E. That is so, but this cannot happen unless Treasury bills are contracted in proportion.

S. Can it not? Could not the Treasury get a larger proportion of its bills taken up outside the banking system by accepting a lower price?

E. Certainly not Socrates—that would cause a rise in the short term rate and . . .

S. Yes, yes—I remember, you told me about the short term rate. So that contraction of the cash base is not a *sufficient* condition for monetary contraction simply because the authorities choose to adopt a certain interest rate policy rather than because of any change in the nature of the monetary system?

E. That is so.

S. Now tell me about 'the liquidity position as a whole', on which I understand the Committee places great emphasis. How does the Committee define liquidity?

E. Well, the Committee doesn't actually *define* liquidity anywhere, Socrates, but it appears to mean 'the ease or difficulty encountered by spenders in their efforts to raise money for the purpose of spending on goods and services' (para. 389). Raising money in this context includes both selling assets and borrowing.

S. This is a most comprehensive definition of the monetary influence on demand but it gives no indication of its elements or manifestations, nor do I understand how the authorities 'act' upon it as stated in your third proposition. I can see, for example, that constraints on spending might result in spenders holding financial assets in excess of normal requirements, but the authorities can't take these away from them by *monetary* measures—except by encashing them! I would have thought that the quantity of money together with the strength of the desire to hold on to it *was* a critical factor and that the power of the authorities to influence the situation rested upon their power to control its supply. How else can the authorities act on 'the liquidity position as a whole'?

E. By 'operations on the structure of interest rates which, for institutional reasons, change the liquidity of financial operators' (para. 394).

S. Oh dear! I thought it was the other way round.

E. I think that the difficulty stems from the use of the term liquidity by the Committee in two very different ways.

S. Quite so. It has often seemed to me that there is much to be said for the establishment of a permanent 'inquisition' on the use of terms by professional economists. But pray continue.

E. The important point is that it is through changes in the value of financial assets that monetary action affects demand.

S. Indeed? But according to your second proposition the Committee allows very little strength to the 'interest incentive' effect on spending?

E. That is so.

S. That I understand to mean the response by spenders to changes in the *cost* of obtaining funds.

E. That is my understanding too.

S. But is not a change in the value of financial assets simply one form of a change in the cost of obtaining funds? There is no difference, is there, between a fall in the price which can be obtained for a bond you already hold and a fall in the price at which you can sell a new bond of your own?

E. I agree.

S. If the Committee does not believe that spenders respond to changes in the cost of obtaining funds how do such changes affect demand?

E. According to the Committee through their effect on lenders. A rise in interest rates means that financial institutions can only expand their lending by selling securities at a loss.

S. I know that banks substitute advances for securities when circumstances are favourable, and vice versa, but are there any other institutions which normally act in this way?

E. Not *normally*. Perhaps the point should be made more general. Financial institutions operate by borrowing and lending on different terms: it is thus that they affect the liquidity of spenders. A change in interest rates will inhibit operations because of the increased costs of the financial institutions.

S. Pray why can these financial institutions not pass on the increased cost by raising their lending rate?

E. There are institutional reasons why rates cannot be thus adjusted.

S. What are these institutional reasons?

E. There are certain conventions and agreements regarding rates. Thus the bank's lending rate to the discount houses and the bank's advances rate are related to Bank-rate; they do not reflect what the market will bear.

S. I see. So this 'control' only works to the extent that financial institutions maintain conventions which, in the circumstances in which the control is required, would restrict their profits?

E. As to the effect on profits I am unable to speak—the profits of the banks was not a subject into which the Committee thought it should pry.

S. Did the Committee consider that your financial institutions are flexible and adaptable?

E. Yes, indeed—there are several statements which reflect this view.

S. In that case, is not the 'control' on which the Committee places so much emphasis rather unreliable?

E. Should this prove to be the case Socrates the Committee suggests the device of raising the minimum liquidity ratio of the banks, and similar restrictions on other lenders.

S. Does the Committee specify what assets would qualify as liquid assets in the case of the banks?

E. No, I'm afraid it doesn't, but the context would seem to imply that it had in mind those assets which are at present included in 'liquid assets'.

S. This would include commercial bills?

E. It would.

S. Would it not be possible for the banks to satisfy a higher liquidity ratio by the simple device of lending by way of bill (directly or indirectly) instead of by advances, as they used to do in the past?

E. Within limits—yes.

S. Is there any reason to suppose the limits are narrow?

E. No, I think not, from what the Committee says about the increase in bill finance during the recent credit squeeze (para. 165).

S. So that this control, also, depends on the institutions concerned keeping to present conventions in circumstances in which it would not be in their interest to do so because it would divert business into other financial channels?

E. In the Committee's view such a control would need to be accompanied by restrictions on other financial institutions because they all contribute, as does trade credit, to the 'general liquidity position', but the Committee 'shuddered' at the thought of this.

S. Yes, I follow that—in terms with which I am familiar the banking system determines the volume of money and the other financial institutions and trade credit influence its velocity.

E. Those are not terms which commend themselves to the Committee, Socrates. With regard to velocity the Committee states 'we have not made more use of this concept because we cannot find any reason for supposing, or any experience in monetary history indicating, that there is any limit to the velocity of circulation' (para. 391). Are you feeling ill Socrates?—you have gone quite pale.

S. How in the name of Aristotle can the question as to whether or not velocity has an absolute limit have any bearing whatever on its validity or utility as a concept? Am I to be asked to abandon the concept of velocity in physics for the same reason?

E. I think the Committee may have meant . . .

S. As to this historical generalization would your Committee maintain its position to the extent of claiming that you could manage today with the same quantity of money as you had under your first Queen Elizabeth?

E. I doubt it Socrates.

29

APPRAISAL OF MONETARY MANAGEMENT

J. KAREKEN*

THAT the monetary authorities should have waited as long before acting as they did in each of the economic recoveries of the period 1955–67, until there had been an actual loss of reserves, is far from clear. By acting sooner, they might have done better.

Possible reasons for the British approach

What is clear, though, is that, having delayed, they were largely compelled to seek quick results. This may explain the restriction of consumer loan terms in 1955, 1960, and again in 1965. Consumer demand seems to change quickly when loan terms are changed, even more quickly than when personal income tax rates are changed.

This desire for quick results may also explain why the monetary authorities imposed a loan ceiling on banks in 1955, why they called for special deposits in 1960, and why in 1965 they called for special deposits and imposed loan ceilings on bank and nonbank intermediaries. They may have believed, perhaps rightly, that it takes a long time to change the total of financial institutions' loans to the private sector of the economy by changing Bank rate and official holdings of Treasury securities—longer than it takes by simply telling institutions what to do.

Yet there would seem to be another reason why the monetary authorities proceeded as they did in 1955, 1960, and 1965, and in 1956–57, 1961 and 1966, as well: an aversion to high interest rates.

* Extract reprinted from Kareken, J., 'Monetary policy', Chap. II in Caves, R. (ed.), *Britain's Economic Prospects* (London, 1968), pp. 83–9, by permission of the author and publisher. J. Kareken is Associate Professor of Economics at the University of Minnesota.

Imposing more restrictive limiting consumer installment loan terms is a way of reducing the flow of consumer credit and aggregate demand, one that does not involve an increase in interest rates. Making requests of banks is a way of controlling loans and, hopefully, aggregate demand but without an increase in interest rates. Then, too, although bank loans may decrease following a call for special deposits, interest rates do not necessarily increase. What happens to interest rates when a call is made depends on what the Bank does to the banking system's cash. If the Bank does not provide the cash needed to meet a call, interest rates increase. If, however it does provide the cash, there is essentially no increase in rates. Nonbank loan rates may increase, but the increase is relatively small—smaller than when the Bank does not provide the cash to meet the call.

In a description of the special deposits scheme which the Bank submitted to the Radcliffe Committee, there appears the following passage:

> The special deposits would properly bear interest in order not to penalize the banks while this portion of their previously earning assets was set aside in this 'sterilized' form. The cash required by the banks to make the deposits would be provided by the Bank of England . . . normally by the purchase of Treasury bills, or possibly of stock maturing in the near future which was widely held as a money market asset.[1]

No less instructive is this next passage, taken from an official description of how calls are made: 'As the Bank Return indicates, the counterpart of Special Deposits normally takes the form of an increase in the amount of government securities in the Banking Department of the Bank of England.'[2] Apparently, then, the Bank has all along thought of its special deposits scheme as a way of controlling bank lending, but one which involves no increase in interest rates.[3]

[1] Bank of England, 'Some Possible Modifications in Technique', p. 42, para. 35.

[2] 'The Procedure of Special Deposits', *Bank of England Quarterly Bulletin*, vol. 1, no. 1, December 1960, p. 18.

[3] The Bank believes that deliberately selling Treasury bonds to decrease bank loans and deposits is unwise and that evidently loans and deposits do not decrease when it sells Treasury bills. [See Reading 14]. The Bank's belief cannot explain, however, why the monetary authorities proceeded as they did in 1960–61 or in 1965–66. Had they been willing to see sufficient increases in interest rates, the Bank could have managed just by calling for special deposits. It was not necessary to engage in open market operations, which according to the Bank would have been unwise or a waste of effort. The Bank did call for special deposits in 1960–61

How the monetary authorities proceeded in 1955–57, 1960–61, and 1965–66, and late 1967, too, is consistent with a continuing aversion to high interest rates. Nor should it seem strange that having listed the numerous Bank rate increases of the period 1955–67, I should now put forward an aversion to high interest rates as an explanation of the monetary authorities' behaviour. Instead of making requests of financial institutions in, say, 1964–65, the monetary authorities could have increased Bank rate and market interest rates more than they did. What needs explaining therefore is why there were not further increases in interest rates in 1955–57, 1960–61, and 1964–66.

There is another plausible explanation besides an aversion to high rates: a persistent doubt, widely shared by British policy makers, that changes in interest rates affect domestic demand. This doubt would account for the monetary authorities having increased interest rates, if only to protect official reserves, and at the same time called for special deposits or imposed loan ceilings. Attributing this doubt to Treasury and Bank officials is not unreasonable. Ever since that inspired (but possibly misguided) group of Oxford economists asked businessmen whether a change in interest rates mattered at all, doubters have far outnumbered the faithful. Possibly this was not true, at least in official councils, in the years immediately after the Conservative party came to office (October 1951); but the 1955–56 experience, rashly interpreted perhaps, evidently made doubters of many of the official faithful.[4] The Radcliffe Committee—charged, it will be recalled, with inquiring into the working of the British monetary system—does seem to have been appointed by a disappointed and despairing Chancellor of the Exchequer.

I wonder whether doubt about the domestic impact of an increase in interest rates helps explain how the monetary authorities proceeded in 1964–66 and in late 1967. It is clear from the loan priorities announced in November 1964 that by then, if not before, they had become dedicated to maintaining the output of investment goods, housing included. They cannot have been unaware that building societies, which account for a large portion of British residential mortgage loans, are sometimes a little slow in adjusting

and in 1965–66; but the authorities made requests of financial institutions too, and these requests cannot be explained by the Bank's belief.

[4] Dow, J. C. R., *The Management of the British Economy 1945–60* (Cambridge, 1964), pp. 66–70.

their share (deposit) and loan rates, and that therefore an increase in market interest rates diverts the flow of funds from mortgage loans and reduces the output of housing.[5] They may have proceeded as they did because they feared that still higher market interest rates would cut housing output further. By 1964 it may also have been clearer than it was that domestic demand for plant and equipment is not completely unaffected by a change in interest rates. Even the Radcliffe Committee had found instances of a 7 per cent Bank rate having affected demand for plant and equipment (and inventory).[6] The official view may also have been influenced by a shift in professional opinion in recent years, both in the United Kingdom and in the United States. It is still not known how much British domestic plant and equipment demand is affected by a change in rates,[7] but possibly by late 1964 the monetary authorities had become more aware of the risk of increasing interest rates. They do seem to have become more dedicated to economic growth. It is not unreasonable to suggest that by late 1964 the monetary authorities had acquired yet another reason for being averse to increasing interest rates.

Equity and efficiency

If they were averse to increasing interest rates, it does not follow that the monetary authorities should have proceeded as they did

[5] The Radcliffe Committee made this point. See the Committee *Report*, pp. 100–1, paras. 291–4. It is curious that on occasion the monetary authorities have exerted influence on the building societies to keep their share rates down. They did in 1957 (p. 102, para. 296, in the *Report*) and in 1965. This suggests that they have been more concerned with keeping rates down, presumably for appearance's sake, than with maintaining the output of housing. It would seem that if the monetary authorities encouraged the building societies to be quick in response to increases in market interest rates, the output of housing would not decrease as much as it has in the past. But it is almost certainly true that the interest elasticity of the demand for housing is relatively high, and that, whatever institutional arrangements are, a government anxious to encourage the output of housing should not force an increase in interest rates to restrict aggregate demand.

[6] *Radcliffe Report*, p. 159, para. 452. I mention the Radcliffe findings with misgivings, being unconvinced that the way to find out about the effects of a change in government economic policy is by asking businessmen and housewives.

[7] Published statistical studies of British plant and equipment demand are, to say the least, few and far between. A great deal of econometric research has been started, though, and coming years should bring not only a surge of publications, but also a deeper understanding of what determines British plant and equipment demand.

when in their judgement domestic restraint was appropriate. It is at least arguable, on grounds of equity and efficiency, that running a larger fiscal surplus would have been better than imposing more restrictive limits on consumer loan terms and loan ceilings.[8]

There apparently is no denying that consumer demand changes, and almost immediately, when limiting consumer installment loan terms are changed. Consumer demand has quickly decreased when the monetary authorities have increased minimum down payment ratios and decreased maximum repayment periods. But with a restrictive change in limiting consumer loan terms, high-income spending units suffer less, one suspects, than low-income units. They are less dependent than low-income units on borrowed funds; they can look to their own resources, whereas low-income units cannot. They can look with greater confidence to lending officers of financial institutions. Imposing a personal income surtax would perhaps have been more equitable than imposing more restrictions limiting consumer installment loan terms.[9]

It is not only on grounds of equity, however, that one can object to how the monetary authorities proceeded. Imposing loan ceilings is a capricious and uncertain way of reducing aggregate demand. As the monetary authorities have thought, imposing loan ceilings makes spending impossible. The firm or household wanting to spend beyond its means suddenly finds that finance is unavailable and so withdraws from the goods market. But, even assuming this is what happens, there is no guarantee that those units rationed out of the goods market are the ones whose expenditures would have been least productive (or less satisfying). To be more specific, it is hard to believe that the firms rationed out of the goods market are the large, well-established ones, and that the households rationed out

[8] Running a larger fiscal surplus might have required acting sooner, but it is not apparent that doing so would typically have been bad. See Chap. 1 [Caves, R. (ed.), *Britain's Economic Prospects* (London, 1968)].

[9] There is the possibility that in 1964–66 the authorities saw the problem as being to reduce not consumer demand but consumer demand for durables. They may have decided consumer demand for durables was becoming excessive, and that with resources being immobile it would have been 'inefficient' to reduce total consumer demand. One can reasonably be skeptical, though, that to keep the price level stable it is necessary to reduce whatever demand happens to be excessive. The authorities may have wanted to maintain the supply of British durables in foreign markets, and for this reason imposed more restrictive limiting consumer loan terms. Whatever the target level of consumer spending for durables, there presumably is some personal income surtax rate which, given the values of all other policy variables, assures the appropriate demand.

are the relatively prosperous ones with established banking connections.[10]

That some spending units (firms particularly) can find their way around loan ceilings, the authorities would certainly admit, for British experience shows as much.[11] When in mid-1960 the authorities in effect requested banks to limit their private sector loans, firms responded by issuing more commercial bills. Thus in 1965 banks were requested to limit their holdings of commercial bills as well as their loans. Also in 1965 ceilings were imposed on the loans not only of banks but of other institutional lenders as well.

Attempting to limit aggregate demand by imposing ceilings on loans is an unending task. In the end it is not enough simply to impose ceilings on the loans of all financial institutions. They are a convenience, not a necessity, to a significant portion of the nonfinancial sector that can finance itself by the sale of Treasury securities to financial institutions. At any one time, it is not known how the private sector will find a way around loan ceilings, but to assume that a way will be found seems more reasonable than that one will not. This suggests that imposing loan ceilings is a highly uncertain way of limiting aggregate demand. If there is an immediate reduction in aggregate demand, a subsequent increase is also likely. The size of this subsequent increase must be largely unknown, and this hardly recommends the imposition of loan ceilings as a reliable way of reducing aggregate demand.[12]

[10] See the *Radcliffe Report*, p. 162, para. 459.

[11] Or better, around effective loan ceilings. Without a satisfactory loan demand equation (which unfortunately I was unable to produce), it is impossible to be sure, but it would seem that British institutional lenders have largely complied with the direct requests made of them. Thus, there was a decrease in bank loans outstanding after mid-1955, although real output continued to increase through December. And there was only a modest increase over the second half of 1956, in spite of a rather sharp increase in real output. (The mini-recession ended in mid-1956). The September 1957 request was made just as a recession was beginning, so the subsequent decrease in bank loans outstanding is proof of nothing; and the indirect request of mid-1961, which was followed by a decrease in bank loans outstanding, also coincided with the start of a small recession. The requests of late 1964 and mid-1965 came, though, when real output was still increasing, and the rate of growth of bank loans decreased appreciably, so again there would seem to have been some effect. I might also note here that the requests of late 1964 and mid-1965 appear to have checked the growth of nonbank intermediary loans to U.K. residents, although not the growth of total loans and deposits. But it may not have been intended that loans to nonresidents, made perhaps to finance British exports, be held down.

[12] The monetary authorities would acknowledge that the imposition of loan

There will perhaps be objections to my argument that imposing loan ceilings is a capricious way of financing aggregate demand. There was no attempt in 1965–66 or in late 1967 to reduce productive business loans. As the establishment of loan priorities shows, the attempt was made to reduce only unproductive business loans. But everything that has been said about the capriciousness of imposing loan ceilings applies to consumer loans as well as business loans. It is no defence of a policy that only the consumer sector was capriciously dealt with. Moreover, it is surely a little presumptuous to claim knowledge of the difference between productive and unproductive business loans. Is a lathe or a new plant necessarily more productive than an office building or a business take-over? The monetary authorities requested that banks and other financial institutions make only productive business loans; but this is no guarantee that only relatively productive loans were made.

If, as has been suggested, imposing loan ceilings (and loan priorities) is an uncertain and capricious way of reducing aggregate demand, and if imposing more restrictive consumer loan terms is an inequitable way, then the Government would have done better, when restraint was called for, to impose still higher personal income tax rates or to cut public consumption still more. Imposing a greater fiscal surplus is the economically straightforward way of reconciling the desire to keep interest rates unchanged, possibly to maintain output of investment goods, housing included, and the desire to keep the price level stable (or exchange rates fixed).

ceilings is only briefly effective, but would stress that there is an immediate effect. Is the effect more immediate, however, than when tax rates are increased?

THE INSTRUMENTS OF MONETARY POLICY AND THE GENERALIZED TRADE-OFF FUNCTION FOR BRITAIN, 1955–1968[1]

DOUGLAS FISHER*

Introduction

RESEARCH on a number of topics having to do with British monetary policy has been hampered by inadequate disclosure by the monetary authorities concerning almost every facet of their policies. We do not know, for certain, what their objectives are, aside from rather vague pronouncements emphasizing the balance of payments; and we certainly have very little idea of how they might weight their objectives, given the all-too-apparent conflicts between them. Further than this, there is even some uncertainty about their instruments, as to both their nature and their intended and actual effects. With respect to the latter, the problem of disentangling effects is complicated by the so-called 'package deal' approach, in which more than one instrument is fired off at a time, and by the qualitative nature of many of the alleged instruments.

In a recent paper, I have made a beginning on the problem, with the following results.[2] It was discovered that the only apparent monetary policy during the 1951 to 1964 period was conducted in Bank Rate and that none of the monetary quantities tested, especially broad and narrow money and the liquid assets ratio,

* Reprinted from *The Manchester School*, vol. 32, no. 3, September 1970, pp. 209–22, by permission of the author and publisher. Douglas Fisher is at the University of Essex.

[1] I wish to thank J. Michael Parkin, Michael Sumner, Charles A. E. Goodhart, and the referee for their helpful comments.

[2] Fisher, Douglas, 'The Objectives of British Monetary Policy, 1951–1964', *Journal of Finance*, vol. 23, December 1968.

could be interpreted as instruments of monetary policy. Further than this, the authorities exhibited themselves as willing to accept a surprisingly high amount of unemployment per billion dollars of foreign reserves, especially in what were identified as crisis periods in which the trade-offs between the two objectives reached 2·78 per cent of the labour force per billion dollars of gold and convertible currencies; on average, it was 1·07 per cent.

The results of that paper were preliminary in several senses, not the least of which was the use of consumption data rather than income data in order to maintain a reasonably consistent series. In fact, from 1955 it is possible to employ income data in the calculations; and, of more interest, it is possible to evaluate some aspects of the role of Special Deposits and of hire purchase controls as instruments of monetary policy, tests which could produce no satisfactory results in the earlier study. An advantage arises both on account of having more data, in general, and on account of more frequent use of these techniques, in particular, in recent years. Further, other more complete monetary data were employed in order to see what might have developed in the form of open market operations, a matter which was not taken up in the earlier study, again because of the lack of consistent data.

It turns out that Special Deposits and hire purchase controls are, in fact, instruments of monetary policy, at least insofar as the single equation form adopted here is identified adequately. However, peculiarities arise, not the least of which is a perverse reaction by Special Deposits to the balance of payments situation, a finding in agreement with some earlier work by N. J. Gibson. One consequence of finding other instruments is that we must calculate, at the least, the *average trade-offs* of monetary policy in order to generalize about the judgement of the monetary authorities; another is that some of the earlier findings need to be qualified. There is an advantage incurred too: we will obtain a set of coefficient values and functional forms which will be useful in other areas of research such as in the development of macroeconomic models of the British economy. Along these lines the meaning of the reaction coefficients is spelled out more fully than it was in the earlier paper.

The instruments of British policy

We will assume for the British authorities the following short run policy function, which relates an instrument (I_{ti}) to four possible objectives, not otherwise identified for the present (O_{j-1t}):

$$I_{ti} = a_i + b_{1i}I_{t-1i} + \sum_{j=2}^{k} b_{ji}O_{j-1t} \qquad i = 1, \ldots, n \text{ instruments} \quad (1)$$

The point to be emphasized here, from the beginning, is that in this model the instruments are the dependent variables and the objectives are the independent variables; in other words, we argue that changes in the objectives induce the monetary authorities to adjust their instruments, in the short run—the model is short run because of the presence of I_{t-1} as an independent variable.[2]

It is not possible to be entirely precise about the apparent objectives of the British monetary authorities, but the most likely candidates taken from the official and professional literature are the following, without their quantitative values:

B: the level of gold and convertible currencies plus the IMF position
P: the rate of change of prices
G: the rate of growth of gross domestic product
U: the level of unemployment as a per cent of the labour force

In fact, these and other versions of *B*, *P*, *G* and *U* were tried along with the ones above; and the set which emerged as actual objectives —that is, the set on which the various instruments were successfully regressed—was the following, in which no growth variable attempted had any apparent influence on monetary policy:

B: the level of gold and convertible currencies
P: the price level in index numbers
U: the level of unemployment as a per cent of the labour force

These emerge as objectives, then, in an approximate sense—approximate, first, because there are underlying factors which these in turn are proxies for; and, second, because the objectives are discovered only in practise by, you might say, revealed

[2] Two other studies are the original sources for the model employed here, in its non-general form; they are Reuber, G. L., 'The Objectives of Canadian Monetary Policy, 1949–61: Empirical Trade-Offs and the Reaction Function of the Authorities', *Journal of Political Economy*, vol. 72, April 1964, pp. 109–32, and Dewald, W. G., and Johnson, H. G., 'An Objective Analysis of the Objectives of American Monetary Policy, 1952–61', in Carson, Deane (ed.), *Banking and Monetary Studies* (Homewood, Illinois, 1963), pp. 171–89.

preference, so that no weight is given to what might have been desired under a different institutional environment.[3]

There are several aspects of Equation (1) which need to be emphasized before we consider the results of testing it on the British data. More importantly, the coefficients of that equation are not econometrically *identified* as the tastes of the monetary authorities but represent the tastes of the authorities modified by their understanding of how the economic system works. We will accordingly refer to the coefficients as representing their *judgements*. In the Appendix a fairly simple model of the system is attributed to the authorities and then an expression for the optimum set of instruments is derived. What this reveals is that at the least the regression coefficients of Equation (1) contain elements reflecting

(I) the authorities' tastes,

(II) the authorities' views as to

- (i) the links between the ultimate instruments (e.g., Bank Rate), and the intermediate financial variables (e.g., the money stock), and
- (ii) the links between the intermediate financial variables and the final variables (e.g., the level of unemployment).

Furthermore, the coefficients of Equation (1) will be *biased* estimates of the authorities' judgements of (i) and (ii) insofar as the authorities conceive of

(III) exogenous variables (e.g., Autonomous Investment) affecting the final variables.

For the purposes of this paper we do not need to distinguish among the elements of (I) and (II). The presence of bias introduced by ignoring (III) does not depend on whether there *is* an influence of exogenous elements on the final variables but only on whether or not the authorities *think* there is. This raises questions of identification which are outside the scope of the single equation model of this paper.

Table 1, which follows, presents the results of testing Equation (2), a specific version of (1), on the British data, taken quarterly, from 1955 to the end of 1968. Six 'instruments' are recorded.

$$I_{ti} = a_i + b_{1i} I_{t-1i} + b_{2i} B_t + b_{3i} P_t + b_{4i} U_t \qquad i = 1, \ldots, 6 \text{ instruments} \qquad (2)$$

[3] The use of the price *level* instead of the rate of change of prices can be justified in this way, although its appearance is not very satisfying. The results of one test are given in footnote 4.

It is not easy to interpret these results directly because of the presence of the lagged dependent variable in the regression equation, a matter which is dealt with below; but there are some preliminary matters, having to do with sign and significance, which are best discussed in connection with the full results of Table 1.[4] It is, in fact, very clear that the three formal instruments, Bank Rate, Special Deposits, and hire purchase controls show generally firm and consistent relations with the objectives, a fact which is very reassuring for the calculations which are to follow. The one important exception—that is to say, the one case in which the reaction of the monetary authorities appears to be *destabilizing*—is the relation between Special Deposits and the level of gold and convertible currencies (B): in this case, an improvement in the balance of payments position induces the authorities to respond with a further call for Special Deposits, a reaction which can be judged destabilizing if one is prepared to argue that the primary affect is on interest rates or on domestic spending (perhaps by restraining the money supply). This last, it is usually argued, has not been the purpose of Special Deposit controls during the period studied here.[5] On the other hand, a t-value of 1·13 is not especially significant either, indicating, perhaps, that one can minimize the importance of this 'exception'.

With regard to the 'instruments' in the bottom half of the table, a few comments will suffice to dispose of them. In the first place, the liquid assets ratio, an item which the authorities *influence* rather than determine (like the money stock), shows, if anything, a perverse reaction by the authorities. The two interest rates, one short term and one long term, obviously are linearly related to the changes in Bank Rate and indicate, again, no apparent influence other than that of Bank Rate, on the structure of interest rates.

[4] The result of running the same equation with the rate of change of prices instead of the level of prices, is to get a markedly worse fit. Since the objectives are *approximately* identified by the fit of the equation, the more sensible rate of change of prices, which is also a more sensitive indicator, must be *provisionally* rejected. For purposes of comparison, the result for Hire Purchase, with the substitution suggested, is

$$HP_t = 16{\cdot}533 + 0{\cdot}735\, HP_{t-1} - \underset{(0\cdot74)}{2{\cdot}387}\, B_t + \underset{(1\cdot00)}{1{\cdot}645} \left(\frac{P}{\overline{P}}\right)_t - \underset{(1\cdot07)}{2{\cdot}560}\, U_t$$

$$R^2 = 0{\cdot}791$$

[5] Gibson, N. J., 'Special Deposits as an Instrument of Monetary Policy', *Manchester School*, vol. 32, September 1964, pp. 239–59, and Dow, J. C. R., *The Management of the British Economy, 1945–60* (Cambridge, 1964).

There were no signs of any open market operations, and none were expected. Examination of the stocks of broad and narrow money as instruments would not have provided any readily identifiable information, unless the policy function worked in these cases; and, as the tables notes, it did not. The instruments in the top half of the table, because they are in principle determined solely by the authorities, are identified in this single equation form; but as we will see below, the coefficients are not easy to interpret.

If we solve Equation (1) for the *long run* values of the coefficients, we can get some idea of the overall magnitude of the reactions of the authorities; these recalculations will be unencumbered by the differences in timing apparent from the widely different values for b_1 illustrated in Table 1. Algebraically, we assume $I_{ti} = I_{t-1i}$ and divide through by $1 - b_{1i}$ to get Equation (3)

$$I_{ti} = \frac{a_i}{1 - b_{1i}} + \sum_{j=2}^{k} \frac{b_{ji}}{1 - b_{1i}} O_{j-1t} \qquad i = 1, \ldots, n \text{ instruments} \tag{3}$$

which we will write as

$$I_{ti} = a'_i + \sum_{j=2}^{k} b'_{ji} O_{j-1t} \qquad i = 1, \ldots, n \text{ instruments} \tag{4}$$

After this recalculation of the coefficients of Table 1, along with the elimination of the results for the unidentified instruments for the reasons suggested above, we are left with the pure reaction coefficients collected in Table 2.

The results for Bank Rate in Table 2 are, understandably, the most likely to be representative of the direction of British monetary policy. They indicate, taking the perverse side of things, that the British authorities raise the level of Bank Rate by 123 basis points whenever there is a loss of one billion dollars of gold and convertible currencies; raise the level by 19 basis points in order to dampen a change in the level of prices of one index number (a fairly mild response), and react to an increase in the amount of unemployment of 1 per cent of the labour force by lowering Bank Rate by 138 basis points. The strength of this latter result, indicating an adjustment (calculated by holding B and P constant) might be found surprising to some observers of the British economy; but it is verified in my other study, referred to above. Other than this, the relative unimportance of the price level compared with either of the other objectives is mirrored in the Special Deposit and hire purchase

TABLE 1

The policy function of the British monetary authorities—Quarterly data, 1955–1968 (t-value in parentheses)

Instrument	Coefficient of lagged term (b_1)	B (b_2) $ billion	P (b_3) Index numbers	U (b_4) Per cent of labour force unemployed	R^2
Bank Rate	0·447300	−0·679	0·103094	−0·761225	0·734
		(2·72)	(2·00)	(2·85)	
Special deposits	0·913677	13·485	0·994879	−28·592992	0·954
		(1·13)	(2·30)	(2·96)	
Hire purchase	0·701095	−4·173	0·193536	−5·049883	0·803
		(1·31)	(1·97)	(2·02)	
Liquid assets ratio	0·667032	−0·003	0·000664	−0·007420	0·784
		(0·73)	(1·12)	(2·14)	
Treasury bill rate	0·522942	−0·333	0·073417	−0·759528	0·755
		(1·31)	(1·40)	(2·80)	
2½% Consol	0·750198	−0·141	0·013329	−0·142505	0·945
		(1·48)	(0·81)	(1·62)	

Notes: 1. Other instruments and combinations attempted, either without significant or without different results were: broad money; narrow money; bankers' deposits in the Bank of England; securities in the Banking Department of the Bank of England; bankers' deposits, special deposits, plus currency in the hands of the public; the yield on the 4 per cent Consol; the yield on the 2½ per cent Treasury perpetuity.

2. All data, except special deposits and hire purchase variable (per cent down payment on motor cars), were seasonally adjusted by a four-quarter moving average; and all are available, in either form, from the author.

TABLE 2

Long run reaction coefficients (British monetary instruments, 1955 to 1968, Quarterly)

Instrument	b_2'	b_3'	b_4'
Bank Rate	−1·228	0·186	−1·377
Special deposits	156·216	11·525	−331·233
Hire purchase	−13·961	0·647	16·895

variables, a result which buoys our confidence in the method employed in this paper.

The Special Deposits variable, on the other hand, seems to present some difficulties here. We know that, in all likelihood, changes in Special Deposits are not meant to affect the money stock but to put pressure on the liquid assets ratio.[6] We do not observe that the latter behaves as an instrument but that is not necessarily evidence against the line of influence suggested because the single equation model used here is surely not identified when the liquid assets ratio is studied: in particular, the influences of banks, and the suppliers of liquid assets other than the government, as well as the public cannot be dismissed out of hand. In other words, generally, the monetary authorities influence, but cannot be presumed to determine, the liquid assets ratio. All of this does not help to explain why the relation between Special Deposits and the balance of payments variable is perverse; indeed, this finding cannot be explained directly but must be presumed to be either an echo effect of some sort, implied by the correlations between the objectives, a result of the differences in the lag structure, to be studied below, or a random result of no importance in practice.

The generalized trade-off function

We cannot average the results of Table 2 for they are stated in units of measurement of the independent variables. An approach to the reconciliation of the obvious 'package' nature of the three proper instruments of that table—one which, in effect, estimates the implicit judgement of the monetary authorities—is to calculate the trade-off functions for each of the instruments. In a general form, we would begin by writing the total differential equation relating changes in the instruments to changes in the objectives; this is represented by Equation (5)

$$dI_{ti} = \sum_{j=1}^{k} \frac{\partial I_{ti}}{\partial O_{jt}} dO_{jt} \qquad i = 1, \ldots, n \text{ instruments} \tag{5}$$

[6] Gibson, N. J., op. cit. It is conceivable that the purpose of Special Deposits is to impose a tax on the profits of banks since (probably) bank profits rise during squeezes (particularly when the squeeze does not mean an actual reduction in bank advances). Whether or not the authorities take this unusual view of things is a matter of fact; but, at least, it is not likely to be a matter which would explain the results here since interest rate measures (from which the higher bank earnings

We have estimates of the partial derivatives in Table 2; and if we take Equation (5) at the maximum—that is, if we assume that the actual change in the instrument is zero, which is clearly the optimum from the point of view of the monetary authorities—we obtain an overall trade-off function for each instrument, as in Equation (6).[7]

$$\sum_{j=1}^{k} b'_{ji}\, dO_{jt} = O \qquad (6)$$

We are now in a position to compare—among the instruments—the judgement of the monetary authorities implicitly revealed in their changes of policy instruments under their (assumed) complete control. Equation (6) provides, for example, the *function* giving the per cent of the labour force unemployed which is equivalent to one billion dollars of foreign reserves and a one index number rise of the price level. Let us take this point of view in order to deal with concrete results: in Table 3 are illustrated the results of calculating Equation (6) and dividing through by b'_4, the estimated coefficient of the per cent of the labour force unemployed.[8]

The first row in Table 3 indicates that the monetary authorities, implicitly, reckon that a billion dollars of gold and convertible currencies is worth 0·89 of 1 per cent of the labour force unemployed and that one index number of inflation is worth 0·14 of 1 per cent of unemployment (which is to say, is not worth very much). It should be emphasized that we are expressing the judgement of the authorities in an alternative cost form; the interpretation of the table is quite straightforward as a consequence, for we are saying, for example, that the authorities would accept a drop of unemployment of 0·89 of 1 per cent of the labour force in lieu of one billion dollars of foreign reserves. They would accept, following Equation (6), in the sense of leaving the policy instrument unchanged in such a case.

flow) have the expected relation with the balance of payments variable. The reason the lag, discussed below, might be partly explained is that bank profits seem to get very large just after the squeeze is ended.

[7] Solved for pairs of trade-offs, as in Reuber, op. cit., Dewald and Johnson, op. cit., and Fisher, op. cit., we get, for example,

$$\frac{dP_t}{dB_t} = -\frac{b'_2}{b'_3}$$

and so on, for all the combinations of the instruments possible, and their converses.

[8] The actual equation employed in this case is

$$dU = -\frac{b'_2}{b'_4}\,dB - \frac{b'_3}{b'_4}\,dP$$

for each of the three instruments reported.

TABLE 3

Trade-off coefficients for British monetary policy 1955–1968 (all entries in per cent of labour force unemployed)

Instrument	Balance of payments ($1 billion)	Price level (1 index number)
Bank Rate	−0·892	0·135
Special deposits	0·472	0·035
Hire purchase	−0·826	0·038
Average 1, 2, 3	−0·415	0·069
Average 1, 3	−0·859	0·086

We see again, in Table 3, the relative unimportance of the price level in comparison with the other two objectives; and we see that there are interesting differences between the values of the authorities as expressed by the three different samples. We are not able, really, to neglect these differences, primarily because the assumptions of our model leave us with no other choice. That is, the revealed preferences of the authorities are deemed to be the actual preferences of the authorities, *ceteris paribus*.[9]

This, then, leaves us with the problem of which among the various possibilities would best represent the generalized trade-off function of the British monetary authorities for this period. It seems to me that we have three choices: the values expressed by the Bank Rate function, which we can refer to as the 'announced preference function'; the values expressed by the average of the three results, which we can refer to as 'the revealed preference function'; and the values expressed by the average of Bank Rate and hire purchase, which we can refer to as the 'compromise preference function'. We can hardly settle the matter once and for all here; but the arguments of this paper, as well as the findings of the next section on the lag structure of the authorities' decisions, strongly suggest that we

[9] *Ceteris paribus* covers other instruments, both non-quantitative and fiscal, in the monetary authorities' arsenal. See the Appendix for a more complete discussion of the issues.

accept the 'compromise preference function' as the actual function of the authorities; and, accordingly, it is presented as Equation (7) here.

$$du = -0{\cdot}859\ dB + 0{\cdot}086\ dP \qquad (7)$$

The structure of lags

In our comments above we noted that the prominent peculiarity, the perverse effect of a change in foreign reserves on the Special Deposits required of commercial banks, might be due to lags. In fact, the lags implied in the equations fitted do differ materially, and the estimated lag is the longest for Special Deposits. Table 4 illustrates the lags, looked at in two ways; the parameter used in these calculations is the value of the coefficient attached to the lagged value of the dependent variable because it gives the percentage influence of past values of the dependent variable on the policy instrument.[10]

The calculations run as follows. We get the percentage of the influence registered by the 8th quarter by calculating the value of the 8th term in the following infinite series.

$$(1 - b_1), (1 - b_1^2), (1 - b_1^3), \ldots \qquad (8)$$

TABLE 4

The lags implicit in the behaviour of the British monetary authorities, 1955–1968

Instrument	Value of b_1	Amount of effect on the instrument after 8 quarters	Weighted average lag (in quarters)
Bank Rate	0·447	0·998	0·81
Special deposits	0·914	0·513	10·63
Hire purchase	0·701	0·942	2·34

[10] When there is serial correlation in the errors of Equation (2), the coefficient of the lagged dependent variable will be biased upward. Of course the measured serial correlation is not statistically significant, but the measures themselves are biased, leaving us with no simple resolution short of a reformulation. Nevertheless, we should point out that the lags in Table 3 are probably *overstated*, so that from this point of view the estimates shown there are upper limits.

We get the 'weighted average lag' from the following formula, which will be recognized as a conventional multiplier.

$$\text{Weighted average lag} = \frac{b_1}{1 - b_1} \tag{9}$$

The conclusions are somewhat striking. Bank Rate is adjusted rapidly, on average in less than a quarter of a year, while Special Deposits are adjusted, on average, with a lag of better than two and a half years. Indeed, as noted, the length of the lag for Special Deposits is quite enough to explain the perverse results of Table 1. It is also sufficient to have produced the perverse *effects* of Special Deposits on the economy that others have found, the perversity being the result of poor timing rather than of any technical defect in the Special Deposits instrument. It also does not appear that these instruments are part of the same package, in contradiction to Dow's argument.

Conclusions

Let me emphasize that these results do not imply anything about the net impact of monetary policy during the period. What is estimated, most clearly, are the judgements of the authorities, and what is discovered is that there seems to be some difference between *announced* and actual (revealed) judgements. It is not possible to take a position as to whether these differences are mistakes either of the authorities or of the estimating procedure; and, accordingly, I cannot assume them away.

It would be interesting to see what happens when these results, or the forms of the model, are employed in other, more completely identified models where the actions of the authorities might influence the results, as indeed, is intended. One of the advantages, perhaps the principal advantage of Equation (7), is that the tastes of the authorities are in a mathematical form especially designed to be used in other studies. It seems likely that the estimates of the demand for money, for one, might be influenced by alternative specifications of the authorities' taste function; and, of course, full econometric models might well include some cognizance of this factor as well as the structural factors emphasized in the Appendix.

APPENDIX

An explanation of the results

Actually, in deriving Equation (7), I have not illuminated the meaning of the coefficients there. In particular the revealed judgements of the authorities include certain structural parameters —that is to say Equation (7) (or its predecessors) is a 'reduced form' equation for which the structural model has not so far been made explicit. Let us tackle that job now; the model is adapted from that of John H. Wood.[11] We will not attempt to go back to the reaction model but will, instead, derive Equation (7) directly.

The British monetary authorities, one hopes, have a model of the British economy similar to the following. That is, it can be asserted that the authorities explain short run *changes* in the endogenous variables of the system in terms of three sets of exogenous and predetermined variables, as illustrated in Equation System (10); it is here given the *dimensions* of the problem in hand.

$$\begin{aligned}
dy_t &= \sum_{i=1}^{4} b_{iy}\, dM_{it} + \sum_{i=5}^{8} b_{iy}\, dO_{it-1} + \sum_{i=9}^{n} b_{iy}\, dE_{it} \\
dP_t &= \sum_{i=1}^{4} b_{ip}\, dM_{it} + \sum_{i=5}^{8} b_{ip}\, dO_{it-1} + \sum_{i=9}^{n} b_{ip}\, dE_{it} \\
dB_t &= \sum_{i=1}^{4} b_{ib}\, dM_{it} + \sum_{i=5}^{8} b_{ib}\, dO_{it-1} + \sum_{i=9}^{n} b_{ib}\, dE_{it} \\
dU_t &= \sum_{i=1}^{4} b_{iu}\, dM_{it} + \sum_{i=5}^{8} b_{iu}\, dO_{it-1} + \sum_{i=9}^{n} b_{iu}\, dE_{it}
\end{aligned} \qquad (10)$$

Now in each of the equations of this system, change in an endogenous variable (elsewhere called an approximate objective) is attributed by the authorities to three different influences. The variables denoted M_t are intermediate financial variables through which monetary policy operates; in Britain, a likely list includes the following: money stock, short term interest rate, liquid assets ratio, bank advances. The variables denoted dO_{it-1} are the lagged values of the endogenous variables; they are consequently assumed to be predetermined in this model. The last $n - 8$ variables in the authorities' system are exogenous variables; in this case they would include such things as autonomous investment and consumption,

[11] Wood, John H., 'A Model of Federal Reserve Behaviour', *in* Horwich, George (ed.), *Monetary Process and Policy: A Symposium* (Homewood, Illinois, 1967).

the real balance of trade, and, somewhat unrealistically, the effect of treasury policy in this system.[12]

Let us express this system in matrix notation, with the dimensions of the parameter matrices below them; the terms in first difference form are vectors of appropriate dimension; the dependent variables are now identified by the vector dO_t.

$$dO_t = \underset{4\times 4}{B_1} dM_t + \underset{4\times 4}{B_2} dO_{t-1} + \underset{4\times n-8}{B_3} dE_t \tag{11}$$

Now each of the ultimate instruments (I) in the authorities' system—Bank Rate, Special Deposits, hire purchase controls, and, let us add, policy directives—will be presumed to work through each of the intermediate variables (e.g., the money stock) in the system. We will continue to think in linear terms, and the result is Equation (12), in its matrix version.

$$dM_t = \underset{4\times 4}{F} dI_t \tag{12}$$

So far, all of this is *objective* information—that is to say, so far, we simply have a general model which we attribute to the monetary authorities.[13] The word objective was emphasized in the last sentence for we must recognize that the model is the monetary authorities' *view* of the working of the system; this, of course, is one of the weaknesses of the revealed preference approach—the authorities might be misinformed after all. Now we must have an equation describing their 'loss' function. Let us assume that the authorities minimize the following quadratic disutility function; the W_i are the authorities' 'values' in *weight* form, and the asterisk indicates *desired* changes of the objectives.

$$U_t = \sum_{i=1}^{4} W_i (dO^*_{it} - dO_{it})^2 \tag{13}$$

Let us expand Equation (13); the result is (14)

$$U_t = \sum_{i=1}^{4} W_i dO^{2*}_{ti} - 2 \sum_{i=1}^{4} W_i dO^*_{it} dO_{it} + \sum_{i=1}^{4} W_i dO^2_{it} \tag{14}$$

[12] This is unrealistic because monetary policy and fiscal policy are worked out jointly between the Bank of England, the Treasury, and the ruling political party whose neck, ultimately, is on the line.

[13] We really ought to introduce subjective constraints on the changes in the instruments (since an upward change of 10 per cent, from 7 to 17 per cent, of Bank Rate might easily bring down the Government). The immediate consequence would be to require more instruments than objectives, a matter which we will neglect here.

which is, in matrix form

$$U_t = dO_t'^* W dO_t^* - 2dO_t' W dO_t^* + dO_t' W dO_t \qquad (15)$$

In Equation (15), W is a 4×4 diagonal matrix of the original taste coefficients. We can now substitute (12) into (11) and the result into (15). We get Equation (16) consequently, where the terms in the square brackets are vectors of order 4×1.

$$U_t = dO_t^{*\prime} W dO_t^* - 2[B_1(F dI_t) + B_2 dO_{t-1} + B_3 dE_t]' W dO_t^* + [B_1(F dI_t) + B_2 dO_{t-1} + B_3 dE_t]' W [B_1(F dI_t) + B_2 dO_{t-1} + B_3 dE_t] \qquad (16)$$

Let us rewrite this equation, contracting the exogenous and predetermined parts into $B_{23} dE_t^*$, in order to achieve some economy. The result is Equation (17)

$$U_t = dO_t^{*\prime} W dO_t^* - 2[B_1 F dI_t + B_{23} dE_t^*]' W dO_t^* + [B_1 F dI_t + B_{23} dE_t^*]' W [B_1 F dI_t + B_{23} dE_t^*] \qquad (17)$$

To differentiate this with respect to dI—that is, in order to find the optimal strategy—we must expand the system, as in Equation (18); here we note that only four terms contain the instrument vector (dI_t).

$$U_t = dO_t^{*\prime} W dO_t^* - 2(B_1 F dI_t)' W dO_t^* - 2(B_{23} dE_t^*)' W dO_t^* + (B_1 F dI_t)' W (B_1 F dI_t) + (B_1 F dI_t)' W (B_{23} dE_t^*) + (B_{23} dE_t^*)' W (B_1 F dI_t) + (B_{23} dE_t^*)' W (B_{23} dE_t^*) \qquad (18)$$

The differentiation then produces Equation (19), directly.

$$\frac{\partial u_t}{\partial dI_t} = -2(B_1 F)' W dO_t^* + 2(B_1 F)' W (B_1 F dI_t) + 2(B_1 F)' W (B_{23} dE_t^*) \qquad (19)$$

Equation (19), you will note, is a generalized form of Equation (5); to proceed to a generalized trade-off function, like Equation (7), one would follow the same route as above, perhaps by direct estimation or, as I did, by averaging. The result of the exercise of this section, however, is to make it quite clear what is contained in the trade-off coefficients. That is to say, the following matrices were all included in 'judgements' in the earlier results of this paper.

F: a matrix of links between instruments and intermediate variables.

B_1: a matrix of links between intermediate variables and objectives.

W: the taste coefficients proper.

In other words, we have included the monetary authorities' view of the world along with their tastes. And, there is one other problem: the trade-off coefficients are going to be biased unless there is no influence from both the exogenous and the predetermined variables. The first problem is inescapable so we will have to live with it, and the second is an empirical problem which is outside the scope of the present enquiry.

31

BALANCE SHEET ANALYSIS OF MONEY AND THE CONCEPT OF DOMESTIC CREDIT EXPANSION

M. J. Artis *and* A. R. Nobay*

The latest Letter of Intent to the IMF describes government economic policy in terms of a new monetary concept—that of domestic credit expansion (DCE), for which a ceiling value of £400 million for the financial year has been fixed. The new concept seems to have deposed that of the money supply, for which the previous Letter of Intent had contained a commitment. But both Letters give targets for the 'borrowing requirement', which is, of course, negative—i.e. in surplus—in the latest Letter.

The three items—the DCE, increase in money supply, and the borrowing requirement—can be shown to be arithmetically related to one another within the framework of a balance sheet analysis involving the Government and banking sectors; and the first part of this section is taken up with a demonstration, essentially, of this point.

The important question raised by the Government's novel commitment to a ceiling figure for DCE is, however, that of the operational significance attached to the concept. Clearly, the IMF and the British Government regard the concept as being of some importance. But it is not so apparent why they should do so. Although the May issue of *Economic Trends* contained an article entitled 'Money supply and domestic credit', which was presumably designed to clarify this issue, the article was not in our view a

* Extract reprinted from Artis, M. J., and Nobay, A. R., 'Two aspects of the monetary debate', *National Institute Economic Review*, no. 49, August 1969, pp. 42–51, by permission of the authors and publisher. M. J. Artis is at the National Institute of Economic and Social Research and is editor of its *Economic Review*; A. R. Nobay is at Southampton University.

complete success. It leaves the reader unclear what the significance of the concept is supposed to be.

The second part of this section therefore looks at the possibilities. Of these, there are broadly two: firstly, DCE may be viewed as a kind of *ex ante* money supply, adapted for an open economy, and fundamental in just the way that the money supply is in simple quantity theory models, to the economy. Here some earlier studies published by the IMF are of assistance in clarifying the issues, and we summarise and criticise the analysis deployed in those studies. The other possibility is that DCE is to be regarded as no more than a useful summary statistic whose quick availability provides forecasters with another useful check on the progress of the economy and the validity of their predictions. In either case, we conclude, the lack of published information about the relevant relationships is most disquieting.

Balance sheet analysis

Regular presentation of a balance sheet analysis interlinking the Government and banking sectors began with the June 1966 issue of the Central Statistical Office's *Financial Statistics* under the title 'Factors determining changes in money supply'. It was based upon an analysis for earlier years published by Bell and Berman in the journal *Economica* [1]. It may, for convenience, be called the 'old presentation'; for with the June 1969 issue of *Financial Statistics*, a 'new' presentation appeared, recast so as to give prominence to the concept of DCE. The title of the new presentation was changed to 'Domestic credit expansion and changes in money supply'.

The old presentation: formation of the money supply

The basis for the old presentation of the 'factors determining changes in money supply' lies in the application to the banking system of the simple accounting concept of equality between assets and liabilities. Its application can be readily appreciated by imagining a very simple banking system. This would be one in which the only liabilities of banks are their deposits, where these deposits are held only by residents of the country concerned, and where the corresponding bank assets comprise only lending to the non-bank domestic sectors—the Government and the non-bank private sector. It is easy to see that in such a case a change in bank deposits must have an identical counterpart in a change in assets, that is, in lending to one or both of the non-bank domestic sectors. If then, money supply is defined as (non-bank) residents' holdings of bank deposits plus notes and coin,[1] it follows that a change in money supply can be arithmetically identified with a change in lending to the Government (by way of a change in non-banks residents' holdings of notes and coin and of bank lending to the Government) plus bank lending to the private (non-bank) sector. This simple identity is the core of the balance sheet analysis of changes in money supply; but in practice, because the actual banking system violates some of the assumptions made in the simple example set out above, the accounting identities can only be maintained by introducing various balancing allowances.[2]

Demonstrating the asset-counterpart of changes in money supply is an unexceptionable and straightforward exercise in accounting. The 'old' presentation, however, went one step further than this, adding a special 'twist' to the analysis. It invited the reader to start with the government borrowing requirement (net balance),[3] to deduct from this that part of the requirement met by non-bank sectors, to give as a residual the increase in bank holdings of government debt. By adding to this the increase in bank lending to other sectors a statement could be obtained of the increase in bank assets, which—apart from institutional complications[4]—would be equal to the change in residents' deposits; together with the change in non-bank holdings of notes and coin, this would give the change in money supply. Table I represents an attempt to set out the steps involved in the old presentation, noting the consolidations and adjustments incorporated in the published analysis.

[1] It is usual to exclude government holdings of bank deposits (and notes and coin) from the definition of money supply. We can suppose government bank deposits are held at a Central Bank, which is not part of the banking system for the purposes of this example. (As a matter of fact, the operational, official, British definition of money supply does not exclude government holdings of deposits with the commercial banks—which are quite substantial in absolute amount.)

[2] The main complications arise from the existence of bank liabilities other than deposits, from holdings of deposits by non-residents (and lending to non-residents) and holdings by banks of non-financial assets and liabilities of other banks.

[3] This can be described as the total amount the Government borrows *minus* any increase in the gold and foreign exchange reserves. An increase in the latter gives rise to a financing requirement (the reserves are 'bought' or 'sold' for sterling), but involves an addition of assets of an equal amount. It can be conveniently thought of as the change in central government financial indebtedness to all other sectors.

[4] As in footnote 2 above.

TABLE I

Basis for the 'old' presentation: 'factors determining changes in money supply'

(1) Total government borrowing
minus
(2) (i) Increase in government debt held by non-residents
(ii) Increase in notes and coin held by non-bank residents
(iii) Increase in other government debt held by non-bank residents
equals
(3) Increase in government debt held by banks
plus
(4) (i) Increase in bank lending to non-government domestic sectors[(a)]
(ii) Increase in bank lending to non-residents
(iii) Increase in holdings of bank shares
equals
(5) Increase in total bank financial assets[(b)]
plus
(6) Increase in total bank non-financial assets
equals
(7) Increase in total bank assets[(b)]
minus
(8) Increase in total non-deposit liabilities of banks
equals
(9) Increase in total net bank deposits
minus
(10) Increase in non-residents' holdings of net bank deposits
equals
(11) Increase in residents' net bank deposits

Increase in money supply = (11) + (2)(ii)

[(a)] Excluding direct loans to banks.
[(b)] Excluding items in transit and inter-bank deposits.

Notes: The table sets out the CSO presentation without the consolidations which are actually employed. In practice, the CSO presentation consolidates items (4)(ii) and (10) into a net figure, and similarly items (4)(iii), (6) and (8); it deducts from both (1) and (2)(i) the change in foreign exchange reserves, and does not give separate figures for (5) or (7) as a result of the consolidations described.

As the figures of lending and financial and total assets exclude items in transit and inter-bank deposits, the resultant figures of deposits are of net deposits. The split of net deposits between non-bank residents and non-residents, however, requires an allocation of items of transit between the two.

'Government' means 'central government' and includes the Issue Department of the Bank of England.

It is clear from this account that the table of 'factors determining changes in money supply' was essentially a piece of *ex post* accounting arithmetic. It did not, in itself, contain any behavioural 'message'; it did not, for example, show the relevance or otherwise of the controversy concerning the 'old' and 'new' orthodoxies about the means of controlling the supply of money. From this point of view, issue could be taken [5] with the title of the table, as promising something which an *ex post* accounting analysis could not provide. Furthermore, the 'twist' imparted to the analysis by the incorporation of the net borrowing requirement as, so to speak, its starting point, [6] probably encouraged the idea that the rate of advance in money supply was to be directly associated with the size of the borrowing requirement. [7]

An association between the government net borrowing requirement and the change in money supply might well be thought a good starter as an hypothesis, but as such it would imply judgements about the economic relationships involved, and about the policies pursued by the authorities.

[5] And was—see Sheppard ([4], p. 302, n. 2).

[6] The note to the table claimed that it 'provides a statistical framework for analysing the impact of government borrowing, the balance of payments and the transactions of the banking sector on the money supply'. In practice the balance of payments did not figure usefully in the tables as changes in reserves were consolidated in the figures for the government net balance and for the acquisition of government debt by the overseas sector. Details of the transactions of the banking system were limited to the overall change in bank lending to Government and to private sectors, and the change in deposits.

[7] On the occasion when an alternative presentation was given (as a supplementary table in the March 1968 issue of *Financial Statistics*), the footnotes offered a further hostage to the criticism that *ex post* accounting identities were being given a determining (i.e. *ex ante*) character. This alternative presentation was certainly cast in terms which suggested a primary determining role for the Government's net borrowing requirement and bank lending to the private sector. The reader was invited first to add together the central government net balance and bank lending to other sectors, then to deduct lending by the overseas sector to the Government and banking sector and lending by the non-bank domestic sector to the Government (excluding currency), so reaching a figure of the increase in money supply (subject to minor adjustments for institutional complications). A footnote remarked that 'In this presentation the acquisition of government debt by the banking system does not appear as it is regarded as a dependent variable'. It is in fact a residual in a set of accounting identities. More generally, Sheppard [4] has directed criticism of the formative article by Bell and Berman [1] (the basis for the old CSO presentation) primarily along the lines that they muddled, or tended to muddle, the *ex post* accounting 'explanation' of changes in money supply with *ex ante* economic and behavioural explanation.

TABLE 2

Redemption of marketable government and government-guaranteed debt, and the net borrowing requirement

£ million

	Redemptions[a]	Net borrowing requirement
1959	894	121
1960	648	307
1961	796	220
1962	1,241	−79
1963	994	148
1964	779	423
1965	1,100	597
1966	993	521
1967	1,600	1,134
1968	1,033	751

Source: CSO, *Financial Statistics*.
[a] Excluding sinking fund purchases.

The 'net balance' is in the first place a statement only of the change in net indebtedness of the Government—possibly a better term than borrowing 'requirement'—since despite its name the latter does not correspond to net sales of government debt, except when 'sales' are defined to include increases in cash claims on the Government, as in the form of notes and coin. It obviously does not itself convey anything about the composition of the net increase in government borrowing, either as between changes in holdings of debt by different sectors of the economy (including the overseas sector) or as between types of debt instrument. These are, however, of obvious significance in the determination of money supply. The monetary authorities can in principle choose, or not, to sell debt to the non-bank sector in amounts which exceed or fall short of the borrowing requirement.[8] Nor of course does the net balance in itself account in any

[8] The point has been made in this connection that the monetary authorities typically face in a given year the necessity to redeem for cash, or to convert, maturing loans in amounts often much larger than the net borrowing requirement (Table 2). In a *proximate* sense, the cash redemption of maturing issues does of course lead to increased bank deposits and money supply, and whether or not to offer conversion issues is certainly an important matter for decision by the

TABLE 3

Central government net borrowing requirement and the increase in money supply

£ million

	Central government borrowing requirement	Increase in money supply[a]
1954	4	268
1955	136	−248
1956	42	81
1957	170	228
1958	80	274
1959	121	578
1960	307	182
1961	220	262
1962	−79	311
1963	148	697
1964	423	597
1965	597	915
1966	521	536
1967	1,134	1,309
1968	751	986

Source: CSO, *Financial Statistics*; Bell and Berman [1], p. 153, Table 93.

[a] Figures may not be strictly comparable owing to changes in coverage.

way for changes in bank lending to other sectors of the economy, or for banks' decisions about the size of their portfolio of government securities. But it is precisely the province of monetary policy to influence these various elements; through appropriate use of monetary policy a given borrowing requirement can in principle be made compatible with any of a very large range of changes in money supply.

monetary authorities. However, since the terms of conversion must in general be consistent with the broad interest rate policy of the monetary authorities, it is really the latter which is important rather than whether particular issues are redeemed for cash or converted. However, the size of maturing issues is partly an index of the size of the total national debt outstanding; this may clearly be of great importance. The large size of the debt may imply that intervention to defend a particular short run interest policy on government stock has to be quantitatively large, involving large changes in money supply as a consequence.

Thus it is not a matter for surprise to find years in which the borrowing requirement and changes in money supply have different signs; nor that the coefficient of determination between the two works out at substantially less than 1.[9] Even if it were otherwise, the point still stands that the relationship of the net borrowing requirement to changes in money supply is one dependent upon a complex set of judgements about economic relationships and policy attitudes. These comments, however, concern only a possible misconception fostered by the arrangement and title of the old presentation. There is no need to labour them further. On the contrary, it should certainly be stated that the accounting framework employed (one among many possible) can be viewed in a scientifically positive way: as a quite useful receptacle for judgements about those relationships (and policies) which really do determine the change in money supply. It can, for example, be used as a forecasting framework.

The 'new' presentation: DCE

As an accounting concept, DCE can be described as just a further rearrangement of the basic monetary balance sheet underlying the 'old' presentation.[10]

It is simplest to begin by considering again a very simple banking system, abstracting from the institutional complications which exist in practice. We again suppose a banking system whose only liabilities are deposits, the only holders of which are residents, and which lends only to domestic borrowers; and we again define the money supply as deposits plus notes and coin. Then as before we start with a situation in which changes in money supply can be decomposed into changes in notes and coin, and changes in bank lending to Government and other sectors. A simple further elaboration is to imagine that the banking system is the custodian of the foreign reserves which it holds as assets. Then in any period, the change in bank assets can be split between lending to the Government and other sectors, and changes in reserves. So a change in money supply can be decomposed into a change in reserves, a

[9] Over the years 1954–68, for which the figures are shown in Table 3, the coefficient of determination (R^2) works out at 0·65.

[10] In fact, when the new presentation was introduced the compilers took the opportunity to elaborate further the basic balance sheet structure. Most important, they replaced the concept of the central government borrowing requirement by that of the public sector borrowing requirement, bringing in the nationalized industries and local authorities. This step could, of course, have been taken without introducing DCE at the same time.

change in other bank assets (lending) and a change in holdings of note and coin. Then one could, as a matter of definition, describe the change in money supply as being composed of two elements: (i) a change in reserves and (ii) a residual, which might be labelled 'changes in money of internal origin' or 'domestic credit expansion'. And 'domestic credit expansion' could be described as (i) the change in money supply less change in reserves or as (ii) the change in bank lending to private and government sectors plus change in non-bank lending to the Government by way of holdings of notes and coin. The two ways of measuring DCE—as a corrected money supply, or as a lending total, are of course identically equal.

The actual computation of DCE in the CSO presentation departs from the above in two main conceptual respects (there are a good many institutional complications). Firstly, the decision has been taken to treat an increase in government borrowing overseas as equivalent to a fall in reserves; and secondly, in practice, the CSO presentation emphasizes the definition of DCE as a lending total at the expense of its definition as corrected money supply.

The procedure of treating an increase in government borrowing overseas as a fall in reserves can be justified to the extent that such borrowing in fact occurs to prevent a fall in the recorded reserves, government borrowing and reserves together playing the role of residual finance in the balance of payments.[11]

Let us define $\Delta\bar{R}$, as the difference between any increase in reserves, ΔR, and any increase in government borrowing overseas ΔB^O; i.e.

$$\Delta\bar{R} = \Delta R - \Delta B^O$$

Then, breaking the change in money supply into its domestic component (DCE = ΔD) and its overseas component, $\Delta\bar{R}$, we have:

$$\Delta M = \Delta D + \Delta\bar{R}$$

whence

$$\Delta D = \Delta M - \Delta\bar{R} \qquad (1)$$

We can approach the change in money supply by a different route, namely that ΔM can be defined as the sum of the change in

[11] Cf. 'Money supply and domestic credit', *Economic Trends*, May 1969, p. xxii, n. 7, where this appears to be the justification offered. It would not be correct, however, to infer that all government borrowing overseas has this deliberate character, even though the 'objective effect' of any such borrowing is a *ceteris paribus* increase in reserves.

bank liabilities (deposits) ΔDP, and the change in notes and coin held by the public, ΔNC. Thus:

$$\Delta M = \Delta DP + \Delta NC \tag{2}$$

But ΔDP is equal, in this simplified model, to the sum of the changes in bank lending to the private sector ΔA^B and the public sector ΔB^B, so that:

$$\Delta M = \Delta A^B + \Delta B^B + \Delta NC \tag{3}$$

From (1) and (3) it follows that

$$\Delta D = \Delta A^B + \Delta B^B + \Delta NC - \Delta \bar{R} \tag{4}$$

which is to say that domestic credit expansion can be viewed as the change in the lending by the banking system to private and government sectors, together with lending by the non-bank public to the government sector by way of notes and coins plus the net change in lending to the Government by the overseas sector.

When the various institutional complications are introduced, the identities (1) and (4) can only be preserved by including appropriate adjustment items. The manner in which these have been introduced in the CSO presentation substantially preserves the 'purity' of the DCE definition set out in (4)—that is, as a sum of defined lending by defined sectors—but at the (inevitable) cost of infecting the definition set out in (1). This is not, perhaps, of very great importance. But it does have the effect that bank purchases of public (or private) sector debt which are underpinned by issues of bank capital are treated as increasing the domestic credit expansion, although such an operation is no different in principle from a purchase of debt by, say, a hire purchase finance company or any other non-bank domestic unit.[12]

The operational significance of DCE

As an accounting concept, DCE can be viewed either as a lending total or as a corrected money supply.

[12] That is, assuming that it is the character of the liability issued against the purchase of debt which is significant, and not the classification of the issuing institution as a bank or non-bank. It is—as suggested below in the text—the *monetary* character of bank liabilities which makes their lending significant in the theoretical framework of DCE.

DCE as a lending total

The *Economic Trends* article introducing the concept of DCE and, indeed, certain details of the accounting presentation of the concept (as already indicated) seem to place a rather heavy emphasis on DCE as a lending figure. Indeed, the very title of the concept seems to betray the same emphasis.

It is, however, impossible to see any operational significance in this view of the concept. As a total, it is simply the sum of arbitrarily defined lending by certain arbitrarily chosen sectors to other arbitrarily chosen sectors. It naturally provokes such questions as 'Why is not overseas lending to the private sector included?—or for that matter lending by, say, a hire purchase company to the Government in the form of treasury bills?' It is difficult to see any answer to such questions which does not bring in the significance of DCE as a corrected money supply concept. Here at least there is a coherent rationale available.

DCE as 'corrected' money supply

The treatment of DCE as a variant of the money supply 'corrected' for the balance of payments is a more promising one. In the first place monetary analysis, using the concept of DCE from this point of view, was fully worked out in two studies which appeared some time ago in IMF *Staff Papers*.[13] It is not necessary to assume that the DCE concept will be used in the conduct of British economic policy precisely in the manner indicated by those studies; but they do give us at least the opportunity of seeing how the concept might conceivably be used in the present British context. Secondly, although the article in *Economic Trends* does not leave any very clear and distinct impression as to how the authors consider the concept of DCE should be used, they do not rule out its use in this context. For example, it is claimed that 'as a matter of statistical presentation the total of DCE, unlike the money supply, is not directly affected by receipts for external transactions' and it is further noted that 'a change in receipts from external transactions . . . does not directly affect its total if other things remain equal'. And attention is drawn at one point to the 'relatively narrow range' within which the ratio of money GNP to money supply has been moving—a key point.[14]

[13] Polak, J. J. [**27**], and Polak, J. J., and Boissoneault, L. [**3**].

[14] But one which seems to be betrayed by a later footnote in the same article [16, p. xxii, n. 2].

The IMF analysis is a variant of the quantity theory approach, and like that approach assumes as a first approximation a constant (income) velocity of circulation. Unlike the quantity theory, however, it does not view the money supply as an appropriate variable to regard as exogenous, at least in an open economy. Rather, a change in the money supply is viewed as the sum of two components: domestic credit creation (ΔD), which is regarded as exogenous at least in a policy sense,[15] and the change in reserves (ΔR). The change in reserves is regarded as the difference between 'autonomous' items (for convenience, labelled 'exports'—X), and endogenous items ('imports'—I), which are systematically linked to the level of income. So the change in money supply in any period is the algebraic sum of two exogenous factors—domestic credit creation and 'exports' and one endogenous factor, 'imports'. If a constant (income) velocity of money is assumed, then we are at liberty to use a constant time period equal in length to the turnover period of money, with the convenience that in such a period, the change in money income is equal to the change in money supply.

In symbols, all we have so far stated is that:

$$\Delta M = \Delta D + \Delta R \tag{5}$$

$$\Delta R = X - I \tag{6}$$

$$\Delta Y = \Delta M \tag{7}$$

In addition, it is assumed that there is a simple proportional relationship between imports and income, as that:

$$I = mY \tag{8}$$

The end-result of this analysis is the proposition that an increase in domestic credit creation must lead, in equilibrium, to an equal rise in imports and fall of reserves. Equilibrium is reached where income is neither expanding nor contracting so that money supply also is static (from (7), $\Delta Y = \Delta M = 0$). If there is domestic credit creation at this point, stability of money supply can only be attained if reserves are falling (from (5), if $\Delta M = 0$, $\Delta D = -\Delta R$). If this equilibrium is disturbed by an increase in domestic credit expansion ($\Delta D'$) then a process of income expansion is set in train. The only

[15] Although ΔD, as recorded in time series might well appear to be endogenous—brought about, for example, by a rise in investment and increased demand for bank advances—it is still exogenous inasmuch as, *in principle*, the authorities could have prevented it.

'leakage' in this process is through imports; and the new position of equilibrium will not be attained until the extra autonomous 'injection' is balanced by extra 'leakage',[16] i.e. where the import level has increased sufficiently to balance the expansion in domestic credit. With exports at their original level, reserves will then be falling at a rate faster than in the original equilibrium position by the amount of the extra domestic credit creation.[17] The new equilibrium level of income will be $(1/m)\,\Delta D'$ higher, and the money supply will have increased by the same amount.[18]

The analysis can be turned into one which will allow quantification. In the article by Polak and Boissoneault **[3]** the authors first derived average figures for income velocity and for the marginal propensity to import, and then proceeded to calculate actual imports from knowledge of the autonomous factors ('exports' in the balance of payments and domestic credit expansion).[19] These calculations were carried out for 39 countries over a varying period of time, mostly about 18 years, using annual data. In a final stage of the analysis, allowance was made for the changes in velocity and in the import relationship, as a means of allocating the residuals between the calculated and actual imports to these two proximate causes.

The statistical study was not set out as a definitive test of the application of the model to any particular country, but rather as a test of its general applicability, and the results for the United Kingdom included on the study were certainly rather mixed.[20]

[16] The more familiar closed economy Keynesian case is where savings = investment.

[17] The new equilibrium situation is where $\Delta D' + \Delta D = -\Delta R$.

[18] Although at the new equilibrium ΔM will again be 0, the level of M will have been increased by the cumulative sum of the (diminishing) differences between ΔD and I in the interim periods before imports have attained their new equilibrium.

[19] As $\Delta M = \Delta D + X - I$ it follows that $\Delta D + X = \Delta M + I$ and it was in fact the statistical equivalent of the RHS of the latter equation that the authors employed as the sum of 'autonomous' factors. They noted in this connection that it might seem odd to make imports depend upon an expression for autonomous factors which itself includes imports. But, they argued, 'Imports have undone part of the effects of the autonomous increase in money; to get a proper measure of the autonomous expansionary factors, the money that was taken out by imports has to be added back to the observed increase in money' [op. cit., p. 352].

[20] The main results for the U.K. were set out in graphical form [op. cit., pp. 412–3] but a run of data was set out in a form suitable for replication of the calculations for part of the period covered. Results were given graphically for the years 1950–58; of these, results can be replicated from the data provided for the

We have not been able to carry out any further investigations of our own with the definition of DCE now officially sponsored, as the currently available run of figures is no more than for three years.

Put crudely, the IMF model asserts that an excessive DCE spills over into imports. It would seem to follow that there is a direct connection (via imports) between the size of DCE and the size of the balance of payments deficit or surplus.

If, indeed, it is the case that the importance currently attached to DCE by the Government is derived from a model of this type, then it is necessary to draw attention to certain weaknesses of it. They are of two kinds: the first concerns the stability of the imports/income and money/income relationships; the second concerns the question which variables should properly be treated as autonomous (exogenous) and which induced (endogenous).

In the theoretical exposition 'imports' are just those external transactions which are related to domestic income. When it comes to estimating the coefficients of the model one can only use some figure for actual imports of goods and services. The ratio of actual imports to actual GDP, whether measured in current prices or constant prices, is not constant. One has to ask, of course, just how stable 'stable' should be. Presumably sufficiently stable to give a good forecast in terms of the margins of error regarded as tolerable in economic forecasting. If this is the test, then the National Institute's recent experience—using rather more sophisticated forms of import equation—is not altogether encouraging.

It is often unclear what exactly is being claimed in the assertion that the income velocity of money is roughly constant. One possibility is to compare the magnitude of variations in velocity, translated into a money supply equivalent, with the actual changes in money supply. This has been done for recent years in the United Kingdom in Table 4. It can be seen that the monetary equivalent of velocity variations is often substantial in relation to money supply changes—sometimes larger and frequently of the opposite sign. Of course, the particular figures which emerge depend upon the choice of variable described as 'income', and 'money' and the period chosen. The notes to the table explain the particular choice of variables but a range of other choices with equal plausibility

years 1953–58. Replication of the calculations for these years indicates an average error of nearly 4 per cent (that is, averaging the unweighted sum of proportional errors without regard to sign) in the computation of yearly imports, and the error in the earlier years was very clearly much larger than this.

TABLE 4

Variations in the income velocity of circulation, 1963–68

(A) Annual figures

Year	(1) GNP at market prices £ million	(2) Money supply £ million	(3) Income velocity (3) = (1) ÷ (2)	(4) Percentage change in velocity % +/−	(5) Monetary equivalent of change in velocity £ million +/−	(6) Change in money supply £ million
1963	30,678	10,745	2·85	—	—	—
1964	33,296	11,426	2·91	+2·07	+222	+681
1965	35,734	12,165	2·94	+0·80	+91	+739
1966	37,942	12,974	2·92	−0·44	−53	+809
1967	39,710	13,759	2·89	−1·31	−170	+785
1968	42,424	15,091	2·81	−2·60	−357	+1,332

(B) Quarterly figures (seasonally adjusted)

Year and quarter		Monetary equivalent of change in velocity £ million +/−	Change in money supply £ million +/−	Year and quarter		Monetary equivalent of change in velocity £ million +/−	Change in money supply £ million +/−
1963	I	+383	+40	1966	I	−203	+323
	II	+303	+244		II	+156	+26
	III	−15	+106		III	+89	+140
	IV	+24	+295		IV	+157	+38
1964	I	−36	+82	1967	I	−58	+192
	II	+145	+166		II	−193	+278
	III	−153	+236		III	−305	+535
	IV	+193	+103		IV	−334	+281
1965	I	+5	+156	1968	I	+159	+361
	II	−101	+297		II	−287	+312
	III	+127	+184		III	+364	+103
	IV	−84	+261		IV	−24	+385

Source: CSO, *Financial Statistics*: *Economic Trends*.

Notes: As indicated in part (A) of the table, the monetary equivalent of the change in velocity is calculated by applying the percentage changes in velocity between two periods (years or quarters) to the money supply of the previous period. The money supply definition employed is the official one, and includes some changes in coverage. Seasonally adjusted levels of both GNP and money supply were estimated by the method of ratios to moving averages; the resultant series for the seasonally adjusted change in money supply differs from that given in *Financial Statistics*, where it is calculated independently of levels.

could have been made. The period 1963 to 1968 used in the tables is in general more favourable to the 'constant velocity' case than earlier periods, say the 1950s. But the figures shown in Table 4 could hardly be described as reassuring, since they suggest that a given change in money supply might be offset or effectively increased by as much as one quarter or one third by changes in velocity. Such variations in velocity are normally explicable in Keynesian terms and do not, in the framework of such models, necessarily imply that monetary policy is useless. The case seems to be otherwise for models which incorporate the assumption that the income velocity is constant.

The direct link between DCE and imports in the IMF model depends upon the constancy of two ratios. But as we have seen there can be a considerable variation in each ratio, which is not reassuring.

Finally the IMF analysis regards domestic credit expansion as exogenous, on the grounds that it is under the control of the monetary authorities. This characterization of DCE, whilst acceptable within the confines of a pure model, may be misleading in other contexts, and in two ways. First, it may be completely erroneous in the sense that the monetary authorities in fact simply do not have the degree of control required or implied. We have not inquired further into this in the current British context; but it may be hazarded that past statements by Bank of England spokesmen about the behaviour of the gilt-edged market (if they are a fair assessment) make the issue of control a more than nominal one. Secondly, the assumption of exogeneity of DCE may be confusing in statistical work; the problem here is that whilst the monetary authorities may have the ability to control DCE in (almost) whatever way they like, they may in practice have followed policies which make DCE statistically endogenous. Hence a study which shows a partial association between DCE and (say) imports may only prove that some third factor (income?)—given the policy actually followed by the authorities—determined both.

The Letter of Intent

The Letter of Intent, published on 24 June, stated that the Government's 'objectives and policies imply a domestic credit expansion' in the fiscal year 1969/70 of 'not more than £400 million'. It also stated the Government's intention to ensure that the quarterly course of domestic credit expansion was consistent with 'the intended result for the year as a whole, and to take action as appropriate to this end'.

There is no room for ambiguity about the fact that government policy is tied to a ceiling for DCE.[21] But there is a great deal of ambiguity about the precise nature of this commitment. In particular it is not clear what status the concept of DCE has either in forecasting or in policy-making. Two quite distinct and opposite possibilities may be envisaged; one is that the DCE figure is regarded purely as a passive indicator, and the other that it is regarded as a dominating influence upon the economy.

In the first case, DCE would be used simply as a check that an economic forecast made in some more elaborate way is working out as expected. The point is simply that monetary statistics become available very quickly whereas other statistics used in forecasting, e.g., industrial production or employment only become available after longer delays, in some cases of many months. When a forecast is made it is theoretically possible to work out from it what should be the future course of DCE and then to compare this with the actual movement of DCE, quarter by quarter as the monetary statistics come in. Thus 'an early warning' would be given that the economy was deviating from the forecast path. Economists and policy makers are always searching for a forecasting philosophers' stone of this kind. Bank clearings have been considered for this role and a certain amount of research has been conducted and published concerning the relationship between bank clearings and the rest of the economy. However as an early warning signal bank clearings had only rather a short run before it was found that they did not work very well. It is doubtful whether any one single and infallible indicator will ever be found. Meanwhile not much on this score can be said about DCE on its current definition until research is done to establish the reliability of its performance.

If, however, DCE were to be confined to this role of a mere signal, then whenever there was a departure of the actual DCE from the projected, one would not talk of taking steps to correct DCE itself so much as taking steps to correct those elements in the underlying forecast, e.g., consumption or investment, which were getting out of line. Yet the Letter of Intent gives the impression that the ceiling figure on DCE is in itself an important policy commitment; and the treatment the concept has been given is certainly

[21] We do not know what margin 'for contingencies' is allowed for by the ceiling—i.e. what central figure the authorities are working to.

disproportionate to that deserved by the discovery of another useful indicator for the forecaster's use. Rather, it would seem that DCE is being regarded, not just as an indicator, but as a dominating influence on the economy in its own right.

But the grounds on which such a view is held are not known. If we follow the lines of the IMF analysis DCE is seen as a kind of *ex ante* money supply, and can be incorporated in an interesting variant of the quantity theory of money. But if so it suffers from precisely the defects of that theory: money is regarded as important to the exclusion of other factors; the transmission mechanism is unclear; assumptions are involved which casual inspection reveals to be unjustified.

Whatever may be the case (and a 'mixed' view is possible), what is required and what is missing, is some detail—or even a sketch—of the relationships involved, and their goodness of fit, and the transmission mechanism which is thought to relate DCE to the economy. In the meantime, the impression has been given that the policy reaction to a tendency for DCE to exceed its ceiling will be increased monetary restrictiveness; which might or might not, be in fact appropriate.

One is forced to conclude that at best the new policy departure has not been justified by publication of the kind of information required. At worst it might involve a harmful gearing of policy to an irrelevant magnitude.

REFERENCES

[1] Bell, G. L., and Berman, L. S., 'Changes in the money supply in the United Kingdom 1954 to 1964', *Economica*, N.S., vol. 33, no. 130, May 1960.

[2] Polak, J. J., 'Monetary analysis of income formation and payments problems', IMF *Staff Papers*, November 1967.

[3] Polak, J. J., and Boissoneault, L., 'Monetary analysis of income and imports and its statistical operation', IMF *Staff Papers*, April 1960.

[4] Sheppard, D. K., 'Changes in the money supply in the United Kingdom, 1954 to 1964: A comment', *Economica*, N.S., vol. 35, no. 139, August, 1968.

32

MONETARY MANAGEMENT IN THE UNITED KINGDOM

[Text of a speech by the Governor of the Bank of England*]

Introduction

This evening I want to say something about the operation of monetary policy in Britain and its place in economic management as a whole. Since the war all governments of the United Kingdom have accepted responsibility for aiming to achieve full employment, growth, relatively stable prices and external balance. Monetary policy has an inescapable part to play in pursuit of these aims. Whatever its stance it will have implications of some sort for demand and prices and the balance of payments. However, it is only one of several levers which policy-makers may pull. Policies adopted in other fields—fiscal policy especially—will affect the contribution to be made by monetary policy and can either ease or complicate its task.

The conduct of monetary policy is never a simple matter. Our understanding of the links between the financial world on the one hand and the real world of output and spending on the other is far from perfect. There is a wide divergence of view about how effective monetary policy is in influencing spending and through what particular channels it should primarily aim to operate. A further complication lies in its potentially strong impact on international capital flows, which can undermine the achievement of its own internal objectives as well as make for difficulties in the management of our foreign exchange reserves.

* Text of the Jane Hodge Memorial Lecture delivered by the Governor of the Bank of England at the University of Wales, Institute of Science and Technology, on 7 December 1970. Reprinted from the *Bank of England Quarterly Bulletin*, vol. 11, no. 1, March 1971, pp. 37–47.

However, whatever may be the possibilities or the difficulties of operating monetary policy, I want to stress one very important point—often neglected or glossed over in abstract discussion. This is that monetary policy is conducted within a particular framework of institutions and markets. This framework provides opportunities, of course, but it also creates constraints. It is an important responsibility of the central bank to foster the growth and efficiency of the financial system as a whole; and its aims in these directions may, from time to time, clash with the immediate goals of monetary policy. From this potential clash there arises a rather wider problem of monetary management.

Deposit banks

For these reasons, I want to begin my survey of monetary management by looking at the institutional structure. To do this thoroughly would, of course, mean casting my net very wide. The range of institutions and activities which can be called financial and which are in one way or another affected by monetary policy is enormous. To avoid making inordinate claims on your time I shall therefore concentrate on the central part of our financial system—and that part over which the Bank of England has most direct influence—the banking system.

It was not so many years ago that domestic banking in this country was conducted virtually entirely by the deposit banks; that is, primarily, the London clearing banks. The asset structure of these banks is largely conditioned by the part that they have historically played in operating the money transmission service of the country; and this has meant that they have developed broadly similar asset portfolios and have come to observe similar minimum ratios for cash and liquid assets. The liquidity ratio was formalized as an aid to credit control when monetary policy entered a more active phase in 1951. In addition the rates which the clearing banks pay on deposit accounts and charge to borrowers vary fairly closely in line with Bank rate.

Cash ratio

These conventions should enable the authorities not only to regulate the cost of the banks' lending but also, in principle, to control its availability by influencing the total of their deposits and of their cash and liquid assets through open-market operations. In practice no attempt has been made to use the cash ratio for this purpose. To do so would have meant making major institutional changes in the system. It would also have been likely to produce large fluctuations in short-term interest rates with unwelcome consequences not merely for the money markets, but for many areas (such as the housing mortgage markets) of wider economic significance. These considerations have led the authorities to continue with the present system under which Treasury bills are always interchangeable with cash through the mechanism of the discount market. In this way dislocations which the uneven pattern of Exchequer spending and receipts might otherwise cause in monetary conditions are smoothed out, while the ready marketability of Treasury bills as the residual source of government finance is ensured. This arrangement, coupled with the use of Bank rate, has given the authorities control over most domestic short-term interest rates.

Liquidity ratio

Nor has the liquid assets ratio been a reliable fulcrum for regulating the expansion of the clearing banks' lending. For many years after the war this was not surprising. The limiting outlets for private spending during the war and the pressing need of the Government for finance had made the banks little more than intermediaries for channelling savings into official debt. In 1945 the clearing banks' advances amounted to only 17 per cent of their gross deposits and throughout the fifties there was no choice but direct restrictions when their lending had to be restrained. The real transformation in their balance sheets came during the boom at the end of that decade; and when the economy entered its next phase of expansion in 1963, there was some doubt whether their liquid assets base would be able to support the growth of credit that would be needed. At that time the ratio was lowered from 30 to 28 per cent, still somewhat higher perhaps than would have been necessary on prudential grounds alone. It was then too that the clearers' conventions on interest rates again became a live issue. In the event by the mid-sixties their advances had risen to 50 per cent of deposits while their holdings of gilt-edged had fallen to less than 12 per cent.

This structure has changed little since then and there is no question that at times during the last dozen years the clearing banks' credit base has been under pressure. Even so their holdings of gilt-edged have generally provided them with sufficient latitude to make short-run adjustments. Almost throughout the post-war period, until very recently, the Exchequer was adding, often on a substantial scale, to its domestic borrowing rather than reducing it; and this made it more difficult to contain the banks' lending by debt management alone.

Special deposits

Because of the difficulty of bearing on the credit base with any precision through open-market operations alone, the possibility of introducing a variable liquidity ratio was explored in the late fifties. The outcome, in 1958, was the Special Deposit scheme, which is essentially similar to a variable liquidity ratio.

While a call for Special Deposits can affect the attitudes of the banks to new lending straight away, there is likely to be some delay before the full effect is seen on the level of advances. In the meantime, and depending on their liquidity position, the banks may sell some investments. But it is open to the authorities—and the banks understand this—to ensure that the whole adjustment by the banks is not completed by such sales of gilts. The initial call for Special Deposits can be supplemented by open-market operations, by action on interest rates or, in due course, by further calls for Special Deposits.

Other banks

So far I have been talking of the deposit banks. Only some dozen years ago the other banks in London accounted for little more than 10 per cent of the deposits held with the banking sector as a whole. Since then—and excluding funds placed among themselves in the inter-bank market—their deposits have increased twenty times to over £17,000 million. This phenomenal expansion came after the widespread move to the convertibility of currencies at the end of 1958 and has been associated with the growth of the Euro-dollar market. But, although the bulk of this business is in foreign currencies, these banks have increasingly attracted sterling deposits from British companies and expanded their sterling lending. Their resident sterling deposits, other than on inter-bank account, are now approaching £3,000 million. This represents around 20 per cent of such deposits with the whole banking sector.

These banks are not a homogeneous group. There are the accepting houses, for example; there are head offices of British banks with extensive branch networks abroad; there is an ever-growing number of branches and subsidiaries of foreign banks; and, a most interesting development, there are the subsidiaries of the clearing banks themselves.

I sometimes feel that the clearing banks attract more than their fair share of criticism for being—it is alleged—unadventurous and slow to react to a changing world. Yet from small beginnings the clearing banks' subsidiaries have grown rapidly to account for well over 10 per cent of deposits with these 'other' banks as a whole. If we consider sterling business only, their performance has been even more striking. In the past five years the clearing banks' subsidiaries have increased their sterling resources fivefold; and in the course of doing so they have gained over one third of all the growth in the sterling resources of these 'other' banks as a group. I wonder whether those who like to characterize the clearing banks as sleeping giants are really aware of all these developments.

The heavy involvement of the 'other' banks in both sterling and foreign currency deposit taking carries implications for the play between domestic and external interest rates and for international capital flows. Local authorities look to these banks for temporary money and the price asked will at times be strongly influenced by Euro-dollar rates and by the cost of obtaining forward cover in the foreign exchange market. The relationship between rates in the conventional money market, which are effectively determined by the authorities, and rates in the relatively new parallel markets, where our influence is less direct, is one of the problems currently concerning us.

I have already referred to the common code and liquidity conventions observed by the deposit banks. In general, the growing number of 'other' banks observe no such conventions: considerations of banking prudence are largely satisfied by ensuring a broad correspondence between the maturity of assets and the maturity of liabilities. The relatively new and efficient markets in local authority and inter-bank debt, to which I have already referred, enable these banks to adjust their balance sheets to this end very flexibly. The structure of these banks' assets varies very widely, and their liquidity ratios, calculated on almost any basis, range from the very small to the very large indeed.

This diversity of asset structure underlines the problem which has faced us in recent years of devising an effective and reasonably equitable system of credit control, based on liquidity or other asset ratios. In 1967 a scheme of Cash Deposits—analogous to Special Deposits, but designed to bear on earnings as well as liquidity—was worked out for periods of less severe restraint. But circumstances have not yet allowed us to activate this particular scheme. We have been compelled to resort to ceiling controls for relatively prolonged periods—despite their manifest disadvantages.

Lending ceilings

It may seem paradoxical that direct requests should have been used more, rather than less, intensively once the deposit banks' excess liquidity had run off and the Special Deposits scheme had been set up. The reason lies in the circumstances of the sixties, which allowed so little leeway for policy. The external situation was a constant and pressing source of anxiety. Confidence was generally weak, and domestic demand had to be held back both before and after devaluation to encourage the transfer of resources into exports, and to limit imports. Broadly speaking, lending ceilings and guidelines have been in force since 1965. These have applied to lending on commercial bills as well as advances. The leading hire purchase finance houses have been subject to the same restrictions as the banks; and other financial institutions have been asked to bear the objectives of policy closely in mind.

The advantages of ceiling controls are clear enough. They are unequivocal, both for the banks and their customers; their coverage can be extended in equity to competing financial institutions; and they work quickly. But their drawbacks are not less obvious, notably in checking competition and innovation within the banking sector and encouraging the diversion of credit flows through other channels.

All this amounts to saying that quantitative restrictions should be used only when severe restraint is necessary. We are far from happy that we have had to use them so severely and for so long, not only because of their inherent disadvantages but also because of the strain which their prolonged use places upon the very happy cooperative—as distinct from legalistic—relationship which exists in this country between the central bank and the commercial banks. I am a great believer in our system of voluntary cooperation, in which both sides recognize their common interest in the successful development of the economy. And I believe that it is an economical and efficient system in which one side is not continually looking for loopholes in the control and the other side continually trying to plug them. For all that, the longer ceiling restrictions are in force, the greater the strain upon the system. We must all hope that an improvement in our economic conditions such as would permit us to move towards a less restrictive régime will not be too long delayed.

Changing views of monetary policy

From my remarks so far it may be seen that the operation of monetary policy in Britain has developed in a very pragmatic way. The environment conditions policy; and the environment has a habit of changing. So too does opinion about the importance of monetary policy in regulating demand and about the way in which it makes its impact. And recent discussion on these counts has been very lively indeed.

At the end of the war it was widely believed that interest rates should be kept low to finance reconstruction as well as to ease the servicing of a greatly increased national debt; and it was some while before it was universally accepted that a slump was not after all inevitable. A fairly comprehensive system of physical controls had been maintained to suppress inflation; and the doctrines of Keynes, at least as interpreted by his followers—it is interesting to speculate on what Keynes himself would have prescribed had he lived to see the shape of the post-war world—had led to a totally new emphasis on fiscal policy. The active drive for cheap money was succeeded by a period in which monetary policy went into limbo. There was general scepticism about its relevance.

The prolongation of controls, however, and the austere budgetary strategy of the time began to generate a reaction in which rising prices and the vulnerability of the reserves also played a part. At the end of 1951 monetary policy again entered an active phase. Having been at 2 per cent almost constantly since 1932, Bank rate was to be varied forty times in the next nineteen years. The changed economic climate and the dismantling of physical controls made it essential to revive monetary policy, but undoubtedly too much was expected of it in the early fifties. Although it has the great advantage over fiscal policy that it can be operated and modified on a day-to-day basis, it is by no means as smooth, speedy or flexible in its effects as is often assumed. As its limitations became more apparent, the need was felt for a reappraisal; and this led to the appointment of the Radcliffe Committee.

You will recall the main lines along which that Committee reported in 1959. They saw changes in interest rates as having a limited and slow effect on capital spending but a potentially significant impact on lending by financial institutions. The money supply was only part of a wider concept of liquidity. People could realize assets, or borrow, as well as run down money balances; and their willingness to do so would be conditioned by prospective income flows. It was on the structure of interest rates therefore that policy should act, chiefly to restrict the availability of credit. In line with this thinking, bank deposits were less important than bank advances. This qualified view of monetary policy, and of the money supply in particular, was to be strongly contested. Even before the Committee was appointed, there had been academic reaction across the Atlantic to the tendency to relegate money to a minor role. In the following years, first in the United States and more recently in this country the monetarist school of thought steadily gained ground.

Monetarist controversy

It is easy to caricature the opposing theories, for some extreme positions have been taken; but it is fair to add that nowadays there are plenty of intermediate positions too. In simplified terms, those who attach only minor importance to the money supply regard financial assets as close substitutes for money, and real assets as a rather different category. On this view a change in the money stock will be associated with only a relatively slight shift in interest rates and people will be content to hold less money in relation to incomes. There will be some effects on spending—through changes in the cost of capital, in the availability of credit and in existing wealth; but the impact will not be pronounced and could more certainly be achieved by acting directly on interest rates in the first place.

On the other hand, those who attach major importance to the money supply see holdings of money as a substitute for a broader range of both financial and real assets, on which the return cannot be generalized. On this view a change in money balances will be associated with erratic movements in interest rates and will then largely be made good by adjustments in spending, for people will be reluctant to hold less money in relation to incomes. In this case policy could exert a strong influence on demand by acting directly on the money supply.

Much work—including some in the Economic Section of the Bank—has been done to test these theories by trying to establish, through associations between the money stock and interest rates, whether or not money and financial assets are in fact close substitutes. One major difficulty is that changes in interest rates are undoubtedly coloured by expectations about the future course both of the rates themselves and of price inflation. The real, as distinct from the nominal, rates of interest that may be in people's minds when they decide to spend or invest cannot be at all closely estimated statistically.

Subject to this qualification, the evidence supports neither extreme. It suggests that changes in the amount of money may have some consequences for money incomes but that in the short run the relationship is neither strong nor predictable. Although the association between changes in money stock and money incomes is undoubtedly strong in the long run, so that movements in the money stock may be useful as an indicator of movements in income, this fact tells us nothing about causation. In particular, since the authorities have not operated in a strictly monetarist way over the past twenty years but have broadly accommodated the rising demand for money balances as incomes rose, statistical associations derived from this period cannot tell us what would happen if policies were radically different.

Official attitudes to monetary policy

Yet, though the argument has not yet been conclusive, it has already served a useful purpose in provoking a general reappraisal of attitudes. The liabilities of the banks have always been significant for policy, of course, since deposits are a key factor in the determination of advances; and it is important that this aspect should not be neglected even if lending ceilings are in force. In recent years, however, we have certainly given more attention than formerly to the growth of monetary aggregates in evaluating policy. These include not only the money supply but also what has come to be known as D.C.E., or domestic credit expansion. Movements in the money supply are influenced among other things by the balance of payments and by inflows and outflows of foreign funds. D.C.E. is some measure—in an arithmetical sense—of the internal factors associated with changes in the money stock, before these are overlaid by external influences. It is thus, in an open economy like ours, sometimes a more useful indicator than the money supply.

But, although there has been some shift of emphasis in recent years, this should be seen in perspective. I certainly accept that such aggregates as the money supply and D.C.E. can be useful indicators of monetary conditions and the impact of policy generally. In particular, it is not a simple matter in an inflationary age to judge the level of interest rates most appropriate to the thrust of policy; and the growth of the monetary aggregates may offer some guidance in this respect. But to focus solely on the money supply or D.C.E. among the financial, let alone the economic, variables is not enough. It is essential to the understanding of monetary processes and their implications to look much more widely at the stocks of financial assets held throughout the financial sector—and indeed throughout the economy as a whole—and at the financial flows between all the major sectors. We have been concentrating much effort on this in the Bank and shall continue to do so.

Gilt-edged market

In short, while we are keeping a close watch on developments in the monetary aggregates, we are looking at them as guidelines for overall policy rather than as targets. I doubt whether it would be possible to force through a predetermined volume of sales even at the cost of marked instability in interest rates; but even if it were possible, to attempt it would in many circumstances be both damaging and purposeless. For expectations play a large and unpredictable role in investors' decisions. Even when the Government is running a large revenue surplus, as at present, maturities of nearly £2,000 million a year require careful handling if adequate refinance is to be forthcoming. By the same token it would be mistaken to put much weight on short-term deviations in the path of the money supply or D.C.E., which can reflect not only these factors but also bunching in bank lending as well as purely random influences.

There has been much argument about our tactics in the gilt-edged market. There is no need, I think, to go over all the ground here. I suspect, however, that people do not always make a clear distinction between our tactics and our ends. Apart from the needs of government finance, our main end is to achieve the degree of monetary restraint judged to be appropriate to the economic situation and the overall direction of policy. Any particular degree of restraint in any particular circumstances will involve a certain level and pattern of interest rates which will have to be accepted. The burden of high interest rates on the Exchequer and balance of payments, though always a consideration, is not a foremost one. Rising nominal rates can often be illusory when seen in real terms; and to hold rates artificially low can only create a consistently weak market and lead to steady monetization of the debt. It is this last consideration which has perhaps become more important in our minds recently as inflation has accelerated. Consequently unprecedentedly high nominal rates have seemed appropriate and our tactics in market management have become more flexible so that the market has been allowed to make sharper adjustments than in the past.

While we at the Bank naturally do not mind constructive and well-informed criticism of our market tactics—indeed we welcome it if it can help us towards improving the way we do our job—there is, I think, a real danger in much of the argument and criticism that is actually deployed. Many people apparently believe, or appear to believe, that a purely tactical change in the relatively arcane sphere of operations in the gilt-edged market can magically and painlessly do wonders for the real economy. It cannot be emphasized too strongly or too often that attacking a severe inflation simply by holding down the growth of the money supply means reducing real activity: or in more homely terms a lot of bankruptcies and unemployment. Thus the proper questions for discussion in a situation such as the present are first how much reduction in real activity is appropriate; and secondly how much weight should be placed on monetary policy in achieving it?

But in general it should be recognized that excessive reliance on monetary policy is bound to place severe strains on financial markets and the financial position of companies and may have serious effects on the nation's productive investment and housebuilding. At the same time it will have implications for external capital flows; and this raises doubt about how far monetary policy can in any case be pushed in an open economy without frustrating, at least in part, the authorities' objectives both domestically and externally.

External aspects

Sterling, like all currencies which are used internationally, is sensitive to capital flows, whether arising out of changes in yield differentials or from speculation on exchange rate adjustments. Exchange controls have limited the movement of resident funds; but leads and lags, transfers over intra-company accounts and switching by the banks in London are all important potential channels for capital movements. Meanwhile the growth of the Euro-dollar market has seen a vast increase over recent years in the volume and mobility of international funds.

It is true that movements of interest sensitive funds will tend to slow down once investors have adjusted their portfolios and, in the case of covered transactions, as the forward rate reacts; but an attempt to offset them by further monetary action can renew the process. In Britain there has on the whole been little conflict of this kind since the war. During the sixties, for instance, when economic conditions generally pointed to the maintenance of high interest rates, arbitrage movements were often submerged by speculative flows which in themselves worked to tighten liquidity. But the dilemma has not been uncommon abroad; and it is one with which in future we may have to reckon ourselves now that the balance of payments is on a sounder basis.

Speculative flows present a special problem. There are a variety of techniques that can be used in an attempt to discourage arbitrage flows. These include attempting to change the relationship between short and long-term interest rates; intervention in the forward market; and the kind of specific measures applied by Germany and Switzerland in the face of speculative movements during the sixties. In practice, however, it is not simple to sustain an artificial relationship between short and long rates. Nor is it necessarily a straightforward matter to identify the nature of capital flows and to determine whether they would be susceptible to intervention in the forward market. Yet, once committed, it is impossible to withdraw from the market without intensifying speculation if the judgement should prove wrong.

As banks and corporations become more internationally-minded and sophisticated in their financial operations, the difficulties of conducting monetary policy in an open economy are not going to diminish. Recent years have underlined the pervasive influence, largely transmitted through the Euro-dollar market, that credit conditions in the United States can have elsewhere in the world. For all these reasons we shall have to think hard over the next few years about the effects of our monetary policies on the rest of the world and the limitations imposed on us by the monetary policies of other important countries. It will be important to develop further the international cooperation and interdependence which has already been taken further than many would have thought possible a generation ago.

Forward view

I have tried to give a broad survey of the problems and possibilities of monetary management in Britain in the changing environment of the past twenty-five years. Before concluding, I should like to take a brief look forward.

The most pressing economic problem, not only for this country but in virtually all the major industrialized nations in the years ahead, is likely to be that of cost inflation. Much thought and discussion about this problem will be necessary, not merely among policy-makers, but among all the elements and individuals of our societies. Whatever role is assigned to monetary policy, there will doubtless be need to evolve our techniques and our thinking as we have done in the past. One obvious example of the necessity to adjust which has already made itself felt is the importance of distinguishing between nominal and real rates of interest.

Whatever our success in coping with inflation, the familiar problems of demand management will obviously continue with us. Here, to the extent that the financial position of the public sector remains under firm control and the balance of payments remains in surplus (and in my belief these two areas are very closely related), the strains on monetary policy and the institutional framework in which it operates could be significantly eased.

If this should prove to be the case, we may be able to make more progress with an aspect of monetary management to which I referred at the beginning of my talk, fostering the growth of an efficient and competitive financial system. As I have emphasized, our aims in this direction have in recent years been frequently in conflict with the need to maintain strict control over bank lending. It is true that, despite the heavy and unwelcome quantitative controls which we have imposed, the banking world has certainly not ceased to evolve. I have referred to the rapid growth of the subsidiaries of the clearing banks and of many other forms of British and foreign banks; and to the growth and development of new markets both in sterling and foreign currency. Individual banks have extended the range of their services in many ways and, by merging among themselves and forming international ties, have been able to match the financial needs of ever-growing industrial groupings and multi-national concerns.

I have no doubt that the banks will want to innovate further and in all sorts of ways. The clearers are experimenting rather more with term loans, for example, which afford them closer control over their advances. They recently increased the margin between their lending rates and Bank rate; and it may be that they will want to widen it further, or change their practices on interest rates completely. Developments of these kinds could lead to some breaking down of the line between the deposit banks and that other very heterogeneous group which, for want of a better term, we call simply the 'other' banks. In these circumstances credit allocation could come to be determined more by price than by physical rationing throughout the banking sector.

The way in which the banking system evolves will be conditioned by credit control, and is bound to have implications for credit control. Some developments could make life easier, others could complicate it. In principle it is important that control should not be imposed and stifle innovation; but rather should allow innovation to take place and then adapt to it. We may hope that in the fullness of time a greater use of such mechanisms as Special and Cash Deposits, buttressed perhaps by the acceptance of greater variability of short-term interest rates, could lead to a more flexible framework for monetary management.

33

CHRONOLOGY OF MONETARY POLICY ACTIONS: 1960–1970[1]

DATE	INSTRUMENT	DETAILS[2]
1960		
21 January	Bank rate raised by 1 per cent	New rate: 5 per cent
28 April	(i) Hire purchase controls re-introduced	10 or 20 per cent minimum down payments; 2 years' maximum repayment period
	(ii) Special Deposits called for	1 per cent of gross deposits from London Clearing Banks; ½ per cent from Scottish Banks
	(iii) Other groups of banks informed of call for Special Deposits and made aware of policy to restrain lending	
23 June	(i) Bank rate raised by 1 per cent	New rate: 6 per cent
	(ii) Special Deposits called for	1 per cent of gross deposits from London Clearing Banks; ½ per cent from Scottish Banks
27 October	Bank rate reduced by ½ per cent	New rate: 5½ per cent
8 December	Bank rate reduced by ½ per cent	New rate: 5 per cent
1961		
19 January	Hire purchase controls relaxed	Maximum repayment period extended from 24 to 36 months
25 July	(i) Bank rate raised by 2 per cent	New rate: 7 per cent
	(ii) Special Deposits called for	1 per cent of gross deposits from London Clearing Banks; ½ per cent from Scottish Banks
	(iii) Bank of England requests reduction in rate of growth of advances, with discrimination in favour of exports and against advances for personal consumption, hire purchase, and	Circularized institutions include: London Clearing and Scottish banks; Association of Overseas Banks Accepting Houses Committee and other banks; the Finance Houses and

DATE	INSTRUMENT	DETAILS[2]
1961		
25 July	speculative building. Restraint of advances is not to be offset by lending on commercial bills	Industrial Bankers' Associations; the British Insurance Association[3]
5 October	Bank rate reduced by ½ per cent	New rate: 6½ per cent
2 November	Bank rate reduced by ½ per cent	New rate: 6 per cent
1962		
8 March	Bank rate reduced by ½ per cent	New rate: 5½ per cent
22 March	Bank rate reduced by ½ per cent	New rate: 5 per cent
26 April	Bank rate reduced by ½ per cent	New rate: 4½ per cent
31 May	(i) Release of Special Deposits	1 per cent of gross deposits to London Clearing Banks; ½ per cent to Scottish Banks
	(ii) Some relaxation of advances requests; qualitative discrimination re-emphasized	Institutions circularized those receiving the original request for restraint on 25 July 1961
4 June	Hire purchase controls relaxed	Minimum down payment required reduced to 10 per cent for all goods except cars (which remained at 20 per cent)
27 September	Release of Special Deposits	1 per cent of gross deposits to London Clearing Banks; ½ per cent to Scottish Banks
4 October	Requests for credit restraint lifted	
29 November	Release of Special Deposits	1 per cent of gross deposits to London Clearing Banks; ½ per cent to Scottish Banks
1963		
3 January	Bank rate reduced by ½ per cent	New rate: 4 per cent
16 October	Minimum liquid assets ratio of the London Clearing Banks reduced from 30 to 28 per cent	First cast as a temporary measure for the period to April 1964, then extended indefinitely
1964		
27 February	Bank rate raised by 1 per cent	New rate: 5 per cent
July	Hire purchase controls relaxed	Minimum down payment on shop and office furniture down from 20 to 10 per cent
23 November	Bank rate raised by 2 per cent	New rate: 7 per cent. New rate announced on a Monday
8 December	Bank of England requests reduction in rate of increase of advances other than those for exports and investment	Circularized institutions include: London Clearing Banks; British Insurance Association; Building Societies Association;

DATE	INSTRUMENT	DETAILS[2]
1694		
8 December		Hire purchase organizations, and National Association of Pension Funds
1965		
29 April	Special Deposits called for	1 per cent of gross deposits from London Clearing Banks; ½ per cent from Scottish Banks
5 May	Bank of England re-emphasizes the discrimination required in lending; lending by way of advances, acceptances and commercial bills restricted until 31 March 1966, to a level not more than 5 per cent above March 1965 figures	Circularized institutions include all those receiving the request for restraint on 8 December 1964, and additionally the London Discount Market Association and Discount Houses not members of that Association
3 June	(i) Bank rate reduced by 1 per cent	New rate: 6 per cent
	(ii) Hire purchase controls tightened	Minimum down payment raised to 15 per cent (from 10 per cent) on most goods, to 25 per cent (from 20 per cent) on cars
27 July	(i) Hire purchase controls tightened	Maximum repayment period reduced to 30 months
	(ii) Bank of England re-emphasizes need for restraint and discrimination in lending, to favour exports	Main banking organizations circularized
1966		
1 February	Bank of England requests that existing limits on lending be retained beyond 31 March, until further review	All organizations included in the request of May 1965 circularized
7 February	Hire purchase controls tightened	Minimum down payment on most goods raised to 25 per cent; maximum repayment period reduced to 24 months (27 months for cars)
12 July	Bank of England again renews lending limits	
14 July	(i) Bank rate raised by 1 per cent	New rate: 7 per cent
	(ii) Special Deposits called for	1 per cent of gross deposits from the London Clearing Banks;

DATE	INSTRUMENT	DETAILS[2]
1966		
14 July		½ per cent from the Scottish Banks
	(iii) Hire purchase controls tightened	Minimum down payment on cars increased from 25 to 40 per cent, on furniture from 15 to 20 per cent; and on other durables from 25 to 33⅓ per cent. The repayment period reduced to 24 months for cars and furniture
9 August 1 November	Banks reminded of priorities	
1967		
26 January	Bank rate reduced by ½ per cent	New rate: 6½ per cent
16 March	Bank rate reduced by ½ per cent	New rate: 6 per cent
11 April	(i) Credit limits for lending by London Clearing Banks and Scottish Banks removed; guidance on direction of lending restated	Special Deposit calls to be regarded in future as routine policy device (announced in Budget speech)
	(ii) Hire purchase terms on motor cycles relaxed	Minimum down payment on motor cycles reduced to 25 per cent (from 40 per cent), maximum repayment period lengthened to 27 months (from 24 months)
4 May	Bank rate reduced by ½ per cent	New rate: 5½ per cent
7 June	Hire purchase controls relaxed	Minimum down payment on cars reduced from 40 to 30 per cent, maximum repayment period lengthened from 24 to 30 months
29 August	Hire purchase controls relaxed	Minimum down payments reduced from 30 to 25 per cent for cars; from 20 to 15 per cent for furniture; from 33⅓ to 25 per cent for appliances. Maximum repayment period lengthened from 24 to 30 months for furniture and appliances; from 30 to 36 months for cars; from 27 to 36 months for motor cycles
19 October	Bank rate raised by ½ per cent	New rate 6 per cent
9 November	Bank rate raised by ½ per cent	New rate 6½ per cent

DATE	INSTRUMENT	DETAILS[2]
1967		
18 November	(i) Bank rate raised by 1½ per cent	New rate 8 per cent
	(ii) Banks asked to impose a ceiling on lending with the exception of special fixed-rate and other export finance, the special fixed-rate ship-building loans, and loans to the public sector	Within the ceiling, priority to be given to finance underpinning an improved balance of payments. The upward trend in lending to persons to be halted; personal loans related to purchase of goods to which hire purchase controls apply should only be made available on similar terms. Bridging finance for personal house purchase to continue to be made available
	(iii) Hire purchase controls on cars tightened	Minimum deposit raised to 33⅓ per cent (from 25 per cent) and maximum repayment period shortened to 27 months (from 36 months)
1968		
21 March	Bank rate reduced by ½ per cent	New rate: 7½ per cent
23 May	Banks requested to restrict total private sector lending within a ceiling of 104 per cent of the November 1967 level (for the clearing banks approximately the level already reached in May 1968)	Discrimination requested in favour of advances underpinning an improved balance of payments and, in particular, against the granting of advances to support the import of manufactured goods or stockbuilding of imports. Lending by Clearing and Scottish Banks to local authorities should return to normal levels
30 August	Restatement of restrictions	Increased lending to exporters to be met by reductions to other groups
19 September	Bank rate reduced by ½ per cent	New rate: 7 per cent
1 November	Hire purchase regulations tightened	Minimum deposit on cars raised from 33⅓ to 40 per cent; maximum period of repayment reduced from 27 to 24 months. For all items with previous 25 per cent minimum deposit and maximum repayment period of 30–36 months, the provisions

DATE	INSTRUMENT	DETAILS[2]
1968		
1 November		became 33⅓ per cent deposit, 24 months' repayment period. The minimum deposit for furniture and mattresses raised from 15 to 20 per cent, repayment period reduced from 30 to 24 months
22 November	Clearing and Scottish Banks asked to restrict lending, exclusive of special fixed-rate export finance, to 98 per cent of the November 1967 level, by March 1969. Other banks requested to restrict lending to 102 per cent of the November 1967 level by March 1969	All banks asked to be restrictive in financing imports and payment of import deposits. Curtailment of non-priority lending should fall particularly on lending for personal consumption. Members of the Finance Houses Association and large non-member finance houses asked to observe comparable restraints on lending
1969		
31 January	Reminder of the 98 per cent advances limit to be reached by mid-March	Priorities restated
27 February	(i) Bank rate raised by 1 per cent (ii) Further reminder of the advances limit to be achieved by mid-March	New rate: 8 per cent
15 April	Budget speech reminder of the limit	Measure for enforcement of the limit intimated
31 May	Further reminder of the advances limit	As a penalty for non-compliance with the advances limit, the rate of interest on Special Deposits was halved from 2 June
1970		
5 March	Bank rate reduced by ½ per cent	New rate: 7½ per cent
14 April	(i) London Clearing and Scottish Banks' restricted lending and finance houses' restricted lending to grow by 5 per cent over year to 31 March 1971. Lending by other banks to grow by 7 per cent over same period (ii) Special Deposits called for	½ per cent of gross deposits from

DATE	INSTRUMENT	DETAILS[2]
1970		
14 April		the London Clearing Banks; ¼ per cent from the Scottish Banks. Full rate of interest restored.
15 April	Bank rate reduced by ½ per cent	New rate: 7 per cent
28 July	London Clearing and Scottish Banks requested to slow down growth of advances	
29 October	Special Deposits called for	1 per cent of gross deposits from the London Clearing Banks, ½ per cent from the Scottish Banks

SOURCE: *Quarterly Bulletin of the Bank of England*; *Board of Trade Journal*.

[1] The table covers changes in Bank rate, lending 'requests', calls for, and releases of Special Deposits, and alterations in hire purchase controls. It reports detail of the most important aspects of these changes but does not carry full detail in all cases (especially where hire purchase controls are concerned). Similar coverage for earlier periods can be found in Dow, J. C. R., *The Management of the British Economy 1945–60*, (Cambridge, 1964), Chap. IX, p. 253.

[2] Changes in hire purchase regulations are covered in greater detail, for the period 1948–66, in the *National Institute Economic Review*, no. 35, February 1966, p. 83, and for the period 1966–7, in the *National Institute Economic Review*, no. 42, November 1967, p. 19.

[3] References, here and subsequently in this table, to the institutions circularized about lending restraints are to those explicitly named in the *Quarterly Bulletin of the Bank of England* and are not exhaustive.

AUTHOR INDEX

SUBJECT INDEX